THIS BOOK IS THE PROPERTY OF THE

R██████ ████ ██████

And is Loaned to the Pupil on the Following Conditions

1 - It is not to be taken from the school room without the consent of the teacher.

2 - If lost, defaced, or otherwise injured; the pupil shall pay the teacher its full cost.

Teachers Shall Enforce the above Rules Strictly

Number ██████████ Issued .... 19......

TO WHOM LOANED	CONDITION	DATE LOANED	DATE RETURNED

Integrated 2 Mathematics

Authors

Senior Authors

Rheta N. Rubenstein

Timothy V. Craine

Thomas R. Butts

Kerry Cantrell

Linda Dritsas

Valarie A. Elswick

Joseph Kavanaugh

Sara N. Munshin

Stuart J. Murphy

Anthony Piccolino

Salvador Quezada

Jocelyn Coleman Walton

McDougal Littell/Houghton Mifflin

Evanston, Illinois

Boston   Dallas   Phoenix

Authors

Senior Authors

Rheta N. Rubenstein Associate Professor of Education, University of Windsor, Windsor, Ontario

Timothy V. Craine Assistant Professor of Mathematical Sciences, Central Connecticut State University, New Britain, Connecticut

Thomas R. Butts Associate Professor of Mathematics Education, University of Texas at Dallas, Dallas, Texas

Kerry Cantrell Mathematics Department Head, Marshfield High School, Marshfield, Missouri

Linda Dritsas Mathematics Coordinator, Fresno Unified School District, Fresno, California

Valarie A. Elswick Mathematics Teacher, Roy C. Ketcham Senior High School, Wappingers Falls, New York

Joseph Kavanaugh Academic Head of Mathematics, Scotia-Glenville Central School District, Scotia, New York

Sara N. Munshin Mathematics Teacher, Theodore Roosevelt High School, Los Angeles, California

Stuart J. Murphy Visual Learning Specialist, Evanston, Illinois

Anthony Piccolino Assistant Professor of Mathematics and Computer Science, Montclair State College, Upper Montclair, New Jersey

Salvador Quezada Mathematics Teacher, Theodore Roosevelt High School, Los Angeles, California

Jocelyn Coleman Walton Educational Consultant, Mathematics K-12, and former Mathematics Supervisor, Plainfield High School, Plainfield, New Jersey

All authors contributed to the planning and writing of the series. In addition to writing, the Senior Authors played a special role in establishing the philosophy of the program, planning the content and organization of topics, and guiding the work of the other authors.

Field Testing The authors give special thanks to the teachers and students in classrooms nationwide who used a preliminary version of this book. Their suggestions made an important contribution to its development.

ISBN: 0-395-64439-9   23456789 VH 98 97 96 95

Welcome to Integrated Mathematics 2!

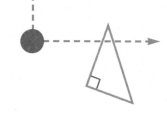

Building on Experience

Integrated Mathematics 2 builds on the mathematical topics and problem solving techniques in *Integrated Mathematics 1*. The Topic Spiraling chart on page xiii shows how mathematical concepts are spiraled over the three years of the *Integrated Mathematics* program, so that you continually build on what you have learned.

Mathematical Strands

You can learn more with *Integrated Mathematics* because the mathematical topics are integrated. Over a three-year period, this program teaches all the essential topics in a contemporary Algebra 1/Geometry/Algebra 2 sequence, plus many other interesting topics.

➤ Algebra and Geometry are taught in each of the three years.

➤ Topics from Logical Reasoning, Measurement, Probability, Statistics, Discrete Mathematics, and Functions are interwoven throughout.

AB

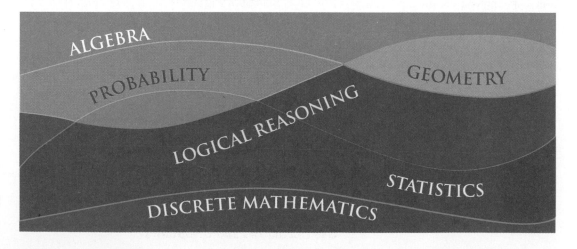

$$= y^3$$

(x, y)

Course Goals

This new program has been written to prepare you for success in college, in careers, and in daily life in the 21st century.

It helps you develop the ability to:

➤ **Explore and solve mathematical problems**

➤ **Think critically**

➤ **Work cooperatively with others**

➤ **Communicate ideas clearly**

Advantages of this Program

Integrated Mathematics develops clear understanding of topics and strong problem solving skills by giving you opportunities to:

➤ **Get actively involved in learning**

➤ **Study meaningful mathematics**

➤ **See connections among different branches of mathematics**

➤ **Try a wide variety of types of problems, including real-world applications and long-term projects**

➤ **Use calculators and computers**

Contents

Unit 3   Linear Systems and Matrices

Unit
Project
3

Unit 4   Quadratic Functions and Graphs

Unit Project 4
Fountains **184**

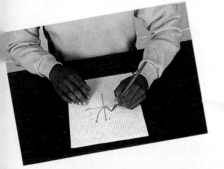

Unit 7   Logic and Proof

Table of Contents

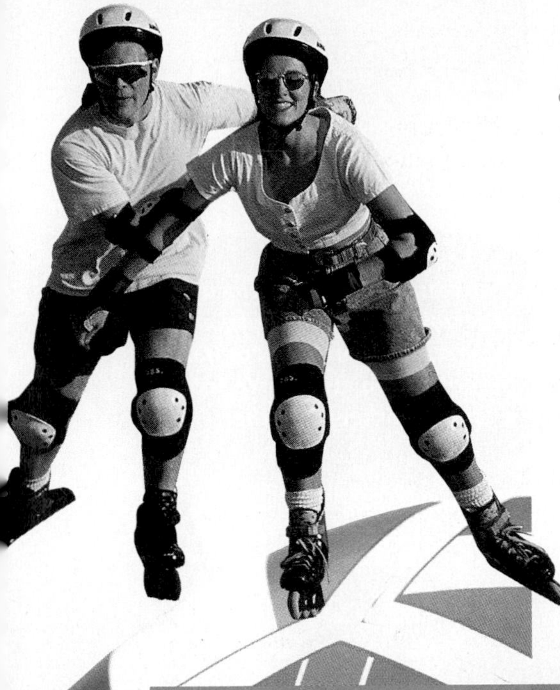

Student Resources

Integrated Mathematics Topic Spiraling

This chart shows how mathematical strands are spiraled over the three years of the *Integrated Mathematics* program.

	Course 1	Course 2	Course 3
Algebra	Linear equations Linear inequalities Multiplying binomials Factoring expressions	Quadratic equations Linear systems Rational equations Complex numbers	Polynomial functions Exponential functions Logarithmic functions Parametric equations
Geometry	Angles, polygons, circles Perimeter, circumference Area, surface area Volume Trigonometric ratios	Similar and congruent figures Geometric proofs Coordinate geometry Transformational geometry Special right triangles	Inscribed figures Transforming graphs Vectors Triangle trigonometry Circular trigonometry
Statistics, Probability	Analyzing data and displaying data Experimental and theoretical probability Geometric probability	Sampling methods Simulation Binomial distributions	Variability Standard deviation z-scores
Logical Reasoning	Conjectures Counterexamples If-then statements	Inductive and deductive reasoning Valid and invalid reasoning Postulates and proof	Identities Contrapositive and inverse Comparing proof methods
Discrete Math	Discrete quantities Matrices to display data Lattices	Matrix operations Transformation matrices Counting techniques	Sequences and series Recursion Limits

What Students are Saying...

Who has the **BEST IDEAS** about how mathematics should be taught? **Students** and **teachers**, of course! That is why preliminary versions of this book were tried out by thousands of students and their teachers in **CLASSROOMS NATIONWIDE**. The suggestions from these students and teachers have been incorporated into this book.

Here is what some of the students who have already studied this course have said.

Our class liked the Explorations, especially collecting data and using calculators and computers to make predictions. We learned a lot by working together.

$$\frac{k}{x}$$

$\angle C$

I feel more comfortable with mathematics since being in this course. I am willing to try harder problems because I feel confident.

This year started off with interesting, new topics. We didn't have to spend a lot of time on boring review. Once we got into the course, I realized how much I remembered from last year.

Get Involved

This course may be different from ones you have taken before. In this course you will be

➤ **TALKING** about mathematics

➤ working *together* to explore ideas

➤ gathering **DATA**

➤ looking for **patterns**

➤ making and testing **predictions**

➤ using *calculators* or **computers**.

Your ideas and viewpoints are important. Sharing them with others will help everyone learn more. So don't hold back. Jump right in and get involved.

............................➤

Guide to Your Course

The next ten pages will give you an overview of the organization of your book and a preview of what you will be learning in the course. They will help you get off to a good start.

Before I started Integrated Mathematics, I could hardly wait to take my last math class. Now I'm looking forward to math next year.

Your Ideas are Important!

2^x

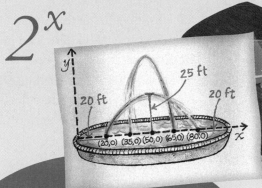

This course showed me that math really does relate to everyday life — in sports, music, jobs, health, nature, and lots of other places.

$m \parallel n$

I used to just sit back and listen in math class. Now I get involved. I think and talk and write about math.

Figures with...

2 pairs of parallel sides	4 ≅ sides	4 right angles	4 ≅ sides and 4 right angles	4 pr. of consecutive ≅ sides	4 sides
#2					
#11					
#3					

Unit Projects

Each unit begins with a project that sets the stage for the mathematics in the unit. The project gives you a chance to **apply** what you are *learning* right away. As you study the unit, you will gather the **INFORMATION** and develop the SKILLS to complete the project. The first three pages of each unit help you get started.

Project Theme

Each project has a theme, like mysteries, that relates the mathematics of the unit to daily life and to careers.

unit **7**

Logic and Proof

How good a detective are you? What clues can you find in this picture that could help you determine WHODUNIT? For instance, what day and time did the crime likely take place? Can you tell whether the writer was left-handed or right-handed? What do you think the message on the paper means? Does it look as if anything was removed from the desk?

whoDUNit?

Mystery stories have been popular in many countries for centuries. Among the mystery writers whose books have served as the basis for TV programs or movies are British author Agatha Christie and French author Maurice Leblanc. In their stories the mystery is solved by the police or by detectives like Jane Marple and Arsène Lupin.

Unit Project **7**

Write a Mystery Story

Your project is to write a mystery story. To structure your story, you will need an outline that contains all the clues you give the reader. Your outline should show how the clues fit together to point to the solution of your mystery. As you outline your story, use two of the techniques of logical argument presented in the unit.

Also include in your story a travel itinerary and applications of at least two of the postulates and theorems about angles and parallel lines that you study in the unit.

When all the groups have completed their stories, have the members of another group read your group's story. Ask them to evaluate it according to the following criteria.

? Does the reader want to continue reading in order to solve the mystery?

? Does the reader have enough clues to solve the mystery?

? Does solving the mystery challenge, surprise, or inform the reader?

In **real life** not all mysteries are solved by amateur, police, or private detectives. Specialists in many fields use logic and reasoning to solve mysteries.

archaeology

Archaeologists dig for evidence of the existence of a mythic empire like the Toltec empire in central Mexico.

art history

Art historians are able to date paintings by determining the elements contained in the paint.

law enforcement

Forensic, or legal, scientists analyze the DNA in samples of blood or hair to determine if they came from a suspect in the case.

362

363

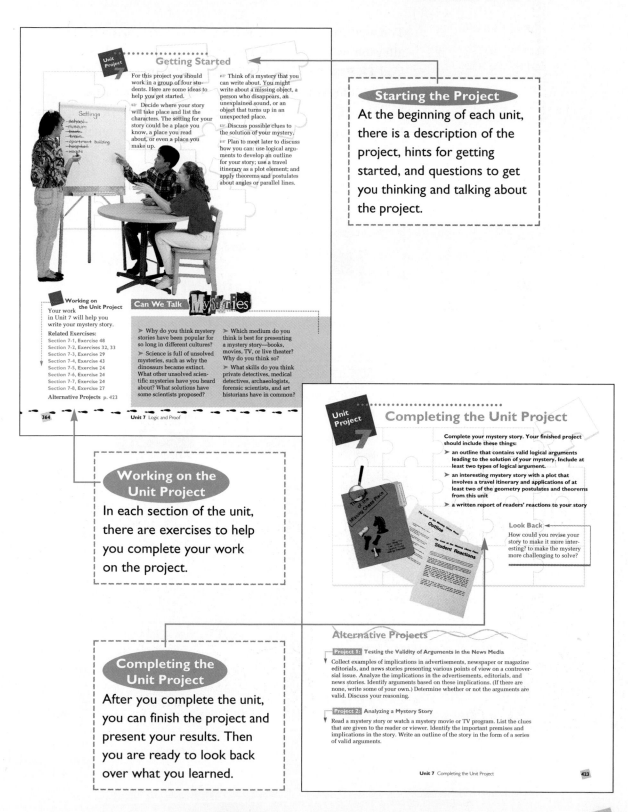

Getting Started

For this project you should work in a group of four students. Here are some ideas to help you get started.

☞ Decide where your story will take place and list the characters. The setting for your story could be a place you know, a place you read about, or even a place you make up.

Settings
- school
- museum
- boat
- train
- apartment building
- hospital
- woods

☞ Think of a mystery that you can write about. You might write about a missing object, a person who disappears, an unexplained sound, or an object that turns up in an unexpected place.

☞ Discuss possible clues to the solution of your mystery.

☞ Plan to meet later to discuss how you can: use logical arguments to develop an outline for your story; use a travel itinerary as a plot element; and apply theorems and postulates about angles or parallel lines.

Working on the Unit Project

Your work in Unit 7 will help you write your mystery story.

Related Exercises:
Section 7-1, Exercise 48
Section 7-2, Exercises 32, 33
Section 7-3, Exercise 29
Section 7-4, Exercise 43
Section 7-5, Exercise 24
Section 7-6, Exercise 24
Section 7-7, Exercise 24
Section 7-8, Exercise 27

Alternative Projects p. 423

Can We Talk Mysteries

▶ Why do you think mystery stories have been popular for so long in different cultures?

▶ Science is full of unsolved mysteries, such as why the dinosaurs became extinct. What other unsolved scientific mysteries have you heard about? What solutions have some scientists proposed?

▶ Which medium do you think is best for presenting a mystery story—books, movies, TV, or live theater? Why do you think so?

▶ What skills do you think private detectives, medical detectives, archaeologists, forensic scientists, and art historians have in common?

Starting the Project
At the beginning of each unit, there is a description of the project, hints for getting started, and questions to get you thinking and talking about the project.

Working on the Unit Project
In each section of the unit, there are exercises to help you complete your work on the project.

Completing the Unit Project
After you complete the unit, you can finish the project and present your results. Then you are ready to look back over what you learned.

Completing the Unit Project

Complete your mystery story. Your finished project should include these things:

▶ an outline that contains valid logical arguments leading to the solution of your mystery. Include at least two types of logical argument.

▶ an interesting mystery story with a plot that involves a travel itinerary and applications of at least two of the geometry postulates and theorems from this unit

▶ a written report of readers' reactions to your story

Look Back
How could you revise your story to make it more interesting? to make the mystery more challenging to solve?

Alternative Projects

Project 1: Testing the Validity of Arguments in the News Media

▼ Collect examples of implications in advertisements, newspaper or magazine editorials, and news stories presenting various points of view on a controversial issue. Analyze the implications in the advertisements, editorials, and news stories. Identify arguments based on these implications. (If there are none, write some of your own.) Determine whether or not the arguments are valid. Discuss your reasoning.

Project 2: Analyzing a Mystery Story

▼ Read a mystery story or watch a mystery movie or TV program. List the clues that are given to the reader or viewer. Identify the important premises and implications in the story. Write an outline of the story in the form of a series of valid arguments.

Section Organization

The organization of material within sections is patterned after the way that you learn: Ideas are introduced. You **EXPLORE** them, **think** about them, and TALK about them with other students. You check that you UNDERSTAND them by working through some sample problems. Before going on, you pause and **look back** at what you have learned.

Focus This is what you will be doing in the lesson.

Application A problem situation connects the mathematics you will be studying to real-world applications.

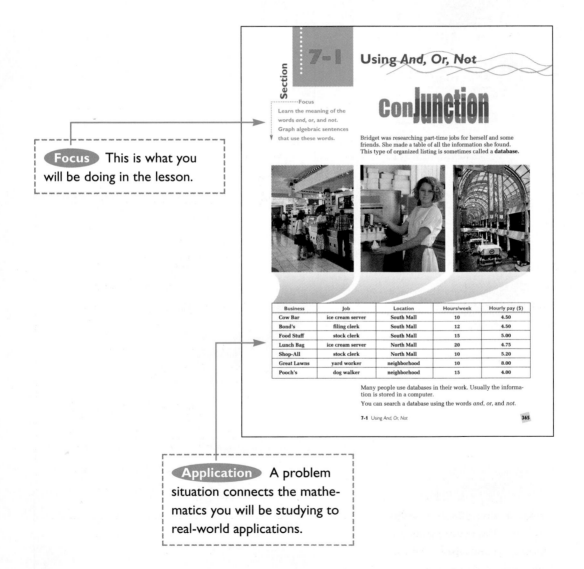

Section 7-1

Using *And, Or, Not*

Focus
Learn the meaning of the words *and, or,* and *not.*
Graph algebraic sentences that use these words.

ConJunction

Bridget was researching part-time jobs for herself and some friends. She made a table of all the information she found. This type of organized listing is sometimes called a **database.**

Business	Job	Location	Hours/week	Hourly pay ($)
Cow Bar	ice cream server	South Mall	10	4.50
Bond's	filing clerk	South Mall	12	4.50
Food Stuff	stock clerk	South Mall	15	5.00
Lunch Bag	ice cream server	North Mall	20	4.75
Shop-All	stock clerk	North Mall	10	5.20
Great Lawns	yard worker	neighborhood	10	8.00
Pooch's	dog walker	neighborhood	15	4.00

Many people use databases in their work. Usually the information is stored in a computer.

You can search a database using the words *and, or,* and *not.*

7-1 *Using And, Or, Not*   365

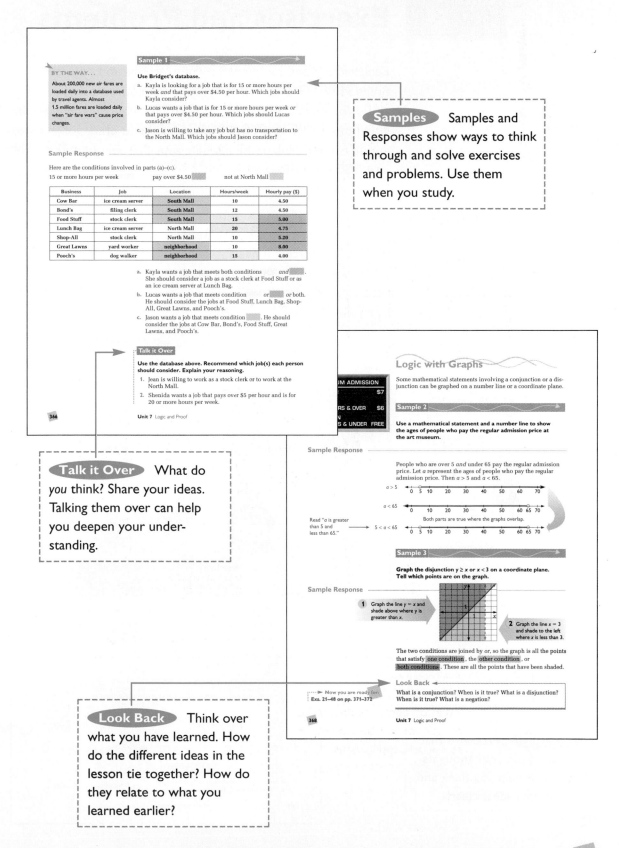

BY THE WAY...

About 200,000 new air fares are loaded daily into a database used by travel agents. Almost 1.5 million fares are loaded daily when "air fare wars" cause price changes.

Sample 1

Use Bridget's database.

a. Kayla is looking for a job that is for 15 or more hours per week *and* that pays over $4.50 per hour. Which jobs should Kayla consider?

b. Lucas wants a job that is for 15 or more hours per week *or* that pays over $4.50 per hour. Which jobs should Lucas consider?

c. Jason is willing to take any job but has no transportation to the North Mall. Which jobs should Jason consider?

Sample Response

Here are the conditions involved in parts (a)–(c).

15 or more hours per week   pay over $4.50   not at North Mall

Business	Job	Location	Hours/week	Hourly pay ($)
Cow Bar	ice cream server	South Mall	10	4.50
Bond's	filing clerk	South Mall	12	4.50
Food Stuff	stock clerk	South Mall	15	5.00
Lunch Bag	ice cream server	North Mall	20	4.75
Shop-All	stock clerk	North Mall	10	5.20
Great Lawns	yard worker	neighborhood	10	8.00
Pooch's	dog walker	neighborhood	15	4.00

a. Kayla wants a job that meets both conditions   and   . She should consider a job as a stock clerk at Food Stuff or as an ice cream server at Lunch Bag.

b. Lucas wants a job that meets condition   or   or both. He should consider the jobs at Food Stuff, Lunch Bag, Shop-All, Great Lawns, and Pooch's.

c. Jason wants a job that meets condition   . He should consider the jobs at Cow Bar, Bond's, Food Stuff, Great Lawns, and Pooch's.

Talk it Over

Use the database above. Recommend which job(s) each person should consider. Explain your reasoning.

1. Jean is willing to work as a stock clerk or to work at the North Mall.

2. Shenida wants a job that pays over $5 per hour and is for 20 or more hours per week.

366   **Unit 7** Logic and Proof

Samples Samples and Responses show ways to think through and solve exercises and problems. Use them when you study.

Talk it Over What do *you* think? Share your ideas. Talking them over can help you deepen your understanding.

Look Back Think over what you have learned. How do the different ideas in the lesson tie together? How do they relate to what you learned earlier?

Logic with Graphs

Some mathematical statements involving a conjunction or a disjunction can be graphed on a number line or a coordinate plane.

UM ADMISSION

$7

RS & OVER $6

S & UNDER FREE

Sample 2

Use a mathematical statement and a number line to show the ages of people who pay the regular admission price at the art museum.

Sample Response

People who are 5 *and* under 65 pay the regular admission price. Let *a* represent the ages of people who pay the regular admission price. Then $a > 5$ and $a < 65$.

Both parts are true where the graphs overlap.

Read "*a* is greater than 5 and less than 65." $5 < a < 65$

Sample 3

Graph the disjunction $y \geq x$ or $x < 3$ on a coordinate plane. Tell which points are on the graph.

Sample Response

1 Graph the line $y = x$ and shade above where y is greater than x.

2 Graph the line $x = 3$ and shade to the left where x is less than 3.

The two conditions are joined by *or*, so the graph is all the points that satisfy one condition , the other condition , or both conditions . These are all the points that have been shaded.

Now you are ready for:
Exs. 21–48 on pp. 371–372

Look Back

What is a conjunction? When is it true? What is a disjunction? When is it true? What is a negation?

368   **Unit 7** Logic and Proof

Section Organization

xix

Exercises and Problems

Each section has a wide variety of exercises and problems. Some **practice** and **EXTEND** the concepts and skills you have learned. Others apply the concepts to everyday situations and **explore connections** to other subject areas and to careers. The problems help you sharpen your **THINKING** and **problem solving skills**.

Reading After you read the section, try the Reading exercise. It helps you check that you understand what you have read.

Connections to... Mathematics is a part of many different subject areas, including history, literature, science, music, driver education.

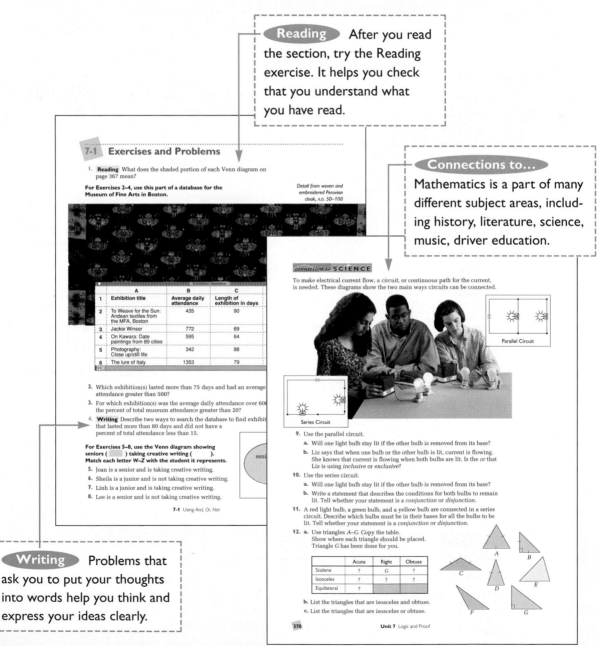

Writing Problems that ask you to put your thoughts into words help you think and express your ideas clearly.

Exercises and Problems

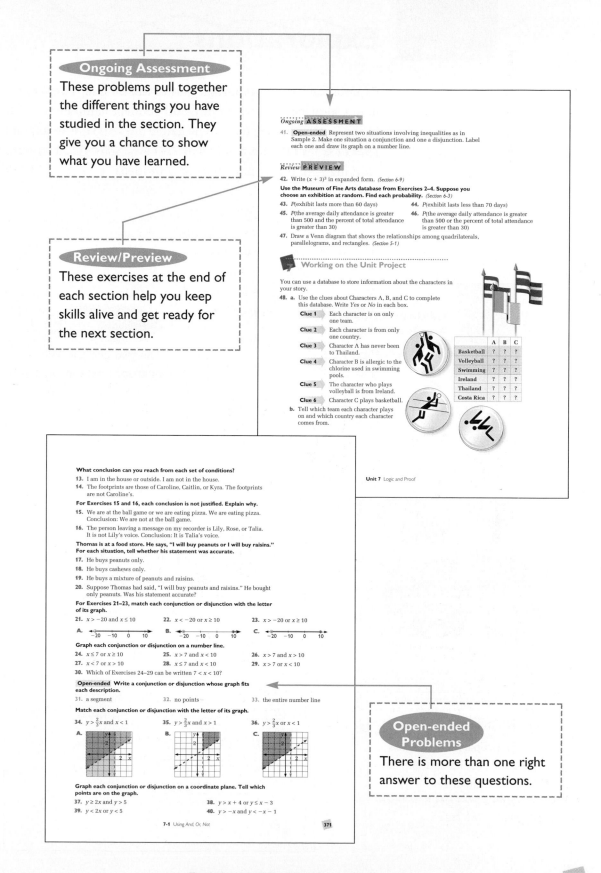

Ongoing Assessment

These problems pull together the different things you have studied in the section. They give you a chance to show what you have learned.

Review/Preview

These exercises at the end of each section help you keep skills alive and get ready for the next section.

Ongoing **ASSESSMENT**

41. **Open-ended** Represent two situations involving inequalities as in Sample 2. Make one situation a conjunction and one a disjunction. Label each one and draw its graph on a number line.

Review **PREVIEW**

42. Write $(x + 3)^3$ in expanded form. *(Section 6-9)*

Use the Museum of Fine Arts database from Exercises 2–4. Suppose you choose an exhibition at random. Find each probability. *(Section 6-3)*

43. P(exhibit lasts more than 60 days)

44. P(exhibit lasts less than 70 days)

45. P(the average daily attendance is greater than 500 and the percent of total attendance is greater than 30)

46. P(the average daily attendance is greater than 500 or the percent of total attendance is greater than 30)

47. Draw a Venn diagram that shows the relationships among quadrilaterals, parallelograms, and rectangles. *(Section 5-1)*

Working on the Unit Project

You can use a database to store information about the characters in your story.

48. **a.** Use the clues about Characters A, B, and C to complete this database. Write *Yes* or *No* in each box.

Clue 1 ▸ Each character is on only one team.

Clue 2 ▸ Each character is from only one country.

Clue 3 ▸ Character A has never been to Thailand.

Clue 4 ▸ Character B is allergic to the chlorine used in swimming pools.

Clue 5 ▸ The character who plays volleyball is from Ireland.

Clue 6 ▸ Character C plays basketball.

	A	B	C
Basketball	?	?	?
Volleyball	?	?	?
Swimming	?	?	?
Ireland	?	?	?
Thailand	?	?	?
Costa Rica	?	?	?

b. Tell which team each character plays on and which country each character comes from.

Unit 7 Logic and Proof

What conclusion can you reach from each set of conditions?

13. I am in the house or outside. I am not in the house.

14. The footprints are those of Caroline, Caitlin, or Kyra. The footprints are not Caroline's.

For Exercises 15 and 16, each conclusion is not justified. Explain why.

15. We are at the ball game or we are eating pizza. We are eating pizza. Conclusion: We are not at the ball game.

16. The person leaving a message on my recorder is Lily, Rose, or Talia. It is not Lily's voice. Conclusion: It is Talia's voice.

Thomas is at a food store. He says, "I will buy peanuts or I will buy raisins." For each situation, tell whether his statement was accurate.

17. He buys peanuts only.

18. He buys cashews only.

19. He buys a mixture of peanuts and raisins.

20. Suppose Thomas had said, "I will buy peanuts and raisins." He bought only peanuts. Was his statement accurate?

For Exercises 21–23, match each conjunction or disjunction with the letter of its graph.

21. $x > -20$ and $x \le 10$

22. $x < -20$ or $x \ge 10$

23. $x > -20$ or $x \ge 10$

A. (number line −20 to 10) B. (number line −20 to 10) C. (number line −20 to 10)

Graph each conjunction or disjunction on a number line.

24. $x \le 7$ or $x \ge 10$

25. $x > 7$ and $x < 10$

26. $x > 7$ and $x > 10$

27. $x < 7$ or $x > 10$

28. $x \le 7$ and $x < 10$

29. $x > 7$ or $x < 10$

30. Which of Exercises 24–29 can be written $7 < x < 10$?

Open-ended Write a conjunction or disjunction whose graph fits each description.

31. a segment

32. no points

33. the entire number line

Match each conjunction or disjunction with the letter of its graph.

34. $y > \frac{2}{3}x$ and $x < 1$

35. $y > \frac{2}{3}x$ and $x > 1$

36. $y > \frac{2}{3}x$ or $x < 1$

A. (graph) B. (graph) C. (graph)

Graph each conjunction or disjunction on a coordinate plane. Tell which points are on the graph.

37. $y \ge 2x$ and $y > 5$

38. $y > x + 4$ or $y \le x - 3$

39. $y < 2x$ or $y < 5$

40. $y > -x$ and $y < -x - 1$

7-1 Using And, Or, Not

Open-ended Problems

There is more than one right answer to these questions.

371

Exercises and Problems

Explorations

Explorations are an important part of this course. They will help you discover, understand, and connect mathematical ideas. In the Explorations, you will be gathering **data**, looking for **patterns**, and making **generalizations**. You will be working with others and sharing your ideas.

Exploration Goal This is the question you will be investigating in the Exploration.

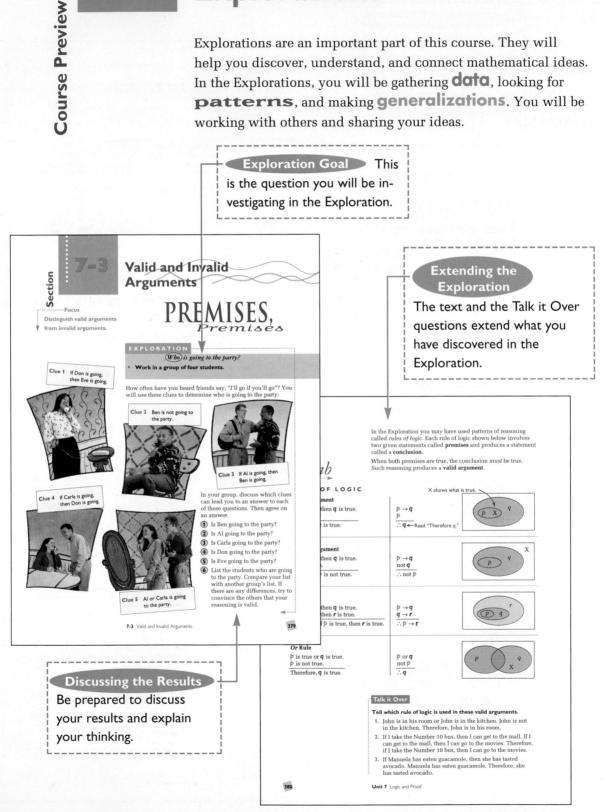

Extending the Exploration
The text and the Talk it Over questions extend what you have discovered in the Exploration.

Discussing the Results
Be prepared to discuss your results and explain your thinking.

Review and Assessment

With this book you review and ASSESS YOUR PROGRESS as you go along. In each unit there are one or two Checkpoints for self-assessment, plus a thorough Unit Review and Assessment at the end.

Unit 7 REVIEW AND ASSESSMENT

Tanya is working on a science project on the construction of balls used in different sports. She made this database.

7-1

Ball	Diam. (cm)	Mass (g)	Interior Construction	Exterior Construction
baseball	7.3	145	rubber or cork wrapped with yarn	leather cover
basketball	24.0	596	inflated rubber	leather or rubber cover
lacrosse	6.4	143	solid rubber	solid rubber cover
soccer	22.0	425	inflated shell	leather cover
tennis	6.5	57	hollow	cloth cover
volleyball	21.0	270	inflated rubber	leather or rubber cover

For Questions 1 and 2, find every ball that makes each statement true.

1. The ball has a diameter less than 10 cm and a mass greater than 140 g.

2. The ball has a diameter less than 10 cm or a mass greater than 140 g.

3. Use a mathematical statement and a graph to describe the range of diameters that are greater than that of a lacrosse ball and less than that of a basketball.

4. For Exercises 1 and 2, which statement is an example of a conjunction? a disjunction?

5. Is this statement *True* or *False* for the balls in the database? Each ball with a leather cover has a mass over 100 g.

7-2

6. Write the converse of the statement in Question 5 and decide if it is *True* or *False*. If it is false, give a counterexample.

7. Draw a Venn diagram for the statement in Question 5.

For Questions 8 and 9, decide if the argument is *valid* or *invalid*. If the argument is valid, tell which rule of logic was used. If the argument is invalid, tell why.

7-3

8. If a triangle is equilateral, then it is equiangular. Triangle *QRS* is not equiangular. Therefore, triangle *QRS* is not equilateral.

9. I will be home this afternoon or I will be at work. I will be at work. Therefore, I will not be home this afternoon.

10. **Open-ended** Write a valid argument using the chain rule.

11. Write the two implications in this biconditional using symbols and using words: $x^2 = 36 \leftrightarrow x = 6$

7-4

12. Is the biconditional in Question 11 *True* or *False*? If it is false, rewrite it so it is true.

13. **Writing** Tell how you know that a biconditional is true.

424   **Unit 7** Logic and Proof

Assessment Matches Learning

The Checkpoint and unit Review and Assessment questions are like the ones in the text and the Exercise and Problem sets.

IDEAS AND (FORMULAS)

(ALGEBRA)

Postulates of Algebra

➤ Addition Property of Equality: If the same number is added to equal numbers, the sums are equal. *(p. 402)*

$$a = b \rightarrow a + c = b + c$$

➤ Subtraction Property of Equality: If the same number is subtracted from equal numbers, the differences are equal. *(p. 402)*

$$a = b \rightarrow a - c = b - c$$

➤ Multiplication Property of Equality: If equal numbers are multiplied by the same number, the products are equal. *(p. 402)*

$$a = b \rightarrow ac = bc$$

➤ Division Property of Equality: If equal numbers are divided by the same nonzero number, the quotients are equal. *(p. 402)*

$$a = b \text{ and } c \neq 0 \rightarrow \frac{a}{c} = \frac{b}{c}$$

➤ Reflexive Property: A number is equal to itself. *(p. 402)*

$$a = a$$

➤ Substitution Property: If values are equal, one value may be substituted for the other. *(p. 402)*

$$a = b \rightarrow a \text{ may be substituted for } b.$$

➤ Distributive Property: An expression of the form $a(b + c)$ is equivalent to $ab + ac$. *(p. 402)*

$$a(b + c) = ab + ac$$

GEOMETRY

Postulates and Theorems of Geometry

➤ If two angles are supplements of the same angle, then they are equal in measure. *(p. 409)*

➤ If two angles are complements of the same angle, then they are equal in measure. *(p. 409)*

➤ If the sides of an angle form a straight line, then the angle is a straight angle with measure 180°. *(p. 410)*

➤ For any segment or angle, the measure of the whole is equal to the sum of the measures of its non-overlapping parts. *(p. 410)*

➤ Vertical angles are equal in measure. *(p. 411)*

➤ If two parallel lines are intersected by a transversal, then:
  * corresponding angles are equal in measure. *(p. 416)*
  * alternate interior angles are equal in measure. *(p. 417)*
  * co-interior angles are supplementary. *(p. 417)*

➤ If a quadrilateral is a parallelogram, then:
  * consecutive angles are supplementary. *(p. 419)*
  * opposite angles are equal in measure. *(p. 419)*

426   **Unit 7** Logic and Proof

Topic Overview

To give you an overview of the unit, the summary is organized by math topic strands. A list of Key Terms is included.

Technology

In this course you will see many different ways that **CALCULATORS** and **COMPUTERS** can make exploring ideas and solving problems easier.

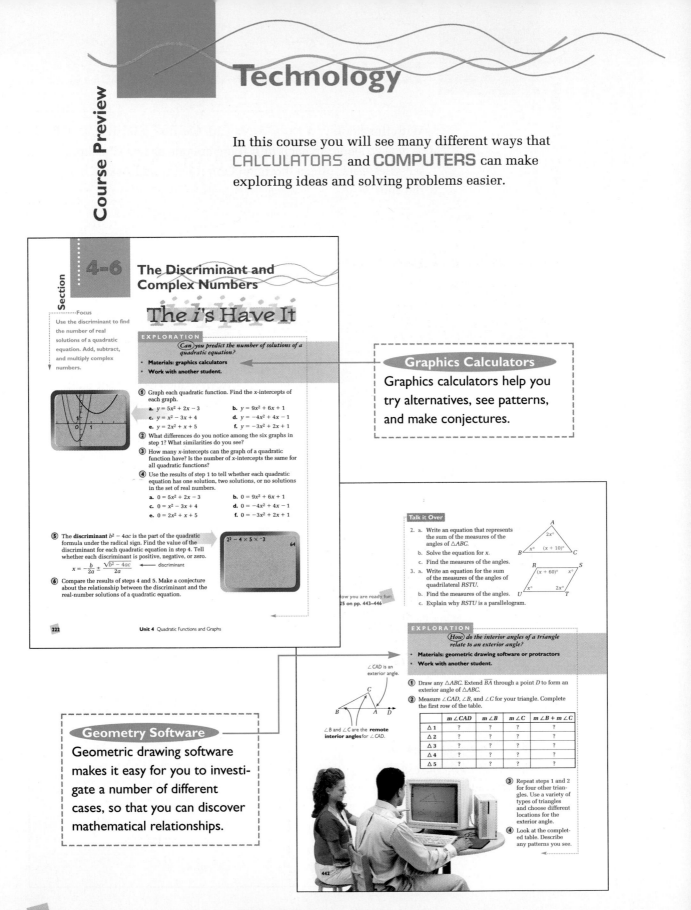

Section 4-6

The Discriminant and Complex Numbers

The *i*'s Have It

Focus
Use the discriminant to find the number of real solutions of a quadratic equation. Add, subtract, and multiply complex numbers.

EXPLORATION

Can you predict the number of solutions of a quadratic equation?

• **Materials: graphics calculators**
• **Work with another student.**

① Graph each quadratic function. Find the *x*-intercepts of each graph.

a. $y = 5x^2 + 2x - 3$ b. $y = 9x^2 + 6x + 1$
c. $y = x^2 - 3x + 4$ d. $y = -4x^2 + 4x - 1$
e. $y = 2x^2 + x + 5$ f. $y = -3x^2 + 2x + 1$

② What differences do you notice among the six graphs in step 1? What similarities do you see?

③ How many *x*-intercepts can the graph of a quadratic function have? Is the number of *x*-intercepts the same for all quadratic functions?

④ Use the results of step 1 to tell whether each quadratic equation has one solution, two solutions, or no solutions in the set of real numbers.

a. $0 = 5x^2 + 2x - 3$ b. $0 = 9x^2 + 6x + 1$
c. $0 = x^2 - 3x + 4$ d. $0 = -4x^2 + 4x - 1$
e. $0 = 2x^2 + x + 5$ f. $0 = -3x^2 + 2x + 1$

⑤ The **discriminant** $b^2 - 4ac$ is the part of the quadratic formula under the radical sign. Find the value of the discriminant for each quadratic equation in step 4. Tell whether each discriminant is positive, negative, or zero.

$$x = -\frac{b}{2a} \pm \frac{\sqrt{b^2 - 4ac}}{2a} \longleftarrow \text{discriminant}$$

⑥ Compare the results of steps 4 and 5. Make a conjecture about the relationship between the discriminant and the real-number solutions of a quadratic equation.

$2^2 - 4 \times 5 \times {}^-3$

64

222   **Unit 4** Quadratic Functions and Graphs

Graphics Calculators

Graphics calculators help you try alternatives, see patterns, and make conjectures.

Talk it Over

2. a. Write an equation that represents the sum of the measures of the angles of △ABC.
   b. Solve the equation for *x*.
   c. Find the measures of the angles.

3. a. Write an equation for the sum of the measures of the angles of quadrilateral *RSTU*.
   b. Find the measures of the angles.
   c. Explain why *RSTU* is a parallelogram.

Now you are ready for:
25 on pp. 443–446

EXPLORATION

How do the interior angles of a triangle relate to an exterior angle?

• **Materials: geometric drawing software or protractors**
• **Work with another student.**

① Draw any △ABC. Extend $\overline{BA}$ through a point *D* to form an exterior angle of △ABC.

② Measure ∠CAD, ∠B, and ∠C for your triangle. Complete the first row of the table.

∠CAD is an exterior angle.

∠B and ∠C are the **remote interior angles** for ∠CAD.

	m ∠CAD	m ∠B	m ∠C	m ∠B + m ∠C
△ 1	?	?	?	?
△ 2	?	?	?	?
△ 3	?	?	?	?
△ 4	?	?	?	?
△ 5	?	?	?	?

③ Repeat steps 1 and 2 for four other triangles. Use a variety of types of triangles and choose different locations for the exterior angle.

④ Look at the completed table. Describe any patterns you see.

442

Geometry Software

Geometric drawing software makes it easy for you to investigate a number of different cases, so that you can discover mathematical relationships.

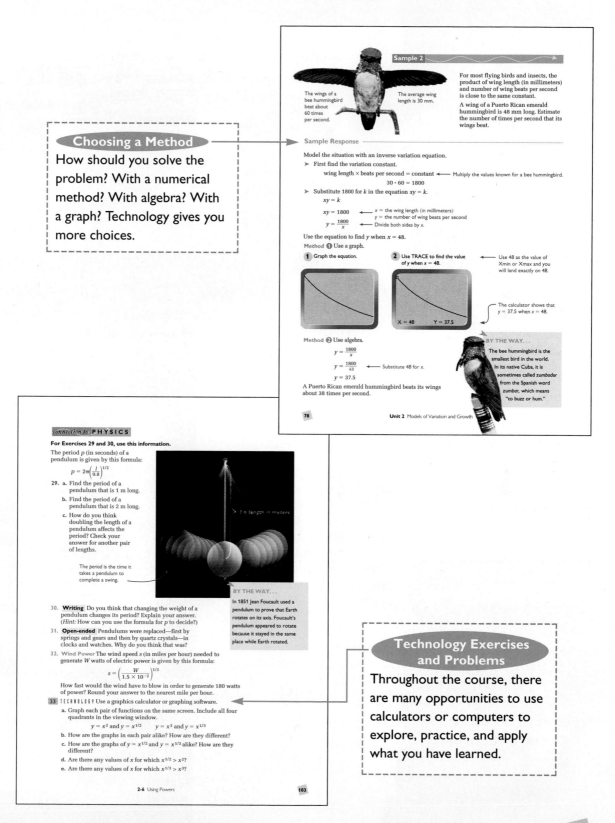

Choosing a Method

How should you solve the problem? With a numerical method? With algebra? With a graph? Technology gives you more choices.

Sample 2

The wings of a bee hummingbird beat about 60 times per second.

The average wing length is 30 mm.

For most flying birds and insects, the product of wing length (in millimeters) and number of wing beats per second is close to the same constant.

A wing of a Puerto Rican emerald hummingbird is 48 mm long. Estimate the number of times per second that its wings beat.

Sample Response

Model the situation with an inverse variation equation.

➤ First find the variation constant.

wing length × beats per second = constant ◄── Multiply the values known for a bee hummingbird.

$$30 \cdot 60 = 1800$$

➤ Substitute 1800 for k in the equation $xy = k$.

$$xy = k$$

$$xy = 1800 \quad \longleftarrow \quad x = \text{the wing length (in millimeters)}$$
$$ \quad\quad y = \text{the number of wing beats per second}$$

$$y = \frac{1800}{x} \quad \longleftarrow \quad \text{Divide both sides by } x.$$

Use the equation to find y when $x = 48$.

Method ❶ Use a graph.

❶ Graph the equation.

❷ Use TRACE to find the value of y when $x = 48$. ◄── Use 48 as the value of Xmin or Xmax and you will land exactly on 48.

X = 48   Y = 37.5

The calculator shows that $y = 37.5$ when $x = 48$.

Method ❷ Use algebra.

$$y = \frac{1800}{x}$$

$$y = \frac{1800}{48} \quad \longleftarrow \quad \text{Substitute 48 for } x.$$

$$y = 37.5$$

A Puerto Rican emerald hummingbird beats its wings about 38 times per second.

BY THE WAY...

The bee hummingbird is the smallest bird in the world. In its native Cuba, it is sometimes called *zumbador* from the Spanish word *zumbar*, which means "to buzz or hum."

78   **Unit 2** Models of Variation and Growth

---

connection to **PHYSICS**

For Exercises 29 and 30, use this information.

The period p (in seconds) of a pendulum is given by this formula:

$$p = 2\pi \left(\frac{l}{9.8} \right)^{1/2}$$

29. **a.** Find the period of a pendulum that is 1 m long.
   b. Find the period of a pendulum that is 2 m long.
   c. How do you think doubling the length of a pendulum affects the period? Check your answer for another pair of lengths.

The *period* is the time it takes a pendulum to complete a swing.

l = length in meters

BY THE WAY...

In 1851 Jean Foucault used a pendulum to prove that Earth rotates on its axis. Foucault's pendulum appeared to rotate because it stayed in the same place while Earth rotated.

30. **Writing** Do you think that changing the weight of a pendulum changes its period? Explain your answer. (*Hint:* How can you use the formula for p to decide?)

31. **Open-ended** Pendulums were replaced—first by springs and gears and then by quartz crystals—in clocks and watches. Why do you think that was?

32. **Wind Power** The wind speed s (in miles per hour) needed to generate W watts of electric power is given by this formula:

$$s = \left(\frac{W}{1.5 \times 10^{-2}} \right)^{1/3}$$

How fast would the wind have to blow in order to generate 180 watts of power? Round your answer to the nearest mile per hour.

33. **TECHNOLOGY** Use a graphics calculator or graphing software.
   a. Graph each pair of functions on the same screen. Include all four quadrants in the viewing window.

$$y = x^2 \text{ and } y = x^{1/2} \qquad y = x^3 \text{ and } y = x^{1/3}$$

   b. How are the graphs in each pair alike? How are they different?
   c. How are the graphs of $y = x^{1/2}$ and $y = x^{1/3}$ alike? How are they different?
   d. Are there any values of x for which $x^{1/2} > x^2$?
   e. Are there any values of x for which $x^{1/3} > x^3$?

2-6 Using Powers   103

Technology Exercises and Problems

Throughout the course, there are many opportunities to use calculators or computers to explore, practice, and apply what you have learned.

unit 1

Sampling and Reasoning

RECYCLING

Like buried time capsules, the landfills of America wait to be dug up by future generations of archaeologists. That newspaper tossed into the trash 12 years ago is still quite readable today. Those uneaten hot dogs and ears of corn from a family picnic are still with us many years later.

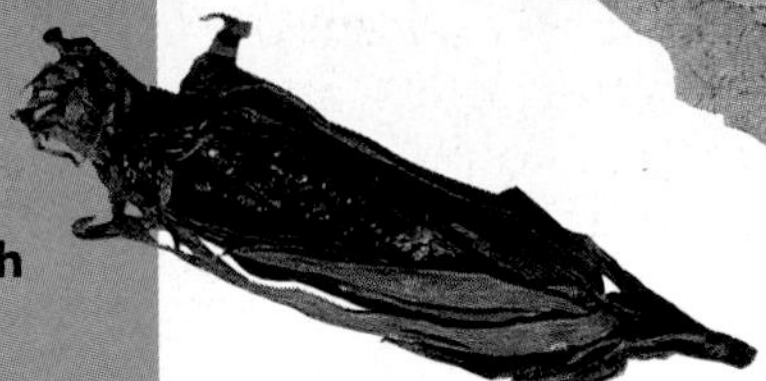

Corn buried 1971

reduce

People all over the world are looking for ways to **REUSE** nonconsumable items rather than throw them away, to **REDUCE** the amount of trash produced and **RECYCLE** more of it.

Associations that support recycling have sprung up in Canada, Brazil, and Europe. Japan recycles about a third of its trash. In the United States, the number of communities with recycling programs jumped from 50 to 4000 between 1990 and 1993!

discard

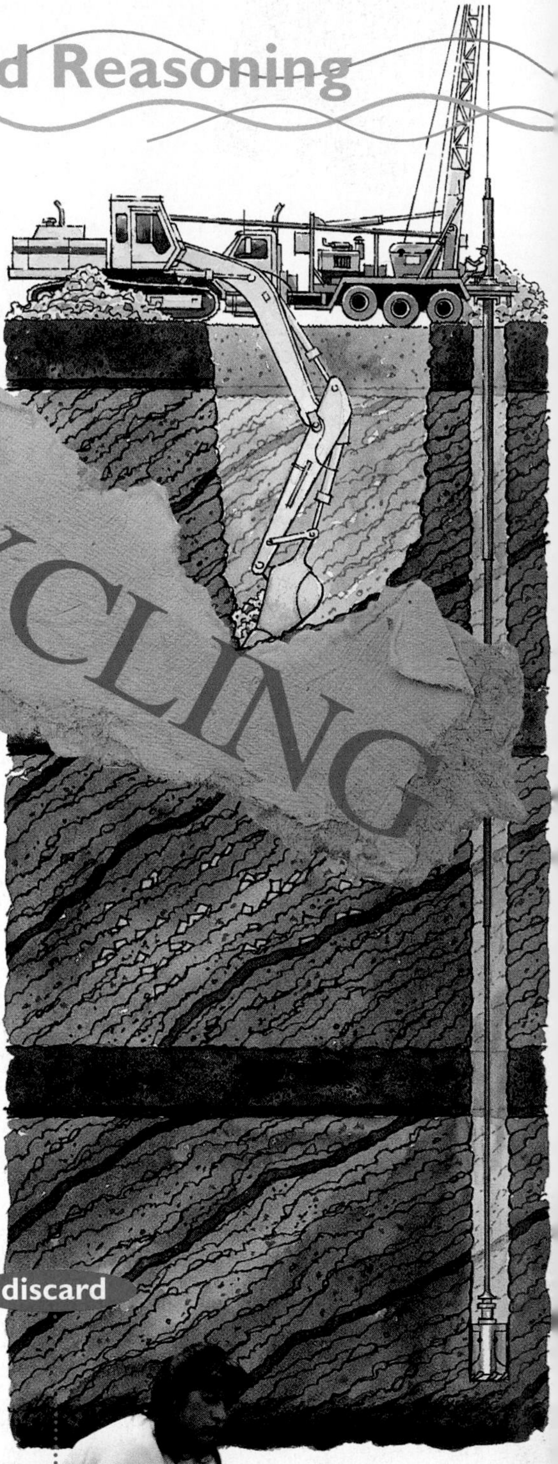

Landfills admit no light, no air, and very little moisture, so trash decomposes slowly.➤

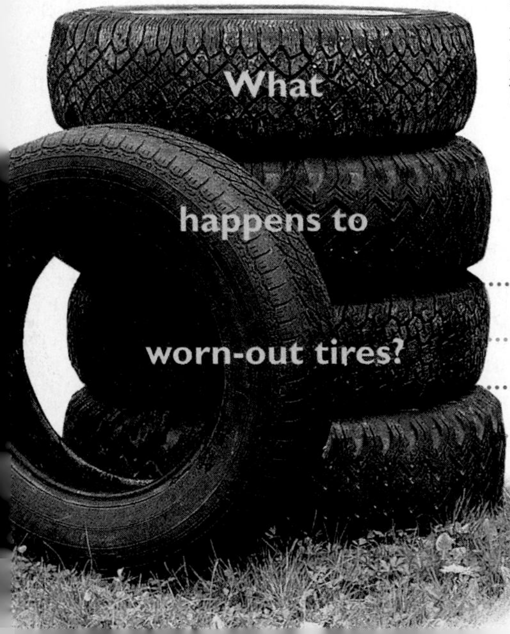

What
happens to
worn-out tires?

reuse

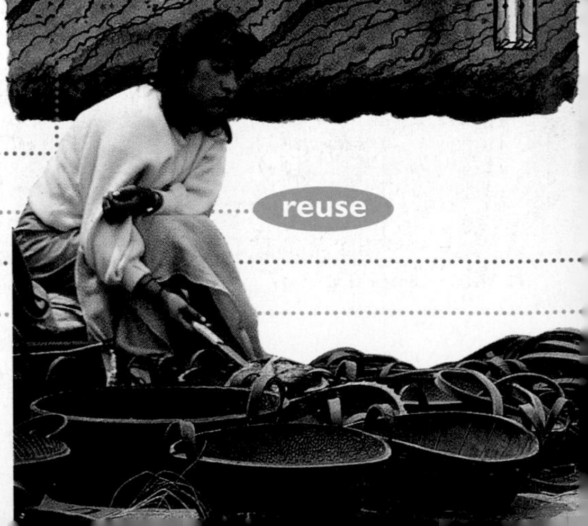

In Ecuador, used tires become market baskets.➤

Disposal Proposal

Your project is to develop a proposal for reducing the amount of trash produced by the students in your school. First, you will need to survey students about their attitudes toward recycling and reuse. Then you will obtain a sample of the trash from a classroom and analyze its contents.

In this unit, you will learn about surveys, sampling, and reasoning. You will use your findings from the survey and sample analysis to make a display or plan an event to persuade students to throw away less and recycle and reuse more. You may build a three-dimensional model for a display case, make a series of posters, organize an assembly program, present a humorous skit, or make an announcement over the public-address system.

Your presentation should include your survey questions, a summary of the results, and a graph showing the contents of the classroom trash sample.

A glass recycling station in Portugal ➤

products

Take a **pile of trash**—car tires, used plastic foam cups, old canvas, empty milk jugs, cardboard boxes, old file folders. Add a dash of technology and you have ... brand-new shoes!

Recycling creates new products out of old. You can buy sweaters made from soft drink bottles and even sea-green stationery made from old paper money.

The rubber in tires can be used to make everything from hockey pucks to handbags.➤

recycle

create

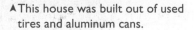

▲This house was built out of used tires and aluminum cans.

1

Getting Started

For this project you should work in a group of four students. Here are some ideas to help you get started.

☞ Discuss what questions to ask on your reduce/reuse/recycle survey. Decide whether you will survey all the students in the school or only a sample. If you use a sample, plan to meet later to choose a sampling method and a sample size.

☞ Set a date and time for collecting a sample of classroom trash. Plan to wear rubber gloves and bring along trash bags for the trash you remove from wastebaskets.

☞ Think about how to get students' attention and convince them of the need to change. Plan to meet later to discuss how to use reasoning to construct good arguments that will help students understand the problem.

☞ Choose an effective format—written, visual, or dramatic—for communicating your findings and recommendations to all the students in your school.

Survey Questions
1) Do you recycle newspapers?
2) Do you recycle aluminum cans?

Can We Talk RECYCLING

Working on the Unit Project

Your work in Unit 1 will help you develop a disposal proposal for your school.

Related Exercises:
Section 1-1, Exercise 26
Section 1-2, Exercise 25
Section 1-3, Exercise 28
Section 1-4, Exercises 24–26
Section 1-5, Exercises 31, 32
Section 1-6, Exercise 44
Section 1-7, Exercise 33

Alternative Projects p. 52

➤ Where do you think most of the trash comes from in your school? What type of trash do you think is the most common?

➤ Is recycling practiced in your city or town? If so, what types of materials are picked up at curbside and what types do you bring to a collection center?

➤ About 50% of the trash in an average landfill is paper. Do you think that half of any pile of trash is paper? Why or why not?

➤ What other products do you know about that are made of recycled materials? How do the prices and the quality of these products compare with those made from all new materials?

➤ What do you think archaeologists can learn about the lifestyle of a culture by examining its trash?

A recycling center in France ➤

Surveys and Samples

Stamp
of Approval

In 1992 the United States Postal Service asked the public its opinion on this issue: Should a young Elvis or an older Elvis picture be used on a commemorative stamp?

A survey in a popular magazine showed pictures of the two stamps. Voters marked their choices on postcards. The young Elvis stamp was chosen by 851,200 people. The older Elvis stamp was chosen by 277,723 people.

There are about 250 million people living in the United States, but less than 2 million people voted on the Elvis stamp issue.

A complete group is a **population**. The population of the United States is about 250 million.

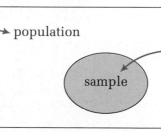

population

sample

A part of a group is a **sample**. The sample that sent in an Elvis stamp ballot included 1,128,923 people.

According to a network news report, by the end of the first week of voting 300,000 ballots were received. 78% were for the young Elvis; 17% were for the older Elvis.

Talk it Over

1. What do you think the other 5% of the ballots showed at the end of the first week?

2. What percent of the final results were for the young Elvis? the older Elvis?

3. Were the results at the end of the first week a good indication of the final results? Explain your reasoning.

Every ten years, the United States government gathers data about the entire population of the country. This process is called a *census* because every member of the population is included.

A census is expensive and requires lots of planning. It is more common for people who collect information to take a survey of a sample of a population.

Many surveys ask questions that can be answered with either a "yes" or a "no."

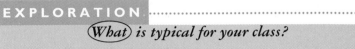

EXPLORATION

What is typical for your class?

• **Work with the whole class.**

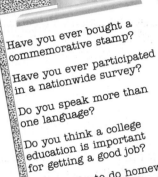

Have you ever bought a commemorative stamp?

Have you ever participated in a nationwide survey?

Do you speak more than one language?

Do you think a college education is important for getting a good job?

Do you like to do homework?

① Take a survey of your class. Use one yes-no question from the list at the left, or make up one of your own.

② Find the total number of people who answered "yes" to your survey question. Find the total who answered "no."

③ What percent of the answers were "yes"? What percent were "no"?

④ Do you think that your results accurately reflect the views of your school population? Explain why or why not.

Talk it Over

4. How might the results of your survey be different if you had taken the survey of a retirement community? of people at a video arcade?

5. Why do you think yes-no or multiple-choice questions are often used on surveys?

6. Suppose you want to predict how someone in your school might answer the question you used in the Exploration. Choose the letter of the sample size you think will give you the most representative response. Explain your choice.

   a. 20 people   b. 200 people   c. 2 people

7. What are some factors to consider when you are making a survey? Make a list.

Surveys (or polls) are used to predict such things as election results, the popularity of new products, or opinions of television shows. Based on the results, information is projected for the entire population.

Sample

Suppose everyone in the United States had to choose an Elvis stamp. Use the results of the Elvis stamp ballot to estimate the number who would select the young Elvis.

Sample Response

Problem Solving Strategy: Use a proportion.

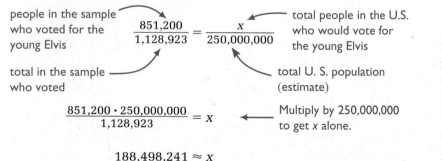

people in the sample who voted for the young Elvis → $\dfrac{851,200}{1,128,923} = \dfrac{x}{250,000,000}$ ← total people in the U.S. who would vote for the young Elvis

total in the sample who voted ↗   total U. S. population (estimate) ↘

$\dfrac{851,200 \cdot 250,000,000}{1,128,923} = x$ ← Multiply by 250,000,000 to get x alone.

$188,498,241 \approx x$

About 188,500,000 people would choose the young Elvis stamp.

75% of the voters chose the young Elvis.

Look Back

A city planner wants to know if a stoplight is needed at a street corner. What population should the planner consider? What is a sample that the planner might use? Write a short survey that the planner could give the people in that sample.

Exercises and Problems

1. **Reading** About what percent of the United States population voted for one Elvis stamp or the other?

2. **Reading** Complete each <u>?</u> using a key word from this section. A part is to the whole as a <u>?</u> is to the <u>?</u>.

For Exercises 3–5, use the survey results below.

3. Do the results show the views of a *sample* of consumers or of the entire *population* of consumers?

4. Why is it more reasonable to survey a sample of the population than to take a census to collect this information?

5. **a.** Write two multiple-choice questions that could have been used in this survey.

   b. Would you be able to find each average percent of increase shown based on the responses to your questions? Why or why not?

recycled plastic packaging: 6.1%

gasoline with $\frac{1}{3}$ less pollutants: 7.4%

recycled paper products: 6.0%

detergents with $\frac{1}{3}$ less pollutants: 7.3%

A survey of 1413 people has shown that consumers want to buy products that are safe for the environment, even if the products are more expensive. The diagram shows the average percent of increase consumers will pay.

6. **Opinion Polls** Suppose that 63% of the people in a sample said that they supported a plan to pay for a new school. Because sampling never gives perfect measures, the actual results could be different by up to 3% in either direction. This is called the *margin of error.*

   a. What is the largest percent of the population that might support the plan? What is the smallest percent?

   b. Write an inequality to describe the percent of the population that might support the plan.

   c. Graph the inequality from part (b) on a number line.

7. At a preview of a movie, 6 people out of 500 walk out. Suppose 600,000 people see the movie. Estimate the number of people who walk out.

8. In a 125-seat section of a baseball park, 38 people bought programs. The park holds 54,000 people. Estimate the total number of programs sold.

9. **Wildlife** In part of a shoreline reserve, there are 45 nesting adult sanderlings and 17 sanderling chicks. There are 120 nesting adult sanderlings in the reserve. Estimate the total number of sanderling chicks.

BY THE WAY...

Amy Gustafson is a chemical engineer whose work involves designing *biodegradable* plastics, such as the plastic film she is holding. The base for this clear, flexible, water-repelling film is corn starch.

10. **a. Research** Find out the number of students in your school.

   b. Use the results of the Exploration on page 4 to estimate the total number of students in your school who would answer "yes" to the question you used in the Exploration.

   c. Group Activity Ask the question of at least 10 students who are not in your mathematics class. Combine the data your class collects and estimate the total number of students in your school who would answer "yes" to the question.

   d. Compare your answers to parts (b) and (c). Suppose you asked another 20 students. How do you think the results would change?

11. **a. Research** Find the results of a survey in a magazine or a newspaper.

   b. Identify at least two reasons why a sample was used, rather than the entire population.

   c. Use the data in the survey to project the results for the population of the United States.

   d. Describe who could use the information from the survey and how they might use it.

connection to **HISTORY**

12. In the late 1700s, Thomas Paine estimated that one person in sixteen in England was over 50 years old. He concluded that 420,000 people were then over 50. What number does it appear that he was using for the population of England?

13. **Writing** England did not have a formal census until 1801, so Paine had to rely on rough estimates of the population.

   Write about how a historian might estimate the population of a country 200 years ago.

14. **Open-ended** The passage at the right is from *The Rights of Man*, by Thomas Paine. In it, he describes the method he used to estimate the number of people over 50 years old.

   Do you think this method gave Paine a good estimate of the number of people over 50 years old? Why or why not?

"To form some judgment of the number of those above fifty years of age, I have several times counted the persons I met in the streets of London, men, women, and children, and have generally found that the average is about one in sixteen or seventeen."

15. The diagram shows that part of the population of polygons is the sample of squares. Choose another sample from this population and draw a diagram that shows the sample and the population.

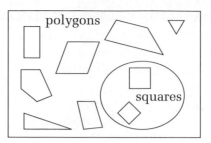

16. Suppose that the population is the set of all real numbers. A sample of that set might be the even integers.

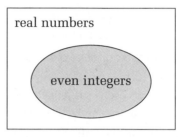

   a. Name at least two other sets that could be samples of this population.

   b. Draw a diagram that shows the population, the set of even integers, and the samples that you described in part (a).

Ongoing **ASSESSMENT**

17. **Open-ended** Describe two situations where a sample might be used. Give the advantages and disadvantages of using a sample in each case.

Review **PREVIEW**

Solve. *(Toolbox Skill 13)*

18. $3x + 7 = 13$ **19.** $-8x - 1 = 3$ **20.** $14 - \frac{1}{2}x = 26$

21. Make a table of values to graph the equation $y = 0.25x - 2$. Find the slope and the intercepts of the graph. *(Toolbox Skills 20, 21, and 24)*

Assume that the needle on the spinner is equally likely to land on each section. Find each probability. *(Toolbox Skill 7)*

22. $P(2)$ **23.** $P(\text{odd})$

24. $P(\text{less than 3})$ **25.** $P(8)$

Working on the Unit Project

26. **Group Activity** Write a first draft of your survey with a minimum of ten questions about reducing, reusing, and recycling trash at your school. Describe the student population that might participate in your survey. Tell whether you would take a census or take a survey of a sample of the population. Explain your choice.

Simulation

Give it a Spin

HOW TO MAKE A SPINNER

Draw a large circle with five equal sections labeled as shown.

Make a pointer out of a paper clip.

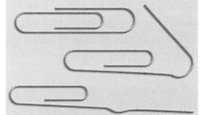

Use a pencil to hold the pointer at the center of the circle.

EXPLORATION

How can you describe a sample without actually choosing it?

- **Materials: spinner (look to the left), paper clip**
- **Work in a group of four students.**

The 1870 census recorded that 80% of the total population of the United States, age 10 years or older, was literate (able to read and write in some language).

1 **a.** What is 80% of 10 people? If you could choose 10 people at random from the population in 1870, how many literate people would you be likely to get?

b. What is 80% of 25 people? If you could choose 25 people at random from the population in 1870, how many literate people would you be likely to get?

2 It is unlikely that exactly 80% of any sample will be literate, and it is difficult to find the records to do a historical survey of a sample of the United States population in 1870. However, you can use an experiment to find the number of people in a sample who are literate.

a. Make a spinner as described at the left.

b. Discuss with your group why the blue shaded sections represent 80% of the circle.

Continued on next page.

9

③ Each student spins the spinner 25 times. Tally the results.

	Number of landings on a blue section	Number of landings on a yellow section	Total number of spins	Percent of total that landed on a blue section
Student 1	?	?	25	?
Student 2	?	?	25	?
Student 3	?	?	25	?
Student 4	?	?	25	?
Total	?	?	100	?

④ Tally the results for the entire class. Which is closer to 80%, the percent for your group or the percent for the whole class?

When you use an experiment based on a real-life situation to answer a question, you are using **simulation.** Each run of the experiment is called a **trial.** Simulation experiments may use physical models (like a spinner or a coin) or computer programs.

Simulation allows people to test new ideas, procedures, and equipment while saving time and money. For example, pilots may use flight simulators to learn about flying under dangerous conditions without actually putting themselves or their airplanes in danger.

Student Resources Toolbox
p. 637 *Probability*

heads

tails

·····▶ Now you are ready for:
Exs. 1–11 on pp. 12–13

Talk it Over

1. The theoretical probability that a person chosen at random from the population of 1870 is literate is 0.8. What is the experimental probability that you found in the Exploration?

2. Suppose that you guess the answer to a true-false question. The probabilities that you are right or wrong are equal. Decide whether you could use each of these methods to simulate whether or not you answer correctly.

   a. Toss a coin. You are correct if it lands with heads facing up.

   b. Use the spinner at the right. You are correct if the spinner lands on a shaded section.

   c. Roll a die. You are correct if the outcome is an even number.

3. Suppose you run 20 trials of an experiment. Would you expect the average of the results to be *more accurate* or *less accurate* than the average of the results of 200 trials?

Probability and Simulation

The simulation in the Exploration is based on an observation of a population. Some simulations are based on other facts.

Sample

There are two traffic lights on a school bus route. On the route to school the probability that the first light is red is $\frac{1}{3}$, and the average wait is 1 min. The probability that the second light is red is $\frac{1}{2}$, and the average wait is 2 min.

On average, how long will the school bus be stopped at a light?

Sample Response

Problem Solving Strategy: Use simulation.

Step 1 Make a **tree diagram** to show the possibilities at each light.

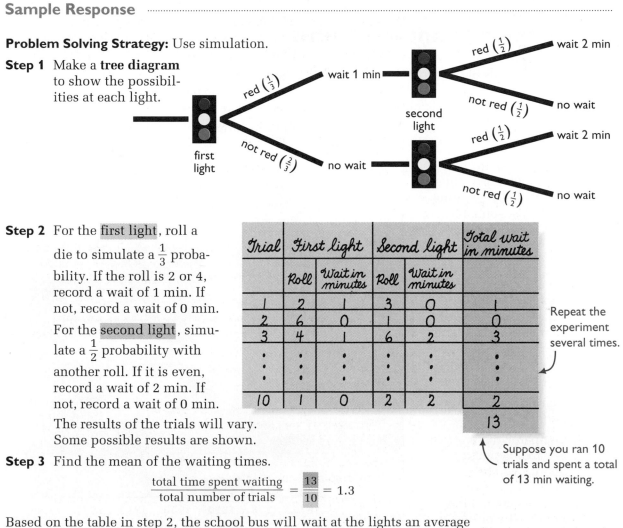

Step 2 For the first light, roll a die to simulate a $\frac{1}{3}$ probability. If the roll is 2 or 4, record a wait of 1 min. If not, record a wait of 0 min.

For the second light, simulate a $\frac{1}{2}$ probability with another roll. If it is even, record a wait of 2 min. If not, record a wait of 0 min.

The results of the trials will vary. Some possible results are shown.

Trial	First light		Second light		Total wait in minutes
	Roll	Wait in minutes	Roll	Wait in minutes	
1	2	1	3	0	1
2	6	0	1	0	0
3	4	1	6	2	3
⋮	⋮	⋮	⋮	⋮	⋮
10	1	0	2	2	2
					13

Repeat the experiment several times.

Suppose you ran 10 trials and spent a total of 13 min waiting.

Step 3 Find the mean of the waiting times.

$$\frac{\text{total time spent waiting}}{\text{total number of trials}} = \frac{13}{10} = 1.3$$

Based on the table in step 2, the school bus will wait at the lights an average of 1.3 min each day on the route to school.

4. In the Sample, the probability that the first light is red is $\frac{1}{3}$. Why does the probability that it is not red equal $\frac{2}{3}$?

5. In the Sample, a roll of 2 or 4 was used to represent a wait at the first stoplight. Would the experiment be different if a roll of 1 or 5 was used to represent a wait? Explain why or why not.

Look Back

How could you simulate a 50% probability with a physical model? a 25% probability? a $\frac{1}{6}$ probability?

▶ Now you are ready for:
Exs. 12–25 on pp. 14–15

1-2 Exercises and Problems

1. How many trials of the experiment in the Exploration did each individual do? How many trials did each group do? Do you think that the results would have been more accurate if you had done fewer trials? more trials?

2. **Reading** Give two reasons to use simulation instead of a real-life experiment.

3. a. **History** Use the graph. About what percent of the people graduating from high school in 1900 were female?

   b. Use your answer to part (a). If you could choose 20 high school graduates at random from the high school graduates in 1900, how many females would you be likely to get?

   c. Use simulation to answer the question in part (b).

   d. Compare your answers to parts (b) and (c). Should you be surprised if the two answers are not the same? Why or why not?

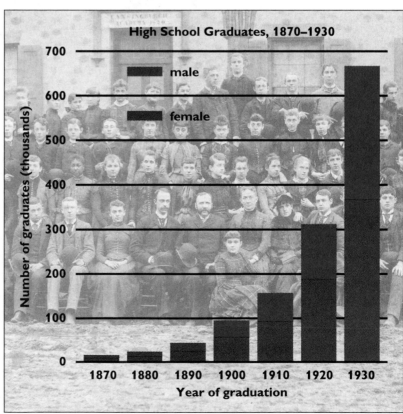

High School Graduates, 1870–1930

male

female

Number of graduates (thousands)

700
600
500
400
300
200
100
0

1870 1880 1890 1900 1910 1920 1930

Year of graduation

Traffic Safety **For Exercises 4–12, suppose that 60% of all people normally wear seat belts.**

4. **Writing** Explain how the spinner at the right could be used to simulate how many people in a sample wear seat belts.

5. Suppose you want to know how many people out of 20 are likely to wear seat belts. Would 20 trials give you enough data? Why or why not?

6. a. **Using Manipulatives** Draw a large circle with five equal sections. Use the circle and a paper clip to make a spinner as shown.

   b. Spin the pointer 10 times and tally the results. Repeat this until you have 5 samples of 10 spins each.

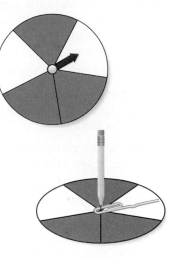

Use the results of Exercise 6 to estimate the probability of each event.

7. Exactly 6 out of 10 people normally wear seat belts.

8. Out of 10 people, 6 or fewer normally wear seat belts.

9. Approximately 50–70% of the people in a sample of 10 people normally wear seat belts.

10. All the people in a sample normally wear seat belts.

11. **Group Activity** Work with the whole class.

Combined Results of Simulation About Wearing a Seat Belt

Number of seat belt wearers in sample	0	1	2	3	4	5	6	7	8	9	10
Number of samples	?	?	?	?	?	?	?	?	?	?	?

   a. Combine your data from Exercise 6. In a table like the one above, tally the number of samples that have 0, 1, 2, 3, 4, 5, 6, 7, 8, 9, or 10 seat belt wearers.

   b. What observations can you make about the data in the table? Is there a pattern in the data?

   c. What is the greatest number of seat belt wearers in any sample?

   d. What is the least number of seat belt wearers in any sample?

   e. What is the mean of the number of seat belt wearers in the samples? Is this about what you would expect it to be? Explain why or why not.

   f. What is the given probability that a person chosen at random normally wears a seat belt? What is the experimental probability found by your class?

Student Resources Toolbox
p. 635 *Data Displays and Measures*

12. Suppose that it is equally probable that a seat belt wearer is male or female. Use a coin and the spinner from Exercise 6. Let heads represent females and tails represent males.

Coin	Spinner	Result
heads	unshaded	female, no seat belt
heads	shaded	?
tails	unshaded	?
tails	shaded	?

a. Copy and complete the table.

b. **Using Manipulatives** Do 20 trials of an experiment to predict how many people out of 20 might be female seat belt wearers.

c. Based on the given information, what is the probability that a person chosen at random will be a female seat belt wearer?

d. Compare your answers to parts (b) and (c). Should you be surprised if the two answers are not the same? Why or why not?

13. In the parking lot of a shopping mall there is a 25% probability that a driver can find a parking spot close to the entrance. There is a 100% probability of finding a space farther away.

Assume that a driver first looks for a space close to the entrance.

It takes an average of 3 min to find a parking spot close to the entrance, but only an average of 1 min to find a spot farther away.

a. Use simulation to estimate the average time needed to find a parking spot.

b. The owner of the mall wants parking spots available in less than 2 min. How often did this occur in your simulation?

14. **Research** Find out how simulators are used in training pilots, drivers, surgeons, or for another use. Describe the factors that are simulated. Give some reasons why a simulator is used instead of real-life training.

15. You are going to take a ten-question true-false test. This is an unusual test. There are no test questions and the results are based on guessing.

a. On a piece of paper, write the numbers from 1 to 10. For each question number write *True* or *False*.

b. Flip a coin to find the answer for the first question. If the result is heads, your answer is correct. If the result is tails, your answer is incorrect. Continue this way for the ten questions and write the number you have correct at the top of the paper.

c. **Group Activity** Record the results for the whole class. Make a chart or graph to show how the scores are distributed in your class.

d. Suppose that 50% is a passing score on the test. Do you think that a true-false test is a good way to see if a student understands a topic? Explain why or why not.

Start

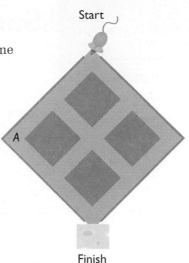

A

Finish

16. **Open-ended** A mouse goes through this maze. Assume that the mouse always heads toward the cheese. Also assume that at every intersection with a choice, the probability that the mouse will turn is equal to the probability that the mouse will go straight.

Use simulation to estimate the probability that the mouse will go through the corner marked *A* on the maze to get to the cheese. Describe your method.

Review **PREVIEW**

17. On a list of best-selling books, three out of twenty are mysteries. Estimate the number of mysteries in a catalog of 750 best-selling books. *(Section 1-1)*

Simplify. *(Toolbox Skill 10)*

18. $-x + 5y - 4x + 7$

19. $5a^2 + 8b - 4ab + 7a^2$

20. $10n - 8mn + 3mn - n$

Graph each inequality on a number line. *(Toolbox Skill 14)*

21. $x > 0$

22. $x < 2.5$

23. $x \geq -4$

24. $x \leq 4$

Working on the Unit Project

25. Suppose that 50% of the people in your school recycle newspapers and that 30% of the newspaper recyclers also recycle aluminum cans. Design a simulation to estimate about what percent of the people in your school are likely to recycle both newspapers and aluminum cans.

Sampling Methods

Focus
Learn about different ways
to select a sample.

Take Your PICK

A drama teacher plans to choose four students from the drama club to be in a publicity photo. How could the teacher choose the four students?

The teacher could put the names of all the students in a box, mix the names, and pull out four names without looking. This is an example of a random sample.

The teacher could choose the four students in the first row. This is an example of a convenience sample.

The teacher could mix the names of the girls and choose two. Then do the same for the boys. This is an example of a stratified random sample.

The teacher could choose a group of four students, such as the four students in the back left corner. This is an example of a cluster sample.

The teacher could choose every third student, beginning in the front row and counting left to right. This is an example of a systematic sample.

Types of Samples

 In a **random sample,** each member of the population has an equally likely chance of being selected. The members of the sample are chosen independently of each other.

 A sample that is chosen so that it is easy for the researcher is called a **convenience sample.**

 For a **stratified random sample,** the population is divided into subgroups, so that each population member is in only one subgroup. Then individuals are chosen randomly from each subgroup.

 A sample that consists of items in a group, such as a neighborhood or a household, is called a **cluster sample.** The group may be chosen at random. However, this is not a random sample because the items in the group are not chosen independently of each other.

 A **systematic sample** is obtained using an ordered list of the population, then selecting members systematically from the list. The point at which to start in the list is usually chosen at random.

Sample 1

The drama coach for a large high school wants to know how students feel about acting. The coach randomly chooses 100 boys and 100 girls to complete a survey.

a. Classify the sample as *random, convenience, stratified random, cluster,* or *systematic.* Explain your choice.

b. Are any groups likely to be underrepresented? If so, which ones?

Sample Response

a. Stratified random; the subgroups are *boys* and *girls*, and students are chosen randomly from within each subgroup.

b. No group is likely to be underrepresented.

Random, stratified random, and systematic samples are generally preferred since they are usually representative of the population.

A sample that overrepresents or underrepresents part of the population is called **biased.** For example, the teacher discussed on page 16 could choose the four soccer players in the drama club. This is an example of a *biased cluster sample.*

1. Kenesha Williams wants to estimate how many hours of sports each resident of her town watches on television each week. She surveyed people attending a baseball game in her town. What group is likely to be underrepresented in her sample?

2. A school district supervisor wants to know how students feel about cafeteria food. The supervisor randomly chooses a school in the district, then randomly chooses a classroom in the school, then gives a survey to the students in the classroom.

    a. What type of sample is this? Is it likely to be biased? Why or why not?

    b. Suppose the supervisor chooses 20 classrooms by this method. Is the overall sample likely to be biased? Why or why not?

3. A sports director sent an all-male team to represent the class at the Super Sports rally. The director said that this was a random sample. How is that possible?

Give an example of each type of sample.

4. systematic   5. convenience   6. cluster

▶ Now you are ready for:
Exs. 1–10 on pp. 20–21

Random Sampling

TECHNOLOGY NOTE

You can use the random number generator on a calculator to help you choose a random sample. The generator may be a second function on a scientific calculator. It may be on the MATH menu of a graphics calculator.

You can get only an estimate of how a population behaves or thinks by surveying a sample. For example, the exact percent of the population who watch a TV show could be found only by surveying every viewer.

One way you can get better and more representative results from a survey is to use larger random samples. Another way is to take a survey of several random samples rather than just one.

You do not have to pull names out of a box to select a random sample. When the population is large, it is easier to use other methods.

Sample 2

Suppose you want to give a survey about bicycle riding to 40 sophomores. You have a list of the names of the 200 sophomores in your school. Describe how to use the list to obtain a random sample.

Number the sophomores from 1 to 200.

Generate random numbers from 1 to 200, and give the survey to the students whose numbers you generate.

Method ❶ Use a calculator.

Most scientific and graphics calculators will produce a random number between 0 and 1.

➤ Produce a random number on a calculator.

➤ Multiply the number by 201 to get a number between 0 and 201.

➤ Use the integer part of the number, which will be a number from 1 to 200 if you ignore values less than 1.

➤ Give the survey to the student whose number you have generated.

➤ Repeat this process until 40 students are chosen. Ignore duplicates.

Method ❷ Use a physical model.

You could use a random number table, but a telephone book provides a good approximation of a list of random numbers if you ignore the exchanges (the first three digits).

➤ Begin as described at the left.

➤ Then give the survey to the student whose number you have chosen. Ignore numbers over 200.

➤ Continue down the column, and into the next if necessary, until 40 students are chosen. Ignore duplicates.

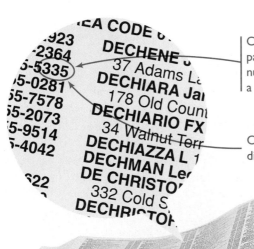

Choose a position on a page, such as the third number from the top in a middle column.

Consider the last three digits as a number.

Look Back ←

Do you think a random sample from your class could contain only girls? Do you think that this sample would represent your class as a whole? Explain why or why not.

·······➤ **Now you are ready for:**
Exs. 11–28 on pp. 21–22

1. a. **Reading** Name three different sampling methods.

   b. **Writing** Describe how the methods you listed in part (a) are alike. How are they different?

For each situation:

a. Classify each sample as *random, convenience, stratified random, cluster,* or *systematic.* Explain your choice.

b. Tell which groups, if any, are likely to be underrepresented.

2. For a sample of households, an environmental group dials the first number on every tenth page of the white pages in the telephone book.

3. A general interest magazine conducts a poll that asks teen readers questions about dating.

4. A college professor selects 100 high school students in a summer mathematics and science workshop as the sample for a study about high school students.

5. **Open-ended** A group of 30 students from your school is randomly selected to discuss future school events, such as dances. Eight of the students say they do not want to attend and are dropped from the sample.

connection to **LITERATURE**

In *The Crystal Desert*, David Campbell describes an underwater diving project in Antarctica. For the project he collected small shellfish called *amphipods*.

> Today I will descend to about fifteen meters to collect the tiny amphipods that skitter over the ocean floor and hide beneath the boulders that have been dropped by the icebergs passing overhead. ...
> I want representative samples of both diseased and healthy animals. A baited trap would attract only those amphipods with strong appetites, which are necessarily the healthy ones. A trawl net or bottom grabber would favor the slow and sick animals that couldn't escape, biasing the sample toward the unhealthy ones. So I use a simple hand-held net, purchased in a tropical fish store in New York.

6. What types of samples does David Campbell want to avoid?

7. How do you think David Campbell will proceed with the net to get a representative sample?

8. Do you think that David Campbell will be able to predict the percent of the amphipod population that is healthy from his sample?

9. **Writing** Suppose you surveyed the first 50 students who entered the school cafeteria at lunch. Would that sample be representative of all the people who use the cafeteria? Explain why or why not.

10. Which is more likely to give accurate results, a random sample of 50 students chosen from a class of 300, or a random sample of 50 students chosen from a class of 100? Why?

Use a glossary or dictionary as a population. Select 13 words to obtain each of these types of samples. Explain your method.

11. cluster sample

12. convenience sample

13. systematic sample

14. stratified random sample

15. Use a glossary as a population. Tell how you could select a random sample of 13 words from the glossary.

16. **Research** Use the stock market report in a daily newspaper. Select a random sample of 30 stocks.

17. Use the phone extensions shown or select 20 extensions randomly from a telephone book.

7679	2225	7870
0517	1121	1523
9750	1903	8262
5324	9493	2274
1466	0251	8970
0723	8458	1963
3139	4472	

a. Change each extension into an ordered pair. For example, the extension 4460 becomes the ordered pair (44, 60).

b. Graph the ordered pairs on a scatter plot.

c. Describe the scatter plot. Does it show a *positive correlation,* a *negative correlation,* or *no correlation*? Explain what type of correlation, if any, you would expect to see in the scatter plot.

Student Resources Toolbox
p. 632 *Data Displays and Measures*

d. Describe how you would expect the graph of a random sample of ordered pairs to look.

For Exercises 18–20, use the numbers −5, −4, −3, −2, −1, 0, 1, 2, 3, 4, and 5 as the population for *x*.

18. a. Solve $3x - 1 = x + 5$.

　　b. Suppose you randomly choose a number from the population. What is the probability that it is a solution of the equation in part (a)?

19. a. Solve $x^2 = 1$.

　　b. Suppose you randomly choose a number from the population. What is the probability that it is a solution of the equation in part (a)?

20. a. Solve $3x - 5 \geq -8$.

　　b. Suppose you randomly choose a number from the population. What is the probability that it is a solution of the inequality in part (a)?

21. **Research** Find out how juries are selected in your area. Are any random sampling techniques used? Is a jury selected from the entire population, or are some groups not included?

Ongoing ASSESSMENT

22. **Writing** Describe a method that you could use to find a random sample of 25 books from your school library.

Review PREVIEW

23. Suppose that one eighth of all Americans live below the poverty level. Use simulation to answer this question: If you could choose 50 Americans at random, how many would likely be below the poverty level? Describe your method. *(Section 1-2)*

Simplify. *(Toolbox Skill 10)*

24. $(-6m)(12m)$ 　　　　**25.** $(5w)(-2x)(3y)$ 　　　　**26.** $9x - 2(x + 3)$

27. A recent poll of 200 people from a town of 10,000 found that 140 people approve of the mayor's performance. The actual results could be different by up to 3% in either direction. Estimate the interval for the number of people in the town who approve of the mayor's performance. *(Section 1-1)*

Working on the Unit Project

28. Consider the survey that you wrote for Exercise 26 in Section 1-1. Choose the sample size and the type of sample that you would like to use. Explain your choices.

1-4 Cautions in Using Statistics

In Line WITH THE FACTS

Survey: Rights of Citizens

Do you think that in-line skaters should be able to move freely throughout the city?

Survey: High-Speed Dangers

Should in-line skaters be allowed to endanger the safety of pedestrians by skating on sidewalks?

Talk it Over

1. Compare the two survey questions. How are they alike? How are they different?

2. Suppose the two questions were given to two different unbiased samples of people. What results would you expect?

3. Create another version of this question. What do you think the response would be?

4. How could the question be written to avoid influencing the results?

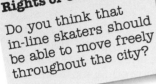

When you give a survey, asking unbiased questions is as important as choosing an unbiased sample. Even multiple-choice questions can be interpreted in different ways.

Talk it Over

Use the survey questions below.

5. Which set of choices is less precise? Why?

6. a. Could you find the mode of the answers to the question on the left? the mean? the median?

   b. Could you find the mode of the answers to the question on the right? the mean? the median?

How many days per week should in-line skaters be allowed to skate on the street?	How many days per week should in-line skaters be allowed to skate on the street?
a) every day b) some days c) not very many days d) no days	a) zero e) four b) one f) five c) two g) six d) three h) seven

X Lab

CAUTIONS IN USING STATISTICS

These are some important factors to consider about surveys:

➤ how the questions are worded

➤ how the survey is distributed

➤ how the responses are collected

➤ how the results are presented

➤ how the results are interpreted

The managing editor of a fashion magazine wants to find out what parts of the magazine people like to read. The editor sends a survey to 800 subscribers. Three weeks later, 68 surveys have been returned.

Writing Describe some problems with this method of surveying.

Sample Response

By using only the subscribers as the population, the director will not find out what people who buy the magazine in stores think. Also, the sample contains only people who were interested enough to return the surveys, so people who have strong opinions or who have more time to read may be overrepresented.

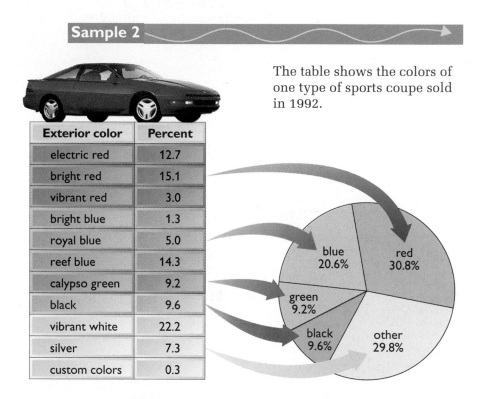

The table shows the colors of one type of sports coupe sold in 1992.

Exterior color	Percent
electric red	12.7
bright red	15.1
vibrant red	3.0
bright blue	1.3
royal blue	5.0
reef blue	14.3
calypso green	9.2
black	9.6
vibrant white	22.2
silver	7.3
custom colors	0.3

The circle graph was used in a report of the data. Do you think that the graph presents a misleading picture of the data? Why or why not?

Sample Response

Yes. The graph leads you to think that blue may be the second most popular color of this model. The category called "Other" hides information that may give a different impression of the data.

Look Back ◀─────────────

When you use data from a survey, you need to consider what might have influenced the results. Here are some questions to ask.

➤ How was the sample chosen?

➤ What was the population?

➤ What was the sample size?

In your own words, what are three more questions that you might have about a survey?

1-4 Exercises and Problems

For Exercises 1–6, use this survey.

1. Decide whether each question is worded so that it will not influence the response.

2. Could you find the median of the answers to the first question? to any of the questions?

3. Write at least four more questions that will help you find out if students are satisfied with your school. Make sure that your questions are worded so that they will not influence the results.

4. **a.** Decide how to choose a sample of people in your school and how you will give them the survey. Describe the method you chose.

   b. **Research** If possible, give the survey to the sample of people you have chosen.

5. What biases might be reflected in the results of the survey?

6. Suppose you give the survey during a final exam week. Explain how this might influence the results.

School Satisfaction Survey
(Please circle the appropriate response.)

1) How long have you been enrolled in this school district?
   a) since I started school
   c) 2–3 years
   b) This is my first year.
   d) 4 or more years

2) How many times have you been tardy to your classes this week?
   a) 0
   c) 2–3
   b) 1
   d) 4 or more

3) How many hours did you spend on homework during the last week?
   a) less than 1
   c) between 2 and 3
   b) from 1 to 2
   d) 3 or more

4) How satisfied are you with the choices of classes available to you?
   a) All the classes I want are available.
   b) Most of the time I am satisfied with the classes available.
   c) There are many classes I would like to take, but cannot get into.
   d) There are not enough _____classes.
       (Write the type of class in the blank.)

7. **Reading** Describe how the wording of a survey question can lead to a biased sample. Give an example.

8. **Open-ended** Do you think it matters whether a survey is given in person, over the phone, or in written form? Which kind of survey would you prefer to take? Which kind of survey would you prefer to give? Explain.

Writing For Exercises 9–12, describe some problems with each method of surveying. Then write one question that you would like to ask the people who gave the survey.

9. **Market Research** A marketing firm selects a sample for a survey on toothpaste by calling numbers randomly chosen from a telephone book. People who do not want to participate are listed as "no opinion."

10. A teen magazine conducts a survey about the presidential candidates for the next election. The Republican and Democratic candidates are listed along with several popular singers and actors. More than 25,000 people respond to the survey.

11. Television rating sheets are sent to 10,000 viewers four times a year. At the end of a ten-week period, about 30-50% of the viewing diaries are returned and the results are studied.

12. A radio station surveys its audience by asking people to call the station between 9 A.M. and noon on a weekday.

13. **Basketball** The table shows the salaries of the players on a professional basketball team. Do you think that the graph presents a misleading picture of the data? Why or why not?

Annual Salaries (thousands of dollars)		
	A	**B**	**C**
1	360	1000	2260
2	225	915	2000
3	215	850	2000
4	120	650	
5	50		
6	50		

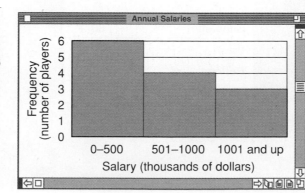

14. Sam has to graph the equation $y = x^2$ for his homework. He makes this table and draws this graph.

   a. Explain why Sam's graph is not accurate.

   b. Describe Sam's mistake in terms of what you know about sampling.

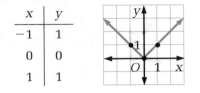

x	y
−1	1
0	0
1	1

15. **Research** Find an example of a study whose results could be interpreted in more than one way. Describe possible biases or sampling errors in the study. Give an example of a different conclusion that could be drawn from the study.

16. The table below shows the total number of bicycles in eight countries.

   a. Create a graph that gives a misleading picture of the data.

   b. Explain how your graph is misleading.

   c. **Research** Find the population of each country in the table in 1992. How many bicycles did each country have per person?

Bicycles Owned in 1992	
Country	Number of bicycles in millions
China	450
India	200
United States	120
Japan	73
Germany	60
Brazil	20
Holland	15
United Kingdom	15

17. **Group Activity** Work with another student.

a. Each person should write a four-question survey on music likes and dislikes. You may want
to look at music magazines for ideas. Then write
a short description of how you could give the
survey to a sample of students in your school.

b. Exchange surveys and descriptions and read
each other's work. Discuss any factors that may
influence the results of the survey.

c. Use your surveys to create eight questions that
will not influence the results of the survey. Decide how you can give the survey to the sample.

d. If possible, give the survey to the sample and present the results in a
table or graph.

e. After reviewing the results, describe what you would change in your
questions or method.

········
Review PREVIEW

18. To give a survey to a grocery store's customers, the store manager randomly chooses one section of one aisle of the store and asks each person who
buys something in that section to complete the survey. What type of
sampling is this? *(Section 1-3)*

Find the missing length in each right triangle. *(Toolbox Skill 31)*

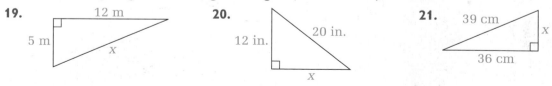

19.
12 m

5 m
x

20.
20 in.

12 in.

x

21.
39 cm
x

36 cm

Decide which of the given numbers are solutions of each inequality.
(Toolbox Skill 14)

22. $12x + 4 \geq 10$;   0.25, 0.5, 1.75

23. $-3y - 14 < 4$; $-7, -6, 0$

········

Working on the Unit Project

24. Consider the survey that you wrote for Exercise 26 in Section 1-1. Might
any of the questions you wrote influence the results of the survey? If so,
rewrite the questions.

25. Consider the sample size and the type of sample that you chose for
Exercise 28 in Section 1-3. Do you think your sample will give an
accurate representation of the student population? If not, choose a larger
or better type of sample.

26. Select the students to include in your sample. Give them your survey.

1. **Writing** Suppose you want to convince your cafeteria manager to add a certain food to the cafeteria menu. How could you use a survey to convince the manager? What questions might be on the survey? Describe a sampling technique you could use.

2. At Huron High School, 45 of 180 students chosen at random play sports. There are 760 students in the entire school. Estimate the total number of students who play sports.

     1-1

3. In a recent election, two thirds of the voters were at least 60 years old. Describe two different ways to simulate the percent of voters under 60.

     1-2

For Exercises 4 and 5, classify the sample selected in each situation as *random, convenience, stratified random, cluster,* **or** *systematic.*

     1-3

4. To win a door prize at a dance, each of the 170 students attending the dance writes his or her name on a piece of paper. The pieces are put in a box, mixed, and one name is drawn.

5. The owner of a sandwich shop studies sales of food sold between 1 P.M. and 2 P.M. and food sold between 6 P.M. and 7 P.M.

6. Before ordering new cake pans, the owner of a bakery surveys customers to find out whether circular or rectangular cakes are preferred at weddings. Here are two questions on the survey.

     1-4

Which shape is more appealing?	Which shape tastes better?
a) circular, because it is traditional	a) circular, because each piece will have more frosting
b) rectangular, because the decorators can be more creative	b) rectangular, because some pieces will have extra frosting

    a. Explain why the questions are biased.

    b. Rewrite each question so it is not biased.

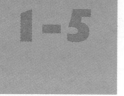
Inductive Reasoning

Focus

Apply inductive reasoning to many situations. Learn that inductive reasoning does not always lead to a good conclusion.

Base It On
EXPERIENCE

Rosario looked in the mirror one morning and noticed a rash on her face. It occurred to her that she might be allergic to a new facial soap she had used the night before, but then she noticed the rash on her legs as well. She decided to go see her doctor.

BY THE WAY...

In 1990, Dr. Antonia Novello became the first woman and the first Hispanic to hold the position of Surgeon General. She chose a career in medicine after struggling with a serious health problem throughout her childhood and into her early twenties.

Dr. Gutierrez asked Rosario some questions, looked at her rash, and decided that Rosario was allergic to penicillin. Dr. Gutierrez made observations and used past experience to reach this diagnosis.

In mathematics, a guess based on past experience is called a **conjecture.** When you make a conjecture based on several observations, you are using **inductive reasoning.**

Inductive reasoning is used in other careers besides medicine. A mechanic could use inductive reasoning when repairing cars. A store owner uses inductive reasoning when deciding what to reorder based on what has sold well in the past.

Inductive reasoning is often used to solve problems in mathematics.

Sample 1

Writing **Do you think the sum of any two odd numbers is even or odd? Explain your reasoning.**

Sample Response

Problem Solving Strategy: Use inductive reasoning.

Aaron Freed

Question: Is the sum of two odd numbers even or odd?

Method: I made a table with sums of odd numbers and looked for a pattern.

Odd	Odd	Sum	Odd or Even
1	3	4	even
35	35	70	even
101	321	422	even
−155	173	18	even
−3001	−1077	−4078	even
3,400,879	10,657	3,411,536	even

I used a calculator to try negatives and large numbers.

I always got an even sum.

Conjecture: I tried many pairs of odd numbers and the sum was never odd. I think that the sum of two odd numbers is always even.

Talk it Over

1. In Sample 1, does inductive reasoning show that the sum of two odd numbers is always even? Explain.
2. Do you think the sum of any three odd numbers is *even* or *odd*? Explain your reasoning.

Sample 2

Make a conjecture about a relationship among the exterior angles of a polygon.

Problem Solving Strategy: Use inductive reasoning.

Draw several polygons. Measure the exterior angles and make a table.

An **exterior angle** of a polygon is an angle formed by extending a side of the polygon.

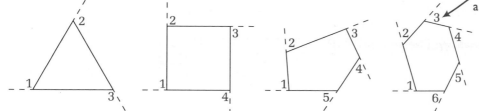

What do you know about angle measure relationships? You know that the measures of the interior angles of a triangle have a *sum* of 180°. Maybe there is a relationship among the sums of the external angle measures. Include a sum column in your table.

Polygon	∠1	∠2	∠3	∠4	∠5	∠6	Sum
triangle	120°	120°	120°	—	—	—	360°
square	90°	90°	90°	90°	—	—	360°
pentagon	85°	75°	85°	55°	60°	—	360°
hexagon	75°	60°	60°	60°	40°	65°	360°

Conjecture: The sum of the measures of the exterior angles of a polygon is 360°.

Talk it Over

3. Is it a good idea to test only regular polygons when you are making a conjecture? Why or why not? (*Note:* In a regular polygon, all the sides are the same length and all the angles are equal in measure.)

4. Is the conjecture in Sample 2 true for interior angles? Why or why not?

Shortcomings of Inductive Reasoning

Movie executives sometimes use inductive reasoning. Based on past experience, they predict which movies will be popular in the future. They are not always correct. For example, the sequel of a hit movie is not always as popular as the original.

You cannot *prove* that a conjecture is true just by using inductive reasoning. For example, in Samples 1 and 2 it would be impossible to test all the possibilities. However, you can *disprove* a conjecture by finding any example that does *not* work, a **counterexample.**

Tell whether you think the inequality $x \leq x^2$ is *True* or *False*. If you think it is false, give a counterexample.

Sample Response

Problem Solving Strategy: Use a table.

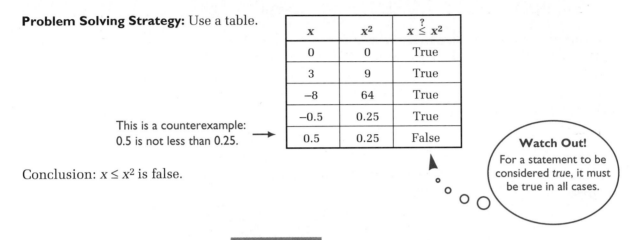

x	x^2	$x \overset{?}{\leq} x^2$
0	0	True
3	9	True
−8	64	True
−0.5	0.25	True
0.5	0.25	False

This is a counterexample:
0.5 is not less than 0.25.

Conclusion: $x \leq x^2$ is false.

Watch Out!
For a statement to be considered *true*, it must be true in all cases.

Talk it Over

5. How many counterexamples are needed to disprove a conjecture?

6. Suppose you are using inductive reasoning to make a conjecture about triangles. What types of triangles should you test to check your conjecture?

7. Tell whether you think the inequality $|x| > x$ is *True* or *False*. If it is false, give a counterexample.

Look Back

Can you use inductive reasoning to show that a conjecture is *always* true? *sometimes* true? *never* true? Why or why not?

1-5 Exercises and Problems

1. **Reading** What kinds of numbers should you test to support a conjecture about an algebraic statement?

Open-ended For Exercises 2 and 3, make a conjecture about each situation.

2. When Sarah visited Michelle, she played with Michelle's cat. After a while, Sarah's eyes began to itch and water. The next week Sarah visited another friend who also had a cat. On her way home, Sarah noticed that her eyes were very itchy and watery. Two days later, the neighbor's cat came and rubbed against Sarah. Again, her eyes began to itch and water.

3. In the cartoon Shing is wondering why he has been called to the principal's office. Should he be worried? Why or why not?

4. Julia was walking down a hallway in her school. She noticed that a boy was seated in the chair closest to the door in each of the five classrooms that she passed. She made this conjecture.

   "In each classroom a boy is seated in the chair closest to the door."

   a. Is her conjecture an example of inductive reasoning? Explain.

   b. Do you think her conjecture is correct for the rest of the classrooms in the school? Why or why not?

5. When Marvin turned 25 years old, he bought a new red car. He had never gotten a speeding ticket before that time. During the first six months after buying the car, he got three speeding tickets.

   a. What conjecture might Marvin make about red cars?

   b. Are the officers who issued the tickets likely to make the same conjecture? Why or why not?

   c. What observations might Marvin make to test his conjecture?

   d. What about Marvin's behavior could have changed after he bought the car?

   e. Do you think your conjecture in part (a) is valid? Why or why not?

Predict the next number in each pattern.

6. 4, 12, 36, 108, _?_ 324

7. 1, 1, 2, 3, 5, 8, 13, _?_ 21

8. $1 = 1^2$
   $1 + 3 = 2^2$
   $1 + 3 + 5 = 3^2$
   $1 + 3 + 5 + 7 = $ _?_ 4^2

9. $1 \cdot 11 = 11$
   $11 \cdot 11 = 121$
   $111 \cdot 111 = 12321$
   $1111 \cdot 1111 = $ _?_ 1234321

10. On a test, Morgan Philips asked her students to tell whether the diagonals of a quadrilateral are *always*, *sometimes*, or *never* equal in length. Here is a wrong answer that she received.

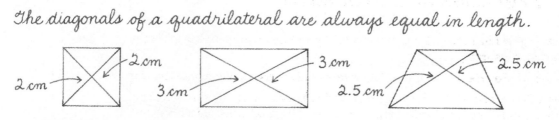

The diagonals of a quadrilateral are always equal in length.

   a. What other kinds of quadrilaterals might the student have tested?

   b. What advice might you give the student?

11. **Writing** Do you think the product of any two odd numbers is *even* or *odd*? Explain.

12. **Writing** Suppose you extend a ray that bisects an angle of a triangle so that it passes through the opposite side. Do you think it will bisect the opposite side? Explain your reasoning.

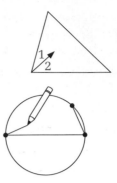

13. Suppose you draw a triangle with its vertices on a circle and with one side that is a diameter of the circle. Make a conjecture about the angle opposite the diameter.

14. Make a conjecture about the value of the product of any two numbers between 0 and 1.

For Exercises 15–18, tell whether you think each statement is *True* or *False*. If you think it is false, give a counterexample.

15. $-x < x$ False

16. $x \geq \dfrac{1}{x}$

17. $2(x + 3) > 2x + 1$ True

18. For any whole number n, $n^2 + n + 11$ is a prime number.

19. **Group Activity** Work with another student to explore the sum of the angle measures of a polygon. Each of you should use a different one of the two methods shown and try a few different polygons. How do the methods compare? What do you think is the formula for the sum of the angle measures of a polygon?

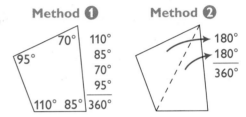

There was a cholera epidemic in London in 1854. Dr. John Snow made a map to study the epidemic. Using the map and inductive reasoning, he was able to find the cause of the epidemic and take steps to end it.

For Exercises 20–23, use the map.

20. What do the dots on the map represent?
    Deaths from cholera

21. How many water pumps are shown on the map?   Eleven

22. Based on the map, what do you think might have been the cause of the epidemic?
    something with the water and people

23. What do you think Dr. Snow did in order to end the epidemic?
    Cleaned water and/or added more water pumps

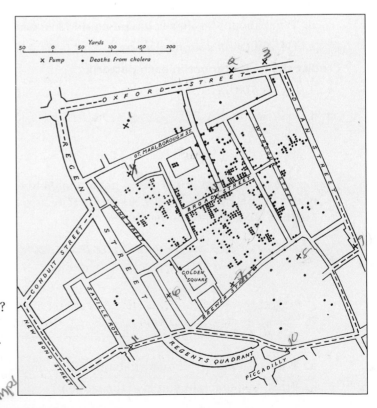

24. TECHNOLOGY Use a graphics calculator or graphing software.

Alternative Approach Use graph paper. Make a table of values and draw the graphs as indicated in part (a). Cover up all but the first quadrant for part (d).

Student Resources Toolbox
p. 649 *Graphs, Equations, and Inequalities*

a. Graph $y = -x + 2$ and $y = x^2$ together on the same axes. Use this viewing window: $-10 \le x \le 10$ and $-10 \le y \le 10$.

b. What is the shape of each graph?

c. Do the graphs intersect? If so, where?

d. Use a new viewing window: $0 \le x \le 10$ and $0 \le y \le 10$. How does this affect what appears on the graph?

e. What false conjecture might someone make by looking only at the viewing window used in part (d)?

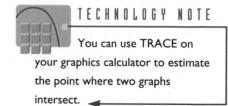

TECHNOLOGY NOTE

You can use TRACE on your graphics calculator to estimate the point where two graphs intersect.

Ongoing ASSESSMENT

25. **Group Activity** Work with another student.

a. Each of you should make two conjectures, one about even and odd numbers and another about equilateral triangles.

b. Use inductive reasoning to test each other's conjectures.

Review PREVIEW

26. A school tries to find out what parents think about school dances by calling the homes of students chosen at random. All the calls are made between 11 A.M. and 1 P.M. Describe a problem with this method of surveying. *(Section 1-4)*

Identify the dependent variable and the control variable in each situation. *(Toolbox Skill 19)*

27. Evy is writing his final essay for English class. The longer the test, the more paper he uses.

28. If she is making breakfast for all the people in her family, Dania uses more eggs.

Use the distributive property to complete each __?__. *(Toolbox Skill 10)*

29. __?__ $(m + n + 1) = 2m + 2n + 2$ **30.** __?__ $(2a - 3b + 1) = 10a - 15b + 5$

Working on the Unit Project

31. **Research** You will need rubber gloves and a trash bag. Take a sample of the trash in one classroom. Can you use it to predict the amount of trash produced by the entire school in one day? Explain why or why not.

32. Use the results of your survey or some additional sampling to estimate the amount of materials students in your school reuse, recycle, or throw away each day.

Deductive Reasoning

Play by the Rules ✓

·······Focus

Write if-then statements in
other ways and draw simple
conclusions from them.
Learn the difference
between inductive and
deductive reasoning. Apply
deductive reasoning to
many situations.

EXPLORATION

How can you use your class to visualize if-then statements?

- **Divide the class into four teams.**

(1) In your team, decide on two rules for grouping the students in your class. Write your rules in this form.

If ..., then you are in Group A.
If ..., then you are in Group B.

(2) Are any students in your class in both groups? If so, how many?

(3) Are any students in your class in neither group? If so, how many?

(4) The diagrams shown are **Venn diagrams.** They are used to show relationships between groups. Decide which Venn diagram can be used to illustrate your rules and make a large copy of it.

(5) Take turns with the other teams in your class. Have your classmates stand up. Without telling your team's rules, arrange your classmates into Groups A and B. Write each student's name on your Venn diagram. Have the other teams try to guess your rules.

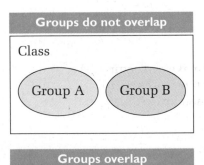

Groups do not overlap

Class

Group A   Group B

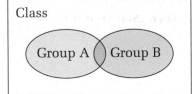

Groups overlap

Class

Group A   Group B

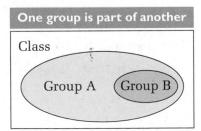

One group is part of another

Class

Group A   Group B

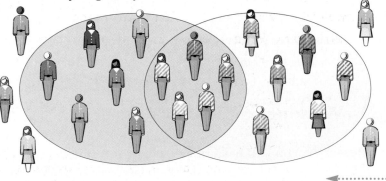

In the Exploration, you used *deductive reasoning* to decide which students belonged in each group. **Deductive reasoning** involves using facts, definitions, logic, and accepted rules and properties to reach conclusions.

Use the Venn diagram to tell whether each statement about the students in the class is *True* or *False*.

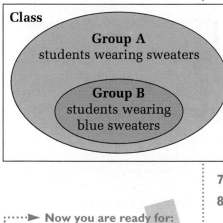

Class

Group A
students wearing sweaters

Group B
students wearing
blue sweaters

1. Janice is wearing a blue sweater. Janice is in Group B.
2. Lyle is wearing a blue sweater. Lyle is in Group A.
3. If a student is wearing a sweater, then the student is wearing a blue sweater.
4. If a student is not wearing a sweater, then the student is not wearing a blue sweater.
5. If a student is not wearing a blue sweater, then the student is not wearing a sweater.
6. Reword the statement in question 4 using the word *all*.
7. Reword the statement in question 4 using the word *every*.
8. The **converse** of an if-then statement is formed by interchanging the "if" and "then" parts. Which statements are converses of each other in questions 3–5?

▶ Now you are ready for:
Exs. 1–20 on pp. 41–42

Inductive versus Deductive

You use *inductive* reasoning to make conjectures based on a sample of cases. You use *deductive* reasoning to show that statements are true based on general rules.

Sample 1

Show that if two integers are odd, then their sum is even.

Sample Response

Problem Solving Strategy: Use deductive reasoning.

Step 1 Write variable expressions for any two odd integers.

Let m and n be any integers.

Then $2m$ is even and $2n$ is even. ← Any integer that is 2 times another integer is even.

So, $2m + 1$ is odd and $2n + 1$ is odd. ← Any integer that is 1 more than an even integer is odd.

Step 2 Add the two odd integers.

$(2m + 1) + (2n + 1) = 2m + 2n + 2$

$= 2(m + n + 1)$ ← Use the distributive property.

Step 3 Interpret the result.

$2(m + n + 1)$ is 2 times another integer, so it is even. Therefore the sum of any two odd integers is even.

Talk it Over

9. Suppose a and b represent integers.

    a. How can you show that $2a + 4b + 6$ represents an even integer?

    b. How can you show that $2a + 4b + 7$ represents an odd integer?

In Sample 2 of Section 1-5 on pages 32–33, you saw how inductive reasoning was used to make a conjecture about the exterior angles of a polygon. Here you will see that the conjecture is true based on deductive reasoning.

Sample 2

Show that the sum of the exterior angle measures of any polygon is 360°.

Sample Response

Problem Solving Strategy: Use deductive reasoning.

Step 1 Think about what facts you know about the angles of a polygon.

You saw in Exercise 19 on page 36 that the sum of the *interior* angle measures of a polygon is $180(n - 2)$, where n is the number of sides.

Step 2 See if there is a relationship between interior and exterior angle measures of a polygon. Use a diagram.

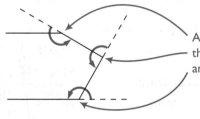

At each vertex, the sum of the interior and exterior angle measures is 180°.

There are n vertices in an n-gon. The sum of all the angle measures, interior plus exterior, is 180n.

Step 3 Subtract the interior angle measures from the sum of all the angle measures.

$$\text{Sum of exterior angle measures} = 180n - 180(n - 2)$$
$$= 180n - 180n + 360$$
$$= 360$$

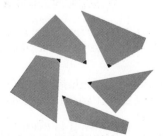
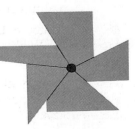

Look Back

In Sample 2 of Section 1-5 on pages 32–33, you saw how inductive reasoning was used to make a conjecture about the sum of the exterior angle measures of a polygon. In Sample 2 of this section, you saw how deductive reasoning was used to show that the sum is always 360°. Compare the reasoning in the two cases.

▶ Now you are ready for:
Exs. 21–44 on pp. 43–44

1-6 Exercises and Problems

1. Use the two rules your group wrote for the Exploration on page 38.
   a. Rewrite each rule using the word *all*.
   b. Rewrite each rule using the word *every*.
   c. Write the converse of each rule.

The Venn diagram shows how students responded to a survey about using after-school time on five specific activities. For Exercises 2–9, tell whether each statement about the students in the survey is *True* or *False*.

2. All students listen to music.

3. Some students watch TV.

4. If a student works at a job, then the student watches TV.

5. If a student watches TV, then the student does volunteer work.

6. Every student who watches movies watches TV.

7. Some students who watch movies do volunteer work.

8. Some students who do volunteer work also work at a job.

9. All students who do not watch TV do not do volunteer work.

10. Pick three statements from Exercises 2–9. Write the converse of each statement. Tell whether the converse is *True* or *False* about the students in the survey.

11. Write one statement about the Venn diagram that is true about *all* students, a second statement that is true about *some* students, and a third statement that is true for *no* students.

12. Draw a Venn diagram that shows the relationships among these groups: triangles, geometric figures, polygons, and three-dimensional figures.

13 TECHNOLOGY Use a graphics calculator or graphing software.

Alternative Approach Work in a group of three students. Make tables and use graph paper. Each student should graph two different equations in part (a).

a. Graph each equation.

$$y = 3x - 4 \qquad y = x^2 \qquad y = -2x + 5$$
$$y = 3x^2 \qquad y = -5x \qquad y = x - 3$$

b. How could you group the equations in part (a) according to your graphs? Make a Venn diagram that shows your groupings. Label each loop with the name of its group.

c. Write two if-then statements that are true based on your diagram.

Career Emergency medical technicians (EMTs) follow established procedures when they respond to emergencies. A procedure is shown for responding to someone who has had exposure to the cold.

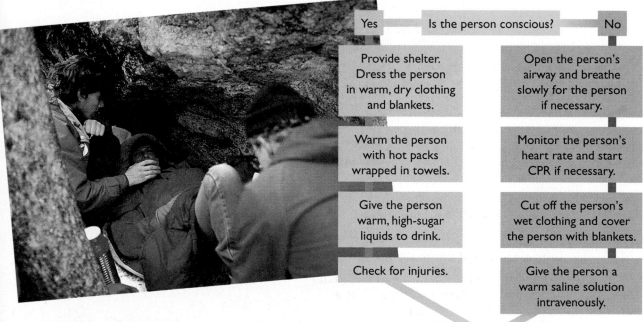

Yes — Is the person conscious? — No

Provide shelter. Dress the person in warm, dry clothing and blankets.	Open the person's airway and breathe slowly for the person if necessary.
Warm the person with hot packs wrapped in towels.	Monitor the person's heart rate and start CPR if necessary.
Give the person warm, high-sugar liquids to drink.	Cut off the person's wet clothing and cover the person with blankets.
Check for injuries.	Give the person a warm saline solution intravenously.

GO TO THE HOSPITAL.

14. What is the first thing an EMT should check about a person who has had exposure to the cold?

15. What should an EMT do first if a person exposed to the cold is not conscious?

16. What are the two things an EMT should do for a person exposed to the cold whether or not the person is conscious?

For Exercises 17–20, use deductive reasoning to reach a conclusion.

17. Rachel is older than Michelle and Hector is younger than Michelle.

18. If a person is in Sacramento, then that person is in California. If a person is in California, then that person is in the United States.

19. If the base angles of a triangle are equal in measure, then the triangle is isosceles. If the triangle is isosceles, then the sides opposite the base angles are equal in measure.

20. $x = 3 + 2$ and $3 + 2 = 5$

21. **Reading** Suppose x represents an integer.

    a. Do you know whether x is even or odd? If so, which is it?

    b. Do you know whether $2x$ is even or odd? If so, which is it?

    c. Do you know whether $2x + 1$ is even or odd? If so, which is it?

Replace each ? with a phrase that makes a true statement.
(Note: You may have to first decide whether the converse is true.)

22. If Alta Perez is at school, then she will teach mathematics third period. Alta Perez is at school. Therefore, ? .

23. If it is raining, then physical education class will be held indoors. It is raining. Therefore, ? .

24. If a quadrilateral is a square, then its sides are equal in measure. In quadrilateral $ABCD$, $AB \neq CD$. Therefore, ? .

25. All isosceles triangles have at least two sides equal in measure. No two sides of $\triangle PQR$ are equal in measure. Therefore, ? .

26. If $3x + 5 = 14$, then $x = 3$. But, $x \neq 3$. Therefore, ? .

27. If $5x - 7 > -17$, then $x > -2$. But, $x \leq -2$. Therefore, ? .

28. If a triangle is equilateral, then all three sides are equal in measure. The three sides of $\triangle ABC$ are equal in measure. Therefore, ? .

29. If a quadrilateral is a rectangle, then its four angles are right angles. The angles of quadrilateral $MNOP$ are right angles. Therefore, ? .

Use deductive reasoning to show that each statement is true.

30. The difference of two odd numbers is even.

31. The product of two odd numbers is odd.

Student Resources Toolbox
p. 641 *Algebraic Expressions*

32. The product of an odd and an even number is even.

33. Vertical angles are equal in measure.

34. The sum of the measures of the acute angles of a right triangle is 90°.

35. **Literature** An old Sufi tale tells about an elephant that is put on exhibit in a darkened room. Those who go to the exhibit must rely on touch to describe the elephant.

    a. Tell whether each conclusion was reasonable based upon the observations. Write *Yes* or *No*.

    b. How might the observers have worked together to give a more consistent description?

    c. **Writing** Write a moral for this story using ideas and vocabulary from this unit.

A. water spout B. fan
C. pillar   D. throne

43

36. **Group Activity** Work with another student.

   a. Work together to solve this puzzle using deductive reasoning.

   Hana is thinking of a number. If you subtract the number of quarters in a dollar from the number, multiply by the number of days in a week, and add the number of weeks in a year, then the result is 17. What is the number?

   b. Each student should write a number puzzle like the one in part (a).

   c. Use deductive reasoning to solve each other's puzzle.

Review **PREVIEW**

37. Do you think that the inequality $-x \leq x^2$ is true? Use inductive reasoning to support your answer. *(Section 1-5)*

Identify each type of space figure and find its surface area. *(Toolbox Skill 28)*

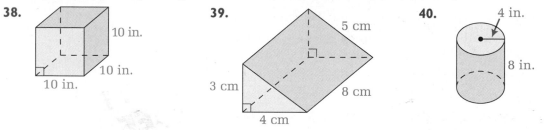

38.

10 in.
10 in.
10 in.

39.

5 cm
3 cm
8 cm
4 cm

40.

4 in.
8 in.

For Exercises 41–43: *(Toolbox Skills 21, 23, and 24)*

a. **Find the slope and the vertical intercept of each graph.**

b. **Write an equation for each line.**

41.

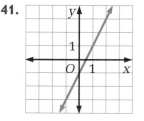

42.

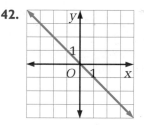

43.

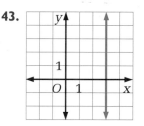

 Working on the Unit Project

44. What conclusions can you reach from the results of your recycling survey? Are you using *inductive* or *deductive* reasoning when you reach those conclusions? Explain.

Errors in Reasoning

········Focus

**Recognize errors in
mathematical and logical
reasoning.**

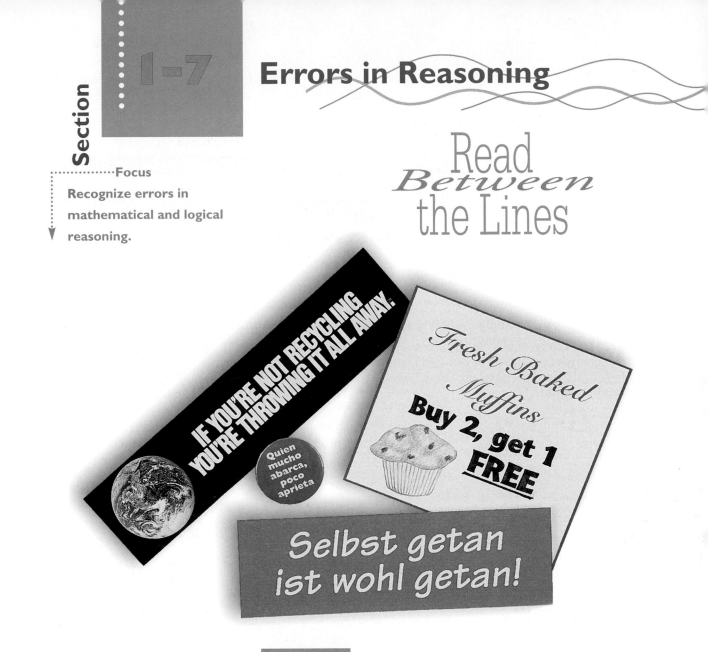

IF YOU'RE NOT RECYCLING,
YOU'RE THROWING IT ALL AWAY.

Quien mucho abarca, poco aprieta

Fresh Baked
Muffins
**Buy 2, get 1
FREE**

*Selbst getan
ist wohl getan!*

Talk it Over

1. Which statement means "If you wish a thing done well, do it yourself"? Which means "If you overextend yourself, you will accomplish little"?

2. What does the "it" refer to on the recycling bumper sticker? What conclusion might you draw from the bumper sticker?

3. Suppose the statement "If you buy two of something, then you get another one free" is true. Is the converse of this statement true? Why or why not?

4. Give an example of a false statement that has a true converse.

One common error in reasoning is to assume that the converse of a true statement is also true. It is a good idea to look at the converse and see if you can think of a counterexample.

Sample 1

If two triangles are congruent, then the corresponding angles are equal in measure.

a. Write the converse of this statement.

b. Is the converse true? Why or why not?

Sample Response

a. If the corresponding angles of two triangles are equal in measure, then the triangles are congruent.

b. The converse is not always true. It is only true when the corresponding sides of the triangles have the same length. A picture can show a counterexample.

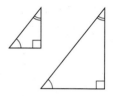

When you solve an equation, your steps are supported by valid mathematical reasoning. If one of your steps is invalid, you may reach an incorrect solution. An example of an invalid step is to divide by zero. Division by zero is *undefined*.

Sample 2

Writing Amalia and Cassandra used two different methods to solve $2x - 4 = 3x - 6$. One student reached an invalid conclusion. Which conclusion is wrong? Which step leads to the invalid conclusion?

Amalia's Method

$$2x - 4 = 3x - 6$$
$$2x - 4 + 6 = 3x - 6 + 6$$
$$2x + 2 = 3x$$
$$2x + 2 - 2x = 3x - 2x$$
$$2 = x$$

Conclusion: The solution is 2.

Cassandra's Method

$$2x - 4 = 3x - 6$$
$$2(x - 2) = 3(x - 2)$$
$$\frac{2(x - 2)}{x - 2} = \frac{3(x - 2)}{x - 2}$$
$$2 = 3$$

Conclusion: The equation has no solution.

Cassandra's conclusion is wrong.

When Cassandra divided both sides of the equation by $x - 2$, she made the assumption that $x - 2$ was not 0. Before she can conclude that the equation has no solution, Cassandra needs to see whether the original equation has a solution when $x - 2 = 0$.

The statement $x - 2 = 0$ is true when $x = 2$. If Cassandra substitutes 2 for x in the original equation, the statement is true. The correct solution is 2.

Talk it Over

5. Substitute 2 for x in the original equation of Sample 2. What is the true statement you get?

6. The information in the graph is used to make a prediction about the future finances of FirstGene Labs. Nathan and Gavin each made a prediction.

FirstGene Labs Accounting Report

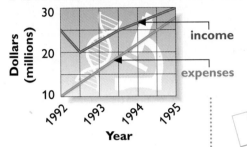

income

expenses

Nathan's Prediction:
The future for this company is very good. The company made $5 million more in 1995 than it did in 1992. Its income continues to increase steadily.

Gavin's Prediction:
This business is heading for bankruptcy! The company's expenses are rising faster than its income. By 1996 the company will be spending more than it earns.

a. Which prediction do you think is more likely to be correct? Why?

b. A company's profit is its income minus its expenses. In what year did FirstGene Labs have the biggest profit? the smallest profit?

c. Based on your answers to part (b), which student's prediction do you support?

Look Back

Darcy reads that if a figure is a square, then it is a quadrilateral. What is the converse of this statement? Is the converse true? Why or why not?

1. **Reading** In *Talk it Over* question 6, both students used the same graph to arrive at different conclusions. What information from the graph did Nathan use to make his prediction? What information from the graph did Gavin use?

For Exercises 2–7:

a. **Tell whether each statement is *True* or *False*. If it is false, give a counterexample.**

b. **Write the converse of each statement.**

c. **Tell whether the converse of each statement is *True* or *False*. If it is false, give a counterexample.**

2. If you live in California, then you live on the west coast.

3. If $|n| > 0$, then $n > 0$ for all n.

4. If $x > 0$, then $x^2 > 0$ for all x.

5. If two sides of a triangle are congruent, then the triangle is isosceles.

6. If the sum of two angles of a triangle is $90°$, then the triangle is a right triangle.

7. If a figure is a square, then it has four equal sides.

For Exercises 8–10, tell whether each conclusion is valid. Write *Yes* or *No*. If not, give a counterexample.

8. If Sejal runs under 3 min, then she will win the race. Sejal won the race. Conclusion: She ran under 3 min.

9. If the girls' basketball team wins Friday's game, then they will be in the championships. The girls' basketball team is in the championships. Conclusion: They won Friday's game.

10. If Liu answers the phone, then she is home. Liu is home. Conclusion: She answers the phone.

11. Lewis tries to convince his friend that $1 = 2$. He uses the steps below to show his reasoning. Explain the error in his reasoning.

Think about two equal positive numbers a and b. You can write $a = b$.

$$a = b$$
$$ab = b^2 \qquad \longleftarrow \text{Multiply both sides by } b.$$
$$ab - a^2 = b^2 - a^2 \qquad \longleftarrow \text{Subtract } a^2 \text{ from both sides.}$$
$$a(b - a) = (b + a)(b - a) \qquad \longleftarrow \text{Factor each side.}$$
$$a = (b + a) \qquad \longleftarrow \text{Divide both sides by } (b - a).$$
$$a = (a + a) \qquad \longleftarrow \text{Since } a = b, \text{ substitute } a \text{ for } b.$$
$$a = 2a$$
$$\frac{a}{a} = \frac{2a}{a} \qquad \longleftarrow \text{Divide both sides by } a.$$
$$1 = 2$$

12. **a. Research** Find an advertisement for cigarettes. What is the Surgeon General's warning?

   b. What type of images and people appear? Are the visual image and the written message contradictory? If so, how?

   c. Which image do you think the advertiser expects people to notice? How effective is the advertiser in promoting the product?

   d. Why do you think the advertisement may lead people to draw an incorrect conclusion?

13. **Research** Find an article about the effects of cigarette smoking on a person's health. Write about the main ideas of the article. Present some of the information in a graph.

For Exercises 14–18, use the three graphs.

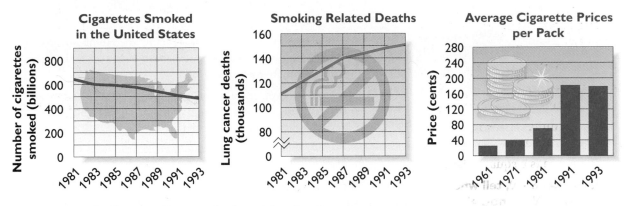

14. How might the two line graphs be misleading?

15. Give an example of an incorrect conclusion that someone might make from the graphs.

16. **Writing** Write a convincing argument to explain why the number of cigarettes smoked in a year has decreased.

17. **Writing** Write a convincing argument to explain why the number of smoking-related deaths has risen even though the number of cigarettes smoked in a year has decreased.

18. **Writing** Write at least three questions that you would like to ask the surveyor about the information in the graphs.

19. **Computer Programming** The first time Nituna ran her computer program, she had an error in line 40. She noticed that the program worked for a little while because the program printed $\frac{1}{2}$ and 2. Then she saw her error. Explain the error in line 40.

Program

```
10 REM Nituna Abeyto
20 REM Program 1
30 For I = 1 to 10
40 Let X = I / (3 - I)
50 Print X
60 Next I
70 End
```

Output

```
RUN
1
2
2
ERROR LINE 40
]
```

20. Since 1975, the number of bicycles in the world has increased and the number of rhinoceros in the world has decreased.

Can you conclude that the number of bicycles has increased *because* the number of rhinoceros has decreased? Explain why or why not.

connection to **LITERATURE**

The story of *The Phantom Tollbooth* by Norton Juster is about Milo, a young boy who travels with his dog, Tock, and his friend Humbug.

In the distance a beautiful island covered with palm trees and flowers beckoned invitingly from the sparkling water.

"Nothing can possibly go wrong now," cried the Humbug happily, and as soon as he'd said it he leaped from the car...and sailed all the way to the little island.

"And we'll have plenty of time," answered Tock, who hadn't noticed that the bug was missing—and he, too, suddenly leaped into the air and disappeared.

"It certainly couldn't be a nicer day," agreed Milo, who was too busy looking at the road to see that the others had gone. And in a split second he was gone also.

He landed next to Tock and the terrified Humbug on the tiny island...."Pardon me," said Milo to the first man who happened by; "can you tell me where I am?"

"To be sure," said Canby; "you're on the Island of Conclusions. Make yourself at home. You're apt to be here for some time."

"But how did we get here?" asked Milo, who was still a bit puzzled by being there at all.

"You jumped, of course," explained Canby. "That's the way most everyone gets here. It's really quite simple: every time you decide something without having a good reason, you jump to Conclusions whether you like it or not. It's such an easy trip to make that I've been here hundreds of times."

21. When the Humbug, Tock, and Milo see a beautiful island in the distance, each character makes a statement that causes him to jump to Conclusions. Explain why each character's statement is not necessarily true.

22. **Open-ended** Give an example of a situation from your life when someone jumped to the wrong conclusion. Describe how you think the person reached the conclusion.

Traffic Safety **For Exercises 23–26, use the graphs on seat belt use and traffic fatalities.**

23. What relationship is implied by the graphs?

24. Is there a direct correlation between seat belt use and the change in traffic fatalities?

25. Do the graphs support the conclusion that the *cause* of the decrease in traffic fatalities was the increase in seat belt use? Explain why or why not.

26. Besides seat belt use, what other factors might have contributed to the drop in traffic fatalities?

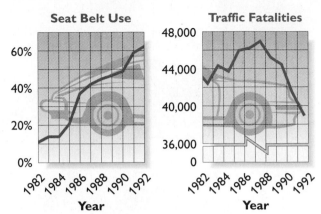

Seat Belt Use

Traffic Fatalities

Year

Year

Ongoing **ASSESSMENT**

27. **Writing** Write a true if-then statement about the relationship among the sides of right triangle $\triangle ABC$. Write the converse of your statement. Is the converse also true? Why or why not?

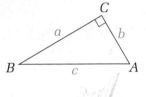

Review **PREVIEW**

28. Draw a Venn diagram that shows that if a student is in a biology class, then the student is in a science class. *(Section 1-6)*

For Exercises 29 and 30, copy each graph. Then shade the side that will give you the graph of the given inequality. *(Toolbox Skill 25)*

29. $x - 2y \geq -2$

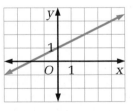

30. $x + 4y \leq 4$

For Exercises 31 and 32, draw a graph of each situation. Tell whether each graph represents a function. Write *Yes* or *No*. *(Toolbox Skill 19)*

31. Doug Weber borrowed $12,000 from his mom for college. Each month he pays her $300.

32. Every week Jennika learns how to play two new songs on the piano.

Working on the Unit Project

33. Gather your survey and trash-sampling results. Come to a final decision about the form in which you will present your findings and recommendations. Start to think about the recommendations you will make.

Completing the Unit Project

Now you are ready to complete your disposal proposal.

Your completed disposal proposal should include these things:

➤ a copy of your survey of students' attitudes about trash disposal

➤ a written summary of the survey results

➤ a graph showing the contents of the classroom trash sample you analyzed

➤ your findings and recommendations in the form of a skit, a poster, a display, or a script for an assembly program or a public-address announcement designed to convince students to accept your disposal proposal

Look Back ◄

How did the use of surveys and sampling help you prepare your proposal for reducing waste in your school?

Alternative Projects

Project 1: Conclusions in Advertisements

Cut out newspaper and magazine advertisements that make claims based on surveys. Present your answers to these questions visually.

Do the ads tell you anything about their sampling methods? Would anything about the ads lead you to make errors in statistical reasoning or errors in deduction? Were the ads as effective after you analyzed them as they were when you first looked at them?

Project 2: Simulating Survey Results

Pick a topic that you find interesting and that you would like to ask people about. Design a survey for which you can simulate the results using dice, coins, number cubes, spinners, or random numbers. Use simulation to predict the results of the survey, and then conduct the survey. Write a report that compares the results of your simulation with the results of the survey.

1. Why would a business use a sample instead of a census to learn about its customers' needs?

1-1

2. A radio station in Middletown surveyed 50 people and found that 18 of them prefer listening to classical music. Predict how many of the 4000 people in the town prefer classical music.

3. On average, a school counselor spends 10 min with each freshman, 6 min with each sophomore, 5 min with each junior, and 15 min with each senior during registration. The probability is equal that a freshman, sophomore, junior, or senior will come to the counselor's office.

1-2

Use simulation to estimate the total time that the counselor spends with 10 students chosen randomly. Describe the method that you used.

STUDENT	Class	Time spent
1	?	?
2	?	?
3	?	?
⋮	⋮	⋮

For Exercises 4–7, tell whether each method would produce a random sample of a school audience of 400 students. Write *Yes* or *No*.

1-3

4. The students in the back row are selected.

5. Select the students whose birth dates are multiples of four.

6. The 20 tallest students are selected.

7. Assign each girl in the audience a number from 1 through 200; assign each boy a number from 201 through 400. Use a random number table to select 20 numbers between 1 and 400 for the sample.

8. **Writing** Discuss three different sampling methods. Give examples of each method. Tell whether you think that each method might influence the results.

9. A manager at a television station wants to know audience reaction to its news show. The manager telephones viewers at home and surveys those who are 35–49 years old. Describe at least two problems with this method of surveying.

1-4

10. A report on music preferences concluded that "most students 18–21 years old that we surveyed listen to music more than four hours a day." What are two questions you might ask about the survey?

11. **Writing** Suppose you draw a segment that corresponds to a height of a triangle. An example is shown. Do you think it will always bisect the corresponding base? Explain your reasoning.

1-5

12. Do you think the sum of any two multiples of 4 is also a multiple of 4? Explain your reasoning.

13. On a bus trip home from school, Marvella noticed that two students got off at each of the first four bus stops. She predicts that two students will get off at every bus stop.

    a. Do you agree with her prediction? Why or why not?

    b. Suppose Marvella attends a school in which every student has a brother or sister also attending. Does this affect whether you agree or disagree with her prediction? Why or why not?

14. Use deductive reasoning to show that the sum of two even numbers is even.

1-6

For Questions 15–17, tell whether each statement about the singing groups is *True* or *False*.

15. If a student is in the Chorus, then the student is also in the Freshman Singers.

16. If a student is in the Freshman Singers, then the student is not in the Chorus.

17. No students are in both the Chorus and Madrigal Singers.

18. Reword the statement in Question 16 using the word *none*.

Singing Groups at Barr High School

Freshman Singers

Chorus

Madrigal Singers

1-7

For Questions 19–21:

a. Tell if each statement is *True* or *False*. If it is false, give a counterexample.

b. Write the converse of each statement.

c. Tell if the converse of each statement is *True* or *False*. If it is false, give a counterexample.

19. If you arrive after most people at the movie, you sit in the front row.

20. If two lines that intersect form right angles, the lines are perpendicular.

21. If $\dfrac{1}{x+1}$ is a rational number, then x is an integer.

22. **Open-ended** Make a conjecture about triangles. Explain your reasoning.

23. **Self-evaluation** Discuss how the ways that you might use data, statistics, or reasoning have changed. Do you accept most statements as true, or do you look for bias or errors in reasoning? Give examples.

24. **Group Activity** Your group will create an advertisement for a product, such as shampoo or an automobile.

    a. In your ad, make a claim based on a survey that could have been conducted before creating the product.

    b. What kind of sampling might be used for the survey in part (a)? (Remember, you want survey results that give a favorable impression.)

    c. What photographs might you feature in the ad?

    d. What if-then statements might you include in the ad?

IDEAS AND (FORMULAS)$=x^2$

ALGEBRA

➤ A proportion can be used to estimate population values from sample values. *(p. 5)*

➤ The expression $2n$ can be used to represent an even integer. $2n + 1$ represents an odd integer. *(p. 39)*

STATISTICS & PROBABILITY

➤ Censuses and surveys are used to collect information. Surveys cost less and involve only samples of a population. *(p. 4)*

➤ Simulations make it possible to answer questions about real-life situations that are otherwise difficult to explore. *(p. 10)*

➤ Rolling a die, spinning a spinner, and tossing a coin are common methods of simulating. *(p. 10)*

➤ There are many different types of samples: random, convenience, stratified random, cluster, and systematic. Random samples tend to be the most representative. *(pp. 16–17)*

➤ Larger samples give more reliable results. *(p. 18)*

➤ You can generate random numbers from a computer, a calculator, or a list of numbers such as telephone numbers. *(p. 19)*

➤ The way a survey is written and conducted affects the results. *(p. 24)*

LOGICAL REASONING $p \leftrightarrow q$ *if - then*

➤ Inductive reasoning is based on several observations. *(p. 31)*

➤ You cannot *prove* a conjecture by inductive reasoning, but you can *disprove* one by finding a counterexample. *(p. 33)*

➤ You can use if-then statements to draw conclusions. *(p. 38)*

➤ You can use a Venn diagram to determine whether an if-then statement is true or false. *(p. 39)*

➤ You can use deductive reasoning to show that statements are always true based on facts, definitions, logic, and accepted rules and properties. *(pp. 38–39)*

➤ One common error in deduction is assuming that the converse of a true statement is also true. *(p. 46)*

➤ Division by zero is undefined and can lead to an error in reasoning. *(p. 46)*

Key Terms

- **population** (p. 3)
- **trial** (p. 10)
- **convenience sample** (p. 17)
- **systematic sample** (p. 17)
- **inductive reasoning** (p. 31)
- **Venn diagram** (p. 38)

- **sample** (p. 3)
- **tree diagram** (p. 11)
- **stratified random sample** (p. 17)
- **biased** (p. 17)
- **exterior angle** (p. 33)
- **deductive reasoning** (p. 38)

- **simulation** (p. 10)
- **random sample** (p. 17)
- **cluster sample** (p. 17)
- **conjecture** (p. 31)
- **counterexample** (p. 33)
- **converse** (p. 39)

unit 2

Models of Variation and Growth

For the California gull, the best fast food place around is a place called Mono Lake. The air there is so thick with brine flies that all a gull needs to do to get a square meal is to open its beak. The number of brine flies has been estimated at 4000 per square foot of shore.

ECOSYSTEMS

Mono Lake was named by the Yokut people, a group of Native Americans who lived west of the lake. *Mono* means "brine fly" in their language.

To the average visitor, the most attractive feature of Mono Lake may be the **tufa**, calcium carbonate formations that rise above the lake like castle towers.

MONO MEANS BRINE FLY

CALIFORNIA

Mono Lake

San Francisco

Los Angeles

calcium carbonate

Be a Park Guide

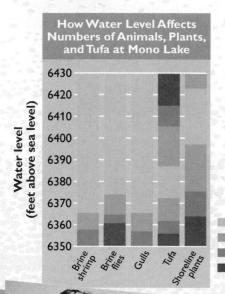

How Water Level Affects Numbers of Animals, Plants, and Tufa at Mono Lake

Water level (feet above sea level)

6430
6420
6410
6400
6390
6380
6370
6360
6350

Brine shrimp · Brine flies · Gulls · Tufa · Shoreline plants

- No change
- Slight drop
- Severe drop
- Complete elimination

In many salt lakes, the water level has dropped over time, bringing changes in the salt concentration. In this project, you will apply models of variation and growth to understand the ecosystem of a salt lake.

You will use what you learn to prepare to become a park guide at Mono Lake. Your role as a park guide is to educate, entertain, and satisfy the curiosity of visitors to Mono Lake. You should be ready to point out the major features of the ecosystem, describe how it has changed, predict how it may change in the future, and answer visitors' questions.

On a set of note cards you will record the points you plan to address in your guided tour. You can use the cards to rehearse your talk. The cards will also serve as a data bank for answering questions.

To scientists, called **limnologists**, who study the ecosystems of lakes and ponds, salt lakes have a special appeal. They are easier to model than fresh water ones because they support only a few types of plants and animals.

Mono Lake has no fish but supports huge numbers of brine shrimp, brine flies, and gulls and shore birds.

Another important salt lake lies in Africa, between Lake Victoria and Mt. Kilimanjaro in northern Tanzania. **Lake Natron** is the breeding ground for many of the world's six million flamingos.

studies

Lake Natron

TANZANIA

AFRICA

Limnologists from the University of California at Santa Barbara check oxygen and temperature levels in Mono Lake.

Getting Started

For this project you should work with another student. Here are some ideas to help you get started.

☞ Discuss with your partner what features of the Mono Lake ecosystem you will point out and describe during a tour of Mono Lake.

☞ Plan to meet again later to discuss how you can apply models of variation and growth in your guided tour. At that time you may consider using some of the following ideas from the "Working on the Unit Project" exercises: how a drop in the water level of a salt lake affects the saltiness of the water, the size of bird populations, the aquatic life, and the formation of tufa.

☞ Think about what questions visitors to Mono Lake may ask.

CALIFORNIA STATE PARK SYSTEM

Welcome to MONO LAKE California

ECOSYSTEMS

Working on the Unit Project

Your work in Unit 2 will help you prepare to be a Mono Lake park guide.

Related Exercises:
Section 2-1, Exercises 30–32
Section 2-2, Exercise 43
Section 2-3, Exercises 32, 33
Section 2-4, Exercise 42
Section 2-5, Exercises 35–37
Section 2-6, Exercise 43
Section 2-7, Exercise 33

Alternative Projects p. 113

Can We Talk

➤ Why do you think no fish live in either Mono Lake or Lake Natron?

➤ What factors influence the water level of a lake? Which are natural causes and which are due to human activity?

➤ Which do you think is more important, providing water for people or protecting natural ecosystems?

➤ Some of the fresh water that used to run into Mono Lake is being used to provide drinking water for the population of Los Angeles. What kind of conservation steps can Los Angeles residents take to reduce their water usage?

➤ What effect do you think global warming might have on a salt lake?

Functions and Graphs

trail Mix

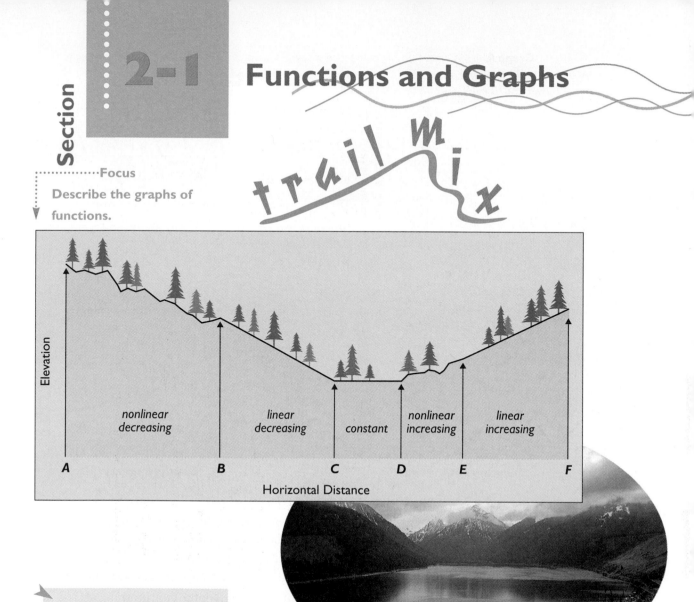

Elevation

*nonlinear
decreasing*

*linear
decreasing*

constant

*nonlinear
increasing*

*linear
increasing*

A **B** **C** **D** **E** **F**

Horizontal Distance

BY THE WAY...

The Nez Perce, a Native American people, spent part of each summer along Wallowa Lake. In their language, a "wallowa" is a support for a fish trap used to catch salmon. An important Nez Perce leader, Chief Joseph, may have been born at Wallowa Lake.

Talk it Over

1. This path along Wallowa Lake in Oregon has uphill, down-hill, and flat parts. Suppose you are hiking along the path from left to right. In your own words, describe how the path changes.

2. Using the terms in the diagram, how would you describe the graph over the interval between points *A* and *C*?

3. Name the endpoints of an interval on the horizontal axis where the graph has each characteristic.

   a. increasing

   b. linear

   c. linear increasing

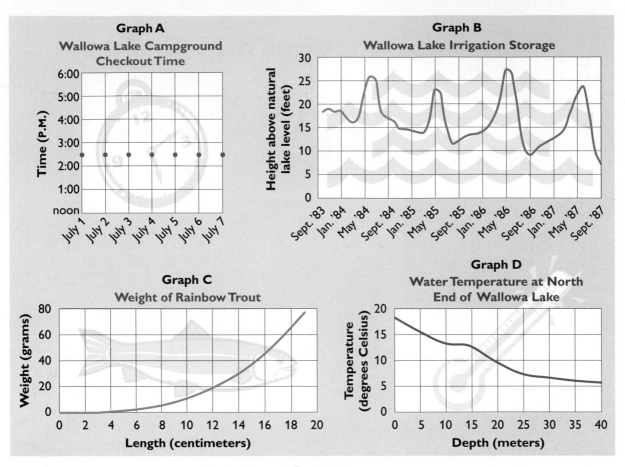

Graph A
Wallowa Lake Campground Checkout Time

Graph B
Wallowa Lake Irrigation Storage

Graph C
Weight of Rainbow Trout

Graph D
Water Temperature at North End of Wallowa Lake

4. Use graphs A–D.

  a. The graph of a straight line is **linear.** Which graphs are linear throughout? Which are nonlinear throughout?

  b. Which graphs are increasing throughout? Which are decreasing throughout? Which are constant throughout?

  c. Which graphs show discrete data? continuous data?

5. From graph A, what can you say about the checkout time for Wallowa Lake Campground during the first week of July?

6. Can you use graph B to predict the water level for October 1987? Why or why not?

7. From graph C, estimate the weight of a rainbow trout that is 18 cm long.

8. From graph D, can you tell if the temperature changes at the same rate from the surface down to a depth of 40 m? Explain.

9. Graphs can have different characteristics over different intervals. Using this idea and the terms in the diagram on page 59, describe the characteristics of graph D.

10. Remember that a **function** is a relationship in which there is *only one* value of the *dependent variable* for each value of the *control,* or *independent, variable.* Do you think graphs A–D are graphs of functions? Why or why not?

Student Resources Toolbox
p. 649 *Graphs, Equations, and Inequalities*

Growth and Decay

Graphs of functions can be examples of *growth, decay,* or a *constant* depending on whether the value of the dependent variable continually increases, decreases, or remains the same when the value of the control variable increases.

TYPES OF GRAPHS

A **growth graph** is increasing throughout.

y

As *x* increases, *y* increases.

O x

A **decay graph** is decreasing throughout.

y

As *x* increases, *y* decreases.

O x

A **constant graph** is linear and horizontal.

y

As *x* increases, *y* stays the same.

O x

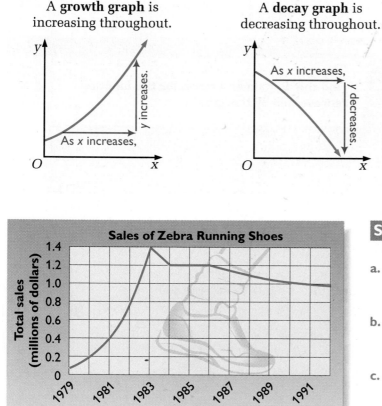

Sales of Zebra Running Shoes

Total sales (millions of dollars)

1.4 1.2 1.0 0.8 0.6 0.4 0.2 0

1979 1981 1983 1985 1987 1989 1991

Year

Sample 1

a. Use the terms *linear* or *nonlinear* and *increasing, decreasing,* or *constant* to describe the graph.

b. Is this a *growth graph*, a *decay graph*, or *neither*? Explain your choice.

c. **Writing** Based on the graph, do you think Zebra Company stock is a good investment? Why or why not?

Sample Response

a. Between 1979 and 1983: nonlinear and increasing.
Between 1983 and 1984: linear and decreasing.
Between 1984 and 1986: constant.
Between 1986 and 1992: nonlinear and decreasing.

b. Neither, because the graph is sometimes increasing, sometimes decreasing, and sometimes constant.

c. Zebra Company stock does not look like a good investment. The graph shows that sales were not increasing over the last nine years shown.

Now you are ready for:
Exs. 1–17 on pp. 63–64

11. What is the least value of the control variable shown for the graph in Sample 1 on page 61? What is the greatest value?

12. Estimate the least value and the greatest value of the dependent variable in Sample 1.

For any function, the **domain** is all the values of the control variable for which the function is defined. The **range** is all the values of the dependent variable over the domain.

Sample 2

Find the domain and range for the function represented by this graph.

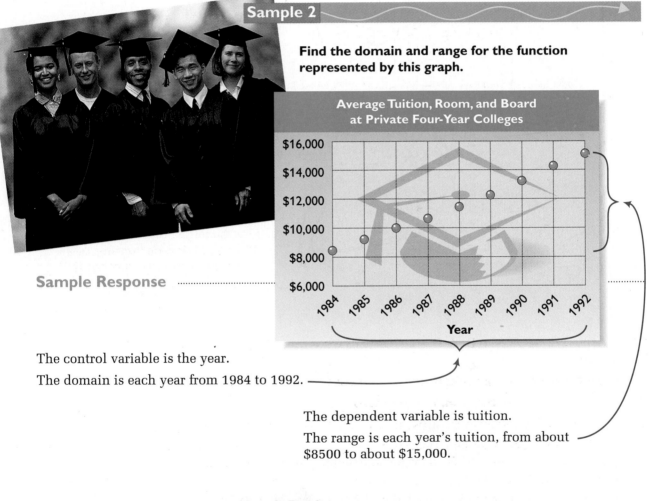

Average Tuition, Room, and Board at Private Four-Year Colleges

Sample Response

The control variable is the year.

The domain is each year from 1984 to 1992.

The dependent variable is tuition.

The range is each year's tuition, from about $8500 to about $15,000.

Look Back

Give the characteristics of growth graphs and decay graphs, and of linear graphs and nonlinear graphs.

······► Now you are ready for: Exs. 18–32 on pp. 65–66

Exercises and Problems

1. **Reading** Give the characteristics of a constant graph.

Use the terms *linear* or *nonlinear* and *increasing, decreasing,* or *constant* to describe each graph.

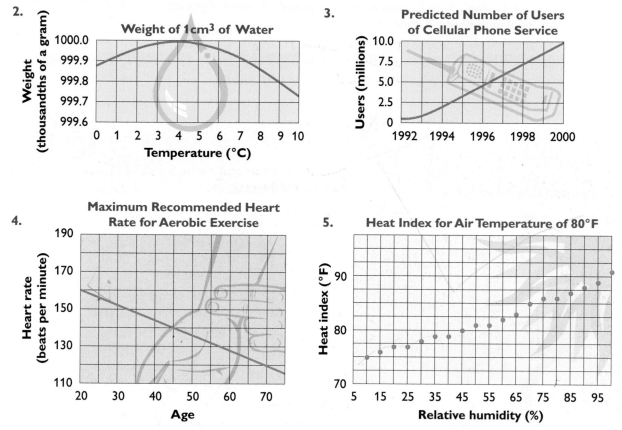

2.

Weight of 1cm³ of Water

3.

Predicted Number of Users of Cellular Phone Service

4.

Maximum Recommended Heart Rate for Aerobic Exercise

5.

Heat Index for Air Temperature of 80°F

6. Which of the graphs in Exercises 2–5 are growth graphs? Explain your choices.

7. Is the graph of $x = 4$ a constant graph? Why or why not?

For Exercises 8–11, use the graphs in Exercises 2–5.

8. **Physics** At what temperature between 0°C and 10°C is water the heaviest?

9. **Writing** Inez Barco is planning to invest some money. Based on the graph, would you advise her to invest some money in cellular phone service? Why or why not?

10. **Fitness** Boris Aronsky checks his pulse during a high-intensity/low-impact aerobics class. He counts 27 beats in 10 seconds. Boris is 26 years old. Is Boris's heart rate above or below the suggested maximum?

11. **Meteorology** When the air temperature reaches 80°F, does it always feel like 80°F? Explain your answer. (*Note:* The Heat Index is how hot it feels due to the combined effect of temperature and humidity.)

12. a. **Writing** Describe how the graph of the height of a person might look over the person's lifetime.

   b. **Research** Find out what your height was at various ages from your day of birth through today. Graph the data. How well does your graph match your description in part (a)?

Tell whether each graph is an example of *linear growth, nonlinear growth, linear decay, nonlinear decay, a constant,* or *none of these.*

13.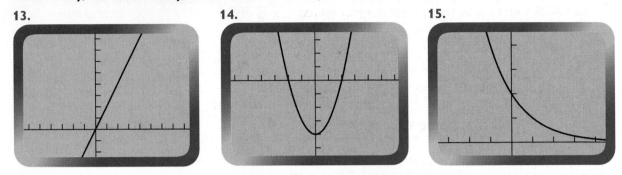

14.

15.

Career Some directors use graphs to analyze a movie as it is being filmed.

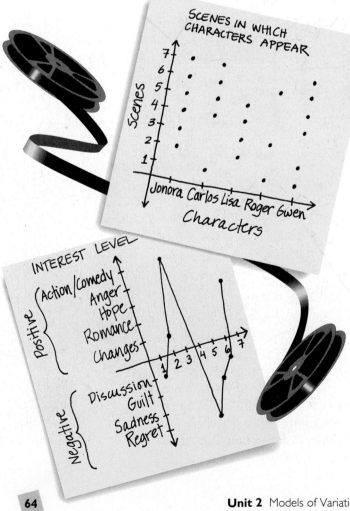

SCENES IN WHICH CHARACTERS APPEAR

Scenes

Jonora Carlos Lisa Roger Gwen

Characters

INTEREST LEVEL

(Action/Comedy) Positive
Anger
Hope
Romance
Changes

1 2 3 4 5 6 7

Discussion
Guilt
Sadness
Regret

Negative

16. **Open-ended** Suppose a director made the first graph to look at the impact of the characters.

   a. Which character do you think has the least impact? Why?

   b. **Writing** What changes, if any, do you think the director should make in order to increase the impact of the character in part (a)?

17. Suppose a director made the second graph to chart a movie's emotional high points and low points. The numbers represent the scenes.

   a. How many strong "highs" are there? How many strong "lows"?

   b. **Writing** What changes, if any, do you think the director should make to increase the emotional impact of the movie?

18. Find the domain and range for the functions represented by graphs C and D on page 60.

19. a. What does the formula $C = 2\pi r$ represent in the study of geometry?

   b. Graph the function. Use r for the control variable and C for the dependent variable. (*Note:* If you are using a graphics calculator, use x and y instead.)

   c. Use the terms *linear* or *nonlinear* and *increasing*, *decreasing*, or *constant* to describe your graph.

   d. Is the graph of $C = 2\pi r$ a *growth graph*, a *decay graph*, or *neither?* Explain your choice.

   e. **Writing** Does the domain of the function $C = 2\pi r$ include negative values? Does the range? Why or why not?

20. Repeat Exercise 19 with the formula $A = \pi r^2$.

Student Resources Toolbox
p. 657 *Formulas and Relationships*

---

connection to DRIVER'S EDUCATION

Under certain conditions the distance a car travels once the driver has decided to stop the car is given by the function in the photograph.

21. a. Graph the function. Use s for the control variable and d for the dependent variable.

   b. Use the terms *linear* or *nonlinear* and *increasing*, *decreasing*, or *constant* to describe your graph.

   c. Is your graph a *growth graph*, a *decay graph*, or *neither?* Explain your choice.

   d. How does the graph show that the stated relationship between stopping distance and speed is a function?

   e. Suppose the top speed for a car is 110 mi/h. Find the domain and range for the stated stopping distance relationship.

$d = 0.05s^2 + s$, where d is the stopping distance in feet and s is the speed of the car in miles per hour

Open-ended Describe a situation that can be modeled by each type of graph.
Sketch a graph for your situation.

22. linear graph   **23.** nonlinear graph   **24.** decay graph   **25.** constant graph

Review **PREVIEW**

26. Gabriel read this advertisement for a pain-relief medication. He was surprised to learn that three fourths of doctors recommend this medication. What is Gabriel's error in reasoning? *(Section 1-7)*

"Three out of four doctors who use this medication recommend it."

27. Make a scatter plot of the data and draw a fitted line. *(Toolbox Skill 1)*

x	113	187	245	310	332	405	559	621
y	237	369	498	632	668	812	1120	1260

For Exercises 28 and 29, tell whether each statement is *True* or *False*.
(Toolbox Skill 21)

28. The slope of a horizontal line is 0.

29. The slope of a vertical line is negative.

Working on the Unit Project

30. a. Make a scatter plot of this data for Mono Lake. Graph salt content as a function of the water level in the lake.

  b. Describe the graph.

31. When the concentration of salt in a lake is greater than three percent by weight, the lake is a *salt lake.*

  a. Find the percent of salt by weight for each of the water levels of Mono Lake shown in the table. One liter of water weighs 1 kg, or 1000 g.

  b. Graph the concentration of salt as a function of water level.

  c. Describe the graph.

32. About 40 in. of water evaporates from Mono Lake each year.

  a. Sketch the graph of the changing water level due to evaporation as a function of time.

  b. Is the function an example of *linear growth, nonlinear growth, linear decay, nonlinear decay,* or a *constant*?

Water level (feet above sea level)	Salt content (grams per liter)
6417	51.3
6414	54.0
6410	56.3
6407	58.1
6403	60.2
6380	89.3
6378	86.8
6377	91.6
6376	89.3
6375	93.4
6373	97.7
6372	99.4

Linear Models and Direct Variation

Focus

Review linear functions, slope of a line, and direct variation.

Exercise makes your heart beat faster. To keep your workout safe, you must make sure your heart does not beat too fast.

Health and fitness experts use this formula to find the *maximum target heart rate* during aerobic exercise:

$$h = -0.8a + 176$$

heart rate in → beats per minute

age in years

This formula is a *mathematical model* of the relationship between age and maximum target heart rate during exercise. Functions, tables, graphs, equations, and inequalities that describe a situation are called **mathematical models.**

AGE	TARGET ZONE	NUMBER OF HEARTBEATS IN 10 SECONDS
20	120-160	20-27
25	117-156	20-26
30	114-152	19-25
35	111-148	19-25
40	108-144	18-24
45	105-140	18-23
50	102-136	17-23
	99-132	17-22
	28	16-21

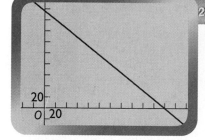

a	h
0	176
10	168
20	160
30	152
40	144

Talk it Over

1. How does the maximum target heart rate change with age?

2. How does the formula show that the maximum target heart rate is always under 176 beats per minute?

3. **a.** What is a reasonable domain for this function?

   b. Find the range for the function over this domain.

4. This table of values and this graph also model the relationship between age and maximum target heart rate.

   a. In the table, the value of *a* increases by 10. How does the value of *h* change?

   b. Is the graph *linear* or *nonlinear*?

   c. Is the graph *increasing, decreasing,* or *constant*?

   d. Is the graph a *growth graph,* a *decay graph,* or *neither*? Explain your choice.

The target heart rate formula on page 67 is an example of a **linear function.** Its graph is a line. The function is written in **slope-intercept form.**

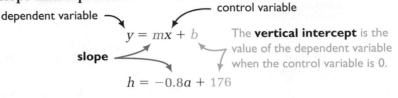

dependent variable

control variable

$$y = mx + b$$

The **vertical intercept** is the value of the dependent variable when the control variable is 0.

slope

$$h = -0.8a + 176$$

X\. Lab

SLOPE OF A LINE

$$\text{slope} = \frac{\text{vertical change}}{\text{horizontal change}}$$

$$m = \frac{y_2 - y_1}{x_2 - x_1}$$

The slope of a horizontal line is 0.

The slope of a vertical line is undefined.

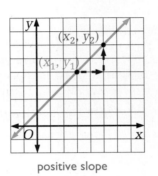

positive slope

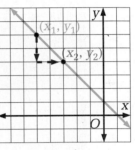

negative slope

There is exactly one line through any two points. You can use slope to find an equation for the line through any two points.

Sample 1

Write an equation for the line through the points (10, 7) and (−6, −1).

Sample Response

Use the slope-intercept form of the equation of a line.

Step 1 Find the slope.

$$m = \frac{y_2 - y_1}{x_2 - x_1}$$ ⟵ Write the slope formula.

$$m = \frac{-1 - 7}{-6 - 10}$$ ⟵ Substitute the coordinates of **(10, 7)** and **(−6, −1).**

$$m = \frac{-8}{-16}$$

$$m = \frac{1}{2}$$

Step 2 Find the vertical intercept.

$$y = mx + b$$ ⟵ Write the slope-intercept form of the equation of a line.

$$7 = \frac{1}{2} \cdot 10 + b$$ ⟵ Substitute the value of the **slope** and the **coordinates of a point.**

$$7 = 5 + b$$

$$2 = b$$

Step 3 Substitute the values you found for m and b.

$$y = mx + b$$

$$y = \frac{1}{2}x + 2$$

·····▶ Now you are ready for:
Exs. 1–26 on pp. 70–72

Sample 2

Ashanthi is on a pledge-walk to raise money. She is an experienced walker who maintains a steady pace of 4 mi/h.

   a. Write an equation that models the distance she walks.

   b. Draw a graph that models the distance she walks.

Sample Response

a. Let D = the distance in miles.

Let t = the time in hours.

Distance = rate × time

$$D = 4t$$

b. Make a table of values or use a graphics calculator. Use y for the dependent variable and x for the control variable.

y = 4x	
x	**y**
0	0
1	4
2	8
3	12
4	16

⟵ Time and distance are both nonnegative.

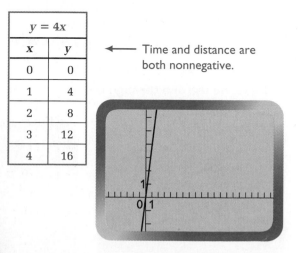

The part of the graph in the first quadrant models the distance she walks.

In Sample 2 on page 69, the distance Ashanthi walks *varies directly with* the time she walks. The equation that models the distance is $D = 4t$. An equation in the general form

$$y = kx$$

is called a **direct variation** equation. The value of k ($k \neq 0$) is called the **variation constant.**

BY THE WAY...

Hubble's Law is an important direct variation equation used by astronomers. The law states that the more distant galaxies are moving faster.

Talk it Over

5. Compare the equations $y = kx$ and $y = mx + b$. Explain why direct variation is a linear function.

6. What is the variation constant in the equation in Sample 2?

7. What is the vertical intercept of the graph in Sample 2?

8. In Sample 2 the slope of the graph is the walking rate, 4 mi/h. If Ashanthi walks at a rate of 3 mi/h instead, how does the graph change?

9. Suppose Ashanthi gets credit for the 2.5 mi she walks to the starting line of the pledge-walk. How does the graph change?

Look Back

How does the graph of a linear function change when the slope increases or decreases? when the vertical intercept increases or decreases?

······▶ Now you are ready for:
Exs. 27–43 on pp. 72–74

2-2 Exercises and Problems

1. **Reading** What is the vertical intercept of the graph of the maximum target heart rate formula on page 67?

For each pair of points in Exercises 2–7:

a. **Find the slope of the line through the points.**

b. **Describe the line through the points as *increasing, decreasing, or constant*.**

2.

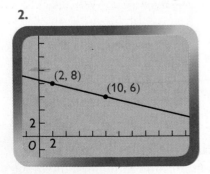

3.

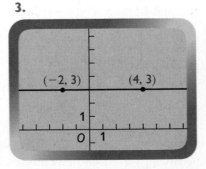

4.

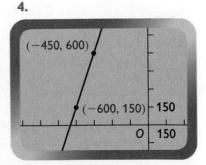

5. (0, 6) and (−2, 0)

6. (−7, 3) and (5, −1)

7. (5, −12) and (11, −12)

For Exercises 8–13, write an equation for the line through each pair of points.

8. (0, 1) and (2, 9)

9. (1, 1) and (4, 10)

10. (8, 5) and (−4, 2)

11. (2, 1) and (4, −3)

12. (−1, −3) and (−3, 5)

13. (3, −7) and (0, −9)

14. The graphs show the coordinates of two points on the same line.

Round the coordinates to the nearest hundredth. Then find the slope of the line.

15. Let c = the cost of a tune-up.

Let s = the number of spark plugs needed.

Choose the letter of the equation that models the price information shown in the advertisement. Then find the cost of tuning up a car that needs eight spark plugs.

a. $c = 40s + 2.29$

b. $s = 2.29c + 40$

c. $c = 2.29s + 40$

d. $s = 40c + 2.29$

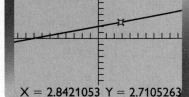

For Exercises 16 and 17, use the diagrams.

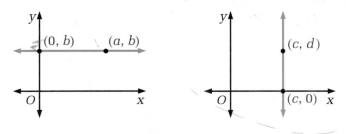

16. Show that the slope of a horizontal line is 0.

17. Show that the slope of a vertical line is undefined.

18 TECHNOLOGY Use a graphics calculator.

TECHNOLOGY NOTE

See the Technology Handbook, pp. 604–606.

a. Enter the maximum target heart rate equation, $h = -0.8a + 176$.

b. Set the window to show the domain and range you found in question 3 on page 67. Graph the equation you entered.

c. Use TRACE to find the coordinates of two points on the line. Round the coordinates to the nearest thousandth.

d. Find the change in x and the change in y between your two points.

e. Use your answers to part (d) to find the slope of the line. Compare your answer to the value of m in the equation you entered.

f. Repeat parts (c)–(e) for two more pairs of points. Try two points that are far apart and two points that are close together. Do you get about the same value for the slope each time?

19. **Writing** Here are two new forms of an equation of a line. Use them to answer the questions.

point-slope form: $y - y_1 = m(x - x_1)$

two-point form: $y - y_1 = \dfrac{y_2 - y_1}{x_2 - x_1}(x - x_1)$

a. Use the slope-intercept form, the point-slope form, and the two-point form to write an equation of the line through the points (5, 11) and (−10, −1). Which method do you prefer? Why?

b. Explain why the point-slope form is equivalent to the definition of slope. Why is "point-slope form" an appropriate name?

c. Explain how to combine the point-slope form with the definition of slope to write the two-point form. Why is "two-point form" an appropriate name?

For each equation:

a. Identify the slope and the vertical intercept of the graph.

b. Graph the equation.

c. Use the term *increasing, decreasing,* **or** *constant* **to describe the graph.**

20. $y = 2x - 3$ **21.** $y = 7x$ **22.** $y = -5x - 4$

23. $y = x + 3.7$ **24.** $y = -4.2$ **25.** $y = -\dfrac{3}{5}x + 2$

26. **Writing** Explain how you can use the slope of a line to tell if the line represents an *increasing*, a *decreasing*, or a *constant* function.

27. Choose the letters of the direct variation equations.

   a. $y = 3x$ **b.** $y = x - 3$ **c.** $y = 3$ **d.** $\dfrac{y}{x} = 3$

28. Choose the letters of the graphs that show direct variation.

   a.   **b.**   **c.**   **d.**

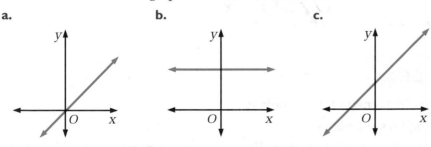 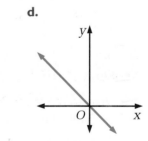

29. **Open-ended** Describe a real-world situation that fits a direct variation model.

30. Nora Ramond works as a service station attendant. She earns a weekly salary of $280.00 plus $10.50 per hour for overtime over 40 hours.

a. Write an equation that you can use to find Nora's weekly earnings.

b. What do you think is a reasonable domain for the function?

c. Find the range for the domain you gave in part (b).

d. Graph the function.

       Unit 2 Models of Variation and Growth

e. What is the vertical intercept of the graph? Explain the meaning of the vertical intercept in terms of the situation.

f. What is the slope of the graph? Explain the meaning of the slope in terms of the situation.

31. **Fitness Training** Damon Carson exercises on a cross-country skiing machine. One day he recorded the distances shown by the machine at various times.

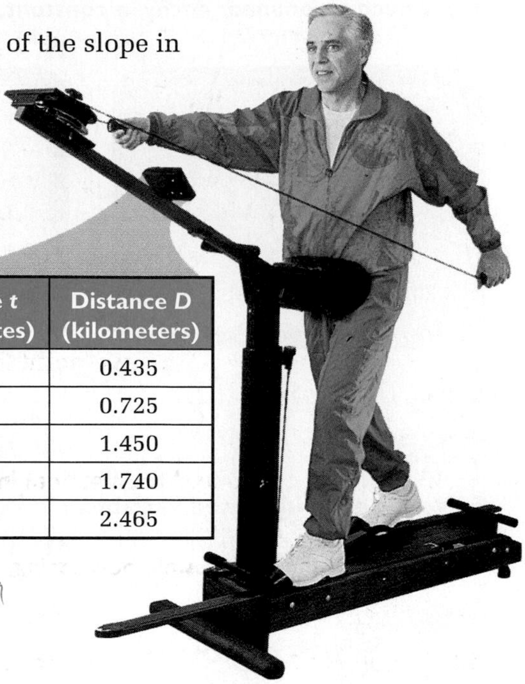

a. Find the ratio $\frac{D}{t}$ for each pair of data values.

b. Is direct variation a good model for the data? If so, what is the variation constant?

c. Write an equation that models the situation.

d. Graph your equation.

Time t (minutes)	Distance D (kilometers)
3	0.435
5	0.725
10	1.450
12	1.740
17	2.465

e. Predict the distance the machine will show after 25 min.

f. How long will Damon Carson need to exercise for the machine to show a distance of 4.5 km?

32. $\overleftrightarrow{AB}$ crosses the x-axis at a 52° angle. The vertical intercept is 2.

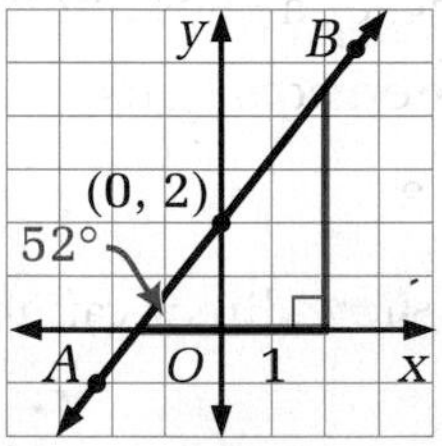

a. Explain why the slope of $\overleftrightarrow{AB}$ has the same value as tan 52°.

b. Write an equation of $\overleftrightarrow{AB}$.

Student Resources Toolbox
p. 659 *Trigonometry*

• • • • • • • • • •
Ongoing **ASSESSMENT**

33. **Group Activity** Work in a group of three students.

TECHNOLOGY Use a graphics calculator.

a. Each of you should write equations of three lines that have vertical intercepts between −5 and 5. Be sure to include these three types of graphs: *growth, decay,* and *constant.* Do not show your list to anyone.

b. Choose one student to go first. That student graphs one of his or her equations on the calculator.

c. Another member of the group identifies the vertical intercept of the graph shown on the calculator and states which type of graph it is.

d. Continue around the group until each group member has entered all three of his or her equations.

e. Discuss any errors and how to avoid them.

Tell whether each graph is an example of *linear growth, nonlinear growth, linear decay, nonlinear decay, a constant,* or *none of these.* (Section 2-1)

34.

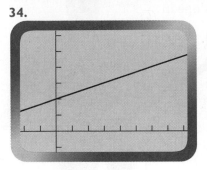

35.

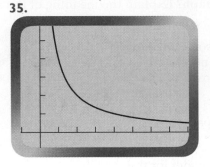

36.

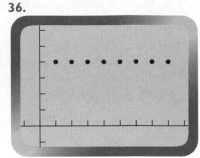

Solve. *(Toolbox Skill 13)*

37. $\frac{x}{4} - 4 = 8$

38. $7y = 3y - 56$

39. $2h = 5(h + 15)$

Solve for each indicated variable. *(Toolbox Skill 15)*

40. $A = lw$, for l

41. $V = Bh$, for h

42. $D = rt$, for r

Working on the Unit Project

43. The table shows one scientist's model of the rate at which water must flow into Mono Lake in order to keep the water level at the heights shown.

Inflow (cubic feet per second)	Water level (feet above sea level)
127	6390
110	6380
93	6370
76	6360
59	6350
42	6340
26	6330

a. Make a scatter plot of the data.

b. Draw a fitted line.

c. Is the function an example of *linear growth* or *linear decay?* Explain.

d. Is the function an example of direct variation? Explain.

e. Write an equation of the fitted line.

f. Use your equation from part (e) to predict the rate of inflow needed to maintain the water level at 6430 ft above sea level. At this water level, gulls will breed at the same high levels as they did in 1987.

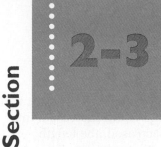

Inverse Variation

One's Loss Is Another's Gain

EXPLORATION .....

*What kinds of rectangles have an area of
36 square units?*

- **Materials: 36 small squares of paper of the same size,
graph paper, scissors**

- **Work with another student.**

① Use the squares to build as many
rectangles as you can with area
36 square units.

② Copy and complete the table of the
lengths and widths of your rectangles.

List both the
4 × 9 and the
9 × 4 rectangles.

width	length
4	9
9	4
⋮	⋮

③ Make a scatter plot of the data
in the table. Use width as the
control variable.

④ Cut each square in half to form two
rectangles. Make at least two new
rectangles with area 36 square units.
Add these to your table and your
scatter plot.

⑤ Describe what happens to the
lengths of rectangles with area
36 square units:

a. as the widths become very small

b. as the widths become very large

⑥ Describe the shape of the scatter plot.

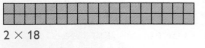

1 × 36

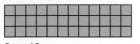

2 × 18

3 × 12

4 × 9

6 × 6

The area of the rectangles in the Exploration was constant while the length and width varied. When the width increased, the length decreased. When the width decreased, the length increased. This is an example of *inverse variation.*

$$lw = 36$$

When two quantities have a constant nonzero product, their relationship is called **inverse variation.**

You can say that the width *varies inversely with* the length of the rectangle. You can also say that the length varies inversely with the width of the rectangle.

Talk it Over

1. Suppose you want to graph all the possible dimensions for rectangles with area 36 square units. Should you connect the points on your scatter plot with straight lines or a curve? Explain your choice.

2. How is inverse variation different from direct variation? How is it like direct variation?

Sample 1

Is inverse variation a good model for the data in the table? If it is, write an equation that models the data.

x	y
25.2632	0.4750
25.8947	0.4634
26.5263	0.4524
27.1579	0.4419
27.7895	0.4318

Sample Response

Multiply the data in each row to see if the product is constant.

x	y	xy	
25.2632	0.4750	12.00002	
25.8947	0.4634	11.99960398	
26.5263	0.4524	12.00049812	All the products are very close to 12.
27.1579	0.4419	12.00107601	
27.7895	0.4318	11.9995061	

Inverse variation is a good model for the data.

The equation $xy = 12$ models the data.

3. The data in Sample 1 are all positive. In which quadrant(s) does a scatter plot of the data appear?

4. Look at these other pairs of numbers that satisfy the equation in Sample 1: $(-12, -1), (-6, -2), (-4, -3), (-1, -12),$ $(-2, -6), (-3, -4)$. In which quadrant(s) does a scatter plot of these data appear?

The graph of inverse variation is a shape made of two curves, called a **hyperbola.** To graph inverse variation on a graphics calculator, you first rewrite the equation $xy = k$ as $y = \dfrac{k}{x}$.

X₍ℓab

INVERSE VARIATION

The equation has these forms ($k \neq 0$, $x \neq 0$):

$$xy = k \quad \text{or} \quad y = \frac{k}{x}$$

⬑ variation constant

You read them as follows:

"y varies inversely with x,"
or
"y is proportional to $\dfrac{1}{x}$."

The graph is a hyperbola.

when k is positive   when k is negative

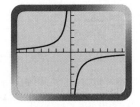

5. Explain why there are two curves in the graph of $xy = 12$.

6. Explain how to rewrite the equation $xy = k$ as $y = \dfrac{k}{x}$.

7. How does changing the sign of k affect the graph of $y = \dfrac{k}{x}$?

8. How do you think increasing the value of k changes the graph of $y = \dfrac{k}{x}$? To check your answer, graph $y = \dfrac{1}{x}$, $y = \dfrac{2}{x}$, and $y = \dfrac{4}{x}$ on the same calculator or computer screen.

·····▶ Now you are ready for:
Exs. 1–7 on pp. 79–80

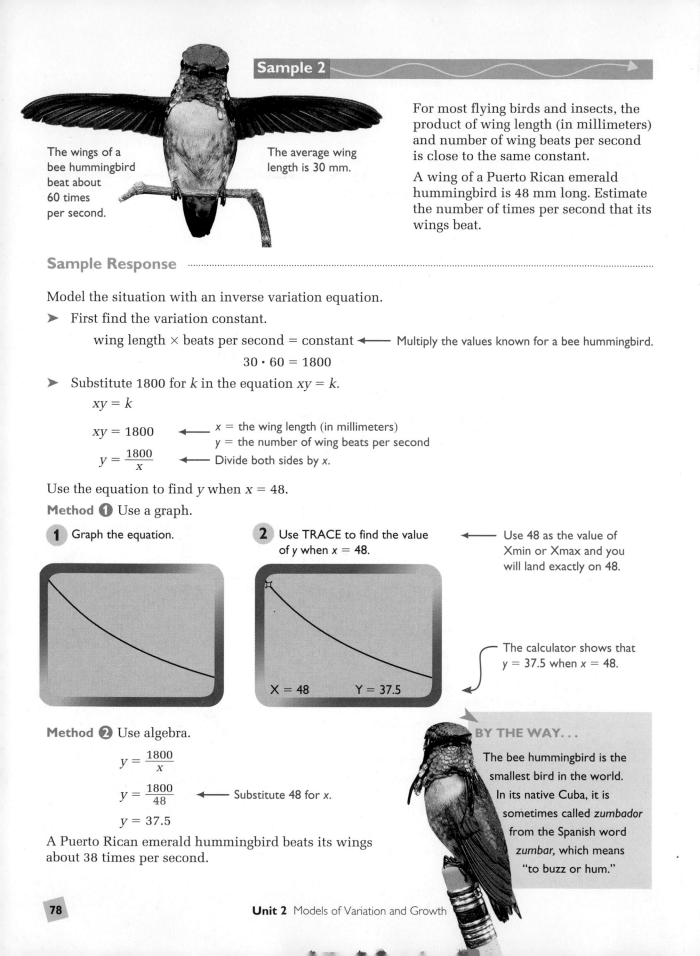

The wings of a
bee hummingbird
beat about
60 times
per second.

The average wing
length is 30 mm.

For most flying birds and insects, the product of wing length (in millimeters) and number of wing beats per second is close to the same constant.

A wing of a Puerto Rican emerald hummingbird is 48 mm long. Estimate the number of times per second that its wings beat.

Sample Response

Model the situation with an inverse variation equation.

➤ First find the variation constant.

wing length × beats per second = constant ⟵ Multiply the values known for a bee hummingbird.

$$30 \cdot 60 = 1800$$

➤ Substitute 1800 for k in the equation $xy = k$.

$$xy = k$$

$$xy = 1800 \quad \longleftarrow \quad \begin{array}{l} x = \text{the wing length (in millimeters)} \\ y = \text{the number of wing beats per second} \end{array}$$

$$y = \frac{1800}{x} \quad \longleftarrow \quad \text{Divide both sides by } x.$$

Use the equation to find y when $x = 48$.

Method ❶ Use a graph.

1 Graph the equation.

2 Use TRACE to find the value of y when $x = 48$. ⟵ Use 48 as the value of Xmin or Xmax and you will land exactly on 48.

X = 48   Y = 37.5

The calculator shows that $y = 37.5$ when $x = 48$.

Method ❷ Use algebra.

$$y = \frac{1800}{x}$$

$$y = \frac{1800}{48} \quad \longleftarrow \quad \text{Substitute 48 for } x.$$

$$y = 37.5$$

A Puerto Rican emerald hummingbird beats its wings about 38 times per second.

BY THE WAY...

The bee hummingbird is the smallest bird in the world. In its native Cuba, it is sometimes called *zumbador* from the Spanish word *zumbar*, which means "to buzz or hum."

······▶ **Now you are ready for:**
Exs. 8–33 on pp. 80–82

Look Back ◀────────────────

Describe how you can tell when a set of data, a graph, or an equation is an example of inverse variation.

2-3 Exercises and Problems

1. In the Exploration, in which quadrant(s) was your scatter plot?

2. **Reading** Suppose x and y are any two numbers.

   a. In which quadrants is the graph of $xy = 12$?

   b. In which quadrants is the graph of $xy = -12$?

3. Dividers separate a box for juice glasses into 48 square regions. The dimensions of the box are 4 glasses wide by 12 glasses long.

   a. Make a table of the dimensions of some other one-layer boxes that will hold 48 of the same type of juice glass.

   b. Write an equation that relates the width and length of each box.

Is inverse variation a good model for each set of data? Why or why not? If it is, write an equation that models the data.

4.

x	y
0.4228	4.9670
0.4438	4.7319
0.4648	4.5184
0.4858	4.3231
0.5067	4.1441
0.5277	3.9793

5.

x	y
1.7895	0.9762
2.0000	0.9093
2.2105	0.8023
2.4211	0.6598
2.6316	0.4541
2.8421	0.2950

6. a. Draw a circle with a diameter between 8 cm and 10 cm.

   b. Draw a *chord* of length 7 cm. (A *chord* is a segment with endpoints on the circle.) The chord divides the circle into two regions. Label the smaller region X and the larger region Y.

   c. Mark a dot 5 cm along the chord. Draw 5 different chords that pass through the dot.

   d. Measure to the nearest millimeter the part of each chord that lies in region X and the part of each chord that lies in region Y. Record these lengths in a table as x and y.

   e. Make a scatter plot of the data in your table. Describe it.

   f. Is your graph an example of inverse variation? If it is, what is the constant product?

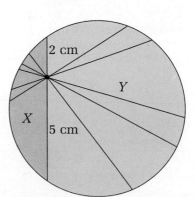

2 cm

Y

X

5 cm

7. **Writing** Repeat Exercise 6 but mark the dot halfway along the 7 cm chord. Make a conjecture about how the placement of the dot affects the results. Test your conjecture by marking the dot somewhere else along the 7 cm chord. Summarize your observations.

For Exercises 8–10, rewrite the equation in the form $y = \dfrac{k}{x}$.

8. $xy = 18$

9. $xy = -7$

10. $x = \dfrac{2}{y}$

For Exercises 11–13, find y when x = 6.

11. $y = \dfrac{72}{x}$

12. $x = \dfrac{51}{y}$

13. $xy = 3$

14. A rectangle has length 42 cm and width 22 cm. Find the length of another rectangle of equal area whose width is 12 cm.

15. Some college students want to share an apartment off campus. The rent will be $600 per month. The maximum number of tenants allowed is 6.

   a. **Writing** Explain why the relationship between each student's share of the monthly rent and the number of students is an example of inverse variation. Assume that each student pays the same amount.

   b. How many people would have to share the rent of the apartment to make the cost $120 per month?

16. When a seesaw is balanced, each person's weight varies inversely with the distance from the center support. If a person who weighs 90 lb sits at one end of a 12 ft seesaw, how far from the support must a 120 lb person sit in order to balance the seesaw?

For Exercises 17 and 18, use the equation in Sample 2 to estimate how many times the wings beat per second.

17. sphinx moth with wing length 20 mm

18. wandering albatross with wing length 1.5 m

20 mm

1.5 m

BY THE WAY...

The wandering albatross has the largest wingspan of any living bird.

METHOD OF TRAVEL	Rate (miles per hour)	Time (hours)
backpacking	3	?
cross-country skiing	4	?
bicycling	10	?
car: slow & scenic	25	?
car: moderate	45	?
car: speed limit	55	?

19. Suppose you are planning a camping trip to a lake 12 mi away.

   The equation $rt = 12$ describes the relationship between r, the rate of travel, and t, the time it takes to get to the lake.

   a. Rewrite the equation $rt = 12$ so you could enter it on a graphics calculator.

   b. Complete the table.

   c. What is a reasonable domain for the function? Why?

For Exercises 20 and 21, use this information.

The length of a sound wave, or wavelength, varies inversely with the frequency of the wave. The speed of sound is the variation constant. When the wavelength is in meters and the frequency is in number of waves per second, the speed of sound is given in meters per second.

20. a. The speed of sound in air is 343 m/s. Write an equation showing how frequency *f* and wavelength *w* are related when sound travels in air.

The frequency of A above middle C is 440 waves per second.

The frequency of A below middle C is 220 waves per second.

middle C

    b. What is the wavelength in air of A above middle C?

    c. What is the wavelength in air of A below middle C?

21. a. The speed of sound in water is 1497 m/s. Write an equation showing how frequency and wavelength are related when sound travels in water.

    b. What is the wavelength in water of A above middle C?

    c. What is the wavelength in water of A below middle C?

22. a. **Open-ended** Make a table of data for an inverse variation.

    b. Write an equation that describes the data in your table. Identify the control variable and the dependent variable.

    c. Draw a graph of your data.

Ongoing **ASSESSMENT**

23. **Open-ended** Suppose you are helping a friend with homework over the telephone. Describe how the graph of an inverse variation is like other types of graphs you have worked with and how it is different.

24. Choose the letters of the direct variation equations. *(Section 2-2)*

    a. $y = 6$ **b.** $y = 6x$ **c.** $y = 6x - 6$ **d.** $\frac{y}{x} = 6$

Graph each inequality. *(Toolbox Skill 25)*

25. $y \geq 4$ **26.** $x < 2$ **27.** $y \leq 3x + 2$ **28.** $y > \frac{1}{2}x - 1$

Find the volume of each figure. In Exercises 29 and 31, find the surface area also. *(Toolbox Skill 28)*

29.

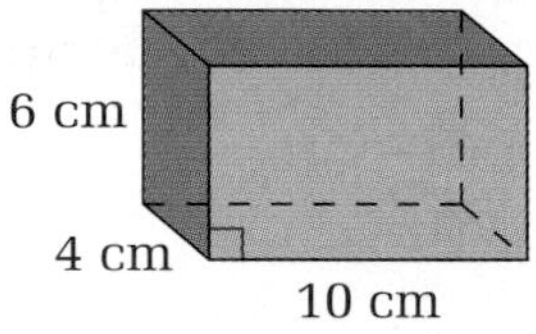

6 cm

4 cm

10 cm

30.

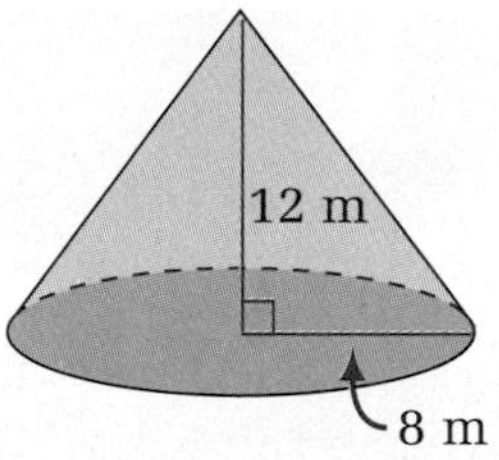

12 m

8 m

31.

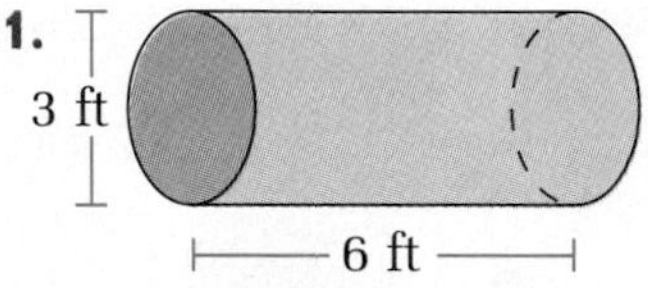

3 ft

6 ft

Working on the Unit Project

32. The graph shows scientists' predictions of the salt content of Mono Lake when the water level drops to the levels in the graph.

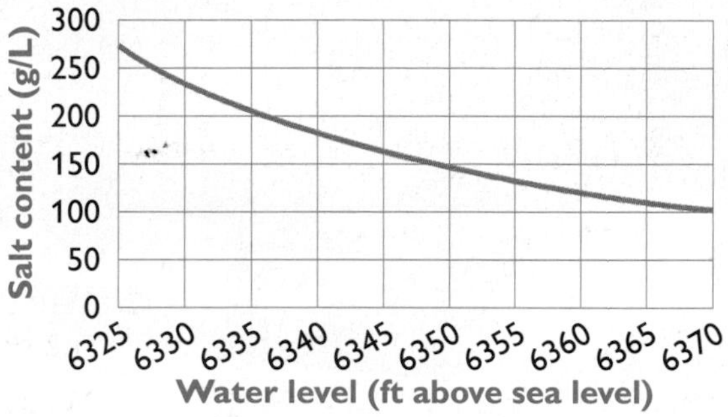

    a. Describe the graph.

    b. Does the graph show inverse variation? How do you know?

Salt content (g/L)

300
250
200
150
100
50
0

6325 6330 6335 6340 6345 6350 6355 6360 6365 6370

Water level (ft above sea level)

33. Over the next several days, you will do this experiment to learn how tufa form.

    a. Mix five different concentrations of salt water. Add 1–5 teaspoons of salt to a cup of hot tap water in clear glasses labeled 1–5.

    1   2   3   4   5

    b. Each day observe the growth of the salt deposits on the bottoms of the glasses and record the water level. (Some evaporation will take place.)

    c. **Writing** Describe the relationship between the rate of growth of the salt deposits and the salt concentration.

    d. **Writing** Describe the relationship between the size of the salt deposits and the salt concentration.

1. **Writing** Describe a situation that can be modeled by this graph. Describe the characteristics of the graph over four intervals. Copy the graph and add scales and labels on the axes.

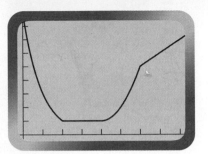

For Exercises 2–4, use the heart rate graph.   2-1

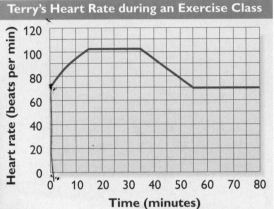

Terry's Heart Rate during an Exercise Class

2. What is the control variable? What is the dependent variable?

3. What is the domain of the function? What is the range?

4. Use the terms *linear* or *nonlinear* and *increasing, decreasing,* or *constant* to describe the graph.

5. The coordinates of two points are (3, 21) and   2-2
(−1, −11).

   a. Find the slope of the line through the points.

   b. Find the vertical intercept of the line.

   c. Write an equation of the line.

   d. Find the value of x when $y = 7$.

6. Use the equation $xy = 10$.   2-3

   a. Write the equation in the form $y = \frac{k}{x}$.

   b. Graph the equation over a domain of −10 to 10.

   c. Describe the graph.

   d. Find the value of y when $x = 2.5$.

   e. Find the value of x when $y = 8$.

Surface Area and Volume of Spheres

around and *round*

Focus

Find the surface area and volume of spheres, and use the fact that all spheres are similar.

Talk it Over

Suppose you have an orange that is almost perfectly round. Suppose you also have the materials shown here: string, a vegetable peeler, scissors, aluminum foil, and a ruler.

1. The *surface area* of the orange is the area of the skin of the orange. Suggest how to estimate the surface area of the orange in at least three ways—using string, using a peeler, and using the aluminum foil.

2. The *volume* of the orange is everything inside the skin. Suggest how to use any of the materials in question 1 to estimate the volume of the orange in at least two different ways.

3. How could you use any of the materials shown to measure the radius of an orange?

4. Imagine packing a round object into a cylinder that is just tall and just wide enough to contain it. What is the volume of this cylinder? (Remember that the formula for the volume of a cylinder is $V = \pi r^2 h$.) About how much of the cylinder is filled by the object?

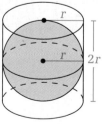

An orange is shaped like a *sphere*. A **sphere** is a round space figure. The *radius of a sphere* is the distance from its center to its surface. The *diameter of a sphere* is twice the radius.

SURFACE AREA AND VOLUME OF A SPHERE

Surface Area	**Volume**	
$S.A. = 4\pi r^2$	$V = \frac{4}{3}\pi r^3$	

measured in *square units*

measured in *cubic units*

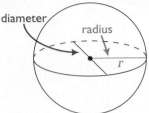

The terms **radius** and **diameter** refer to the segments shown and to the lengths of those segments.

Sample 1

The radius of a field hockey ball is about 3.7 cm.

a. Find its surface area to the nearest square centimeter.

b. Find its volume to the nearest cubic centimeter.

Sample Response

a. **Problem Solving Strategy:** Use a formula.

$$S.A. = 4\pi r^2 \quad \longleftarrow \text{Write the formula for the surface area of a sphere.}$$
$$= 4\pi(3.7)^2 \quad \longleftarrow \text{Substitute 3.7 for } r.$$
$$\approx 172.03$$

The surface area of a field hockey ball is about 172 cm².

b. **Problem Solving Strategy:** Use a formula.

$$V = \frac{4}{3}\pi r^3 \quad \longleftarrow \text{Write the formula for the volume of a sphere.}$$
$$= \frac{4}{3}\pi(3.7)^3 \quad \longleftarrow \text{Substitute 3.7 for } r.$$
$$\approx 212.17$$

The volume of a field hockey ball is about 212 cm³.

For calculations involving π, give your answers to the nearest tenth unless told otherwise.

Talk it Over

5. Why is surface area measured in square units and volume measured in cubic units?

6. How close is the estimate you made in question 4 to the formula for the volume of a sphere?

7. How can you use the formula for the surface area of a sphere if you know the diameter instead of the radius?

Volume = 14 cm³

What is the radius of this spherical bubble?

Sample Response

Problem Solving Strategy: Use a formula.

$$V = \frac{4}{3}\pi r^3$$ ← Write the formula for the volume of a sphere.

$$14 = \frac{4}{3}\pi r^3$$ ← Substitute 14 for V.

$$14 \approx 4.19 r^3$$

$$3.34 \approx r^3$$ ← Divide both sides by 4.19.

$$\sqrt[3]{3.34} \approx r$$ ← Find the cube root.

$$1.49 \approx r$$

The radius of the bubble is about 1.5 cm.

Student Resources Toolbox
p.647 *Solving Equations and inequalities*

Talk it Over

8. The surface area of a basketball is about 1810 cm².

   a. Describe how to find the radius of a basketball using the surface area information.

   b. How is solving this problem different from Sample 2?

········► **Now you are ready for:**
Exs. 1–19 on pp. 87–89

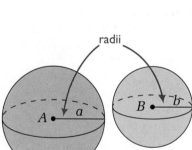

radii

Sphere A is similar to sphere B. (Spheres are named by their centers.)

Similar Spheres

All spheres have the same shape, so all spheres are similar. The ratio of the surface areas of two spheres is the ratio of the squares of the corresponding radii.

$$\frac{\text{surface area of sphere } A}{\text{surface area of sphere } B} = \frac{(\text{radius of sphere } A)^2}{(\text{radius of sphere } B)^2} = \frac{a^2}{b^2}$$

Also, the ratio of the volumes of two spheres is the ratio of the cubes of the corresponding radii.

$$\frac{\text{volume of sphere } A}{\text{volume of sphere } B} = \frac{(\text{radius of sphere } A)^3}{(\text{radius of sphere } B)^3} = \frac{a^3}{b^3}$$

Talk it Over

9. Is the ratio of the squares of the diameters of two spheres the same as the ratio of the squares of their radii? Why or why not?

10. Is the ratio of the cubes of the diameters of two spheres the same as the ratio of the cubes of their radii? Why or why not?

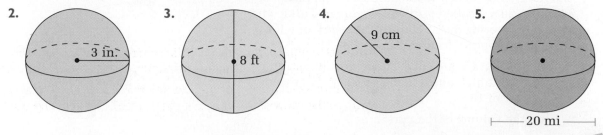

Sample 3

To the nearest 10 mi, the diameter of Earth is about 7930 mi. The diameter of the moon is about 2160 mi. Compare the volumes of Earth and the moon.

7930 mi

2160 mi

Sample Response

Assume that Earth and the moon are spheres. The ratio of their volumes is the ratio of the cubes of their diameters.

$$\frac{\text{volume of Earth}}{\text{volume of the moon}} = \frac{(\text{diameter of Earth})^3}{(\text{diameter of the moon})^3}$$

$$= \frac{7930^3}{2160^3}$$

$$\approx 50$$

The volume of Earth is about 50 times the volume of the moon.

Look Back ←

Use the formula for the surface area of a sphere to write the ratio of the surface areas of two spheres, one with radius a and the other with radius b. Write the ratio in simplified form. Is it what you expect? Do the same with the ratio of the volumes.

·····► **Now you are ready for:**
Exs. 20–42 on pp. 89–90

2-4 **Exercises and Problems**

1. **Reading** Look at the formulas for the surface area and the volume of a sphere on page 85. How are the formulas alike? How are they different? How are they like other formulas you know for area and volume?

Find the surface area and the volume of each sphere.

2.

3 in.

3.

8 ft

4.

9 cm

5.

20 mi

2-4 Surface Area and Volume of Spheres

87

Sports Complete the table.

	Type of Ball	Diameter (cm)	Radius (cm)	Surface Area (cm²)	Volume (cm³)
6.	basketball	24.0	?	?	?
7.	soccer ball	22.0	?	?	?
8.	large softball	13.0	?	?	?
9.	tennis ball	6.5	?	?	?
10.	golf ball	4.3	?	?	?
11.	table tennis ball	3.7	?	?	?

Find the radius of each sphere with the given surface area or volume.

12. S.A. = 36π in.²   **13.** $V = 36\pi$ cm³   **14.** $V = 288\pi$ ft³   **15.** S.A. = 100π m²

Architecture Round houses are built by people all over the world, from the frozen Arctic to sunny Polynesia to the windswept plains of Central Asia. Round houses are warmer in cold climates, are cooler in hot climates, and can withstand high winds.

16. The Inuit people of the Arctic use blocks of snow to build igloos in the shape of a *hemisphere,* or half a sphere. The thick snow walls and the round shape help to hold heat inside an igloo. Suppose an igloo is 15 ft in diameter.

   a. Find the amount of floor space in the igloo to the nearest square foot.

   b. Find the surface area of the igloo to the nearest square foot and its volume to the nearest cubic foot.

   c. Suppose you build a snow house with a square floor, flat walls, and a flat roof. Your house is as tall as the igloo and has the same amount of floor space. Find the surface area and volume of your snow house.

   d. What is the ratio of the surface areas of the igloo and your snow house? What is the ratio of their volumes?

   e. **Writing** Use the fact that heat loss is proportional to surface area to explain why hemispherical houses are built in the Arctic.

17. The traditional homes of the herders of the plains of Central Asia are called *yurts*. A Kirghiz or Turkic yurt has a felt covering over a round framework of willow poles. Curved poles form a domed roof.

   a. Find the surface area of a Turkic yurt with walls that are 7 ft high and a hemispherical dome with a diameter of 18 ft.

   b. Find the volume of the yurt in part (a).

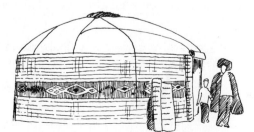

18. The outside of a baseball is made of two congruent pieces of stitched leather. Find the area of one piece. The diameter of a baseball is about 7.5 cm.

19. When a bubble gum bubble bursts, it leaves 9 in.² of gum on Sara's face. Assume the bubble was a sphere whose surface area was twice the area of gum on Sara's face. Estimate the diameter of the bubble.

20. Sphere Q has radius 12 units. Sphere R has radius 8 units.

 a. What is the ratio of the diameters of the spheres?

 b. What is the ratio of the surface areas of the spheres?

 c. What is the ratio of the volumes of the spheres?

connection to **E A R T H   S C I E N C E**

 Career Geologists use a series of nested spheres to model the interior of Earth.

 Writing Use the diagram to predict which layer in each pair has the greater volume. Explain how you made your choice.

21. the crust or the inner core

22. the upper mantle or the outer core

Complete the table. Round volumes to the nearest billion cubic kilometers.

> volume of crust = volume of outer sphere − volume of inner sphere
> $$= \frac{4}{3}\pi(6353)^3 - \frac{4}{3}\pi(6340)^3 \approx 7{,}000{,}000{,}000$$

	Layer	Radius of outer sphere (km)	Radius of inner sphere (km)	Volume (billion km³)
23.	crust	6353	6340	?
24.	upper mantle	6340	5710	?
25.	lower mantle	5710	3420	?
26.	outer core	3420	1600	?
27.	inner core	1600	0	?

28. Compare your results in Exercises 23, 24, 26, and 27 with your predictions in Exercises 21 and 22. Do the results surprise you? Why or why not?

29. Astronomy Jupiter has a diameter of about 88,846 mi and Earth has a diameter of about 7926 mi.

 a. Find the ratio of their surface areas.　　　　**b.** Find the ratio of their volumes.

In *Journey to the Centre of the Earth*, written by Jules Verne and published in 1864, Axel reluctantly accompanies his uncle, Professor Lidenbrock, on a trip down a secret passage that leads to the center of Earth.

Today we know that the radius of Earth is about 3963 mi.

30. By Axel's reasoning, how long would it actually take Axel and his uncle to reach the center of Earth?

31. Find the ratio of the surface area of Earth to the surface area found with Axel's estimate of Earth's radius.

32. Find the ratio of the actual volume of Earth to the volume found with Axel's estimate of Earth's radius.

> *Journey to the Centre of the Earth*
>
> " ... I want to be able to draw a map of our journey, a sort of vertical section of the globe ... [said Professor Lidenbrock]."
>
> "That will be very interesting, Uncle, but are your observations sufficiently precise .... ?"
>
> "Yes. ... I estimate that we have come 213 miles ... and we are at a depth of 48 miles."
>
> "Uncle," I said, "admitting that your calculations are correct, will you allow me to draw a vigorous conclusion from them?"
>
> "Conclude away, my boy."
>
> "... the radius of the earth is about ... 4,800 miles [and] we have done forty-eight ... And this at a cost of 213 miles diagonally ... In about twenty days ... If we keep on like that, it will take us ... nearly five and a half years, to reach the centre! ... Not counting the fact that ...we shall come out ... on the earth's circumference long before we reach the centre."
>
> "To blazes with your calculations!" retorted my uncle angrily.

Ongoing ASSESSMENT

33. **a.** **Using Manipulatives** Find an orange that is close in shape to a sphere. Using any materials you have at home, estimate the surface area and the volume of the orange *without using the formulas.*

b. Use the formulas to see how close your estimates are to the actual surface area and volume of the orange.

c. **Writing** Describe the methods you used in part (a).

Review PREVIEW

34. Choose the letters of the inverse variation equations. *(Section 2-3)*

a. $y = 5x$　　　**b.** $y = \dfrac{x}{5}$　　　**c.** $5 = xy$　　　**d.** $y = \dfrac{5}{x}$

Suppose you choose one marble from a bag that contains 2 green marbles, 3 red marbles, and 3 blue marbles. Find each probability. *(Toolbox Skill 7)*

35. P(green marble)　　　**36.** P(red marble)　　　**37.** P(blue marble)

Tell whether or not each equation shows direct variation. If it does, identify the variation constant. *(Section 2-2)*

38. $y = 196x$　　　**39.** $y = 1.4x + 27$　　　**40.** $\dfrac{y}{x} = 13$　　　**41.** $y = 35$

2 Working on the Unit Project

42. **Research** To learn more about the ecosystems of salt lakes, you may want to read selected chapters from these books:

➤ *East African Mountains and Lakes* by Leslie Brown

➤ *Planet Earth: Rivers and Lakes* by Lawrence Pringle and the Editors of Time-Life Books

Direct Variation with Powers

Focus
Model and apply relationships in which one quantity is proportional to the square or the cube of another quantity.

EXPLORATION

How do the graphs of some formulas from geometry compare?

- **Materials: graphics calculators or graphing software**
- **Work in a group of three students.**

As a group, decide which formula each of you will work with.

$$C = \pi d \qquad\qquad \text{S.A.} = 4\pi r^2 \qquad\qquad V = \frac{4}{3}\pi r^3$$

① Answer these questions about your formula.

    a. What does each of the variables mean?

    b. What is the control variable? the dependent variable?

② Replace the control variable in your formula with *x* and the dependent variable with *y*. Then graph your formula. Sketch the graph in your notebook.

    ③ Answer these questions about your graph.

        a. Is it *linear* or *nonlinear*?

        b. Is it a *constant graph,* a *growth graph,* a *decay graph,* or *none of these*?

        c. Does it pass through the point (0, 0)?

        d. Is it the graph of a function?

④ Answer these questions with the other members of your group.

    a. How are the formulas alike? How are they different?

  b. How are the graphs alike? How are they different?

Direct Variation with the Square

In the formula S.A. $= 4\pi r^2$, the dependent variable, the surface area, varies directly with the square of the control variable, the radius. The relationship between the variables is called **direct variation with the square.**

$$\text{S.A.} = 4\pi r^2 \qquad \text{variation constant}$$

DIRECT VARIATION WITH THE SQUARE

The equation has this form:

$$y = kx^2$$

variation constant
$(k \neq 0)$

You read this as follows:

"y varies directly with x^2,"
or
"y is proportional to x^2."

The graph is a curve called a *parabola*.

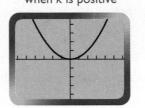

when k is positive   when k is negative

Talk it Over

1. How does changing the sign of k affect the graph of $y = kx^2$?

2. How do you think increasing the value of k changes the graph of $y = kx^2$? To check your answer, graph $y = \frac{1}{2}x^2$, $y = x^2$, and $y = 2x^2$ on the same screen.

Videotapes of basketball games show that some players leap as high as 3 ft.

Sample 1

BY THE WAY...

The great basketball player Michael Jordan appeared to have an impossibly long hang time because he released the ball *on the way down,* instead of at or before the peak of his leap.

The leap height of a basketball player varies directly with the square of the "hang time." When the leap height is in feet and the hang time is in seconds, the variation constant is 4.

What is the hang time for a leap height of 3 ft? Round your answer to the nearest hundredth of a second.

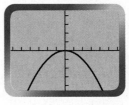

"Hang time" is how long the player is in the air.

Sample Response

Problem Solving Strategy: Use an equation.

Let $L =$ the leap height in feet.

Let $t =$ the hang time in seconds.

$$L = 4t^2 \quad \longleftarrow \text{ L varies directly with } t^2. \text{ The variation constant is 4.}$$

$$3 = 4t^2 \quad \longleftarrow \text{ Substitute 3 for } L.$$

$$0.75 = t^2 \quad \longleftarrow \text{ Divide both sides by 4.}$$

$$\sqrt{0.75} = t \quad \longleftarrow \begin{array}{l}\text{The hang time cannot be negative.}\\ \text{Find the positive square root.}\end{array}$$

$$0.87 \approx t$$

The hang time is about 0.87 second.

The pole vault is a track and field event. From a running start, the athlete uses a springy pole to leap over a high crossbar.

Sample 2

The height reached by a pole-vaulter varies directly with the square of the speed of the athlete at the moment the pole is stuck in the ground. If one pole-vaulter reaches a height of 16 ft with a speed of 32 ft/s, how high does a second pole-vaulter leap with a speed of 35 ft/s? Round the answer to the nearest foot.

Sample Response

Problem Solving Strategy: Use an equation.

Step 1 Model the situation with an equation that represents direct variation with the square.

Let $h =$ the height in feet.
Let $s =$ the speed in feet per second.

$$h = ks^2$$

Sergei Bubka set an Olympic pole vault record in 1988 for the USSR. In 1992 he set a world record by reaching a height of 20 ft 1 in.

Step 2 Find the variation constant.

$$16 = k(32^2) \quad \longleftarrow \text{ Substitute 16 for } h \text{ and 32 for } s.$$

$$0.016 \approx k \quad \longleftarrow \text{ Divide both sides by } 32^2.$$

Step 3 Find the height when the speed is 35 ft/s.

$$h \approx (0.016)(35^2) \quad \longleftarrow \text{ Substitute 0.016 for } k \text{ and 35 for } s.$$

$$\approx 19.6$$

A pole-vaulter with a speed of 35 ft/s leaps about 20 ft.

leap height

······► **Now you are ready for:**
Exs. 1–14 on pp. 96–97

Direct Variation with the Cube

In the formula $V = \frac{4}{3}\pi r^3$, the dependent variable, the volume, varies directly with the cube of the control variable, the radius. The relationship between the variables is called **direct variation with the cube**.

$$V = \frac{4}{3}\pi r^3 \qquad \text{variation constant}$$

X · Lab

DIRECT VARIATION WITH THE CUBE

The equation has this form:

$$y = kx^3$$

variation constant
$(k \neq 0)$

You read this as follows:

"y varies directly with x^3,"
or
"y is proportional to x^3."

The graph is a curve through the origin.

when k is positive   when k is negative

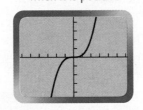 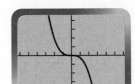

Talk it Over

3. How does changing the sign of k affect the graph of $y = kx^3$?

4. How do you think increasing the value of k changes the graph of $y = kx^3$? To check your answer, graph $y = \frac{1}{2}x^3$, $y = x^3$, and $y = 2x^3$ on the same screen.

Sample 3

The number of watts of power generated by a windmill varies directly with the cube of the wind speed in miles per hour.

How fast must the wind be blowing for this windmill to produce 200 watts of power? For this windmill, the variation constant is 0.015. Round your answer to the nearest mile per hour.

Sample Response

Problem Solving Strategy: Use a formula.

Let W = the power in watts.

Let s = the wind speed in miles per hour.

$W = 0.015s^3$ ◄──── W varies directly with s^3. The variation constant is 0.015.

Method ❶ Use algebra.

$$W = 0.015s^3$$
$$200 = 0.015s^3 \quad \text{◄──── Substitute 200 for } W.$$
$$13{,}333.33 \approx s^3 \quad \text{◄──── Divide both sides by 0.015.}$$
$$\sqrt[3]{13{,}333.33} \approx s \quad \text{◄──── Find the cube root.}$$
$$23.71 \approx s$$

The wind speed must be about 24 mi/h.

Method ❷ Use a graph.

Replace the control variable with x and the dependent variable with y.

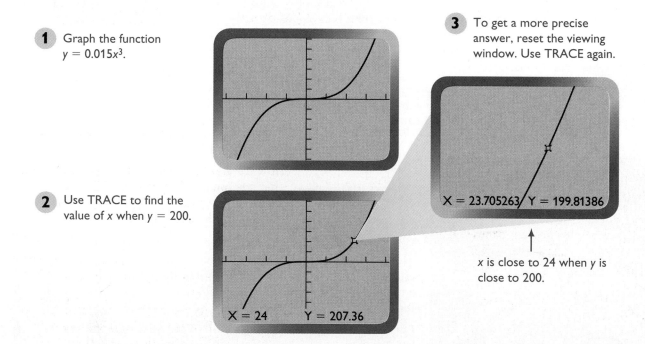

1 Graph the function $y = 0.015x^3$.

2 Use TRACE to find the value of x when $y = 200$.

X = 24   Y = 207.36

3 To get a more precise answer, reset the viewing window. Use TRACE again.

X = 23.705263   Y = 199.81386

x is close to 24 when y is close to 200.

The wind speed must be about 24 mi/h.

> **Look Back** ◄─
>
> How are the graphs and equations for direct variation, direct variation with the square, and direct variation with the cube alike? How are they different?

······► **Now you are ready for:**
Exs. 15–37 on pp. 97–98

2-5 Direct Variation with Powers

2-5 Exercises and Problems

1. **Reading** In which quadrant(s) does the graph of $y = kx^2$ appear when k is positive? when k is negative?

2. Suppose you repeat the Exploration using the formulas for the perimeter of a square ($P = 4s$), the area of a square ($A = s^2$), and the volume of a cube ($V = s^3$). Without graphing, predict how your group's answers will compare.

3. Make a concept map for all the variation models presented in this unit.

For each equation in Exercises 4–7, find the values of x when $y = 15$. Round decimal answers to the nearest tenth.

4. $y = \pi x^2$ 5. $y = 4\pi x^2$ 6. $y = 4x^2$ 7. $y = 5.7x^2$

For Exercises 8 and 9, write an equation that models each situation. Use k to represent the variation constant.

8. The surface area, S.A., of a hemisphere varies directly with the square of the diameter, d.

9. The energy, E, of a moving car varies directly with the square of its speed, s.

10. The amount of material needed to cover a ball varies directly with the square of the radius. It takes about 172 cm² of material to cover a ball with a radius of 3.7 cm. What is the radius of a ball that needs 366 cm² of material to cover it?

11. The area of a square varies directly with the square of the diagonal. A square with a diagonal of 9 in. has an area of 40.5 in.². What is the area of a square with a diagonal of 14 in.?

connection to **DRIVER'S EDUCATION**

When a car goes around a curve on a flat road, the car will stay on the road only if the force between the car and the road is great enough. The force, in pounds, needed to accelerate a car around a curve varies directly with the square of the speed of the car in feet per second.

For Exercises 12 and 13, the value of the variation constant is 1.3.

12. Suppose that when the road is dry, the maximum force between the car and the road is 2250 lb. How fast can the car take the turn? Round your answer to the nearest mile per hour. (*Hint:* 1 ft/s ≈ 0.68 mi/h)

13. Suppose that when the road is wet, the maximum force between the car and the road is 1500 lb. How fast can the car take the turn? Round the answer to the nearest mile per hour.

14. The distance an object falls varies directly with the square of the time the object is in the air. When distance is measured in feet and time is measured in seconds, the variation constant is 16.

   a. Write an equation for the distance an object falls as a function of time. Use d for distance and t for time.

   b. **Skydiving** A skydiver jumps from an airplane at an altitude of 15,000 ft. The parachute opens at an altitude of 3000 ft. Use your equation to calculate how long the skydiver has been in the air when the parachute opens.

For each equation in Exercises 15–18, find the value of x when $y = 15$. Round decimal answers to the nearest tenth.

15. $y = \frac{4}{3}\pi x^3$ 16. $y = -x^3$ 17. $y = 3.7x^3$ 18. $y = -4x^3$

Wind Power For Exercises 19–21, use this information.

The power generated by a windmill is given by the equation $W = ks^3$, where W is power measured in watts and s is the wind speed in miles per hour.

19. One windmill has a variation constant of 0.013. How fast must the wind be blowing for the windmill to produce 170 watts of power?

20. How does the power output from a windmill change if the variation constant is increased?

21. How does the power output from a windmill change if the wind speed is halved?

For Exercises 22 and 23, use the formula for the volume of a sphere.

22. What is the radius of a sphere with volume 282 in.^{3}?

23. a. How does the volume of a sphere change when the radius doubles?

   b. How does the volume of a sphere change when the radius is halved?

24. **Biology** Suppose the height of an animal is h.

   a. The strength of an animal's bones varies directly with h^2. Model this relationship with an equation. Use s as the variation constant.

   b. The weight of an animal varies directly with h^3. Model this relationship with an equation. Use w as the variation constant.

   c. Explain why, as the height of the animal increases, its body weight increases much faster than the strength of its bones.

Ongoing **ASSESSMENT**

25. **Writing** Explain how to test a graph or data set of an unknown function to decide whether it shows direct variation, inverse variation, direct variation with the square, direct variation with the cube, or none of these.

BY THE WAY...

No gorilla could ever be as big as the movie monster King Kong. Its skeleton could not support its weight.

Find the surface area and volume of a sphere with each radius. *(Section 2-4)*

26. $r = 7$ cm

27. $r = 1.9$ in.

28. $r = 62$ cm

Use the Pythagorean theorem to find the missing side of each right triangle.
(Toolbox Skill 31)

29. leg: 6   leg: ?
hypotenuse: 10

30. leg: 5   leg: ?
hypotenuse: 13

31. leg: 7   leg: 24
hypotenuse: ?

Evaluate each expression for the given value of the variable. Round decimal answers to the nearest tenth. *(Toolbox Skill 9)*

32. x^4, when $x = 2.2$

33. $\frac{9}{5}hk^2$, when $h = 15$
and $k = 2$

34. $4x^5$, when $x = 3$

Working on the Unit Project

To study the evaporation of water from a lake, you can use a cylinder or a cone as a simple geometric model of the lake.

35. Suppose the cylinder at the right is filled to the top with salt water. Due to evaporation, the water level in the cylinder drops one inch each day for nine days.

   a. Graph the volume of the water as a function of time. Use the formula $V = \pi r^2 h$ for the volume of a cylinder. The variable r is the radius of a circular base and h is the height of the cylinder.

   b. Describe your graph.   **c.** What is the domain?   **d.** What is the range?

36. Repeat Exercise 35 for the cone at the right. Use the formula $V = \frac{1}{3}\pi r^2 h$ for the volume of a cone. (*Hint:* As the water level drops, the length of the radius remains half the height of the cone.)

37. **Writing** Suppose the water in the cylinder and the cone in Exercises 35 and 36 is equally salty before any evaporation takes place. Will it still be equally salty after water has evaporated for nine days? Why or why not?

Focus

Use negative, zero, and fractional exponents.

Using Powers

The Powers *that be*

EXPLORATION

(What) *definition of negative and zero exponents does your calculator use?*

- **Materials: scientific or graphics calculators**
- **Work with another student.**

Table 1		
2^{-1}	?	$\frac{1}{2}$
2^{-2}	?	$\frac{1}{4}$
2^{-3}	?	$\frac{1}{8}$
2^{-4}	?	$\frac{1}{16}$
2^{-5}	?	$\frac{1}{32}$

1. **a.** To complete the second column of Table 1, use a calculator to find the value of the expression in the first column.

   b. Use your calculator to show that the decimals you wrote in the second column are equal to the fractions in the third column.

   c. What definition of x^{-n} do you think your calculator uses? Check that this definition works for 8^{-1}, 3^{-2}, and $(-5)^{-3}$.

Table 2	
1^0	?
2^0	?
3^0	?
4^0	?
5^0	?

2. **a.** To complete Table 2, use a calculator to find the value of the expression in the first column.

   b. What definition of x^0 do you think your calculator uses? Check that your calculator also uses this definition for negative values of x.

3. To see if your definitions for x^{-n} and x^0 work when $x = 0$, use your calculator to evaluate 0^{-1}, 0^{-2}, and 0^0. What happens? Why do you think this happens?

X (. △ab →

ZERO AND NEGATIVE EXPONENTS

Zero Exponent Rule

$a^0 = 1$ when $a \neq 0$

Negative Exponent Rule

$a^{-n} = \dfrac{1}{a^n}$ and $\dfrac{1}{a^{-n}} = a^n$ when $a \neq 0$

Simplify $6b^0a^{-4}$. Write the answer with positive exponents.

Sample Response

$$6b^0a^{-4} = 6 \cdot 1 \cdot a^{-4}$$ ⟵ Use the zero exponent rule.

$$= 6\left(\frac{1}{a^4}\right)$$ ⟵ Use the negative exponent rule.

······▶ Now you are ready for:
Exs. 1–11 on p. 102

$$= \frac{6}{a^4}$$

Exs. 1–11 on p. 102

EXPLORATION

What definition of $x^{1/2}$ and $x^{1/3}$ does your calculator use?

• **Materials: scientific or graphics calculators**
• **Work with another student.**

① Use a calculator to complete the table.

② **a.** Compare the numbers in the last two columns of your completed table. Make a conjecture about the meaning of $x^{1/2}$. Use your calculator to test your conjecture for several more values of x.

x	$\sqrt{x}$	$x^{1/2}$
1	?	?
2	?	?
3	?	?
4	?	?
5	?	?

b. Does your definition work for negative values of x? Why or why not?

③ Make a conjecture about the meaning of $x^{1/3}$. Use your calculator to test your conjecture for several positive values of x and several negative values of x. Do your results support your conjecture?

In the Exploration, you found that square roots and cube roots can be expressed using fractional exponents.

X ◁ab

FRACTIONAL EXPONENTS

exponential form   radical form

$$x^{1/2} = \sqrt{x} \text{ when } x \geq 0$$

⎰ The exponent $\frac{1}{2}$ means the nonnegative square root.

$$x^{1/3} = \sqrt[3]{x}$$

⎰ The exponent $\frac{1}{3}$ means the cube root.

Simplify.

1. $81^{1/2}$

2. $27^{1/3}$

3. $(-8)^{1/3}$

4. Let $a = 9$ and $b = 16$. Find the value of $a \cdot b^{1/2}$ and of $(ab)^{1/2}$. How do the values compare?

The radical form of the expression $(2y)^{1/3}$ is $\sqrt[3]{2y}$. Rewrite each expression in the form indicated.

5. $(5x)^{1/2}$ in radical form

6. $4\sqrt[3]{n}$ in exponential form

Sample 2

You can use the formula below to estimate the speed v (in feet per second) that a roller coaster car must travel in order to stay on a vertical loop of track with radius r (in feet).

$$v = (32r)^{1/2}$$

About how fast must a roller coaster car travel on a vertical loop of track with radius 23 ft? Round your answer to the nearest foot per second.

Watch Out!
To find the square root of a product, you first multiply and then find the square root.

Loop-and-screw roller coaster, Seibuen Park, Saitama Prefecture, Japan

Sample Response

Problem Solving Strategy: Use a formula.

$v = (32r)^{1/2}$

$= (32 \cdot 23)^{1/2}$ ⟵ Substitute 23 for r.

$= 736^{1/2}$

≈ 27.13 ⟵ Use the exponent key on your calculator.

The speed of the roller coaster car must be about 27 ft/s.

BY THE WAY...

The Moonsault Scramble coaster at the Fujikyu Highland Park, near Kawaguchi Lake, Japan, is 207 ft tall. When it was built, it was the tallest above-ground roller coaster in the world.

······▶ **Now you are ready for:**
Exs. 12–43 on pp. 102–104

Look Back ◀

Summarize the meaning of each type of exponent: positive integer, negative integer, zero, one half, and one third.

2-6 Exercises and Problems

BY THE WAY. . .

The idea of zero arose separately in ancient India, Iraq, and Central and South America.

1. **Reading** For what value(s) of x does $x^0 \neq 1$?

Simplify. Write answers with positive exponents.

2. $-4s^0 r^{-3}$

3. $\dfrac{45u^{-5}}{9}$

4. $(2 + x^0)(y^{-6})$

5. $(4m^{-2})(3n^{-4})$

6. $(b^0 c^{-1})(d^4)$

7. $\dfrac{4}{v^{-2}}$

8. $\dfrac{4 + 7g^0}{h^{-3}}$

9. $\dfrac{15n^{-5}}{p^{-4}}$

10. To understand the zero and negative exponent rules, Le Ly looked at powers of 2. She noticed a pattern.

   a. Describe the pattern that Le Ly noticed.

   b. When Le Ly continues the pattern, what will she write for 2^0? for 2^{-1}? for 2^{-2}?

   c. Does Le Ly's method work for bases other than 2?

$$2^4 = 16$$
$$2^3 = 8 \Big) \div 2$$
$$2^2 = 4 \Big) \div 2$$
$$2^1 = 2 \Big) \div 2$$
$$2^0 =$$
$$2^{-1} =$$
$$2^{-2} =$$

11. **Writing** Explain why $\dfrac{1}{a^{-n}} = a^n$ when a is not equal to zero.

Simplify.

12. $49^{1/2}$

13. $64^{1/2}$

14. $125^{1/3}$

15. $(-27)^{1/3}$

Rewrite each expression using fractional exponents.

16. $3\sqrt{a}$

17. $-2\sqrt[3]{x}$

18. $\sqrt[3]{3ab}$

19. $\sqrt{s} \cdot \sqrt[3]{t}$

20. $\sqrt{5x}$

21. $7\sqrt{8x}$

22. $-9\sqrt{p} \cdot \sqrt[3]{4q}$

23. $\sqrt{\dfrac{s}{2}}$

Rewrite each expression in radical form.

24. $5x^{1/2}$

25. $-6w^{1/3}$

26. $(3j)^{1/3}$

27. $\left(\dfrac{4}{r}\right)^{1/2}$

28. a. The formula $V = \dfrac{4}{3}\pi r^3$ gives the volume of a sphere

   of radius r. By solving the formula for r, show that $r = \left(\dfrac{3V}{4\pi}\right)^{1/3}$.

   b. Find the radius of a sphere with volume 200 cm³.

   c. Will the sphere in part (b) fit inside a cube with an edge that is 6 cm long?

For Exercises 29 and 30, use this information.

The period p (in seconds) of a pendulum is given by this formula:

$$p = 2\pi\left(\frac{l}{9.8}\right)^{1/2}$$

29. a. Find the period of a pendulum that is 1 m long.

   b. Find the period of a pendulum that is 2 m long.

   c. How do you think doubling the length of a pendulum affects the period? Check your answer for another pair of lengths.

> The *period* is the time it takes a pendulum to complete a swing.

l = length in meters

BY THE WAY...

In 1851 Jean Foucault used a pendulum to prove that Earth rotates on its axis. Foucault's pendulum appeared to rotate because it stayed in the same place while Earth rotated.

30. Writing Do you think that changing the weight of a pendulum changes its period? Explain your answer. (*Hint:* How can you use the formula for p to decide?)

31. Open-ended Pendulums were replaced—first by springs and gears and then by quartz crystals—in clocks and watches. Why do you think that was?

32. Wind Power The wind speed s (in miles per hour) needed to generate W watts of electric power is given by this formula:

$$s = \left(\frac{W}{1.5 \times 10^{-2}}\right)^{1/3}$$

How fast would the wind have to blow in order to generate 180 watts of power? Round your answer to the nearest mile per hour.

33 TECHNOLOGY Use a graphics calculator or graphing software.

   a. Graph each pair of functions on the same screen. Include all four quadrants in the viewing window.

   $y = x^2$ and $y = x^{1/2}$ $y = x^3$ and $y = x^{1/3}$

   b. How are the graphs in each pair alike? How are they different?

   c. How are the graphs of $y = x^{1/2}$ and $y = x^{1/3}$ alike? How are they different?

   d. Are there any values of x for which $x^{1/2} > x^2$?

   e. Are there any values of x for which $x^{1/3} > x^3$?

34. a. Find each value and arrange in order from least to greatest:

7^0 7^3 $(-7)^3$ 7^{-3} $(-7)^{-3}$ $7^{1/3}$ $(-7)^{1/3}$

b. Writing Suppose your friend was absent when Section 2-6 was discussed. Explain to your friend why $a^n > a^{-n}$ when n is positive and $a > 1$.

c. Writing Explain to your friend why $a^3 > a^{1/3}$ when $a > 1$.

Write an equation that models each situation. Use *k* to represent the variation constant. *(Section 2-5)*

35. The area of a square room varies directly with the square of the length of the room.

36. The volume of a globe varies directly with the cube of its radius.

Tell whether each statement is an example of *inductive reasoning* or *deductive reasoning*. *(Section 1-6)*

37. Stephen King's new novel must be a horror story since all his previous best-selling novels have been horror stories.

38. If the measures of two angles of a triangle are 35° and 56°, then the measure of the third angle is 89°.

Simplify. *(Toolbox Skill 9)*

39. $18 \cdot 2^3$ **40.** $120 \cdot 4^2$ **41.** $5^4 \cdot 3^2$ **42.** $(2^4 \cdot 3^3)^2$

Working on the Unit Project

This exercise will help you to see how a drop in the water level of a lake affects the sizes of populations of animals living in the water.

43. In 1985, one cubic foot of water in Mono Lake held 1.9×10^3 brine shrimp. There were about 8.4×10^{10} cubic feet of water in the lake.

a. In 1985 about how many brine shrimp were there in Mono Lake?

b. One brine shrimp weighs about 2.7×10^{-3} oz. What was the approximate total weight of brine shrimp in Mono Lake in 1985?

c. In 1985 the depth of Mono Lake was about 50 ft. Suppose the water level dropped 15 ft. About how much less water would be in the lake? Assume that the lake is a cylinder.

d. About how many fewer shrimp can the lake hold at the water level in part (c)?

e. About how many pounds do the brine shrimp in part (d) weigh?

This brine shrimp is about 8 times actual size.

Doubling and Halving

····Focus
Explore situations
in which quantities
repeatedly double
or split in half.

way **2** *go!*

EXPLORATION

How fast do numbers grow as they double?

- **Materials: newspapers, rulers**
- **Work with another student.**

Table 1

Number of tears	Area of each piece
0	
1	
2	
3	
⋮	

Table 2

Number of tears	Number of pieces
0	1
1	2
2	
3	
⋮	

① Read step 2. Predict how many times you will be able to tear the stack of newspaper pieces.

② **a.** Unfold a sheet of newspaper. Measure its area. Copy Table 1 and record the area in the first row.

b. Fold the sheet of newspaper in half. Tear along the fold so that you have two pieces. What is the area of each piece? Record the area in Table 1.

c. Stack the pieces of newspaper on top of each other. Fold the stack in half and tear along the fold. Copy Table 2 and record the number of pieces. Record the area of each piece in Table 1.

d. Repeat part (c) until you cannot tear the stack again. Extend Tables 1 and 2 as needed to record the number of pieces and the area of each piece.

③ Suppose you could tear the stack as many times as you predicted in step 1. How many pieces would you have?

④ Measure the height of your stack of pieces of newspaper. Estimate how tall the stack would be if you could make ten tears.

The Daily Herald

Wednesday, October 19, 1995

Vol. 274, No. 49   28 pages   30 cents

Town Landfill Hits 50,000 Cubic Meters

Volume Doubling Every 3 Years

At a special town meeting yesterday, the town council announced that the amount of trash in the town's landfill had reached the 50,000 cubic meter mark. Further, a consulting firm hired by the town discovered that the volume of the landfill is doubling every three years.

Last year the town council hired the consulting firm to study the town's trash disposal program. At present, 80 percent of the town's trash goes into the landfill. To prevent an impending "trash crisis" in which the landfill can no longer accommodate the town's trash, the firm made the following recommendations:

- Institute a curbside recycling program for newspaper, glass, plastic, and aluminum cans.
- Construct a plant that converts trash to electricity.
- Develop a public-service campaign to encourage the re-use of such items as paper grocery bags and

recycling program could immediately increase the volume's doubling period to four years."

In response, townspeople expressed various opinions. Many were concerned about the cost of the program and the potential increase in property taxes required to finance it.

Others were quite enthusiastic about the recommendations and called for the immediate establishment of a timetable for their implementation. Some of those present were concerned about the inconvenience of sorting items for recycling. This objection was countered by statistics citing general satisfaction with similar programs in other parts of the state.

Overall, the response to the recommendations was positive. A motion was passed to extend the consultants' contract for a six-month period. During this time a detailed implementation program would be worked out and presented for approval

Doubling

Suppose it always takes the same amount of time for a quantity to double. This amount of time is called the **doubling period.**

The volume of the landfill in the newspaper headline has a doubling period of three years. The table shows the relationship between the *number of* doubling periods and the volume.

Number of 3-year doubling periods	Volume V (cubic meters)
0	$50{,}000 \times 2^0 = 50{,}000$
1	$50{,}000 \times 2 = 50{,}000 \times 2^1 = 100{,}000$
2	$100{,}000 \times 2 = 50{,}000 \times 2 \times 2 = 50{,}000 \times 2^2 = 200{,}000$
3	$200{,}000 \times 2 = 50{,}000 \times 2 \times 2 \times 2 = 50{,}000 \times 2^3 = 400{,}000$
4	$400{,}000 \times 2 = 50{,}000 \times 2 \times 2 \times 2 \times 2 = 50{,}000 \times 2^4 = 800{,}000$
⋮	⋮
n	(previous volume) $\times 2$ = (original volume) $\times$ (n factors of 2) = V

Sample 1

Suppose the volume of the landfill in the newspaper headline continues to double every three years. Find the volume 24 years from now.

Sample Response

First find the number of doubling periods.

$$\text{total time} \longrightarrow \quad \frac{24 \text{ years}}{3 \text{ years}} = 8 \longleftarrow \text{number of doubling periods}$$
$$\text{doubling period} \longrightarrow$$

Then use an equation.

$$V = 50{,}000 \cdot 2^n \longleftarrow \begin{array}{l}\text{The equation gives the volume } V \\ \text{after } n \text{ three-year doubling periods.}\end{array}$$

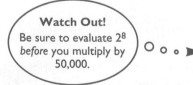

Watch Out!
Be sure to evaluate 2^8 *before* you multiply by 50,000.

$$= 50{,}000 \cdot 2^8 \longleftarrow \text{Substitute 8 for } n.$$

$$= 50{,}000 \cdot 256$$

$$= 12{,}800{,}000$$

The volume of the landfill will be 12.8 million m³.

Unit 2 Models of Variation and Growth

Talk it Over

1. **a.** What do you think the volume of the landfill was three
   years before the newspaper report?

   b. What value of *n* would you use to represent the time
   three years before the newspaper report? Find the value
   of *V* for this value of *n*.

   c. Find the value of *V* for $n = -2$. What does this quantity
   represent?

2. To graph the equation $V = 50{,}000 \cdot 2^n$, plot the points in the
   table on page 106 and the points you found in question 1.

   a. Is the graph *linear* or
   nonlinear? Does it show
   growth or *decay*?

   b. What does the vertical
   intercept represent?

   c. Does the graph ever
   touch the horizontal
   axis? Why or why not?

   d. What part of the graph
   do you think models the
   volume of the landfill? Explain.

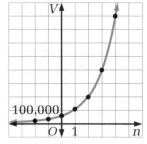

The equation $V = 50{,}000 \cdot 2^n$ from Sample 1 represents an
exponential function. The general form is $y = ab^x$, where $a > 0$,
$b > 0$, and $b \neq 1$.

EXPONENTIAL FUNCTIONS WITH BASE 2

┌─ *x* is the number of doubling periods.

$$y = a \cdot 2^x$$

a is the original amount when
$x = 0$. The value of *a* cannot
equal 0.

y is the amount after
x doubling periods.

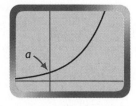

······► Now you are ready for:
Exs. 1–11 on p. 110

Halving

Look at the data you recorded in Tables 1 and 2 in the Exploration.
The doubling of the number of pieces of newspaper after each tear
is an example of **exponential growth.** The decrease in the area of
each piece is an example of **exponential decay.**

3. Use the data you recorded in Table 1 of the Exploration. Write an equation for the area A of one piece of your newspaper after n tears.

4. a. Suppose you could continue tearing the stack of newspaper pieces. Would the area of one piece ever be zero? Explain.

   b. Explain what your answer to part (a) means about the graph of the equation you wrote in question 3. Graph your equation in question 3.

An exponential function with base $\frac{1}{2}$ models a quantity that is halved again and again in equal time periods. The amount of time it takes for the quantity to divide in half is called the **half-life.**

X Lab

EXPONENTIAL FUNCTIONS WITH BASE $\frac{1}{2}$

x is the number of half-lives.

$$y = a\left(\frac{1}{2}\right)^x$$

y is the amount after x half-lives.

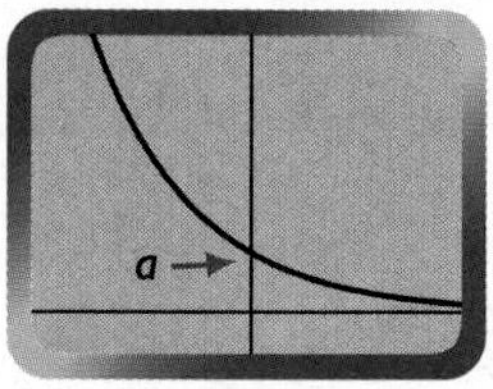

a is the original amount when $x = 0$. The value of a cannot equal 0.

You can use the function $y = a\left(\frac{1}{2}\right)^x$ to model the decay of *radioactive* substances. As a substance gives off radiation, the amount of radioactive material decreases exponentially. Each radioactive substance has a specific half-life.

Radioactive iodine is used by doctors to diagnose and treat some thyroid problems.

Sample 2

One form of radioactive iodine has a half-life of about 8 days.

a. Write an equation that models the exponential decay of 500 g of this form of radioactive iodine.

b. How long will it be before only 50 g of the radioactive iodine is left?

Sample Response

a. Let x = the number of 8-day half-lives.

Let y = the amount (in grams) of radioactive iodine.

$$y = a\left(\frac{1}{2}\right)^x$$ ◄——— Use an exponential function with base $\frac{1}{2}$.

$$y = 500\left(\frac{1}{2}\right)^x$$ ◄——— The original amount is 500 g. Substitute 500 for a.

The equation $y = 500\left(\frac{1}{2}\right)^x$ models the exponential decay of 500 g of this form of radioactive iodine.

b. **Method ❶**

Problem Solving Strategy: Use a table.

Use the equation from part (a) to make a table of values.

Number of half-lives	Amount of radioactive iodine (g)
0	500
1	250
2	125
3	62.5
4	31.25

50 occurs between the 3rd and 4th half-lives.

Since the half-life is 8 days, there will be 50 g of this form of radioactive iodine left after $8 \cdot 3 = 24$ days and before $8 \cdot 4 = 32$ days.

Method ❷

Problem Solving Strategy: Use a graph.

Use a graphics calculator. Trace the graph of the equation in part (a).

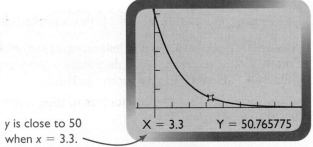

y is close to 50 when $x = 3.3$.

X = 3.3   Y = 50.765775

Since x is the number of 8-day half-lives, there will be 50 g of this form of radioactive iodine left after about $8(3.3) = 26.4$ days.

Look Back ◄————

Describe how to recognize a table that represents an exponential function with base 2. Describe how to recognize a graph that represents an exponential function with base $\frac{1}{2}$.

······► **Now you are ready for:**
Exs. 12–33 on pp. 110–112

1. **a.** Use the data you recorded in Table 2 in the Exploration. Write an equation to model the data.

   b. Graph your equation from part (a).

2. Suppose the thickness of the sheet of newspaper you used in the Exploration is 2.2×10^{-3} in.

   a. Write an equation to model the height h of your stack of newspaper pieces after n tears.

   b. What would be the height of the stack if you could make 15 tears?

3. **Reading** The newspaper article shown on page 106 quotes an environmental engineer:

   Find the landfill's volume 24 years from now, if the doubling period is four years. Compare your answer to the answer in Sample 1.

   > "An aggressive recycling program could immediately increase the volume's doubling period to four years."

For Exercises 4–7, use the equation $y = 58 \cdot 2^x$. Find the value of y for each value of x.

4. $x = 0$ 5. $x = 5$ 6. $x = 10$ 7. $x = 20$

Tell if each graph represents an exponential function with base 2. Write *Yes* or *No*. Explain your answer.

8.
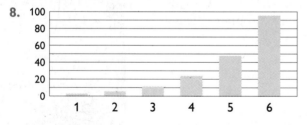

9.
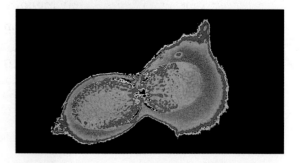

10. **Biology** A type of bacteria reproduces by dividing into two bacteria every 20 min. If you start with one bacterium, how many bacteria will there be after one hour? after two hours?

11. **Open-ended** Make up a situation that can be modeled by the equation $y = 100 \cdot 2^x$.

Number of tears	Area of each piece (in.²)
0	600
1	300
2	150
3	75
4	37.5
5	18.75

For Exercises 12 and 13, use the area data that Lydia and Al recorded when they did the Exploration using a sheet of newspaper with dimensions 20 in. × 30 in.

12. **a.** Describe the change in the area of one piece each time they tear the stack.

   b. Lydia modeled their data with the equation $A = 600\left(\frac{1}{2}\right)^n$. Explain how she might have arrived at this equation.

13. a. Graph the equation $A = 600\left(\frac{1}{2}\right)^n$. Include points with negative

   n-coordinates. Which points on the graph represent areas of Lydia's and Al's pieces of newspaper?

   b. **Writing** Compare the graph of the equation $A = 600\left(\frac{1}{2}\right)^n$ to the graph

   of the equation $V = 50{,}000 \cdot 2^n$ shown on page 107. How are they alike? How are they different?

For Exercises 14 and 15, use the information in Exercises 12 and 13. Suppose Lydia and Al are able to continue tearing their stack of newspaper pieces.

14. Use a table to find the number of tears after which the area of each piece is less than 1 in.^{2}

15 TECHNOLOGY Use a graphics calculator to find the number of tears after which the area of each piece is less than 0.1 in.^{2}

16. a. Graph the equation $y = 4\left(\frac{1}{2}\right)^x$.

   b. Use your graph to estimate the value of x when $y = 3$.

17. One form of radium decays exponentially with a half-life of 1600 years.

   a. Use an equation to model the exponential decay of 120 g of this form of radium.

   b. How long will it take 120 g of the radium to decay to 5 g of radium?

18. Sports There are 64 teams in the first round of an NCAA basketball championship. In each round, every team in the round plays a game against one other team in the round. Only the winning teams advance to the next round.

   a. Explain why the number of teams in each round can be modeled by an equation that represents exponential decay.

   b. Write an exponential equation that you can use to find the number of teams in any round.

   c. What does the exponent in your equation represent?

19. Demographics Brunei is a tiny, thinly populated country with a high standard of living. In 1989, the population of Brunei was 345,000. It was doubling approximately every nine years. Suppose the population has continued to grow at the same rate.

   a. Write an equation that models the population growth.

   b. In what year will the population exceed 5,000,000?

   c. Do you think the population can continue to double every nine years? Why or why not?

In area, Brunei is only a little larger than Delaware.

20. **Using Manipulatives** Begin with a sheet of typing paper with dimensions 8.5 in. × 11 in. Follow these steps:

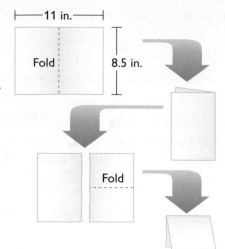

Step 1 Fold the paper in half so that the short sides meet, and then tear the paper in half along the fold.

Step 2 Take one of the pieces and fold it in half so that the short sides meet, and then tear along the fold.

Step 3 Repeat step 2 until you can no longer fold and tear.

a. After how many tears is the area of the smallest piece of paper less than 1 in.^{2}?

b. What are the dimensions of the smallest piece of paper?

Ongoing **ASSESSMENT**

21. **Writing** Use Lydia's and Al's area data from Exercise 12 on page 110.

Part (b) of Exercise 12 gives the equation $A = 600\left(\frac{1}{2}\right)^n$ as Lydia's

model of the data. Al says they can model the data with the equation $A = 600 \cdot 2^{-n}$. Do you agree with him? Explain your reasoning.

Review **PREVIEW**

Simplify. Write answers with positive exponents. *(Section 2-6)*

22. $(6y^0)(6x^{-4})$

23. $\dfrac{7y^{-6}}{x^4}$

24. $(2n^3)^0$

Find the slope of each line. *(Section 2-2)*

25. $y = 3x - 5$

26. $y = 5$

27. $y = -\frac{1}{2}x + 4$

28. $x = -2$

What name best describes each shape? *(Toolbox Skill 27)*

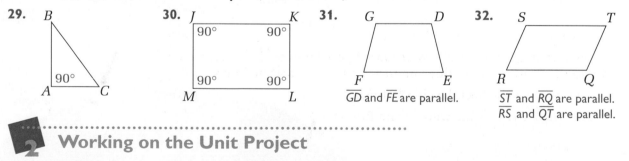

29. B, $90°$, A, C

30. J $90°$ K $90°$, $90°$ M $90°$ L

31. G D, F E
$\overline{GD}$ and $\overline{FE}$ are parallel.

32. S T, R Q
$\overline{ST}$ and $\overline{RQ}$ are parallel.
$\overline{RS}$ and $\overline{QT}$ are parallel.

Working on the Unit Project

33. Between 1942 and 1992, the salinity of Mono Lake has doubled. *Salinity* is the number of grams of salt per liter of water. In 1942 the salinity of Mono Lake was about 51.3 g/L.

Suppose the salinity doubles at regular intervals.

a. What would be the doubling period for the salinity?

b. After two more doubling periods, what would be the salinity?

Now you are ready to make a set of note cards for your Mono Lake guided tour.

Your note cards should include these things:

➤ **a description of the major features of the Mono Lake ecosystem**

➤ **historical information about changes in the ecosystem**

➤ **predictions about the future of the ecosystem**

➤ **interesting details to enliven your tour**

➤ **backup information for answering visitors' questions**

Look Back ←

How did the use of mathematical models help you to better understand an ecosystem?

Alternative Projects

Project 1: Tropical Rain Forest

Research tropical rain forest ecosystems. Apply the models of variation and growth you learn about in this unit to write a report that includes:

➤ how rain forests affect the global climate

➤ how logging affects the world's rain forests

Project 2: Population Growth

Obtain population data for your state as far back as possible. Analyze the data. Determine whether or not there is a constant doubling period. Graph the data and use it to predict population changes for the next 20 years. If professional forecasts are available, compare them with your predictions. What factors account for any differences between the various professional forecasts and your predictions?

For Questions 1–3, use the graph.   2-1

1. Name the dependent and control variables.

2. What is the domain of the function represented by the graph? What is the range?

3. Use the terms *linear* or *nonlinear* and *increasing*, *decreasing*, or *constant* to describe the graph.

[Graph: Freshman enrollment (thousands) on vertical axis, ranging 370 to 430; years 1984–1991 on horizontal axis]

4. A line contains two points with coordinates (8, 29) and (−1, 2).   2-2

   a. What is the slope of the line?   b. What is the vertical intercept of the line?

   c. Write an equation of the line.   d. Find the value of x when $y = 14$.

   e. **Writing** Explain why the equation you wrote can be used to model the mail-order charge when the shipping charge is $3 per CD plus a handling charge of $5.

Writing Is *direct variation* or *inverse variation* a good model for   2-2, 2-3
the data in each table? Explain how you made your decision.

5.

x	y
4.4	4.96
4.6	5.04
4.8	5.12
5.0	5.20

6.

x	y
5.4	2.27
5.5	2.23
5.6	2.19
5.7	2.15

7. a. Rewrite the equation $xy = 144$ so that it can be entered   2-3
   on a graphics calculator.

   b. Find y when $x = 20$.

8. What is the volume of a sphere with radius 3 in.?   2-4

9. The ratio of the radii of two spheres is 3:5.

   a. What is the ratio of the surface areas of the two spheres?

   b. The surface area of the larger sphere is 100 ft². What is the surface area of the smaller sphere?

Use this information for Questions 10–12.   2-5

In flight, the weight of birds, insects, and aircraft is carried by the wings. The equation $w \approx (9 \times 10^{-5})s^2$ relates the wing loading w (g/cm²) and the minimum speed s (km/h) for level flight.

Wing loading is the weight supported by each square unit of wing surface.

10. What type of variation is modeled by the equation?

11. Estimate the minimum flying speed for an insect with $w = 0.02$ g/cm².

12. Estimate the wing loading for an aircraft with a minimum flying speed of 80 km/h.

Simplify. Write answers with positive exponents.

2-6

13. x^9y^{-1} **14.** $\dfrac{5^0}{g^{-2}}$ **15.** $(5r)(-4t^{-3})$ **16.** $(2^{-6})(3^0)$

17. Another way of writing the equation relating speed and wing loading from Questions 10–12 is $s = 105.4w^{1/2}$. Find the minimum speed required for level flight with a wing loading of 0.1 g/cm^2.

18. **Writing** Describe the important characteristics of the graph of an exponential function with base 2.

2-7

19. The graph models the decay of a form of radioactive bismuth. The half-life is five days.

a. What was the original amount of the radioactive substance?

b. Estimate the number of days after which less than $\frac{1}{10}$ of the original amount is left.

c. Write an exponential equation that models the decay of this form of radioactive bismuth.

d. Find the amount of radioactive bismuth left after one year.

20. **Self-evaluation** What have you added to your understanding of direct variation as a result of your work in this unit?

21. **Group Activity** Work in a group of three to six students.

a. Sit in a circle. Choose someone to write each of these phrases on a separate sheet of paper.

direct variation   inverse variation
varies with the square   varies with the cube
exponential growth (doubling)   exponential decay (half-life)

b. Each of you should choose a sheet of paper at random. Put aside the papers not chosen.

On your paper, write an equation that is an example of the type of function named there. Also write down a reasonable domain for the function. Then pass your paper clockwise.

c. Look at the equation written on the paper you receive. On the same piece of paper, sketch a graph of the equation over the domain stated on the paper. Again pass your paper clockwise.

d. Describe a situation that is modeled by the equation and the graph on the paper you receive. Be sure to include values for at least two points.

IDEAS AND (FORMULAS)$= x^2$

ALGEBRA $)x^2$

$(x$

➤ The graphs of functions can be examples of linear growth, nonlinear growth, linear decay, nonlinear decay, or a constant. *(p. 61)*

➤ Graphs of functions can have different characteristics over different intervals. *(p. 61)*

➤ Functions, tables, graphs, equations, and inequalities can be used as mathematical models of situations. *(p. 67)*

➤ Linear functions can be written in slope-intercept form $y = mx + b$: *(p. 68)*

$$\underset{\text{variable}}{\text{dependent}} = \text{slope} \times \underset{\text{variable}}{\text{control}} + \underset{\text{intercept}}{\text{vertical}}$$

➤ The slope m of the line between (x_1, y_1) and (x_2, y_2) is: *(p. 68)*

$$m = \frac{y_2 - y_1}{x_2 - x_1}$$

➤ In a direct variation situation, two quantities have a constant ratio. An algebraic model for "y varies directly with x" is $y = kx$ when $k \neq 0$. *(p. 70)*

➤ In an inverse variation situation, two quantities have a constant product. An algebraic model for "y varies inversely with x" is $y = \frac{k}{x}$ when $k \neq 0$ and $x \neq 0$. *(pp. 76–77)*

➤ A model for "y varies directly with x^2" is $y = kx^2$ when $k \neq 0$. The model represents direct variation with the square. *(p. 92)*

➤ A model for "y varies directly with x^3" is $y = kx^3$ when $k \neq 0$. The model represents direct variation with the cube. *(p. 94)*

➤ The following rules apply to the exponent zero and negative exponents when $a \neq 0$. *(p. 99)*

$$a^0 = 1 \qquad a^{-n} = \frac{1}{a^n} \text{ and } \frac{1}{a^{-n}} = a^n$$

➤ Square roots and cube roots can be expressed using fractional exponents: $x^{1/2} = \sqrt{x}$ when $x \geq 0$, and $x^{1/3} = \sqrt[3]{x}$. *(p. 100)*

➤ Exponential functions with base 2, such as $y = a \cdot 2^x$ when $a \neq 0$, model the doubling of a quantity in equal time periods. *(p. 107)*

➤ Exponential functions with base $\frac{1}{2}$ model the halving of a quantity in equal time periods. *(p. 108)*

➤ Functions in the form $y = a\left(\frac{1}{2}\right)^x$ when $a \neq 0$ model the decay of radioactive substances. *(p. 108)*

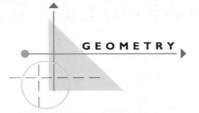

GEOMETRY

➤ Through any two points there is exactly one line. *(p. 68)*

➤ The graph of inverse variation is a hyperbola in Quadrants I and III or Quadrants II and IV. *(p. 77)*

➤ For a sphere with radius r: Surface Area (S.A.) = $4\pi r^2$ *(p. 85)*

   Volume (V) = $\frac{4}{3}\pi r^3$ *(p. 85)*

➤ All spheres are similar space figures. *(p. 86)*

➤ The ratio of the surface areas of two spheres is the ratio of the squares of their radii. *(p. 86)*

The ratio of the volumes of two spheres is the ratio of the cubes of their radii. *(p. 86)*

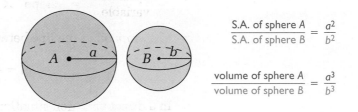

$$\frac{\text{S.A. of sphere } A}{\text{S.A. of sphere } B} = \frac{a^2}{b^2}$$

$$\frac{\text{volume of sphere } A}{\text{volume of sphere } B} = \frac{a^3}{b^3}$$

➤ The graph of direct variation with the square is a parabola. *(p. 92)*

➤ The graph of direct variation with the cube is a curve through the origin. *(p. 94)*

Key Terms

- **linear** (p. 60)
- **decay graph** (p. 61)
- **range** (p. 62)
- **slope-intercept form** (p. 68)
- **direct variation** (p. 70)
- **hyperbola** (p. 77)
- **diameter of a sphere** (p. 85)

- **doubling period** (p. 106)
- **exponential decay** (p. 107)

- **function** (p. 60)
- **constant graph** (p. 61)
- **mathematical model** (p. 67)
- **slope** (p. 68)
- **variation constant** (p. 70)
- **sphere** (p. 84)
- **direct variation with the square** (p. 92)

- **exponential function** (p. 107)
- **half-life** (p. 108)

- **growth graph** (p. 61)
- **domain** (p. 62)
- **linear function** (p. 68)
- **vertical intercept** (p. 68)
- **inverse variation** (p. 76)
- **radius of a sphere** (p. 85)
- **direct variation with the cube** (p. 94)

- **exponential growth** (p. 107)

FOOD

Imagine cookouts without ketchup, corn on the cob, or potatoes. Dessert without chocolate or vanilla flavoring. Thanksgiving dinner without turkey, cranberry sauce, sweet potatoes, or pumpkin pie. That would be our fate if the people native to the Americas had not been cultivating wild plants and domesticating wild animals over thousands of years.

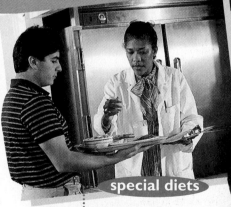

special diets

Nutritionists plan high-carbohydrate menus for athletes in training, school lunches for growing children, and special diets for people with health problems. They also show families how to create nutritious meals on a budget.

Create a Daily Menu

Your project is to create a day's menu for three people with different activity levels and different body weights. Each person's meals must supply a healthful balance of nutrients and all the Calories needed for one day but without too many extra Calories. After you have completed the "Working on the Unit Project" exercises for Section 3-1, you will be able to determine a person's daily Calorie requirements as a function of body weight and activity level. Using this information, the Food Guide Pyramid, the serving size table on page 120, and a Calorie chart, your group will plan three menus. Then you will learn how to analyze and adjust the nutritional content of your menus.

activity level ➤   LIGHT   MODERATE   STRENUOUS

The Food Guide Pyramid shows you how to eat right. As you move up the pyramid, you need less of the foods at each level.

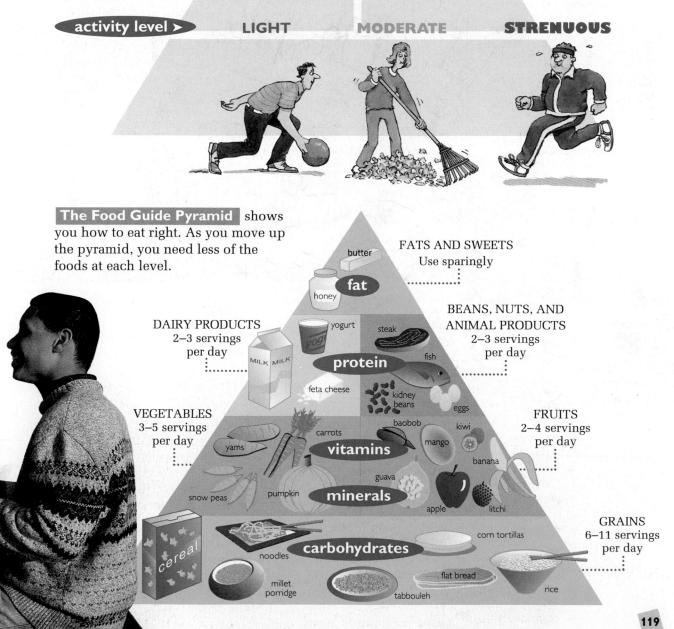

FATS AND SWEETS
Use sparingly

butter

honey   fat

DAIRY PRODUCTS
2–3 servings
per day

yogurt

MILK MILK

protein

steak

fish

BEANS, NUTS, AND
ANIMAL PRODUCTS
2–3 servings
per day

feta cheese

kidney beans

eggs

VEGETABLES
3–5 servings
per day

carrots

baobob

kiwi

mango

vitamins

yams

banana

guava

minerals

apple

litchi

FRUITS
2–4 servings
per day

snow peas   pumpkin

cereal

noodles

carbohydrates

corn tortillas

flat bread

rice

millet
porridge

tabbouleh

GRAINS
6–11 servings
per day

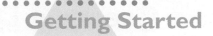

Getting Started

For this project you should work in a group of three students. Here are some ideas to help you get started.

☞ Make a list of foods from the five food groups shown that are eaten in your communities and in other countries.

☞ Plan to learn more about foods around the world by looking at cookbooks and restaurant menus.

☞ Discuss how you will illustrate your group's menus.

☞ Make plans to obtain a Calorie chart.

☞ Plan to meet again after completing the "Working on the Unit Project" exercises for Section 3-1 to choose body weights and activity levels for which to plan your menus.

Serving sizes for each food group
Grains
1 slice of bread
1 ounce of dry cereal
$\frac{1}{2}$ cup cooked cereal, rice, or pasta
Vegetables
1 cup raw leafy vegetables
$\frac{1}{2}$ cup of others
$\frac{3}{4}$ cup juice
Fruits
1 medium apple, etc.
$\frac{1}{2}$ cup cooked
$\frac{3}{4}$ cup juice
Dairy Products
1 cup milk or yogurt
$1\frac{1}{2}$ oz cheese
Beans, Nuts, Meat
2–3 oz cooked lean fish, poultry, or meat
$\frac{1}{2}$ cup cooked beans
1 egg
2 tbsp nut butter

Can We Talk FOOD

Working on the Unit Project

Your work in Unit 3 will help you create a daily menu.

Related Exercises:

Section 3-1, Exercise 32
Section 3-2, Exercise 29
Section 3-3, Exercise 38
Section 3-4, Exercise 38
Section 3-5, Exercise 35
Section 3-6, Exercise 26
Section 3-7, Exercise 27
Section 3-8, Exercise 26

Alternative Projects p. 180

➤ On a typical day, do you eat many different foods or only a few that you like? Which levels of the food pyramid do they come from?

➤ How can the way food is prepared affect the nutritional content of the food? Are there any foods that you like prepared in a variety of ways? Which ones?

➤ How do the sizes of the servings shown in the table above compare with those you eat?

➤ What activities do you participate in? Would you describe your overall activity level as light, moderate, or strenuous?

➤ In your family or community, what are some favorite foods? Are special foods served on holidays and birthdays? Are recipes passed down from generation to generation?

Systems and Graphs

At the Crossroads

·····Focus
Solve systems of linear
equations by graphing
and graph systems of
linear inequalities.

FitnessPLUS
Initiation Fee $50
Monthly Fee $60

BODYWORKS
INITIATION FEE $225
MONTHLY FEE $35

Cost of membership		
	FitnessPLUS	**Bodyworks**
5 months	?	?
10 months	?	?

Talk it Over

1. Candra Reeves wants to join a health club. Use the rate sheets at the left to fill in this table.

2. Which health club membership will cost less if Candra joins for five months? for ten months?

You can write two equations to compare the costs of belonging to each health club.

Let $c =$ the total cost of membership.   Let $n =$ the number of months of membership.

	total cost	=	initiation fee	+	the monthly fee times n
FitnessPLUS:	c	=	50	+	$60n$
Bodyworks:	c	=	225	+	$35n$

Two or more equations that state relationships between the same variable quantities are called a **system of equations.** Since the two cost equations are linear, they are a **linear system.**

Talk it Over

3. Without graphing, identify the slope and the vertical intercept of the graph of each cost equation. Explain the meaning of each number in terms of the total cost of belonging to each health club.

4. Find the cost of a seven-month membership for each health club. What do you notice?

A **solution of a system of equations** is an ordered pair whose coordinates make all the equations true. One method of solving a system of equations is *solving by graphing*.

Graphing both equations on the same axes helps you "see" the solution.

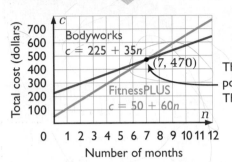

The coordinates of the intersection point make both equations true. The solution (n, c) is $(7, 470)$.

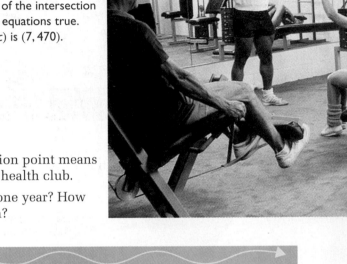

Talk it Over

5. Explain what each coordinate of the intersection point means in terms of the cost of a membership for each health club.

6. Which health club costs less to belong to for one year? How can you use the graph to answer this question?

Student Resources Toolbox
pp. 652–653 *Graphs, Equations, and Inequalities*

Sample 1

Solve this system of equations by graphing: $v + w = 3$
$w = \frac{2}{3}v - 5$

Sample Response

Method ❶ Graph the equations of the system by hand.

Note: When either variable may be the control variable, let the letter that occurs earlier in the alphabet be the control variable.

To graph $v + w = 3$, use the line's vertical intercept (find w when $v = 0$) and the line's **horizontal intercept** (find v when $w = 0$).

To graph $w = \frac{2}{3}v - 5$, start at the vertical-intercept -5 and then use the slope $\frac{2}{3}$ to find a second point.

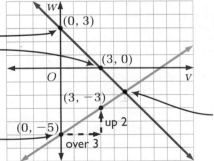

Estimate the coordinates of the intersection point. The lines intersect at about $(4.8, -1.8)$.

The solution (v, w) is about $(4.8, -1.8)$.

Method 2 Use a graphics calculator.

Enter the equations in slope-intercept form. Use x for the control variable and y for the dependent variable.

Then use ZOOM and TRACE to find the coordinates of the intersection point to the nearest tenth.

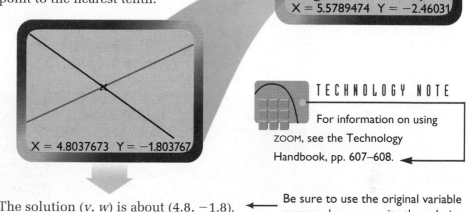

$y = -x + 3$

$y = \frac{2}{3}x - 5$

X = 5.5789474 Y = -2.46031

X = 4.8037673 Y = -1.803767

TECHNOLOGY NOTE

For information on using ZOOM, see the Technology Handbook, pp. 607–608.

The solution (v, w) is about $(4.8, -1.8)$. ◄──── Be sure to use the original variable names when you write the solution.

Sample 2

Writing To use a locker at FitnessPLUS you can pay either $45 per year or $5.25 per month. How many months per year do you have to use a locker to make it worth paying the yearly rate? Explain, using this graph.

Sample Response

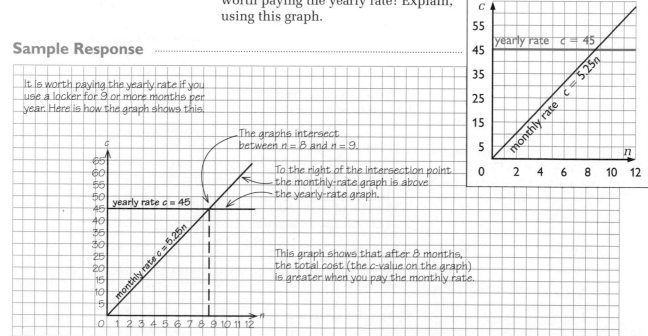

It is worth paying the yearly rate if you use a locker for 9 or more months per year. Here is how the graph shows this.

The graphs intersect between $n = 8$ and $n = 9$.

To the right of the intersection point the monthly-rate graph is above the yearly-rate graph.

This graph shows that after 8 months, the total cost (the c-value on the graph) is greater when you pay the monthly rate.

yearly rate $c = 45$

monthly rate $c = 5.25n$

7. Use the graph in Sample 2 to estimate $c = 5.25n$
the solution of this system of equations. $c = 45$

8. Do you need to know the exact solution of the system in order to answer the question asked in Sample 2? Explain.

······► Now you are ready for:
Exs. 1–14 on pp. 125–127

Systems of Inequalities

Sonya is budgeting for her trip to Japan. She plans to spend no more than $50 (about 5000 yen) for lunch and dinner each day.

■ Talk it Over

9. Let l = dollars spent for lunch. $l + d \leq 50$
Let d = dollars spent for dinner. $l \geq 0$
                                        $d \geq 0$

Explain why you can use this **system of inequalities** to describe the possible combinations of Sonya's daily lunch and dinner costs.

10. Which of the labeled points on the graph make the inequality $l + d \leq 50$ true? make $l \geq 0$ true? make $d \geq 0$ true?

11. Which of the labeled points make all three inequalities true? Describe the region of the coordinate plane that contains all points that are possible combinations of Sonya's daily lunch and dinner costs.

The graph of the points that make all the inequalities in a system true is called the **solution region** of the system of inequalities.

Student Resources Toolbox
p. 654 *Graphs, Equations, and Inequalities*

Sample 3

Graph this system of inequalities: $y \geq -x + 4$
                                          $2x - y > -2$

1 Graph the inequality $y \geq -x + 4$.

Graph $y = -x + 4$ as a *solid line*.

Test the point $(0, 0)$.
$$y > -x + 4$$
$$0 \overset{?}{>} -0 + 4$$
$$0 > 4 \text{ (false)}$$

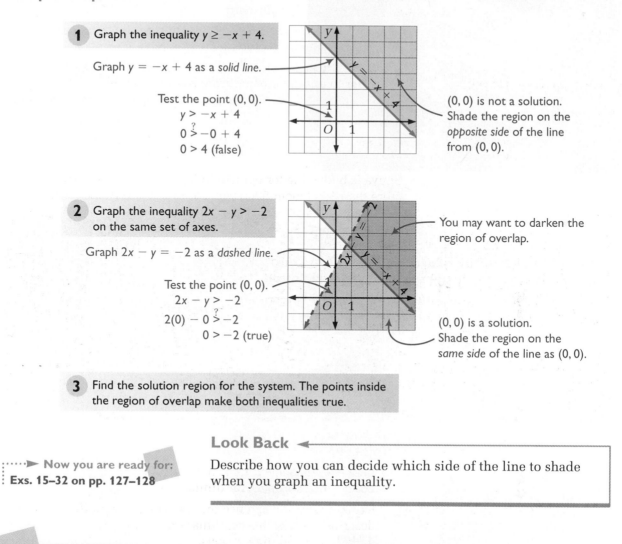

$(0, 0)$ is not a solution.
Shade the region on the *opposite side* of the line from $(0, 0)$.

2 Graph the inequality $2x - y > -2$ on the same set of axes.

Graph $2x - y = -2$ as a *dashed line*.

Test the point $(0, 0)$.
$$2x - y > -2$$
$$2(0) - 0 \overset{?}{>} -2$$
$$0 > -2 \text{ (true)}$$

You may want to darken the region of overlap.

$(0, 0)$ is a solution.
Shade the region on the *same side* of the line as $(0, 0)$.

3 Find the solution region for the system. The points inside the region of overlap make both inequalities true.

Look Back

···▶ **Now you are ready for:**
Exs. 15–32 on pp. 127–128

Describe how you can decide which side of the line to shade when you graph an inequality.

3-1 Exercises and Problems

1. **Reading** What is the solution of a system of equations? How is the solution related to the graphs of the equations?

Estimate the solution of each linear system.

2.
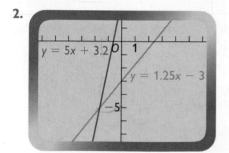

$y = 5x + 3.2$
$y = 1.25x - 3$

3.
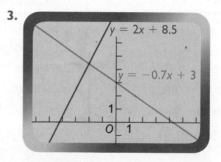

$y = 2x + 8.5$
$y = -0.7x + 3$

FotoRite
Frequent Buyers' Club
save over 10¢ per print
Club Membership Cost: $15.00
Member cost per print: $.25
Non-member cost per print: $.40

4. Use the information on the Frequent Buyers' Club card.

   a. Write an equation for the total cost for a club member to have n prints made. Write an equation for the total cost for a non-member to have n prints made.

   b. Graph the system of equations in part (a).

   c. Use your graph to find the solution of the system of equations. Explain the meaning of the solution in this situation.

Solve each system of equations by graphing.

5. $y = x$
   $y = 1.8x + 3$

6. $a - b = 1$
   $b = -4a$

7. $2x + 5y = 5$
   $y = \frac{2}{5}x + 5$

8. $n = 0.5p + 1$
   $n = 0.2p + 2$

Public Transportation For Exercises 9 and 10, use this information about public transportation fares in Boston.

Bus and subway riders can either pay single-ride fares or buy monthly passes at the prices shown. A *combo pass* lets you ride both the bus and the subway.

$20
(Single ride: $.60)

$46

$27
(Single ride: $.85)

9. **Writing** Suppose you ride the bus every day and you sometimes ride the subway. How many times per month must you ride the subway to make it worth buying a combo pass? Explain, using this graph to support your answer.

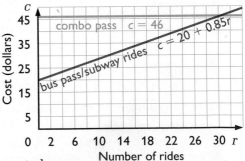

10. Yukiko is trying to decide whether to buy a combo pass or to buy a subway pass and then pay the single-ride fare when she rides the bus.

    a. Write a system of equations that models Yukiko's choices.

    b. Graph the system of equations that you wrote in part (a).

    c. Suppose Yukiko usually rides the bus 20 times per month. Should she buy a combo pass? How does your graph support your answer?

11. a. Open-ended Describe a real-world situation that can be modeled by this linear system. $y = 0.99x + 1.49$ $y = 0.89x + 1.99$

   b. Without graphing, tell how the slope and vertical intercept of the graph of each equation in part (a) are related to the situation you described.

12. a. Solve this system of equations by graphing. $y = 3$ $y = 8x - 1$

   b. Solve the equation $3 = 8x - 1$ for x.

   c. Describe what the system in part (a) has in common with the equation in part (b). Explain how to use the system to solve the equation.

   d. Write a system of equations that you can use to solve $4x = x - 12$.

13. Candra Reeves is considering another health club.

   a. Write a cost equation for Neighborhood Health Club.

   b. Compare the equation you wrote for part (a) with the equations on page 121. Which of the equations has the graph with the greatest slope? the greatest vertical intercept?

   c. Graph all three equations on the same axes.

   d. Suppose Candra Reeves plans to join a health club for three months. Which plan is the cheapest? Suppose she plans to join for seven months. Which plan is the cheapest? Explain how the graph supports your answers.

Neighborhood Health Club

Initiation Fee $120
Monthly Fee $50

14. a. Solve this system of equations by graphing. $y = x^2 + 4$ $y = 4$

   b. Is the system in part (a) a linear system? Explain why or why not.

Graph each system of inequalities.

15. $y \leq 3x - 3$
$y > -\frac{1}{2}x + 2$

16. $y < 3x$
$3y - 2x \geq 9$

17. $x < 2$
$y < x + 5$
$x + 2y > -2$

18. $y - 3x \geq 5$
$2y + 5x < 7$

19. a. Write an equation for each side of this trapezoid.

   b. Write a system of inequalities that describes the shaded region.

   c. Choose a point inside the shaded region and show that its coordinates make all your inequalities in part (b) true.

Graph each system of inequalities. Write the specific name of the shape of each solution region.

20. $2x + y \leq 4$
$y \geq -3$
$x \geq -1$

21. $y \geq -1$
$y \leq x + 1$
$3x + 2y \leq 16$
$y \leq 2$

22. $3 < x < 5$
$0 < y < 2$

23. $-4 \leq x \leq 2$
$-3 \leq y \leq 1$

24. **Writing** Describe how to solve this system of equations by graphing: $y = -x + 8$
$x - 2y = -22$

25. Radium-226 decays exponentially with a half-life of 1600 years. Use an equation to model the exponential decay of 100 g of radium-226. *(Section 2-7)*

Rewrite each expression using a fractional exponent. *(Section 2-6)*

26. $\sqrt{8x}$ **27.** $-5\sqrt[3]{t}$ **28.** $\sqrt[3]{7m}$

Solve. *(Toolbox Skill 13)*

29. $15 = \frac{8}{5}m + 3$ **30.** $7(a + 10) = -14$ **31.** $4(6 - 3n) = -6 + 2n$

Working on the Unit Project

32. a. Calories in food come from carbohydrates, protein, and fat. About 10% of your daily Calories should come from protein.

Let c = grams of carbohydrate.
Let f = grams of fat.

Explain why you can use the equation

$$4c + 9f = 0.9 \times \text{daily Calories}$$

to model the possible combinations of amounts of fats and carbohydrates that you should eat in one day.

carbohydrate
4 Cal/g

protein
4 Cal/g

fat
9 Cal/g

b. Your daily Calorie needs depend on your weight and your activity level.

Daily Calorie needs = Activity rating × weight (lb)

Estimate your daily Calorie needs on two activity levels: light and strenuous.

c. Use the two numbers you found in part (b) to write two equations like the one shown in part (a).

d. Graph the two equations you wrote in part (c) on the same axes.

Activity Rating	Activity Level	
14	light	walking casually, bowling, doing auto repair
15	moderate	walking briskly, climbing stairs, doing yard work
16	strenuous	moving heavy objects, dancing, jogging

e. Suppose you want your daily intake of fats and carbohydrates to be no more than you need for strenuous activity and no less than you need for light activity. Shade the region of your graph that shows the combinations of amounts of fats and carbohydrates you can consider.

f. Dietitians recommend that your daily fat intake be less than 30% of your total daily Calories. Pick several points in the shaded region of your graph. Which of them show combinations of fats and carbohydrates that meet this goal?

g. Write down at least two ideas about a healthy diet from this exercise that you may want to remember when you create menus for your project.

Solving Systems by Substitution

"My point, exactly"

Bakeerah brought this ad to school to discuss with her math class. The class wondered if using an electronic bulb really would save money as the ad claims. They wrote and graphed these two equations, where x is the number of days of use and y is the total cost.

Electronic bulb: $y = 24 + 0.01x$
Twenty 100-watt bulbs: $y = 15 + 0.04x$

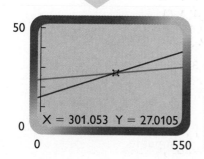

X = 301.053   Y = 27.0105

Talk it Over

1. Use the information in the ad to explain how the two cost equations represent the situation.

2. Use the graph of the system of equations. About how many days do you have to use one electronic bulb before it becomes cheaper than using twenty 100-watt bulbs? Explain.

3. Are the TRACE values shown on the calculator screen an exact solution of the system of cost equations? Explain.

You can use algebra to find the exact solution of the system of cost equations. At the intersection point of the graphs of the equations, *the y-values are the same.*

Replace *y* in one equation with the expression for *y* from the other equation.

$$y = 24 + 0.01x$$
$$y = 15 + 0.04x$$

Use the *two* equations in *x* and *y* to write *one* equation that you can solve for *x*.

$$24 + 0.01x = 15 + 0.04x$$

This method of solving a system of equations is called *solving by substitution.*

Talk it Over

4. Solve the third equation shown above for *x*. Compare the answer to your answer for question 2 on page 129.

5. Substitute the value of *x* you found in question 4 into each cost equation. What value do you get for *y*?

Sample 1

Solve this system of equations by substitution: $x - 2y = -11$
$x + y = 4$

Sample Response

1 Solve the second equation for *x*.

$$x + y = 4 \quad\blacktriangleright\quad x = 4 - y$$

2 Substitute $4 - y$ for *x* in the first equation.

$$x - 2y = -11$$
$$4 - y - 2y = -11$$

3 Solve the new equation for *y*.

$$4 - 3y = -11$$
$$-3y = -15$$

This is the *y*-value of the solution. ⟶ $y = 5$

$$x + y = 4$$
$$x + 5 = 4$$
$$x = -1$$

4 To find the *x*-value, substitute 5 for *y* in either of the original equations.

The solution (x, y) is $(-1, 5)$.

Talk it Over

6. Check that the solution found in Sample 1 makes both equations true.

7. Graph the equations $x - 2y = -11$ and $x + y = 4$ on one set of axes. Explain how to use your graph to check that the solution found in Sample 1 is reasonable.

Unit 3 Linear Systems and Matrices

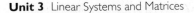

GLORY

12:30 3:00 5:30 8:00 10:30

ADULTS $7 CHILDREN $4

Movie theaters keep track of how many tickets they sell. For a 5:30 showing, this movie theater sold 272 tickets and took in $1694. How many of each type of ticket were sold?

Sample Response

Problem Solving Strategy: Use a system of equations.

You know two totals — the number of tickets sold and the amount of money taken in. Each total comes from sales of both adults' and children's tickets.

1 Write an expression for each total in terms of two variables. A table may help you organize the information.

	Number of tickets sold	Dollar amount taken in
Adult	a	$7a$
Child	c	$4c$
Total	$a + c$	$7a + 4c$

2 Use what you know about the totals to write a system of equations.

$$a + c = 272$$
$$7a + 4c = 1694$$

3 Solve the system by substitution.

$a + c = 272 \longrightarrow c = 272 - a$ ← Solve one equation for c in terms of a.

$7a + 4c = 1694$ ← Substitute $272 - a$ for c in the other equation and solve for a.

$7a + 4(272 - a) = 1694$

$7a + 1088 - 4a = 1694$

$3a + 1088 = 1694$

$3a = 606$

$a = 202$

$a + c = 272$ ← To find c, substitute 202 for a in either of the original equations.

$202 + c = 272$

$c = 70$

The solution (a, c) of the system is $(202, 70)$.

There were 202 adults' tickets and 70 children's tickets sold.

Look Back

For each linear system, tell how you would begin solving by substitution. Which equation would you solve for what variable?

a. $3x - y = 5$
$4x + y = 9$

b. $3a - 5b = 10$
$a + 7b = 12$

c. $r + 2t = 5$
$2r + t = -2$

1. **a.** Estimate the solution of this system of equations by graphing:
   $$y = x - 4$$
   $$y = \frac{1}{3}x - 9$$
   b. Solve the system in part (a) using substitution.

Solve each system of equations by substitution.

2. $y = 4x$
   $y = -x - 15$

3. $b = a + 5$
   $b = 3a - 1$

4. $y = \frac{1}{2}x$
   $y = \frac{5}{2}x + 8$

5. $x - y = 1$
   $x + y = -1$

6. $c + 2d = 12$
   $c + d = 2$

7. $f - 3g = 9$
   $5f + g = -3$

8. Choose one of the systems of equations you solved in Exercises 2–7.
   Check your solution by solving the system by graphing.

9. Melissa and Bjorn started solving Exercise 5 two different ways.

   a. Describe how their methods are different.

   b. Will they get the same results? Explain why or why not.

   c. **Writing** Which method do you think is easier for solving this system of equations? Do you think that the same method is best for all systems of equations? Explain why or why not.

melissa Andrews

$x - y = 1 \rightarrow x = 1 + y$
$x + y = -1$

$1 + y + y = -1$
$1 + 2y = -1$

Bjorn Storesund

$x - y = 1$
$x + y = -1 \rightarrow y = -1 - x$

$x - (-1 - x) = 1$
$x + 1 + x = 1$

10. **a.** Solve this system of equations by substitution:
    $$F = 1.8C + 32$$
    $$F = C$$

    b. You can use the first equation in part (a) to convert a temperature in degrees Celsius (C) to a temperature in degrees Fahrenheit (F). Explain what the solution of the system of equations represents.

Use a system of equations to answer each question.

11. Use the information shown on the refrigerator price tags. After how many years of use is the cost of the Cold-air the same as the cost of the Cool-spot?

12. **Investment** Theo and Mona Northrop have saved $5500. They want the amount they invest in a mutual fund to be three times the amount they leave in their savings account. How much money should the Northrops put in the mutual fund?

13. Tickets to the school play cost $2.50 for general admission or $2.00 for students. On opening night, 319 tickets were sold. The total receipts were $694. How many of each kind of ticket were sold?

COOL-SPOT SALE
$970
Average cost of electricity per year
$68

Sale!
COLD-AIR
$1000
Average cost of electricity per year
$64

Use a system of equations to find *x* and *y* in each situation.

14.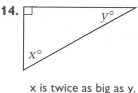

x is twice as big as y.

15.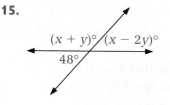

$(x + y)° \quad (x - 2y)°$

$48°$

Student Resources Toolbox
p. 655 *Formulas and Relationships*

16. **Reading** Here is another way to solve the problem in Sample 2.

   a. Explain how the entry for number of children's tickets sold is related to the solution on page 131.

   b. Explain how the equation
   $$7a + 4(272 - a) = 1694$$
   is related to the solution on page 131.

	Number of tickets sold	Dollar amount taken in
Adult	a	$7a$
Child	$272 - a$	$4(272 - a)$

$ from adults + $ from children = 1694

$$7a + 4(272 - a) = 1694$$

17. **Movie Salaries** In 1916, Mary Pickford's contract stated that her earnings that year would be half the profits of all her movies that year, plus $340,000 in bonuses. Charlie Chaplin's contracted salary that year was $670,000.

   a. Write an equation for Mary Pickford's earnings. Let *s* represent her earnings and *p* represent the profits of all her movies.

   b. Write an equation for Charlie Chaplin's salary. Let *s* represent his salary.

   c. What would the profits of Mary Pickford's movies have to be in order for her earnings to equal Charlie Chaplin's salary?

BY THE WAY...

Mary Pickford was a good businesswoman as well as a popular actress. "It took longer to make one of Mary's contracts than it did to make one of Mary's pictures," said her studio boss.

WHO'S PAID MOST?

Two of the highest paid actors in Hollywood are Sylvester Stallone and Jack Nicholson. For his work on *Rocky V*, Stallone was said to have received about $27 million plus 35% of the film's gross earnings. This puts Sly in the same income bracket as Nicholson, who is believed to have made a cool $60 million for his role as the Joker in *Batman*.

18. a. **Movie Salaries** Use the information in this article to write a system of equations that represents the earnings of Sylvester Stallone from *Rocky V* and the earnings of Jack Nicholson from *Batman*.

   b. Suppose both actors' earnings were the same. Use your system of equations from part (a) to find the gross earnings of *Rocky V*.

Ongoing ASSESSMENT

19. **Group Activity** Work with another student.

    a. Each of you should write a system of inequalities whose solution region is a right triangle. Then trade papers.

    b. Graph the system of inequalities that you were given. Find the coordinates of the vertices of the triangle.

    c. Find the area of the right triangle.

    d. Trade papers again and check each other's work.

Student Resources Toolbox
p. 657 *Formulas and Relationships*

Review PREVIEW

20. Graph this system of inequalities: $3x + 5y > -10$ *(Section 3-1)*
                                     $y \le 3$

Expand each product. *(Toolbox Skill 11)*

21. $x(-3x + 4)$ 22. $(x - 9)(x + 6)$ 23. $-5x(x - 10)$ 24. $(2x - 7)(3x + 8)$

Without graphing, find the slope of each line. *(Toolbox Skill 15, Section 2-2)*

25. $y = \frac{1}{4}x + 6$ 26. $y = \frac{2}{3}$ 27. $-3x + y = 11.5$ 28. $x = -9$

Working on the Unit Project

29. This graph is based on the information in Exercise 32 on page 128. These are the equations of the three lines.

    strenuous: $f = 0.53w$
    moderate: $f = 0.50w$
    light: $f = 0.47w$

    a. Explain what the graph shows.

    b. Suppose you solved this system of equations by substitution:

        $f = 0.47w$
        $w = 120$

    Tell what the solution means in this situation.

    c. Write a system of equations whose solution gives a recommended maximum daily fat intake for a moderately active 150 lb adult.

    d. Solve the system of equations you wrote in part (c). Explain the meaning of each coordinate of the solution.

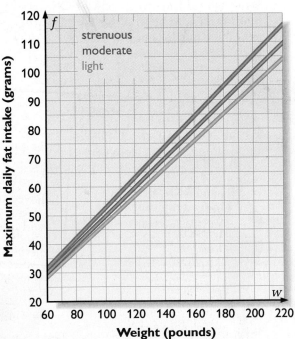

Slopes and Systems

Hit the Slopes

Focus

Understand and use the relationships between the slopes of parallel and perpendicular lines.

EXPLORATION

Can you predict whether two lines will intersect?

- **Materials: graphics calculator or graph paper**
- **Work with another student.**

① Use these equations.

$$y = 3x \qquad y = 3x + 3 \qquad y = 3x - 4$$

a. How are the equations alike? How are they different?

b. Graph the equations on the same set of axes.

c. Describe the graphs. How are they alike? How are they different?

② **a.** Write an equation of another line with the same slope as the line $y = 3x$.

b. Predict whether the line will intersect the graphs in step 1.

c. Test your prediction by graphing your equation on the same set of axes that you used in step 1.

③ **a.** Write an equation of a line that you think will intersect all the graphs in step 1.

b. Graph your equation on the same set of axes that you used in step 1. Check whether the graph intersects the other lines.

④ For each linear system, predict whether the lines will intersect if you graph the equations on the same set of axes.

a. $y = -2x + 1$ **b.** $y = -2x + 7$ **c.** $y = x - 5$
    $y = -4x - 4$ $x - y = 8$ $2x - 2y = 16$

⑤ Test your predictions in step 4 by graphing each system of equations. Discuss any unexpected results.

The graphs of two equations in a linear system can be related in one of three ways. You can use the relationship between the two graphs to tell how many solutions the system has.

TYPES OF LINEAR SYSTEMS

Two intersecting lines **One solution**	**One line** **Many solutions**	**Parallel lines** **No solutions**
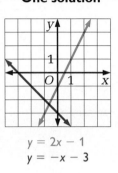	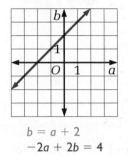	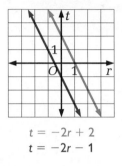
$y = 2x - 1$ $y = -x - 3$	$b = a + 2$ $-2a + 2b = 4$	$t = -2r + 2$ $t = -2r - 1$

A linear system that has one or more solutions is called a **consistent system.**

A linear system that has no solutions is called an **inconsistent system.**

Sample 1

Use this system of equations: $4x - y = 2$
$3y = 12x - 6$

a. Without graphing, describe the relationship between the graphs of the equations.

b. Tell whether the system of equations has *no solution, one solution,* or *many solutions*. Identify the system as *consistent* or *inconsistent.*

Sample Response

a. Write both equations in slope-intercept form.

$$4x - y = 2 \qquad\qquad\qquad 3y = 12x - 6$$
$$-y = -4x + 2 \qquad\qquad \frac{3y}{3} = \frac{12x}{3} - \frac{6}{3}$$
$$y = 4x - 2 \qquad\qquad\qquad y = 4x - 2$$

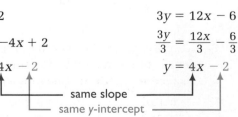

same slope
same y-intercept

The graphs of the equations are one line.

▶ **Now you are ready for:**
Exs. 1–15 on pp. 139–140

b. The system of equations has many solutions, because the graphs are one line. The system is consistent.

(How) are the slopes of perpendicular lines related?

- **Materials: graph paper, protractor**
- **Work in a group of three students.**

① Each of you should copy one of these segments on graph paper. Put one endpoint at the edge of your paper.

Segment A	Segment B	Segment C

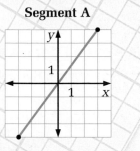

② Find the slope of your segment.

③ Fold the graph paper so that the endpoints of your segment meet.

④ Unfold the paper. Trace the fold line. Find its slope.

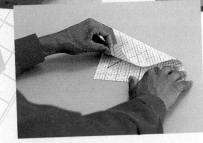

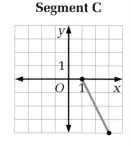

	Slope of segment	Slope of fold line
Segment A	?	?
Segment B	?	?
Segment C	?	?

⑤ Record your group's results from steps 2 and 4 in a table like this. Discuss any patterns that you see.

⑥ Look again at your graph paper. What do you think is the measure of the angle formed by each segment and its fold line? Use a protractor to check your guess.

⑦ Use your group's results from steps 5 and 6 to make a conjecture about how the slopes of any two perpendicular lines are related.

1. Use your conjecture from the Exploration. What do you think is the slope of a line perpendicular to the line $y = 5x - 4$? to the line $y = -\frac{3}{4}x + 7$?

2. What is the slope of a horizontal line? What is the slope of a vertical line? Does your conjecture from the Exploration apply to horizontal and vertical lines? Explain.

X $_($ $\triangle ab$

PARALLEL LINES AND PERPENDICULAR LINES

When the slope of a line is m, the slope of a parallel line is m.

When the slope of a line is m, $(m \neq 0)$, the slope of a perpendicular line is $-\frac{1}{m}$.

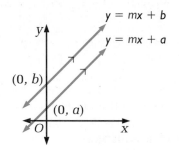

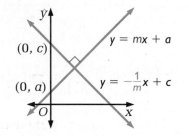

Sample 2

Write an equation of the line p that goes through the point $(-6, -1)$ and is perpendicular to the line $y = -2x - 3$.

Sample Response

Drawing a picture may help you understand the problem.

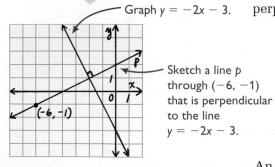

Graph $y = -2x - 3$.

Sketch a line p through $(-6, -1)$ that is perpendicular to the line $y = -2x - 3$.

To write an equation of line p, you need to know the slope. The slope of $y = -2x - 3$ is -2, so the slope of the perpendicular line p is $-\left(\frac{1}{-2}\right)$ or $\frac{1}{2}$.

$y = mx + b$ ← Use slope-intercept form.

$-1 = \frac{1}{2}(-6) + b$ ← p goes through $(-6, -1)$ and has slope $\frac{1}{2}$.

$-1 = -3 + b$

$2 = b$

An equation of the perpendicular line p is $y = \frac{1}{2}x + 2$.

┌─────────────────────────┐
│ **Talk it Over**   │
└─────────────────────────┘

3. Explain how you can use the graph in Sample 2 to check that $\frac{1}{2}$ and 2 are reasonable values for m and b in the equation for the perpendicular line p.

4. Describe how to find an equation of the line that goes through the point $(-6, -1)$ and is *parallel* to the line $y = -2x - 3$.

5. Find an equation of the line that goes through the point $(4, 3)$ and is perpendicular to the line $y = 3$.

Look Back ◄────────

▶ **Now you are ready for:**
Exs. 16–38 on pp. 140–141

Suppose the equations of a linear system are in slope-intercept form. Describe how to tell if the system of equations is consistent or inconsistent.

3-3 Exercises and Problems

1. Which linear system in step 4 of the Exploration on page 135 has equations whose graphs are parallel lines? Write equations of two more lines that are parallel to the lines in this system.

2. **Reading** Describe three ways in which the graphs of two linear equations can be related.

For each system of equations:

a. **Without graphing, describe the relationship of the graphs of the equations.**

b. **Tell whether the system of equations has *no solution, one solution,* or *many solutions*. Identify the system as *consistent* or *inconsistent*.**

3. $y = 4x + 2$
   $y = 4x - 2$

4. $p = 4n - 2$
   $5p = 20n - 10$

5. $3v + 2w = -6$
   $5v - 2w = -10$

6. $3y = 2x - 1$
   $12y = 8x - 4$

7. a. Find the slope of $\overline{AB}$, of $\overline{BC}$, of $\overline{CD}$, and of $\overline{AD}$.

   b. What type of polygon is $ABCD$? Explain how you know.

8. a. Graph these equations on the same set of axes.

   $y = x + 2$ $y = x - 3$ $y = 1$ $y = -3$

   b. What type of polygon do the lines form? Explain how you know.

   c. Find the area of the polygon.

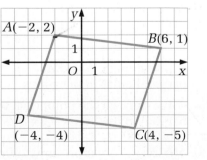

Without graphing, tell whether each line is parallel to, intersects, or is the same line as the line $2x - 5y = 10$.

9. $5y = 2x + 10$

10. $4x = 10y + 20$

11. $6x = 10 + 10y$

12. $x - 2.5y = 5$

13. **Movie Salaries** At one time, Arnold Schwarzenegger's fee for a film was reported to be between $10 million and $13 million, plus 15% of the profits.

   a. Suppose his fee was $10 million, plus 15% of the profits. Use two variables to write an equation for this fee.

   b. Suppose his fee was $13 million, plus 15% of the profits. Use the same two variables to write an equation for this fee.

   c. Graph the equations from parts (a) and (b) on the same set of axes.

   d. Describe your graph. Is your system of equations *consistent* or *inconsistent*?

14. **Economics** To find a country's trade balance with Japan, you subtract the value of the products that the country *buys from* Japan from the value of the products that the country *sells to* Japan.

   a. Describe the slope of the graph for Indonesia from 1990 to 1992. Do the same for China. Explain what the slopes mean in terms of Japan's trade balance with each of the two countries.

   b. Repeat part (a) for Malaysia and China from 1988 to 1989.

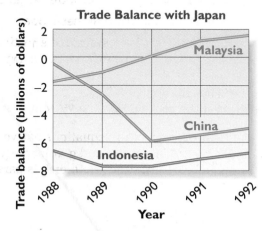

15. **Research** In a newspaper, magazine, or another textbook, find a graph that contains two lines. Describe the information that the graph shows. Tell if the graph represents a system that is *consistent* or *inconsistent*.

16. a. Use the table that you made in step 5 of the Exploration on page 137. For each segment, find this product:

$$\text{slope of segment} \times \text{slope of fold line}$$

   b. Use your results in part (a) to make a conjecture about the product of the slopes of two perpendicular lines.

17. Find the slope of a line that is perpendicular to the line $-3x + y = \frac{1}{2}$.

18. Find the slope of a line that is parallel to the line $4x + 5y = -10$.

Write an equation of the line that fits each description.

19. a line through the point $(-3, 2)$ and parallel to the line $y = -4x + 1$

20. a line through the point $(4, 7)$ and parallel to the line $y = 2$

21. a line through the point $(-3, 2)$ and perpendicular to the *y*-axis

22. a line through the point $(-2, 6)$ and perpendicular to the line $y = -2x + 2$

23. a line through the point $(-4, 0)$ and parallel to the line $y = 3x - 9$

24. a line through the point $(0, 5)$ and perpendicular to the *x*-axis

25. **Writing** You know how to find an equation of these lines:

   ➤ a line through a given point and *perpendicular* to a given line
   ➤ a line through a given point and *parallel* to a given line

How are the procedures alike? How are they different?

For Exercises 26 and 27, tell what type of polygon $ABCD$ is. Explain how you know.

26. $A(-8, 3)$, $B(2, 5)$, $C(3, 0)$, $D(-2, -1)$

27. $A(-4.8, 3.6)$, $B(-0.8, 5.6)$, $C(2.8, -1.6)$, $D(-1.2, -3.6)$

28. Write an equation of the line that goes through $(-3, 2)$ and is parallel to the line that goes through $(6, -3)$ and $(3, 1)$.

29. Two lines rise from left to right and cross the x-axis at an angle of $45°$. One line goes through the point $(-1, 0)$ and the other line goes through the point $(2, 1)$.

    a. Find the slope of each line. (*Hint:* See Exercise 32 on page 73.)

    b. Write an equation for each line.

    c. Tell whether the system of equations you wrote in part (b) has *no solution, one solution,* or *many solutions.*

Ongoing ASSESSMENT

30. **Open-ended** Write equations of two parallel lines. Graph and label them l_1 and l_2. Write and graph an equation of a line that is perpendicular to l_1. Label it l_3. Tell whether l_3 is parallel or perpendicular to l_2.

Review PREVIEW

Solve each system of equations. *(Section 3-2)*

31. $a + b = 10$
    $3a + 2b = 40$

32. $5x - y = 15$
    $x - 4y = 22$

33. $2k + 3n = 10$
    $10k - 3n = -4$

34. Tell whether you think the inequality $x < 2x$ is true for all values of x. If not, give a counterexample. *(Section 1-5)*

Solve. *(Toolbox Skill 13)*

35. $6(3y - 4) = 3$

36. $9 = -3(5 - 2x)$

37. $-8(-3 - 5n) = 0$

Working on the Unit Project

38. **Research** Does your family have recipes that are passed down from generation to generation? Choose an old family recipe or the recipe for a favorite food. Find the fat, protein, carbohydrate, and Calorie content of each ingredient. You can find tables that give this information about foods in these sources:

    ➤ *The New Laurel's Kitchen* by Laurel Robertson, Carol Flinders, and Brian Ruppenthal (vegetarian only)

    ➤ *Nutrition Almanac* by Lavon J. Dunne

    ➤ *Nutritive Value of Foods,* Home and Garden Bulletin Number 72, United States Department of Agriculture

Gallina en Pepitoria
Puerto Rico (Chicken in Almond Sauce)

3½-pound chicken
½ cup (2 oz) blanched almonds
2-inch piece stick cinnamon
¼ cup olive oil
½ cup tomato,
2 cups chicke
2 eggs

2 tsp lime or lemon juice
4 whole cloves
1 clove garlic, chopped
1 medium onion, chopped
¼ tsp white pepper

Solving Systems by Addition-or-Subtraction

Disappearing Act

Focus

Solve systems of equations using addition-or-subtraction and choose a method for solving a system of equations.

Talk it Over

People in ancient China used red and black counting rods arranged in a checkerboard pattern to solve linear systems. The diagram shows this linear system:

$$4x - 3y = 11$$
$$-5x + 2y = -12$$

1. What number does each group of counting rods represent?

2. How are the colors red and black used?

3. Compare the diagram to the modern way of writing the linear system. How are they alike? How are they different?

4. Explain why it is not easy to solve the linear system by substitution. (This system of equations is solved in Sample 3.)

A horizontal rod stands for 10.

Two vertical rods stand for 2.

The Chinese book *Nine Chapters on the Mathematical Art* (completed before the first century A.D.) contains the first known use of the *addition-or-subtraction method* for solving a linear system. This method involves combining the like terms of the two equations to make a new equation with just one variable.

Here are two ways to begin solving a linear system:

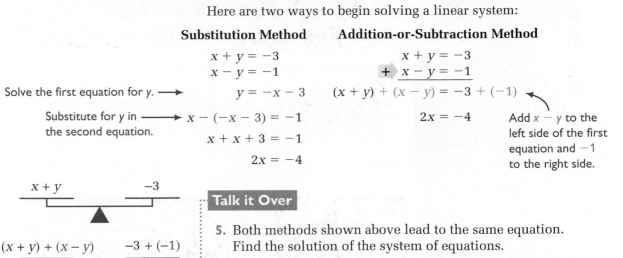

Substitution Method	**Addition-or-Subtraction Method**

$$x + y = -3$$
$$x - y = -1$$

Solve the first equation for y. ⟶ $y = -x - 3$

Substitute for y in ⟶ $x - (-x - 3) = -1$
the second equation.
$$x + x + 3 = -1$$
$$2x = -4$$

$$x + y = -3$$
$$+ \quad x - y = -1$$
$$(x + y) + (x - y) = -3 + (-1)$$
$$2x = -4$$

Add $x - y$ to the left side of the first equation and -1 to the right side.

| $x + y$ | -3 |

| $(x + y) + (x - y)$ | $-3 + (-1)$ |

| $2x$ | -4 |

Talk it Over

5. Both methods shown above lead to the same equation. Find the solution of the system of equations.

6. Compare the number of steps needed in each method to reach the equation $2x = -4$. Which method do you think is easier to use for this system of equations? Why?

7. The balance scales show the addition-or-subtraction method. Why do the scales remain balanced?

Sample 1

Solve by the addition-or-subtraction method.

a. $3y = 2x + 2$
   $3y = x - 2$

b. $5a + 2b = 23$
   $7a - 2b = 13$

Sample Response

You can compare the coefficients of the like terms to decide which operation will *eliminate* one of the variables.

a. The coefficients of y are *the same*.
   Subtract to eliminate the y-terms.

$$3y = 2x + 2$$
$$- \quad 3y = \quad x - 2$$
$$0 = x + 4$$

$3y - 3y$ ↗ $2x - x$ ↑ $2 - (-2)$ ↘

$$0 = x + 4$$
$$-4 = x$$

Solve the new equation.

$$3y = -4 - 2$$
$$3y = -6$$
$$y = -2$$

Substitute in one of the original equations to find the other variable.

The solution (x, y) is $(-4, -2)$.

b. The coefficients of b are *opposites*.
   Add to eliminate the b-terms.

$$5a + 2b = 23$$
$$+ \quad 7a - 2b = 13$$
$$12a + 0 = 36$$

$5a + 7a$ ↗ $2b + (-2b)$ ↑ $23 + 13$ ↘

$$12a = 36$$
$$a = 3$$

$$5(3) + 2b = 23$$
$$15 + 2b = 23$$
$$2b = 8$$
$$b = 4$$

The solution (a, b) is $(3, 4)$.

Multiplying Before Using Addition-or-Subtraction

Sometimes the equations in a system of equations do not have any like terms with the same or opposite coefficients. You can change the coefficients by multiplying both sides of either equation by a constant.

Sample 2

The readouts on the stair machine and the treadmill tell Raquel how many Calories she burns. How many minutes should she spend on each machine if she exercises for 30 min and wants to burn 200 Cal?

Sample Response

Problem Solving Strategy: Use a system of equations.

Let x = the number of minutes on the stair machine.
Let y = the number of minutes on the treadmill.

Write two equations that relate x and y.

$$x + y = 30$$ ⟵ Raquel exercises for 30 min.

$$5.7x + 7.3y = 200$$ ⟵ Raquel wants to burn a total of 200 Cal.

To make the coefficients of the x-terms the same, multiply both sides of the first equation by 5.7.

$$5.7(x + y) = 5.7(30)$$ ⟶ $$5.7x + 5.7y = 171$$

$$-\ \underline{\quad 5.7x + 7.3y = 200\quad}$$ ⟵ Subtract to eliminate the x-terms.

$$-1.6y = -29$$

$$y = 18.125$$

$$y \approx 18$$ ⟵ Round to the nearest minute.

$$x + 18 = 30$$ ⟵ Substitute 18 for y in the first equation to find x.

$$x = 12$$

Watch Out!
Be sure that for *each* pair of like terms, you *subtract* the term of the second equation from the term above it.

Raquel should spend about 12 min on the stair machine and about 18 min on the treadmill.

·····▶ **Now you are ready for:**
Exs. 1–18 on pp. 147–148

Talk it Over

8. In Sample 2, suppose you multiply both sides of the first equation by -5.7 instead of 5.7. How does this change the other steps of the solution?

9. Describe the steps you can take if you choose to eliminate y in solving the system of equations in Sample 2.

10. Describe the first step you would take to solve this system of equations.

$$5s + 2t = 11$$
$$-10s - 6t = -18$$

To solve the system of equations shown on page 142, you need to change the coefficients of both equations.

Sample 3

Solve this system of equations: $4x - 3y = 11$
$-5x + 2y = -12$

Sample Response

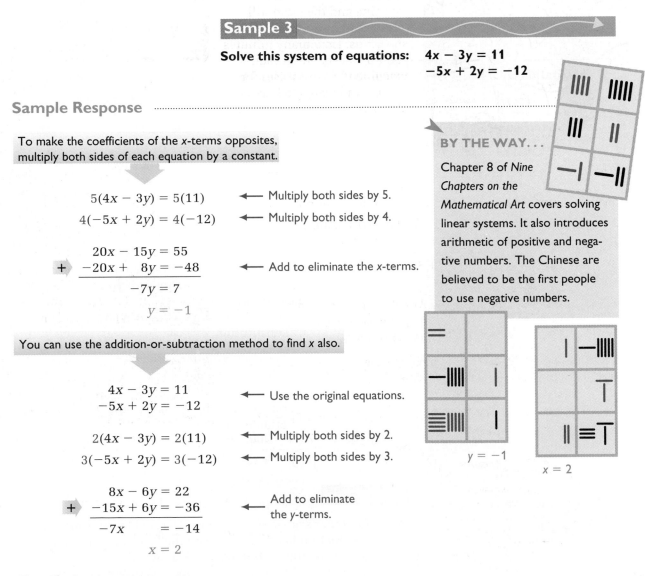

To make the coefficients of the x-terms opposites, multiply both sides of each equation by a constant.

$$5(4x - 3y) = 5(11)$$ ◀── Multiply both sides by 5.
$$4(-5x + 2y) = 4(-12)$$ ◀── Multiply both sides by 4.

$$+\ \begin{array}{r} 20x - 15y = 55 \\ -20x + 8y = -48 \end{array}$$ ◀── Add to eliminate the x-terms.
$$-7y = 7$$
$$y = -1$$

You can use the addition-or-subtraction method to find x also.

$$4x - 3y = 11$$
$$-5x + 2y = -12$$ ◀── Use the original equations.

$$2(4x - 3y) = 2(11)$$ ◀── Multiply both sides by 2.
$$3(-5x + 2y) = 3(-12)$$ ◀── Multiply both sides by 3.

$$+\ \begin{array}{r} 8x - 6y = 22 \\ -15x + 6y = -36 \end{array}$$ ◀── Add to eliminate the y-terms.
$$-7x = -14$$
$$x = 2$$

The solution (x, y) is $(2, -1)$.

BY THE WAY...

Chapter 8 of *Nine Chapters on the Mathematical Art* covers solving linear systems. It also introduces arithmetic of positive and negative numbers. The Chinese are believed to be the first people to use negative numbers.

$y = -1$

$x = 2$

You now know three methods for solving a system of equations. Here are some suggestions for choosing which method to use.

X·Lab

CHOOSING A METHOD TO SOLVE A LINEAR SYSTEM

You might solve by...	when...
graphing	➤ an approximate solution is acceptable. ➤ you want to tell when one quantity is greater than or less than another quantity. ➤ the lines are easy to graph by hand, or a graphics calculator is available. ➤ you want to check that a solution found by another method is reasonable.
substitution $b = a + 5$ $b = 3a - 1$	➤ at least one equation is solved for one of the variables. ➤ at least one equation has a variable with coefficient 1.
addition-or-subtraction	➤ the like terms of the two equations are in the same order and on the same side of the equation. ➤ the coefficients of at least one pair of like terms in the two equations are the same or are opposites. ➤ no variable in either equation has a coefficient of 1.

Helen Marvelli

$$y = \boxed{4x - 2}$$
$$3y = 12x - 6$$

$$3(4x - 2) = 12x - 6$$
$$12x - 6 = 12x - 6$$
$$12x - 6 - 12x = 12x - 6 - 12x$$
$$-6 = -6$$

Remember that not all systems have exactly one solution. What happens if you use algebra to solve a system that has no solution or many solutions? For this system, Helen chose solving by substitution.

You can see that this equation is true for all values of x.

You end up with a *true* statement without variables. This means that the system is consistent and has many solutions.

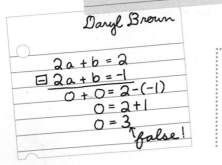

Daryl Brown

$$2a + b = 2$$
$$\boxminus \ 2a + b = -1$$
$$0 + 0 = 2 - (-1)$$
$$0 = 2 + 1$$
$$0 = 3 \quad \text{false!}$$

Talk it Over

11. For another system of equations, Daryl chose the addition-or-subtraction method. Compare the last line of her work with the last line of Helen's work above. How are they alike? How are they different? What do you think Daryl's result means?

Tell which method you would use to solve each system of equations. Give a reason for your choice.

12. $c = 6d + 7$
$12d - 2c = -14$

13. $w = \frac{2}{3}v + 2$
$w = \frac{2}{3}v - 1$

14. $2x + y = 17$
$2x - 5y = 11$

15. Solve the system in question 12. Explain the result.

Look Back ◄

Samples 1, 2, and 3 show how to use addition-or-subtraction to solve four different systems of linear equations. Explain the differences in how you apply the method in each case.

·····► **Now you are ready for:**
Exs. 19–38 on pp. 148–150

3-4 Exercises and Problems

1. a. Reading Sample 1 shows how to use addition-or-subtraction to solve a system of equations. How do you decide whether to add or subtract?

  b. To solve the system in Exercise 2, will you add or subtract? Why?

Solve each system of equations.

2. $-3a - 5b = -17$
$3a + 8b = 5$

3. $p - 6q = 14$
$2p + 6q = 10$

4. $-2c + 9d = 35$
$6c + 7d = 65$

5. $-5m + 3n = 12$
$5m - 8n = 23$

6. $7j - 3k = -14$
$2j + 3k = 32$

7. $y = 4x + 5$
$y = 2x - 7$

8. $2x + y = 5$
$3x - 2y = 4$

9. $4w - v = 15$
$-2w + 6v = -2$

10. Open-ended Write two different systems of equations that both have (2, 3) as a solution.

11. A problem in *Nine Chapters on the Mathematical Art* can be represented by this system of equations. Solve the system.

$9x - y = 11$
$6x - y = -16$

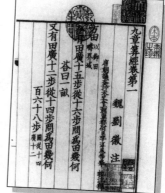

For Exercises 12–15, use a system of equations to solve each problem.

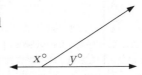

12. Fitness Liam burns 8.3 Cal/min when using a rowing machine, and 5.9 Cal/min when using an exercise bike. He plans to exercise for 45 min and wants to burn 300 Cal. How many minutes should he spend on each machine?

13. x is 15 more than four times y. Find the measure of each angle.

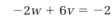

14. The difference between x and y is 12. Find the measure of each angle.

15. Each of two sides of a triangle is 8 in. longer than the third side. The perimeter is 43 in. How long is each side of the triangle?

Career **For Exercises 16–18, use this information on jewelry making.**

Some jewelers make the gold that they use from pure gold and a combination of other metals. The *karat* of the gold depends on the percent of pure gold used.

Karat	24	22	18	14	10
% pure gold	100	91.7	75	58.3	41.7

Note: Weights of precious metals are given in *pennyweights* (abbreviated dwt), where 20 dwt = 1 ounce.

16. A jeweler has on hand some 14-karat gold and some 24-karat gold. The jeweler needs to know how much of each to use to make 8 dwt of 18-karat gold for a bracelet ordered by a customer.

   a. Let x = the amount of 14-karat gold needed (dwt). Let y = the amount of 24-karat gold needed (dwt).

   Explain the meaning of each equation in this system of equations. (*Hint:* Use the information in the table above.)

   $$x + y = 8$$
   $$0.583x + 1y = 0.75(8)$$

   b. Solve the system of equations in part (a). Give the values of x and y to the nearest tenth. Explain the meaning of the solution.

17. How much 10-karat gold and how much 22-karat gold should be combined to make 10 dwt of 14-karat gold?

18. How much 24-karat gold should be added to 50 dwt of 14-karat gold to make 18-karat gold? How much 18-karat gold will there be?

Solve each system of equations.

19. $3x - 2y = 2$
    $10x - 3y = -8$

20. $2r + 2t = -14$
    $-5r + 3t = -45$

21. $4a + 15b = 10$
    $3a + 10b = 5$

22. $3u + 2v = -6$
    $5u - 4v = 1$

23. The Broadcast Club at Curie High School plans to spend $200 on tapes and CDs for the school radio station. Cherub Records offers to sell them tapes for $6 and CDs for $12. At Flower's Music, tapes cost $8 and CDs cost $10.

   a. Use this graph. What do the variables t and c represent? Which line represents Cherub Records? Flower's Music?

   b. Use the graph to estimate the solution of the system of equations.

   c. Solve the system using addition-or-subtraction.

   d. For which values of t is it cheaper to buy at Cherub Records? For which values of t is it cheaper to buy at Flower's Music?

   e. **Writing** Do you think the system is easier to solve by *graphing* or by *addition-or-subtraction*? Explain your choice.

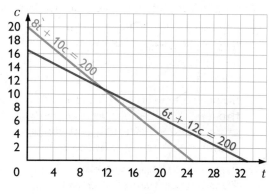

Writing Tell what method you would use to solve each system of equations. Give a reason for your choice.

24. $y = 2x + 13$
$3x + y = 15$

25. $5k - 3n = -4$
$6k - 5n = 1$

26. $-4a + b = 10$
$4a + 2b = -1$

27. $y = \frac{1}{2}x + 6$
$y = -2x + 1$

28. Dan solved a system of equations using the addition-or-subtraction method.

   a. Explain his solution.

   b. Write each equation in the system in slope-intercept form. What do you know about the graphs of the equations? What type of system is this?

Solve each system of equations. If there is no solution, write *no solution*.

29. $3a - 2b = 24$
$6a - 4b = -6$

30. $y = 9x - 3$
$4x + 2y = 5$

31. $2x + 9y = 20$
$5x + 6y = 17$

32. $3r - 3s = 18$
$r = s + 6$

Dan O'Brien

$2x + 3y = 1$
$4x + 6y = -2$

$2(2x + 3y) = 2(1)$

$4x + 6y = 2$
$4x + 6y = -2$ *(Subtract)*
$0 = 4$ ALWAYS FALSE!

Ongoing ASSESSMENT

33. **Group Activity** Work in a group of three students.

   Use this system of equations: $y = 3x + 14$
                                          $2y = -x + 7$

   a. Solve the system of equations by substitution, addition-or-subtraction, and graphing. Each of you should use a different method.

   b. With your group, decide which method you think is best for solving the system. Give a reason for your choice.

Review PREVIEW

34. Write an equation of the line that goes through the point $(-3, 2)$ and is parallel to the line $y = -2x + 2$. *(Section 3-3)*

Use the information in the table to find each probability. *(Toolbox Skill 6)*

35. Suppose a resident of Maine is picked at random. What is the probability that the person lives on a farm?

36. Suppose a resident of a farm in the New England states is picked at random. What is the probability that the person lives in Maine?

37. Suppose a resident of the New England states is picked at random. What is the probability that the person lives on a farm?

Populations of the New England States (1990)		
State	Total population (thousands)	Farm population (thousands)
Connecticut	3287	686
Maine	1228	680
Massachusetts	6016	947
New Hampshire	1109	544
Rhode Island	1003	140
Vermont	563	382

38. For a backpacking trip, Selena wants to make a snack of raisins and peanuts so that the mix has half her daily allowances for protein and fat. Her daily allowances are 55 grams of protein and 73 grams of fat. How many cups of each food should she use? Round to the nearest half cup.

	protein (g)	fat (g)
raisins (**1 cup**)	4	1
peanuts (**1 cup**)	38	70

Unit 3 CHECKPOINT

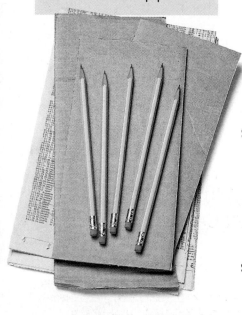

1. Writing Use this system of equations: $y = \frac{1}{2}x + 1$
$$10y = -5x - 3$$

Does the system have *no solution, one solution,* or *many solutions*? Explain how you can tell without graphing the system.

2. The town of Reedsville pays \$400 per ton to dispose of cardboard waste. If the town rents a cardboard compactor for \$350, then they will pay only \$80 per ton to dispose of cardboard waste.   **3-1**

   a. Write a system of equations that models the town's costs for each cardboard waste disposal plan.

   b. Graph the system of equations in part (a).

   c. Which disposal plan is cheaper if the town has one ton of cardboard waste? if the town has two tons of cardboard waste? Explain how the graph supports your answers.

3. Graph this system of inequalities: $y \le -2x + 1$
$$y > 1.5x - 3$$

Solve each system of equations by substitution.   **3-2**

   4. $y = 3x - 1$ **5.** $x + y = 461$
       $y = -5x + 3$ $6x + 5y = 2530$

6. Write an equation of the line that goes through (2, 5) and is parallel to the line $y = -3x + 4$.   **3-3**

7. Write an equation of the line that goes through (−2, 0) and is perpendicular to the line $y = -3x + 4$.

Solve each system of equations.   **3-4**

   8. $4y = 3x + 1$ **9.** $2y = 12x + 4$ **10.** $3x - y = -1$
      $-8y = -3x - 5$ $-y = -6x - 2$ $4x - y = 4$

11. Tell what method you would use to solve this system. Give a reason for your choice. $y = -5x$
                                                           $2x + y = 9$

3-5 Matrix Operations

~On the Menu~

Focus
Use matrices to represent data sets and use matrix operations.

Real-world data that belong to more than one category are often displayed in a table or *matrix*.

Bombay House
Luncheon Specials
Monday – Friday, 11:00 – 2:00

	Curry	Kurma
Chicken	$3.75	$4.25
Lamb	$4.00	$4.50
Shrimp	$5.25	$5.75

In mathematics a **matrix** is an arrangement of numbers, called **elements,** in rows and columns. (*Note:* The plural of *matrix* is *matrices*.)

The numbers in a matrix are written inside large square brackets ([ ]).

Write category labels outside the brackets.

The element 4.25 is in row 1, column 2.

$$P = \begin{array}{c} \text{chicken} \\ \text{lamb} \\ \text{shrimp} \end{array} \begin{bmatrix} 3.75 & 4.25 \\ 4.00 & 4.50 \\ 5.25 & 5.75 \end{bmatrix}$$

curry   kurma

3 rows

You can name a matrix with a single capital letter.

2 columns

The number of rows and the number of columns, *in that order,* are the **dimensions** of the matrix. The dimensions of this price matrix are 3 × 2, read "three by two."

1. In which row and column is the price for an order of lamb curry?

Bombay House

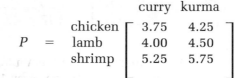

$$P = \begin{array}{c} \text{chicken} \\ \text{lamb} \\ \text{shrimp} \end{array} \begin{array}{cc} \text{curry} & \text{kurma} \\ \begin{bmatrix} 3.75 & 4.25 \\ 4.00 & 4.50 \\ 5.25 & 5.75 \end{bmatrix} \end{array}$$

BY THE WAY...

Curry dishes are cooked with curry powder, which is a combination of the spices cumin, tumeric, and coriander. Kurma dishes are cooked with yogurt, cream, almonds, and sweet spices.

2. What does the element in row 3, column 2 of the price matrix represent?

3. Suppose the owner of Bombay House wants to expand the menu to show prices for vegetable curry and vegetable kurma. What would be the dimensions of the new price matrix?

4. Use the original price matrix P. Suppose the owner wants to raise prices at Bombay House by 4%.

   a. Explain why the owner can multiply each price by 1.04 in order to find the new price.

   b. What will be the dimensions of the new price matrix?

To multiply the matrix P by the number 1.04, you multiply each element of P by 1.04.

Multiplying a matrix by a number is called *scalar multiplication*.

$$1.04P = 1.04\begin{bmatrix} 3.75 & 4.25 \\ 4.00 & 4.50 \\ 5.25 & 5.75 \end{bmatrix} = \begin{bmatrix} 1.04(3.75) & 1.04(4.25) \\ 1.04(4.00) & 1.04(4.50) \\ 1.04(5.25) & 1.04(5.75) \end{bmatrix} = \begin{bmatrix} 3.90 & 4.42 \\ 4.16 & 4.68 \\ 5.46 & 5.98 \end{bmatrix}$$

Sample 1

	A	B	C	D	E
		rock/pop	jazz	classical	other
1		rock/pop	jazz	classical	other
2	CDs	1913	139	333	388
3	tapes	843	61	119	164

February Sales

Bill Chee uses spreadsheet software to keep track of sales data at his music store. In March, he hopes to increase sales in all categories by 7%.

a. Write the February sales data in a matrix.

b. Use scalar multiplication to find how many of each type of recording in each category the store needs to sell to meet the March sales goal.

a. Give the matrix a name and include category labels.

February Sales

$$A = \begin{array}{c} \\ \text{CDs} \\ \text{tapes} \end{array} \begin{array}{cccc} \text{rock/pop} & \text{jazz} & \text{classical} & \text{other} \\ \left[\begin{array}{cccc} 1913 & 139 & 333 & 388 \\ 843 & 61 & 119 & 164 \end{array}\right] \end{array}$$

b. To increase each element of the February sales matrix by 7%, multiply the matrix A by 1.07.

Method ❶ Use arithmetic.

You can leave off the category labels while you do the calculations.

$$1.07A = \textbf{1.07}\left[\begin{array}{cccc} 1913 & 139 & 333 & 388 \\ 843 & 61 & 119 & \textbf{164} \end{array}\right]$$

Multiply each element of A by 1.07.

$$= \left[\begin{array}{cccc} (1.07)1913 & (1.07)139 & (1.07)333 & (1.07)388 \\ (1.07)843 & (1.07)61 & (1.07)119 & \textbf{(1.07)164} \end{array}\right]$$

$$= \left[\begin{array}{cccc} 2046.91 & 148.73 & 356.31 & 415.16 \\ 902.01 & 65.27 & 127.33 & \textbf{175.48} \end{array}\right]$$

Enter each result in the corresponding position of the product matrix.

Method ❷ Use a graphics calculator.

Enter the February sales matrix in matrix A. Then find $1.07A$.

```
1.07[A]
        [ 2046.91 148.7...
          902.01  65.2...
```

Write the answer as a matrix with labels.

Recordings are sold in whole units. Round off each element to the nearest whole number.

March Sales Goals

$$\begin{array}{c} \\ \text{CDs} \\ \text{tapes} \end{array} \begin{array}{cccc} \text{rock/pop} & \text{jazz} & \text{classical} & \text{other} \\ \left[\begin{array}{cccc} 2047 & 149 & 356 & 415 \\ 902 & 65 & 127 & 175 \end{array}\right] \end{array}$$

TECHNOLOGY NOTE

To see all the elements of a matrix, you may need to use the arrow keys to scroll right and left. For more information on using the matrix functions of a graphics calculator, see the Technology Handbook, p. 609.

Talk it Over

5. How many jazz tapes does Bill Chee hope to sell in March?

6. In Sample 1, what are the dimensions of the February sales matrix A? What are the dimensions of the matrix $1.07A$?

7. Will the dimensions of a matrix M and a scalar multiple of M always be the same? Explain.

▶ Now you are ready for:
Exs. 1–13 on pp. 155–157

Matrix Addition and Subtraction

When two matrices have the same dimensions, you can add or subtract the matrices by adding or subtracting the elements in corresponding positions.

Sample 2

These spreadsheets show the January and February sales at the music store in Sample 1. Find the total sales in each category for January and February combined. Write the answer as a matrix.

January Sales

	A	B	C	D	E
1		rock/pop	jazz	classical	other
2	CDs	1837	131	319	393
3	tapes	839	63	127	158

February Sales

	A	B	C	D	E
1		rock/pop	jazz	classical	other
2	CDs	1913	139	333	388
3	tapes	843	61	119	164

Sample Response

1 Write the January and February data in matrices.

January Sales

$$B = \begin{array}{c} \\ \text{CDs} \\ \text{tapes} \end{array} \begin{bmatrix} \text{rock/pop} & \text{jazz} & \text{classical} & \text{other} \\ 1837 & 131 & 319 & 393 \\ 839 & 63 & 127 & 158 \end{bmatrix}$$

February Sales

$$A = \begin{array}{c} \\ \text{CDs} \\ \text{tapes} \end{array} \begin{bmatrix} \text{rock/pop} & \text{jazz} & \text{classical} & \text{other} \\ 1913 & 139 & 333 & 388 \\ 843 & 61 & 119 & 164 \end{bmatrix}$$

2 To find the total sales in each category, add the matrices.

$$B + A = \begin{bmatrix} 1837 & 131 & 319 & 393 \\ 839 & 63 & 127 & \mathbf{158} \end{bmatrix} + \begin{bmatrix} 1913 & 139 & 333 & 388 \\ 843 & 61 & 119 & \mathbf{164} \end{bmatrix}$$

Add the elements in corresponding positions.

$$= \begin{bmatrix} (1837 + 1913) & (131 + 139) & (319 + 333) & (393 + 388) \\ (839 + 843) & (63 + 61) & (127 + 119) & (\mathbf{158} + \mathbf{164}) \end{bmatrix}$$

$$= \begin{bmatrix} 3750 & 270 & 652 & 781 \\ 1682 & 124 & 246 & \mathbf{322} \end{bmatrix}$$

Enter each result in the corresponding position of the sum matrix.

3 Write the answer as a matrix with labels.

January/February Sales

$$\begin{array}{c} \\ \text{CDs} \\ \text{tapes} \end{array} \begin{bmatrix} \text{rock/pop} & \text{jazz} & \text{classical} & \text{other} \\ 3750 & 270 & 652 & 781 \\ 1682 & 124 & 246 & 322 \end{bmatrix}$$

Unit 3 Linear Systems and Matrices

8. How many classical CDs were sold in January/February?

9. You can subtract matrices by subtracting elements in corresponding positions. Use matrices B and A in Sample 2:

$$A - B = \begin{bmatrix} 1913 & 139 & 333 & \mathbf{388} \\ 843 & 61 & 119 & 164 \end{bmatrix} - \begin{bmatrix} 1837 & 131 & 319 & \mathbf{393} \\ 839 & 63 & 127 & 158 \end{bmatrix}$$

$$= \begin{bmatrix} 76 & 8 & 14 & \mathbf{-5} \\ 4 & -2 & -8 & 6 \end{bmatrix} \longleftarrow 388 - 393 = -5$$

a. Explain the meaning of the matrix $A - B$ in terms of sales at Bill Chee's music store.

b. What do the negative numbers in the matrix $A - B$ mean?

MATRIX OPERATIONS

Scalar multiplication

➤ To multiply matrix A by a constant c, multiply each element of A by c.

Matrix addition or subtraction

➤ To add or subtract two matrices, add or subtract the elements that are in corresponding positions.

➤ Matrices can be added or subtracted only if they have the same dimensions.

······➤ Now you are ready for:
Exs. 14–35 on pp. 157–158

Look Back ◄──────────

How is scalar multiplication like matrix addition or subtraction? How is it different?

3-5 Exercises and Problems

1. **Reading** How many elements does a matrix with dimensions 3×4 have?

What are the dimensions of each matrix?

2. $\begin{bmatrix} 4 & 7 \\ 8 & 2 \end{bmatrix}$

3. $\begin{bmatrix} 67 & 32 & 18 & 5 & 0 \\ 53 & 12 & 6 & 41 & 11 \\ 2 & 8 & 0 & 4 & 72 \end{bmatrix}$

4. $\begin{bmatrix} 6 \\ 17 \\ 3 \end{bmatrix}$

5. $\begin{bmatrix} 0 & 25 & 16 & 70 \end{bmatrix}$

This duck is being banded as part of a program to estimate the nesting duck population in Central Oregon.

connection to **BIOLOGY**

For Exercises 6–10, use this information.

Biologists use *capture-recapture models* to estimate how many animals are in an area. The biologists repeatedly capture, tag, and release samples of the animals. They use a *capture-history matrix* to keep track of which animals are captured each time.

Suppose this capture-history matrix records the results of five samples of a duck population.

Each column represents a time when biologists captured a sample of ducks.

Each row of the matrix represents a duck.

Capture-History Matrix

$$\begin{array}{c} \\ \text{duck } A \\ \text{duck } B \\ \text{duck } C \end{array} \begin{array}{ccccc} 1 & 2 & 3 & 4 & 5 \\ \left[\begin{array}{ccccc} 1 & 0 & 0 & 1 & 0 \\ 1 & 0 & 1 & 0 & 1 \\ 0 & 1 & 0 & 0 & 1 \end{array}\right] \end{array}$$

The element "0" means the duck was not captured.

The element "1" means the duck was captured.

6. What are the dimensions of the capture-history matrix?

7. What do the dimensions mean in this situation?

8. How many times was duck *A* captured?

9. Which duck was captured the greatest number of times?

10. What does the element in row 3, column 4 mean in this situation?

11. **Sales** A sports store is planning a 20% off sale on all basketball, cycling, and running clothes and shoes.

    a. Write the price data in a matrix.

    b. Explain why you can multiply each price by 0.80 to find each sale price.

    c. Use scalar multiplication to find the sale price of each item.

    d. What is the sale price of cycling shorts?

Original Price (Dollars)			
	Basketball	**Cycling**	**Running**
Shirts	9.99	16.99	10.99
Shorts	16.99	9.99	9.99
Shoes	64.99	59.99	54.99

12. **Baking** Use this table from a box of biscuit mix.

	MIX	**MILK**	**SUGAR**	**EGGS**	**SHORTENING**
Biscuits	1⅓ cups	½ cup	none	none	none
Muffins	1⅓ cups	¾ cup	¼ cup	1	2 tablespoons
Coffee Cake	1⅓ cups	½ cup	¼ cup	1	none

    a. Write the ingredients table as a matrix.

    b. Multiply the ingredients matrix by 3.

    c. What does scalar multiplication by 3 mean in this situation?

13. **Open-ended** Describe a situation that can be represented by a matrix for which scalar multiplication does *not* give a sensible answer.

Simplify.

14. $\begin{bmatrix} -1 & 0 \\ 3 & -5 \end{bmatrix} + \begin{bmatrix} 4 & -6 \\ 1 & 0 \end{bmatrix}$

15. $\begin{bmatrix} 2.4 & -1.3 \\ 5.2 & 1.8 \\ -3.1 & 2.7 \end{bmatrix} - \begin{bmatrix} 1.3 & 6.2 \\ 7.1 & 0.5 \\ -2.1 & -4.0 \end{bmatrix}$

16. $5 \begin{bmatrix} -3 \\ 4 \\ 0 \end{bmatrix} + \begin{bmatrix} 15 \\ -7 \\ -9 \end{bmatrix}$

17. $3 \begin{bmatrix} 2 \\ 0 \\ 11 \end{bmatrix} + 2 \begin{bmatrix} 4 \\ 13 \\ 9 \end{bmatrix}$

18. Is it possible to add the matrices $\begin{bmatrix} 12 & 14 & 2 & 5 \\ 76 & 42 & 9 & 1 \\ 18 & 7 & 58 & 3 \end{bmatrix}$ and $\begin{bmatrix} 56 & 11 \\ 5 & 3 \\ 0 & 3 \end{bmatrix}$?

    Explain why or why not.

19. **Business** In March, Bill Chee sold 2082 rock/pop CDs, 143 jazz CDs, 327 classical CDs, 423 other CDs, 865 rock/pop tapes, 64 jazz tapes, 149 classical tapes, and 167 other tapes at his music store.

    a. Organize the data in a matrix with dimensions 2×4.

    b. Did Bill Chee reach his sales goal for March?
    (See Sample 1 response on page 153.)

    c. Use the music sales data in Sample 2 on page 154. What are the total sales at Bill Chee's music store for the first quarter of the year?

20. Use the matrices $B = \begin{bmatrix} 14 & 48 & 18 \\ 5 & 30 & 2 \end{bmatrix}$ and $D = \begin{bmatrix} 56 & 48 & 13 \\ 80 & 36 & 1 \end{bmatrix}$.

    a. Find $B + D$ and $D + B$. Does the order in which you add two matrices matter? Explain why or why not.

    b. Find $B - D$ and $D - B$. Does the order in which you subtract two matrices matter? Explain why or why not.

21. **Basketball** Use the two win-loss tables.

**Top Three Western Conference Teams
1989–1990 Basketball Season**

	HOME GAMES			AWAY GAMES	
	WINS	LOSSES		WINS	LOSSES
LA Lakers	37	4	LA Lakers	26	15
Utah	36	5	Utah	19	22
Portland	35	6	Portland	24	17

    a. Write the information in each table in a 3×2 matrix.

    b. Add the matrices in part (a).

    c. What does the sum of the matrices mean in this situation?

    d. Subtract the matrices in part (a).

    e. What does the difference of the matrices mean in this situation?

For Exercises 22 and 23, use these matrices.

Women in the Labor Force (millions)

	All Women			Women with Children	
	married	other*		married	other*
1989	30.5	24.7	1989	16.4	5.5
1990	31.0	25.2	1990	16.5	5.7
1991	31.1	25.2	1991	16.6	5.8

* widowed, divorced, separated, or single

22. **Writing** Does adding the matrices give a meaningful result in this situation? Why or why not?

23. **Writing** Does subtracting the matrices give a meaningful result in this situation? Why or why not?

Ongoing **ASSESSMENT**

24. **Open-ended** Write a five-question quiz on this section. Include questions using scalar multiplication and addition or subtraction of matrices.

Review **PREVIEW**

Solve each system of equations. If there is no solution, write *no solution*. *(Section 3-4)*

25. $-4w + 6v = -1$
    $4w - 9v = 13$

26. $2c + d = 15$
    $4c + 2d = 39$

27. $8a - b = -3$
    $7a + b = -2$

28. $3x - 5y = 22$
    $5x - 4y = 28$

Simplify. Write answers with positive exponents. *(Section 2-6)*

29. $3^{-2}c^{-5}d^4$

30. $\dfrac{8^0 m^3}{n^{-4}}$

31. $(6a^{-3})(-3b^2)$

32. $\dfrac{27x^{-3}y^0}{3}$

Tell whether each diagram shows a *dilation*, a *rotation*, a *reflection*, or a *translation*. *(Toolbox Skills 33, 34, 35, 36)*

33.

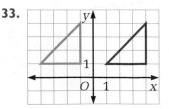

34.

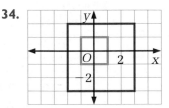

Working on the Unit Project

35. For one day's breakfast, lunch, and dinner, record the number of servings you eat from each of these food groups: grains, vegetables, fruits, milk products, and other protein foods (meats, beans, etc.). Organize the information in a 5 × 3 matrix. (See page 120 for suggested serving sizes.)

3-6

Matrices and Transformations

Dilate and Translate

This textile designer is using a type of computer drawing program called a *computer-aided design* (CAD) system. The drawing program lets her experiment with the position or size of any figure she draws.

Any change made to the size or position of a figure is called a **transformation.** The transformation on the computer screen is a size change or **dilation.** A dilation may be either an *enlargement* or a *reduction.*

You can also show a dilation on a coordinate plane.

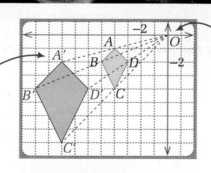

Point A′ (read "A prime") is the **image** of point A after an enlargement.

The **center of dilation** is the intersection point of lines drawn through corresponding points on the original figure and its image.

Talk it Over

1. What point is the center of dilation for the dilation above?

2. Find the **scale factor** for the dilation:

   $$\text{scale factor} = \frac{\text{length on image}}{\text{length on original}}$$

Student Resources Toolbox
p. 663 *Transformations*

3. How do the coordinates of each vertex of A′B′C′D′ compare with the coordinates of the corresponding vertex of ABCD?

To show how the coordinates of any point (x, y) of a polygon are transformed, you can write

$$P(x, y) \rightarrow P'(x', y').$$

For a dilation with center at the origin and a scale factor of 2,

$$P(x, y) \rightarrow P'(2x, 2y).$$

Some computer programs that run CAD systems or other computer drawing programs use matrices to represent the points of a figure. Scalar multiplication can represent a dilation.

Represent the point (x, y) as a 2 x 1 matrix.

$$P \quad \begin{bmatrix} x \\ y \end{bmatrix}$$

Multiply by the scale factor to represent a dilation with center at the origin.

$$2\begin{bmatrix} x \\ y \end{bmatrix} = \begin{bmatrix} 2x \\ 2y \end{bmatrix}$$
$$\quad P \qquad P'$$

Talk it Over

4. How do you write the point $(-3, 8)$ as a matrix?

5. Matrices can also be used to represent the vertices of a polygon. The matrix $\begin{bmatrix} -2 & 3 & 3 & -2 \\ 5 & 5 & 3 & 3 \end{bmatrix}$ represents rectangle *PQRS*.

   a. Describe the relationship between the coordinates of the vertices of *PQRS* and the matrix.

   b. Write a matrix to represent $\triangle UVW$.

(Graph at left shows points $P(-2, 5)$, $Q(3, 5)$, $S(-2, 3)$, $R(3, 3)$, $W(5, 1)$, $U(1, -2)$, $V(5, -2)$.)

Sample 1

Find the coordinates of the vertices of $\triangle DEF$ after a dilation with scale factor $\frac{1}{4}$ and center at the origin. Write the answer as a matrix.

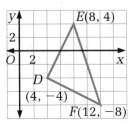

(Graph shows $E(8, 4)$, $D(4, -4)$, $F(12, -8)$.)

Sample Response

1 Write the coordinates of the vertices of $\triangle DEF$ in matrix form.

$$\begin{array}{ccc} D & E & F \end{array}$$
$$\begin{bmatrix} 4 & 8 & 12 \\ -4 & 4 & -8 \end{bmatrix}$$

Each column of the matrix represents a vertex of the triangle.

2 Multiply the matrix of vertices by the scale factor.

$$\frac{1}{4}\begin{bmatrix} 4 & 8 & 12 \\ -4 & 4 & -8 \end{bmatrix} = \begin{bmatrix} \frac{1}{4}(4) & \frac{1}{4}(8) & \frac{1}{4}(12) \\ \frac{1}{4}(-4) & \frac{1}{4}(4) & \frac{1}{4}(-8) \end{bmatrix}$$

Use scalar multiplication.

$$\begin{array}{ccc} D' & E' & F' \end{array}$$
$$= \begin{bmatrix} 1 & 2 & 3 \\ -1 & 1 & -2 \end{bmatrix}$$

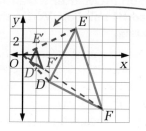

Draw a line through each vertex and its image to check the center of dilation.

$OE' = \frac{1}{4}OE$, so the scale factor is $\frac{1}{4}$.

Translations

Student Resources Toolbox

p. 662 *Transformations*

A **translation** is a transformation that moves each point of a polygon the same distance in the same direction.

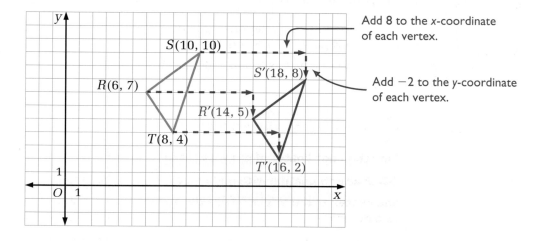

Add 8 to the *x*-coordinate of each vertex.

Add −2 to the *y*-coordinate of each vertex.

This translation slides $\triangle RST$ 8 units right and 2 units down. You can write

$$P(x, y) \rightarrow P'(x + 8, y - 2)$$

to show the change in the coordinates of each point of $\triangle RST$.

You can also use matrix addition to represent the translation.

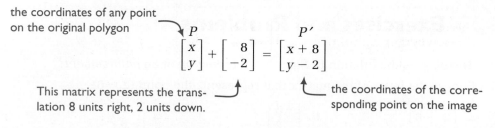

the coordinates of any point on the original polygon

P P'

$$\begin{bmatrix} x \\ y \end{bmatrix} + \begin{bmatrix} 8 \\ -2 \end{bmatrix} = \begin{bmatrix} x + 8 \\ y - 2 \end{bmatrix}$$

This matrix represents the translation 8 units right, 2 units down.

the coordinates of the corresponding point on the image

Find the coordinates of the vertices of polygon JKLM after a translation 1 unit left and 4 units up. Write the answer as a matrix.

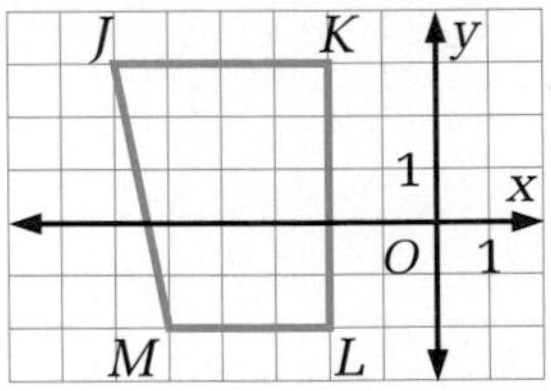

Sample Response

1 Write the coordinates of the vertices in matrix form.

$$\begin{array}{cccc} J & K & L & M \\ \begin{bmatrix} -6 & -2 & -2 & -5 \\ 3 & 3 & -2 & -2 \end{bmatrix} \end{array}$$

2 Add a matrix that will move each point 1 unit left and 4 units up.

Add −1 to each x-coordinate.

Subtracting 1 is the same as adding −1.

$$\begin{bmatrix} -6 & -2 & -2 & -5 \\ 3 & 3 & -2 & -2 \end{bmatrix} + \begin{bmatrix} -1 & -1 & -1 & -1 \\ 4 & 4 & 4 & 4 \end{bmatrix} = \begin{bmatrix} -6-1 & -2-1 & -2-1 & -5-1 \\ 3+4 & 3+4 & -2+4 & -2+4 \end{bmatrix}$$

Add 4 to each y-coordinate.

$$= \begin{array}{cccc} J' & K' & L' & M' \\ \begin{bmatrix} -7 & -3 & -3 & -6 \\ 7 & 7 & 2 & 2 \end{bmatrix} \end{array}$$

Talk it Over

6. Write the ordered pair for each vertex of $J'K'L'M'$.

7. Check the results of Sample 2 by sketching $JKLM$ and $J'K'L'M'$ on a coordinate plane.

Look Back

Suppose you write the coordinates of the vertices of a polygon as a matrix. What operation should you perform on the matrix to show a dilation? a translation?

3-6 Exercises and Problems

1. **Reading** Is the dilation in Sample 1 a *reduction* or an *enlargement*?

2. Choose the letter of the matrix that represents the point $(2, -6)$.

   a. $\begin{bmatrix} 2 & -6 \end{bmatrix}$
   b. $\begin{bmatrix} -6 \\ 2 \end{bmatrix}$
   c. $\begin{bmatrix} 2 \\ -6 \end{bmatrix}$
   d. $\begin{bmatrix} -6 & 2 \end{bmatrix}$

3. Choose the letter of the matrix that represents △EFG.

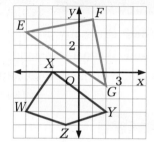

a. $\begin{bmatrix} -4 & 3 \\ 1 & 4 \\ 2 & -1 \end{bmatrix}$ **b.** $\begin{bmatrix} 3 & 4 & -1 \\ -4 & 1 & 2 \end{bmatrix}$

c. $\begin{bmatrix} -3 & 4 & -1 \\ 4 & 1 & 2 \end{bmatrix}$ **d.** $\begin{bmatrix} -4 & 1 & 2 \\ 3 & 4 & -1 \end{bmatrix}$

4. Write a matrix that represents quadrilateral WXYZ.

Find the coordinates of each vertex of △PQR after each transformation. Write each answer as a matrix.

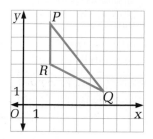

5. a dilation with scale factor 2 and center at the origin

6. a translation 3 units right and 2 units up

7. a dilation with scale factor $\frac{1}{3}$ and center at the origin

8. a translation 2 units left and 3 units down

For Exercises 9–12, write each transformation in matrix form.

9. a translation 4 units right and 3 units up of polygon EFGH with vertices E(−3, 2), F(−1, −1), G(−2, −4), and H(−4, −3).

10. a dilation with center at the origin and scale factor 2 for △TUV with vertices T(4, 1), U(1, 4), and V(4, 3)

11. 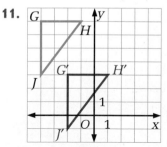 **12.**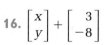

Writing Describe the transformation represented by each matrix expression.

13. $3\begin{bmatrix} x \\ y \end{bmatrix}$ **14.** $\begin{bmatrix} x \\ y \end{bmatrix} + \begin{bmatrix} 5 \\ 4 \end{bmatrix}$ **15.** $\frac{1}{2}\begin{bmatrix} x \\ y \end{bmatrix}$ **16.** $\begin{bmatrix} x \\ y \end{bmatrix} + \begin{bmatrix} 3 \\ -8 \end{bmatrix}$

17. Draw the image of polygon MNPQ under the transformation represented by the matrix expression $2\begin{bmatrix} x \\ y \end{bmatrix} + \begin{bmatrix} -1 \\ 3 \end{bmatrix}$.

18. a. Add these matrices: $\begin{bmatrix} x \\ y \end{bmatrix} + \begin{bmatrix} 0 \\ 0 \end{bmatrix}$

b. **Writing** Describe the transformation represented by the matrix expression in part (a).

c. How could you represent the same transformation using scalar multiplication?

19. **a.** **Open-ended** Draw any polygon on a coordinate plane.

  b. **Open-ended** Write a translation and a dilation in matrix form.

  c. Draw the image of the polygon after each transformation.

Use matrices *A* and *B*. *(Section 3-5)*

20. What are the dimensions of each matrix?

$$A = \begin{bmatrix} 16 & 28 & 30 & 17 \\ 63 & 20 & 40 & 5 \end{bmatrix}$$

21. **a.** Add these matrices.

  b. What element is in the first row, third column of the matrix in part (a)?

$$B = \begin{bmatrix} 58 & 33 & 4 & 44 \\ 150 & 110 & 170 & 200 \end{bmatrix}$$

22. **a.** Multiply matrix *A* by 7.

  b. What element is in the second row, second column of the matrix in part (a)?

Solve each equation for the indicated variable. *(Toolbox Skill 15)*

23. $4x + 3y = 16$, for y **24.** $-2x + 5y = 21$, for x **25.** $x + 4y = 39$, for y

Working on the Unit Project

26. Phelton kept a record of everything he ate one day.

For each meal, Phelton made a matrix that shows the number of Calories and the grams of protein, carbohydrate, and fat in the foods from each level of the Food Guide Pyramid (see page 119).

Breakfast

	Cal	pro.(g)	carb.(g)	fat(g)
fats/sweets	108	0.2	28	0
milk/protein	121	8	12	5
fruits/vegetables	83	1	19	0.4
grain foods	200	7	42	2

Lunch

	Cal	pro.(g)	carb.(g)	fat(g)
fats/sweets	99	0.2	0.4	11
milk/protein	437	35	16	25
fruits/vegetables	81	0.3	21	0.5
grain foods	112	4	24	0.6

Dinner

	Cal	pro.(g)	carb.(g)	fat(g)
fats/sweets	84	0.6	16	0.3
milk/protein	264	28	12	11
fruits/vegetables	298	8	50	1
grain foods	0	0	0	0

For Phelton's diet that day, find the total number of Calories and nutrients provided by the foods in each category. Write the answer as a matrix.

Matrix Multiplication

········Focus

Recognize when matrices can be multiplied and find the product of two matrices.

$$\begin{bmatrix} \text{Rows} \\ \text{Rows} \\ \text{Rows} \\ \text{Rows} \end{bmatrix} \text{ by } \begin{bmatrix} \text{COLUMNS} & \text{COLUMNS} & \text{COLUMNS} & \text{COLUMNS} \end{bmatrix}$$

At the Park High School spring fair, the student council sold bunches of flowers to raise money to buy books for the school library. These matrices show data about sales on Saturday.

Flower Prices (per bunch)

	carnations	irises	roses
price ($)	3	6	8

Flower Sales

	Saturday
carnations	52
irises	34
roses	20

Talk it Over

1. How much money did the student council raise on Saturday?

2. Describe how you found the answer to question 1.

The process you used to find the amount of money raised is called *matrix multiplication*. All matrix multiplication is based on multiplying a *row* by a *column*.

Multiply the flower-prices and flower-sales matrices on page 165.

Sample Response

Abbreviate carnations, irises, and roses C, I, and R.

Multiply the first elements.   Multiply the second elements.   Multiply the third elements.

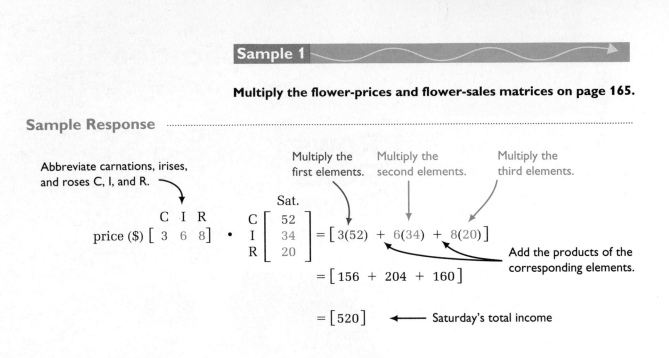

$$\text{price (\$)} \begin{array}{ccc} \text{C} & \text{I} & \text{R} \\ [\,3 & 6 & 8\,] \end{array} \cdot \begin{array}{c} \text{Sat.} \\ \begin{array}{c} \text{C} \\ \text{I} \\ \text{R} \end{array} \begin{bmatrix} 52 \\ 34 \\ 20 \end{bmatrix} \end{array} = [\,3(52) + 6(34) + 8(20)\,]$$

Add the products of the corresponding elements.

$$= [\,156 + 204 + 160\,]$$

$$= [\,520\,] \quad \longleftarrow \quad \text{Saturday's total income}$$

Talk it Over

$$[\,2 \quad 1 \quad 0 \quad -5\,] \begin{bmatrix} -1 \\ 0 \\ 8 \\ 3 \end{bmatrix}$$

3. In Sample 1, explain the meaning of each of these numbers: 156, 204, 160, and 520.

4. Multiply the two matrices shown at the left.

5. Do you think the result of multiplying a one-row matrix by a one-column matrix will always be a single number? Explain.

Multiplying a 2 × 3 matrix by a 3 × 2 matrix involves *four* multiplications of a row and a column. You arrange the results in a 2 × 2 *product matrix*.

Multiply matrices *L* and *R* to find the product matrix *P*.

L is the prices matrix expanded to show the profit from each bunch sold.

R is the sales matrix expanded to show data about sales on Sunday.

Left matrix *L*   Right matrix *R*   Product matrix *P*

$$\begin{array}{c} \text{price (\$)} \\ \text{profit (\$)} \end{array} \begin{array}{ccc} \text{C} & \text{I} & \text{R} \\ \begin{bmatrix} 3 & 6 & 8 \\ 2 & 3 & 4 \end{bmatrix} \end{array} \cdot \begin{array}{c} \text{Sat. Sun.} \\ \begin{array}{c} \text{C} \\ \text{I} \\ \text{R} \end{array} \begin{bmatrix} 52 & 50 \\ 34 & 41 \\ 20 & 15 \end{bmatrix} \end{array} \quad P = LR \quad \begin{array}{c} \text{income (\$)} \\ \text{profit (\$)} \end{array} \begin{array}{cc} \text{Sat. Sun.} \\ \begin{bmatrix} ? & ? \\ ? & ? \end{bmatrix} \end{array}$$

Multiply each row of *L* by each column of *R* and enter the result in the appropriate column of *P*.

1 Multiply row 1 of *L* by column 1 of *R*.

Use the results of Sample 1:

(row 1 of *L*) • (column 1 of *R*) = 520   ← Saturday's total income

The result belongs in
row 1, column 1 of *P*.

$$P = \begin{array}{c} \text{income (\$)} \\ \text{profit (\$)} \end{array} \begin{array}{cc} \text{Saturday} & \text{Sunday} \\ \left[\begin{array}{cc} 520 & ? \\ ? & ? \end{array}\right] \end{array}$$

2 Multiply row 1 of *L* by column 2 of *R*.

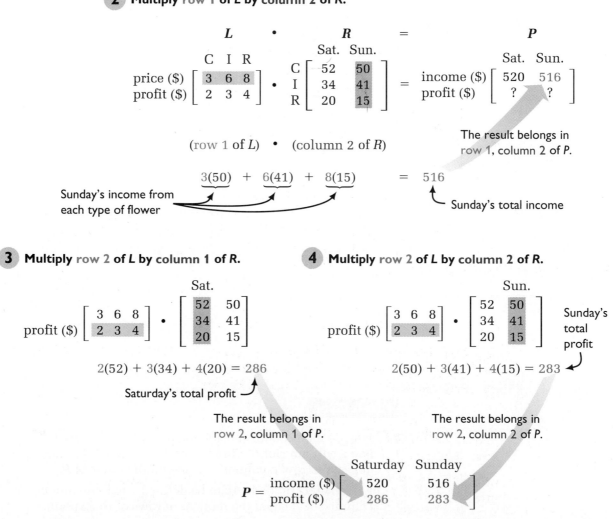

(row 1 of *L*) • (column 2 of *R*)

Sunday's income from
each type of flower

$$3(50) \;+\; 6(41) \;+\; 8(15) \;=\; 516$$

Sunday's total income

The result belongs in
row 1, column 2 of *P*.

3 Multiply row 2 of *L* by column 1 of *R*.

$$\text{profit (\$)} \begin{bmatrix} 3 & 6 & 8 \\ 2 & 3 & 4 \end{bmatrix} \cdot \begin{array}{c} \text{Sat.} \\ \begin{bmatrix} 52 & 50 \\ 34 & 41 \\ 20 & 15 \end{bmatrix} \end{array}$$

$$2(52) + 3(34) + 4(20) = 286$$

Saturday's total profit

The result belongs in
row 2, column 1 of *P*.

4 Multiply row 2 of *L* by column 2 of *R*.

$$\text{profit (\$)} \begin{bmatrix} 3 & 6 & 8 \\ 2 & 3 & 4 \end{bmatrix} \cdot \begin{array}{c} \text{Sun.} \\ \begin{bmatrix} 52 & 50 \\ 34 & 41 \\ 20 & 15 \end{bmatrix} \end{array} \begin{array}{c} \text{Sunday's} \\ \text{total} \\ \text{profit} \end{array}$$

$$2(50) + 3(41) + 4(15) = 283$$

The result belongs in
row 2, column 2 of *P*.

$$P = \begin{array}{c} \text{income (\$)} \\ \text{profit (\$)} \end{array} \begin{array}{cc} \text{Saturday} & \text{Sunday} \\ \left[\begin{array}{cc} 520 & 516 \\ 286 & 283 \end{array}\right] \end{array}$$

MATRIX MULTIPLICATION

➤ To multiply a *row* of matrix L by a column of matrix R, add the products of the corresponding elements of the row and the column.

$$L \quad \cdot \quad R \quad = \quad P$$

$$\begin{bmatrix} - & - \\ a & b \\ - & - \end{bmatrix}\begin{bmatrix} - & - & c & - \\ - & - & d & - \end{bmatrix} = \begin{bmatrix} - & - & - & - \\ - & - & ac+bd & - \\ - & - & - & - \end{bmatrix}$$

➤ To find the matrix product LR, multiply each *row* of L by each *column* of R, and enter the result in the corresponding position (*row*, *column*) of the product matrix P.

·······➤ **Now you are ready for:**
Exs. 1–9 on pp. 170–171

Dimensions of a Matrix Product

It is helpful to consider the dimensions of the product matrix when you begin the multiplication. For example:

Multiply the matrix L times the matrix R.

$$\underset{\text{of } L}{3 \text{ rows}} \quad \text{times} \quad \underset{\text{of } R}{4 \text{ columns}} \quad \text{gives} \quad \underset{\text{elements of } P}{3 \cdot 4 = 12}$$

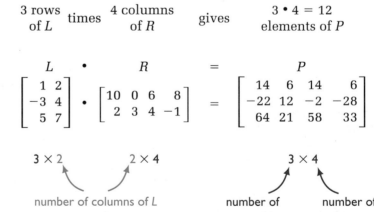

$$L \quad \cdot \quad R \quad = \quad P$$

$$\begin{bmatrix} 1 & 2 \\ -3 & 4 \\ 5 & 7 \end{bmatrix} \cdot \begin{bmatrix} 10 & 0 & 6 & 8 \\ 2 & 3 & 4 & -1 \end{bmatrix} = \begin{bmatrix} 14 & 6 & 14 & 6 \\ -22 & 12 & -2 & -28 \\ 64 & 21 & 58 & 33 \end{bmatrix}$$

Notice how the dimensions of the three matrices are related.

$3 \times 2 \qquad 2 \times 4 \qquad\qquad 3 \times 4$

number of columns of L
equals
number of rows of R

number of
rows of L

number of
columns of R

Talk it Over

6. Use the matrix multiplication above. Choose a row r of L and a column c of R. Find the product. Check that the result appears in row r, column c of the product matrix P.

7. For a matrix product AB to be defined, must the number of columns of A equal the number of rows of B? Explain.

Find the product of these two matrices.

$$A = \begin{bmatrix} 8 \\ 12 \\ -3 \\ 4 \end{bmatrix} \qquad B = \begin{bmatrix} 1 & 0 & 5 & 7 \\ 2 & 12 & -2 & 10 \end{bmatrix}$$

Sample Response

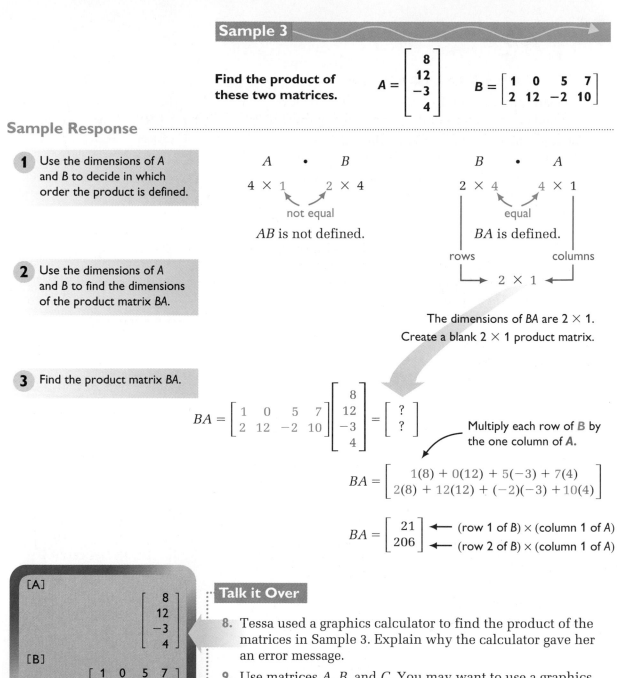

1 Use the dimensions of A and B to decide in which order the product is defined.

$$A \quad \bullet \quad B$$
$$4 \times 1 \qquad 2 \times 4$$
not equal

AB is not defined.

$$B \quad \bullet \quad A$$
$$2 \times 4 \qquad 4 \times 1$$
equal

BA is defined.

rows   columns
2×1

2 Use the dimensions of A and B to find the dimensions of the product matrix BA.

The dimensions of BA are 2×1.
Create a blank 2×1 product matrix.

3 Find the product matrix BA.

$$BA = \begin{bmatrix} 1 & 0 & 5 & 7 \\ 2 & 12 & -2 & 10 \end{bmatrix} \begin{bmatrix} 8 \\ 12 \\ -3 \\ 4 \end{bmatrix} = \begin{bmatrix} ? \\ ? \end{bmatrix}$$

Multiply each row of **B** by the one column of **A**.

$$BA = \begin{bmatrix} 1(8) + 0(12) + 5(-3) + 7(4) \\ 2(8) + 12(12) + (-2)(-3) + 10(4) \end{bmatrix}$$

$$BA = \begin{bmatrix} 21 \\ 206 \end{bmatrix} \begin{matrix} \leftarrow \text{(row 1 of B)} \times \text{(column 1 of A)} \\ \leftarrow \text{(row 2 of B)} \times \text{(column 1 of A)} \end{matrix}$$

[A]
$$\begin{bmatrix} 8 \\ 12 \\ -3 \\ 4 \end{bmatrix}$$

[B]
$$\begin{bmatrix} 1 & 0 & 5 & 7 \\ 2 & 12 & -2 & 10 \end{bmatrix}$$

[A] [B]

ERROR

Talk it Over

8. Tessa used a graphics calculator to find the product of the matrices in Sample 3. Explain why the calculator gave her an error message.

9. Use matrices A, B, and C. You may want to use a graphics calculator.

$$A = \begin{bmatrix} 3 & 1 \\ 5 & 2 \end{bmatrix} \quad B = \begin{bmatrix} -6 & 4 \\ 0 & -9 \end{bmatrix} \quad C = \begin{bmatrix} 8 & 1 \\ 5 & 7 \end{bmatrix}$$

Find each product: AB, BA, AC, CA, BC, and CB.

10. Does the order in which you multiply two matrices affect the product? Use the results in question 9 to explain your answer.

MATRIX MULTIPLICATION

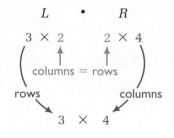

➤ The matrix product LR is defined only if
  the number of columns of L = the number of rows of R.

➤ The dimensions of the matrix product LR are
  (the number of rows of L) × (the number of columns of R).

➤ Matrix multiplication is not commutative, so order matters.
  In general, $AB \neq BA$.

Look Back ←

> ····➤ **Now you are ready for:**
> **Exs. 10–27 on pp. 171–173**

Suppose two matrices can be added. Can they *always*, *sometimes*, or *never* be multiplied? Explain.

3-7 Exercises and Problems

1. A sushi bar sells four types of sushi. These matrices show the prices per piece and the number of pieces sold Tuesday night.

a. What is the total income from all the tuna sushi sold Tuesday night?

b. What does the product (1.75)(19) represent?

c. Multiply the sushi-prices and sushi-sales matrices.

Sushi Prices (per piece)

salmon tuna egg eel

price ($) $\begin{bmatrix} 1.50 & 2.00 & 1.00 & 1.75 \end{bmatrix}$

Sushi Sales

number sold

$\begin{matrix} \text{salmon} \\ \text{tuna} \\ \text{egg} \\ \text{eel} \end{matrix} \begin{bmatrix} 36 \\ 23 \\ 30 \\ 19 \end{bmatrix}$

Multiply each pair of matrices.

2. $\begin{bmatrix} 4 & 6 \end{bmatrix} \begin{bmatrix} 2 \\ 12 \end{bmatrix}$

3. $\begin{bmatrix} \frac{1}{3} & 0 & -\frac{4}{3} & 2 \end{bmatrix} \begin{bmatrix} 6 \\ \frac{2}{3} \\ 3 \\ -1 \end{bmatrix}$

4. $\begin{bmatrix} 1.2 & 2 & 0 \end{bmatrix} \begin{bmatrix} 2 \\ 4.1 \\ 7.8 \end{bmatrix}$

5. **Writing** Explain why it is not possible to multiply the matrices $\begin{bmatrix} 6 & 8 & 0 \end{bmatrix}$ and $\begin{bmatrix} 4 \\ 0 \end{bmatrix}$.

6. **Reading** Look at the row and column labels of the matrices in Sample 2.

a. What do you notice about the column labels of the left matrix L and the row labels of the right matrix R?

b. How are the row and column labels of the product matrix P related to the row and column labels of the left matrix L and the right matrix R?

BY THE WAY...

Between 1987 and 1993 the use of stair-climbing machines in the United States rose about 960%.

The number of Calories that you use during exercise depends on many things, including your weight and level of fitness.

7. a. Multiply these two matrices.

$$\text{Cal/min} \begin{array}{ccc} \text{ski} & \text{bike} & \text{stairs} \\ \left[7 \quad 4 \quad 6 \right] \end{array}$$

number of minutes

$$\begin{array}{c} \text{ski machine} \\ \text{exercise bike} \\ \text{stair machine} \end{array} \begin{bmatrix} 15 \\ 10 \\ 5 \end{bmatrix}$$

b. Explain what the product you found in part (a) represents.

8. Use matrices *C*, *D*, and *P*.

C

Calories Used per Minute

$$\begin{array}{c} \\ \text{Mike} \\ \text{Robin} \end{array} \begin{array}{ccc} \text{ski} & \text{bike} & \text{stairs} \\ \left[\begin{array}{ccc} 7 & 4 & 6 \\ 9 & 5 & 8 \end{array} \right] \end{array}$$

D

Number of Minutes

$$\begin{array}{c} \\ \text{ski machine} \\ \text{exercise bike} \\ \text{stair machine} \end{array} \begin{array}{cc} \text{Mon.} & \text{Wed.} \\ \left[\begin{array}{cc} 15 & 10 \\ 10 & 10 \\ 5 & 10 \end{array} \right] \end{array}$$

P

Calories Used per Day

$$\begin{array}{c} \\ \text{Mike} \\ \text{Robin} \end{array} \begin{array}{cc} \text{Mon.} & \text{Wed.} \\ \left[\begin{array}{cc} ? & ? \\ ? & ? \end{array} \right] \end{array}$$

a. How many Calories does Robin use while exercising on Wednesday? Which row(s) and column(s) do you use to answer this question?

b. Find the product *CD* to complete the product matrix *P*.

9. These two matrices represent a transformation and a quadrilateral.

T

Transformation matrix

$$\begin{bmatrix} 0 & 1 \\ -1 & 0 \end{bmatrix}$$

Q

$$\begin{array}{c} \\ x\text{-coordinate} \\ y\text{-coordinate} \end{array} \begin{array}{cccc} O & B & C & D \\ \left[\begin{array}{cccc} 0 & 0 & ? & ? \\ 0 & 5 & ? & ? \end{array} \right] \end{array}$$

a. Complete matrix *Q*, the matrix that represents quadrilateral *OBCD*.

b. Find the product matrix *TQ*.

$$TQ = \begin{array}{c} \\ x\text{-coordinate} \\ y\text{-coordinate} \end{array} \begin{array}{cccc} O' & B' & C' & D' \\ \left[\begin{array}{cccc} ? & ? & ? & ? \\ ? & ? & ? & ? \end{array} \right] \end{array}$$

Student Resources Toolbox
p. 662 *Transformations*

c. Graph *O'B'C'D'*. What type of transformation does *T* represent?

Find the product of each pair of matrices.

10. $A = \begin{bmatrix} 2 & -1 \\ 1 & \frac{1}{5} \\ -3 & 0 \end{bmatrix}$ $B = \begin{bmatrix} -1 & 0 & -3 \\ 1 & \frac{2}{5} & 4 \end{bmatrix}$

11. $A = \begin{bmatrix} 1.1 & 3.0 & 2.2 & -0.5 \end{bmatrix}$ $B = \begin{bmatrix} 0.1 & 5.1 \\ 2.3 & -3 \\ 0.2 & 2 \\ 0 & 4 \end{bmatrix}$

12. $A = \begin{bmatrix} -5 & -2 \\ 3 & 1 \end{bmatrix}$ $B = \begin{bmatrix} 1 & 2 \\ -3 & 5 \end{bmatrix}$

13. $A = \begin{bmatrix} 1 \\ -1 \end{bmatrix}$ $B = \begin{bmatrix} 20 & 26 \\ 60 & 20 \\ 35 & 15 \end{bmatrix}$

14. Consumer Economics Matrix *A* shows a shopping list of items that Saul Wilson buys every week. Matrix *B* shows the price of each item at each of three stores in his town.

Items on List

	number
loaf of bread	2
8 oz yogurt	20
$A =$ dozen eggs	2
half-gallon milk	5
box of cereal	3

Price ($)

	loaf of bread	8 oz yogurt	dozen eggs	$\frac{1}{2}$-gal milk	box of cereal
Store 1	1.89	0.75	1.50	1.49	2.29
$B =$ Store 2	1.89	0.79	1.40	1.35	2.39
Store 3	1.89	0.69	1.10	1.60	2.59

a. Describe how to find the total cost of the items on Saul's list at Store 3.

b. Should you find the product *AB* or the product *BA* to show the total cost at each store? What will the dimensions of the product matrix be?

c. Find the product matrix that you chose in part (b).

d. At which store is the total cost the least?

15. Codes *Cryptographers* invent codes for sending messages. Some codes use numbers to represent letters of the alphabet. Matrices are sometimes used to make numerical codes more difficult to break.

a. Write a message that contains exactly nine letters.

b. Rewrite your message using numbers to represent the letters of the alphabet. Use 1 for A, 2 for B, 3 for C, and so on.

c. Write a 3 × 1 matrix containing the first three numbers you wrote in part (b). Write a second 3 × 1 matrix for the next three numbers and a third 3 × 1 matrix for the last three numbers.

d. Choose one of these matrices to be your *coding matrix*. Multiply each of the matrices you wrote in part (c) by your coding matrix.

$$A = \begin{bmatrix} 0 & 1 & 3 \\ 0 & 0 & 2 \\ 1 & 3 & 0 \end{bmatrix} \quad B = \begin{bmatrix} 5 & 0 & 10 \\ 2 & 6 & 0 \\ 0 & 1 & 1 \end{bmatrix}$$

e. Use the elements of the product matrices in part (d) to write your coded message. Save your messages and matrices for use in Exercise 16 on page 179.

TOP SECRET

20-15-16-19-5-3-18-5-20

$$\begin{bmatrix} 20 \\ 15 \\ 16 \end{bmatrix} \quad \begin{bmatrix} 19 \\ 5 \\ 3 \end{bmatrix} \quad \begin{bmatrix} 18 \\ 5 \\ 20 \end{bmatrix}$$

$$\begin{bmatrix} 63 \\ 32 \\ 65 \end{bmatrix} \quad \begin{bmatrix} 14 \\ 6 \\ 34 \end{bmatrix} \quad \begin{bmatrix} 65 \\ 40 \\ 33 \end{bmatrix}$$

63-32-65-14-6-34-65-40-33

Is the product of each pair of matrices defined? If so, give the dimensions of the product matrix.

16. $\begin{bmatrix} 3 & -2 \\ 0 & 4 \end{bmatrix}\begin{bmatrix} 7 & 4 & 2 \\ 1 & 3 & 9 \\ 0 & 0 & 7 \end{bmatrix}$

17. $\begin{bmatrix} 4 & -6 \end{bmatrix}\begin{bmatrix} 8 & 5 & 2 \\ 7 & 5 & -4 \end{bmatrix}$

18. $\begin{bmatrix} 8 & -6 & 4 & 2 \\ 1 & -1 & 0 & 9 \end{bmatrix}\begin{bmatrix} -2 \\ 5 \end{bmatrix}$

Ongoing ASSESSMENT

19. Writing Give an example of a pair of matrices *A* and *B* for which *AB* and *BA* are both defined. Explain why both products are defined.

Review PREVIEW

20. Find the coordinates of the vertices of △*PQR* after a dilation with scale factor $\frac{3}{5}$ and center at the origin. *(Section 3-6)*

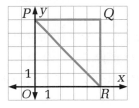

Use the distributive property to rewrite each expression. *(Toolbox Skill 10)*

21. $\frac{1}{4}(a + 12b)$

22. $-6(2m - 2n)$

23. $3(-4y^2 + 2y)$

Solve each system of equations. *(Sections 3-1, 3-2, 3-4)*

24. $5x - 3 = y$
$y = 6x + 8$

25. $a + 3b = 4$
$4a - 16 = -12b$

26. $4v + 15w = 7$
$-3v - 4w = 2$

1 tablespoon honey

1/2 cup strawberries

Working on the Unit Project

27. Pauline kept a record of what she ate for breakfast one morning as shown at the right. Then she found the nutritional content of each food and recorded it in the matrix below.

3/4 cup orange juice

3/4 cup 2% milk

3/4 cup oatmeal

Nutritional Content

	oatmeal 1 cup	honey 1 tablespoon	2% milk 1 cup	orange juice 1 cup	strawberries 1 cup
protein (g)	6	0.1	8.12	1.74	0.91
fat (g)	2.4	0	4.68	0.5	0.55
carbohydrate (g)	25.2	17.8	11.7	25.8	10.4

a. Write the contents of Pauline's breakfast in a matrix *B* that you can multiply by the nutritional-content matrix *A*.

b. Use matrix multiplication to find how many grams of each nutrient Pauline's breakfast provided. Write the answer as a matrix.

Section 3-8

Focus

Use technology to find inverse matrices and use inverse matrices to solve systems of equations.

Using Technology and Matrices with Systems

The inverse is key

EXPLORATION

Can two matrices behave like reciprocals?

- **Materials: graphics calculator**
- **Work with another student.**

1 Find each matrix product.

a. $\begin{bmatrix} 1 & 0 \\ 0 & 1 \end{bmatrix}\begin{bmatrix} -5 \\ 3 \end{bmatrix}$

b. $\begin{bmatrix} 6 & 2 \\ 0 & -3 \end{bmatrix}\begin{bmatrix} 1 & 0 \\ 0 & 1 \end{bmatrix}$

2 What do you notice about your answers in step 1? In what way is the matrix $\begin{bmatrix} 1 & 0 \\ 0 & 1 \end{bmatrix}$ like the number 1?

3 Multiply this pair of 2 × 2 matrices in both orders.

a. $\begin{bmatrix} 5 & 10 \\ 0.5 & 3 \end{bmatrix}\begin{bmatrix} 0.3 & -1 \\ -0.05 & 0.5 \end{bmatrix}$

b. $\begin{bmatrix} 0.3 & -1 \\ -0.05 & 0.5 \end{bmatrix}\begin{bmatrix} 5 & 10 \\ 0.5 & 3 \end{bmatrix}$

4 What do you notice about your answers in step 3? In what way is this pair of matrices like the pair of numbers 3 and $\frac{1}{3}$?

You know that two numbers whose product is the number 1 are called *reciprocals*. Two 2 × 2 matrices whose product is the matrix $\begin{bmatrix} 1 & 0 \\ 0 & 1 \end{bmatrix}$ are called **inverse matrices**. The symbol A^{-1} is used to represent the inverse of matrix A.

The matrix $\begin{bmatrix} 1 & 0 \\ 0 & 1 \end{bmatrix}$ is sometimes called the 2 × 2 *identity matrix*. The product of this matrix and any other 2 × 2 matrix B is the matrix B.

Unit 3 Linear Systems and Matrices

Use a graphics calculator to find the inverse of this matrix.
$$\begin{bmatrix} -8 & 1 \\ -6 & 2 \end{bmatrix}$$

Sample Response

Enter the elements of the matrix $\begin{bmatrix} -8 & 1 \\ -6 & 2 \end{bmatrix}$ as matrix A on a graphics calculator. Then find A^{-1}.

The inverse is $\begin{bmatrix} -0.2 & 0.1 \\ -0.6 & 0.8 \end{bmatrix}$.

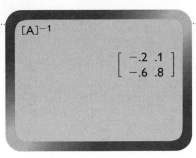

$[A]^{-1}$

$\begin{bmatrix} -.2 & .1 \\ -.6 & .8 \end{bmatrix}$

Talk it Over

1. Use A and A^{-1} from Sample 1. Use matrix multiplication to check that $A^{-1}A = AA^{-1} = \begin{bmatrix} 1 & 0 \\ 0 & 1 \end{bmatrix}$.

TECHNOLOGY NOTE

If matrix A does not have an inverse, you will get an ERROR message when you try to use a graphics calculator to find A^{-1}.

Not all 2 × 2 matrices have inverses. Use a graphics calculator to find the inverse of each matrix, if it exists.

2. $B = \begin{bmatrix} 6 & 2 \\ -1 & -3 \end{bmatrix}$

3. $C = \begin{bmatrix} 8 & 10 \\ 4 & 5 \end{bmatrix}$

Solving Systems Using Matrices

You can write a linear system as a **matrix equation** by using the left and right sides of the equations as the elements of two matrices.

$-8x + y = 10$
$-6x + 2y = 16$

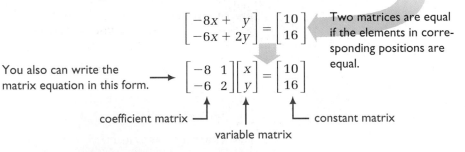

$$\begin{bmatrix} -8x + y \\ -6x + 2y \end{bmatrix} = \begin{bmatrix} 10 \\ 16 \end{bmatrix}$$

Two matrices are equal if the elements in corresponding positions are equal.

You also can write the matrix equation in this form. $\begin{bmatrix} -8 & 1 \\ -6 & 2 \end{bmatrix}\begin{bmatrix} x \\ y \end{bmatrix} = \begin{bmatrix} 10 \\ 16 \end{bmatrix}$

coefficient matrix — variable matrix — constant matrix

Talk it Over

4. Use matrix multiplication to explain why the two forms of the matrix equation above are equivalent.

5. To solve a matrix equation, you must get the variable matrix by itself on one side of the equation. What do you think is the first step of solving the matrix equation above?

Suppose a matrix equation is in the form $A\begin{bmatrix} x \\ y \end{bmatrix} = B$. These steps show that you can solve the equation by finding $A^{-1}B$.

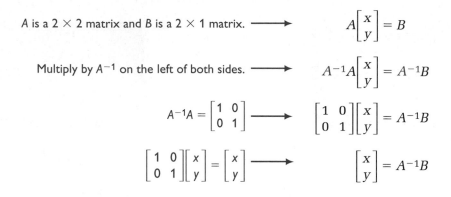

A is a 2 × 2 matrix and B is a 2 × 1 matrix. ⟶ $A\begin{bmatrix} x \\ y \end{bmatrix} = B$

Multiply by A^{-1} on the left of both sides. ⟶ $A^{-1}A\begin{bmatrix} x \\ y \end{bmatrix} = A^{-1}B$

$A^{-1}A = \begin{bmatrix} 1 & 0 \\ 0 & 1 \end{bmatrix}$ ⟶ $\begin{bmatrix} 1 & 0 \\ 0 & 1 \end{bmatrix}\begin{bmatrix} x \\ y \end{bmatrix} = A^{-1}B$

$\begin{bmatrix} 1 & 0 \\ 0 & 1 \end{bmatrix}\begin{bmatrix} x \\ y \end{bmatrix} = \begin{bmatrix} x \\ y \end{bmatrix}$ ⟶ $\begin{bmatrix} x \\ y \end{bmatrix} = A^{-1}B$

Talk it Over

Use this linear system and matrix equation from page 175.

$-8x + y = 10$ $\begin{bmatrix} -8 & 1 \\ -6 & 2 \end{bmatrix}\begin{bmatrix} x \\ y \end{bmatrix} = \begin{bmatrix} 10 \\ 16 \end{bmatrix}$
$-6x + 2y = 16$

6. Use the results of Sample 1 and what you learned above to solve the matrix equation.

7. Check that the x- and y-values of your answer in question 6 are a solution of the linear system.

Sample 2

Use the matrix functions of a graphics calculator to solve this linear system.

$8.3x = 2y + 3$
$y = 6.4x - 15$

Sample Response

1 Write both equations in the form $ax + by = c$.

$8.3x - 2y = 3$
$-6.4x + y = -15$

2 Write the system as a matrix equation.

$\begin{bmatrix} 8.3 & -2 \\ -6.4 & 1 \end{bmatrix}\begin{bmatrix} x \\ y \end{bmatrix} = \begin{bmatrix} 3 \\ -15 \end{bmatrix}$

$A\begin{bmatrix} x \\ y \end{bmatrix} = B$

3 On a graphics calculator, enter the coefficient matrix as matrix A and the constant matrix as matrix B.

4 Check that A^{-1} exists.

$[A]^{-1}$

$$\begin{bmatrix} -.2222222222\ldots \\ -1.4222222222\ldots \end{bmatrix}$$

You can scroll to the right if you want to see the rest of A^{-1}.

5 Find $A^{-1}B$.

$[A]^{-1}[B]$

$$\begin{bmatrix} 6 \\ 23.4 \end{bmatrix}$$

The solution of the matrix equation is $\begin{bmatrix} 6 \\ 23.4 \end{bmatrix}$.

The solution of the linear system is (6, 23.4).

Look Back

Explain how to solve a matrix equation in the form $A\begin{bmatrix} x \\ y \end{bmatrix} = B$.

Give an example.

3-8 Exercises and Problems

1. Use the results of the Exploration to find this matrix product without multiplying. $\begin{bmatrix} 1 & 0 \\ 0 & 1 \end{bmatrix}\begin{bmatrix} -3 & 9 \\ -6 & 4 \end{bmatrix}$

2. Are the matrices $\begin{bmatrix} 7 & -5 \\ 4 & -3 \end{bmatrix}$ and $\begin{bmatrix} 3 & -5 \\ 4 & -7 \end{bmatrix}$ inverses? Explain why or why not.

▓ TECHNOLOGY **Use a graphics calculator to find the inverse of each matrix, if it exists. Round each element to the nearest hundredth.**

3. $\begin{bmatrix} 0 & -1 \\ 3 & 2 \end{bmatrix}$

4. $\begin{bmatrix} 2 & 2 \\ 6 & 5 \end{bmatrix}$

5. $\begin{bmatrix} 3.6 & 0.6 \\ 2.4 & 0.4 \end{bmatrix}$

6. $\begin{bmatrix} 4 & 0 \\ 0 & 4 \end{bmatrix}$

7. **Writing** Ramona wrote a system of equations as a matrix equation. Explain why her matrix equation does not represent the system. (*Hint:* Multiply the matrices on the left side of the equation.)

> Ramona Peregrino
>
> $\begin{aligned} 2x + 3y &= -1 \\ x + 5y &= -4 \end{aligned}\Bigg\} \longrightarrow \begin{bmatrix} 2 & 1 \\ 3 & 5 \end{bmatrix}\begin{bmatrix} x \\ y \end{bmatrix} = \begin{bmatrix} -1 \\ -4 \end{bmatrix}$

8. **Reading** Read the solution of the matrix equation $A\begin{bmatrix} x \\ y \end{bmatrix} = B$ at the top of page 176. What are the dimensions of A^{-1}? of $A^{-1}A$? of $A^{-1}B$?

9. $2x + 2y = -1$
$6x + 5y = -2$

10. $5y = -4.3x - 1$
$7.6x + 10y = -1$

11. $5y = -0.5x + 20$
$0.2y = -2.02x - 35$

12. $y = -2x + 5$
$y = x - 2$

connection to **CHEMISTRY**

13. For a chemistry lab, Sergio and Odessa need a solution that is 45% methanol and 55% water. They have 250 mL of a solution that is 10% methanol and 90% water. They must add enough pure methanol to the solution to increase the concentration of methanol to 45%.

Sergio drew this diagram.

Odessa used Sergio's diagram to write this system of equations.

$250 + x = y$
$0.10(250) + 1x = 0.45y$

a. Explain the meaning of each of Odessa's equations.

b TECHNOLOGY Solve Odessa's system of equations using inverse matrices.

c. Explain the meaning of each coordinate of the solution of Odessa's system of equations.

14. Use the matrix equation shown at the right.

$$\begin{bmatrix} 3 & -1 \\ -6 & 2 \end{bmatrix} \begin{bmatrix} x \\ y \end{bmatrix} = \begin{bmatrix} 0 \\ 4 \end{bmatrix}$$

a TECHNOLOGY Use a graphics calculator to decide if the coefficient matrix has an inverse.

b. Write a linear system that the matrix equation represents.

c. Graph the system. Tell whether it is *consistent* or *inconsistent*.

15. a. Multiply these two 3 × 3 matrices.

b. How is the product in part (a) like the product of two 2 × 2 inverse matrices?

$$\begin{bmatrix} 1 & -3 & -1 \\ -0.5 & 2 & 1 \\ -0.5 & 3 & 1 \end{bmatrix} \begin{bmatrix} 2 & 0 & 2 \\ 0 & -1 & 1 \\ 1 & 3 & -1 \end{bmatrix}$$

c. Multiply these two 3 × 3 matrices. What do you notice?

$$\begin{bmatrix} 1 & 0 & 0 \\ 0 & 1 & 0 \\ 0 & 0 & 1 \end{bmatrix} \begin{bmatrix} 2 & 0 & 2 \\ 0 & -1 & 1 \\ 1 & 3 & -1 \end{bmatrix}$$

d TECHNOLOGY The matrices in part (a) are an example of a pair of 3 × 3 inverses matrices. Use a graphics calculator to find the inverse of this 3 × 3 matrix in the same way that you find the inverse of a 2 × 2 matrix.

$$\begin{bmatrix} 2 & 1 & -1 \\ 0 & 2 & -2 \\ 0 & 1 & 0 \end{bmatrix}$$

16. Codes Use the coded message, the coding matrix, and the other matrices that you wrote for Exercise 15 on page 172.

Decoding your message involves using the inverse of your 3 × 3 coding matrix.

a. T E C H N O L O G Y Use a graphics calculator to find the inverse of your coding matrix. (See Exercise 15 on page 178.)

b. Group Activity Trade your coded message and the inverse matrix you found in part (a) with another student. Write the coded message you receive as three 3 × 1 matrices. Multiply each of the three 3 × 1 matrices by the inverse matrix you receive.

c. Rewrite the product matrices in part (b) using letters. Use A for 1, B for 2, and so on. Compare the decoded message with your partner's original message.

BY THE WAY...

Jim Sanborn is a sculptor whose artwork carries encoded messages. In *The Code Room*, the message is encoded and written in the Cyrillic alphabet. The word *Medusa* is a key to unraveling part of the code.

Ongoing **ASSESSMENT**

17. Group Activity Work in a group of four students.

a. Each of you should solve this linear system using a different method: *graphing, substitution, addition-or-subtraction,* or *inverse matrices.* Compare your solutions and correct any mistakes.

$$2x + 5y = -1$$
$$x + 3y = -1$$

b. Decide with your group which method you think is easiest to use for this system.

Review **PREVIEW**

Multiply each pair of matrices. *(Section 3-7)*

18. $\begin{bmatrix} 1 & -2 \\ 7 & -1 \end{bmatrix}\begin{bmatrix} 25 \\ 7 \end{bmatrix}$

19. $\begin{bmatrix} 2 & 15 & 1 \end{bmatrix}\begin{bmatrix} 9 & 14 \\ 3 & -8 \\ 0 & 4 \end{bmatrix}$

20. $\begin{bmatrix} 0 \\ 11 \end{bmatrix}\begin{bmatrix} -5 & 3 \end{bmatrix}$

21. Use deductive reasoning to reach a conclusion. *(Section 1-6)*

If you are in Port Moresby, then you are in Papua New Guinea.
If you are in Papua New Guinea, then you are south of the equator.

Evaluate $x^2 + 3x + 14$ for each value of x. *(Toolbox Skill 9)*

22. $x = 4$ **23.** $x = -3$ **24.** $x = 0$ **25.** $x = \frac{2}{3}$

Working on the Unit Project

26. Describe one way that you will use a linear system and one way that you will use matrices in revising and presenting your menus.

Completing the Unit Project

Now you are ready to complete your menus. Your finished project should include these things:

➤ three different daily menus for people with different body weights and activity levels

➤ a description of how each menu was developed and refined. You should also show how you used linear systems to analyze the menus.

➤ an analysis of the nutritional content of each menu and an explanation of how each fulfills the requirements of the Food Guide Pyramid and other nutritional guidelines explored in the "Working on the Unit Project" exercises throughout this unit

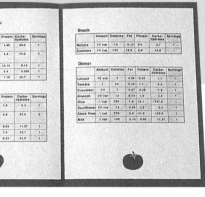

Look Back

How has learning about nutrition and exercise changed your ideas about what you should eat and how much you should exercise?

Alternative Projects

Project 1: Using Matrices for Secret Codes

Prepare a classroom display on secret codes. Do some library research to learn about the history of secret codes and about the contributions of mathematician Lester S. Hill, who was one of the first people to apply matrices to this field.

Also include in your display an example of the use of 2 × 2 matrices to code/decode a secret message using the methods introduced in Exercise 15 on page 172 and Exercise 16 on page 179 for 3 × 1 matrices. (Be sure to check that your coding matrix has an inverse.)

Project 2: Create a Daily Menu for a Person with Special Nutritional Needs

Research the special nutritional needs of a young child, a senior citizen, or a person on a restricted diet due to a health problem such as heart disease or diabetes. Carry out the project described on page 119 for someone in this category.

1. ABC Auto Repair charges $93 for parts and $42 per hour of labor for a repair job. Bob's Auto Shop charges a flat fee of $225 for the same job. **3-1**

   a. Write a system of equations to represent the situation.

   b. Graph the system of equations in part (a).

   c. Which estimate is cheaper if the job takes two hours? Four hours? Explain how the graph supports your answers.

2. Graph this system of inequalities: $y \le -2x + 1$
   $$0.5x - y < 2$$

3. **Investment** Lee Wong invested $3000, some in certificates of deposit (CDs) and some in a money market fund. The CDs paid 4% annual interest and the fund paid 2% annual interest. Her total annual income from interest was $101. How much money did she invest in CDs? **3-2**

For Questions 4 and 5, use equations A–C. **3-3**

   A. $2y - 8 = 8x$ **B.** $4x - y = 1$ **C.** $2y = 8x - 2$

4. Without graphing, tell which pair(s) of equations will make a system of equations with many solutions. Explain how you know.

5. Without graphing, tell which pair(s) of equations will make an inconsistent system of equations. Explain how you know.

6. Write an equation of the line that goes through the point (1, 8) and is perpendicular to the line $y = \frac{1}{3}x + 2$.

Solve each linear system. Use a different method for each system. **3-4**

7. $y = 2x - 3$
   $2y - 4x = -6$

8. $3x + 2y = 7$
   $-4x - y = -11$

9. $y = 13$
   $8x - 3 = y$

10. **Open-ended** Write a 3×5 matrix that represents the amount that three students paid for their lunches each day one week. **3-5**

11. Betty's Boutique is having a 20% off sale.

    a. Use scalar multiplication to write a matrix representing 20% of the pre-sale prices. Then use matrix subtraction to find the sale prices.

    b. Multiply the pre-sale prices matrix by 0.8. Compare your answer to your answer in part (a).

Pre-Sale Price ($)

	Juniors	Misses	Tall
turtlenecks	12	15	20
sweaters	35	40	50
jeans	40	40	50

Find the coordinates of the vertices of △ABC after each transformation. Write each answer as a matrix. **3-6**

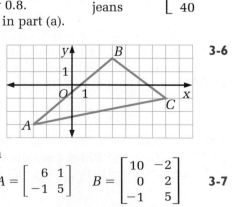

12. a dilation with scale factor $\frac{1}{3}$ and center at the origin

13. a translation 1 unit left and 2 units down

14. Find the product of these two matrices: $A = \begin{bmatrix} 6 & 1 \\ -1 & 5 \end{bmatrix}$ $B = \begin{bmatrix} 10 & -2 \\ 0 & 2 \\ -1 & 5 \end{bmatrix}$ **3-7**

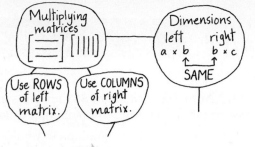

15. **Writing** Jennifer started this concept map for matrix multiplication. Complete her map or create a new one. Describe the ideas your map shows.

16 T E C H N O L O G Y Use the matrix functions of a graphics calculator to solve this linear system.

$$-x - y = -5$$
$$2x - 15y = 3$$

3-8

17. **Self-evaluation** What method (*graphing, substitution,* or *addition-or-subtraction*) would you prefer to use to solve this linear system? Why? Describe the difficulties you find with the methods you do not prefer.

$$y = 10x + 5$$
$$y = -2x - 3$$

18. **Group Activity** Work with another student.

   a. Choose a point P. One student should write the equation of the line that goes through P and is parallel to $y = 2x$. The other student should write the equation of the line that goes through P and is perpendicular to $y = 2x$.

   b. Write an equation of a line that intersects both lines from part (a) and does not go through P.

   c. Graph the three equations that you wrote in parts (a) and (b). What are the coordinates of the vertices of the triangle formed by the lines? Write the answer as a matrix.

   d. Each of you should write a transformation in matrix form. Use each other's matrix to transform the triangle in part (c). What are the new coordinates of the vertices?

IDEAS AND (FORMULAS)=X^2 $_5P_5$

ALGEBRA $)X^2$ $(\times$

➤ To solve a linear system by graphing, estimate the intersection point of the graphs of the equations. *(p. 122)*

➤ You can use the graphs of the equations of a linear system to compare the quantities represented by the equations. *(p. 123)*

➤ To solve a system of equations by substitution, solve one equation for one variable. Replace that variable in the other equation with the resulting expression. *(p. 130)*

➤ The graphs of the equations of a linear system can be intersecting lines, the same line, or parallel lines. You can use the relationship of the graphs to tell how many solutions the system has, and whether the system is consistent. *(p. 136)*

➤ You can use the slope-intercept form of the equations of a linear system to recognize several characteristics of the system without graphing the lines or solving the system. *(p. 136)*

➤ When the slope of a line is m, the slope of a parallel line is m and the slope of a perpendicular line is $-\frac{1}{m}$. *(p. 138)*

➤ To solve a linear system by addition-or-subtraction, combine the like terms of the equations to make a new equation with just one variable. You may need to multiply both sides of one or both equations by a constant. *(pp. 143–145)*

DISCRETE 3!
T⟵ T 3•2•1= **MATH** ▶
$_5P_5$

➤ You can use matrices to organize data that belong to more than one category. *(p. 151)*

➤ Scalar multiplication involves multiplying each element of a matrix by the same number. *(pp. 152–153, 155)*

➤ You add or subtract two matrices with the same dimensions by adding or subtracting the elements in corresponding positions. *(pp. 154–155)*

➤ To multiply a row of matrix *L* by a column of matrix *R*, add the products of the corresponding elements of the row and the column. *(pp. 165–166)*

➤ To find the matrix product *LR*, multiply each row of *L* by each column of *R*. Enter the result in the corresponding row-column position of the product matrix. *(pp. 166–168)*

➤ The matrix product *LR* is defined only if the number of columns of *L* equals the number of rows of *R*. *(pp. 168, 170)*

➤ The matrix product *LR* has the same number of rows as *L* and the same number of columns as *R*. *(pp. 168, 170)*

➤ Generally, matrix multiplication is not commutative. *(p. 170)*

➤ You can use a matrix equation to represent a linear system. The solution of the equation $A\begin{bmatrix} x \\ y \end{bmatrix} = B$ is $A^{-1}B$. *(pp. 175–176)*

GEOMETRY ▶

➤ You can use scalar multiplication to represent a dilation with center at the origin. *(pp. 159–160)*

➤ You can represent a translation with matrix addition. *(p. 161)*

.........**Key Terms**

- **system of equations** (p. 121)
- **horizontal intercept** (p. 122)
- **consistent system** (p. 136)
- **element of a matrix** (p. 151)
- **transformation** (p. 159)
- **center of dilation** (p. 159)
- **inverse matrices** (p. 174)

- **linear system** (p. 121)
- **system of inequalities** (p. 124)
- **inconsistent system** (p. 136)
- **dimensions of a matrix** (p. 151)
- **dilation** (p. 159)
- **scale factor** (p. 159)
- **A^{-1}** (p. 174)

- **solution of a system of equations** (p. 122)
- **solution region** (p. 124)
- **matrix** (p. 151)
- **scalar multiplication** (p. 155)
- **image** (p. 159)
- **translation** (p. 161)
- **matrix equation** (p. 175)

FOUNTAINS

Have you ever seen water play leapfrog? In a fountain at Epcot Center, the water almost seems to be alive. It jumps and plays like a sprightly puppy.

water arcs

The effect of air resistance on the flow of water has to be considered by people who design fountains. To produce water arcs of the desired height and width, **fountain designers** must determine how fast the water should flow and at what angle it should come out of the nozzle.

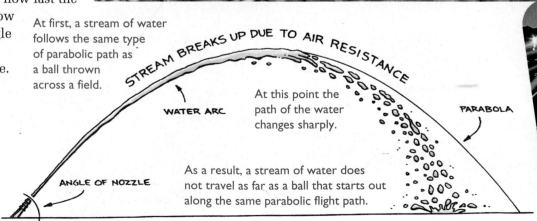

At first, a stream of water follows the same type of parabolic path as a ball thrown across a field.

STREAM BREAKS UP DUE TO AIR RESISTANCE

WATER ARC

At this point the path of the water changes sharply.

PARABOLA

ANGLE OF NOZZLE

As a result, a stream of water does not travel as far as a ball that starts out along the same parabolic flight path.

Design a Fountain

Your project is to design a fountain for a park in your community. Include at least two intersecting water arcs in your fountain. Each water arc should meet these requirements: ················>

STARTING POINT
ground level

HEIGHT
between 30 ft and 60 ft

WATER SPEED
between 6 ft/s and 70 ft/s

ANGLE
between 15° and 75°

For this range of angles, a parabola is a reasonable model for a water arc. To determine the angle and water speed of each parabolic water arc, you will use an equation given in the "Working on the Unit Project" exercises for the unit.

Make a poster to display your fountain design. Include a sketch of your fountain as well as graphs of the paths of the water arcs.

FOUNTAINS AROUND THE WORLD

Buenos Aires, Argentina

Brisbane, Australia

Portland, Oregon

Paris, France

Kyoto, Japan

Getting Started

For this project you should work in a group of four students. Here are some ideas to help you get started.

☞ In your group, decide where you will locate your fountain. What size would be appropriate for the location? Who will visit your fountain?

☞ An equation for the path of a parabolic water arc is stated and applied in the "Working on the Unit Project" exercises throughout the unit. Plan to meet later to discuss how to use this equation to design your fountain.

Moroccan Embassy, Spain

Madrid, Spain

Hong Kong

FOUNTAIN PLAN

Location:

Size:

Visitors:

Working on the Unit Project

Your work in Unit 4 will help you design your fountain.

Related Exercises:

Section 4-1, Exercises 37–40
Section 4-2, Exercise 29
Section 4-3, Exercise 39
Section 4-4, Exercise 45
Section 4-5, Exercise 52
Section 4-6, Exercise 53
Section 4-7, Exercise 30

Alternative Projects p. 236

Can We Talk FOUNTAINS

➤ To the ancient Greeks, water was one of the four basic elements along with earth, air, and fire. Today, water is known to be essential for life. How is water used by people and other living things?

➤ Some of the earliest fountains were built around 4000 B.C. in what is now Iran. These fountains may have been used to decorate gardens. What other uses for fountains do you know about?

➤ Where else besides fountains have you seen water arcs? Which of these water arcs are natural and which are made by people?

➤ A rainbow is a different kind of water arc. It is formed when tiny droplets of water in the air act like prisms, separating light into the various colors within it. When and where have you seen a rainbow? What legends or stories do you know in which a rainbow is important?

Graphing Quadratic Functions

Focus

Understand how the coefficients of a quadratic function influence its graph: the direction it opens, its vertex, its line of symmetry, and its y-intercept.

Here's Looking at ⋃

The water cannon is about 10 ft above the river.

On the north bank of the Chicago River, the Water Arc sprays recirculated water across the river toward a terrace along the south bank. The curve of water is big enough for boats to sail under.

The path of the water is an example of a **parabola,** a curve that can be modeled with a quadratic function. A **quadratic function** is a function that can be written in the **standard form**

$$y = ax^2 + bx + c, \text{ where } a \neq 0.$$

The path of the Water Arc can be modeled using the function

$$y = -0.006x^2 + 1.2x + 10.$$

Talk it Over

1. Use a graphics calculator or software to graph the function. The water cannon is about 10 ft above the river surface.

   a. What point on your graph represents the water cannon?

   b. What is the greatest height the water reaches?

   c. How far across the river does the water reach?

2. What happens to the graph if you change the coefficient of x^2 in the equation from -0.006 to 0.006? Describe the new graph.

BY THE WAY...

The Water Arc sprays at a rate of 2100 gallons per minute with a water pressure of 375 pounds per square inch.

ORIENTATIONS OF PARABOLAS

When a is negative, the graph of $y = ax^2 + bx + c$ is a parabola that opens down.

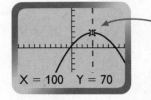

X = 100   Y = 70

The **vertex** is on the line of symmetry. Here it is a **maximum**.

$y = -0.006x^2 + 1.2x + 10$

When a is positive, the graph of $y = ax^2 + bx + c$ is a parabola that opens up.

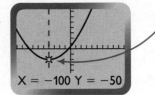

X = -100   Y = -50

Here the vertex is a **minimum**.

$y = 0.006x^2 + 1.2x + 10$

The formula for the line of symmetry is $x = -\dfrac{b}{2a}$.

Sample 1

Use the function $y = -3x^2 + 2x + 1$.

   a. Tell whether the graph opens *up* or *down*.

   b. Tell whether the vertex is a *maximum* or a *minimum*.

   c. Find an equation for the line of symmetry.

   d. Find the coordinates of the vertex.

Sample Response

The function $y = -3x^2 + 2x + 1$ is in the form $y = ax^2 + bx + c$.

a. The value of a is -3. It is negative, so the graph opens down.

b. Because the graph opens down, the vertex is a maximum.

c. $x = -\dfrac{b}{2a}$ ⟵ Write the formula for the line of symmetry.

$x = -\dfrac{2}{2(-3)}$ ⟵ Substitute **2** for b and **−3** for a.

$x = \dfrac{1}{3}$

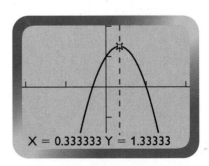

X = 0.333333   Y = 1.33333

d. The vertex lies on the line of symmetry, so $x = \dfrac{1}{3}$.

$y = -3x^2 + 2x + 1$ ⟵ Write the original function.

$y = -3\left(\dfrac{1}{3}\right)^2 + 2\left(\dfrac{1}{3}\right) + 1$ ⟵ Substitute $\dfrac{1}{3}$ for x.

$y = 1\dfrac{1}{3}$ ⟵ This is the y-value of the vertex.

······▶ **Now you are ready for:**
Exs. 1–20 on pp. 190–191

The coordinates of the vertex are $\left(\dfrac{1}{3}, 1\dfrac{1}{3}\right)$.

The vertex is one point that helps you sketch a parabola.

The intercepts, where the parabola crosses the x-axis and y-axis, also help you sketch a graph.

Here are graphs of the Water Arc.

One x-intercept is about −8.

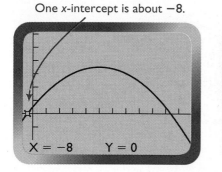

X = −8   Y = 0

The y-intercept is 10.

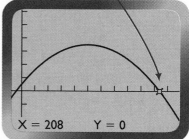

X = 0   Y = 10

The other x-intercept is about 208.

X = 208   Y = 0

You can find the **y-intercept** of an equation by substituting 0 for x in the equation. You can find **x-intercepts** by substituting 0 for y, but for now, you should estimate them from a graph.

Sample 2

Use the function y = x² + 0.5x − 3.74.

a. Find the y-intercept of the graph.

b. Use a graph to estimate the x-intercepts. Check one x-intercept by substitution.

Sample Response

a. $y = x^2 + 0.5x - 3.74$ ←——— Write the function.

$= (0)^2 + 0.5(0) - 3.74$ ←——— Substitute 0 for x.

$= -3.74$

The y-intercept is −3.74.

b. Make a table of values or use a graphics calculator.

The x-intercepts are −2.2 and 1.7.

Check Substitute 1.7 for x and 0 for y.

$y = x^2 + 0.5x - 3.74$

$0 \stackrel{?}{=} (1.7)^2 + 0.5(1.7) - 3.74$

$0 \stackrel{?}{=} 2.89 + 0.85 - 3.74$

$0 = 0$ ✔

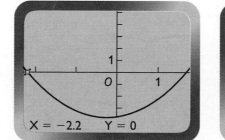

X = −2.2   Y = 0

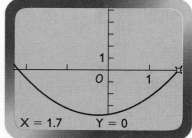

X = 1.7   Y = 0

······▶ Now you are ready for:
Exs. 21–40 on pp. 191–192

Look Back ◀

Explain how you would find the maximum or minimum value of a quadratic function.

4-1 Exercises and Problems

1. **Reading** How are the graph of the Water Arc and the graph in Sample 1 alike? How are they different?

Estimate the vertex of the parabola that describes the movement of each gymnast.

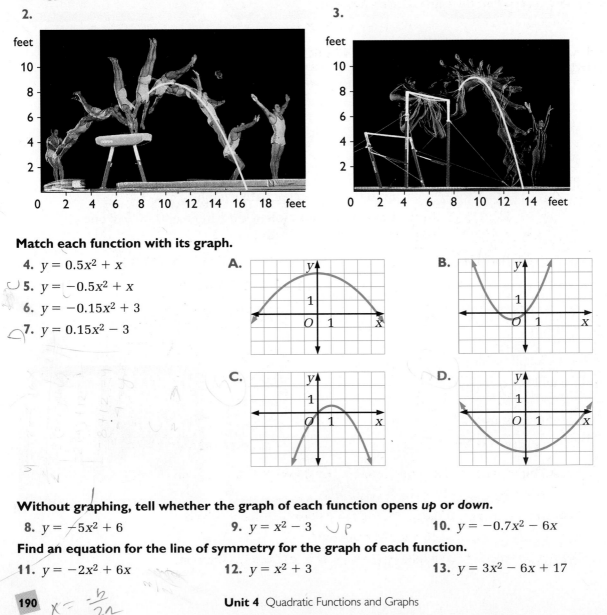

2.

3.

Match each function with its graph.

4. $y = 0.5x^2 + x$

5. $y = -0.5x^2 + x$

6. $y = -0.15x^2 + 3$

7. $y = 0.15x^2 - 3$

A.

B.

C.

D.

Without graphing, tell whether the graph of each function opens *up* or *down*.

8. $y = -5x^2 + 6$

9. $y = x^2 - 3$

10. $y = -0.7x^2 - 6x$

Find an equation for the line of symmetry for the graph of each function.

11. $y = -2x^2 + 6x$

12. $y = x^2 + 3$

13. $y = 3x^2 - 6x + 17$

$x = \dfrac{-b}{2a}$

**Find the coordinates of the vertex of the graph of each function.
Tell whether the vertex is a *maximum* or a *minimum*.**

14. $y = -2x^2 + 12x - 14$ **15.** $y = x^2 + 4x + 3$ **16.** $y = -0.25x^2 - 0.5x + 2.5$

17. Choose one of the equations from Exercises 14–16 and graph it. Label the vertex with its coordinates.

18. Use the function for the Chicago Water Arc on page 187.

    a. Find an equation for the line of symmetry for its graph.

    b. Find the vertex of its graph.

19. **Open-ended** Create three different quadratic functions that have the line $x = 2$ as their line of symmetry. Sketch their graphs.

20. **Writing** How is the graph of $y = ax^2 + bx + c$ affected if a, b, or c is 0? Draw sketches to support your conclusions.

Find the y-intercept of the graph of each function.

21. $y = 2x^2 + x - 3$ **22.** $y = -4x^2 - x + 3$ **23.** $y = \frac{1}{2}x^2 + 3x - 2$

Use the graph to estimate the x-intercepts. Check one x-intercept by substitution.

24. $y = -\frac{1}{3}x^2 + \frac{2}{3}x + 1$

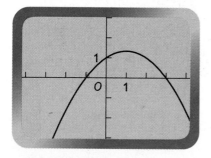

25. $y = \frac{1}{2}x^2 - 2x$

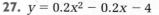
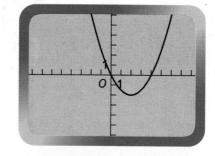

26. $y = -x^2 - 6x - 5$

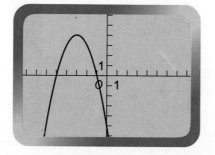

27. $y = 0.2x^2 - 0.2x - 4$

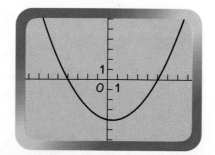

28. a. What do the graphs of the functions $y = -0.006x^2 + 1.2x + 10$ and $y = 0.006x^2 - 1.2x + 10$ have in common?

    b. What do the graphs of the functions $y = 0.006x^2 + 1.2x + 10$ and $y = -0.006x^2 - 1.2x + 10$ have in common?

    c. What point do all four graphs in parts (a) and (b) have in common?

29. **Writing** Explain how to find the *y*-intercept of the graph of the function $y = ax^2 + bx + c$. Choose values for *a*, *b*, and *c* and use them in an example.

Write each system as a matrix equation. *(Section 3-8)*

30. $3x + 2y = 5$
    $4x - y = 3$

31. $4x - 2y = 8$
    $-3x + 5y = -6$

32. $y = 3x - 4$
    $y = -2x + 21$

33. What is the radius of a circle with an area of 50 cm²? *(Toolbox Skill 28)*

Graph each function. *(Toolbox Skill 20)*

34. $y = x^2 + 4$

35. $y = (x - 4)^2$

36. $y = (x + 4)^2$

Working on the Unit Project

Use this function for the path of a water arc whose speed, *v*, is measured in feet per second. Angle *A* is the angle of the nozzle.

$$y = \frac{-16}{v^2(\cos A)^2}x^2 + (\tan A)x$$

37. Suppose a water hose sprays water at an angle of 40° and at a speed of *v* ft/s. Write a function describing the water's path. (Your equation will involve *v*.)

38. Use a graphics calculator.

   a. Graph the equation you wrote in Exercise 37 for these values of *v*: 50 ft/s, 60 ft/s, and 70 ft/s.

   b. As *v* increases how does the maximum height of the water's path change?

   c. As *v* increases how does the distance that the water travels across the ground change?

   d. What do the *x*-intercepts of the graphs represent?

39. Suppose a second water hose sprays water at an angle *A* and at a speed of 65 ft/s. Write an equation describing the water's path. (Your equation will involve angle *A*.)

40. Use a graphics calculator.

   a. Graph the equation you wrote in Exercise 39 for these measures of angle *A*: 25°, 35°, 45°, and 55°.

   b. For which angle *A* is the maximum height of the water the greatest?

   c. For which angle *A* is the distance the water travels across the ground the greatest?

Translating Parabolas

SLIDE —O→VER

EXPLORATION

(How) *do changes in the equation affect the graph of a parabola?*

- **Materials: graphics calculators**
- **Work with another student.**

① Graph $y = x^2$, $y = 2x^2$, $y = 5x^2$, and $y = 12x^2$ on the same axes. What happens to the graph of $y = x^2$ when the coefficient of x^2 is greater than 1?

② Graph $y = x^2$, $y = \frac{1}{2}x^2$, $y = \frac{1}{4}x^2$, and $y = \frac{1}{10}x^2$ on the same axes. What happens to the graph of $y = x^2$ when the coefficient of x^2 is between 0 and 1?

③ How do you think the graphs in steps 1 and 2 will change when the coefficient of x^2 is negative? Check your answer by graphing some examples.

④ Graph $y = 5x^2$, $y = 5x^2 + 3$, and $y = 5x^2 - 3$ on the same axes. How does the graph of $y = 5x^2$ change when you add 3 to $5x^2$? when you subtract 3 from $5x^2$?

⑤ Predict what the graph of $y = 5x^2 - 7$ looks like. Check your answer by graphing.

⑥ Graph each function on the same axes as $y = 2x^2$. Describe how the graph of each function is different from the graph of $y = 2x^2$.

   a. $y = 2(x + 2)^2$ **b.** $y = 2(x - 3)^2$ **c.** $y = 2(x - 6)^2$

⑦ What relationship do you see between the equations in step 6, parts (a)–(c), and their graphs?

⑧ Use what you discovered in steps 4 and 6 to predict what the graph of $y = (x - 7)^2 + 4$ will look like. Sketch your prediction on a piece of paper. Then check your prediction by graphing.

⑨ Describe how the graph of $y = 2(x + 3)^2 - 1$ is different from the graph of $y = x^2$.

The graph of $y = (x + 3)^2 + 2$ is a translation of the graph of $y = x^2$. A translation changes only a graph's position. It does not change a graph's size or shape or the direction in which a graph opens.

Talk it Over

Tell whether the graph of each function is a translation of $y = x^2$.

1. $y = x^2 + 6$ **2.** $y = 3x^2$ **3.** $y = (x - 1)^2$

4. Describe the information you can get about the graph of a parabola from its equation.

Sample 1

Tell how to translate the graph of $y = -0.5x^2$ in order to produce the graph of each function.

    a. $y = -0.5x^2 - 2$ **b.** $y = -0.5(x + 4)^2$ **c.** $y = -0.5(x - 1)^2 + 3$

Sample Response

a. $y = -0.5x^2 - 2$

Translate the graph of
$y = -0.5x^2$
2 units *down*.

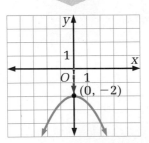

b. $y = -0.5(x + 4)^2$

Translate the graph of
$y = -0.5x^2$
4 units to the *left*.

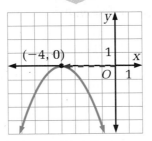

c. $y = -0.5(x - 1)^2 + 3$

Translate the graph of
$y = -0.5x^2$
1 unit to the *right*
and 3 units *up*.

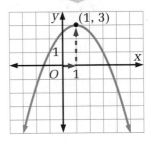

Talk it Over

5. What is the vertex of the graph of $y = 4x^2$? What is the vertex of the graph of $y = 4x^2 + 3$? Describe the change in the position of the vertex when 3 is added to $4x^2$.

6. For each parabola in Sample 1, describe the translation of the vertex.

·····▶ **Now you are ready for:**
: **Exs. 1–11 on pp. 196–197**

Sometimes you want to write a quadratic function in *standard form* before you use it to get information about the graph.

Sample 2

Find the coordinates of the vertex of the graph of $y = 3(x - 4)^2 + 1$.

Sample Response

Method ❶ Use a formula.

The formula for the line of symmetry, $x = -\dfrac{b}{2a}$, gives the x-coordinate of the vertex. You need to write the function in standard form to use the formula.

$$y = 3(x - 4)^2 + 1$$
$$= 3(x - 4)(x - 4) + 1 \qquad \longleftarrow \text{Rewrite } (x - 4)^2.$$
$$= 3(x^2 - 8x + 16) + 1 \qquad \longleftarrow \text{Use the distributive property: } (x - 4)x - (x - 4)4.$$
$$= 3x^2 - 24x + 48 + 1 \qquad \longleftarrow \text{Use the distributive property.}$$
$$= 3x^2 - 24x + 49 \qquad \longleftarrow \text{Combine like terms.}$$

The equation $y = 3x^2 - 24x + 49$ is in the form $y = ax^2 + bx + c$. Find the x-coordinate of the vertex.

$$x = -\frac{b}{2a} \qquad \longleftarrow \text{Use the formula for the line of symmetry.}$$
$$= -\frac{-24}{2(3)} \qquad \longleftarrow \text{Substitute } -24 \text{ for } b \text{ and } 3 \text{ for } a.$$
$$= 4$$

Use this value to find the y-coordinate of the vertex.

$$y = 3(x - 4)^2 + 1 \qquad \longleftarrow \text{Write the original function.}$$
$$= 3(4 - 4)^2 + 1 \qquad \longleftarrow \text{Substitute 4 for } x.$$
$$= 1$$

The coordinates of the vertex are (4, 1).

Method ❷ Use a translation.

The graph of $y = 3(x - 4)^2 + 1$ is a translation of the graph of $y = 3x^2$. Translate the vertex of $y = 3x^2$ to the right 4 units and up 1 unit to find the vertex of $y = 3(x - 4)^2 + 1$.

$$(0, 0) \qquad \longleftarrow \text{Write the vertex of the parabola } y = 3x^2.$$
$$(0 + 4, 0 + 1) \qquad \longleftarrow \text{The vertex is translated 4 units right and 1 unit up.}$$
$$(4, 1)$$

The coordinates of the vertex are (4, 1).

7. In Method 1 of Sample 2, does it matter whether you distribute the 3 before you expand $(x - 4)^2$? Why or why not?

8. Graph $y = 3(x - 4)^2 + 1$ and $y = 3x^2 - 24x + 49$ on the same set of axes. What do the graphs tell you about the two functions?

Look Back

In the Exploration, you discovered that changes to the function $y = x^2$ can move its graph up, down, left, or right. Describe a way to remember the effect that each change in the function has on the graph.

⋯⋯▶ **Now you are ready for:**
Exs. 12–29 on pp. 197–198

4-2   Exercises and Problems

1.   **Reading** Which of the parabolas in the Exploration are translations of the graph of $y = x^2$?

2. Without graphing, list the functions in order from the one with the narrowest graph to the one with the widest graph.

$$y = \frac{2}{3}x^2 + 1 \qquad y = 12x^2 - 5 \qquad y = 0.01x^2 \qquad y = 5x^2 + 8$$

3. Without graphing, list the functions in order beginning with the one whose graph has the vertex farthest to the left.

$$y = \frac{2}{3}(x + 1)^2 \qquad y = 12(x - 5)^2 \qquad y = 0.01(x - 3)^2 \qquad y = 5(x + 8)^2$$

For Exercises 4–7, tell how to translate the graph of $y = -3x^2$ in order to produce the graph of each function.

4. $y = -3(x + 7)^2$

5. $y = -3(x - 2)^2 + 3$

6. $y = -3(x - 1)^2 - 2$

7. $y = -3(x + 2)^2 + 5$

Each graph is a translation of $y = \frac{1}{3}x^2$. Write a function for each graph.

8.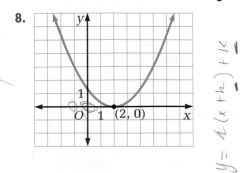

9.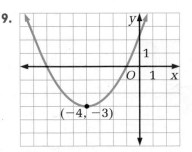

10. Make a concept map to describe the ways the graph of $y = 3x^2$ can be translated. Give examples of at least two functions for each type of translation. Use functions that show vertical translations, horizontal translations, or both vertical and horizontal translations.

11. a. **Using Manipulatives** Make a coordinate grid on graph paper. Place tracing paper on top of the graph paper. Graph $y = \frac{2}{5}x^2$ on your tracing paper.

b. Move the tracing paper so that the parabola is translated up 6 units. What is the y-intercept? the line of symmetry? Rewrite the equation $y = \frac{2}{5}x^2$ to show the translation.

c. Repeat part (b) but translate the original parabola 4 units to the left.

d. Repeat part (b) but translate the original parabola 2 units down and 3 units to the right.

e. Repeat part (b) but reflect the original parabola over the x-axis.

12. **Writing** Jack says that the y-intercept of the graph of $y = 3(x + 1)^2 - 8$ is -8. Lindsey rewrites the function in standard form and says the y-intercept of the graph is -5. Who do you think is right? Why?

For the graph of each function:

a. Find the coordinates of the vertex.

b. Find the y-intercept.

13. $y = (x + 6)^2$

14. $y = (x + 3)^2 - 4$

13 - 19

15. $y = (x - 5)^2 + 2$

16. $y = 2(x + 4)^2 - 18$

17. $y = 5(x - 1)^2 + 11$

18. $y = -4(x - 2)^2 + 9$

19. The equation for the area of a circle is written $A = \pi r^2$.

a. When you rewrite $A = \pi r^2$ using x for the radius and y for the area, you get $y = \pi x^2$. Graph the function $y = \pi x^2$. (Use $\pi \approx 3.14$.)

b. What is a reasonable domain for this function?

20. a. Use the formula $A = \pi r^2$ to find the area of the small circle.

b. Use the formula $A = \pi r^2$ to write an expression for the area of the large circle.

c. Use your answers to parts (a) and (b) to write an equation for the area of the shaded region. Then graph the equation and tell what translation of $y = \pi x^2$ produces the graph.

d. What is a reasonable domain for this function?

e. Estimate the x-intercepts of your graph. What do the x-intercepts represent?

f. Describe the error Yael made in describing the translation of the graph of $y = \pi x^2$ in part (c).

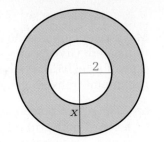

Yael

$y = \pi x^2 - 4\pi$
$y = \pi(x^2 - 4)$
The graph is translated 4 units to the right.

21. **Open-ended** Write three examples of quadratic functions whose graphs fit each description.

a. open down

b. have a narrower opening than $y = x^2$

c. have a wider opening than $y = x^2$

d. have a line of symmetry of $x = 3$

For each function, find the coordinates of the vertex of the graph and tell if the vertex is a *maximum* or a *minimum*. *(Section 4-1)*

22. $y = \frac{1}{2}x^2 + 6x - 5$

23. $y = 5x^2 + 2x + 4$

24. $y = -2x^2 + 12x - 8$

25. Graph the equation $y = 3(2^n)$. Does your graph represent *exponential growth* or *exponential decay*? Explain. *(Section 2-7)*

Solve. *(Toolbox Skill 16)*

26. $x^2 = 169$

27. $x^2 = 784$

28. $x^2 = 64$

Working on the Unit Project

29. **Group Activity** Work with another student. You will need a tape measure and a water hose connected to a faucet outdoors.

a. One person should hold the hose's nozzle as close to the ground as possible at a 45° angle up from the ground.

b. The other person should turn on the water at full force and measure the distance d in feet between the nozzle and the point on the ground where the water lands.

c. Sketch a graph of the path of the water arc on a coordinate plane. Let the origin correspond to the nozzle of the hose. Label the x-intercepts with their coordinates.

Section 4-3

Solving Equations Using Square Roots

Focus

Solve simple quadratic equations by graphing and undoing.

MAKING WAVES

BY THE WAY...

Oceanographers forecast wave patterns so that shipping companies can plan routes. Wave patterns can affect travel time, cargo safety, and passenger comfort.

Oceanographers have identified several kinds of waves. A wave in ocean water that is deeper than half the wavelength is called a *deep water wave.*

The speed of a deep water wave is independent of the depth of the ocean. The relationship between wave speed and wavelength can be modeled with a quadratic function.

$$2\pi C^2 = 9.8L$$

C = wave speed (meters per second)

L = wavelength (meters)

The *wavelength* is the distance from crest to crest.

crest

sea level

For deep water waves, the depth of the water is more than half the wavelength.

A deep water wave has a wavelength of 15 m. Find the wave speed. Use the information on page 199.

Sample Response

$$2\pi C^2 = 9.8L \qquad \longleftarrow \text{Use the equation.}$$

$$2\pi C^2 = (9.8)(15) \qquad \longleftarrow \text{Substitute 15 for } L.$$

$$2\pi C^2 = 147$$

$$\frac{2\pi C^2}{2\pi} = \frac{147}{2\pi} \qquad \longleftarrow \text{Divide both sides by } 2\pi.$$

$$C^2 = \frac{147}{2\pi}$$

$$C = \pm\sqrt{\frac{147}{2\pi}} \qquad \longleftarrow \text{Undo the squaring.}$$

$$C \approx 4.8 \qquad \longleftarrow \text{Find the positive square root.}$$

The wave speed is approximately 4.8 m/s.

Talk it Over

1. In Sample 1, why should you look only for the positive square root?

2. Are $2\pi C^2 = 9.8L$ and $L = \dfrac{2\pi C^2}{9.8}$ equivalent? Why or why not?

3. Is the relationship between L and C an example of direct variation with the square? Why or why not?

Solve $4x^2 - 7 = 21$.

Sample Response

Method ❶ Use algebra.

$$4x^2 - 7 = 21$$

$$4x^2 = 28 \qquad \longleftarrow \text{Add 7 to both sides.}$$

$$x^2 = 7 \qquad \longleftarrow \text{Divide both sides by 4.}$$

$$x = \pm\sqrt{7} \qquad \longleftarrow \text{Undo the squaring.}$$

$$x \approx \pm 2.6$$

The solutions are about 2.6 and about -2.6.

Method ❷ Use a graph.

Rewrite the equation in the form $ax^2 + bx + c = 0$.

$$4x^2 - 7 = 21$$

$$4x^2 - 28 = 0 \quad \longleftarrow \quad \text{Subtract 21 from both sides.}$$

Graph the related function $y = 4x^2 - 28$. Use ZOOM and TRACE to estimate the x-intercepts to the nearest tenth. They are the solutions.

Watch Out!
Unless you know that the value you are looking for is positive, be sure to find both the positive and the negative square root.

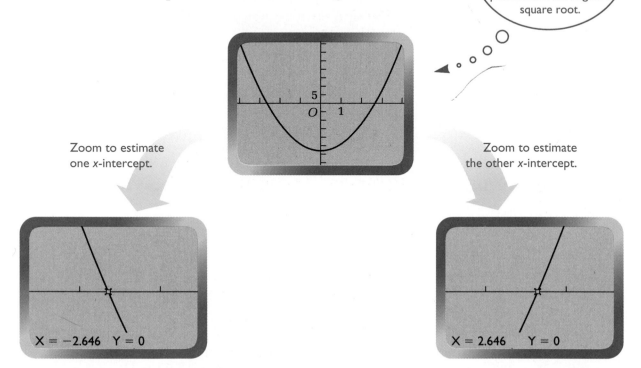

Zoom to estimate one x-intercept.

Zoom to estimate the other x-intercept.

$$X = -2.646 \quad Y = 0$$

$$X = 2.646 \quad Y = 0$$

The solutions are about 2.6 and about -2.6.

The equation $4x^2 - 7 = 21$ is a *quadratic equation*. A **quadratic equation** is one that can be written in the form $ax^2 + bx + c = 0$, where $a \neq 0$. This form is called **standard form**.

When $4x^2 - 7 = 21$ is written as $4x^2 - 28 = 0$, it is in the standard form $ax^2 + bx + c = 0$, where $b = 0$.

The x-intercepts of the graph of $y = ax^2 + bx + c$ are the solutions of the equation $0 = ax^2 + bx + c$.

Talk it Over

4. What is the relationship between the x-intercepts of the graph in Method 2 of Sample 2 and the solutions of the original equation?

5. How is the equation solving process in Sample 1 like the process in Method 1 of Sample 2? How is it different?

Quadratic Equations Involving Parentheses

Operations inside parentheses come first in the order of operations. When you solve quadratic equations by undoing, you reverse the order of operations and undo operations inside parentheses last.

Sample 3

Solve $(x - 3)^2 + 1 = 17$.

Sample Response

$$(x - 3)^2 + 1 = 17$$
$$(x - 3)^2 = 16 \qquad \longleftarrow \text{Subtract 1 from both sides.}$$
$$x - 3 = \pm 4 \qquad \longleftarrow \text{Undo the squaring.}$$
$$x = \pm 4 + 3 \qquad \longleftarrow \text{Add 3 to both sides.}$$

$x = 4 + 3$	*or*	$x = -4 + 3$
$= 7$		$= -1$

The solutions are 7 and -1.

Sample 4

Solve $2(x + 5)^2 - 4 = 18$.

Sample Response

$$2(x + 5)^2 - 4 = 18$$
$$2(x + 5)^2 = 22 \qquad \longleftarrow \text{Add 4 to both sides.}$$
$$(x + 5)^2 = 11 \qquad \longleftarrow \text{Divide both sides by 2.}$$
$$x + 5 = \pm\sqrt{11} \qquad \longleftarrow \text{Undo the squaring.}$$
$$x + 5 \approx \pm 3.3$$
$$x \approx \pm 3.3 - 5 \qquad \longleftarrow \text{Subtract 5 from both sides.}$$

$x \approx 3.3 - 5$	*or*	$x \approx -3.3 - 5$
≈ -1.7		≈ -8.3

The solutions are about -1.7 and about -8.3.

Talk it Over

6. How could you check the solutions in Sample 3?

7. How could you solve the equation in Sample 4 using a graph?

Look Back ←

Describe how to solve a quadratic equation using a graph.
Describe how to solve a quadratic equation by undoing.

4-3 Exercises and Problems

1. **Reading** In Sample 3 on page 202, why should you add 3 to both sides as the last step rather than as the first step?

Use the graph of the related function to estimate the solutions of each equation.

2. $0 = 2x^2 - 3$

3. $0 = 0.5(x + 2)^2$

4. $0 = -(x - 3)^2 + 4$

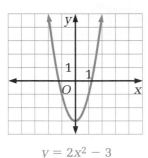

$y = 2x^2 - 3$

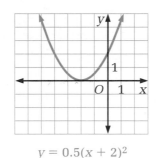

$y = 0.5(x + 2)^2$

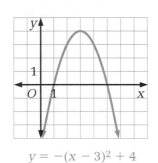

$y = -(x - 3)^2 + 4$

5. Use the graph and the equations in Exercise 4.

   a. Find the mean of the solutions.

   b. Use the graph to find an equation of the line of symmetry.

   c. Write the quadratic function in standard form.

   d. Use the formula $x = -\dfrac{b}{2a}$ to find the equation of the line of symmetry.

   e. Compare the results of parts (a), (b), and (d). What do you notice?

Find the value of x in each figure.

6.   7.   8.

Area = 1600 yd²

362 yd

23 yd

170 yd

3x

115 yd

Solve using mental math.

9. $x^2 = 1600$

10. $x^2 = 144$

11. $x^2 = 49$

12. Compare your answers to Exercises 6 and 9. How are they alike? How are they different?

For each equation, solve by graphing and solve using algebra.

13. $4x^2 - 2 = 10$

14. $(x + 5)^2 = 49$

15. $(x - 1)^2 - 15 = 0$

Solve.

16. $3x^2 + 5 = 32$

17. $(x + 3)^2 = 25$

18. $(x + 5)^2 - 8 = 8$

19. $2(x - 3)^2 = 60$

20. $-2x^2 + 6 = -18$

21. $3(x - 2)^2 = 48$

22. $(x - 2)^2 + 16 = 66$

23. $9(x + 23)^2 - 111 = 987$

24. $25(x - 15)^2 - 27 = 106$

25. Here are samples of two students' work for solving $(x + 2)^2 = 7$.

Charlie Bennett

$(x+2)^2 = 7$

$x+2 = \pm\sqrt{7}$

$x+2 \approx \pm 2.6$

$x \approx 2.6 - 2$

≈ 0.6

OR

$x \approx -2.6 - 2$

≈ -4.6

James Martin

$(x+2)^2 = 7$

$\pm(x+2) = \sqrt{7}$

$\pm(x+2) \approx 2.6$

$x+2 \approx 2.6$

$x \approx 0.6$

OR

$-x-2 \approx 2.6$

$-x \approx 4.6$

$x \approx -4.6$

a. Compare the methods. How are they alike? How are they different?

b. Do both methods give the same results?

c. Which method seems easier to you? Why?

Games Nadine is designing dart boards. If a dart lands on the board, she wants the probability of getting the dart in the unshaded region to be 15%. She assumes that a dart has an equal chance of landing anywhere on a dart board.

For each dart board:

a. **Write an equation in terms of the given variable for the probability P of getting a dart in the unshaded region.**

b. **Solve the equation in part (a) when $P = 15\%$.**

Student Resources Toolbox
p. **639** *Probability*

26.

24 in.

s

s

18 in.

27.

r

24 in.

18 in.

28.

r

r

24 in.

18 in.

29. Science Use this information about deep water waves.

$$2\pi C^2 = 9.8L$$

C = wave speed (meters per second)

L = wavelength (meters)

   a. A deep water wave has a wavelength of 25 m. Find the wave speed.

   b. Convert the wave speed you found in part (a) to kilometers per hour.

30. a. Writing Explain how to solve $2x^2 + 3 = 8$ by using a graph.

   b. Writing Explain how to solve $2x^2 + 3 = 8$ by using algebra.

Ongoing **ASSESSMENT**

31. Writing Lyle solved the equation $0 = 3(x - 2)^2 - 27$ and got the solutions -1 and 5. Based on his solutions to the first equation, he decided that the solutions to the equation $0 = 3(x - 5)^2 - 27$ must be 2 and 8. Do you agree with him? Explain your reasoning.

Review **PREVIEW**

Find the coordinates of the vertex of the graph of each function. *(Section 4-2)*

32. $y = 3x^2 - 1$
       33. $y = -2(x + 15)^2$
       34. $y = -7(x - 2)^2 + 11$

35. Determine whether the conclusion in the following statement is correct. If not, give a counterexample. *(Section 1-7)*

If Sara is sitting in her drama class, then she is in school. Sara is in school. Conclusion: Sara is in drama class.

Find each product. *(Toolbox Skill 11)*

36. $(x + 3)(x - 5)$
       37. $(y - 8)(2y - 4)$
       38. $2(3z + 1)(6z - 9)$

Working on the Unit Project

39. Use the Water Arc equation on page 192 and the data you gathered in Exercise 29 on page 198.

   a. Substitute values you know for $m \angle A$, x, and y in the equation and then solve to find the water speed v.

   b. Use the result of part (a) to help you write an equation for the water's path.

   c. Use the equation you wrote in part (b) to find the maximum height of the water above the ground.

Solving Equations Using Factoring

factor*fiction*

Focus

Solve quadratic equations by factoring.

Area = x^2

Area = x

Area = 1

EXPLORATION

How can algebra tiles help you factor trinomials?

- **Materials: algebra tiles (x^2-tiles, x-tiles, and 1-tiles)**
- **Work in a group of three students.**

A **monomial** is a number, a variable, or the product of a number and one or more variables. A **trinomial** is a sum of three monomials. You can model a trinomial with a set of algebra tiles. The trinomial is an expression for the area covered by the tiles.

Suppose you can build a rectangle with the tiles. The expressions for the length and the width of the rectangle are the factors of the trinomial.

1. **a.** Build a rectangle for $x^2 + 7x + 6$. The tiles should touch but not overlap.

   b. Use the dimensions of the tiles to complete the variable expressions for the length and the width of the rectangle.

   $$\text{Area} = x^2 + 7x + 6 = (x + \underline{?})(x + \underline{?})$$

2. **a.** Build a rectangle for $2x^2 + 5x + 3$. Is building a rectangle more difficult when the coefficient of the x^2-term is greater than one?

   b. Use the dimensions of the tiles to complete the variable expressions for the length and the width of the rectangle.

   $$\text{Area} = 2x^2 + 5x + 3 = (2x + \underline{?})(x + \underline{?})$$

3. Discuss how modeling with algebra tiles can help you factor trinomials.

4. Try to build a rectangle for $3x^2 + 2x + 1$. What is your conclusion about factoring this trinomial?

Factor $2x^2 + 5x + 3$.

Sample Response

Method ❶ Use algebra tiles.

Build a rectangle for $2x^2 + 5x + 3$ with tiles.

The length of the rectangle is $2x + 3$ and the width of the rectangle is $x + 1$.

$2x^2 + 5x + 3 = (2x + 3)(x + 1)$

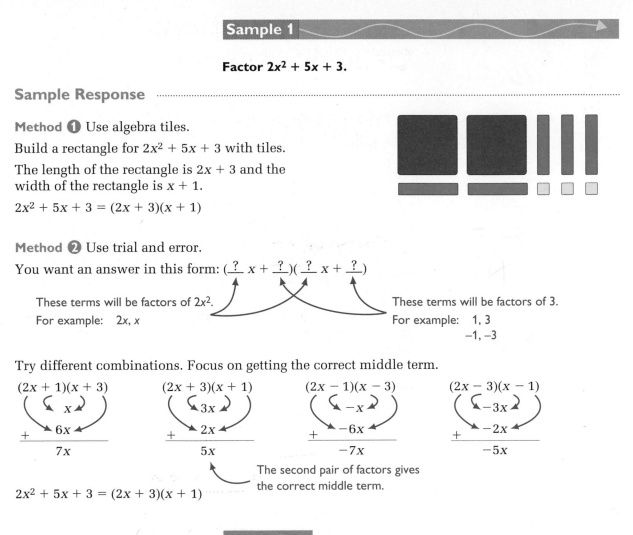

Method ❷ Use trial and error.

You want an answer in this form: $(\underline{?}\, x + \underline{?})(\underline{?}\, x + \underline{?})$

These terms will be factors of $2x^2$.
For example: $2x, x$

These terms will be factors of 3.
For example: $1, 3$
$-1, -3$

Try different combinations. Focus on getting the correct middle term.

$(2x + 1)(x + 3)$
$\quad x$
$+ \quad 6x$
$\overline{\quad 7x}$

$(2x + 3)(x + 1)$
$\quad 3x$
$+ \quad 2x$
$\overline{\quad 5x}$

$(2x - 1)(x - 3)$
$\quad -x$
$+ \quad -6x$
$\overline{\quad -7x}$

$(2x - 3)(x - 1)$
$\quad -3x$
$+ \quad -2x$
$\overline{\quad -5x}$

The second pair of factors gives the correct middle term.

$2x^2 + 5x + 3 = (2x + 3)(x + 1)$

Talk it Over

1. Suppose the trinomial in Sample 1 had been $2x^2 - 5x + 3$. Look at the list of possible factors in the Sample Response. Factor this new trinomial.

2. Suppose the trinomial in Sample 1 had been $2x^2 - 5x - 3$.
   a. What are the factors of the third term, -3?
   b. Factor the trinomial.

3. The first step in factoring any trinomial is to look for common factors in each term of the trinomial. Suppose the trinomial in Sample 1 had been $4x^2 + 10x + 6$.
   a. What is the greatest common factor of each term?
   b. Factor out this common factor: $4x^2 + 10x + 6 = \underline{?}\,(\underline{?})$
   c. Factor completely: $4x^2 + 10x + 6 = \underline{?}\,(\underline{?})(\underline{?})$

4. Which is the correct way to factor $12x^2 + 16x + 5$?
   a. $(6x + 1)(2x + 5)$ b. $(6x + 5)(2x + 1)$ c. $(4x + 5)(3x + 1)$

▸ **Now you are ready for:**
Exs. 1–18 on pp. 210–211

The results of Exercises 17 and 18 on page 211 lead you to these special factoring patterns.

X·Lab

SPECIAL FACTORING PATTERNS

To factor a *difference of two squares*:

$$a^2 - b^2 = (a + b)(a - b)$$

To factor a *perfect square trinomial*:

$$a^2 + 2ab + b^2 = (a + b)^2$$

$$a^2 - 2ab + b^2 = (a - b)^2$$

Examples

$$x^2 - 100 = (x + 10)(x - 10)$$

$$x^2 + 20x + 100 = (x + 10)^2$$

$$x^2 - 20x + 100 = (x - 10)^2$$

Sample 2

Factor $16x^2 - 9$.

Sample Response

Test whether the expression is a difference of two squares. Ask these questions:

Is the expression a difference? Yes.

Is the first term a square? Yes: $16x^2 = (4x)^2$

Is the second term a square? Yes: $9 = 3^2$

$16x^2 - 9 = (4x)^2 - 3^2$

$\quad\quad = (4x + 3)(4x - 3)$ ⟵ Use the pattern: $a^2 - b^2 = (a + b)(a - b)$

Sample 3

Factor $9x^2 - 30x + 25$.

Sample Response

Test whether the trinomial is a perfect square trinomial. Ask these questions:

Is the the first term a square? Yes: $9x^2 = (3x)^2$

Is the last term a square? Yes: $25 = 5^2$

Is the middle term twice the product of $3x$ and 5? Yes: $30x = 2(3x)(5)$

$9x^2 - 30x + 25 = (3x)^2 - 2(3x)(5) + 5^2$

$\quad\quad = (3x - 5)^2$ ⟵ Use the pattern: $a^2 - 2ab + b^2 = (a - b)^2$

Unit 4 Quadratic Functions and Graphs

Solving Equations by Factoring

Some quadratic equations can be solved by factoring and then using the *zero-product property*.

Solve $4x^2 - x = 5$.

Sample Response ....

$$4x^2 - x = 5$$
$$4x^2 - x - 5 = 0$$ ⟵——— Rewrite the equation in standard form.
$$(4x - 5)(x + 1) = 0$$ ⟵——— Factor the trinomial by trial and error.

$4x - 5 = 0$ *or* $x + 1 = 0$ ⟵——— Use the **zero-product property.** When a product of factors is equal to 0, one or more of the factors equals 0.
$4x = 5$ $x = -1$
$x = 1.25$

The solutions are 1.25 and -1.

Solve $5n^2 - 15n - 20 = 0$.

Sample Response ....

$$5n^2 - 15n - 20 = 0$$
$$5(n^2 - 3n - 4) = 0$$ ⟵——— Factor out the greatest common factor.
$$5(n - 4)(n + 1) = 0$$ ⟵——— Factor the remaining trinomial.

$n - 4 = 0$ *or* $n + 1 = 0$ ⟵——— Use the zero-product property.
$n = 4$ $n = -1$

The solutions are 4 and -1.

BY THE WAY...

Factoring was not used to solve quadratic equations until 1631.

Talk it Over

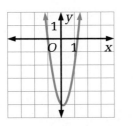

5. In Sample 4, describe how you can check whether 1.25 and -1 are solutions.

6. Use the graph shown at the left to estimate the x-intercepts of the graph of $y = 4x^2 - x - 5$.

7. How do the x-intercepts relate to the solutions of the equation $4x^2 - x - 5 = 0$ in Sample 4?

GUIDELINES FOR FACTORING COMPLETELY

1. Factor out the greatest common factor first.

2. Look for a difference of two squares.

3. Look for a perfect square trinomial.

4. If a trinomial is not a perfect square, use trial and error to look for a pair of factors.

⋯⋯► **Now you are ready for:**
Exs. 19–45 on pp. 211–213

Look Back ◄

Describe how each sample in this section illustrates the guidelines above.

4-4 Exercises and Problems

1. **Reading** When you build a rectangle with algebra tiles to model a trinomial, how do you find the factors of the trinomial from the rectangle?

2. In the Exploration, was there more than one rectangle you could form to represent $2x^2 + 5x + 3$?

3. Use the trinomial $6m^2 - 5m - 4$ and the table at the right.

   a. Complete the first column.

   b. Complete the second column.

   c. Make a table that shows the possible factors of the trinomial and the possible middle terms. Which middle term is correct?

   d. Factor the trinomial.

Factors of $6m^2$	Factors of -4
?, m	1, ?
$3m$, ?	−1, ?
—	2, ?

Factor.

4. $x^2 + 2x - 15$

5. $2x^2 - 7x + 3$

6. $3m^2 + 2m - 21$

7. $7n^2 + 17n + 6$

8. $5x^2 - 14x + 8$

9. $12x^2 - 5x - 3$

10. $4x^2 + 32x + 15$

11. $24z^2 - 14z - 5$

12. $3x^2 - 18x - 48$

13. $6x^2 - 27x + 21$

14. $18x^2 + 14x - 4$

15. $12d^2 - 34d + 20$

16. **Open-ended**

   a. Write a trinomial that cannot be factored.

   b. Make a sketch or build a model of the trinomial to show that you cannot form a rectangle using algebra tiles.

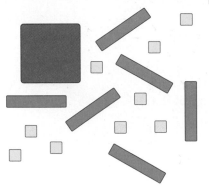

17. Using Manipulatives

a. Model $x^2 + 6x + 9$ using algebra tiles and arrange the tiles to form a rectangle.

b. Make a sketch of your arrangement. What special kind of rectangle is it?

c. Use the dimensions of your rectangle to complete:

$$x^2 + 6x + 9 = (\underline{\ ?\ })(\underline{\ ?\ }) = (\underline{\ ?\ })^2$$

d. The product $3 \cdot 3$ is 9. The product $(-3)(-3)$ is also 9. Use this result to factor the trinomial $x^2 - 6x + 9$.

e. **Writing** The type of trinomial factored in parts (c) and (d) is called a *perfect square trinomial*. Explain how you know when a trinomial is a perfect square trinomial.

18. For parts (a)–(d), find each product.

a. $(x + 1)(x - 1)$ b. $(x + 9)(x - 9)$ c. $(x + 8)(x - 8)$ d. $(x + 6)(x - 6)$

e. What patterns do you notice?

f. Use the patterns to find the product $(x + k)(x - k)$.

19. Writing Which of the special factoring patterns described on page 208 does the diagram model? Explain.

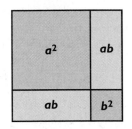

Factor.

20. $x^2 + 4x + 4$ **21.** $x^2 - 14x + 49$ **22.** $16n^2 - 8n + 1$

23. $x^2 - 16$ **24.** $9m^2 - 4$ **25.** $x^2 - 25y^2$

Solve.

26. $0 = 2x^2 - 3x - 5$ **27.** $0 = 9x^2 + 6x - 3$ **28.** $x^2 = 4x + 5$

29. $-1 = x^2 - 2x$ **30.** $2 = 10x^2 + 11x - 4$ **31.** $0 = 8x^2 - 8x - 6$

Match each function with its graph.

32. $y = (x + 1)(x - 2)$

33. $y = 2(x + 1)(x - 2)$

34. $y = -(x + 1)(x - 2)$

35. $y = 0.5(x + 1)(x - 2)$

A.

B.

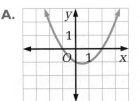

C.

D.

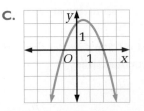

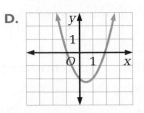

36. a. Factor $ax^2 + bx$.

b. Solve the equation $0 = ax^2 + bx$ for x.

c. What do the two solutions in part (b) represent for the graph of the function $y = ax^2 + bx$?

d. Write an expression for the average of the solutions in part (b).

e. How is your answer to part (d) related to the line of symmetry of the graph of $y = ax^2 + bx$?

f. Explain why the line of symmetry of $y = ax^2 + bx + c$ is also $x = -\frac{b}{2a}$.

37 TECHNOLOGY Use a graphics calculator.

a. Choose one of the equations in Exercises 26–31.

b. On the same set of axes, graph the function related to the equation given in the exercise and the function for the factored form.

c. What do you notice?

Ongoing **ASSESSMENT**

38. Writing A basketball player shoots at a basket that is 10 ft from the floor. The function in the photo gives the distance from the ball to the floor, in feet.

a. Explain how the equation $10 = -16t^2 + 20t + 6$ or $0 = -16t^2 + 20t - 4$ can help you find when the ball is at basket level.

b. Solve $0 = -16t^2 + 20t - 4$ by factoring. Which solution represents the time that the ball passes through the basket?

c. Explain how the equation $0 = -16t^2 + 20t + 6$ can help you find when the ball hits the ground.

d. Solve $0 = -16t^2 + 20t + 6$ by factoring. Which solution makes sense as the time the ball hits the ground?

$d = -16t^2 + 20t + 6$

Review **PREVIEW**

Solve. *(Section 4-3)*

39. $3x^2 - 13 = 14$

40. $(x - 5)^2 = 5$

41. $2(x + 2)^2 - 8 = 10$

For Exercises 42 and 43, assume that the time it takes to travel a distance of 150 mi varies inversely with the speed you are traveling. *(Section 2-3)*

42. Model the situation with an equation.

43. Find the time it would take to travel the 150 miles at 50 mi/h.

44. Use the proportion $\frac{x}{18} = \frac{5}{6}$. *(Toolbox Skill 17)*

a. What are the cross products of the proportion?

b. Solve the proportion.

45. Near the town of Cairo, Illinois, the Mississippi River is 4500 ft across. Suppose an ambitious engineer wants to design a water gun that sprays water across the Mississippi at Cairo. The engineer would like the water arc to reach a maximum height of 1 mi (5280 ft) as shown.

Do parts (a)–(f) to find the necessary water speed v and angle A of the water gun.

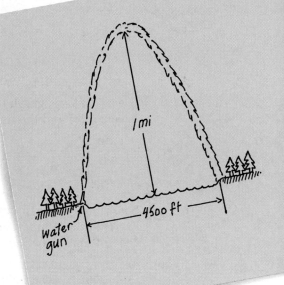

a. Draw the water arc on a coordinate plane, using the location of the water gun for the origin. Label the coordinates of the arc's vertex and two endpoints.

b. Use the graph from part (a) to find the x-intercepts.

c. The equation of a parabola may be written in factored form as $y = a(x - p)(x - q)$, where p and q are the x-intercepts. For the equation of the water arc, you know p, q, and the coordinates of the vertex. Use this information to find a and to write the equation of the water arc in factored form.

d. Rewrite the equation you wrote in part (c) in the standard form $y = ax^2 + bx + c$.

e. Use the fact that $b = \tan A$ to find the angle A at which the water gun should be tilted.

f. Use the fact that $a = \dfrac{-16}{v^2(\cos A)^2}$ to find the water speed v needed to make the arc reach across the Mississippi. Does this speed seem reasonable to you?

Unit 4   **CHECKPOINT**

1. **Writing** Can all quadratic equations be solved by factoring? Explain.

Find the coordinates of the vertex of the graph of each function. Tell whether the vertex is a *maximum* or a *minimum*.   4-1

2. $y = 3x^2 - 6x + 7$ 3. $y = -x^2 + x$

Tell how to translate the graph of $y = 0.5x^2$ to produce the graph of each function.   4-2

4. $y = 0.5(x - 1)^2 + 5$ 5. $y = 0.5(x + 2)^2$

Solve.   4-3, 4-4

6. $7x^2 - 22 = 34$ 7. $3(x + 6)^2 = 33$

8. $2(x - 8)^2 - 25 = 25$ 9. $3x^2 = 31x - 36$

10. $9x^2 + 5 = 30$ 11. $5x^2 + 30x + 45 = 0$

The Quadratic Formula

The Golden Solution

······Focus

Use the quadratic
formula to solve
quadratic equations.

*Mill-owners' Association Building,
Ahmedabac, India.
Designed by Charles Édouard Jeanneret,
known as Le Corbusier.*

Talk it Over

Golden rectangles are often used in art and architecture because
their shape is considered pleasing to the eye. There is a special
relationship between the sides of a golden rectangle.

This ratio is called
the *golden ratio.* →

$$\frac{\text{length of short side}}{\text{length of long side}} = \frac{\text{length of long side}}{\text{length of short side} + \text{length of long side}}$$

1. The rectangle in the photograph is a golden rectangle with
   sides of length 1 and x. Write a proportion to show the
   relationship between the sides.

2. Rewrite the proportion from question 1 using cross products.
   Can you use factoring to solve this equation? Explain.

3. Use a graphics calculator to graph $y = x^2$ and $y = x + 1$. What
   do the points of intersection represent?

4. Use TRACE to approximate the x-values for the points where
   the two graphs intersect. What does the positive x-value
   represent?

5. Another way to solve $x + 1 = x^2$ is to graph $y = x^2 - x - 1$.
   Use TRACE to approximate the x-intercepts of this graph.

6. Describe the relationship between the x-values you found in
   question 4 and the x-intercepts of the graph of $y = x^2 - x - 1$
   that you found in question 5.

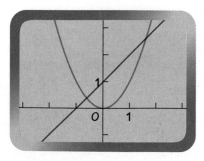

Using the Quadratic Formula

You can use a graph to find approximate solutions of the equation $x + 1 = x^2$. You can also use the quadratic formula.

$X_{(\!\triangle\!}ab$

QUADRATIC FORMULA

The solutions of the quadratic equation $0 = ax^2 + bx + c$, when $a \neq 0$ are given by this formula:

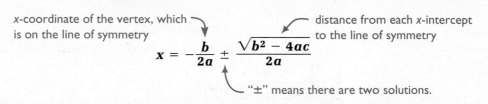

x-coordinate of the vertex, which is on the line of symmetry

distance from each x-intercept to the line of symmetry

$$x = -\frac{b}{2a} \pm \frac{\sqrt{b^2 - 4ac}}{2a}$$

"±" means there are two solutions.

The solutions are:

$$x = -\frac{b}{2a} + \frac{\sqrt{b^2 - 4ac}}{2a} \quad \text{and} \quad x = -\frac{b}{2a} - \frac{\sqrt{b^2 - 4ac}}{2a}$$

Sample 1

Solve $x + 1 = x^2$.

Sample Response

First, write the equation in standard form.

$x + 1 = x^2$

$0 = x^2 - x - 1$ ⟵ This is in the form $0 = ax^2 + bx + c$.

Then use the quadratic formula.

$x = -\dfrac{b}{2a} \pm \dfrac{\sqrt{b^2 - 4ac}}{2a}$ ⟵ Write the quadratic formula.

$= -\dfrac{(-1)}{2(1)} \pm \dfrac{\sqrt{(-1)^2 - 4(1)(-1)}}{2(1)}$ ⟵ Substitute **1** for *a*, −1 for *b*, and −1 for *c*.

$= \dfrac{1}{2} \pm \dfrac{\sqrt{5}}{2}$

$\approx 0.5 \pm 1.12$

$x \approx 0.5 + 1.12 \qquad or \qquad x \approx 0.5 - 1.12$

$\approx 1.62 \qquad\qquad\qquad \approx -0.62$

The solutions are about 1.6 and about −0.6.

BY THE WAY...

In A.D. **628**, the Hindu mathematician Brahmagupta found one of the solutions of a quadratic equation. His method was one which was used to develop the quadratic formula.

Talk it Over

7. Suppose an equation is given as $3x^2 = 2x - 5$. What values of a, b, and c would you use in the quadratic formula?

8. In the equation $2x^2 - 6 = 0$, what is the value of b? Explain.

Sample 2

A cliff diver in Acapulco, Mexico, jumps from about 17 m above the water. His height in meters from the water t seconds after he jumps is given by the function $h = -4.9t^2 + 1.5t + 17$. How long will it take for the diver to reach the water?

Sample Response

$0 = -4.9t^2 + 1.5t + 17$ ← The diver's height when he reaches the water is 0 m. Substitute 0 for h.

$t = -\dfrac{b}{2a} \pm \dfrac{\sqrt{b^2 - 4ac}}{2a}$ ← Use the quadratic formula to find the values for t when $h = 0$.

$= -\dfrac{(1.5)}{2(-4.9)} \pm \dfrac{\sqrt{(1.5)^2 - 4(-4.9)(17)}}{2(-4.9)}$ ← Substitute -4.9 for a, 1.5 for b, and 17 for c.

$\approx 0.15 \pm \dfrac{\sqrt{335.45}}{-9.8}$

$\approx 0.15 \pm -1.87$

$t \approx 0.15 + (-1.87)$ or $t \approx 0.15 - (-1.87)$

≈ -1.72 ≈ 2.02

The diver will reach the water in about 2 seconds.

Talk it Over

9. a. Give a mathematical reason why $t \approx -1.72$ is a valid solution for the equation in Sample 2.

   b. Give a reason why $t \approx -1.72$ is not a valid solution for the situation in Sample 2.

   c. Describe the difference between a valid mathematical solution and a valid solution for a situation.

10. Find the vertex of the parabola given by the function in Sample 2. What does the vertex represent in this situation?

Now you are ready for:
Exs. 20–52 on pp. 218–221

Look Back

When might you choose to use the quadratic formula to solve a quadratic equation? When might you choose to use graphing? What are some advantages of using the quadratic formula?

4-5 Exercises and Problems

1. **Reading** What are golden rectangles? Where are they used?

2. Gabrielle copied her graph of $y = x^2$ and $y = x + 1$ on a piece of graph paper and used one of the intersection points to make the rectangle shown.

   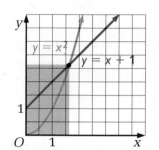

   a. Find the ratio of the longer side of the rectangle to the shorter side. What does this tell you about this rectangle?

   b. Find the ratio of the shorter side of the rectangle to the longer side. How is this ratio related to the ratio you found in part (a)? How is this ratio related to the negative x-value you found in *Talk it Over* question 4?

3. **Research** Look around your home for objects that are in the shape of a golden rectangle. Measure the dimensions to see how close they are to the golden ratio.

> **BY THE WAY...**
>
> When you are standing, your height divided by the distance from the floor to your navel is about 1.618 . . . . the Golden Ratio!

Exercise 4 refers to the *Fibonacci sequence*. The sequence of numbers 1, 1, 2, 3, 5, 8, 13, 21, 34, . . . is known as the Fibonacci sequence.

4. a. What is the next number in the Fibonacci sequence? What rule do you use to get the next number in the sequence?

   b. Complete the table with the correct ratios of the Fibonacci numbers. What do you notice about the ratios?

larger number	2	3	5	8	13	21	34
smaller number	1	2	3	5	8	13	21
ratio of larger to smaller	2	1.5	?	?	?	?	?

Solve using the quadratic formula.

5. $0 = x^2 + 9x + 14$ 6. $0 = x^2 + 7x + 12$ 7. $0 = z^2 - 12z + 27$

8. $0 = 2n^2 + 9n + 4$ 9. $0 = 3x^2 + 5x + 2$ 10. $0 = 2x^2 + x - 3$

11. Solve one of the equations in Exercises 5–10 by factoring and show that the solutions match the results you got by using the quadratic formula.

Solve using cross products and the quadratic formula.

12. $\dfrac{3}{x} = \dfrac{x}{x + 3}$ 13. $\dfrac{5}{x} = \dfrac{x}{x + 5}$ 14. $\dfrac{8}{x} = \dfrac{x}{x + 8}$

15. a. Reading Look at the statement of the quadratic formula on page 215. Why do you think it says $a \neq 0$?

    b. Write an equation in the form $y = ax^2 + bx + c$, where $a = 0$. Describe the graph of this equation. What kind of equations produce this type of graph?

16. a. Using Manipulatives The tiles shown at the right can represent the equation $x^2 + 4x + 1 = 0$. Can you use factoring to solve this equation?

    b. How many more 1-tiles do you need to add to be able to form a square? Add this number to both sides of the equation in part (a). What is the new equation?

    c. Factor the left side of the equation in part (b). How does this expression relate to the square you made with tiles?

    d. Here is what Rodrigo did next. Describe his steps.

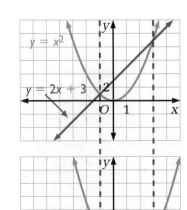

Rodrigo

$$(x+2)^2 = 3$$
$$\sqrt{(x+2)^2} = \pm\sqrt{3}$$
$$x+2 = \pm\sqrt{3}$$
$$x+2-2 = -2\pm\sqrt{3}$$
$$x = -2\pm\sqrt{3}$$

The solutions are:
$$x = -2+\sqrt{3} \text{ and}$$
$$x = -2-\sqrt{3}$$

The method used in Exercise 16 is called *completing the square.* **Use this method to solve each equation.**

17. $x^2 + 6x + 4 = 0$

18. $x^2 + 8x + 10 = 0$

19. $x^2 + 10x + 15 = 0$

Cliff Diving Use the cliff diver equation, $h = -4.9t^2 + 1.5t + 17$, to find the time elapsed for each height above the water. Give your answer to the nearest hundredth of a second.

20. $h = 10$ m   **21.** $h = 6$ m   **22.** $h = 3$ m

23. a. How do the x-coordinates for the points where the line and parabola intersect in the top graph compare to the x-intercepts in the bottom graph?

    b. How does the solution of the equation $0 = x^2 - 2x - 3$ compare with the solution of this system of equations:

$$y = x^2$$
$$y = 2x + 3$$

    c. Writing Use what you observed in parts (a) and (b) to describe two methods for solving the equation $x^2 = 2x + 3$.

Solve each equation by factoring, by graphing, or by using the quadratic formula. Use each method at least once. Explain how you decided which method to use.

24. $2x^2 + 3x + 7 = 9$

25. $6x^2 - 7x - 2 = 0$

26. $-2x^2 = x - 5$

27. $-3x + 1 = 4x^2$

28. $5x^2 - 4 = 3x$

29. $3(x + 1)^2 - 4 = 12$

Use the quadratic formula to find the solutions of each equation.

30. $x^2 - 5x - 8 = 0$

31. $x^2 - 7 = 0$

32. $2x^2 + x = 3$

33. $3x^2 = 9x - 5$

34. $2(x - 1)^2 + 5 = 6$

35. $3(x + 4)^2 - 22 = 14x + 28$

36. Baseball In his first time at bat in a game at Fenway Park, Cecil Fielder hits a baseball toward left center field. The distance in feet, d, and height, h, can be modeled by the equation $h = -0.002d^2 + 0.18d + 4$.

　a. What is the highest point the ball reaches? How far from home plate is the ball when it reaches this height?

　b. Which player is more likely to catch the ball, the shortstop or the center fielder?

37. Baseball In his second time at bat, the equation $h = -0.0015d^2 + 0.5d + 4$ can be used to model the path of the baseball hit by Cecil Fielder. The ball is hit toward the portion of the left field wall that is 347 ft from home plate.

　a. The left field wall in Fenway Park is 37 ft high. Did Cecil Fielder hit the ball over the wall for a home run? Explain.

　b. Along the third base line, the wall is 315 ft from home plate. Assume that the angle between the third base line and the wall is a right angle. Find the value of x in the diagram.

38. a. Open-ended Write a quadratic equation that has the solutions $x = -\dfrac{3}{8} \pm \dfrac{\sqrt{5}}{8}$.

　b. Graph the equation you wrote in part (a). What is the line of symmetry?

　c. Compare the equation for the line of symmetry with the solutions in part (a). Explain how you can find the line of symmetry of the graph from the solutions of the equation.

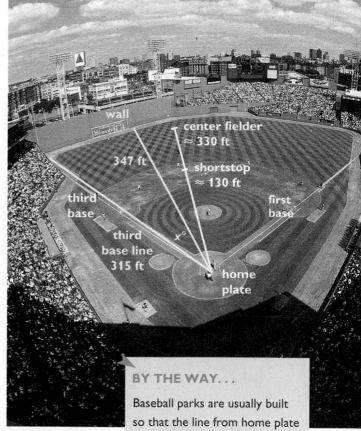

wall

center fielder ≈ 330 ft

347 ft

shortstop ≈ 130 ft

third base

first base

third base line 315 ft

$x°$

home plate

BY THE WAY...

Baseball parks are usually built so that the line from home plate to the pitcher's mound faces east-northeast. This is done so that the batter does not have to look into the sun while trying to hit the ball.

25 ft

?

39. Firefighting A firefighter aims a hose at a window 25 ft above the ground. The equation $y = -0.05x^2 + 2x + 5$ describes the path of the water.

   a. An equation to find the distance between the firefighter and the building is $-0.05x^2 + 2x + 5 = \underline{\ ?\ }$.

   b. Rewrite the equation from part (a) so one side equals zero. Use the quadratic formula to solve the equation. How far from the building is the firefighter?

   c. Suppose the firefighter wants the water to hit a window 20 ft above the ground, without changing the angle of the hose. Find two distances he can stand from the building.

Baron von Münchhausen was famous for telling tall tales. This is part of one of his stories, retold by a great-great-great-great-great-grandniece, Angelita von Münchhausen.

In this story, the Baron tells how he got information about enemy forces in a nearby town.

40. Were the two cannonballs the Baron rode fired at the same time?

41. Did the Baron switch cannonballs exactly halfway between his encampment and the town? If not, was he closer to his encampment or the town?

42. Did the Baron spend more time in the air by switching cannonballs than he would have if he stayed on the first cannonball?

43. Draw a sketch showing what the paths of the cannonballs might have looked like, and what the Baron's flight path was.

THE REAL MÜNCHHAUSEN

Since there was no convenient hill overlooking the town, ... it fell to my lot to provide the necessary reconnaissance. Directing my men to fire our largest cannon at my signal, I climbed a tree just in front of it and hanging by my hands gave the command, "FIRE!" ... Catching the ball between my legs as one would ride a horse, I let go the branch and soared off through the air. ... Below me I could see the astonished faces of my colleagues and the startled look on the faces of the people and soldiers within the town. Just as I flew over, another cannon was fired from within the town walls, and the ball headed straight toward me. I had already seen the disposition of the enemy's forces and would only have met disaster if I had continued to ride the ball until it arrived at its destination. So, as the enemy's ball neared me I quickly changed "horses" in midair and flew back to our own encampment. ... and as the ball passed through a clump of trees I was enabled to seize a branch and thus to descend safely to the ground.

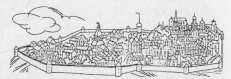

44. a. The height of a football in feet, t seconds after it has been kicked, is given by the equation $h = -16t^2 + 45t + 2.8$. Solve the equation using the quadratic formula. What do the two solutions represent in this situation?

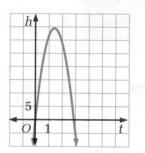

b. **Writing** How are the solutions of a quadratic equation represented on a graph?

Factor each expression. *(Section 4-4)*

45. $x^2 - 5x + 6$ **46.** $2x^2 + 11x + 12$ **47.** $3x^2 - 5x - 8$

48. The president of the student council distributes copies of a survey to every fifth student who enters the cafeteria during the lunch hour. What type of sample is this? *(Section 1-3)*

Find each product. *(Toolbox Skill 11)*

49. $x(2x - 3)$ **50.** $(-5x + 2)(y - 1)$ **51.** $(4k + 9)(7k - 2)$

Working on the Unit Project

52. **Research** Look in books, magazines, or encyclopedias for examples of interesting fountains. Think about whether you can use some of their features in the fountain you are designing.

4-6

The Discriminant and Complex Numbers

The *i*'s Have It

·······Focus

Use the discriminant to find the number of real solutions of a quadratic equation. Add, subtract, and multiply complex numbers.

EXPLORATION

Can you predict the number of solutions of a quadratic equation?

• **Materials: graphics calculators**

• **Work with another student.**

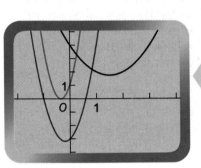

① Graph each quadratic function. Find the *x*-intercepts of each graph.

    a. $y = 5x^2 + 2x - 3$ **b.** $y = 9x^2 + 6x + 1$

    c. $y = x^2 - 3x + 4$ **d.** $y = -4x^2 + 4x - 1$

    e. $y = 2x^2 + x + 5$ **f.** $y = -3x^2 + 2x + 1$

② What differences do you notice among the six graphs in step 1? What similarities do you see?

③ How many *x*-intercepts can the graph of a quadratic function have? Is the number of *x*-intercepts the same for all quadratic functions?

④ Use the results of step 1 to tell whether each quadratic equation has one solution, two solutions, or no solutions in the set of real numbers.

    a. $0 = 5x^2 + 2x - 3$ **b.** $0 = 9x^2 + 6x + 1$

    c. $0 = x^2 - 3x + 4$ **d.** $0 = -4x^2 + 4x - 1$

    e. $0 = 2x^2 + x + 5$ **f.** $0 = -3x^2 + 2x + 1$

⑤ The **discriminant** $b^2 - 4ac$ is the part of the quadratic formula under the radical sign. Find the value of the discriminant for each quadratic equation in step 4. Tell whether each discriminant is positive, negative, or zero.

$$x = -\frac{b}{2a} \pm \frac{\sqrt{b^2 - 4ac}}{2a} \longleftarrow \text{discriminant}$$

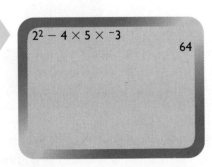

$2^2 - 4 \times 5 \times {}^-3$

64

⑥ Compare the results of steps 4 and 5. Make a conjecture about the relationship between the discriminant and the real-number solutions of a quadratic equation.

Using the Discriminant

Without graphing you can use the discriminant to find out whether or not a quadratic equation has real-number solutions.

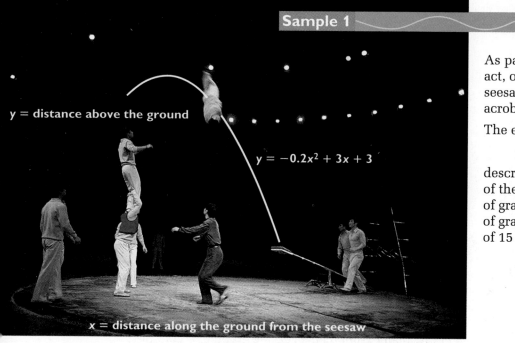

Sample 1

y = distance above the ground

$y = -0.2x^2 + 3x + 3$

x = distance along the ground from the seesaw

As part of a Shanghai Circus act, one acrobat jumps onto a seesaw to propel another acrobat into the air.

The equation

$$y = -0.2x^2 + 3x + 3$$

describes the parabolic path of the flying acrobat's center of gravity. Does her center of gravity ever reach a height of 15 ft above the ground?

Sample Response

Step 1 Decide on a problem solving strategy.

The equation tells you how high off the ground the acrobat's center of gravity is at any point during her flight. Find out whether there are real-number solutions of the equation when $y = 15$.

Step 2 Use the given equation.

$y = -0.2x^2 + 3x + 3$

$15 = -0.2x^2 + 3x + 3$ ⟵ Substitute 15 for y.

$0 = -0.2x^2 + 3x - 12$ ⟵ Write the equation in standard form.

Step 3 Evaluate the discriminant.

$b^2 - 4ac = (3)^2 - 4(-0.2)(-12)$ ⟵ Substitute **-0.2** for a, 3 for b, and **-12** for c.

$= 9 - 9.6$

$= -0.6$

Step 4 Interpret the result.

The discriminant is negative. You cannot find the square root of a negative number in the set of real numbers, so the equation has no real-number solutions. This means that at no time during her flight is the acrobat's center of gravity 15 ft above the ground.

DISCRIMINANTS AND SOLUTIONS

Here are the possible types of solutions for an equation in the form $0 = ax^2 + bx + c$, where a, b, and c are real numbers and $a \neq 0$.

When $b^2 - 4ac > 0$, there are two different real-number solutions.

The graph of $y = ax^2 + bx + c$ has two x-intercepts.

When $b^2 - 4ac = 0$, there is one real-number solution.

The graph of $y = ax^2 + bx + c$ has one x-intercept.

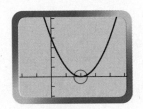

When $b^2 - 4ac < 0$, there are no real-number solutions.

The graph of $y = ax^2 + bx + c$ has no x-intercept.

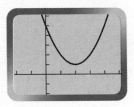

▶ **Now you are ready for:**
Exs. 1–18 on pp. 227–228

Complex Numbers

A quadratic equation with a negative discriminant does not have any real-number solutions. However, such an equation does have solutions in another set of numbers, the *complex numbers*. Physics and engineering are two fields that use complex numbers.

To understand complex numbers, you have to understand the *imaginary unit*.

Calvin and Hobbes   by Bill Watterson

The **imaginary unit** i is defined as follows:

$$i = \sqrt{-1} \quad \text{and} \quad i^2 = -1$$

The square root of a negative number is defined as follows:

$$\sqrt{-a} = i\sqrt{a} \text{ when } a > 0$$

Sample 2

Simplify.

a. $\sqrt{-81}$

b. $\sqrt{-33}$

Sample Response

a. $\sqrt{-81} = i\sqrt{81} = 9i$

b. $\sqrt{-33} = i\sqrt{33} \approx 5.7i$

COMPLEX NUMBERS

A **complex number** is a number of the form $a + bi$, where a and b are real numbers and i is the imaginary unit $\sqrt{-1}$.

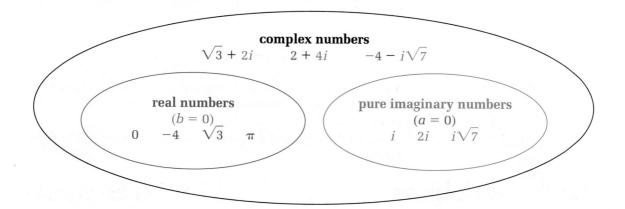

complex numbers
$\sqrt{3} + 2i \qquad 2 + 4i \qquad -4 - i\sqrt{7}$

real numbers
$(b = 0)$
$0 \qquad -4 \qquad \sqrt{3} \qquad \pi$

pure imaginary numbers
$(a = 0)$
$i \qquad 2i \qquad i\sqrt{7}$

Operations with Complex Numbers

You can use what you know about adding like terms and multiplying binomials to do operations with complex numbers.

Simplify.

a. $(9i)(3i)$ b. $(2 + 6i) - (1 - 3i)$ c. $(5 + 7i)(4 + 8i)$

Sample Response

a. $(9i)(3i) = 27i^2$

$\quad\quad\quad\quad\; = 27(-1)$ ←   Substitute −1 for i^2.

$\quad\quad\quad\quad\; = -27$

Watch Out!
Be careful distributing.
Remember that
$-(1 - 3i) = -1 + 3i.$

b. $(2 + 6i) - (1 - 3i) = 2 + 6i - 1 + 3i$

$\quad\quad\quad\quad\quad\quad\quad\;\; = (2 - 1) + (6 + 3)i$ ← Group real parts and group imaginary parts.

$\quad\quad\quad\quad\quad\quad\quad\;\; = 1 + 9i$

c. $(5 + 7i)(4 + 8i) = (5 + 7i)4 + (5 + 7i)8i$

$\quad\quad\quad\quad\quad\quad\quad\;\; = 20 + 28i + 40i + 56i^2$

$\quad\quad\quad\quad\quad\quad\quad\;\; = 20 + 68i + 56(-1)$

$\quad\quad\quad\quad\quad\quad\quad\;\; = 20 + 68i - 56$

$\quad\quad\quad\quad\quad\quad\quad\;\; = -36 + 68i$

Solve $0 = 3x^2 + 2x + 5$.

Sample Response

Use the quadratic formula.

$$x = -\frac{b}{2a} \pm \frac{\sqrt{b^2 - 4ac}}{2a}$$

$$= -\frac{2}{2(3)} \pm \frac{\sqrt{2^2 - 4(3)(5)}}{2(3)}$$ ←   Substitute **3** for a, **2** for b, and **5** for c.

$$= -\frac{2}{6} \pm \frac{\sqrt{-56}}{6}$$

$$= -\frac{1}{3} \pm \frac{i\sqrt{56}}{6}$$

$$\approx -0.33 \pm 1.247i$$

$x \approx -0.33 + 1.247i$ *or* $x \approx -0.33 - 1.247i$

The solutions are about $-0.3 + 1.2i$ and about $-0.3 - 1.2i$.

For questions 1 and 2, use the results of Sample 4.

1. Suppose you graph the function $y = 3x^2 + 2x + 5$ on a coordinate plane. How many x-intercepts will it have?

2. The equation $0 = 3x^2 + 2x + 5$ does not have any real-number solutions. Does $y = 3x^2 + 2x + 5$ have any real-number solutions? Why or why not?

Look Back ←

How can you use the discriminant to tell how many real-number solutions a quadratic equation has?

······▶ **Now you are ready for:**
 Exs. 19–53 on pp. 228–229

4-6 Exercises and Problems

1. **Reading** What is meant by the "discriminant" in the quadratic formula?

2. **Open-ended** Why do you think $b^2 - 4ac$ is called the discriminant?

Use the graph of the related function to tell whether the discriminant for each equation is *positive, negative, or zero*.

3. $0 = 1.5(x + 3)^2$

4. $0 = 0.25(x - 2)^2 - 3$

5. $0 = -x^2 - 1$

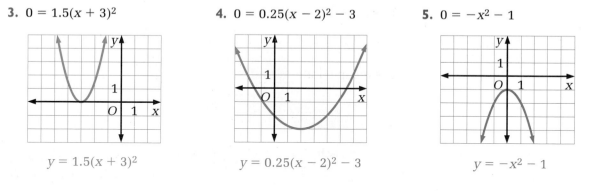

$y = 1.5(x + 3)^2$

$y = 0.25(x - 2)^2 - 3$

$y = -x^2 - 1$

For Exercises 6–14:

a. **Use the discriminant to tell whether each equation has *one solution, two solutions,* or *no solutions* in the set of real numbers.**

b. **Solve each equation that has at least one real-number solution.**

c. **Graph the related quadratic function for each equation that has no real-number solutions.**

6. $x^2 + 2x - 8 = 0$

7. $x^2 - 6x + 9 = 0$

8. $x^2 + 2x + 7 = 0$

9. $2x^2 + 5x + 3 = 0$

10. $3x^2 + x + 2 = 0$

11. $x^2 - 0.25x + 0.125 = 0$

12. $9x^2 + 16x = 12$

13. $-2x^2 + x = 5$

14. $4x^2 - 4x = -1$

15. Use the equation $x^2 + kx + 9 = 0$. Tell what values of k satisfy each condition.

   a. The equation has only one real-number solution.

   b. The equation has two real-number solutions.

   c. The equation has no real-number solutions.

Acrobatics **Use the equation $y = -0.2x^2 + 3x + 3$ from the Shanghai Circus situation in Sample 1.**

16. How high is the acrobat's center of gravity when she is at the halfway point between the edge of the seesaw and the tower of acrobats?

17. When the acrobat's center of gravity is 5 ft above the ground, how far along the ground from her starting point is she?

18. Suppose the equation for the acrobat's center of gravity is $y = -0.2x^2 + 4x + 3$. Will she reach a height of 15 ft?

19. **Writing** Explain how you can use the discriminant to tell whether the solutions of a quadratic equation are real or complex.

Simplify.

20. $\sqrt{-100}$ **21.** $\sqrt{-0.25}$ **22.** $\sqrt{-17}$ **23.** $\sqrt{-83}$

24. $(5i)(7i)$ **25.** $(4i)(-3i)(0.5i)$ **26.** $9i(1 - 8i)$ **27.** $-7i(12 + 3i)$

28. $(8 - 14i) + (10 - 5i)$ **29.** $(-4 + 2i) - (9 - 9i)$ **30.** $(3 + 4i) - (-7 + 11.5i)$

31. $(5 + 4i)(6 - 12i)$ **32.** $(-2 + 8i)(1 + 0.2i)$ **33.** $(4 - 10i)(4 + 10i)$

34. Describe the pattern shown at the right.

$i^1 = i$	$i^5 = i$	$i^9 = i$
$i^2 = -1$	$i^6 = -1$	$i^{10} = -1$
$i^3 = -i$	$i^7 = -i$	$i^{11} = -i$
$i^4 = 1$	$i^8 = 1$	$i^{12} = 1$

Use the result of Exercise 34 to complete each ?.

35. $i^{16} = \underline{?}$ **36.** $i^{99} = \underline{?}$ **37.** $i^{401} = \underline{?}$

Solve.

38. $x^2 - 3x + 5 = 0$ **39.** $25x^2 - 16x + 2 = 0$ **40.** $-3x^2 + x - 5 = 0$

41. $4x^2 + 40x + 100 = 0$ **42.** $-2x^2 + 7x - 12 = 0$ **43.** $6x^2 + 6x + 2 = 0$

44. a. Average the solutions of each equation in Exercises 38–40.

   b. Graph the related quadratic function for each equation that has complex solutions.

   c. What characteristic of each graph that you drew in part (b) is related to your corresponding answer in part (a)?

45. **Group Activity** Work with another student.

    a. Write a quadratic equation in standard form.

    b. Use algebra to decide whether your equation has real-number solutions or complex solutions and find the solutions.

    c. Exchange equations. (Do not exchange your solutions yet.)

    d. Graph the related quadratic function for the equation you received in part (c).

    e. Compare your answers for parts (b) and (d). How are they related?

Tell which method you would use to solve each equation. Then solve.
(Section 4-5)

46. $-(x + 5)^2 + 8 = 3$ **47.** $4x^2 + 12x + 9 = 0$ **48.** $-2x + 7 = 6x^2$

49. A survey of Asa Hirata's students showed that 4 out of 150 students own motorcycles. Estimate the number of students in the total school population of 1200 who own motorcycles. *(Section 1-1)*

Solve each system of equations. *(Sections 3-2, 3-4)*

50. $x + y = 3$
    $y = -2x$

51. $-x + 5y = 8$
    $2x - 10y = -16$

52. $2x + 3y = -4$
    $4x - y = 6$

Working on the Unit Project

53. Michael is designing a fountain with one water arc. His fountain nozzle will spray water at 55 ft/s, and he wants the water arc to reach at least 30 ft into the air. At what angle A should he tilt the nozzle? Do parts (a) and (b) to find out. Use this function from page 192:

$$y = \frac{-16}{v^2(\cos A)^2} x^2 + (\tan A)x$$

    a. Write an equation involving A that describes all the possible water arcs.

    b. Substitute these values for $m \angle A$ into your equation from part (a):

        $m \angle A = 20°, 40°, 60°, 80°$

    Use the discriminant to decide whether each value of $m \angle A$ will produce a water arc that reaches 30 ft high.

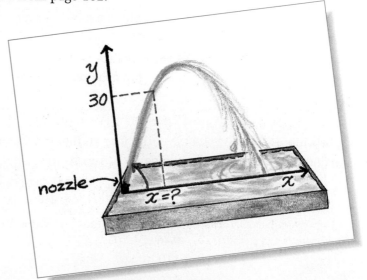

Quadratic Systems

arc rivals

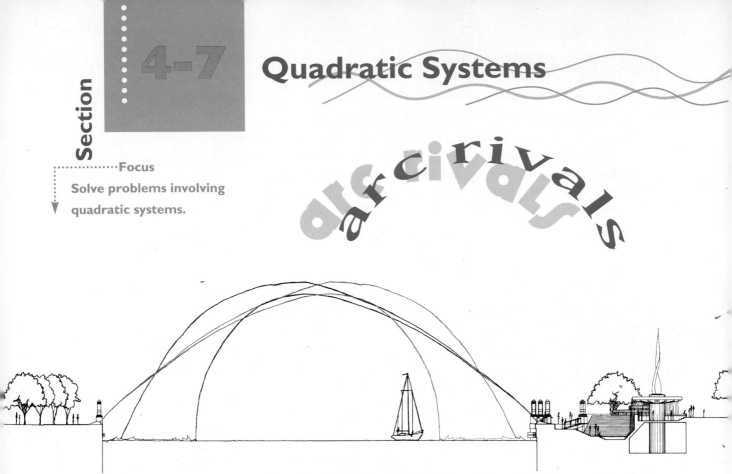

The Water Arc crosses the Chicago River from the north bank toward the south bank. If the designers decided to add a similar arc going in the other direction, where would the water arcs intersect? Assume the river is 220 ft wide.

Sample 1

These equations represent the paths of the two water arcs.

$$y = -0.006x^2 + 1.2x + 10$$
$$y = -0.006x^2 + 1.44x - 16.4$$

Find the point of intersection of the two graphs.

Sample Response

Substitute $-0.006x^2 + 1.44x - 16.4$ for y in the first equation.

$-0.006x^2 + 1.44x - 16.4 = -0.006x^2 + 1.2x + 10$

$1.44x - 16.4 = 1.2x + 10$ ← Add $0.006x^2$ to both sides.

$0.24x = 26.4$

$x = \dfrac{26.4}{0.24}$

$x = 110$

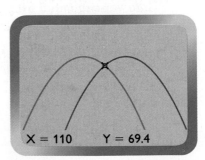

X = 110   Y = 69.4

To find where the arcs intersect, use substitution.

$y = -0.006x^2 + 1.2x + 10$ ← Use one of the original equations.

$= -0.006(110)^2 + 1.2(110) + 10$ ← Substitute 110 for x.

$= -72.6 + 132 + 10$

$= 69.4$

The point of intersection is (110, 69.4).

The water arcs intersect 110 ft from the north bank and 69.4 ft above the river.

Talk it Over

1. Does it make sense that the water arcs intersect 110 ft from the north bank? Explain.

2. Explain why it does not matter which of the two original equations you use to find y after you know x.

3. Substitute x into the other equation to check that you get the same value for y.

4. Check the solution of the system of quadratic equations using a graphics calculator or software.

Two or more quadratic functions with the same variables are called a **quadratic system**. A system of two quadratic functions can be graphed as two parabolas. The points where the parabolas intersect are the real-number solutions of the system.

There will be zero, one, or two real-number solutions, depending on whether the parabolas intersect in zero, one, or two points.

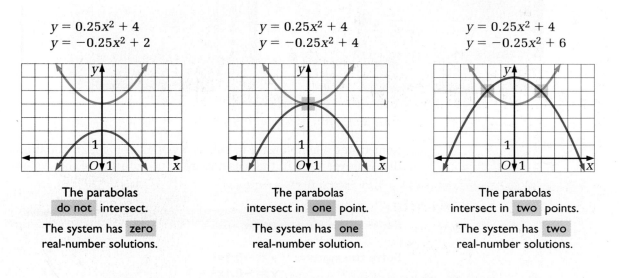

$y = 0.25x^2 + 4$
$y = -0.25x^2 + 2$

The parabolas
do not intersect.

The system has zero
real-number solutions.

$y = 0.25x^2 + 4$
$y = -0.25x^2 + 4$

The parabolas
intersect in one point.

The system has one
real-number solution.

$y = 0.25x^2 + 4$
$y = -0.25x^2 + 6$

The parabolas
intersect in two points.

The system has two
real-number solutions.

You can use algebra to find the solutions of a quadratic system.

Solve the system: $y = x^2 - 5x + 4$
$y = -2x^2 + 7x - 1$

Sample Response

Step 1 Substitute $-2x^2 + 7x - 1$ for y in the first equation.

$-2x^2 + 7x - 1 = x^2 - 5x + 4$

$\qquad 0 = 3x^2 - 12x + 5$ ⟵ Rewrite the equation in standard form.

$\qquad x = -\dfrac{-12}{2(3)} \pm \dfrac{\sqrt{(-12)^2 - 4(3)(5)}}{2(3)}$ ⟵ Substitute **3** for a, **−12** for b, and **5** for c in the quadratic formula.

$\qquad x \approx 2 \pm 1.53$

$x \approx 2 + 1.53 \qquad or \qquad x \approx 2 - 1.53$

$\quad \approx 3.53 \qquad\qquad\qquad\qquad \approx 0.47$

Step 2 Substitute each x-value into one of the original two equations to find the corresponding y-value.

➤ Substitute 3.53 for x.

$\quad y = x^2 - 5x + 4$

$\quad\quad \approx (3.53)^2 - 5(3.53) + 4$

$\quad\quad \approx -1.19$

One solution is about $(3.53, -1.19)$.

➤ Substitute 0.47 for x.

$\quad y = x^2 - 5x + 4$

$\quad\quad \approx (0.47)^2 - 5(0.47) + 4$

$\quad\quad \approx 1.87$

The other solution is about $(0.47, 1.87)$.

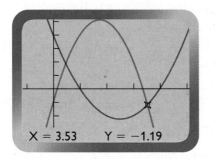

X = 3.53   Y = −1.19

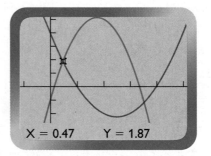

X = 0.47   Y = 1.87

Sometimes when you try to solve a system, you get an equation that is never true. In that case, there is no solution of the system.

Solve the system: $y = -0.1x^2 - 2$
$y = -0.1x^2 + 3$

$-0.1x^2 + 3 = -0.1x^2 - 2$ ⟵— Substitute $-0.1x^2 + 3$ for y in the first equation.

$3 = -2$ ⟵— Add $0.1x^2$ to both sides.

This equation is never true.
There is no solution of the system.

If you graph these equations, you see that the parabolas never intersect. One parabola is always five units above the other.

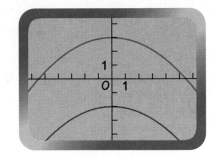

Look Back ⟵—

How is solving quadratic systems similar to solving linear systems? How is it different?

4-7 Exercises and Problems

1. **Reading** Two parabolas are graphed on the same coordinate axes. How many points might the two parabolas have in common?

Solve each system by substitution.

2. $y = 3x^2$
   $y = 3x^2 - 12x + 12$

3. $y = -x^2 + 5$
   $y = -0.5x^2 + 3$

4. $m = n^2 - 3n$
   $m = -2n^2 - 3n$

5. $y = 2x^2 - 4x + 2$
   $y = -2x^2 - 4x - 2$

6. Choose two of the systems from Exercises 2–5 and graph them to check your solutions.

Estimate the solutions of each system of quadratic equations shown.

7. $y = x^2 - 12$
   $y = -x^2 + 6$

8. $y = x^2$
   $y = -x^2 + 4x$

9. $y = \frac{1}{3}x^2$

   $y = -\frac{1}{3}x^2 + 4x - 6$

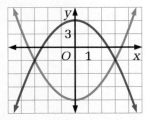

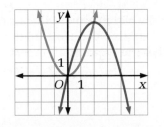

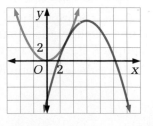

Draw a sketch of each situation.

10. two parabolas that intersect in 2 points

11. two parabolas that intersect in 1 point

12. two parabolas that do not intersect

Solve each system by graphing.

13. $y = x^2 - 2x + 3$
    $y = 0.5x^2 + 3x + 1$

14. $y = 0.7x^2 - 2x$
    $y = 0.7x^2 + 1.5x - 4$

15. $y = x^2 - 4x$
    $y = 0.2x^2 + 6x$

16. $y = -5x^2 + 5x + 2$
    $y = x^2 + 4x - 1$

Write variable expressions for the coordinates of the solutions of each system of equations.

17. $y = ax^2 + b$
    $y = cx^2 + d$

18. $y = ax^2 + bx$
    $y = cx^2 + dx$

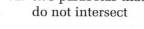

connection to **PHYSICS**

The Waimea Wave water slide near Salt Lake City, Utah, sends riders into the air for a part of their trip. The path depends on the rider's speed at liftoff, which is influenced by the friction between the rider and the waterslide.

Fred Langford, the designer of the slide, had to calculate the parabolic path of a typical rider in order to design protective walls and insure that landings would not be too rough.

Suppose the point of liftoff is at (0, 0). An equation for the path of a rider through the air is $y = -0.025x^2 + x$. An equation for the straight part of the water slide where the rider lands is $y = -x + 34$. (All distances are measured in feet.)

19. **a.** Find the solutions of the system of two equations.

    b. Which of the solutions represents the point of impact where the rider lands?

    c. What are the coordinates of the highest point along the rider's path through the air?

20. If there is more friction, the path of a rider through the air might be represented by the equation $y = -0.028x^2 + x$. How do the two paths compare? Find the coordinates of the new point of impact.

21. Which ride would you prefer, the one with more or less friction?

22. **Open-ended** Write a system of two quadratic equations that has solutions at $(2, 4)$ and $(-2, 4)$.

Review **PREVIEW**

Use the discriminant to tell whether each equation has *one solution*, *two solutions*, or *no solutions* in the set of real numbers. *(Section 4-6)*

23. $x^2 - 5x + 4 = 0$ **24.** $2x^2 + 3x - 5 = 0$ **25.** $-6x^2 - 7x = 3$

26. Solve this system of linear equations. *(Section 3-4)*

$$x + 2y = 14$$
$$-x - y = -2$$

Sketch an example of each figure. Then find each area. *(Toolbox Skill 28)*

27. a rectangle with base = 7 in., height = 6 in.

28. a parallelogram with base = 4.5 m, height = 3 m

29. a trapezoid with base$_1$ = 3 cm, base$_2$ = 5 cm, height = 4 cm

Working on the Unit Project

30. Latricia designed a fountain with two intersecting water arcs. The fountain, shown below, is in a circular pool 100 ft in diameter, and the vertices of the two arcs lie directly above the pool's center.

   a. Write an equation for the wide arc. (*Hint:* Substitute values into the factored form $y = a(x - p)(x - q)$ as you did in Exercise 45 of Section 4-4.)

   b. Latricia designed the narrow arc to have half the width and twice the height of the wide arc. Write an equation for the narrow arc.

   c. Find the points where the arcs intersect.

   d. For what values of x is the narrow arc above the wide arc?

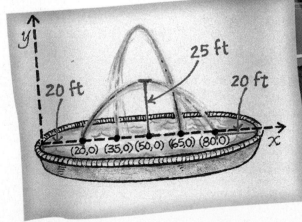

Completing the Unit Project

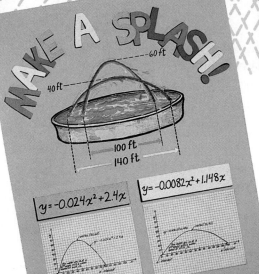

You are now ready to present your fountain design. Your completed poster should include the following:

➤ a detailed sketch of your fountain, including the heights and widths of all water arcs

➤ separate graphs of each of the water arcs. On each graph, write the equation of the arc, the measure of the stream angle, and the water speed. Label the coordinates of the vertex and the x-intercepts.

Look Back ←

Explain how your knowledge of quadratic functions and graphs helped you design your fountain.

Alternative Projects

Project 1: Investigating Water Arcs by Experiment

Punch holes at several different heights in the side of a large can. Place the can on a large sheet of plastic in a sink or shallow tub. Fill the can with water and mark the points where the arcs hit the surface.

Describe the relationship between the height of a hole and how far the water travels. Choose an origin and graph the paths of the water arcs. Write the equations of all the arcs and find the coordinates of the points where pairs of arcs intersect.

Project 2: Using Straight Lines to Draw a Parabola

Follow this procedure to create a parabola with straight lines:

Draw a set of axes on graph paper. Label the axes from 1 to 20. With a ruler, draw lines connecting (0, 20) with (1, 0), (0, 19) with (2, 0), (0, 18) with (3, 0), and so on in this pattern until every labeled point on the vertical axis is connected to a labeled point on the horizontal axis.

Use what you have learned about parabolas in this unit to analyze the parabola formed by straight lines. Discuss the parabola's line of symmetry, vertex, and intercepts, as well as what transformations of $y = x^2$ will produce its graph. If possible, write an equation for the parabola.

Find the vertex and y-intercept of the graph of each function.   4-1

1. $y = 0.5x^2$ **2.** $y = 0.5x^2 + 4$ **3.** $y = 0.5x^2 + 6x + 10$

4. **Open-ended** Write a quadratic equation whose graph opens down and whose line of symmetry is $x = -3$.

Find the vertex of the graph of each function. Tell whether the graph opens *up* or *down*.   4-2

5. $y = -3(x - 3)^2 - 16$ **6.** $y - 1 = -(x - 1)^2$

7. a. **Open-ended** Write an equation for a parabola whose vertex is $(3, 4)$ and opens down.

   b. **Open-ended** Write an equation for a parabola whose vertex is $(3, 4)$, that opens down, and that is wider than the parabola in part (a).

   c. **Writing** Is the parabola in part (b) a translation of the parabola in part (a)? Explain.

Match each function with its graph.

8. $y = -0.25(x + 3)^2$

9. $y = -0.25x^2 - 3$

10. $y = -0.25(x - 3)^2$

11. $y = 0.25x^2 - 3$

A.

B.

C.

D.

Solve by graphing.   4-3

12. $-(x - 4)^2 = 0$ **13.** $2x^2 - 3 = 1$ **14.** $0.2(x + 1)^2 = 4$

Solve by undoing.

15. $5x^2 - 10 = 20$ **16.** $2(x + 5)^2 - 228 = 222$ **17.** $3(x - 2)^2 - 11 = 10$

Factor.   4-4

18. $2x^2 - 3x - 20$ **19.** $4n^2 - 81$ **20.** $16x^2 - 24x + 9$

21. Solve $9x^2 - 15x + 6 = 0$ by factoring.

Solve using the quadratic formula.   4-5

22. $3x^2 + 9x + 10 = 6$ **23.** $-2x^2 = 3x - 5$ **24.** $3(x - 2)^2 = 8$

Use the discriminant to tell whether each equation has *one solution*, *two solutions*, or *no solutions* in the set of real numbers.   4-6

25. $x^2 - 6x = -9$ **26.** $5x^2 + 3 = -9x$ **27.** $4(x + 0.5)^2 - 20 = -21$

Simplify.

28. $4i(3 - 6i)$ **29.** $(8 - 4i) - 6(2 + 9i)$ **30.** $(5 + 7i)(7 - 3i)$

Find all real and complex solutions.

31. $5 - 6x = -6x^2$

32. $0.25x^2 + 3x = -1$

33. $4x^2 + x + 3 = 0$

Solve each system by substitution.

4-7

34. $y = x^2 - 6x + 12$
$y = x^2 + 3$

35. $y = 3x^2 - 5x + 1$
$y = 2x^2 + x + 1$

Solve each system by graphing.

36. $y = -2x^2$
$y = 2x^2 - 3$

37. $y = -0.2x^2 - x + 3$
$y = 0.25x^2$

38. **Self-evaluation** Make a list of the different methods for solving quadratic equations. Which do you think are easier to use? Why?

39. **Group Activity** Work in a group of three students. For each equation in parts (a)–(d), one student should try to solve by factoring, one student should solve by using the quadratic formula, and one student should solve by graphing. Each student should use each method at least once.

a. Solve $3x^2 - 2x - 8 = 0$.

b. Find the x-intercepts of $y = 8x^2 - 14x + 3$.

c. Find the x-intercepts of $y = 2x^2 - 15x + 4$.

d. A pitcher throws a warm-up pitch in a softball game. The path of the ball is modeled by the equation $h = -16t^2 + 12t + 4$ where h represents the height of the ball after t seconds. How long will it take for the ball to hit the catcher's mitt at ground level?

e. For each equation in parts (a)–(d), discuss which solution method you think works best. Give a reason why. Can you decide which method to use by looking at the equation?

IDEAS AND (FORMULAS) $= x^2$

ALGEBRA $(x + = \cdot \cdot \cdot) x^2$

➤ The standard form of the equation for a parabola is $y = ax^2 + bx + c, a \neq 0$. *(p. 187)*

➤ When a is negative, the parabola opens down and has a maximum. When a is positive, the parabola opens up and has a minimum. *(p. 188)*

➤ The formula for the line of symmetry of a parabola is $x = -\dfrac{b}{2a}$. *(p. 188)*

➤ You can solve a quadratic equation by undoing the squaring. *(p. 200)*

➤ You can solve a quadratic equation by graphing the related function and finding the x-intercepts of the graph. *(p. 201)*

➤ You can factor the difference of two squares. *(p. 208)*

$$a^2 - b^2 = (a + b)(a - b)$$

➤ You can factor a perfect square trinomial. *(p. 208)*

$$a^2 + 2ab + b^2 = (a + b)^2 \qquad a^2 - 2ab + b^2 = (a - b)^2$$

➤ You can use the quadratic formula $x = -\dfrac{b}{2a} \pm \dfrac{\sqrt{b^2 - 4ac}}{2a}$ to solve an equation of the form $0 = ax^2 + bx + c$, when $a \neq 0$. *(p. 215)*

➤ The discriminant of a quadratic equation of the form $0 = ax^2 + bx + c$ is $b^2 - 4ac$, when $a \neq 0$. If the discriminant is *positive,* the equation has two real-number solutions. If the discriminant is *zero,* the equation has one real-number solution. If the discriminant is *negative,* the equation has no real-number solutions but has two complex solutions. *(pp. 222, 224)*

➤ Complex numbers can be added, subtracted, and multiplied like binomials. *(p. 226)*

➤ You can solve a system of quadratic equations by substitution. *(p. 230)*

➤ You can solve a system of quadratic equations by graphing them and finding their point(s) of intersection, if any. *(p. 231)*

GEOMETRY

➤ The graphs of parabolas in the form $y = a(x + b)^2 + c$ follow these patterns.

As a gets closer to 0, the parabola gets wider. *(p. 193)*

When b is positive, the graph of $y = ax^2$ is translated b units to the left. When b is negative, the graph is translated b units to the right. *(p. 194)*

When c is positive, the graph $y = ax^2$ is translated c units up. When c is negative, the graph is translated c units down. *(p. 194)*

·········· Key Terms

- **parabola** (p. 187)
- **vertex** (p. 188)
- **y-intercept** (p. 189)
- **monomial** (p. 206)
- **quadratic formula** (p. 215)
- **complex number** (p. 225)
- **quadratic system** (p. 231)

- **quadratic function** (p. 187)
- **maximum** (p. 188)
- **x-intercept** (p. 189)
- **trinomial** (p. 206)
- **discriminant** (p. 222)
- **real number** (p. 225)

- **standard form** (pp. 187, 201)
- **minimum** (p. 188)
- **quadratic equation** (p. 201)
- **zero-product property** (p. 209)
- **imaginary unit** (p. 225)
- **pure imaginary number** (p. 225)

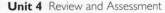

5

Coordinate Geometry and Quadrilaterals

It's only a game, or is it? Many of today's games originally had a serious purpose. Some, like tug of war and hopscotch, were rituals for controlling the weather and other powerful natural forces. Others, such as chess, darts, and shuttlecock, were used to train young people in mental and physical skills.

computers

As a teenager in Moscow in the early 1970s, **Aleksei Pajitnov** played puzzle games to keep busy when he broke his leg. His interest in games continued while he studied applied mathematics and then worked as a programmer at a computer institute. In 1985, in his spare time, Aleksei Pajitnov invented the popular computer game shown above.

LEVEL 2

SCORE 002289 LINES 011

HIGH SCORE 005047

8 8 5 47

6 11 13 4 7 5 9 55

START

TANGRAM (China) Use seven basic pieces to make designs. ④

ALQUERQUE, or el-quirkat (Middle East) Ancestor of checkers. ②

SNAKES AND LADDERS (India) ③ Slide up the ladders toward the 100th square or down the snakes' tails toward square 1.

CAT'S CRADLE (Inuit people of the Arctic) Make complex patterns from looped string. ①

Create a Board Game

Your project is to create a board game for four or more players.

Your group should design and build the board and four or more game pieces, and make up rules for your game. Be sure to tell the number of players, how to choose the order of the players, how moves are determined, and how to win the game.

Like the boards for Alquerque, Go, and Snakes and Ladders, your board should have a coordinate grid.

In the board or the rules you should apply at least three mathematical topics from this unit:

➤ properties of quadrilaterals

➤ the distance formula

➤ the midpoint formula

➤ slopes of perpendicular and parallel lines

➤ transformations

➤ coordinate geometry

◄ Go being played in Kyoto, Japan.

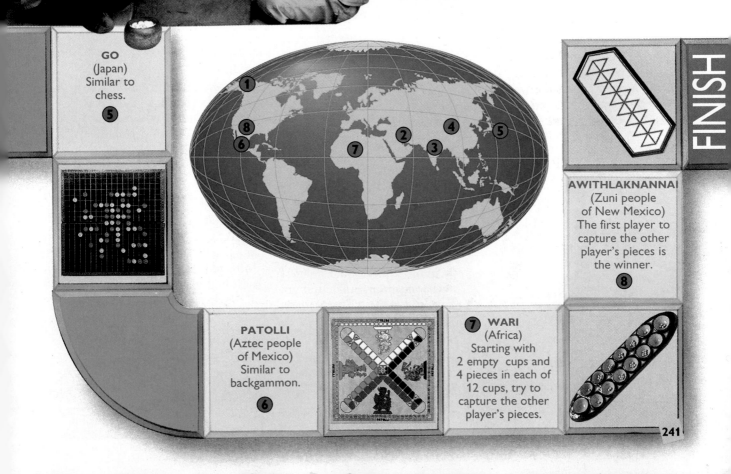

GO
(Japan)
Similar to chess.
5

AWITHLAKNANNAI
(Zuni people of New Mexico)
The first player to capture the other player's pieces is the winner.
8

FINISH

PATOLLI
(Aztec people of Mexico)
Similar to backgammon.
6

7 **WARI**
(Africa)
Starting with 2 empty cups and 4 pieces in each of 12 cups, try to capture the other player's pieces.

For this project you should work in a group of four students. Here are some ideas to help you get started.

☞ Bring in some board games and discuss their features with the members of your group. How are the games alike? How are they different?

☞ Decide what materials you will use to build the board and game pieces.

☞ Discuss ways in which players can decide who will go first, second, and so on.

☞ Your group may wish to talk about the balance between skill and chance in your game.

☞ Plan to meet later to discuss how to include three of this unit's mathematical topics in your game.

GAME PLAN

Size:

Shape:

Goal:

How to play:

Rules:

Can We Talk GAMES

Working on the Unit Project

Your work in Unit 5 will help you create your board game.

Related Exercises:

Section 5-1, Exercises 44–46
Section 5-2, Exercises 39–42
Section 5-3, Exercises 35, 36
Section 5-4, Exercises 42–44
Section 5-5, Exercises 34–40
Section 5-6, Exercises 24, 25

Alternative Projects p. 287

➤ Have you played any of the games pictured here, or any similar games? What do you like best about these or any other board games you have played?

➤ Are there any board games that are played by several generations of your family or in your community? If so, why do you think these games are still popular?

➤ Which of the board games and computer games that you have played use a coordinate grid? How is the grid used in each game?

➤ In what ways are board and computer games alike? How are they different?

➤ In which board and computer games that you have played is winning mainly a matter of luck? In which is ability the most important factor? In which are luck and ability about equally important? How do you know?

➤ What kinds of skills or information do you think you learn from board and computer games? Which skills or information do you think will be helpful in school? at work?

PLAY FAIR!

Quadrilaterals

THE **QUAD**
CLASSIFIED
SQUAD

Focus
Describe characteristics of
quadrilaterals and develop
classification skills.

EXPLORATION

How can quadrilaterals be classified?

• **Work in a group of four students.**

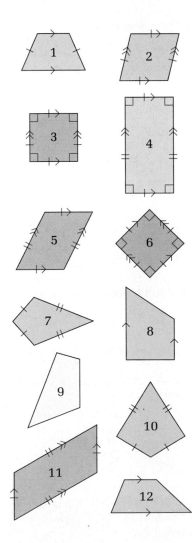

1 Your group will be investigating quadrilaterals. Each of you should make a copy of the table shown to record your results.

2 Look at the twelve numbered quadrilaterals. Which shapes have *two pairs of parallel sides*? Write the numbers of the shapes that fit this description in the appropriate column of the table. — Read "congruent."

Continued on next page.

(3) Repeat step 2 for each of these characteristics.

Remember: Congruent sides are equal in measure.

consecutive sides

- four congruent sides
- four right angles
- four congruent sides and four right angles
- two pairs of consecutive, congruent sides
- four sides

(4) Which shapes are in all six columns? Which are in the fewest columns?

(5) Place each of the words *square*, *quadrilateral*, *rectangle*, and *parallelogram* at the top of the column it best describes. Be sure that the members of your group agree. Use the glossary at the back of this book if necessary.

(6) Read the definitions below. Place each of the words *kite* and *rhombus* at the top of the column it best describes. Be sure that the members of your group agree.

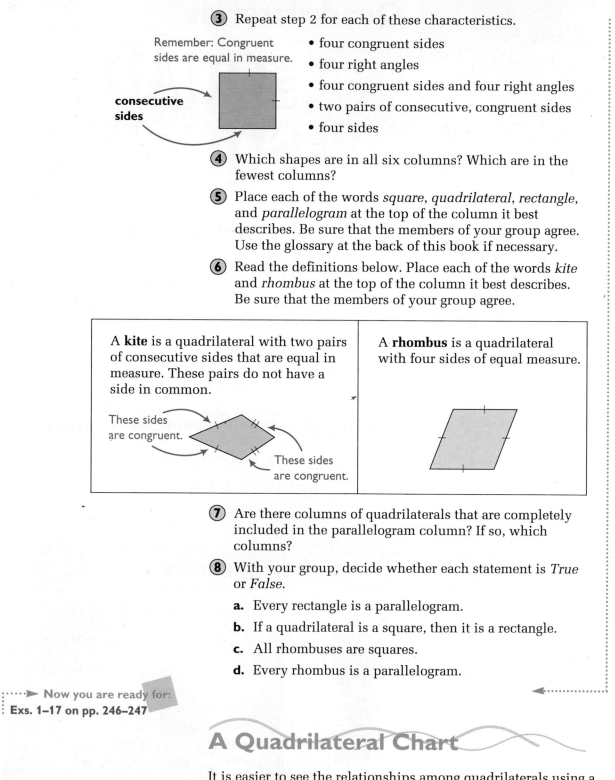

A **kite** is a quadrilateral with two pairs of consecutive sides that are equal in measure. These pairs do not have a side in common.

These sides are congruent.

These sides are congruent.

A **rhombus** is a quadrilateral with four sides of equal measure.

(7) Are there columns of quadrilaterals that are completely included in the parallelogram column? If so, which columns?

(8) With your group, decide whether each statement is *True* or *False*.

    a. Every rectangle is a parallelogram.

    b. If a quadrilateral is a square, then it is a rectangle.

    c. All rhombuses are squares.

    d. Every rhombus is a parallelogram.

▶ Now you are ready for:
Exs. 1–17 on pp. 246–247

A Quadrilateral Chart

It is easier to see the relationships among quadrilaterals using a chart. Each quadrilateral belongs to the family of quadrilaterals linked to it above and has its characteristics.

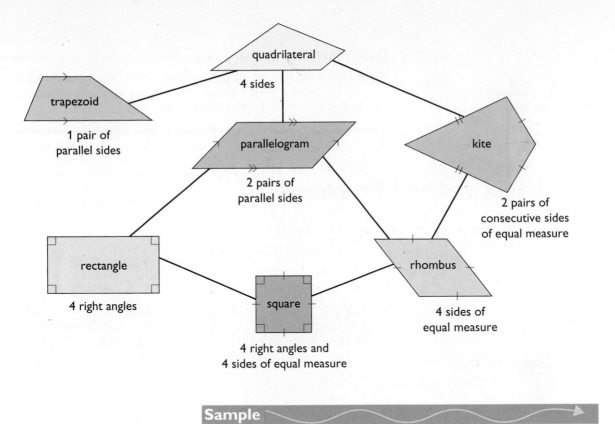

Complete each sentence so that it is a true statement. Be as specific as possible. Use the quadrilateral chart to explain your choice.

a. All rectangles are also __?__.

b. Every rhombus is also a __?__ and a __?__.

Sample Response

a. All rectangles are **parallelograms**. In the chart parallelograms and quadrilaterals are linked to rectangles from above. Parallelograms are more specific.

b. Every rhombus is also a **kite** and a **parallelogram**. In the chart kites, parallelograms, and quadrilaterals are linked to rhombuses from above. Kites and parallelograms are more specific.

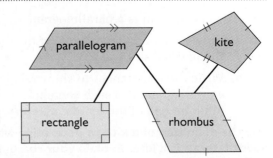

Talk it Over

1. After looking at the quadrilateral chart, Tyler decided that all parallelograms are rectangles. Explain the error he made in using the chart.

2. Do you think that all squares are parallelograms? Why or why not?

····▶ **Now you are ready for:**
: Exs. 18–46 on pp. 248–250

Look Back ◂

What characteristic do all the figures in the quadrilateral chart have in common? Which quadrilaterals are special cases of a parallelogram? Which are special cases of a kite?

····································

5-1 Exercises and Problems

1. Based on the results of the Exploration, choose the letter of the Venn diagram that shows the correct relationship between squares, rectangles, and parallelograms.

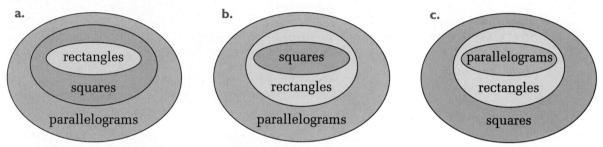

a.

rectangles

squares

parallelograms

b.

squares

rectangles

parallelograms

c.

parallelograms

rectangles

squares

2. **Reading** Use the glossary at the back of this book to find the definitions of *square*, *rectangle*, and *parallelogram*. For each column in your table from the Exploration, tell whether the quadrilaterals in the column fit the definition.

For Exercises 3–7, tell whether each statement is *True* or *False*.

3. All squares are rectangles.

4. Every rectangle is a square.

5. Some parallelograms are rectangles.

6. All parallelograms are quadrilaterals.

7. If a quadrilateral is a parallelogram, then it is a rectangle.

8. **a.** Draw a Venn diagram to show the relationship between kites, rhombuses, and squares.

   b. Write three sentences to show relationships between pairs of shapes in your diagram. For each sentence, use a different pair of shapes and a different one of the words *all*, *every*, and *if-then*.

Use the definition of a kite to determine whether each of these quadrilaterals is a kite. Explain your reasoning.

9.
10 ft
7 ft   7 ft
10 ft

10.
3 m   3 m
2 m   2 m

11.
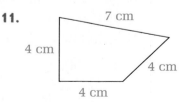
7 cm
4 cm
4 cm
4 cm

12. What characteristic(s) do rhombuses have that not all kites have?

In Thornton Wilder's play, *Our Town,* Rebecca Gibb tells her older brother, George, about a letter received by her friend.

REBECCA: I never told you about that letter Jane Crofut got from her minister when she was sick. He wrote Jane a letter and on the envelope the address was like this: It said: Jane Crofut; The Crofut Farm; Grover's Corners; Sutton County; New Hampshire; United States of America.

GEORGE: What's funny about that?

REBECCA: But listen, it's not finished: the United States of America; Continent of North America; Western Hemisphere; the Earth; the Solar System; the Universe; ... —that's what it said on the envelope.

GEORGE: What do you know!

REBECCA: And the postman brought it just the same.

13. According to the letter, if you live in Grover's Corners then you live in New Hampshire. Write three other true statements using the address on Jane Crofut's letter.

14. Complete the diagram at the right to describe the items included in the address.

15. How would someone address a letter to you using the style on Jane Crofut's letter?

16. **a.** Address a letter to someone who lives in the city of Puebla using the style on Jane Crofut's letter.

    b. Write at least two true statements using the Puebla address.

17. **a.** Address a letter to someone in the country of Morocco using the style on Jane Crofut's letter.

    b. Write at least two true statements using the Morocco address.

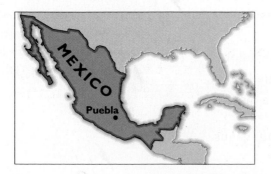

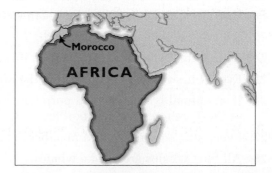

A system of classifying living things by phylum, class, order, family, genus, and species was developed by Carolus Linnaeus in 1758. This chart shows a portion of one of the eleven phyla, the Chordates. Mammals are one of seven classes of Chordates.

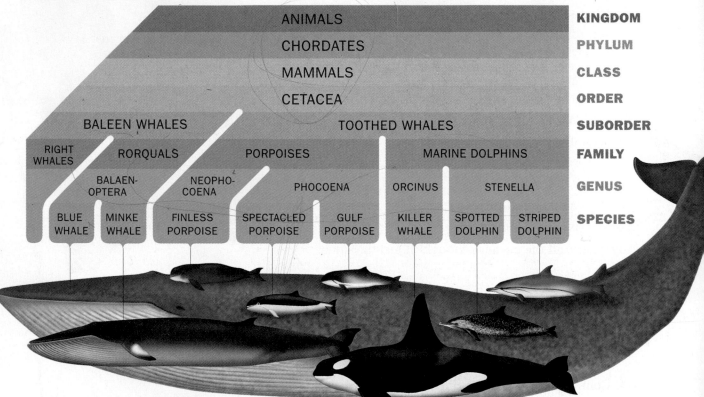

Use the chart for Exercises 18–28.

18. Which species are part of the Porpoise family?

19. Name all the groups that a spotted dolphin belongs to.

20. How is a killer whale like a minke whale?

21. In *Moby Dick*, the author uses the word *Cetacea* to refer to the whale. Why do you think he chose this word?

22. According to the chart, how are members of the Rorqual family different from members of the Porpoise family?

For Exercises 23–28, tell whether each statement is *True or False*.

23. All Baleen whales are Mammals.

24. If an animal is a killer whale, then it is a Marine dolphin.

25. Every blue whale is a member of the Right whale family.

26. If an animal is a spectacled porpoise, then it is a member of the Toothed whales suborder.

27. Every striped dolphin is a member of the *Orcinus* genus.

28. All blue whales are minke whales.

> **BY THE WAY...**
>
> Blue whales, the largest animals on Earth, have *baleen* plates instead of teeth. The plates are made out of the same type of material as human fingernails. In a single day, a blue whale is likely to eat up to eight TONS of krill!

Complete each sentence so that it is a true statement. Be as specific as possible. Use the quadrilateral chart to explain your choice.

29. Every kite is also a _?_.

30. All _?_ are also rhombuses.

31. Every square is also a _?_ and a _?_.

32. All parallelograms are also _?_.

33. If a quadrilateral is a rectangle, then it is also a _?_.

34. When Carly looked in the glossary of a friend's math book, she found this definition.

When Silas looked in another math book, he found this definition.

> *trapezoid:* A quadrilateral with at least one pair of parallel sides.

> **trapezoid:** A quadrilateral with exactly one pair of parallel sides.

a. How are the definitions different?

b. Which of these quadrilaterals are trapezoids if you use the definition Carly found? if you use the definition Silas found?

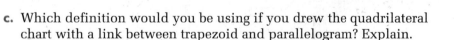

c. Which definition would you be using if you drew the quadrilateral chart with a link between trapezoid and parallelogram? Explain.

35. a. Use the formula $A = \frac{1}{2}h(b_1 + b_2)$ to find the area of trapezoid *ABCD*.

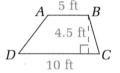

b. Use the formula $A = \frac{1}{2}h(b_1 + b_2)$ to find the area of parallelogram *JKLM*. Do you get the same area if you use $A = bh$?

c. For which types of quadrilaterals can you use the formula $A = \frac{1}{2}h(b_1 + b_2)$ to find the area?

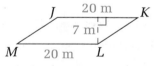

Ongoing **ASSESSMENT**

36. Group Activity Work with at least one other student.

a. Draw and cut out large copies of the quadrilaterals shown. Use paper folding to find the lines of symmetry, if any, for each shape. Draw the lines of symmetry on a copy of the quadrilateral chart.
   • kite   • rhombus   • square   • rectangle   • parallelogram

b. Which figure has no line of symmetry?

c. How do the lines of symmetry for a rhombus compare with the lines of symmetry for a kite?

d. Find the lines of symmetry for a square. How many are there? How are they related to the lines of symmetry for other quadrilaterals?

e. Which figure in the quadrilateral chart has the most lines of symmetry?

Solve each system. *(Section 4-7)*

37. $y = -0.5x^2 + 2$
$y = 0.8x^2 - 4$

38. $y = 0.25x^2 + 2$
$y = -x^2 + 1$

39. $y = x^2 - 3x + 2$
$y = x^2 + 3x + 2$

For Exercises 40–42, write the equation of the line that is perpendicular to each line and goes through the given point. *(Section 3-3)*

40. $y = -\frac{1}{2}x + 6$; $(1, -2)$

41. $y = 5$; $(-2, 5)$

42. $x = -3$; $(-3, 4)$

43. Use the Pythagorean theorem to find the length of the hypotenuse of a right triangle with legs of 7 cm and 24 cm. *(Toolbox Skill 31)*

Working on the Unit Project

As you complete Exercises 44–46, think about how you might use quadrilaterals and their properties in the game you design.

The game of *Alquerque* starts with the pieces arranged on the game board as shown.

① A player moves to any adjacent empty space.

② If the space behind your opponent's piece is empty, your piece may jump over your opponent's piece and into the space. You then remove your opponent's piece.

③ Players are allowed to move in any direction and to make multiple jumps in one turn.

④ The first player to capture all the opponent's pieces wins.

Use the Alquerque board.

44. Do any of the lines form a rhombus that is not a square? If so, draw the rhombus on a copy of the board. If not, explain why not.

45. Some of the lines form a trapezoid. Find one and draw the trapezoid on a copy of the board.

46. Describe the game board to someone who cannot see it.

Pakistan: An Alquerque game in progress.

5-2 The Distance Formula and Quadrilaterals

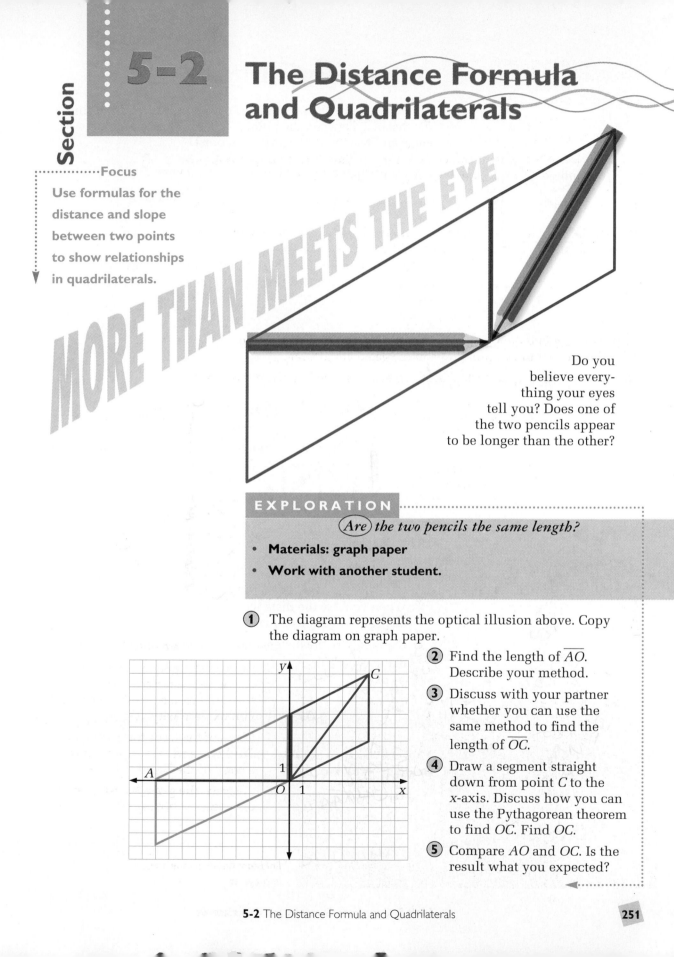

MORE THAN MEETS THE EYE

Do you believe everything your eyes tell you? Does one of the two pencils appear to be longer than the other?

EXPLORATION

(Are) *the two pencils the same length?*

- **Materials: graph paper**
- **Work with another student.**

① The diagram represents the optical illusion above. Copy the diagram on graph paper.

② Find the length of $\overline{AO}$. Describe your method.

③ Discuss with your partner whether you can use the same method to find the length of $\overline{OC}$.

④ Draw a segment straight down from point C to the x-axis. Discuss how you can use the Pythagorean theorem to find OC. Find OC.

⑤ Compare AO and OC. Is the result what you expected?

A Formula for Distance

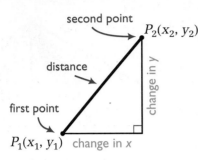

second point

$P_2(x_2, y_2)$

distance

first point

$P_1(x_1, y_1)$ change in x

change in y

When you know the coordinates of two points, you can find the distance between the points. You can draw a right triangle and use the Pythagorean theorem.

$$(\text{distance})^2 = (\text{change in } x)^2 + (\text{change in } y)^2$$

$$\text{distance} = \sqrt{(\text{change in } x)^2 + (\text{change in } y)^2}$$

Distance is positive. Use the positive square root.

To get a general formula, you can write the change in x and the change in y as the differences of the coordinates of the two points.

THE DISTANCE FORMULA

This is the distance d between the points $P_1(x_1, y_1)$ and $P_2(x_2, y_2)$:

$$\textbf{distance} = \sqrt{(\textbf{change in x})^2 + (\textbf{change in y})^2}$$

$$\boldsymbol{d = \sqrt{(x_2 - x_1)^2 + (y_2 - y_1)^2}}$$

Talk it Over

1. Suppose you use the distance formula to find OC in the Exploration. What are the values of x_1, x_2, y_1, and y_2?

2. When you use the distance formula, does it matter if the change in x or the change in y is negative? Explain.

3. Explain why the distance formula can also be written as distance $= \sqrt{(x_1 - x_2)^2 + (y_1 - y_2)^2}$.

Sample 1

Find the distance between the points (−4, 6) and (0, 3).

(−4, 6)

(0, 3)

1

O 1 x

Unit 5 Coordinate Geometry and Quadrilaterals

distance $= \sqrt{(x_2 - x_1)^2 + (y_2 - y_1)^2}$ ⟵ Use the distance formula.

$= \sqrt{(0 - (-4))^2 + (3 - 6)^2}$ ⟵ Substitute **(−4, 6)** for **(x_1, y_1)** and **(0, 3)** for **(x_2, y_2)**.

$= \sqrt{4^2 + (-3)^2}$

$= \sqrt{16 + 9}$

$= \sqrt{25}$

$= 5$

The distance between the two points is 5 units.

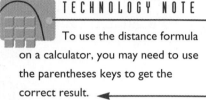

TECHNOLOGY NOTE

To use the distance formula on a calculator, you may need to use the parentheses keys to get the correct result. ◀

Talk it Over

4. Suppose two points lie on a horizontal line. What is the change in y?

5. What is an easy way to find the distance between two points that lie on a vertical line?

Use the diagram.

6. Find JK.   7. Find LM.

······▶ **Now you are ready for:**
Exs. 1–16 on pp. 255–256

Exploring Quadrilaterals on the Coordinate Plane

The definitions of some types of quadrilaterals involve parallel sides or sides of equal measure. The distance formula and the relationship between the slopes of parallel lines can help you identify a specific type of quadrilateral. Remember that two different lines with the same slope are parallel.

Examples of Parallel Lines

same positive slope   same negative slope   slope = 0   undefined slope

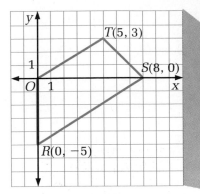

Writing Phelton and Odessa want to include a special design on each family member's Kwanzaa outfit. Phelton made a pattern for the design on graph paper.

For the design to fit together properly, the shape needs to be a trapezoid.

Phelton thinks that sides $\overline{OT}$ and $\overline{RS}$ are parallel, but Odessa does not. Who do you think is correct? Why?

Sample Response

I think Odessa is right. The slopes of the two sides are not equal, so $\overline{OT}$ is not parallel to $\overline{RS}$.

slope of $\overline{OT} = \frac{3-0}{5-0} = \frac{3}{5} = 0.6$

slope of $\overline{RS} = \frac{0-(-5)}{8-0} = \frac{5}{8} = 0.625$

The other pair of opposite sides is not parallel either. Therefore ORST is not a trapezoid.

Perpendicular lines can also help you identify quadrilaterals. Remember that when the slope of a line is m, the slope of a perpendicular line is $-\frac{1}{m}$.

Talk it Over

8. Show that a quadrilateral with vertices $A(-3, 4)$, $B(3, 1)$, $C(6, -5)$, and $D(0, -2)$ is a rhombus.

9. How can you verify that a quadrilateral is a rectangle?

Look Back

How can you remember the distance formula? If you forget it, how can you find the distance between two points?

Now you are ready for:
Exs. 17–42 on pp. 256–258

1. **Open-ended** The picture of the two pencils at the beginning of the section is called an *optical illusion.* Describe another optical illusion you have seen. Why do you suppose your eyes play tricks on you?

For Exercises 2–4, study each optical illusion to answer the question.

2. Are the columns parallel?

3. Which of the two lines continues to the single line?

4. Are the diagonal lines parallel?

5. **Reading** How is the distance formula related to the Pythagorean theorem?

Find the distance between each pair of points.

6. (5, 8) and (10, 4)

7. (−6, 2) and (1, −4)

8. (2, 8) and (−7, 8)

Find each distance.

9. *LM*

10. *GJ*

11. *JL*

12. *GH*

13. *JK*

14. *GM*

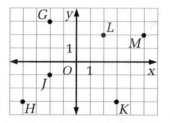

Aviation The length of runway needed for a plane to land safely depends on the plane's weight, the airport's elevation, and the temperature.

15. **a.** The plan for an airport runway system is shown. Estimate the length of each runway: *AB, CD, EF, GH,* and *CJ.*

   b. Suppose a jet needs about 7500 ft to land. Which runways can it land on?

   c. Repeat part (b) for a small plane that needs about 2150 ft to land.

   d. Repeat part (b) for a space shuttle that needs an average of about 9925 ft to land.

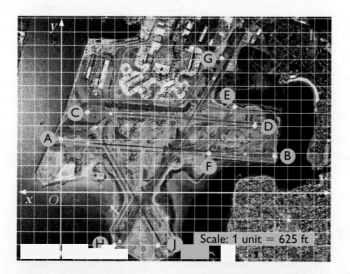

Scale: 1 unit = 625 ft

> **BY THE WAY...**
>
> Planes need more room to take off and land in hot weather and at high elevations. It is not uncommon for a plane in Arizona to unload cargo so that it will have enough runway space to take off.

16. In competitive swimming, when the starter fires a shot, the timers start their watches and the swimmers dive into the water. The time it takes for the sound of the shot to travel to the swimmers and timers can give some swimmers an advantage. To make the contest fair, a correction is made to each swimmer's finishing time.

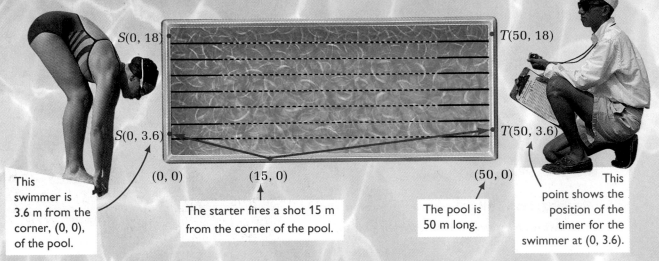

$S(0, 18)$ $T(50, 18)$

$S(0, 3.6)$ $T(50, 3.6)$

$(0, 0)$ $(15, 0)$ $(50, 0)$

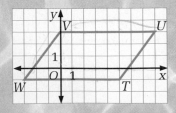

This swimmer is 3.6 m from the corner, $(0, 0)$, of the pool.

The starter fires a shot 15 m from the corner of the pool.

The pool is 50 m long.

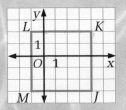

This point shows the position of the timer for the swimmer at $(0, 3.6)$.

For parts (a)–(e), use the diagram above. Assume that sound travels at 346 m/s. Round your answers to the nearest thousandth of a second.

a. Calculate the distance from the starter to the swimmer at $S(0, 3.6)$. Find the time it takes for sound to travel from the starter to the swimmer.

b. Calculate the distance from the starter to the timer at $T(50, 3.6)$. Find the time it takes for sound to travel from the starter to the timer.

c. The positive difference between the two times you found in parts (a) and (b) is the swimmer's advantage. What is this swimmer's advantage?

d. What is the advantage for the swimmer at $(0, 18)$?

e. **Writing** Explain how you think the judges of a swimming competition should use the advantages in order to determine the winner.

> **BY THE WAY...**
>
> At some swimming competitions, horns are placed under each person's starting point so that the signal reaches every swimmer at the same time. Individual electronic timers begin when the horns sound and stop when a swimmer touches a sensor at the end of the pool.

For Exercises 17–19, use the distance formula and slope to show that the quadrilateral is the type specified.

17. Show that *TUVW* is a parallelogram.

18. Show that *EFGH* is a kite.

19. Show that *JKLM* is a square.

Suppose you have a quadrilateral. What do you have to know about its sides to show that it is the special quadrilateral described?

20. a parallelogram   **21.** a kite

22. a trapezoid   **23.** a square

24. Use quadrilateral *GSKP*.

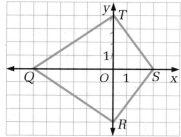

   a. Find the slope of $\overline{GS}$, $\overline{SK}$, $\overline{KP}$, and $\overline{PG}$.

   b. Show that *GSKP* is a trapezoid.

25. a. **Open-ended** Draw a rectangle on a coordinate plane. Give the coordinates of its vertices.

   b. Find the length of each diagonal of your rectangle.

   c. Repeat steps (a) and (b) using a different rectangle.

   d. Make a conjecture about the diagonals of any rectangle.

   e. In part (d), did you use *inductive reasoning* or *deductive reasoning*?

26. **Writing** Jennika thinks that quadrilateral *QRST* is a kite. Do you agree or disagree? Explain your reasoning.

27. Alan claims that quadrilateral *JKLM* is a rhombus. Its vertices are *J*(0, 0), *K*(7, 2), *L*(11, 8), and *M*(4, 6).

   a. Draw *JKLM* on graph paper and measure each side as best you can. Do your measurements indicate that *JKLM* is a rhombus?

   b. Use the distance formula to find the exact length of each of the sides. Do you think that *JKLM* is a rhombus? Why or why not?

   c. Show that *JKLM* is a parallelogram.

   d. **Writing** Look back at parts (a) and (b). Why do you suppose mathematicians prefer to verify information using formulas instead of measurements or drawings?

28. Use quadrilateral *OQRS*.

   a. Show that *OQRS* is a parallelogram.

   b. Show that the opposite sides of *OQRS* are equal in measure.

29. A quadrilateral has vertices *A*(0, 0), *B*(8, 0), *C*(7, 5), and *D*(3, 5).

   a. What type of quadrilateral is *ABCD*?

   b. Find the length of each side to the nearest tenth of a unit.

   c. Use the formula $A = \frac{1}{2}h(b_1 + b_2)$ to find the area of *ABCD*.

   d. Find the perimeter of *ABCD*.

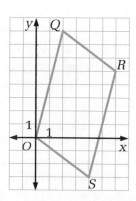

30. Group Activity Work with another student.

  a. Each of you should draw a figure on a coordinate plane that looks like a trapezoid, a parallelogram, a kite, or a rhombus. Try to make your figure an optical illusion. Make it appear to be something it is not.

  b. Label your figure with the coordinates of its vertices.

  c. Trade the figures with each other. Use the distance formula and the slope formula to decide whether the figure you have received is what it appears to be.

Review **PREVIEW**

Tell whether each statement is *True* or *False*. *(Section 5-1)*

31. All kites are parallelograms.

32. Every square is a kite.

For each function, describe how y changes when x is halved. *(Section 2-5)*

33. $y = 4x^2$

34. $y = \dfrac{-3}{x}$

35. $y = \dfrac{2}{5}x^3$

For Exercises 36–38, find the mean of the data points. *(Toolbox Skill 4)*

36. Winter temperatures (°F): 32, −5, 10, −3, 15, 28

37. Ice skating scores: 5.7, 5.9, 5.8, 5.4, 5.7

38. Test scores: 85, 75, 92, 83, 60, 98, 87

Working on the Unit Project

Exercises 39–42 use the *distance-formula game*.

In the distance-formula game, two dice are used to determine a point (x, y) in the coordinate plane. To start, roll the dice to determine the *target point*.

Have each player roll the dice in turn. Record the coordinates rolled. The player whose point is closest to the target point wins the round. The game ends when one player has won three rounds.

39. a. Group Activity Play the game with another student.

  b. List the materials you need to play this game. Describe when and how players use the distance formula.

  c. **Writing** Are the directions for the game clear? How could they be made better?

  d. **Writing** How can you make the directions for your game easy to read and understand?

40. List all the possible target points.

41. How many ways can the distance from a player's point be less than 2 units from the target point (4, 3)?

42. Can two players tie in a round of the game? If so, how could you break the tie?

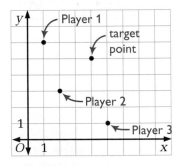

One die represents the y-coordinate…

…and the other represents the x-coordinate.

Focus
Use a formula to find the
midpoint of a segment.

Meet Me Halfway

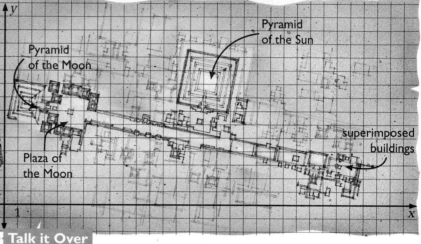

Pyramid of the Sun

Pyramid of the Moon

Plaza of the Moon

superimposed buildings

Talk it Over

1. At Teotihuácan, a Mesoamerican ceremonial center in Mexico, the halfway point along the street connecting the Pyramid of the Moon and the superimposed buildings is directly in front of the Pyramid of the Sun. Estimate the coordinates of the halfway point.

2. What x-coordinate is halfway between 3 and 25? Explain.

3. What y-coordinate is halfway between 7 and 3? Explain.

4. Based on your answers to questions 2 and 3, find more precise coordinates of the halfway point.

The point halfway between the endpoints of a segment is called the **midpoint.** You can find the coordinates of the midpoint of a segment by finding the mean of the x-coordinates and the mean of the y-coordinates.

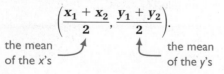

THE MIDPOINT FORMULA

The midpoint of a segment with endpoints (x_1, y_1) and (x_2, y_2) has coordinates

$$\left(\frac{x_1 + x_2}{2}, \frac{y_1 + y_2}{2}\right).$$

the mean of the x's   the mean of the y's

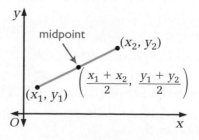

Find the coordinates of the midpoint of the segment whose endpoints are (9, −14) and (3, 4).

Sample Response

Let (x_1, y_1) be $(9, -14)$ and let (x_2, y_2) be $(3, 4)$.

The x-coordinate of the midpoint is $\dfrac{x_1 + x_2}{2} = \dfrac{9 + 3}{2} = 6$.

The y-coordinate of the midpoint is $\dfrac{y_1 + y_2}{2} = \dfrac{-14 + 4}{2} = -5$.

The coordinates of the midpoint are $(6, -5)$.

M is the midpoint of $\overline{AB}$.
Find the coordinates of B.   B is somewhere over here.

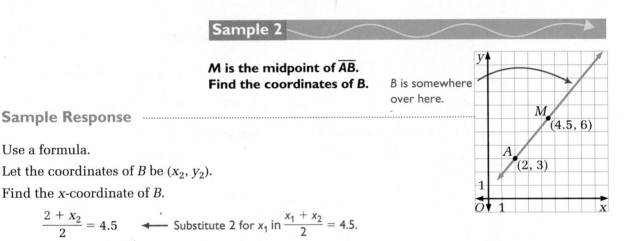

Sample Response

Use a formula.

Let the coordinates of B be (x_2, y_2).

Find the x-coordinate of B.

$\dfrac{2 + x_2}{2} = 4.5$ ⟵ Substitute 2 for x_1 in $\dfrac{x_1 + x_2}{2} = 4.5$.

$2 + x_2 = 9$ ⟵ Multiply both sides by 2.

$x_2 = 7$

Find the y-coordinate of B.

$\dfrac{3 + y_2}{2} = 6$ ⟵ Substitute 3 for y_1 in $\dfrac{y_1 + y_2}{2} = 6$.

$3 + y_2 = 12$ ⟵ Multiply both sides by 2.

$y_2 = 9$

The coordinates of B are $(7, 9)$.

Look Back ⟵

State the distance formula and the midpoint formula in words. How is each formula used?

1. **Reading** Compare the method you used in *Talk it Over* questions 2 and 3 on page 259 to using the midpoint formula. How are they alike? How are they different?

For each graph, find the midpoint of $\overline{AB}$.

2.

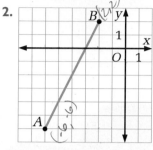

3.

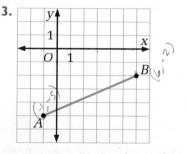

4.

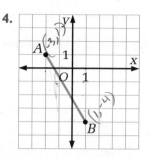

Find the coordinates of the midpoint of each segment whose endpoints are given.

5. $(0, 6)$ and $(-2, 4)$

6. $(-3, 8)$ and $(5, -2)$

7. $(-6, 7)$ and $(1, 3)$

8. $\left(\dfrac{1}{2}, -\dfrac{3}{4}\right)$ and $(-4, 2)$

9. $(4.5, 0.15)$ and $(-1.2, 3.8)$

10. $\left(\dfrac{3}{8}, -\dfrac{2}{3}\right)$ and $\left(\dfrac{1}{4}, -\dfrac{5}{6}\right)$

For Exercises 11–13, M is the midpoint of $\overline{CD}$. Find the coordinates of D.

11. $C(4, -2)$; $M(4, 4)$

12. $C(1, -3)$; $M(-5, 1)$

13. $C(-2, -8)$; $M(2, -3)$

14. Nayati and Blaire each used a formula to show that M is the midpoint of $\overline{FG}$. Here is each person's method.

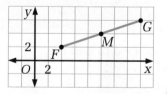

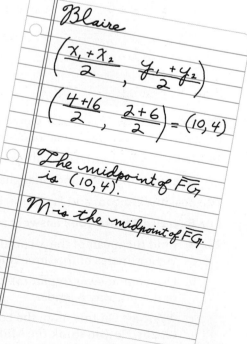

Nayati

$$d = \sqrt{(x_2 - x_1)^2 + (y_2 - y_1)^2}$$

FM $\quad d = \sqrt{6^2 + 2^2} = \sqrt{40}$
MG $\quad d = \sqrt{6^2 + 2^2} = \sqrt{40}$

Since the distance from F to M equals the distance from M to G, M is the midpoint of $\overline{FG}$.

Blaire

$$\left(\frac{x_1 + x_2}{2}, \frac{y_1 + y_2}{2}\right)$$

$$\left(\frac{4 + 16}{2}, \frac{2 + 6}{2}\right) = (10, 4)$$

The midpoint of $\overline{FG}$ is $(10, 4)$.

M is the midpoint of $\overline{FG}$.

a. Explain Nayati's method. Did he show that M is the midpoint of $\overline{FG}$?

b. Explain Blaire's method. Did she show that M is the midpoint of $\overline{FG}$?

c. Which method do you prefer? Why?

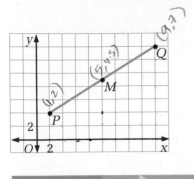

15. Show that $\overline{PQ}$ is twice as long as $\overline{PM}$.

16. **Writing** Explain how finding the midpoint of a segment is like finding the mean of the endpoints.

17. The midpoint formula uses means to divide a segment into two equal parts. Describe a method to divide a segment into three equal parts.

connection to **HISTORY**

The *Midway Islands* have that name because ships used the islands as a halfway stopping point between North America and Asia.

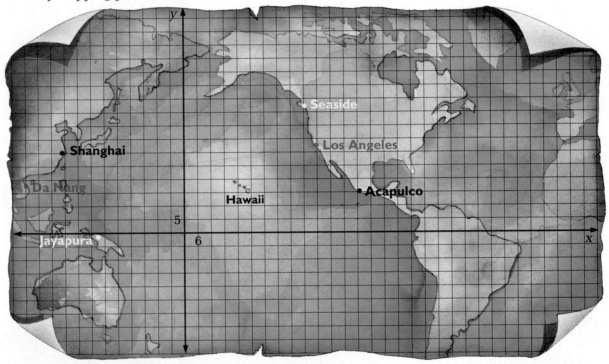

For Exercises 18–20, use the coordinate grid to find the midpoint between each pair of cities.

18. Los Angeles, California, and Da Nang, Vietnam

19. Acapulco, Mexico, and Shanghai, China

20. Seaside, Oregon, and Jayapura, New Guinea

For Exercise 21, use your answers to Exercises 18–20.

21. **a.** Find the mean of the *x*-coordinates and the mean of the *y*-coordinates of the three midpoints.

   b. Use your answer to part (a) to estimate the coordinates of the Midway Islands.

   c. **Writing** On this map, the coordinates of the Midway Islands are (3, 28). Do you think the Midway Islands are "midway" between North American and Asian cities? Explain your reasoning.

BY THE WAY...

The Midway Islands have a total area of only two square miles. Though tiny, these islands were the site of one of the first major United States naval victories in World War II.

262   **Unit 5** Coordinate Geometry and Quadrilaterals

22. Leann found the midpoint of $\overline{AB}$. Then she found the midpoints of $\overline{AC}$ and $\overline{AD}$. Her results are shown.

a. Describe the pattern.

b. What are the next two numbers in the sequence $\frac{1}{2}, \frac{1}{4}, \frac{1}{8}, \ldots$?

A E D   C   B
● ● ●   ●   ●
0 $\frac{1}{8}$ $\frac{1}{4}$ $\frac{1}{2}$ 1

c. Is the sequence of midpoints *continuous* or *discrete*?

d. Will the sequence ever end? Explain.

e. In the fifth century B.C., the Greek mathematician Zeno presented a version of this puzzle that is described below. How does his reasoning relate to Leann's sequence?

f. Do you agree with Zeno's reasoning? Why or why not?

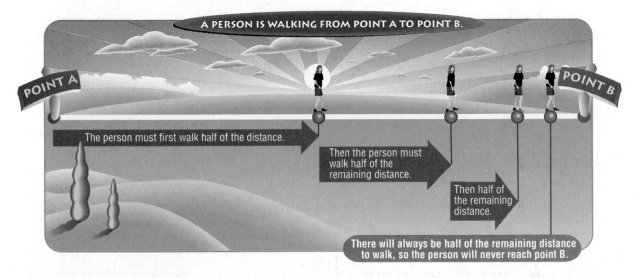

A PERSON IS WALKING FROM POINT A TO POINT B.

POINT A   POINT B

The person must first walk half of the distance.

Then the person must walk half of the remaining distance.

Then half of the remaining distance.

There will always be half of the remaining distance to walk, so the person will never reach point B.

23. a. Show that *LMNO* is a rhombus.

b. Are the diagonals $\overline{LN}$ and $\overline{MO}$ perpendicular to each other? Verify your answer.

c. What is the midpoint of $\overline{LN}$? What is the midpoint of $\overline{MO}$? How do they compare?

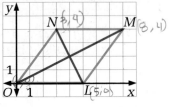

$N(3, 4)$ $M(8, 4)$
$O(0, 0)$ $L(5, 0)$

Ongoing ASSESSMENT

24. Group Activity Work with another student.

a. *P*, *Q*, and *R* are the midpoints of the three sides of $\triangle ABC$. Find the coordinates of *P*, *Q*, and *R*.

b. Show that these lines are parallel: $\overline{QP}$ and $\overline{AB}$, $\overline{RQ}$ and $\overline{BC}$, $\overline{RP}$ and $\overline{AC}$.

c. Find the perimeter of $\triangle PQR$. How does it compare to the perimeter of $\triangle ABC$?

d. How do you think the areas of $\triangle PQR$ and $\triangle ABC$ compare?

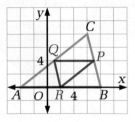

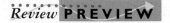

Find the distance between each pair of points. *(Section 5-2)*

25. (5, 10) and (8, 4)   **26.** (−7, 6) and (1, −2)   **27.** (−1, −9) and (4, 3)

Solve. *(Section 4-3)*

28. $3x^2 + 8 = 56$ **29.** $(x - 5)^2 + 6 = 66$ **30.** $-5(x + 2)^2 + 16 = -59$

Tell if the image is a *translation, rotation, dilation,* or *reflection* of the original figure and name the coordinates of the image. *(Toolbox Skills 33–36)*

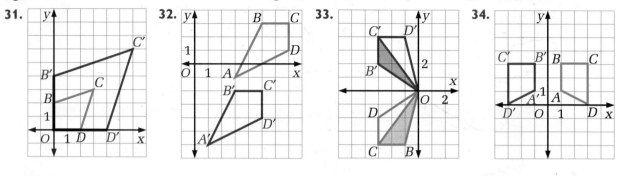

31.   **32.**   **33.**   **34.**

 Working on the Unit Project

People in China developed the puzzle game *tangram* in about 1800. To complete a tangram puzzle, a person must use all seven pieces to form a design. None of the pieces, known as *tans*, may overlap.

35. Make a sketch that shows how to arrange the tans to form one of designs A through I.

36. a. **Writing** Describe how to use midpoints to create a set of tangram pieces from a square.

b. **Writing** Describe how you could use the midpoint formula in the design or play of your game.

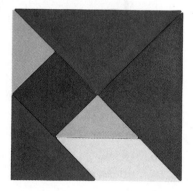

Example

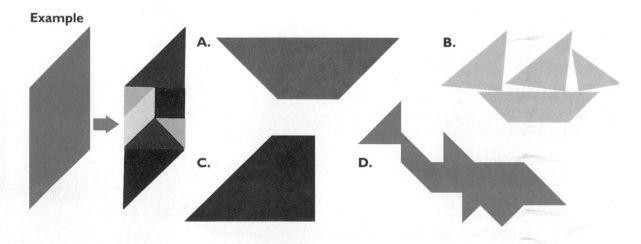

A.

B.

C.

D.

1. **Writing** What properties do you need to show before you can say that a quadrilateral is a parallelogram? a rectangle? a rhombus? a square? What algebra skills do you use? **5-1**

2. Quadrilateral *ABCD* has these vertices: **5-2**

   $A(1, 2)$, $B(12, 4)$, $C(15, -1)$, and $D(4, -3)$

   a. Find the slope of each side of quadrilateral *ABCD*.

   b. What type of quadrilateral is *ABCD*? Why can you make this conclusion?

3. Quadrilateral *WXYZ* has these vertices:

   $W(-4, -1)$, $X(-3, 4)$, $Y(2, 3)$, and $Z(1, -2)$

   a. Find the slope of each side of quadrilateral *WXYZ*.

   b. Find the length of each side of quadrilateral *WXYZ*.

   c. Based on your answers to parts (a) and (b), what type of quadrilateral is *WXYZ*?

For each pair of points A and B:

a. Find the distance between the points.

b. Find the coordinates of the midpoint of $\overline{AB}$. **5-3**

4. $A(5, -2)$ and $B(-7, 0)$
5. $A(3, 0)$ and $B(-4, 12)$
6. $A(-8, -5)$ and $B(12, -6)$
7. $A(3, -1)$ and $B(6, -5)$

For Exercises 8–11, M is the midpoint of $\overline{CD}$. Find the coordinates of D.

8. $C(4, 3)$; $M(-2, 0)$
9. $C(-6, 3)$; $M(-1, 2)$
10. $C(-1, 5)$; $M(3, -2)$
11. $C(3, -2)$; $M\left(\frac{1}{2}, 3\right)$

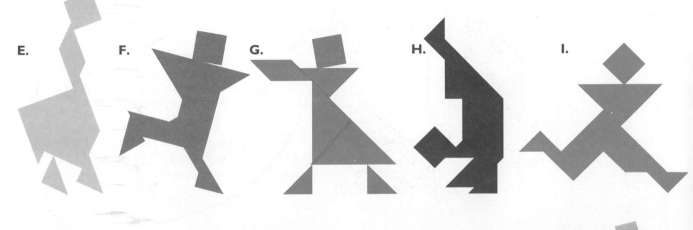

E.   F.   G.   H.   I.

5-4

Coordinates and Transformations

Focus

Transform geometric figures and learn how transformations affect their properties.

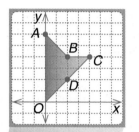

EXPLORATION

How are the coordinates of an image different after a transformation?

- **Work with another student.**

① Danielle is designing a kaleidoscope pattern on her computer. She draws the figure shown. What are the coordinates of points *A*, *B*, *C*, and *D*? Copy the table and record the coordinates in the row labeled *original*.

Transformations	Coordinates of Points			
original	*A*(?, ?)	*B*(?, ?)	*C*(?, ?)	*D*(?, ?)
x-axis reflection	*A'*(?, ?)	*B'*(?, ?)	*C'*(?, ?)	*D'*(?, ?)
y-axis reflection	?	?	?	?
180° rotation	?	?	?	?
270° counterclockwise	?	?	?	?
90° counterclockwise	?	?	?	?
horizontal translation	?	?	?	?
vertical translation	?	?	?	?
horz/vert translation	?	?	?	?

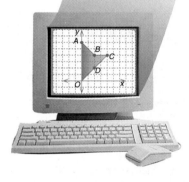

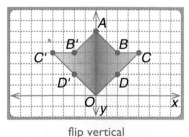

flip vertical

flip horizontal

② Danielle used the *flip vertical* and *flip horizontal* features on her computer. Which type of flip is a **reflection** over the x-axis? over the y-axis?

③ Record the coordinates of each image in your table. How do the coordinates of each image compare to the original coordinates? Discuss any patterns you see.

Unit 5 Coordinate Geometry and Quadrilaterals

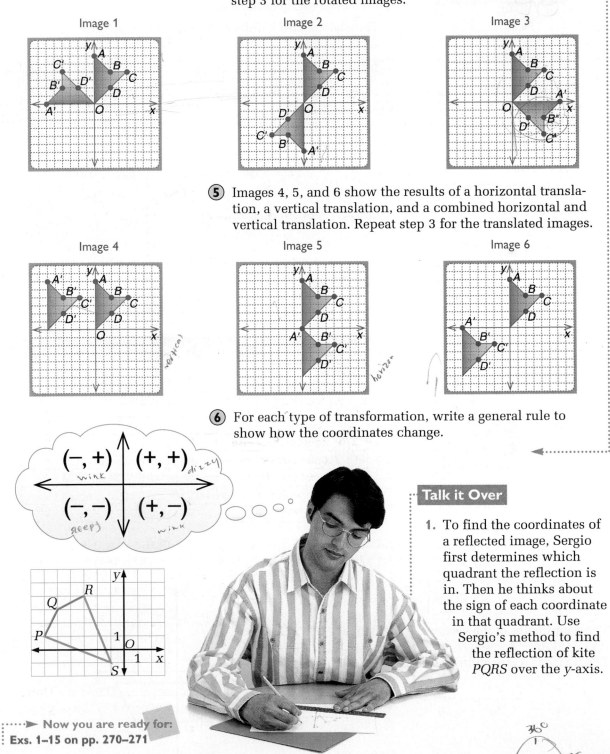

④ Danielle used the *rotate* feature on the computer to create the images below. Which image is a **rotation** of 180°? of 270° counterclockwise? of 90° counterclockwise? Repeat step 3 for the rotated images.

Image 1

Image 2

Image 3

⑤ Images 4, 5, and 6 show the results of a horizontal translation, a vertical translation, and a combined horizontal and vertical translation. Repeat step 3 for the translated images.

Image 4

Image 5

Image 6

⑥ For each type of transformation, write a general rule to show how the coordinates change.

Talk it Over

1. To find the coordinates of a reflected image, Sergio first determines which quadrant the reflection is in. Then he thinks about the sign of each coordinate in that quadrant. Use Sergio's method to find the reflection of kite *PQRS* over the *y*-axis.

······▶ **Now you are ready for:**
Exs. 1–15 on pp. 270–271

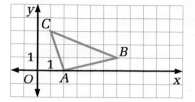

Find the coordinates of the image described.

a. Reflect $\triangle ABC$ over the x-axis.

b. Translate $\triangle ABC$ 3 units right and 2 units down.

Sample Response

a. The image is on the opposite side of the x-axis, so each y-coordinate is the opposite of the original. Each x-coordinate stays the same. The rule is $P(x, y) \rightarrow P'(x, -y)$.

$A(2, 0) \rightarrow A'(2, 0)$

$B(6, 1) \rightarrow B'(6, -1)$

$C(1, 3) \rightarrow C'(1, -3)$

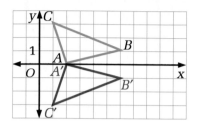

b. Add 3 to each x-coordinate and subtract 2 from each y-coordinate. The rule is $P(x, y) \rightarrow P'(x + 3, y - 2)$.

$A(2, 0) \rightarrow A'(5, -2)$

$B(6, 1) \rightarrow B'(9, -1)$

$C(1, 3) \rightarrow C'(4, 1)$

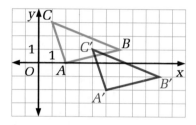

The coordinates of quadrilateral $ABCD$ are listed below in a matrix. Use matrix multiplication to transform $ABCD$. Then sketch $ABCD$ and its image. Describe the transformation.

$$\begin{array}{cccc} A & B & C & D \end{array}$$

$$\begin{bmatrix} 1 & 0 \\ 0 & -1 \end{bmatrix}\begin{bmatrix} 3 & -2 & -3 & 5 \\ 5 & 4 & 1 & 1 \end{bmatrix} \quad \longleftarrow \text{ the } x\text{-coordinates of } ABCD$$
$$\longleftarrow \text{ the } y\text{-coordinates of } ABCD$$

Sample Response

$$\begin{bmatrix} 1 & 0 \\ 0 & -1 \end{bmatrix}\begin{bmatrix} 3 & -2 & -3 & 5 \\ 5 & 4 & 1 & 1 \end{bmatrix} = \begin{bmatrix} 1(3) + 0(5) & 1(-2) + 0(4) & 1(-3) + 0(1) & 1(5) + 0(1) \\ 0(3) + (-1)(5) & 0(-2) + (-1)(4) & 0(-3) + (-1)(1) & 0(5) + (-1)(1) \end{bmatrix}$$

$$= \begin{bmatrix} 3 & -2 & -3 & 5 \\ -5 & -4 & -1 & -1 \end{bmatrix}$$

The coordinates of the vertices of the image of $ABCD$ are $A'(3, -5)$, $B'(-2, -4)$, $C'(-3, -1)$, and $D'(5, -1)$. The image is a reflection over the x-axis.

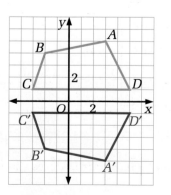

Effects of Transformations

When a geometric figure is transformed, some properties stay the same and some change. The formulas for slope and distance can help you decide which properties stay the same.

Talk it Over

Use the graphs in Sample 1.

2. Find the length of $\overline{AB}$ and of $\overline{A'B'}$ in each image. Does the length of $\overline{AB}$ change when the triangle is reflected? when it is translated?

3. Does $\overline{A'B'}$ have the same slope as $\overline{AB}$ when the triangle is reflected? when it is translated?

4. Suppose you rotated $\triangle ABC$ 90° clockwise around the origin. Would $\overline{AB}$ and $\overline{A'B'}$ be the same length? Would they have the same slope? Explain.

5. Do the results you found in questions 2–4 about $\overline{AB}$ also apply to $\overline{BC}$? Why or why not?

Sample 3

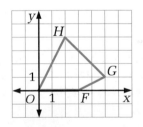

a. Find the coordinates of the image of *OFGH* after a dilation with center at the origin and scale factor 3.

b. Find the length of $\overline{HG}$ and of $\overline{H'G'}$. How do they compare?

c. Find the slope of $\overline{HG}$ and of $\overline{H'G'}$. How do they compare?

Sample Response

a. Multiply each coordinate of the original figure by the scale factor of 3 to get the coordinates of the image.

$$O(0, 0) \rightarrow O'(0, 0)$$
$$F(3, 0) \rightarrow F'(9, 0)$$
$$G(5, 1) \rightarrow G'(15, 3)$$
$$H(2, 4) \rightarrow H'(6, 12)$$

b. Use the formula $d = \sqrt{(x_2 - x_1)^2 + (y_2 - y_1)^2}$.

$$HG = \sqrt{(5 - 2)^2 + (1 - 4)^2} = \sqrt{18} = \sqrt{9 \cdot 2} = 3\sqrt{2}$$

$$H'G' = \sqrt{(15 - 6)^2 + (3 - 12)^2} = \sqrt{162} = \sqrt{81 \cdot 2} = 9\sqrt{2}$$

The length of $\overline{H'G'}$ is three times the length of $\overline{HG}$.

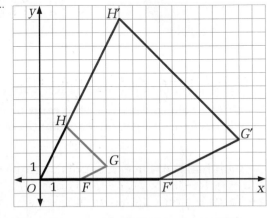

Student Resources Toolbox
p. 642 *Algebraic Expressions*

Continued on next page.

c. The slope of $\overline{HG} = \dfrac{4-1}{2-5} = \dfrac{3}{-3} = -1.$ ◀ Use $H(2, 4)$ and $G(5, 1)$ and the formula $m = \dfrac{y_2 - y_1}{x_2 - x_1}$.

The slope of $\overline{H'G'} = \dfrac{12-3}{6-15} = \dfrac{9}{-9} = -1.$ ◀ Use $H'(6, 12)$ and $G'(15, 3)$.

The slopes are the same.

⋯▶ **Now you are ready for:**
Exs. 16–44 on pp. 272–273

Look Back ◀

Which of the four transformations change the slope of a segment? Which changes the length of a segment?

5-4 Exercises and Problems

Name the transformation that was used to create each design.

Original Figure

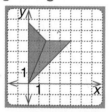

1.

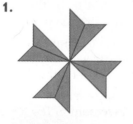

2.

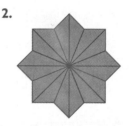

Stamps or coins with errors can be collectors' items. Describe the transformation(s) that may have occurred to cause these errors.

3.

4.

5.

For Exercises 6–8:

a. **Tell what kind of transformation is shown.**

b. **Write a rule to describe what must be done to the coordinates of the original figure to get the coordinates of the image.**

6.

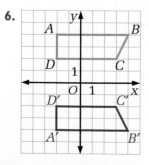

7.

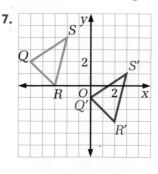

8.

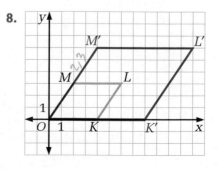

For Exercises 9–14, use quadrilateral *QRST*. Tell what type of transformation is described. Then copy *QRST* and sketch its image.

9. The figure is shifted 2 units right and 5 units down.

10. Each point on the image has the opposite *x*-coordinate and the opposite *y*-coordinate of the corresponding point on the original.

11. The coordinates of the image are three times the corresponding coordinates of the original.

12. Each point on the image has the same *x*-coordinate as the original point, but the opposite *y*-coordinate.

13. Each *x*-coordinate of the image is 4 more than the corresponding *x*-coordinate of the original. The *y*-coordinates are the same in both figures.

14. Each coordinate of the image is two thirds of the corresponding original coordinate.

connection to **EARTH SCIENCE**

15. Geologists believe that all of the world's continents were once connected into one super-continent that is called *Pangaea*. These computer images show the possible path of the continents when the Atlantic Ocean formed.

   a. What types of transformations describe the movement of the continents?

   b. **Open-ended** Describe where you think the continent that you live on will be 100 million years from now.

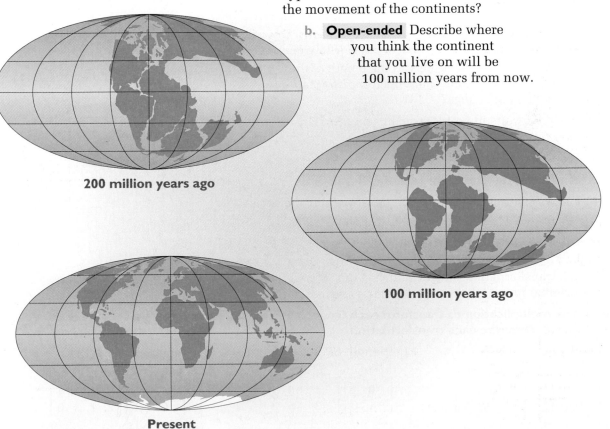

200 million years ago

100 million years ago

Present

For Exercises 16–21, match each rule with the transformation it describes.

16. $(x, y) \rightarrow (x, y - 5)$ **A.** dilation with scale factor 5

17. $(x, y) \rightarrow (y, -x)$ **B.** 90° counterclockwise rotation

18. $(x, y) \rightarrow (x, -y)$ **C.** 180° rotation

19. $(x, y) \rightarrow (-x, -y)$ **D.** 270° counterclockwise rotation

20. $(x, y) \rightarrow (5x, 5y)$ **E.** translation 5 units down

21. $(x, y) \rightarrow (-y, x)$ **F.** reflection over the x-axis

22. **Reading** What properties of a geometric figure may change when a figure is transformed? What formulas can help you decide?

Animators can use many different transformations to animate an image. For each transformation, sketch the image of △ABC and label the coordinates of the vertices. (Save your sketches for Exercises 28 and 29.)

23. reflection over the y-axis

24. translation 2 units left and 5 units up

25. dilation with scale factor 4 and center at O

26. translation 3 units down

27. 90° clockwise rotation around O

For Exercises 28 and 29, use your sketches from Exercises 23–27.

28. **a.** Find the length of $\overline{BC}$.

   b. Find the length of $\overline{B'C'}$ for each transformation.

   c. For which transformations did the length of the segment stay the same? For which transformations did the length change?

   d. Are the results in part (c) true in general? Why or why not?

29. **a.** Find the slope of $\overline{BC}$.

   b. Find the slope of $\overline{B'C'}$ for each transformation.

   c. For which transformations did the slope stay the same? For which transformations did the slope change?

   d. Are the results in part (c) true in general? Why or why not?

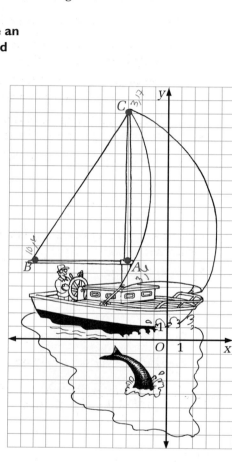

30. Which transformations create an image that is *congruent* to the original image? that is *similar* to the original image?

Use matrix multiplication to transform each figure. Then sketch each figure and its image. Describe each transformation.

31. quadrilateral $ABCD$

$$\begin{array}{cc} & A\ \ B\ \ C\ \ D \\ \begin{bmatrix} -1 & 0 \\ 0 & 1 \end{bmatrix} & \begin{bmatrix} 1 & 2 & 5 & 5 \\ -1 & 2 & 1 & -5 \end{bmatrix} \end{array}$$

32. triangle EFG

$$\begin{array}{cc} & E\ \ \ F\ \ \ G \\ \begin{bmatrix} 0 & 1 \\ -1 & 0 \end{bmatrix} & \begin{bmatrix} -4 & -3 & 1 \\ 2 & 5 & 3 \end{bmatrix} \end{array}$$

33. quadrilateral $JKLM$

$$\begin{array}{cc} & J\ K\ L\ M \\ \begin{bmatrix} -1 & 0 \\ 0 & -1 \end{bmatrix} & \begin{bmatrix} 0 & 1 & 3 & 4 \\ 2 & 4 & 3 & 0 \end{bmatrix} \end{array}$$

For Exercises 34 and 35:

a. Describe each transformation in words.

b. Give a rule, $(x, y) \rightarrow (\ ?\ ,\ ?\ )$, for each transformation.

34. P $\qquad$ P'

$$\begin{bmatrix} x \\ y \end{bmatrix} \rightarrow 2\begin{bmatrix} x \\ y \end{bmatrix}$$

35. P $\qquad$ P'

$$\begin{bmatrix} x \\ y \end{bmatrix} \rightarrow \begin{bmatrix} x \\ y \end{bmatrix} + \begin{bmatrix} 3 \\ -2 \end{bmatrix}$$

Ongoing **ASSESSMENT**

36. **Group Activity** Work with another student.

   a. Each of you should give each other the coordinates of the vertices of a quadrilateral and a rule to describe the coordinates of an image.

   b. Exchange papers and write the coordinates of the image using each other's rule. Then sketch the original figure and its image.

   c. Calculate the lengths of the sides and the slopes of the sides in the original figure and in the image.

   d. Did any properties change? If so, which ones?

Review **PREVIEW**

Find the coordinates of the midpoint of each segment whose endpoints are given. *(Section 5-3)*

37. $(0, 0)$ and $(100, -100)$

38. $(3, 7)$ and $(5, -1)$

39. $(-4, 6)$ and $(1, -2)$

40. Use the equation $y = \dfrac{3}{x^2}$. *(Section 2-5)*

   a. Find the value of y when $x = 7$.

   b. Find the value of x when $y = \dfrac{1}{12}$.

41. Find the length of each side of trapezoid $ABCD$ with vertices $A(0, 1)$, $B(2, 5)$, $C(6, 5)$, and $D(10, 1)$. *(Section 5-2)*

 Working on the Unit Project

Open-ended For Exercises 42 and 43, describe how you could use each transformation. Give examples.

a. translation $\qquad$ b. reflection $\qquad$ c. rotation

42. designing the pattern on your game board

43. directing players' moves in your game

44. **Writing** How could you use transformations to make your game board look the same to all the players?

Coordinates for Triangles and Quadrilaterals

Focus

Represent figures on a coordinate plane using as few variables for coordinates as possible.

Príme POsítíOn

Many cars have two odometers.

One shows how many total miles the car has been driven.

reset button

The trip odometer may be reset to zero to show the distance traveled from a starting point.

34302.6

000 0

Talk it Over

1. Suppose you traveled from Cleveland, Ohio, to Gary, Indiana, and back. Your odometer read 34,302.6 at the beginning of the trip and 34,879.2 at the end. How many miles did you travel?

2. Suppose you set the car's trip odometer to zero at the beginning of a trip from Cleveland to Gary. How will this setting make it easier to find how far you traveled?

3. In a homework problem Luiz and Grace found the slope and the length of the hypotenuse of $\triangle ABC$. Luiz used the given coordinates. Grace first translated the triangle 2 units right and 1 unit up.

    a. Whose calculations look simpler? Why?

    b. Did Grace's translation of the triangle affect its size or shape?

Luiz

$C(1,1)$
$A(-2,-1)$ $B(1,-1)$

slope of $\overline{AC} = \dfrac{1-(-1)}{1-(-2)} = \dfrac{1+1}{1+2} = \dfrac{2}{3}$

length of $\overline{AC} = \sqrt{[1-(-2)]^2 + [1-(-1)]^2}$
$= \sqrt{(1+2)^2 + (1+1)^2}$
$= \sqrt{3^2 + 2^2}$
$= \sqrt{9+4}$
$= \sqrt{13}$

Grace

$C'(3,2)$
$A'(0,0)$ $B'(3,0)$

slope of $\overline{A'C'} = \dfrac{2-0}{3-0} = \dfrac{2}{3}$

length of $\overline{A'C'} = \sqrt{(3-0)^2 + (2-0)^2}$
$= \sqrt{3^2 + 2^2}$
$= \sqrt{9+4}$
$= \sqrt{13}$

Triangles and Quadrilaterals in Standard Position

Any triangle or quadrilateral can be placed with a vertex at (0, 0) and a side along the *x*-axis. This placement is called **standard position**. Calculations of slope and length are often easier when figures are in standard position.

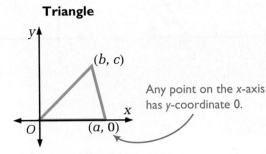

FIGURES IN STANDARD POSITION

Triangle

Any point on the *x*-axis has *y*-coordinate 0.

Use three variables to name the coordinates.

Quadrilateral

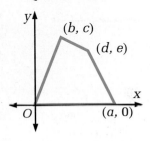

Use five variables to name the coordinates.

Coordinates for Special Quadrilaterals

In trapezoid *OPQR* the sides $\overline{OP}$ and $\overline{RQ}$ are parallel. You can use the coordinates of the vertices of a quadrilateral in standard position to show that the *y*-coordinates of *R* and *Q* are the same. The slopes of the parallel sides, $\overline{OP}$ and $\overline{RQ}$, are equal.

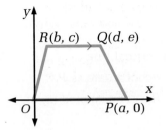

slope of $\overline{OP}$ ⟶ $\dfrac{0-0}{a-0} = \dfrac{e-c}{d-b}$ ⟵ slope of $\overline{RQ}$

$$\frac{0}{a} = \frac{e-c}{d-b}$$

$$0 = e - c$$

$$c = e$$

The numerator on the left side is 0, so the numerator on the right side must equal 0.

Since $c = e$, you can replace *e* with *c*. The coordinates of *Q* are (d, c).

You have just seen that the coordinates of a trapezoid can be named using just four variables. The coordinates of other special quadrilaterals can also be named using fewer than five variables. You will show this in Exercises 22 and 23.

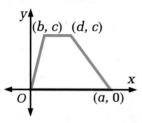

SPECIAL QUADRILATERALS IN STANDARD POSITION

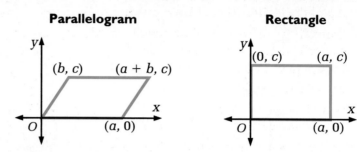

Trapezoid

y
(b, c)   (d, c)

O   (a, 0)   x

Parallelogram

y
(b, c)   (a + b, c)

O   (a, 0)   x

Rectangle

y
(0, c)   (a, c)

O   (a, 0)   x

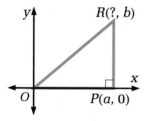

y
S(2, 3)   R(6, 3)

1

O 1   Q(4, 0)   x

Talk it Over

For questions 4 and 5, refer to the diagrams for quadrilaterals in standard position.

4. For parallelogram *OQRS*, what are the values of *a*, *b*, and *c*?

5. The vertices of quadrilateral *OJKL* are *O*(0, 0), *J*(9, 0), *K*(6, 10), and *L*(2, 5). Find the values of *a*, *b*, *c*, *d*, and *e*.

6. Draw a square with one vertex at the origin and one side along the *x*-axis. Label the coordinates using variables. How many different variables do you need for the coordinates?

---

y
R(?, b)

O   P(a, 0)   x

Sample

△*OPR* is a right triangle. Name the missing coordinate without introducing a new variable.

Sample Response

Since there is a right angle at *P*, $\overline{PR}$ is a vertical line.

R is directly above *P* and has the same *x*-coordinate as *P*.

The missing coordinate is *a* and vertex *R* can be labeled (*a*, *b*).

Look Back

How can placing a geometric figure with one vertex at the origin and one side along the *x*-axis be helpful?

1. **Reading** When a triangle is placed in standard position, what are the coordinates of the two vertices that are on the *x*-axis?

For Exercises 2–6, use the map and time zone chart.

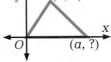

PACIFIC	MOUNTAIN	CENTRAL	EASTERN	USA TIME
				COUNTRY
+2	+1	+0	−1	COSTA RICA
+11	+10	+9	+8	KENYA
−2	−3	−4	−5	TAHITI
$+13\frac{1}{2}$	$+12\frac{1}{2}$	$+11\frac{1}{2}$	$+10\frac{1}{2}$	INDIA

2. Which country is in the same time zone as one region of the United States? How can you tell?

3. **a.** Lorina lives in Seattle, Washington. At 10 A.M. she calls Kenya. What time is it in Kenya?

   b. Arman lives in Dayton, Ohio. At 10 A.M. he calls Kenya. What time is it in Kenya?

   c. Were Lorina and Arman calling Kenya at the same time? Explain your reasoning.

4. Create a table that describes the time zones in the United States if all your calls originate in Tahiti.

5. What is the time difference from Costa Rica to India?

6. How does a caller's "origin" influence how he or she calculates time zone differences?

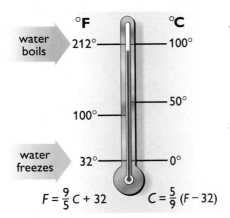

$$F = \frac{9}{5}C + 32 \qquad C = \frac{5}{9}(F - 32)$$

7. **Writing** In 1742, Anders Celsius developed a new temperature scale to make calculations easier.

   a. Explain why calculations are easier on a Celsius scale.

   b. How is the scale Anders Celsius developed like a figure placed in standard position?

8. **a.** **Literature** The title of Ray Bradbury's book *Fahrenheit 451* is based on the Fahrenheit scale. Find the Celsius temperature when the Fahrenheit scale reads 451°.

   b. What would the book's title have been if Bradbury had used the Celsius scale to name his book?

Name each missing coordinate without introducing a new variable.

9. isosceles right triangle

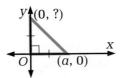

10. right triangle

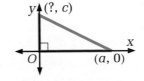

11. triangle

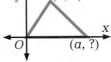

12. rectangle

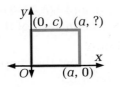

13. trapezoid

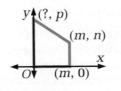

14. parallelogram

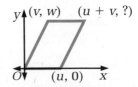

For Exercises 15–17:

a. Describe the transformation needed for each polygon to be in the first quadrant with one vertex at (0, 0).

b. Give the coordinates of the vertices for the image of each polygon.

15.   **16.**   **17.**

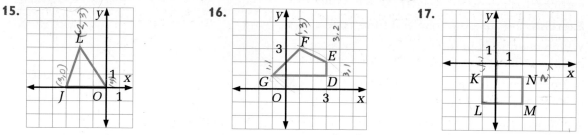

18. Quadrilateral $PQRS$ has vertices $P(0, 0)$, $Q(7, 0)$, $R(8, 4)$, and $S(1, 4)$.

   a. Use slopes to show that $PQRS$ is a parallelogram.

   b. Use the diagram for a parallelogram in standard position. Find the values of a, b, and c.

When polygons are symmetric, you can represent them using fewer variables by placing the axes along lines of symmetry. For Exercises 19–21, name the missing coordinates without introducing a new variable.

19. rectangle   **20.** rectangle   **21.** isosceles triangle

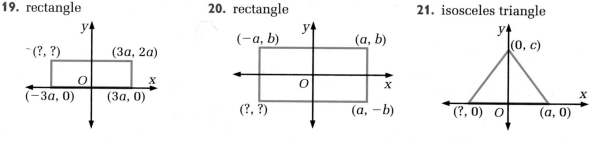

22. Quadrilateral $OEFG$ is a parallelogram.

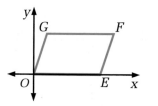

   a. Since $\overline{OG}$ is parallel to $\overline{EF}$, what can you say about the slopes of $\overline{OG}$ and $\overline{EF}$?

   b. **Writing** Since $OEFG$ is a quadrilateral in standard position, the coordinates of its vertices can be written $O(0, 0)$, $E(a, 0)$, $F(d, e)$, and $G(b, c)$. Use the slope of $\overline{OE}$ and of $\overline{GF}$ to show that $e = c$.

   c. Use the slope of $\overline{OG}$ and of $\overline{EF}$ to show that $d = a + b$.

   d. How many different variables do you need to represent the coordinates of the vertices of a parallelogram in standard position?

23. Quadrilateral $OJKL$ is a rectangle.

   a. What is the x-coordinate of L?

   b. **Writing** Since $OJKL$ is also a parallelogram, the coordinates of its vertices can be written $O(0, 0)$, $J(a, 0)$, $K(a + b, c)$, and $L(b, c)$. Tell why the x-coordinate of point K can be written as a instead of the general $a + b$.

   c. How many different variables do you need to represent the coordinates of the vertices of a rectangle in standard position?

24. a. Find the length of $\overline{LM}$ and the length of $\overline{MJ}$.

b. Find the length of $\overline{LK}$ and the length of $\overline{KJ}$.

c. Is *JKLM* a kite? Why or why not?

d. Which of the three variables used to name the coordinates represents a negative number?

25. Suppose that *JKLM* is a rhombus.

a. What is the relationship between $\overline{LK}$ and $\overline{LM}$?

b. Show that $e^2 = b^2$.

c. **Writing** Explain why $e = -b$.

d. Suppose rhombus *JKLM* has the *x*-axis and *y*-axis as lines of symmetry and two vertices at $J(4, 0)$ and $K(0, 3)$. Find the coordinates of the other two vertices.

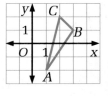

Ongoing **ASSESSMENT**

26. **Writing** Copy the portion of the quadrilateral chart on page 245 that includes these figures: quadrilateral, trapezoid, parallelogram, rectangle, square. Label the coordinates of the vertices for each figure in standard position. Use as few variables as possible. Describe any patterns you see.

Review **PREVIEW**

For each transformation, find the coordinates of the vertices of the image of △*ABC*. *(Section 5-4)*

27. reflection over the *y*-axis

28. translation 1 unit left and 1 unit down

Simplify. *(Section 4-6)*

29. $\sqrt{-25}$ **30.** $\sqrt{-30}$ **31.** $6i(1 - 4i)$ **32.** $(7 - 2i) + (5 - 3i)$

33. Rita made a conjecture that $\frac{1}{x} < x$. Do you think the conjecture is *True* or *False*? Explain. If false, give a counterexample. *(Section 1-5)*

Working on the Unit Project

In the game of Alquerque, the point at the center of the grid is left empty when the pieces are put in place before play begins.

For Exercises 34–39, the point in the center of the board is the origin. What are the coordinates of the vertices of each figure?

34. square *BDFH*   **35.** △*CEA*   **36.** trapezoid *CEOB*

37. △*OGA*   **38.** square *OFGH*   **39.** △*COA*

40. **Open-ended** How could you choose the origin on your game board in order to make it easier to locate points on the board?

Exploring Properties

AMAZING DIAGONALS

Focus

Use coordinate geometry and deductive reasoning to verify some properties of polygons.

EXPLORATION

(How) are the diagonals in special quadrilaterals related?

- Materials: scissors, rulers, protractors
- Work in a group of four students.

Always start with a rectangular piece of paper.

① Each of you should make a different one of these quadrilaterals using paper folding and cutting.

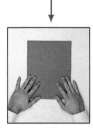 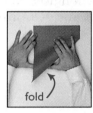  

square

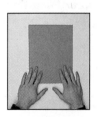  

rhombus

parallelogram

kite

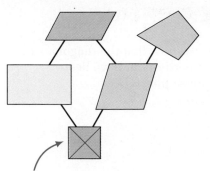

Diagonals have the same midpoint.
Diagonals are perpendicular.
Diagonals are equal in measure.

② The **diagonal** of a polygon is a segment joining two non-consecutive vertices. Show that the square has each of these properties. Use a ruler and a protractor if necessary.

a. The diagonals have the same midpoint.

b. The diagonals are perpendicular to each other.

c. The diagonals are equal in measure.

③ Decide whether each of the other quadrilaterals you made in step 1 has any or all of the properties listed in step 2. The person who made the square should explore the properties of a rectangle.

④ Organize your results from step 3 in a quadrilateral chart like the one at the left.

Verifying Properties with Coordinates

In the Exploration, you used inductive reasoning to support your findings. You can also use coordinates and deductive reasoning to prove conjectures.

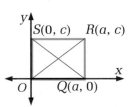

Sample 1

Use the coordinates of a rectangle in standard position to show that the diagonals of every rectangle have each property.

a. The diagonals are equal in measure.

b. The diagonals have the same midpoint.

Sample Response

a. Use the distance formula. Find the length of each diagonal and compare.

$$OR = \sqrt{(a - 0)^2 + (c - 0)^2} = \sqrt{a^2 + c^2}$$

$$SQ = \sqrt{(a - 0)^2 + (0 - c)^2} = \sqrt{a^2 + c^2}$$

These are equal, so the diagonals are equal in measure.

b. Use the midpoint formula. Find the midpoints and compare.

The midpoint of $\overline{OR}$ is $\left(\dfrac{0 + a}{2}, \dfrac{0 + c}{2}\right) = \left(\dfrac{a}{2}, \dfrac{c}{2}\right)$.

The midpoint of $\overline{SQ}$ is $\left(\dfrac{0 + a}{2}, \dfrac{c + 0}{2}\right) = \left(\dfrac{a}{2}, \dfrac{c}{2}\right)$.

The midpoints of the two diagonals are the same. The diagonals *bisect* each other.

▶ Now you are ready for:
Exs. 1–5 on p. 284

Shared Properties

Coordinate geometry can be used to show that the diagonals of special quadrilaterals have the properties you have been exploring. Here is a summary of those properties.

DIAGONALS OF SPECIAL QUADRILATERALS

In a *parallelogram*, the diagonals have the same midpoint.

In a *kite*, the diagonals are perpendicular to each other.

In a *rectangle*, the diagonals are equal in measure.

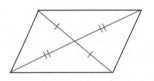

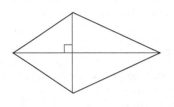

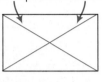

The diagonals are equal in measure.

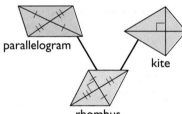

parallelogram

kite

rhombus

Every special quadrilateral shares the properties of the family of quadrilaterals to which it belongs. For example, a rhombus is a kite and a parallelogram. As you saw in the Exploration, its diagonals are perpendicular and have the same midpoint.

Here is another property of special quadrilaterals that is explored in Exercise 4.

OPPOSITE SIDES OF A PARALLELOGRAM

In a *parallelogram*, opposite sides are equal in measure.

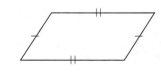

Talk it Over

Use the quadrilateral chart that you made in the Exploration. Name all special quadrilaterals that have each property.

1. The diagonals have the same midpoint.

2. The diagonals are perpendicular to each other.

3. The diagonals are equal in measure.

4. Opposite sides are equal in measure.

B

W

Z

O

C

Properties of Triangles

This sculpture was created by Joan Brossa in 1984. It is one of a series of sculptures around Barcelona, Spain.

Sample 2

Imagine $\triangle OBC$ in the photo. $\overline{WZ}$ connects the midpoints of $\overline{OB}$ and $\overline{CB}$. Show that $\overline{WZ}$ is parallel to $\overline{OC}$ and that it is half as long.

Sample Response

Step 1 Place the triangle in standard position.

Step 2 Use convenient coordinates. Finding midpoints involves dividing by 2, so use variable coordinates that are multiples of 2.

Step 3 Find and label the midpoints.

Step 4 Find each slope.

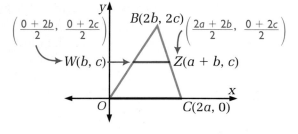

$$\left(\frac{0+2b}{2}, \frac{0+2c}{2}\right) \quad B(2b, 2c) \quad \left(\frac{2a+2b}{2}, \frac{0+2c}{2}\right)$$

$W(b, c) \qquad Z(a+b, c)$

$C(2a, 0)$

The slope of $\overline{WZ}$ is $\dfrac{c-c}{a+b-b} = \dfrac{0}{a} = 0.$

The slope of $\overline{OC}$ is $\dfrac{0-0}{2a-0} = \dfrac{0}{2a} = 0.$

The slopes are equal, so the segments are parallel.

Step 5 Find the length of each segment. Assume that $a > 0$.

$$WZ = \sqrt{(a+b-b)^2 + (c-c)^2} = \sqrt{a^2 + 0^2} = a$$

$$OC = \sqrt{(2a-0)^2 + (0-0)^2} = \sqrt{4a^2 + 0^2} = 2a$$

$WZ = \frac{1}{2}OC$

X$_{(.}$ $\triangle ab$

A PROPERTY OF TRIANGLES

In a triangle, a segment that connects the midpoints of two sides is parallel to the third side and half as long.

$$MN = \tfrac{1}{2}PR$$

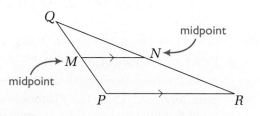

Q

midpoint

M

N ← midpoint

midpoint

P

R

Talk it Over

5. How many segments like $\overline{MN}$ are there for a triangle? Does each segment have the property described above?

······► Now you are ready for:
Exs. 6–25 on pp. 284–286

Look Back ◄────────────────────────────

How can you show that two segments are equal in measure?
that they are parallel? that they are perpendicular?

············

5-6 Exercises and Problems

1. Parallelogram *OUVW* has vertices *O*(0, 0), *U*(10, 0), *V*(12, 5) and *W*(2, 5). Show that the diagonals $\overline{OV}$ and $\overline{UW}$ have the same midpoint.

2. Use the coordinates in the diagram to show that the two diagonals of any parallelogram have the same midpoint.

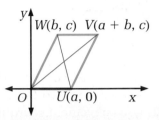

3. Suppose you are trying to convince a friend that the two diagonals of *every* parallelogram have the same midpoint. Which would be more convincing, your computations from Exercise 1 or Exercise 2? Why?

4. Another property of parallelograms is that opposite sides are equal in measure.

   a. Show that this is true for the parallelogram in Exercise 1.

   b. Show that this is true for all parallelograms using the coordinates in Exercise 2.

5. Use the coordinates of *OQRS* in the diagram to show that a square has each property.

   a. $\overline{OR}$ and $\overline{QS}$ have the same midpoint.

   b. $\overline{OR}$ is perpendicular to $\overline{QS}$.

   c. $\overline{OR}$ is equal in measure to $\overline{QS}$.

6. **Reading** Did you use *inductive* or *deductive* reasoning in the Exploration on page 280? in Sample 1 on page 281? in Sample 2 on page 283?

7 T E C H N O L O G Y Use graphing software.

   a. Draw a trapezoid *ABCD* so that no two sides are the same length and $\overline{AB}$ is parallel to $\overline{DC}$. Draw the diagonals and label the point where they intersect *E*.

   b. Measure to find the ratios *AE* to *EC* and *BE* to *ED*. Record your results.

   c. Repeat parts (a) and (b) for five more trapezoids. Describe any patterns you see in your results.

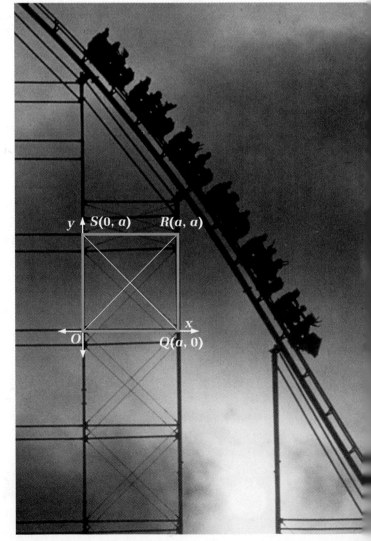

8. In trapezoid *OFGH*, *M* and *N* are the midpoints of $\overline{OH}$ and $\overline{FG}$. Use the coordinates in the diagram.

   a. Find the coordinates of *M* and *N*.

   b. Show that $\overline{MN}$ is parallel to $\overline{OF}$.

   c. Show that $MN = \frac{1}{2}(OF + GH)$.

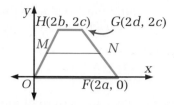

9. The midpoints of the sides of rectangle *LMNO* are *P*, *Q*, *R*, and *S*.

   a. Find the coordinates of *P*, *Q*, *R*, and *S*.

   b. What type of special quadrilateral is *PQRS*?

   c. Use the coordinates you found in part (a) to verify the conjecture you made in part (b).

10. A kite can be represented as shown. Use the diagram to explain why the diagonals of a kite must be perpendicular to each other.

For Exercises 11–14, use the following two statements.

(1) If a parallelogram is a rectangle, then it has diagonals that are equal in measure.

(2) If a parallelogram has diagonals that are equal in measure, then it is a rectangle.

11. What is the relationship between the two statements?

12. **Using Manipulatives** Cut two equal strips of paper. Make them intersect so that a parallelogram is formed by joining their endpoints. What is special about this parallelogram?

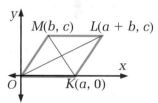

13. Use the diagram to show that statement (2) is true. (*Hint:* Use the distance formula to find *OL* and *KM*, then set them equal. Then show that *OKLM* must be a rectangle.)

14. **Career** Carpenters use geometry to create the frames for buildings, decks, and other projects. Read below about the method carpenters use and decide which statement is being applied.

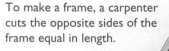

To make a frame, a carpenter cuts the opposite sides of the frame equal in length.

The sides of the frame form a parallelogram but not necessarily a rectangle.

The carpenter "squares up" the parallelogram by adjusting the angle until the two diagonals are equal in measure.

15. Writing Write a quiz that covers all the properties of quadrilaterals and triangles that are covered in Section 5-6.

16. Group Activity Work in a group of four students.

a. Each of you should draw a different quadrilateral on a coordinate grid. Find the midpoints of each side.

b. Join the midpoints to make another quadrilateral. Look for a pattern in your results. Make a conjecture about the type of quadrilateral you get.

c. Use the diagram at the right to verify your conjecture from part (b).

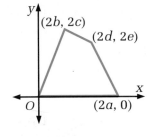

Name the missing coordinates without introducing a new variable. *(Section 5-5)*

17. rectangle

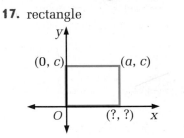

18. right triangle

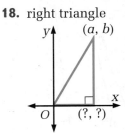

19. parallelogram

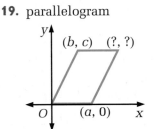

What can you conclude from each statement? *(Section 1-6)*

20. Carlos is taller than Gus and Gus is taller than Ben.

21. If Julie enters the race, then she will win. If she wins, then she will get a prize.

Use this information for Exercises 22 and 23. *(Toolbox Skill 7)*

Kim entered her name in a contest to win a free book at a bookstore. In all, 80 people entered their names. The winner's name will be chosen at random.

22. Find the probability that Kim will win a free book.

23. Find the probability that Kim will not win a free book.

Working on the Unit Project

24. A possible game board pattern is shown. Use what you know about the diagonals of quadrilaterals and coordinate geometry to copy this pattern on a coordinate grid.

25. Open-ended How could you use what you know about the diagonals of quadrilaterals in designing your game board? in directing players' moves?

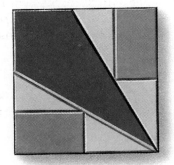

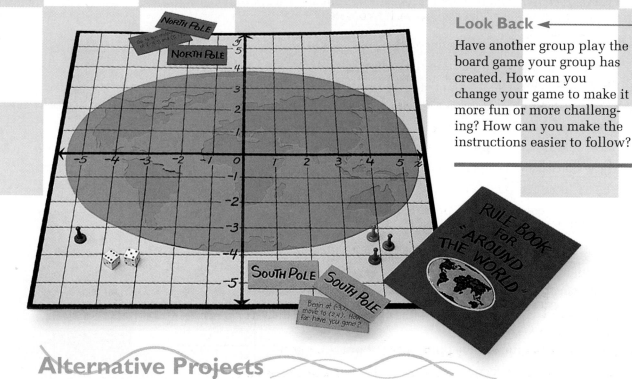

Completing the Unit Project

Unit Project 5

Now you are ready to finish making your game.
Your finished game should include these things:

> a game board that incorporates a coordinate grid

> enough game pieces for at least four players

> dice, cards, or both for determining the moves and the order of play

> clear, complete written instructions for playing the game

Look Back ←

Have another group play the board game your group has created. How can you change your game to make it more fun or more challenging? How can you make the instructions easier to follow?

Alternative Projects

Project 1: Design Your Own House

Design a house for a lot in your neighborhood. Make a siting plan by locating the center of the house and the outer walls. Use properties of quadrilaterals, the distance and midpoint formulas, and coordinate geometry to draw a floor plan. Combine your floor plan and siting plan in a visual display that demonstrates how you created the plans.

Project 2: Treasure Hunt

Design a treasure hunt. Draw a map on a coordinate grid and write clues that use the properties of quadrilaterals, the midpoint and distance formulas, and a coordinate grid.

For Exercises 1–4, tell whether each statement is *True* or *False*. If the statement is false, give a counterexample.   5-1

1. All rhombuses are parallelograms.

2. If a quadrilateral is a rhombus, then it is a kite.

3. Every square is a rhombus.

4. All squares are parallelograms.

5. Make a concept map to show how these shapes are related:
   square, rectangle, quadrilateral, trapezoid, rhombus, kite, parallelogram

6. **a.** Plot the points $A(0, 6)$, $B(2, 5)$, and $C(-3, 4)$.   5-2

   b. Which point is closest to the origin?

   c. Which point is farthest from the origin?

7. Explain how you can use the Pythagorean theorem to help you remember the distance formula.

For Exercises 8 and 9, use the two figures at the right.

8. Show that *FGHJ* is a kite.

9. Show that *MNOP* is a parallelogram.

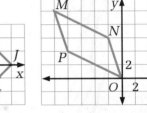

10. The endpoints of $\overline{KL}$ are $K(8, 3)$ and $L(-2, -5)$.   5-3

    a. Find the coordinates of M, the midpoint of $\overline{KL}$.

    b. Suppose L is the midpoint of $\overline{KN}$. Find the coordinates of N.

11. **Open-ended** Create a real-life problem for which you use the distance formula to find the solution. Show how to solve it.

For each transformation in Exercises 12–14, sketch the image of △*ABC* and label the coordinates of the vertices.   5-4

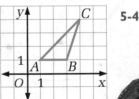

12. reflection over the *y*-axis

13. translation 1 unit up and 8 units left

14. dilation with scale factor 3 and center at *O*

15. In Exercises 12–14, for which transformations did the slope of $\overline{AC}$ change? For which transformations did the length of $\overline{AC}$ *not* change?

16. **Open-ended** Pick any four points in the coordinate plane and draw quadrilateral *PQRS* connecting them. For parts (a) and (b), tell what type of transformation is described and sketch the original and its image.

    a. The image has opposite *x*-coordinates, but the same *y*-coordinates.

    b. The image has opposite *x*-coordinates and opposite *y*-coordinates.

17. **Writing** For figures drawn in the first quadrant, does a reflection over the *x*-axis give you the same image as a 90° clockwise rotation? Explain why or why not.

18. Find the missing coordinate of a parallelogram with vertices (0, 0), (8, 0), (?, 7), and (2, 7). **5-5**

19. A triangle has vertices (0, 0), (6, 0), and (?, 7).

   a. What could the missing coordinate be if the triangle is a right triangle?

   b. What could the missing coordinate be if the triangle is isosceles?

20. Quadrilateral *HIJK* has coordinates $H(-4, -12)$, $I(6, -12)$, $J(5, -8)$, and $K(-5, -8)$.

   a. Sketch the quadrilateral.

   b. Sketch the image of the quadrilateral in standard position.

   c. What kind of quadrilateral is *HIJK*?

21. Plot the points $O(0, 0)$, $Q(4a, 0)$, and $R(2a, 2c)$. Show that $\triangle OQR$ is an isosceles triangle. **5-6**

22. **Self-evaluation** You have seen properties of geometric figures demonstrated with inductive reasoning using numbers for coordinates and with deductive reasoning using variables for coordinates. Which method do you find easier? Which reasoning do you think is better? Why?

23. **Group Activity** Work in a group of five students. Each member of your group should choose one of these shape names: *rectangle*, *kite*, *rhombus*, *parallelogram*, or *trapezoid*.

For each of the properties listed in (a)–(g), discuss with your group members these two questions:

➤ Do *any* quadrilaterals with your shape's name have the given property?

➤ Does *every* quadrilateral with your shape's name have the given property?

   a. two pairs of parallel sides

   b. two pairs of opposite sides that are equal in measure

   c. two pairs of consecutive sides that are equal in measure

   d. diagonals that are equal in measure

   e. diagonals that have the same midpoint

   f. diagonals that are perpendicular

   g. sides that are perpendicular

IDEAS AND (FORMULAS)=X^2

ALGEBRA

> **Measurement** To find the distance between two points, find the change in the x-coordinates and the change in the y-coordinates. *(p. 252)*
> $$\text{distance} = \sqrt{(\text{change in } x)^2 + (\text{change in } y)^2}$$

> **Measurement** The distance d between the points (x_1, y_1) and (x_2, y_2) is given by the formula $d = \sqrt{(x_2 - x_1)^2 + (y_2 - y_1)^2}$. *(p. 252)*

> You can use the distance formula and what you know about the slopes of parallel and perpendicular lines to show that a figure is a certain kind of quadrilateral. *(pp. 253–254)*

> To find the midpoint of a segment, find the mean of the x-coordinates and the mean of the y-coordinates. *(p. 259)*

> You can use a formula to find the midpoint of a segment: If the endpoints of a segment have coordinates (x_1, y_1) and (x_2, y_2), then the midpoint has coordinates $\left(\dfrac{x_1 + x_2}{2}, \dfrac{y_1 + y_2}{2}\right)$. *(p. 259)*

> The distance and slope formulas may be used to show properties of geometric figures. *(p. 281)*

LOGICAL REASONING $p \leftrightarrow q$ · *if - then*

> Special types of quadrilaterals may be organized in a chart. Each quadrilateral is a special case of the quadrilateral(s) it is connected to from above. *(pp. 244–245)*

> You can use the quadrilateral chart to make statements of the form: *All _?_ are _?_* or *Every _?_ is a _?_* or *If a quadrilateral is a _?_, then it is a _?_. (p. 245)*

> A property may be investigated using inductive reasoning by demonstrating the property in many specific cases or with variable coordinates in a general case using deductive reasoning. *(p. 281)*

GEOMETRY

> Dilations affect length, but not slope. Rotations and reflections affect slope, but not length. Translations do not affect slope or length. *(pp. 269–270)*

> **Problem Solving** Placing a figure in standard position on a coordinate plane may make calculations easier. *(p. 275)*

> The vertices of a special quadrilateral can be named using four variables or less. *(p. 276)*

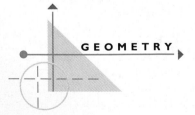

> Coordinate geometry may be used to show that *all* geometric figures of a particular type have certain properties. *(p. 282)*

> Quadrilaterals "inherit" properties of the family to which they belong. *(p. 282)*

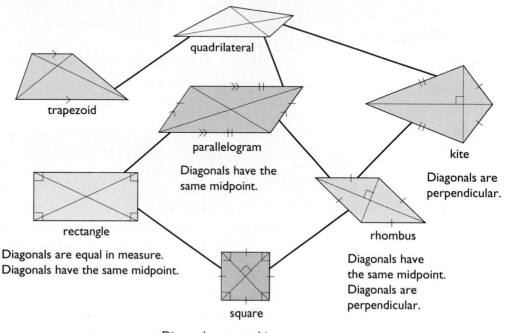

quadrilateral

trapezoid

parallelogram

Diagonals have the same midpoint.

kite

Diagonals are perpendicular.

rectangle

Diagonals are equal in measure.
Diagonals have the same midpoint.

rhombus

Diagonals have the same midpoint.
Diagonals are perpendicular.

square

Diagonals are equal in measure.
Diagonals have the same midpoint.
Diagonals are perpendicular.

> The diagonals of a parallelogram have the same midpoint. The diagonals of a kite are perpendicular to each other. The length of the diagonals of a rectangle are equal in measure. Opposite sides of a parallelogram are equal in measure. *(p. 282)*

> In every triangle, a segment that connects the midpoints of two sides is parallel to and half the length of the third side. *(p. 283)*

Key Terms

- ≅ (p. 243)
- kite (p. 245)
- rotation (p. 267)

- consecutive sides (p. 244)
- midpoint (p. 259)
- standard position (p. 275)

- rhombus (p. 245)
- reflection (p. 266)
- diagonal (p. 281)

Counting Strategies, Probability, Binomials

Can you easily bend your thumb back to touch your wrist? Can you do a back bend? If you can, you are among the small percentage of people who are called *double-jointed* because some of their joints are unusually flexible.

flexibility

A recent study revealed a positive **correlation** between being double-jointed and being a musician. Although rare in the general population, double-jointedness occurs in about 63% of the flutists in the survey and almost 50% of the players of stringed instruments.

music

On the other hand, whether the apparently high incidence of musical talent among scientists and mathematicians represents a positive **correlation** is still an open question.

science

Science & Music
Is there a correlation?

Jamel Lamonté Oeser-Sweat
Age: 17
Science project: medicine
(loofa sponges as source of
bacterial infections)
Musical talent: drums

Develop an Interest Profile

An *interest profile* is a summary of the interests of an individual or the interests common to a group of people.

Your project is to develop two interest profiles that represent a sample of the students in your school. You will make separate profiles for students with birthdays from January 1 through June 30 and from July 1 through December 31.

You will develop and distribute a survey asking students to state their birthday and to rate five school subjects on their level of interest alone.

You will present your profiles in a visual display that includes probabilities based on your survey results. You will describe your profiles in a written report that also contains your survey, a data display of the survey results, and an analysis of your survey.

4 Winners of the 1994 Westinghouse Science Talent Search

Jennifer Yu-Fe Lin
Age: 17
Science project: biology
(factors controlling cell growth)
Musical talent: classical piano

careers

Rajen Arun Sheth
Age: 17
Science project: engineering
(effect of intelligent vehicle/highway
systems on vehicle efficiency)
Musical talent: violin

Jessica Hammer
Age: 17
Science project: psycholinguistics
(how nonverbal cues
affect language learning)
Musical talent: jazz music

What do you want to do when you finish school? **Interest inventory tests** are designed to help people select a career. When you fill out an interest inventory, you are comparing your interests with the interest profiles for various career fields.

Getting Started

Unit Project 6

For this project you should work in a group of four students. Here are some ideas to help you get started.

☞ Think about how you will decide which five of these school subjects to include in your survey:

mathematics, social studies, language arts, science, art, music, physical education, industrial technology, languages, business

☞ In your group, discuss various kinds of sampling methods. Decide which method to use for your survey.

☞ Review the related exercises in the unit. Decide how you will use the answers with your profiles and in your report.

☞ Think about how to create an appropriate data display for your survey results.

☞ Begin to collect drawings and photos for use in your visual display.

Working on the Unit Project

Your work in Unit 6 will help you create your interest profiles.

Related Exercises:

Section 6-1, Exercises 31, 32
Section 6-2, Exercises 40–44
Section 6-3, Exercises 47–52
Section 6-4, Exercises 30, 31
Section 6-5, Exercises 31, 32
Section 6-6, Exercises 29, 30
Section 6-7, Exercises 22, 23
Section 6-8, Exercises 24, 25
Section 6-9, Exercise 32

Alternative Projects p. 358

Can We Talk PROFILES

➤ Do you think the positive correlation between being double-jointed and being a musician reflects a cause-effect relationship between the two characteristics? Why or why not?

➤ Where have you seen other profiles of people?

➤ What are some factors other than interests that affect the choice of a career?

➤ Do you think interest inventory tests can predict whether a person will be successful in a particular career? Why or why not?

Exploring Counting Problems

Let Me COUNT the Ways

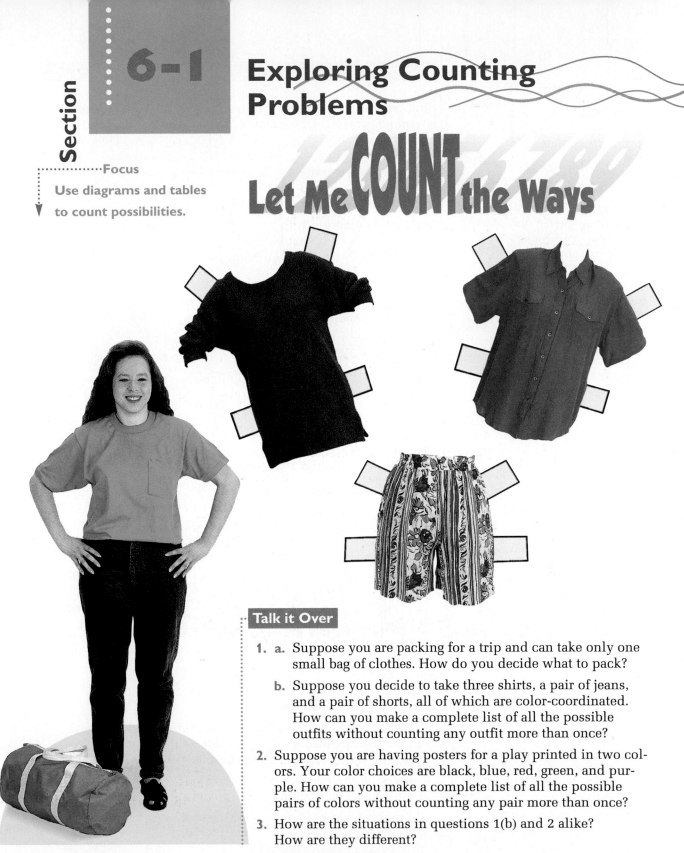

Talk it Over

1. **a.** Suppose you are packing for a trip and can take only one small bag of clothes. How do you decide what to pack?

   b. Suppose you decide to take three shirts, a pair of jeans, and a pair of shorts, all of which are color-coordinated. How can you make a complete list of all the possible outfits without counting any outfit more than once?

2. Suppose you are having posters for a play printed in two colors. Your color choices are black, blue, red, green, and purple. How can you make a complete list of all the possible pairs of colors without counting any pair more than once?

3. How are the situations in questions 1(b) and 2 alike? How are they different?

You can organize information in a systematic way so that you list all possibilities without listing anything more than once.

Sample 1

Suppose you go to a snack bar that has the menu shown and buy a "complete meal." How many different meals are there to choose from?

Sample Response

Problem Solving Strategy: Use a diagram.

Make a **tree diagram** with a column of branches for each category. To keep it simple, label each branch in each category with a single letter. Use a different letter for each item.

Three main dish choices	Two side dish choices	Two drink choices		Outcomes
T	R	L	TRL	tacos, rice, lemonade
		S	TRS	tacos, rice, spring water
	P	L	TPL	tacos, pinto beans, lemonade
		S	TPS	tacos, pinto beans, spring water
B	R	L	BRL	burritos, rice, lemonade
		S	BRS	burritos, rice, spring water
	P	L	BPL	burritos, pinto beans, lemonade
		S	BPS	burritos, pinto beans, spring water
E	R	L	ERL	enchiladas, rice, lemonade
		S	ERS	enchiladas, rice, spring water
	P	L	EPL	enchiladas, pinto beans, lemonade
		S	EPS	enchiladas, pinto beans, spring water

Each of the 12 different possibilities is an **outcome.**

There are 12 different meals to choose from.

Talk it Over

Use the situation in Sample 1.

4. Make another tree diagram in which you select the drink first, the side dish second, and the main dish third. How do the results compare with those in the Sample?

5. Describe another way to find the total number of meals (outcomes) without drawing a tree diagram.

6. An **event** is a set of outcomes. How many outcomes are there for each event?

   a. having a meal with tacos

   b. having a meal with rice

Outcomes from Rolling Dice

Many games use *dice*. Dice are cubes that have a different number of dots from 1 to 6 on each face. A single cube is called a *die*.

Sample 2

Suppose you are playing a board game that involves rolling two dice and counting the number of dots showing on the top of each die. One die is red, the other is white. How many different outcomes are there?

Sample Response

Problem Solving Strategy: Make a table.

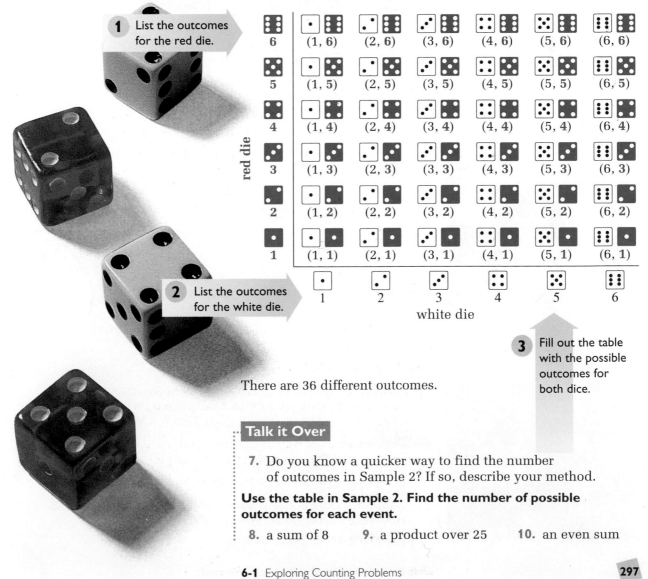

1 List the outcomes for the red die.

2 List the outcomes for the white die.

3 Fill out the table with the possible outcomes for both dice.

There are 36 different outcomes.

Talk it Over

7. Do you know a quicker way to find the number of outcomes in Sample 2? If so, describe your method.

Use the table in Sample 2. Find the number of possible outcomes for each event.

8. a sum of 8   9. a product over 25   10. an even sum

Leaving Out Choices

You do not always have to choose something from every category when you make a selection.

Sample 3

Suppose you are thinking about buying any one, two, or three of the following accessories for a camera: lens, flash, tripod. You will not buy more than one of each type of accessory. How many accessory combinations are possible?

Sample Response

Problem Solving Strategy: Make a systematic list.

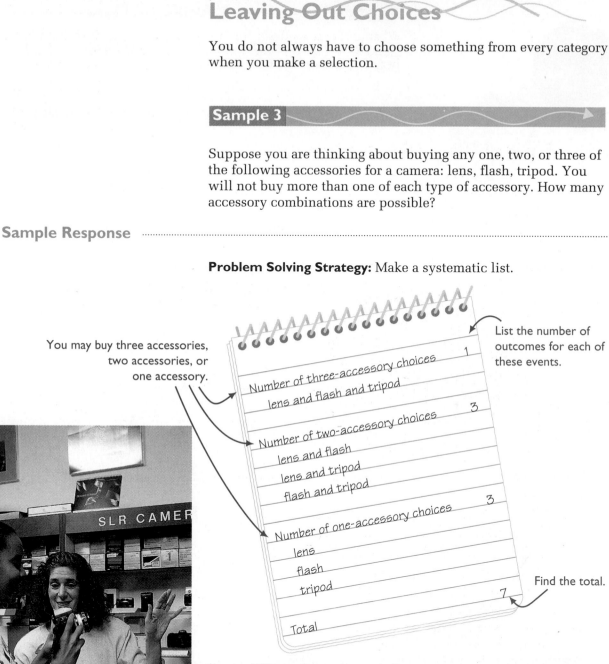

You may buy three accessories, two accessories, or one accessory.

List the number of outcomes for each of these events.

Number of three-accessory choices   1
    lens and flash and tripod

Number of two-accessory choices   3
    lens and flash
    lens and tripod
    flash and tripod

Number of one-accessory choices   3
    lens
    flash
    tripod

    Total   7

Find the total.

Seven different accessory combinations are possible.

Talk it Over

11. How is the situation in Sample 3 different from the situation in Sample 1?

12. Suppose a camera bag is added to the choices in Sample 3. How many different accessory combinations will be possible?

Look Back ←

What are some methods for organizing information to include all possible choices? What are some advantages and disadvantages of each?

6-1 **Exercises and Problems**

Reading Use the table in Sample 2 on page 297. How many outcomes are there for each event when you roll one red die and one white die?

1. rolling exactly one 6

2. rolling exactly one even number

3. rolling two odd numbers

For Exercises 4 and 5, find all the possible outcomes for each situation.

4. Raúl is ordering a shirt. The catalog offers his size in the five colors and two sleeve lengths shown.

T-Shirt: long and short sleeve
Colors: spruce, yellow, white, oatmeal, or purple

Sizes: S, M, L, XL

5. Evetta is buying a telephone. She plans to choose one option, but not both.

Color	white, gray, black
Style	corded, cordless
Options	built-in answering machine, speakerphone

6. **Open-ended** Write a problem that you could solve using this tree diagram. Then solve your problem.

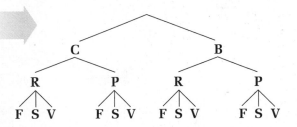

7. Deb drops a nickel, a dime, and a quarter. None lands on its edge. How many possible ways can the coins show heads or tails?

8. Charlotte is playing a board game that involves rolling a pair of dice. The number of spaces that she moves depends on the sum of the dots on the top faces. How many different sums are there?

9. Tobias is playing a board game that involves rolling a pair of dice. The red die shows how many spaces he will move, and the white die shows the category of the question he must answer. How many different outcomes are there?

10. **Writing** Compare Exercises 8 and 9. How are they alike? How are they different?

11. Manuel Arias has four men and four women in his ballet. In how many ways can he assign dance partners that include one man and one woman?

12. A yogurt shop offers raisins, granola, coconut, and walnuts as toppings. A customer may choose one or more toppings. How many choices are there?

13. Amanda rented four videos for the weekend: one drama, two comedies, and one musical. She may watch one, two, three, or all four videos.

    a. Make a diagram to show all of Amanda's choices.

    b. **Writing** Write a story explaining why Amanda might not have watched all four videos and how she decided which videos to watch.

14. Five actresses try out for a play.

    a. In how many ways can the five actresses be cast for these five roles: detective, business executive, salesperson, house cleaner, journalist?

    b. In how many ways can the five actresses be cast if the part of the salesperson is cut?

    c. What if two parts are cut, the salesperson and the journalist?

    d. Describe any patterns you see in your answers to parts (a)–(c).

15. **Consumerism** Suppose you have narrowed your search for a car to five car models, two colors, and the four optional features shown. You are considering all five models and both colors. How many different cars are there to choose from in each case?

sunroof

car stereo system

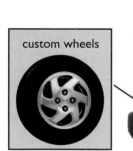

custom wheels

security system

a. You do not want any of the optional features.

b. You want all four optional features.

c. You can afford only one of the optional features.

d. You can afford any two of the optional features.

e. You can afford any number of the optional features, but you are not sure you want them all.

BY THE WAY...

Henry Ford commented about the color choices for the Model T Ford in these words, "Any color — so long as it's black."

Use the coordinate plane.

16. How many segments can be drawn between any two of the five points?

17. How many triangles can be drawn connecting any three of the five points?

18. How many quadrilaterals can be drawn connecting any four of the five points?

19. How many rays can be drawn between any two of the five points?

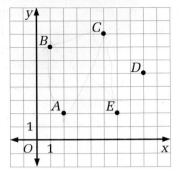

Ongoing ASSESSMENT

20. **Writing** Write and solve a counting problem that you consider challenging. Explain your method for solving it.

Review PREVIEW

Tell whether each statement is *True* or *False*. *(Section 5-6)*

21. The diagonals of a parallelogram are perpendicular and have the same midpoint.

22. The diagonals of a square are equal in measure, have the same midpoint, and are perpendicular.

Simplify. Write each answer with positive exponents. *(Section 2-6)*

23. $(10a^5)(5b^{-2})$

24. $25x^4y^{-3}$

25. $(18m^0)(2n^{-6})$

26. One form of radioactive iodine has a half-life of about 8 days. Make a table to find how long it will be before 600 g of this iodine decays to only 100 g. *(Section 2-7)*

Evaluate each expression for the given values. *(Toolbox Skill 9)*

27. $x(x - 1)(x - 2); x = 3$

28. $ab(b - 7); a = -6, b = 2$

29. $\dfrac{4z}{z - 1}; z = -3$

30. $\dfrac{m(m - 1)}{m - p}; m = -1, p = 7$

Working on the Unit Project

31. List all the different groups of five subjects that you can select from the list on page 294 that include music and art.

32. One part of your survey should consist of questions like this:

    Which subject do you prefer in each pair? Circle one.

    2. a. Music   **b.** Art

    When students have completed this part of the survey, they should have compared each of the five selected subjects with every one of the others. How many questions like this will you need to include in your survey? How did you determine your answer?

Counting and Permutations

REARRANGED
GRANDER ERA

········Focus

Use the multiplication counting principle to find a number of possible arrangements of items.

EXPLORATION

Can you find all possible arrangements of a group of letters?

- **Materials: four index cards**
- **Work with another student.**

1) Print one letter of the word HEAR on each of the index cards. Find all possible four-letter arrangements. The arrangements do not have to form real words. Record your strategies and the arrangements you find.

2) Compare your list of letter arrangements with the list from another group. Compare strategies. Was your list complete? If not, how might you improve your strategy?

3) Make a tree diagram to show all possible four-letter arrangements.

4) In your tree diagram, how many choices are there for the first letter of an arrangement? How many choices for the second letter? for the third? for the fourth? Make a conjecture about how your answers relate to the total number of arrangements.

5) Suppose a fifth letter is added, making the word HEART. Discuss with your partner how you can modify your tree diagram to find all the five-letter arrangements. How many arrangements are there now?

6) Suppose one more letter is added, making the word HEARTS. How many arrangements are there?

X Lab

In the Exploration, you may have noticed that the number of possible letter arrangements was the product of the number of choices you had at each stage of the tree diagram.

MULTIPLICATION COUNTING PRINCIPLE

The number of possible outcomes for an event is found by multiplying the number of choices at each stage of the event.

Sample 1

How many different four-letter arrangements can be made from the letters in the word GRATES? Assume that a letter cannot be used more than once.

Sample Response

Use the multiplication counting principle.

There are 6 choices for the first letter.

There are 4 choices left for the third letter.

$$6 \cdot 5 \cdot 4 \cdot 3 = 360$$

There are 5 choices left for the second letter.

There are 3 choices left for the fourth letter.

There are 360 different four-letter arrangements that can be made.

Talk it Over

1. a. How many different two-letter arrangements can be made from the letters in the word GRATES? Assume that a letter cannot be used more than once.

   b. List one or more of these two-letter arrangements that form an English word. Can you form words from another language besides English with two letters in the word GRATES? If so, what words?

2. a. How many different three-letter arrangements can be made from the letters in the word GRATES? Assume that a letter cannot be used more than once.

   b. List one or more of these three-letter arrangements that form an English word. Can you form words from another language besides English with three letters in the word GRATES? If so, what words?

The symbol **!** is called **factorial** and is used in mathematics in a specific way.

You read the symbol 6! as "six factorial." Here is what it means:

$$6! = 6 \cdot \underline{5 \cdot 4 \cdot 3 \cdot 2 \cdot 1}$$

Start with the positive integer.

Multiply by each next-smaller integer.

······▶ Now you are ready for:
Exs. 1–16 on pp. 306–308

By definition, $0! = 1$.

Permutations

The arrangement of any number of items in a definite order is called a **permutation.** The symbol for the number of different arrangements when n items are arranged r at a time is $_nP_r$.

In the Exploration with HEARTS, 6 letters are arranged 6 at a time. You can use the multiplication counting principle to find the number of possible arrangements.

$$_6P_6 = 6 \cdot 5 \cdot 4 \cdot 3 \cdot 2 \cdot 1 = 720$$

6 items ———— arranged 6 at a time

In Sample 1, 6 letters are arranged 4 at a time.

$$_6P_4 = \underline{6} \cdot \underline{5} \cdot \underline{4} \cdot \underline{3}$$

the number of factors

You can also write this using factorials.

$$_6P_4 = 6 \cdot 5 \cdot 4 \cdot 3 = \frac{6 \cdot 5 \cdot 4 \cdot 3 \cdot 2 \cdot 1}{2 \cdot 1} = \frac{6!}{2!} = \frac{6!}{(6-4)!}$$

This is the difference between the total number of items and the number of items being arranged.

$X_{(} \triangle ab$

PERMUTATIONS OF n ITEMS ARRANGED r AT A TIME

The number of permutations of n items arranged r at a time ($r < n$) is given by this formula.

$$_nP_r = \underbrace{n(n-1)(n-2) \cdots}_{r \text{ factors}} = \frac{n!}{(n-r)!}$$

Example

$$_{10}P_3 = 10 \cdot 9 \cdot 8 = \frac{10!}{(10-3)!} = 720$$

TECHNOLOGY NOTE

See whether your calculator has a factorial key or menu item. Find $(8 - 5)!$. See whether your calculator has a permutation key or menu item. Find $_8P_5$. ◀

Talk it Over

3. What does the symbol $_8P_5$ mean?

4. How do you simplify $(8 - 5)!$?

5. Explain how to find the number of permutations of 8 items arranged 5 at a time.

6. Find the number of three-letter arrangements of the letters in the word ITCH using the multiplication counting principle. Then find the number of three-letter arrangements using the formula $_nP_r = \dfrac{n!}{(n - r)!}$. Compare the methods.

Sample 2

Ching's crossword puzzle clue is "anagram of the word FREE." He knows that an anagram of a word is found by rearranging the letters of the word. (SLIP is an anagram of LIPS.) How many arrangements are there of the letters in the word FREE?

Sample Response

Problem Solving Strategy: Make a systematic list.

Ching notices that FREE looks the same if he interchanges the E's. If he uses the formula $_4P_4$, he will find the number of possible arrangements of the letters of FREE, but some arrangements will be the same. Ching decides to make a systematic list to count the different arrangements.

possibilities			
1st letter	2nd letter	3rd letter	4th letter
f	fr	fre	free
	fe	fer	fere
		fee	feer
r	rf	rfe	rfee
	re	ref	refe
		ree	reef
e	ef	efr	efre
	er	efe	efer
	ee	erf	erfe
		ere	eref
		eef	eefr
		eer	eerf
e̸			

This will be the same. I don't need to count twice! All the arrangements with the first "e" are the same as with the second.

Watch Out!

Think before you use the formula for $_nP_r$. If items are repeated, there are not as many different arrangements. The formula does not apply then.

There are 12 arrangements of the letters in the word FREE.

······► Now you are ready for:
Exs. 17–44 on pp. 308–309

Look Back ◄————

For what situations can you use the multiplication counting principle? How are permutations a special case of the multiplication counting principle?

6-2 Exercises and Problems

1. **Reading** How do you read 9! ? What product does it represent?

2. **Business Travel** A company in New York City keeps travel profiles for its employees. A profile includes the preferred airport of departure, the seating class, and the seating preference.

   La Guardia
   - first class — aisle / window
   - business class — aisle / window
   - coach — aisle / window

   JFK
   - first class — aisle / window
   - business class — aisle / window
   - coach — aisle / window

   a. How many different travel profiles does the tree diagram represent?

   b. How could you use the multiplication counting principle instead of this tree diagram to find the number of different travel profiles possible?

3. There are eight people hiking together. They walk single file on a narrow section of the trail. How many ways can they be lined up on the trail?

4. **Art** Robin is designing a poster for an exhibit of Egyptian art. She wants the border to be a repeated pattern of the four hieroglyphs shown. How many different ways can she arrange the four hieroglyphs in a row?

S   D   L   M

mouth   folded cloth   owl   hand

BY THE WAY...

Egyptian hieroglyphs are pictures, but each one generally represents a letter or a sound. A hieroglyph means what it pictures when it has a *determinative stroke*.

5. a. Suppose you add an "O" to the letters represented by the hieroglyphs. How many different five-letter arrangements can you make?

   b. Suppose you add an "O" and an "E" to the letters represented by the hieroglyphs. How many different six-letter arrangements can you make?

   c. If possible, list one or more words in English or another language that can be formed by the letters in part (a). Do the same for part (b).

6. **a.** In how many different ways can the nine starting players on a baseball team be introduced?

   b. **Writing** Does the number change if the pitcher is always last? Explain.

Find each value.

   7. 2!   **8.** 0!   **9.** 7!   **10.** 1!

11. **Writing** Would you prefer to *make an organized list*, *make a tree diagram*, or *use the multiplication counting principle* to find the number of possible four-letter arrangements of the letters in the word HEARTS? Explain your preference.

12. **License Plates** In California standard license plates have this form.

any digit   any three letters   any three digits
from 1 to 9   except "O"   from 0 to 9

   a. How many different license plates can be created under this system, without letters or digits repeated? with letters or digits repeated?

   b. Why do you think some possible plates are not printed?

   c. **Research** Can you have personalized plates in your state? If so, what restrictions are there on them?

---

connection to **LANGUAGE ARTS**

13. **a.** Use the sentence MY SHOELACE IS UNTIED. How many arrangements of all the words are possible?

   b. Assume you can use a period or a question mark as punctuation. Which arrangements make meaningful sentences?

14. **a.** How many five-word arrangements can you make using these words: SAID, HERE, WAIT, MIMI, NELSON?

   b. Use only commas, a period, and quotation marks as punctuation. Write at least five meaningful sentences using all the words in part (a).

15. **a.** **Open-ended** Write a three-word sentence that has an adjective, a noun, and a verb. How many arrangements of all the words are possible?

   b. Which arrangements make meaningful sentences?

   c. Add two words to your sentence in part (a). One word should be an adverb and the other an adjective. How many arrangements of all the words are now possible?

   d. Write as many meaningful sentences as you can using all the words in part (c).

16. a. Find how many different five-letter arrangements can be made from the letters in the word MOUSE.

b. Find how many different five-letter arrangements can be made from the letters in the word MOOSE.

c. **Writing** Compare the results of parts (a) and (b). How are they different?

Find each value.

17. $\frac{8!}{3!}$

18. $\frac{7!}{(7-3)!}$

19. $_{10}P_4$

20. $_{12}P_3$

How many different permutations are there of all the letters in each word?

21. MAINE

French settlers may have named this state after the French province *Mayne* or used their word for *mainland.*

22. WYOMING

This state got its name from the Native American term *mecheweaming,* which is a term for "at the big flats."

23. IOWA

This state name comes from *ayuxwa,* which is a Native American tribal name. It means "one who puts to sleep."

For Exercises 24–27, find each number of permutations.

24. 8 books, arranged 2 at a time

25. 4 desserts, arranged in a row on a display

26. 7 bushes, arranged 5 in a row along the side of a house

27. a list of 6 students' last names, when no names are repeated

28. There are eight people in a race. First, second, and third places will be awarded. How many different ways could the awards be won?

29. Games Ji Sun is playing a word game and has the tiles C, T, A, and C.

a. List the three-letter permutations.

b. List the two-letter permutations.

c. Using the multiplication counting principle, check that you found all the permutations in parts (a) and (b).

d. How could Ji Sun build on the tiles shown to form another word?

30. Group Activity Work with another student.

a. Agree with your partner on the choice of three colors. One of you writes the colors down in a row and hides them with your hand.

b. One partner guesses the colors in order, and the other tells how many of the guesses are correct. Keep guessing until the correct order is found.

c. Discuss strategies for finding the correct order with the fewest guesses.

d. Repeat the procedure with four colors. Discuss the mathematical reasons why this may take more guesses than using three colors.

31. **Open-ended** Write two words with six letters each. One word should not have any letters repeated. The other should have a single letter repeated. Find how many permutations there are of all the letters in each word. Are the numbers of permutations the same? Why or why not?

Review **PREVIEW**

32. Lani, Eve, Derek, and Peter are four models posing for a photograph. One model is standing on each of four steps. List all the possible ways the models can be arranged on the four steps. *(Section 6-1)*

Factor. *(Section 4-4)*

33. $2x^2 - x - 6$ 34. $9x^2 - 25$ 35. $25x^2 + 20x + 4$

Use a number anywhere on the scale to estimate the probability of each event. *(Toolbox Skill 6)*

36. The sun will not rise next week.

37. You will eat cereal some day next week.

38. You will find a penny on the ground this month.

39. It will snow in your city or town next month.

impossible   unlikely   possible   likely   certain

| 0% | 25% | 50% | 75% | 100% |

| 0 | 0.25 | 0.5 | 0.75 | 1 |

Working on the Unit Project

40. Look back at your answer to Exercise 32 in Section 6-1. In how many different ways can you arrange the questions on the part of your survey in which students compare the five selected subjects with one another?

41. Your survey should consist of one question asking students whether their birthday is in the first or second half of the year, along with the questions mentioned in Exercise 40.

    a. How many questions will your survey have in all?

    b. In how many different ways can you arrange the questions on your survey if the birthday question is the first question?

42. Write your survey. Put the birthday question first.

43. Look at these possible student answers for your survey:

    Student 1: 1. a, 2. a, 3. b ...

    Student 2: 1. a, 2. b, 3. a ...

    How many possible answer lists are there?

44. Distribute your survey.

INTEREST SURVEY

1. In which half of the year is your birthday? Circle one.

   a. January 1—June 30

   b. July 1—December 31

Which subject do you prefer in each pair? Circle one.

2. a. Music   b. Art

3. a. Music   b. Science

···Focus
Find the probability of an
event and of mutually
exclusive events. Relate
probability to odds.

Chances Are

♥ACE

A/re

♥ACE

Playing cards have been used
in many countries around the
world for hundreds of years. The French
introduced the four *suits* in the 1500s.

A standard deck of playing cards consists of 52 cards, with
13 cards in each of four suits: clubs, spades, diamonds, and
hearts. *Face cards* are jacks, queens, and kings.

	A ACE	2 TWO	3 THREE	4 FOUR	5 FIVE	6 SIX	7 SEVEN	8 EIGHT	9 NINE	10 TEN	JACK	QUEEN	KING
Clubs	♣	♣	♣	♣	♣	♣	♣	♣	♣	♣			
Spades	♠	♠	♠	♠	♠	♠	♠	♠	♠	♠			
Diamonds	♦	♦	♦	♦	♦	♦	♦	♦	♦	♦			
Hearts	♥	♥	♥	♥	♥	♥	♥	♥	♥	♥			

Talk it Over

How many of each kind of card are in a standard deck?

1. a 2   **2.** a red card   **3.** a red 2   **4.** a face card

**Jeannine picked one card from a standard deck and Chris picked
one card from another standard deck. They tried to guess each
other's card.**

5. Jeannine gave this clue: "My card is a 2 and it is red." What
are the possible cards that Jeannine could have?

6. Chris gave this clue: "My card is a 2 or it is red." How is his
clue different from Jeannine's? Will it be easier or harder to
guess his card? Why?

7. Can you pick one card that is an ace and a jack from a
standard deck? Why or why not?

In a card game, you are dealing the first card from a well-mixed standard deck. Find the probability of each event.

a. dealing an ace or a jack   **b.** dealing a face card or a spade

Sample Response

Student Resources Toolbox
p. 638 *Probability*

There are 52 possible outcomes.

a. There are 8 favorable outcomes: 4 aces and 4 jacks.

Read as "the probability of an ace or a jack."

$$P(\text{ace or jack}) = \frac{8}{52} \approx 0.15$$

You can also write this as 15%.

b. There are 22 favorable outcomes:
12 face cards and 10 other spades.

Clubs

Spades

Diamonds

You count the jack, queen, and king of spades only once each.

Hearts

$$P(\text{face card or spade}) = \frac{22}{52} \approx 0.42$$

In Sample 1(a) you cannot deal one card that is both an ace and a jack. These two events cannot happen at the same time. That makes the events **mutually exclusive**. Notice this relationship:

$$P(\text{ace or jack}) = \frac{4}{52} + \frac{4}{52} = \frac{8}{52}$$

$P(\text{ace})$ $P(\text{jack})$

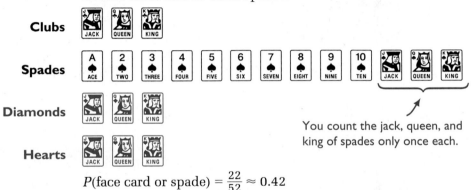

PROBABILITY OF MUTUALLY EXCLUSIVE EVENTS

When two events are mutually exclusive, you can add to find the probability that either one occurs.

For mutually exclusive events A and B:

$$P(A \text{ or } B) = P(A) + P(B)$$

8. Are the events dealing a face card and dealing a spade mutually exclusive? Why or why not?

9. Suppose you are choosing a card from a standard deck.

   a. How many outcomes are there for the event "heart"? for the event "not a heart"?

   b. Are the events "heart" and "not a heart" mutually exclusive? Why or why not?

   c. Find P(heart or not a heart).

Complementary Events

Two events are **complementary events** if they are mutually exclusive and together they include all the possibilities. The events "heart" and "not a heart" are complementary events.

The sum of the probabilities of complementary events is 1.

P(event) $= 1 - P$(not the event)

P(not the event) $= 1 - P$(event)

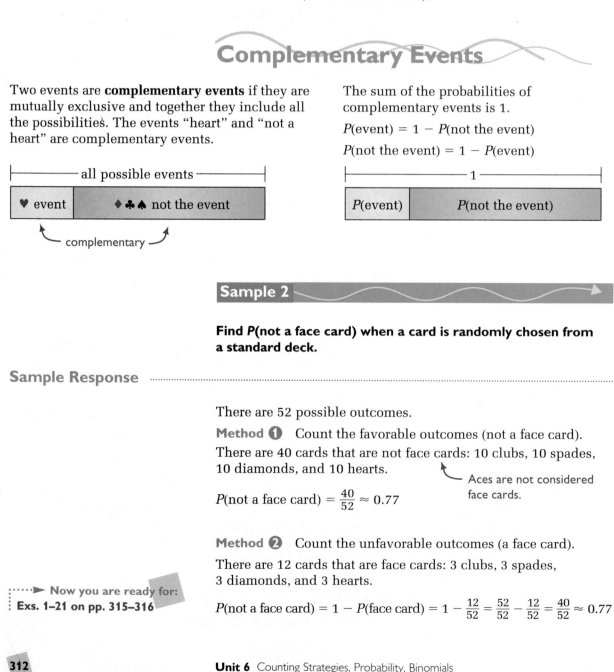

Sample 2

Find P(not a face card) when a card is randomly chosen from a standard deck.

Sample Response

There are 52 possible outcomes.

Method ① Count the favorable outcomes (not a face card).

There are 40 cards that are not face cards: 10 clubs, 10 spades, 10 diamonds, and 10 hearts.

Aces are not considered face cards.

P(not a face card) $= \frac{40}{52} \approx 0.77$

Method ② Count the unfavorable outcomes (a face card).

There are 12 cards that are face cards: 3 clubs, 3 spades, 3 diamonds, and 3 hearts.

······▶ Now you are ready for:
Exs. 1–21 on pp. 315–316

P(not a face card) $= 1 - P$(face card) $= 1 - \frac{12}{52} = \frac{52}{52} - \frac{12}{52} = \frac{40}{52} \approx 0.77$

Counting Techniques and Probability

You can sometimes use the multiplication counting principle and permutations to find the number of possible outcomes when you are finding the probability of an event.

Sample 3

Find the probability that no two people in a group of five people have the same birthday (month and day).

Sample Response

Assume that there are 365 birthdays in a year to choose from.

The number of ways 5 people can have 5 *different* birthdays: 365 dates possible for the first person, 364 for the second, and so on.

$$\frac{\text{number of favorable outcomes}}{\text{number of possible outcomes}} = \frac{365 \cdot 364 \cdot 363 \cdot 362 \cdot 361}{365 \cdot 365 \cdot 365 \cdot 365 \cdot 365} \approx 0.97$$

The number of ways 5 people can have 5 birthdays: 365 dates possible for the first person, 365 dates possible for the second, and so on.

The probability is about 0.97.

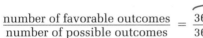
April 1st

June 26th

September 8th

Talk it Over

10. The complement of "no two people" is "at least two people." Use this fact and the result of Sample 3 to find the probability that at least two people in a group of five people have the same birthday.

11. Explain how to find the probability that at least two people in a group of six people have the same birthday.

12. **a.** How likely do you think it is that at least two people in your class have the same birthday?

    b. Write the month and date of your birthday, not the year, on a removable note. At the front of the classroom make a histogram (by month) with the notes for the entire class. Are at least two birthdays the same?

possible outcomes	
favorable outcomes	unfavorable outcomes

Odds

Odds are another way of stating the likelihood of an event. Suppose the *odds against* winning a contest are 5:2 (read "five to two") This means that for every 5 chances of losing, there are 2 chances of winning.

LIKELIHOOD OF AN EVENT

Suppose each outcome of an event is equally likely.

Probability of the event = $\dfrac{\text{number of favorable outcomes}}{\text{number of possible outcomes}}$

Odds in favor of the event = $\dfrac{\text{number of favorable outcomes}}{\text{number of unfavorable outcomes}}$

Odds against the event = $\dfrac{\text{number of unfavorable outcomes}}{\text{number of favorable outcomes}}$

Example Suppose 2 out of 7 outcomes are favorable.

probability = $\dfrac{2}{7} \approx 0.29$

odds in favor = $\dfrac{2}{5}$, or 2:5

odds against = $\dfrac{5}{2}$, or 5:2

In this book, assume that each outcome is equally likely when you toss a coin, roll a die, or spin a spinner with equal sections.

Sample 4

In some ice skating competitions, the order in which the competitors perform is determined by a random drawing. Suppose a competition involves five skaters with different names.

a. Find the probability that the skaters will perform in alphabetical order.

b. Find the odds in favor of the skaters performing in alphabetical order.

Sample Response

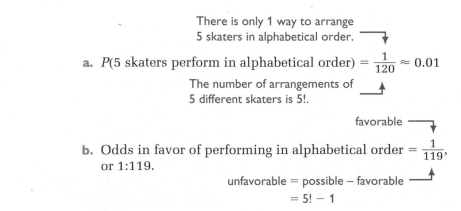

There is only 1 way to arrange 5 skaters in alphabetical order.

a. P(5 skaters perform in alphabetical order) = $\dfrac{1}{120} \approx 0.01$

The number of arrangements of 5 different skaters is 5!.

favorable

b. Odds in favor of performing in alphabetical order = $\dfrac{1}{119}$, or 1:119.

unfavorable = possible − favorable
= 5! − 1

13. For the situation in Sample 4, what are the odds against the five skaters performing in alphabetical order?

14. For the situation in Sample 4, what is the probability that the five skaters will not perform in alphabetical order?

15. Suppose that the probability of an event is 24%. What are the odds in favor of that event? against that event?

Look Back ◄─────────────────────────────────────

What is the relationship between the odds in favor of an event and the odds against an event? How can you find the probability of an event if you know the odds in favor of the event?

·····► Now you are ready for:
Exs. 22–52 on pp. 316–318

6-3 Exercises and Problems

1. a. Reading What two events in Sample 1 are mutually exclusive?

   b. Open-ended Give another example of mutually exclusive events.

2. Reading Are complementary events always mutually exclusive?

Suppose you roll a die. Find each probability.

3. $P(6)$

4. $P(\text{prime})$

5. $P(\text{a factor of } 6)$

6. $P(6 \text{ or prime})$

7. $P(6 \text{ or a factor of } 6)$

8. $P(\text{not a factor of } 6)$

9. Which of the events in Exercises 3–5 are mutually exclusive?

10. Which of the events in Exercises 3–8 are complementary?

11. Suppose $P(\text{rain tomorrow}) = 75\%$. Find $P(\text{no rain tomorrow})$.

12. Suppose the probability of not getting the flu if you get a flu shot is 85%. What is the probability of getting the flu if you get a flu shot?

13. A store selects one student at random from the 2000 students at Plainfield High School to win a graphics calculator. The school has 40 students on its mathematics team. What is the probability that no one on the team will win the calculator?

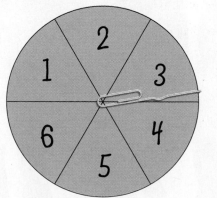

14. a. Writing Write and solve a probability problem about this spinner that involves complementary events.

   b. Using Manipulatives Make a spinner like the one shown. You can unfold a paper clip to use for a pointer and hold it in place with a pencil. Do an experiment to find the experimental probability for the problem you wrote in part (a).

   c. Compare the probabilities you found in parts (a) and (b). Were they exactly the same? Should they be exactly the same? Why or why not?

	Area in square kilometers
Earth	510,066,000
Land	148,429,000
Water	361,637,000
Asia	44,485,900
Africa	30,269,680
North America	24,235,280
South America	17,820,770
Antarctica	13,209,000
Europe	10,530,750
Australia	7,682,300
Pacific Ocean	166,241,000
Atlantic Ocean	86,557,000
Indian Ocean	73,427,000
Arctic Ocean	9,485,000

Student Resources Toolbox
p. 639 *Probability*

connection to **SCIENCE**

Suppose that a meteor that strikes Earth is equally likely to land anywhere on Earth. Find the probability of each event.

15. The meteor lands in an ocean.

16. The meteor does not land in an ocean.

17. The meteor lands in Africa.

18. The meteor does not land in Africa.

19. The meteor lands in South America or North America.

Use the information below for Exercises 20 and 21.

Gwen plans to call Lisa's house on Saturday at a random time between 8:00 A.M. and 12:00 P.M. Gwen does not know that Lisa does not get up until 10:30 A.M. on Saturdays.

20. a. What is the probability that Gwen will call before Lisa gets up?

b. What is the probability that Gwen will call after Lisa gets up?

21. a. Suppose that Lisa's parents leave at 9:15 A.M. on Saturdays to take her brother to play soccer. What is the probability that Gwen will call before Lisa's family leaves?

b. What is the probability that Gwen will call before Lisa's family leaves or after Lisa gets up?

c. What is the probability that Gwen will call after Lisa's family leaves but before Lisa gets up?

22. CD Players Suppose there are 10 songs on a CD. You program the CD player to play the songs at random without any repeats.

a. In how many different orders can 10 songs be played?

b. What is the probability that the songs will be played in the order in which they are arranged on the CD?

23. Ja-Wen, Phelton, Ryan, and Deanna stand in a row to rehearse a song. They are equally likely to stand in any order.

a. What is the probability that they stand in alphabetical order from left to right?

b. What are the odds in favor of them standing in alphabetical order from left to right?

c. No two are the same age. When they stand in alphabetical order from left to right, they are not in order by age. What is the probability that they stand in alphabetical order or in order by age (youngest to oldest) from left to right?

Camp counselors are packing lunches for a hiking trip. Suppose that each item in the menu below is equally likely to be selected and that a meal includes an item from each category.

For Exercises 24–27, find the probability of each event.

24. packing a lunch that includes a turkey sandwich

25. packing a lunch that does not include a turkey sandwich

26. packing a lunch that includes a turkey sandwich, an apple, and milk

27. packing a lunch that includes a turkey sandwich or a lunch that includes an apple

Sandwiches	Fruit	Drink
turkey	banana	milk
tuna	apple	apple juice
vegetarian	orange	lemonade
ham and cheese		

28. Find the odds in favor of the event in Exercise 25.

29. Find the odds against the event in Exercise 26.

connection to **HEALTH**

The data in the diagram are percentages of blood types in the United States. Each blood type can be divided into two categories, positive and negative. This is called the *Rh factor*.

Suppose you choose Person X at random from the population of the United States.

30. **a.** What are the odds in favor of Person X having AB blood?

  b. What are the odds against Person X having AB blood?

31. The odds in favor of Person X having AB negative (AB⁻) blood, which is the least common blood type, are 7 to 993.

  a. What are the odds against Person X having AB⁻ blood?

  b. What is the probability that Person X has AB⁻ blood? AB⁺ blood?

Type O	Type A	Type B	Type AB
46.1%	38.8%	11.1%	3.9%

32. Someone with type O blood is called a *universal donor* because type O blood can be donated to anyone, as long as the Rh factors match.

  a. What are the odds in favor of Person X being a universal donor?

  b. What are the odds against Person X being a universal donor?

  c. Suppose 200 donors are signed up to give blood at a blood drive. How many of them might you expect to be universal donors?

33. **Research** Find out what the term *universal recipient* means. Find the odds in favor of Person X being a universal recipient.

For each number of people:

a. Find the probability that no two birthdays match.

b. Find the probability that at least two birthdays match.

34. 6   **35.** 7   **36.** 8

37. How are the events in parts (a) and (b) of Exercises 34–36 related?

38. How can you find the probability that at least two people in any size group have the same birthday? Describe your method in words or in symbols.

39. How large a group you do need before the probability of having at least two people with the same birthday is 50%?

Ongoing **ASSESSMENT**

40. **Open-ended** A car wash decides to give a free wash to any customer who comes in on his or her birthday. In July and August, the car wash had 10,000 customers and gave 1000 free washes. Do you think this information helps the owner of the car wash predict the number of free washes that will be given during the rest of the year? Why or why not?

Review **PREVIEW**

41. How many different three-letter arrangements can be made from the letters in the word PRICES? How many five-letter arrangements? *(Section 6-2)*

Simplify. *(Section 4-6)*

42. $\sqrt{-81}$ **43.** $(6i)(-2i)(5i)$ **44.** $(6-2i)(4+5i)$ **45.** $(1+8i)-(4-7i)$

46. Rama is dressing a mannequin for a window display. She has a pair of blue slacks, a pair of green slacks, a yellow sweater, and a black sweater to work with. Make a table to show all the ways Rama could dress the mannequin in pants and a sweater. *(Section 6-1)*

 Working on the Unit Project

47. Alphabetize the subject areas included in your survey and number them.

For Exercises 48–51, use your survey results.

a. Find the probability of each event.

b. Find the odds in favor of each event.

48. A person with a birthday in the second half of the year prefers subject 3 to subject 1.

49. A person with a birthday in the first half of the year prefers subject 3 to subject 1.

50. A person with a birthday in the second half of the year prefers subject 2 to subject 4.

51. A person with a birthday in the first half of the year prefers subject 2 to subject 4.

52. **Writing** Are the events in Exercises 48 and 49 mutually exclusive? How do you know?

Compound Events

Before and After

Focus

Find the probability of independent and dependent events.

Every spring, the National Basketball Association (NBA) holds a lottery to find the order in which professional teams can choose new members from college players. The lottery system that was in place from 1990 to 1993 is described at the left.

> Table tennis balls were used to represent each team's entries. The balls were placed in a clear cylinder, thoroughly mixed, and then drawn by vacuum to the top. The ball that came to the top first determined which team got the first choice.
>
> After the first three balls were drawn, a team's win-loss record determined the order, with the team having the worst record getting the next choice.

BY THE WAY...

Orlando won the lottery in both 1992 and 1993. This prompted the NBA Board of Governors to modify the lottery system.

The 11 teams that did not qualify for the professional playoffs participated each year.

1992		1993	
Team standings in reverse order	**Entries**	**Team standings in reverse order**	**Entries**
Minnesota	11	Dallas	11
Orlando	10	Minnesota	10
Dallas	9	Washington	9
Denver	8	Sacramento	8
Washington	7	Philadelphia	7
Sacramento	6	Milwaukee	6
Milwaukee	5	Golden State	5
Charlotte	4	Denver	4
Philadelphia	3	Miami	3
Atlanta	2	Detroit	2
Houston	1	Orlando	1

Each team got from 1 to 11 entries in the lottery. The team with the worst record got the most entries.

Talk it Over

1. How would you find the probability that a particular team wins the lottery (gets the first choice)?

2. What was the probability that the Orlando team would win the lottery in 1992? in 1993?

Compound Events

When you look at the 1992 and 1993 basketball lotteries together, you are looking at a *compound event*. A **compound event** is an event made of two or more events that can happen either at the same time or one after the other. The events can be either *independent events* or *dependent events*.

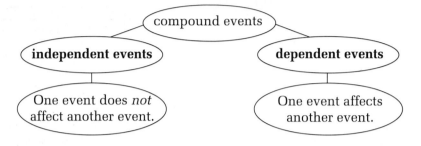

Talk it Over

Tell whether each pair of events is *independent* or *dependent*. Explain.

3. earning grades on your tests and earning your final semester grade

4. selecting a red apple and then a green apple from a bag of 6 red and 4 green apples, if no apples are returned to the bag

5. selecting a red apple and then a green apple from a bag of 6 red and 4 green apples, if the first apple is returned to the bag before the next selection

6. tossing a coin and rolling a die

Sample 1

Suppose you toss a coin and roll a die. Find the probability of getting heads on the coin and "5" on the die, or P(H and 5).

Sample Response

Problem Solving Strategy: Make a table.

Only one outcome has heads and a "5."

Outcomes for rolling a die

		1	2	3	4	5	6
Outcomes for tossing a coin	**H**	H, 1	H, 2	H, 3	H, 4	H, 5	H, 6
	T	T, 1	T, 2	T, 3	T, 4	T, 5	T, 6

The table contains twelve possible outcomes. A set of all possible outcomes, with no repeats, is called a **sample space.**

$$P(\text{H and 5}) = \frac{1}{12} \approx 0.08$$

The diagram shows how you can use the probability of each event in Sample 1 to find the probability of both. Notice that the probability of heads on the coin and "5" on the die can be found by multiplying the probabilities.

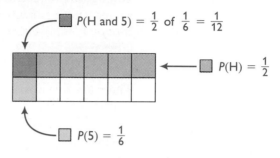

$$P(\text{H and 5}) = P(\text{H}) \cdot P(5) = \frac{1}{2} \cdot \frac{1}{6} = \frac{1}{12} \approx 0.08$$

X·Lab

PROBABILITY OF INDEPENDENT EVENTS

When two events are independent, you can multiply to find the probability that both occur.

For independent events A and B:

$$P(A \textbf{ and } B) = P(A) \cdot P(B)$$

Sample 2

Use the information about the basketball lottery on page 319. What was the probability that the Orlando team would win *both* the 1992 and 1993 lotteries?

Sample Response

First decide if the events are independent or dependent. →

Winning the lottery in 1992 had no effect on the lottery in 1993, so the events are independent. Multiply to find the probability that both events occur.

$P(\text{Orlando would win the 1992 lottery}) = \dfrac{10}{66}$

$P(\text{Orlando would win the 1993 lottery}) = \dfrac{1}{66}$

Add all entries. There are 66 altogether.

$P(\text{Orlando would win in 1992 } and \text{ 1993}) = \dfrac{10}{66} \cdot \dfrac{1}{66} = \dfrac{10}{4356} \approx 0.002$

▶ **Now you are ready for:**
Exs. 1–13 on pp. 323–325

The probability that the Orlando team would win *both* the 1992 and 1993 lotteries was about 0.002.

Dependent Events

With dependent events, the outcome of the first event affects the outcome of the second event. You need to consider this when you figure probabilities.

Sample 3

There are five discs in a CD player. The player has a "random" button that selects songs at random and does not repeat until all songs are played. What is the probability that the first song is selected from disc 3 and the second song is selected from disc 5?

Sample Response

The selection of the first song does affect the possibilities for the second song, so the events are dependent.

1 Find the probability that the first song is selected from disc 3.

$P(\text{disc 3 song}) = \frac{13}{50}$ ← 13 songs on disc 3
← 50 songs altogether

2 Find the probability that the second song is selected from disc 5.

Because songs *cannot* repeat, there is *one less song* possible for the second song.

$P(\text{disc 5 song after disc 3 song}) = \frac{10}{49}$ ← 10 songs on disc 5
← 49 songs left

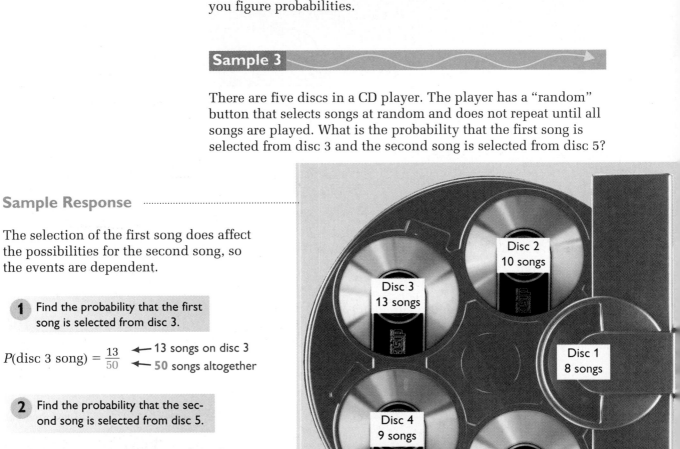

Disc 2
10 songs

Disc 3
13 songs

Disc 1
8 songs

Disc 4
9 songs

Disc 5
10 songs

3 Multiply the probabilities.

$P(\text{disc 3 song, then disc 5 song}) = P(\text{disc 3 song}) \cdot P(\text{disc 5 song after disc 3 song})$

$$= \frac{13}{50} \cdot \frac{10}{49}$$

$$= \frac{13}{245}$$

$$\approx 0.053$$

The probability that the first song is selected from disc 3 and the second song is selected from disc 5 is about 0.05.

PROBABILITY OF DEPENDENT EVENTS

For dependent events A and B:

$$P(A \text{ and } B) = P(A) \cdot P(B \text{ after } A)$$

Talk it Over

7. Explain why the denominators change for each successive event in Sample 3 but not in Sample 2.

8. Suppose songs in Sample 3 can repeat.

   a. Tell whether the choice of a first song and the choice of a second song are *independent* or *dependent* events. Explain.

   b. Find the probability that the first song is selected from disc 3 and the second song is selected from disc 5.

······▶ **Now you are ready for:**
Exs. 14–31 on pp. 325–327

Look Back ◀

What is meant by independent events? How are they different from dependent events? How is the probability that two dependent events will happen different from the probability that two independent events will happen?

6-4 Exercises and Problems

Suppose you roll one red and one blue eight-sided game piece and that each piece is numbered from 1 to 8. Find each probability.

1. $P(\text{red } 8 \text{ and blue } 8)$ 2. $P(\text{red } 1 \text{ and blue } 6)$ 3. $P(\text{even red and blue } 4)$

For Exercises 4 and 5, imagine that you are using the spinner shown.

4. In two spins what is the probability of landing on a "3" then on a "2"?

5. a. Copy and complete this table for the sum of any two spins.

   b. List the sample space for the sum of any two spins.

   c. Which sum is most likely? What is its probability?

   d. What is the probability that the sum is 6?

   e. Which is greater, the probability of an odd sum or an even sum? Explain.

+	1	2	3	3
1	2	3	4	4
2	?	?	?	?
3	?	?	?	?
3	?	?	?	?

connection to SCIENCE

Career Geneticists study how traits are passed from parents to their offspring through *genes*. Genes come in pairs, one from each parent. Sometimes one gene in a pair is considered *dominant* and the other gene is considered *recessive*. It takes two recessive genes to produce a recessive trait, but only one dominant gene to produce a dominant trait.

6. Use the table at the right. Suppose a rabbit with two dominant black-fur genes (BB) mates with a rabbit that has two recessive brown-fur genes (bb). What is the probability that their offspring will have brown fur? black fur?

7. Suppose a rabbit with two dominant black-fur genes (BB) mates with a rabbit that has one dominant and one recessive fur gene (Bb).

   a. Make a table to model this situation.

   b. What is the probability that their offspring will have brown fur? black fur?

8. Repeat Exercise 7 for a rabbit with two recessive brown-fur genes (bb) and a rabbit with one dominant and one recessive fur gene (Bb).

	B	B
b	Bb	Bb
b	Bb	Bb

recessive brown-fur gene

BB   **bb**

dominant black-fur gene

Bb   **Bb**   **Bb**   **Bb**

A rabbit with this pair of genes will have black fur.

Spinner M

Spinner N

9. **Group Activity** Work with another student.

   a. **Using Manipulatives** Make two spinners that match the ones shown.

   b. Predict the most likely sum when spinning both spinners once.

   c. Copy and complete the table for 50 trials. Each of you should spin a different spinner.

Sum	2	3	4	5	6
Tally	?	?	?	?	?

   d. **Writing** Were you surprised by the results? Why or why not?

Make a pointer out of a paper clip.

Basketball **For Exercises 10–12, use the table.**

The lottery system was revised in 1993 so that each team is now assigned combinations of four numbers from 1 to 14 (such as 1, 7, 9, and 12). The team with the worst record is assigned 250 number combinations. The four balls that come to the top first determine which team gets the first choice.

10. Under this system, what is the probability that the first draft pick will go to the team with the worst record? to the team in the lottery with the best record?

11. Under the system described on page 319, what was the probability that the first draft pick would go to the team with the worst record? to the team in the lottery with the best record?

12. Use the standings for 1992 and 1993 from the table on page 319. If the revised system were in place in 1992 and 1993, what would have been Orlando's chances of winning *both* the 1992 and 1993 lotteries?

13. Basketball Marisela's free-throw percentage is 0.700.

    a. Which part of the area diagram below best represents the probability of her making two free throws in a row?

    b. Which part of the tree diagram below best represents the probability of her making two free throws in a row?

    c. What do the other parts of the two diagrams represent?

    d. Find the probability that Marisela makes two free throws in a row.

TEAM STANDINGS IN REVERSE ORDER	Entries
Team 1	250
Team 2	203
Team 3	162
Team 4	126
Team 5	94
Team 6	66
Team 7	44
Team 8	27
Team 9	15
Team 10	8
Team 11	5
TOTAL	1000

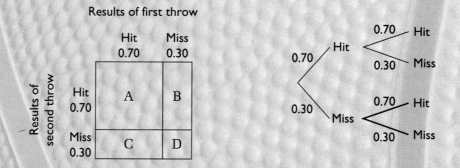

14. **Reading** Give examples from pages 319–322 of a pair of independent events and a pair of dependent events.

15. A bag contains three red marbles and seven blue marbles.

    a. Find the probability of picking two red marbles, if the first marble is returned to the bag before the second is picked.

    b. Find the probability of picking two red marbles, if the first marble is *not* returned to the bag before the second is picked.

Use this situation for Exercises 16–19.

Suppose you are playing a card game with a standard deck of playing cards and are dealt four cards, one after another, from the top of the deck.

16. Are these four events *independent* or *dependent*?

Find each probability.

17. P(four aces)   **18.** P(four hearts)   **19.** P(four face cards)

20. Jury Selection In the Massachusetts jury selection process, about one of every three people called for jury duty actually appears on the given date. These people can then be assigned to one of 10 panels of prospective jurors. Assume that all panels are the same size.

   a. What is the probability that a person called for jury duty appears?

   b. What is the probability that a person called for jury duty appears and is then assigned to Panel 2?

21. Lotteries A state lottery begins with choosing a ball from 30 table tennis balls that are numbered 1 through 30 in a bin. The first ball is put on display and a second ball is then chosen. Find the probability that the 6 is chosen and then the 21 is chosen. Round to the nearest thousandth.

22. Ali flipped a coin to determine the five answers on a true-false quiz. What is the probability that her five answers match all five correct answers?

23. Sharla and her two brothers pick cards at random every weekend to decide who has to clean each room of the house. Suppose it is Sharla's turn to pick her two rooms first. What is the probability that Sharla will have to clean both bathrooms?

(index cards reading: dining room, living room, kitchen, family room, upstairs bathroom, downstairs bathroom)

Ongoing ASSESSMENT

24. **Open-ended** Describe a situation about finding a probability that involves independent events. Change the situation slightly to describe a situation about finding a probability that involves dependent events. Find each probability.

Review PREVIEW

25. A bag contains two green marbles, four white marbles, and four red marbles. One marble is selected at random. *(Section 6-3)*

   a. Find the probability of selecting a white marble.

   b. Find the odds in favor of selecting a white marble.

Solve each equation for the variable shown in red. *(Toolbox Skill 15)*

26. $I = prt$ **27.** $3x - y = 40$ **28.** $mx + ny = p$

29. a. What does the symbol $_9P_2$ mean? *(Section 6-2)*

   b. Find the number of permutations of the letters in the word MARVELOUS arranged two at a time.

....

Use your survey results and the list from Exercise 47 in Section 6-3.

a. **Find the probability of each compound event.**

b. **Tell whether the events in each pair are *independent* or *dependent*.**

c. **Writing Explain how you arrived at your answer to part (b).**

30. A person with a birthday in the first half of the year prefers subject 4 to both subject 2 and subject 5.

31. A person with a birthday in the second half of the year prefers subject 4 to both subject 2 and subject 5.

Unit 6 **CHECKPOINT 1**

1. **Writing** Carl is playing a board game and wants to land on the "Free" space and then on the "Lucky Draw" space. He needs to roll two dice and get a total of 6, followed by a roll that gives a total of 9. Explain how to find the probability that he will roll the totals he needs.

2. John has a new bank card to use at automatic teller machines. For his security code he uses the four digits on the keypad that correspond to the letters in his name.   **6-1**

   a. List the letter arrangements John can use.

   b. Do you think it is a good idea for John to use an arrangement of the letters in his name for a security code? Why or why not?

3. How many seven-letter arrangements can be made from the letters in GRAVITY if you use each letter once?   **6-2**

4. How many permutations are there of 12 birds arranged 3 at a time on a telephone line?

For Exercises 5–7, each letter of the word ALGEBRA is put on one of seven cards. The cards are shuffled and one is chosen at random.   **6-3**

5. Find *P*(vowel). Find *P*(consonant).

6. Are the two events in Exercise 5 mutually exclusive? Are they complementary? Why or why not?

7. What are the odds against choosing a vowel?

8. Suppose a red die and a blue die are tossed. Find *P*(red 6 and blue 1).   **6-4**

9. Suppose you are playing a card game with a standard deck of playing cards and are dealt two cards from the top of the deck. Find *P*(two 3s).

Combinations

Choices, Choices

Focus
Find the number of ways
to select some items from
a group.

Julian likes five of the yogurt flavors at O'Leary's Frozen Yogurt Shop: vanilla, coffee, strawberry, peach, and mocha chip. Here is a partial list of the ways that Julian can order a cone with three scoops from these five flavors. Each scoop is a different flavor.

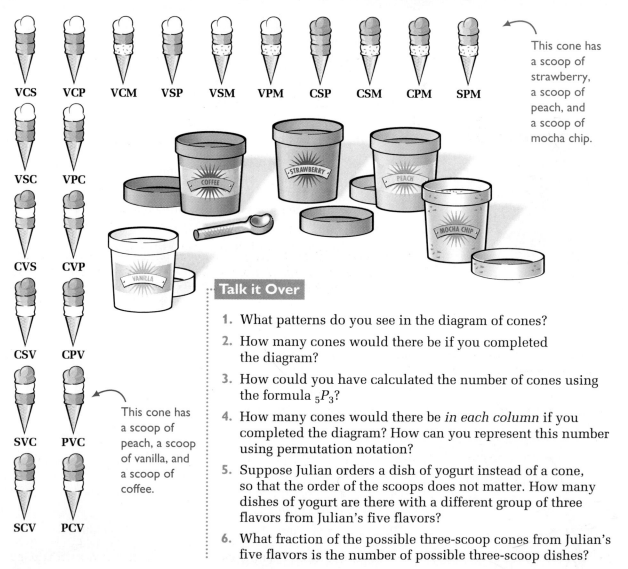

VCS VCP VCM VSP VSM VPM CSP CSM CPM SPM

This cone has a scoop of strawberry, a scoop of peach, and a scoop of mocha chip.

VSC VPC

CVS CVP

CSV CPV

SVC PVC

This cone has a scoop of peach, a scoop of vanilla, and a scoop of coffee.

SCV PCV

Talk it Over

1. What patterns do you see in the diagram of cones?

2. How many cones would there be if you completed the diagram?

3. How could you have calculated the number of cones using the formula $_5P_3$?

4. How many cones would there be *in each column* if you completed the diagram? How can you represent this number using permutation notation?

5. Suppose Julian orders a dish of yogurt instead of a cone, so that the order of the scoops does not matter. How many dishes of yogurt are there with a different group of three flavors from Julian's five flavors?

6. What fraction of the possible three-scoop cones from Julian's five flavors is the number of possible three-scoop dishes?

Order matters when you make a cone. Six different cones can have these flavors.

All dishes that have one peach, one strawberry, and one coffee scoop would be considered the same.

A selection made from a group of items when order is not important is called a **combination.** The symbol for the number of different combinations when n items are selected r at a time is $_nC_r$.

In the situation on page 328, there are 60 permutations of 5 flavors arranged 3 at a time. However, there are only 10 combinations of 5 flavors selected 3 at a time. There is a connection between the number of permutations and the number of combinations.

$$10 = \frac{60}{6} = \frac{_5P_3}{3!} = {_5C_3}$$

Since order does not matter, you have to divide by the number of arrangements of 3 flavors, 3!.

COMBINATIONS OF n ITEMS SELECTED r AT A TIME

The number of combinations of n items selected r at a time $(r < n)$ is given by this formula.

$$_nC_r = \frac{_nP_r}{r!} = \frac{n!}{(n-r)!r!}$$

Example

$$_9C_5 = \frac{_9P_5}{5!} = \frac{9!}{(9-5)!5!} = 126$$

$$_4C_4 = \frac{_4P_4}{4!} = \frac{4!}{(4-4)!4!} =$$

Sample

How many different groups of 3 actresses can be chosen to play the witches in *Macbeth* from these 6 actresses who audition: Val, Carla, Susan, Pat, Mimi, and Rose?

Sample Response

Order does not matter in this situation. You have to find the number of combinations of 6 items selected 3 at a time.

Method ❶

Problem Solving Strategy: Make a systematic list.

Represent each actress with one letter.

VCS	VSP	VPM	VMR	CSP	CPM	CMR	SPM	SMR	PMR
VCP	VSM	VPR		CSM	CPR		SPR		
VCM	VSR			CSR					
VCR									

20 different groups of 3 actresses can be chosen from 6 actresses.

Continued on next page.

Method ②

Problem Solving Strategy: Use a formula.

$$_6C_3 = \frac{6!}{(6-3)!3!} = \frac{6!}{3!3!} = \frac{6 \cdot 5 \cdot 4 \cdot 3 \cdot 2 \cdot 1}{3 \cdot 2 \cdot 1 \cdot 3 \cdot 2 \cdot 1} = 20$$

20 different groups of 3 actresses can be chosen from 6 actresses.

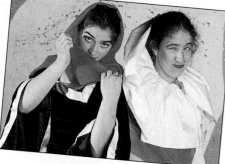

Talk it Over

Celia is choosing two photographs to decorate a bulletin board for a play. She has six good photographs to choose from.

7. How many different pairs of photographs can Celia choose out of six photographs?

8. How many ways can Celia arrange two photographs side by side when she has six to choose from?

9. Is question 7 asking for a number of *permutations* or a number of *combinations*? What about question 8?

Look Back ◄

How are combinations and permutations different? If you know the number of permutations of a group of items, how can you find the number of combinations of those items?

6-5 Exercises and Problems

Reading Tell the meaning of each expression.

1. $_7P_4$
2. $_7C_4$
3. $_8P_5$
4. $_8C_5$

5. Which is smaller, $_8P_5$ or $_8C_5$? How many times smaller? Why?

Find the value of each expression.

6. $_4P_3$
7. $_3C_3$
8. $_3C_0$
9. $_6C_2$
10. $_6C_4$
11. $_9C_3$
12. $_9C_6$
13. $_8P_4$

TECHNOLOGY NOTE
Some calculators have keys or menu items for combinations.

14. Describe any patterns you notice in the number of combinations in Exercises 7–12.

15. **Politics** The Springfield school board has seven members.

a. The board must have three officers: a chairperson, an assistant chairperson, and a secretary. How many different sets of these officers can be formed from this board?

b. How many three-person committees can be formed from this board?

c. Is part (a) asking for a number of *permutations* or a number of *combinations*? What about part (b)?

d. How are your answers to parts (a) and (b) related?

For Exercises 16–18, tell whether each situation is asking for a number of *permutations* **or a number of** *combinations*. **Then answer each question.**

Rubén Eugenio has room for three plants on a windowsill.

16. In how many different ways can three plants be arranged on his windowsill?

17. Suppose Rubén has six plants. How many groups of three plants can he put on his windowsill?

18. Suppose Rubén has nine plants. How many ways can three of these plants be arranged on his windowsill?

19. Security To open a combination lock, you dial a sequence of three numbers called the lock's *combination.* You turn the dial right for the first number, left for the second, and right again for the third.

   a. How many *combinations* are possible for a lock like the one shown?

   b. **Writing** Do you think a lock's combination is like a combination in mathematics? Why or why not?

20. Cheerleading Suppose fifteen people qualify for a college cheerleading squad, six women and nine men.

   a. How many six-member squads can be selected?

   b. Suppose that exactly two members of the six-member squad must be male. How many six-member squads can be selected?

   c. Find the probability of the event in part (b).

21. a. Copy and complete the table.

Numbers of Segments Connecting Points						
Number of points	3	4	5	6	...	n
Ways to connect points					...	—
Number of segments	3	6	?	?	...	?

   b. How are the numbers of segments that can be drawn connecting any two of the points like combinations of items?

22. Music The ten band directors at a summer band camp are planning to give a performance. One of the pieces they want to play calls for a French horn, a tuba, a trombone, and a trumpet. Each of the band directors can play all four instruments. How many different quartets can they have?

23. Business Suppose Carmeta Jackson owns a pizzeria and offers the options shown.

  a. How many ways can a customer order two toppings? three toppings?

  b. If a customer can order from zero to seven toppings, how many different groups of toppings can be ordered?

  c. How many different pizzas can a customer order at her pizzeria?

  d. **Writing** Write a radio advertisement for her pizzeria that includes your answer to part (c).

Ongoing **ASSESSMENT**

24. Group Activity Work with another student.

  a. You should each write one problem that can be solved using permutations and a related problem that can be solved using combinations.

  b. Solve the problems together.

  c. Discuss whether the problems are clearly of one type or the other. Work together to revise them if necessary.

Review **PREVIEW**

25. The athletic director at Piedmont High School picks names from a hat to decide who gets the door prizes at the awards banquet. Suppose the hat contains 15 names on green paper and 35 names on yellow paper. Find the probability of picking 2 names on green paper, if the first name is not returned to the bag before the second is picked. *(Section 6-4)*

Find the area of each figure. *(Toolbox Skill 28)*

26. a trapezoid with $base_1 = 15$ ft, $base_2 = 5$ ft, and height = 9 ft

27. a parallelogram with base = 90 mm and height = 48 mm

Predict the next number or term in each pattern. *(Section 1-5)*

28. 1, 3, 6, 10, 15, _?_   **29.** 5, 15, 45, 135, _?_   **30.** $2x$, $4x$, $16x$, $256x$, _?_

 Working on the Unit Project

31. Suppose your survey included all the subjects listed on page 294. How many interest questions like those described in Exercise 32 on page 301 would appear on your survey?

32. Suppose you want to extend your survey to include all basic courses in each subject area. If there are 23 basic courses, how many interest questions would appear on your survey?

6-6

Pascal's Triangle

Focus

Find patterns in Pascal's triangle. Recognize the elements of Pascal's triangle as combinations.

Shortcuts

This triangular pattern was pictured in a Chinese book entitled *Precious Mirror of the Four Elements* in A.D. 1303. The author, Chu Shih-Chieh, referred to it as "The Old Method." Evidence suggests that it originated with Liu Ju-Hsieh around A.D. 1100.

BY THE WAY...

The Chinese pattern has a modern form named after Blaise Pascal (1623–1662), a French mathematician and essay writer. He explored many of its properties, particularly those related to the study of probability.

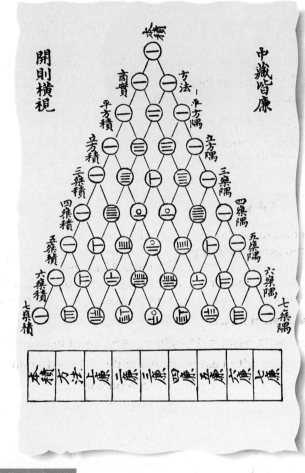

Talk it Over

1. Ignoring the Chinese characters, what symmetry do you see in the triangle?

2. How do the symbols in the first four rows seem to relate to each other?

3. What do you think the symbol ⊢ means?

4. What do you think the symbol ○̲ means?

What patterns do you see in Pascal's triangle?

- **Work with another student.**

(1) Each of you should copy the portion of **Pascal's triangle** shown below. Notice that the first row is row 0 and the first diagonal is diagonal 0.

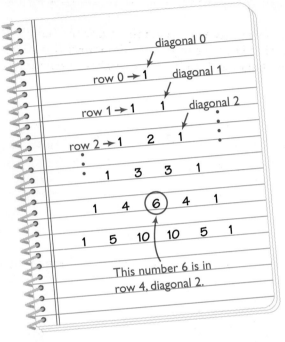

diagonal 0

row 0 → 1   diagonal 1

row 1 → 1   1   diagonal 2

row 2 → 1   2   1

1   3   3   1

1   4   ⑥   4   1

1   5   10   10   5   1

This number 6 is in row 4, diagonal 2.

(2) To locate a number in Pascal's triangle, you specify its row number and diagonal number. Each of you should pick a number in the triangle. Tell your partner its location. Make sure you agree on what number is in that location.

(3) There is a rule for creating each row from the numbers in the row above it. With your partner, figure out the rule and use it to create row 6.

(4) For each row, find the sum of the numbers. What pattern do you see in the sums? Predict the sum of the numbers in row 7.

(5) **a.** Use a formula to calculate these combinations:

$$_4C_0 \qquad _4C_1 \qquad _4C_2 \qquad _4C_3 \qquad _4C_4$$

b. In what row and diagonal of Pascal's triangle do you see each of the results from part (a)?

c. Predict where to find $_3C_2$ in Pascal's triangle. Test your prediction.

(6) Discuss any other number patterns you see in Pascal's triangle. Write down at least one.

Denise finds four different paperback books that she wants to buy but has enough money for only three books. Use Pascal's triangle to find the number of ways she can select three of the four books.

Sample Response

The notation $_4C_3$ represents the number of combinations of three different books that Denise can select from four different books. Locate the number in row 4, diagonal 3, to find the number of combinations.

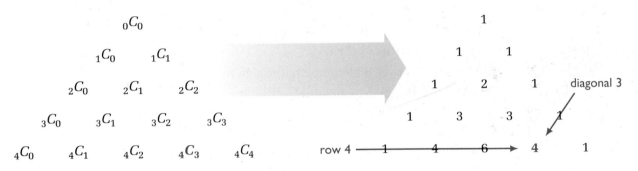

There are four ways Denise can select three of the four books.

X Lab

SOME PROPERTIES OF PASCAL'S TRIANGLE

Each number (except the 1's) is the sum of the two numbers just above it.

The number in row n, diagonal r, is $_nC_r$.

The sum of the numbers in row n is 2^n.

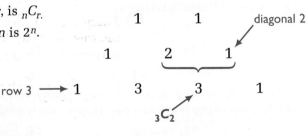

5. How could you use a formula to find the answer to the Sample?

6. For the situation in the Sample, how could you use a formula to find the total number of ways to select no books, one book, two books, or three books?

6-6 Pascal's Triangle

Look Back ←

Choose a row and a number in that row to illustrate each of the properties of Pascal's triangle listed on page 335.

6-6 Exercises and Problems

1. **a. Reading** What number is in row 3, diagonal 3, of Pascal's triangle?

   b. Describe how you could locate the number in Pascal's triangle that is the same as $_{15}C_5$.

   c. Without adding, find the sum of the numbers in row 10.

2. **Group Activity** Work with another student.

   a. Copy the Pascal's triangle shown and complete through row 9.

   b. For each row from rows 2–8, choose one number that is surrounded by six others. Find the product of the six numbers surrounding that number.

   c. Make a conjecture about the product of the six numbers surrounding any number.

```
              1
           1     1
        1     2     1
     1     3     3     1
```

3. Use the triangle you made for Exercise 2(a).

   a. Find the sum of the first five numbers in diagonal 1. Find that number on the next diagonal.

   b. Repeat part (a), using the first six numbers in diagonal 3.

   c. Make a conjecture about how to find the sum of the first n numbers of any diagonal without adding.

4. **Research** Find out what Pascal's law is. Also find all you can about a unit called a *pascal*.

Find each value using Pascal's triangle.

5. $_5C_2$ 6. $_4C_4$ 7. $_6C_5$ 8. $_6C_2$

9. $_7C_1$ 10. $_7C_6$ 11. $_5C_5$ 12. $_6C_3$

13. Use Pascal's triangle to find all the values of n and r for which $_nC_r = 6$.

For Exercises 14–18, suppose you have just a penny, a nickel, and a dime in your pocket. In how many ways can you choose each of the following?

14. no coins   15. exactly one coin   16. exactly two coins   17. three coins

18. **a.** Which row of Pascal's triangle gives you the answers to Exercises 14–17?

   b. How can you use the row you indicated in part (a) to find the total number of ways to choose no coins, one coin, two coins, or three coins?

   c. Reading How could you use a formula to answer part (b)?

19. Nita has six different pens in her book bag. Without looking she grabs three pens at random from the bag. How many three-pen combinations are possible?

20. Career Artists who do printmaking sometimes choose a variety of color combinations for the same design. Suppose the artist who made the prints shown chose from among eight colors. How many different three-color mixtures were possible?

21. Writing Which method did you use to answer Exercise 20? Explain why you chose that method.

22. Suppose you toss four coins. Use Pascal's triangle to find each number.

    a. number of outcomes that have exactly three heads

    b. number of outcomes that have at least three heads

    c. Compare the situations in parts (a) and (b). How are they alike? How are they different?

These cows by Andy Warhol were printed on wallpaper.

Ongoing **ASSESSMENT**

23. Open-ended Choose a row of Pascal's triangle. Describe a situation involving combinations where the solution is a number in that row.

Review **PREVIEW**

24. Use a formula to find the number of possible ways to assign a pair of roommates from a group of 120 women in a college dormitory. *(Section 6-5)*

Without graphing, identify the slope and the vertical intercept of the graph of each function. Then graph each function and tell if it is an *increasing function*, a *decreasing function*, or a *constant function*. *(Section 2-2)*

25. $y = 4x$ **26.** $y = -2x + 3$ **27.** $y = -3$

28. Make a tree diagram that shows all the possible outcomes when you toss three pennies. *(Section 6-1)*

Working on the Unit Project

29. Look back at Exercises 31 and 32 in Section 6-5. Explain how you can use Pascal's triangle to find the answers.

30. a. How could you use your survey results to find out which subject(s) students born in each half of the year find most interesting?

    b. Use the method you described in part (a) to identify the subject(s) students born in each half of the year find the most interesting.

Binomial Experiments with $P = \frac{1}{2}$

IT'S A TOSSUP

Focus

Find probabilities for experiments that have two outcomes for each trial and where the probability of each outcome is one half.

EXPLORATION

What are you likely to get when you toss four coins?

- **Materials: four coins**
- **Work with another student.**

① Copy the table.

Number of heads	0	1	2	3	4	Total tosses
First person's results	?	?	?	?	?	20
Second person's results	?	?	?	?	?	20
Total so far	?	?	?	?	?	40
Another team's results	?	?	?	?	?	40
Total for the two teams	?	?	?	?	?	80
Experimental probability	?	?	?	?	?	—

② One person tosses a group of four coins twenty times. The other person tallies in the table whether there are 0, 1, 2, 3, or 4 heads each time.

③ Change roles and repeat step 2.

④ Total the results of steps 2 and 3.

⑤ Combine results with another team and then calculate the experimental probability of each event to the nearest hundredth. For example:

$$P(0 \text{ heads}) = \frac{\text{total number of times no heads were tossed}}{80}$$

This is the total number of tosses for the two teams.

⑥ Make a graph of the probabilities you found. Label the axes as shown.

⑦ Discuss and summarize your findings.

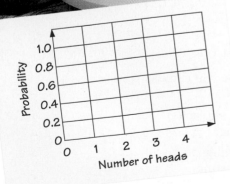

Binomial Experiments

Each time you tossed four coins in the Exploration, you performed a *binomial experiment*, which has the following characteristics.

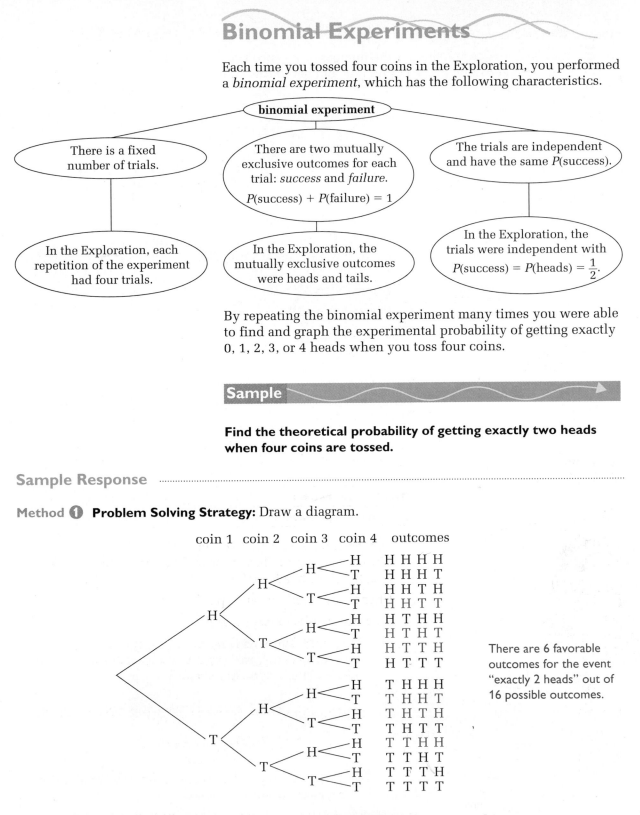

binomial experiment

There is a fixed number of trials.

There are two mutually exclusive outcomes for each trial: *success* and *failure*.
$P(\text{success}) + P(\text{failure}) = 1$

The trials are independent and have the same $P(\text{success})$.

In the Exploration, each repetition of the experiment had four trials.

In the Exploration, the mutually exclusive outcomes were heads and tails.

In the Exploration, the trials were independent with $P(\text{success}) = P(\text{heads}) = \frac{1}{2}$.

By repeating the binomial experiment many times you were able to find and graph the experimental probability of getting exactly 0, 1, 2, 3, or 4 heads when you toss four coins.

Sample

Find the theoretical probability of getting exactly two heads when four coins are tossed.

Sample Response

Method ❶ Problem Solving Strategy: Draw a diagram.

coin 1	coin 2	coin 3	coin 4	outcomes

			H	H H H H
		H	T	H H H T
	H		H	H H T H
		T	T	H H T T
H			H	H T H H
		H	T	H T H T
	T		H	H T T H
		T	T	H T T T
			H	T H H H
		H	T	T H H T
	H		H	T H T H
		T	T	T H T T
T			H	T T H H
		H	T	T T H T
	T		H	T T T H
		T	T	T T T T

There are 6 favorable outcomes for the event "exactly 2 heads" out of 16 possible outcomes.

$$P(\text{exactly 2 heads out of 4}) = \frac{\text{number of favorable outcomes}}{\text{number of possible outcomes}} = \frac{6}{16} = \frac{3}{8} = 0.375$$

Method 2 Use Pascal's triangle.

The number of favorable outcomes is the number of ways you can toss four coins and get two heads, or $_4C_2$. You find this number in row 4, diagonal 2, of Pascal's triangle.

$$_0C_0$$
$$_1C_0 \quad _1C_1$$
$$_2C_0 \quad _2C_1 \quad _2C_2$$
$$_3C_0 \quad _3C_1 \quad _3C_2 \quad _3C_3$$
$$_4C_0 \quad _4C_1 \quad _4C_2 \quad _4C_3 \quad _4C_4$$

$$1$$
$$1 \quad 1$$
$$1 \quad 2 \quad 1$$
$$1 \quad 3 \quad 3 \quad 1$$
$$1 \quad 4 \quad 6 \quad 4 \quad 1$$

The number of possible outcomes is the sum of the number of ways four coins can land. This is the sum of the numbers in row 4 of Pascal's triangle.

$$\underbrace{1 + 4 + 6 + 4 + 1}_{\text{sum of numbers in row 4}} = 16 \qquad \text{or} \qquad 2^4 = 16$$

sum of numbers in row $n = 2^n$

$$P(\text{exactly 2 heads out of 4}) = \frac{\text{number of favorable outcomes}}{\text{number of possible outcomes}} = \frac{6}{16} = \frac{3}{8} = 0.375$$

Talk it Over

1. a. Which of the methods in the Sample do you prefer? Why?

   b. How could you use a formula to find the number of favorable outcomes?

2. Find $P(\text{exactly 1 head})$ when four coins are tossed.

3. Find $P(\text{exactly 2 heads})$ when five coins are tossed.

4. The graph shows the theoretical probability of getting exactly 0, 1, 2, 3, 4, 5, or 6 heads when you toss six coins. Use the graph to estimate the probability of getting four heads when you toss six coins.

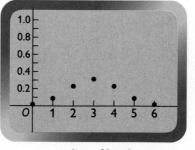

Look Back

How do binomial experiments relate to Pascal's triangle?

1. **Reading** Explain why the experiment in the Sample on page 339 is a binomial experiment.

2. a. **Reading** Use the tree diagram in the Sample on page 339 to complete this table.

Ways of Getting Heads When Tossing Four Coins						
Number of heads	0	1	2	3	4	Total
Number of outcomes	?	?	?	?	?	?
Probability	?	?	?	?	?	?

   b. Make a graph of the probability of each number of heads in part (a).

   c. **Writing** Compare the graph you made in part (b) with the graph you made in step 6 of the Exploration on page 338. How are they alike? How are they different?

Find the probability of the event shown when each group of coins is tossed.

3.

4.

5.

For Exercises 6–8, assume that the birth of a boy and the birth of a girl are equally likely.

6. A three-child family might include 0, 1, 2, or 3 girls.

   a. Why is this a binomial situation?

   b. **Using Manipulatives** Do a simulation. Let heads represent girls and tails represent boys. Toss a group of 3 coins 25 times and tally in a table whether there are 0, 1, 2, or 3 girls in the family.

   c. **Group Activity** Combine results with another student. Then calculate the experimental probability of each event to the nearest hundredth.

   d. Find the theoretical probability of each event.

   e. On the same axes, graph the experimental and theoretical probability of each event. Compare the graphs.

7. Find the probability of a six-child family including exactly three girls.

8. a. Predict whether the probability that a four-child family will include exactly two girls is *50%*, *greater than 50%*, or *less than 50%*. Explain your reasoning.

   b. Find the probability that a four-child family will include exactly two girls.

Rosencrantz and Guildenstern Are Dead by Tom Stoppard is a twentieth century play about two characters from Shakespeare's *Hamlet*. It begins with the title characters on stage. They both have large leather money bags, but Guildenstern's (GUIL) is almost empty and Rosencrantz's (ROS) is almost full.

GUIL *takes a coin out of his bag, spins it, letting it fall.*

ROS: Heads. *He picks it up and puts it in his bag. The process is repeated.*

Heads. *Again.*

Heads. *Again.*

Heads. *Again.*

Heads.

GUIL . . . *flips over two more coins.* . . . ROS *announces each of them as "heads."*

ROS: Eighty-five in a row—beaten the record!

GUIL . . .: And if you'd lost? If they'd come down against you, eighty-five times, one after another, just like that?

ROS . . .: Eighty-five in a row? *Tails?*

GUIL: Yes! What would you think?

ROS (*doubtfully*): Well . . . . Well, I'd have a good look at your coins for a start! . . .

GUIL: It must be indicative of something, besides the redistribution of wealth. . . . each individual coin spun individually (*he spins one*) is as likely to come down heads as tails and therefore should cause no surprise each individual time it does. . . . The equanimity of your average tosser of coins depends upon a law, or rather a tendency, or let us say a probability, or at any rate a mathematically calculable chance, which ensures that he will not upset himself by losing too much or upset his opponent by winning too often.

9. a. In all, 92 coins came down heads 92 times. Based on the experimental results of Rosencrantz and Guildenstern's coin tossing, what is the experimental probability that a tossed coin comes down heads?

  b. What is the theoretical probability that 92 tosses all come down heads?

10. Later in the play Guildenstern makes another wager, "Bet me then. . . . Year of your birth. Double it. Even numbers I win, odd numbers I lose." What is the probability that he will win? Explain.

11. Suppose you select the five answers on a true-false quiz at random.

   a. Why is this a binomial situation?

   b. How many different ways could you answer the five questions?

   c. How many ways could you answer the five questions correctly?

   d. What is the probability of getting all the answers correct?

   e. **Writing** Which method did you use to answer part (b)? part (c)? Tell why you chose each method.

12. Suppose a score of at least 60% is needed to pass a true-false quiz with five questions.

   a. At least how many correct answers are needed to pass?

   b. How many ways can you get at least enough correct answers to pass?

   c. Describe the method you used to get your answer in part (b).

   d. Find the probability of getting at least a 60% on a true-false quiz with five questions by answering randomly.

13. Graph the probabilities associated with getting 0, 1, 2, 3, 4, or 5 questions correct on a true-false quiz with five questions.

14. Marcus makes half of the free-throw shots he attempts in basketball. He shoots four free-throw shots. What is the probability that he will make all four shots?

15. Half of the 70 teachers at Grant High School are married. You need to find 5 chaperones for a dance. If you ask 10 teachers at random to chaperone, what is the probability that you will ask exactly 5 married teachers?

16. Phyllis Hayashibara has a part-time job. There is a 50% chance that she will have to work on any given evening. She has already worked Friday and Saturday evenings. What is the probability that she will have to work on Sunday evening? Explain your answer.

Ongoing ASSESSMENT

17. **Writing** Samantha says that the probability of getting exactly *two* heads when five coins are tossed is the same as the probability of getting exactly *three* heads when five coins are tossed. Do you agree? Why or why not?

Quiz: *Voting Rights*

Mark whether each statement is *True* or *False*.

T F 1. In 1878 Susan B. Anthony succeeded in bringing the 19th Amendment, which guaranteed voting rights to women in the United States, before a senate committee.

T F 2. Carrie Chapman Catt was instrumental in getting the 19th Amendment ratified in 1920.

T F 3. The 15th Amendment guaranteed African Americans the right to vote. The 24th Amendment eliminated poll taxes as an obstacle to voting.

T F 4. In 1893, New Zealand gave women full voting rights.

T F 5. In 1971, United States citizens 18 years of age and over were guaranteed the right to vote.

18. Use Pascal's triangle to find the number of possible ways two students could tie in a six-person race. *(Section 6-6)*

Find the coordinates of each image described. *(Section 5-4)*

19. translation of *QRST* 2 units left and 2 units down

20. dilation of *QRST* with scale factor 2 and center at the origin

21. Suppose you roll a die. *(Section 6-3)*

    a. Find $P(5)$.

    b. Find $P(\text{prime})$.

    c. Are the events in parts (a) and (b) mutually exclusive? Why or why not?

Working on the Unit Project

22. Suppose it is equally likely that a person chosen at random has a birthday in the first or second half of the year.

    a. What is the theoretical probability that a person chosen at random has a birthday in the first half of the year? in the second half of the year?

    b. Find the probability that exactly two of six people chosen at random have a birthday in the second half of the year.

23. Based on your survey results, what is the experimental probability that a person chosen at random has a birthday in the first half of the year? in the second half of the year?

Unit 6   **CHECKPOINT 2**

1. **Writing** Describe how you can use Pascal's triangle to find the number of combinations of five things selected four at a time.

2. **a.** How many different groups of five trophies can you select from nine trophies?   **6-5**

    b. How many different ways can you arrange five trophies in a row?

3. What are the numbers in row 3 of Pascal's triangle? Show how you can find the numbers.   **6-6**

4. Use combination notation to describe the number of ways two items can be chosen from four items. Then use Pascal's triangle to find the number of combinations.

5. Find $P(\text{exactly 3 heads})$ when three coins are tossed.   **6-7**

6. Find $P(\text{exactly 4 heads})$ when five coins are tossed.

6-8

Binomial Experiments with $P \neq \frac{1}{2}$

More Often Than Not

Focus
Find probabilities for binomial experiments where the probability of each outcome is not one half.

The probability of being left-handed is about 10%. These are some notable left-handed people: Monica Seles, Cesar Rosas, and Ken Griffey, Jr.

Sample

Find the probability that exactly two out of three students chosen at random are left-handed.

Sample Response

This is a binomial experiment. There are two outcomes, left-handed and right-handed, and each trial is independent.

Method ❶ Use Pascal's triangle.

Step 1

Find the probability of each outcome that has exactly two left-handed students.

$P(\text{L}) \cdot P(\text{L}) \cdot P(\text{R}) = (0.1)(0.1)(0.9)$
$= 0.009$

You can multiply the probabilities because the events are independent.

Step 2

The number of ways to select two out of three students is found in row 3, diagonal 2.

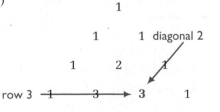

1

1   1 diagonal 2

1   2   1

row 3   1   3   3   1

Step 3

Multiply. The probability of choosing exactly two left-handed students is

$3(0.009) = 0.027.$

Method ❷ Problem Solving Strategy: Draw a diagram.

Step 1 Draw a tree diagram.

A tree diagram with the probability of each branch written on that branch is called a **probability tree diagram.**

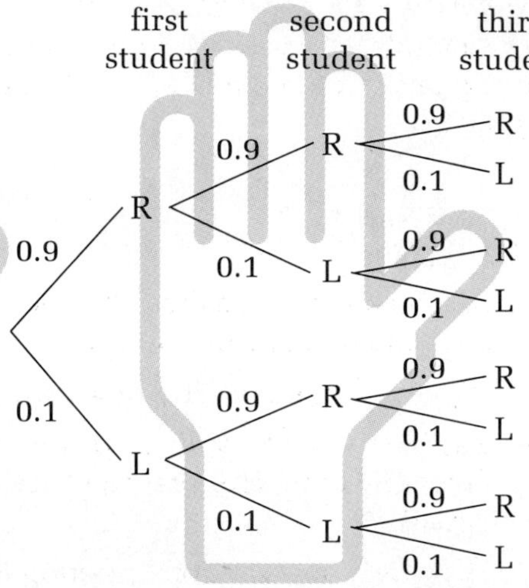

	first student	second student	third student	outcomes	probabilities
	0.9 R	0.9 R	0.9 → R	RRR	$(0.9)(0.9)(0.9) = 0.729$
			0.1 → L	RRL	$(0.9)(0.9)(0.1) = 0.081$
		0.1 L	0.9 → R	RLR	$(0.9)(0.1)(0.9) = 0.081$
			0.1 → L	RLL	$(0.9)(0.1)(0.1) = 0.009$
	0.1 L	0.9 R	0.9 → R	LRR	$(0.1)(0.9)(0.9) = 0.081$
			0.1 → L	LRL	$(0.1)(0.9)(0.1) = 0.009$
		0.1 L	0.9 → R	LLR	$(0.1)(0.1)(0.9) = 0.009$
			0.1 → L	LLL	$(0.1)(0.1)(0.1) = 0.001$

Step 2 Find the probability of each outcome with exactly two left-handed students.

$P(\text{RLL}) = 0.009$ $\qquad$ $P(\text{LRL}) = 0.009$ $\qquad$ $P(\text{LLR}) = 0.009$

Step 3 The probability of choosing exactly two left-handed students is:

$0.009 + 0.009 + 0.009 = 0.027$ ←—— You can add the probabilities because the outcomes are mutually exclusive.

When the outcomes are *not equally likely*, as in the Sample, you cannot divide favorable outcomes by total outcomes to find a probability.

$$\frac{\text{favorable}}{\text{total}} = \frac{3}{8} = 0.375 \neq 0.027$$

Combinations with at least one left-handed student:

RRL   RLL   LLL
RLR   LRL
LRR   LLR
$3(0.081) + 3(0.009) + 0.001$
0.271

"at least one" and "none" are complements.

$P(\text{at least one}) = 1 - P(\text{none})$
$= 1 - P(\text{RRR})$
$= 1 - 0.729$
$= 0.271$

Talk it Over

Use the Sample.

1. Why are the outcomes not equally likely?

2. Show how to use the formula $_3C_2$ to find the number of ways to select exactly two students from three students.

3. Suppose your friend thinks that you can just multiply $(0.1)(0.1)(0.9)$ to find the probability that exactly two out of three students chosen at random are left-handed. How can you show your friend that he or she is mistaken?

4. Two students used information from the tree diagram in the Sample to find the probability that *at least* one out of three students chosen at random is left-handed. Their work is shown at the left. Which method do you prefer? Why?

5. Find the probability that at least two out of three students chosen at random are left-handed.

Experiments with more than two outcomes can be binomial experiments if you consider one outcome to be "favorable" and the remaining outcomes to be "unfavorable."

For example, suppose you roll a die and consider a "1" to be a favorable outcome. Then 2, 3, 4, 5, and 6 are the unfavorable outcomes.

Talk it Over

6. Suppose you roll a die. What is the probability of the favorable outcome, rolling a "1"?

7. What is the probability of not rolling a "1"?

8. Suppose you roll a die three times and consider a "1" to be a favorable outcome. Draw a probability tree diagram for this situation.

9. Use your diagram from question 8. Are the outcomes equally likely? Why or why not?

Look Back ◄

How are binomial experiments with $P \neq \frac{1}{2}$ like binomial experiments with $P = \frac{1}{2}$? How are they different?

6-8 Exercises and Problems

1. **Reading** Why is the answer to the Sample not $\frac{3}{8}$?

For Exercises 2–5, use the special coin described below.

A special coin has been created for a magic trick. The probability of its landing on heads is 0.25 and on tails is 0.75.

2. Draw a probability tree diagram for three tosses of the coin.

3. Find the probability of tossing three consecutive heads.

4. Find the probability of tossing exactly two heads in three tosses.

5. Find the probability of tossing at least two heads in three tosses.

6. Cassandra generally wins three games out of five when she plays table tennis with Alec. What is the probability of her winning at least two of the next five games?

7. Suppose you want to find the probability of rolling at least one "1" on three rolls of a die.

   a. Tell how this problem meets the criteria for a binomial experiment.   independent

   b. Solve the problem. Show your work.

8. **Writing** Compare the two situations represented by the tables below. How are they alike? How are they different?

Ways of Getting Left-handed Students When Selecting Three Students					
Number of "lefties"	0	1	2	3	Total
Number of outcomes	1	3	3	1	8
Probability	0.729	0.243	0.027	0.001	1

Ways of Getting Heads When Tossing Three Coins					
Number of heads	0	1	2	3	Total
Number of outcomes	1	3	3	1	8
Probability	0.125	0.375	0.375	0.125	1

Health The graph shows the range of success rates for some vaccines. All the rates apply to people who have received the minimum number of doses (usually three). All the vaccines protect people through at least the age of ten.

Suppose four children under the age of ten have each had the minimum number of doses of all the vaccines. Find the range of probabilities for each situation.

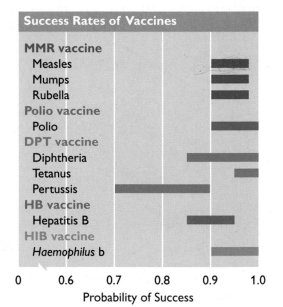

9. All four children are exposed to measles. All four children get the disease.

10. All four children are exposed to polio. None of the children gets the disease.

11. All four children are exposed to mumps. Only one child gets the disease.

12. All four children are exposed to pertussis. At least three children get the disease.

13. Each of the five questions on a multiple-choice test has four choices.

   a. What is the probability of guessing correctly on any single question?

   b. What is the probability of guessing incorrectly on any single question?

   c. Copy and complete the table.

Ways of Getting Correct Answers						
Number correct	0	1	2	3	4	5
Number of outcomes	?	?	?	?	?	?
Probability	?	?	?	?	?	?

   d. Use your completed table to find the probability of getting at least three out of five questions correct just by guessing.

14 T E C H N O L O G Y Mike receives an "A" on tests 90% of the time. You will use a calculator to generate random test results for Mike. You should count any number from 0 to 0.9 as an "A."

Alternative Approach Generate random numbers from a telephone book (see page 19).

   a. Why does it make sense to count numbers from 0 to 0.9 as "A's"?

   b. Generate a group of five random numbers between 0 and 1. Tally in a table whether Mike gets 0, 1, 2, 3, 4, or 5 "A's."

   c. Repeat part (b) for a total of 25 trials.

   d. Find the experimental probability of each event in your table.

   e. Find the theoretical probability of each event in your table.

For Exercises 15–17, use the matrices below.

Colleges must have an idea of how many students will drop out each year in order to decide how many students they can accept. Matrix A contains the drop-out rates by class for each of three colleges. Matrix B contains enrollment figures at the three colleges.

Matrix A

	A	B fresh.	C soph.	D jr.	E sr.
1					
2	College 1	0.22	0.15	0.12	0.08
3	College 2	0.07	0.03	0.02	0.01
4	College 3	0.35	0.22	0.13	0.07
5					
6					

Matrix B

	A	B Coll. 1	C Coll. 2	D Coll. 3
1				
2	fresh.	416	2215	500
3	soph.	324	2060	324
4	jr.	275	1994	252
5	sr.	241	1950	218
6				

15. Find out how many students at each college will drop out. Describe your method.

16. What is the probability that exactly five out of six sophomores chosen at random from College 1 will stay for another year?

17. What is the probability that exactly four out of six freshmen chosen at random from College 3 will stay for another year?

Ongoing **ASSESSMENT**

18. a. **Open-ended** Write and solve a multiple-choice quiz for this section of the unit. Your quiz should have four questions, and there should be five choices for each question.

    b. Find the probability of getting exactly two questions correct just by guessing on your quiz.

19. Find the probability of getting exactly three heads when five coins are tossed. *(Section 6-7)*

Estimate the solutions of each system of quadratic equations shown. *(Section 4-7)*

20. $y = 0.5x^2$
$y = 2x^2 + 3x - 3$

21. $y = x^2 + 0.75$
$y = -x^2 + 1.25$

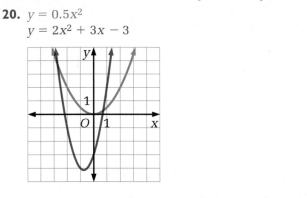
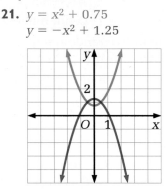

Write and simplify an expression for the volume of each box. *(Toolbox Skills 10, 28)*

22.

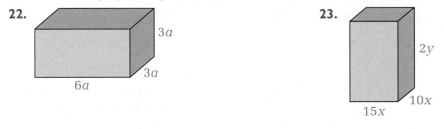

$3a$

$3a$

$6a$

23.

$2y$

$10x$

$15x$

Working on the Unit Project

24. a. Research Find out the number of births in each month over the past few years in your city, town, or county, or at a large hospital in your community.

  b. What is the probability that a person chosen at random from the sample you chose in part (a) has a birthday in the first half of the year? in the second half of the year?

  c. Look back at your answer to Exercise 23 in Section 6-7. Are the probabilities you found in your survey close to the probabilities based on the data you got in part (a)? If not, why do you think there is a significant difference?

25. Use your survey results.

  a. Find the probability that exactly two out of six people chosen at random have a birthday in the second half of the year.

  b. How does your answer to part (a) compare to your answer to part (b) of Exercise 22 in Section 6-7?

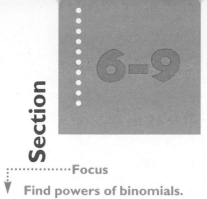
The Binomial Theorem

An expression that can be written as the sum of two monomials, such as $a + b$, is a **binomial.** Here are some powers of binomials:

$$(a + b)^2, (a + b)^3, \text{ and } (a + b)^4$$

You can write these powers in *factored form* or *expanded form*.

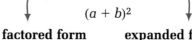

power of a binomial

$$(a + b)^2$$

factored form   **expanded form**

written as a product ⟶ $(a + b)(a + b) = a^2 + 2ab + b^2$ ⟵ written as a sum

You can use models to show these two forms.

Talk it Over

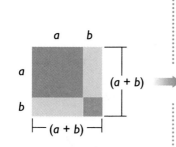

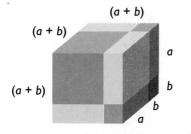

1. Use the area model of $(a + b)^2$. Explain how it shows that the factored form and expanded form are equal.

2. Explain how to use the distributive property to rewrite the product $(a + b)(a + b)$ in expanded form.

Use the volume models below.

3. Explain how you know that each of the three gold prisms in the diagram has a volume of a^2b cubic units.

4. Explain how you know that each of the three green prisms in the diagram has a volume of ab^2 cubic units.

5. Explain how to use the distributive property to rewrite $(a + b)(a + b)(a + b)$ in expanded form.

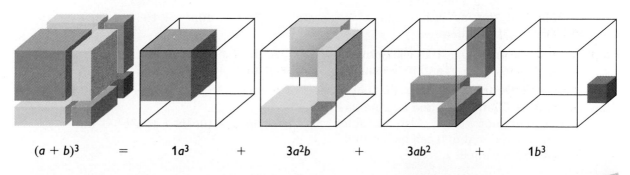

$(a + b)^3$ = $1a^3$ + $3a^2b$ + $3ab^2$ + $1b^3$

Look at the patterns in the following expanded forms of the powers of the binomial $a + b$. Coefficients and exponents of 1 are shown to help you see the patterns.

$$(a + b)^0 = \qquad\qquad 1$$
$$(a + b)^1 = \qquad\qquad 1a^1 + 1b^1$$
$$(a + b)^2 = \qquad 1a^2 + 2a^1b^1 + 1b^2$$
$$(a + b)^3 = 1a^3 + 3a^2b^1 + 3a^1b^2 + 1b^3$$

Talk it Over

6. What pattern do you see in the coefficients?

7. What pattern do you see in the exponents of the a variables? of the b variables?

8. Since $b^0 = 1$ and $a^0 = 1$, you could write

$$(a + b)^2 = 1a^2b^0 + 2a^1b^1 + 1a^0b^2$$

Do the exponents follow the pattern you saw in question 7?

9. Rewrite the expanded form of $(a + b)^3$ using zeros as exponents where appropriate.

The coefficients you use in the expanded form of $(a + b)^n$ are found in the nth row of Pascal's triangle.

Sample 1

Write $(a + b)^5$ in expanded form.

Sample Response

```
        1
      1   1
    1   2   1
  1   3   3   1
1   4   6   4   1
1  5  10  10  5  1
```

Use Pascal's triangle to find the coefficients in the expanded form.

Step 1 Because the power is 5, look at the fifth row of Pascal's triangle. Write the six numbers, leaving space for the variables.

$$1 \quad + 5 \quad + 10 \quad + 10 \quad + 5 \quad + 1$$

Step 2 Write powers of a next to each coefficient, starting with a^5 and decreasing from there.

$$1a^5 \quad + 5a^4 \quad + 10a^3 \quad + 10a^2 \quad + 5a^1 \quad + 1a^0$$

Step 3 Write powers of b next to each power of a, starting with b^0 and increasing from there.

$$1a^5b^0 + 5a^4b^1 + 10a^3b^2 + 10a^2b^3 + 5a^1b^4 + 1a^0b^5$$

Step 4 Simplify. Coefficients and exponents of 1 are usually not written. Also, variables with an exponent of 0 can be omitted because they equal 1.

$$a^5 + 5a^4b + 10a^3b^2 + 10a^2b^3 + 5ab^4 + b^5$$

10. **a.** How many terms are there in the expanded form of $(a + b)^6$?

    b. Write $(a + b)^6$ in expanded form.

··· ► Now you are ready for:
Exs. 1–8 on pp. 354–355

11. How many terms are there in the expanded form of $(a + b)^n$?

The Binomial Theorem

You can rewrite the expanded form in Sample 1 using the $_nC_r$ notation instead of numbers from Pascal's triangle.

$$(_5C_0)a^5b^0 + (_5C_1)a^4b^1 + (_5C_2)a^3b^2 + (_5C_3)a^2b^3 + (_5C_4)a^1b^4 + (_5C_5)a^0b^5$$

This pattern can be generalized.

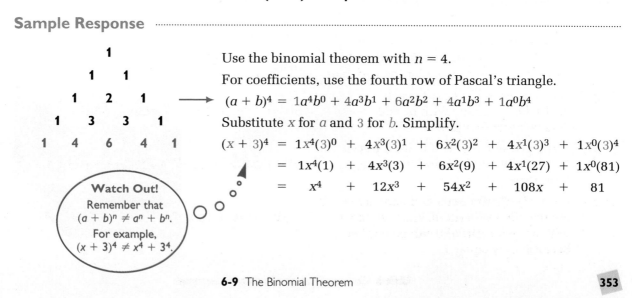

THE BINOMIAL THEOREM

If n is a positive integer, then this is the expanded form of $(a + b)^n$:

$$(_nC_0)a^nb^0 + (_nC_1)a^{n-1}b^1 + (_nC_2)a^{n-2}b^2 + \cdots$$

$$\cdots + (_nC_{n-2})a^2b^{n-2} + (_nC_{n-1})a^1b^{n-1} + (_nC_n)a^0b^n$$

The coefficients of the form $(_nC_r)$ are numbers in the nth row of Pascal's triangle.

Sample 2

Write $(x + 3)^4$ in expanded form.

Sample Response

```
          1
        1   1
      1   2   1
    1   3   3   1
  1   4   6   4   1
```

Use the binomial theorem with $n = 4$.

For coefficients, use the fourth row of Pascal's triangle.

$(a + b)^4 = 1a^4b^0 + 4a^3b^1 + 6a^2b^2 + 4a^1b^3 + 1a^0b^4$

Substitute x for a and 3 for b. Simplify.

$(x + 3)^4 = 1x^4(3)^0 + 4x^3(3)^1 + 6x^2(3)^2 + 4x^1(3)^3 + 1x^0(3)^4$

$\qquad\quad = 1x^4(1) + 4x^3(3) + 6x^2(9) + 4x^1(27) + 1x^0(81)$

$\qquad\quad = x^4 + 12x^3 + 54x^2 + 108x + 81$

Watch Out!
Remember that $(a + b)^n \neq a^n + b^n$.
For example,
$(x + 3)^4 \neq x^4 + 3^4$.

Sample 3

Write $(p - q)^5$ in expanded form.

Sample Response

Use the binomial theorem with $n = 5$.

For coefficients, use the fifth row of Pascal's triangle.

$$(a + b)^5 = 1a^5b^0 + 5a^4b^1 + 10a^3b^2 + 10a^2b^3 + 5a^1b^4 + 1a^0b^5$$

Think of $(p - q)$ as $(p + (-q))$. Substitute p for a and $-q$ for b.

$$
\begin{aligned}
(p - q)^5 &= 1p^5(-q)^0 + 5p^4(-q)^1 + 10p^3(-q)^2 + 10p^2(-q)^3 + 5p^1(-q)^4 + 1p^0(-q)^5 \\
&= 1p^5(q^0) + 5p^4(-q^1) + 10p^3(q^2) + 10p^2(-q^3) + 5p^1(q^4) + 1p^0(-q^5) \\
&= 1p^5q^0 + (-5p^4q^1) + 10p^3q^2 + (-10p^2q^3) + 5p^1q^4 + (-1p^0q^5) \\
&= p^5 \quad - 5p^4q \quad + 10p^3q^2 \quad - 10p^2q^3 \quad + 5pq^4 \quad - q^5
\end{aligned}
$$

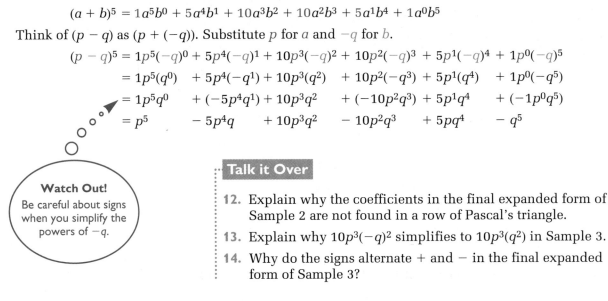

Watch Out!
Be careful about signs when you simplify the powers of $-q$.

Talk it Over

12. Explain why the coefficients in the final expanded form of Sample 2 are not found in a row of Pascal's triangle.

13. Explain why $10p^3(-q)^2$ simplifies to $10p^3(q^2)$ in Sample 3.

14. Why do the signs alternate $+$ and $-$ in the final expanded form of Sample 3?

Look Back

Now you are ready for:
Exs. 9–32 on pp. 355–357

How do you use the patterns in Pascal's triangle and decreasing and increasing powers to write any power of a binomial?

6-9 Exercises and Problems

1. Use the area model to write $(x + 3)^2$ in expanded form.

2. Use the distributive property to write $(x + 7)^2$ in expanded form.

3. **a.** Use the volume model to write $(m + 2)^3$ in expanded form.

   b. Describe the volumes of the eight blocks in the model.

4. **Reading** Where in Pascal's triangle are the coefficients of the terms in the expanded form of $(a + b)^7$?

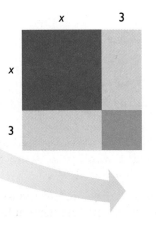

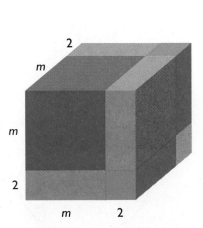

Use Pascal's triangle and patterns of exponents to write each power of a binomial in expanded form.

5. $(c + d)^3$ **6.** $(p + q)^4$ **7.** $(x + y)^5$

8. Write the expanded form of $(a + b)^6$ using $_nC_r$ notation instead of numbers from Pascal's triangle for the coefficients.

Use the binomial theorem to write each power of a binomial in expanded form.

9. $(x + 2)^3$ **10.** $(z + 2)^5$ **11.** $(y - 2)^4$ **12.** $(c + 3)^4$

13. $(x + 3)^3$ **14.** $(x - 3)^3$ **15.** $(a + 1)^{10}$ **16.** $(m - 1)^9$

Will numbers from a row of Pascal's triangle appear in the expanded form of each binomial? Explain why or why not.

17. $(p + q)^6$ **18.** $(p + 2)^3$ **19.** $(p + 2q)^3$

20. Write $(x - 2y)^3$ in expanded form.

21. a. Describe the number pattern for powers of 11 shown below.

			+100000
		+10000	+50000
	+1000	+4000	+10000
+100	+300	+600	+1000
+20	+30	+40	+50
+1	+1	+1	+1
$11^2 = 121$	$11^3 = 1331$	$11^4 = 14641$	$11^5 = 161051$

b. Write the expanded form of $(10 + 1)^6$ using the binomial theorem. Stack the terms to make the next sum in the number pattern. Check your answer by finding 11^6 with a calculator.

c. Explain how the number pattern is related to the expanded form of $(10 + 1)^n$.

22. a. Describe the number pattern for powers of 9 shown below.

			+100000
		+10000	−50000
	+1000	−4000	+10000
+100	−300	+600	−1000
−20	+30	−40	+50
+1	−1	+1	−1
$9^2 = 81$	$9^3 = 729$	$9^4 = 6561$	$9^5 = 59049$

b. Write the expanded form of $(10 - 1)^6$ using the binomial theorem. Stack the terms to make the next sum in the number pattern. Check your answer by finding 9^6 with a calculator.

c. Explain how the number pattern is related to the expanded form of $(10 - 1)^n$. Why do the signs in this pattern alternate + and −?

23. A cube with sides of length $(n + 2)$ is dipped in a bucket of paint and then cut into unit cubes. In this exercise you will find how many of these unit cubes have 0, 1, 2, and 3 faces painted.

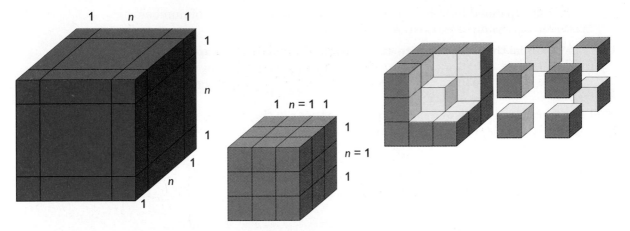

a. Complete the table for values of n from 0 to 3.

n	$n + 2$	Total number of unit cubes	Unit cubes painted on 0 faces	Unit cubes painted on 1 face	Unit cubes painted on 2 faces	Unit cubes painted on 3 faces
0	2	8	0	0	0	8
1	3	27	1	6	?	?
2	4	?	?	?	?	?
3	?	?	?	?	?	?
n	$n + 2$	$(n + 2)^3$	?	?	?	?

b. Complete the table for row n.

c. Explain how the expanded form of $(n + 2)^3$ is related to the entries in row n.

24. You saw that $(a + b)^2$ can be modeled as a *square* made of 4 rectangles, 1 with area a^2, 2 with area ab, and 1 with area b^2.

You also saw that $(a + b)^3$ can be modeled as a *cube* made of 8 prisms, 1 with volume a^3, 3 with volume a^2b, 3 with volume ab^2, and 1 with volume b^3.

A *hypercube* is a four-dimensional cube. Consider a hypercube of length $(a + b)$ on each side.

a. Write a power of a binomial that expresses the "hyper-volume" of the hypercube.

b. If you "explode" the hypercube in the same way that the square and cube were exploded in this section, how many pieces do you expect?

c. How many different "hyper-volumes" will there be among the pieces? What are they?

d. How many pieces do you expect will have each "hyper-volume"? Show how your answer is related to the expanded form of $(a + b)^4$.

25. **a.** If you toss 4 coins, how many different ways can you get exactly 4 heads? exactly 3 heads and 1 tail? exactly 2 heads and 2 tails? exactly 1 head and 3 tails? exactly 4 tails?

    b. Write an expanded form of $(h + t)^4$.

    c. **Writing** How does your expression in part (b) relate to the situation of the possible outcomes when tossing 4 coins? Describe the significance of the coefficients and exponents of each term of the expanded form.

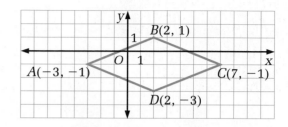

26. Terry misses the school bus 5% of the time. What is the probability that he will miss the bus exactly three out of five days this week? *(Section 6-8)*

27. Show that *ABCD* is a rhombus. *(Section 5-2)*

Tell whether each statement about animals is *True* or *False*. *(Section 1-6)*

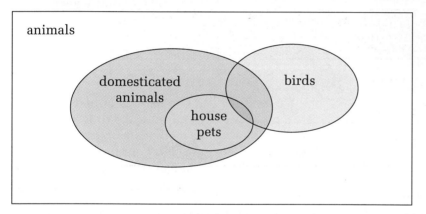

28. If an animal is a house pet, then it is domesticated.

29. Every bird is a domesticated animal.

30. Some domesticated animals are birds.

31. All animals that are not domesticated are not house pets.

Working on the Unit Project

32. **Writing** Use your survey results. Describe any positive or negative correlations between having a birthday in the first or second half of the year and interest in the school subjects included in your survey. If you found no strong correlations, provide a possible explanation.

Completing the Unit Project

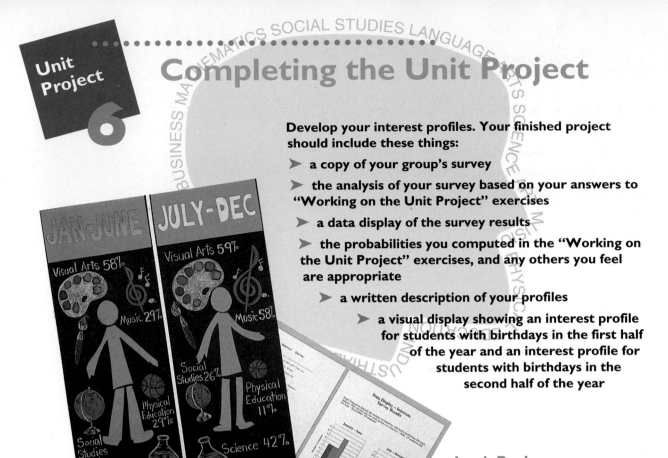

Develop your interest profiles. Your finished project should include these things:

➤ a copy of your group's survey

➤ the analysis of your survey based on your answers to "Working on the Unit Project" exercises

➤ a data display of the survey results

➤ the probabilities you computed in the "Working on the Unit Project" exercises, and any others you feel are appropriate

➤ a written description of your profiles

➤ a visual display showing an interest profile for students with birthdays in the first half of the year and an interest profile for students with birthdays in the second half of the year

Look Back ◄——

If you had the opportunity to improve the procedures or methods you used to develop your profiles, what changes would you make?

Alternative Projects

Project 1: Mendel's Theory of Heredity

Research the principles of heredity developed by Gregor Mendel. Prepare a poster describing the principles. Include a Punnett square and explain how to use it to predict the inheritance of genetic traits.

Project 2: Odds of Winning a Lottery

If your state or a neighboring one runs a lottery, contact the lottery commission to find out the odds of winning, how the odds are computed, and when and how the odds may change. At the same time, interview some people who regularly buy lottery tickets, some who never buy them, and some who only occasionally buy them. Ask them the same questions. Use the information you collected to write an article with the title, "State Lotteries: Fact vs. Fiction."

1. Make a tree diagram to show the possible necklaces from these choices: 28 in., 30 in., or 32 in. long; gold or silver finish; with all blue stones, all red stones, or all green stones.

6-1

One format for making license plates is to use two letters followed by four digits. For Questions 2 and 3, how many different license plates are possible for each situation?

6-2

2. Zero cannot be the first digit and repeats are allowed.

3. Zero cannot be the first digit and repeats are not allowed.

4. There are spaces for 10 bicycles in the rack next to the library. One afternoon 15 people who rode bicycles were there at the same time. Write a mathematical expression for determining the number of ways the bicycles could be arranged in the rack.

For Questions 5–9, use the spinner.

6-3

5. Find P(landing on red).

6. Find P(landing on blue or on an odd).

7. Find P(not landing on green).

8. Find the odds in favor of landing on blue.

9. Find the odds against landing on a 1.

A bag contains twelve buttons as shown.   6-4

10. Find the probability of picking three red buttons if each button is returned to the bag before the next button is picked.

11. Find the probability of picking three red buttons if each button is *not* returned to the bag before the next button is picked.

12. Four is the minimal number of colors you need to shade a map so that no region is the same color as one next to it. Colored pencils are sold in boxes of twelve different colors. How many ways can you select four colors to shade a map so that no region is the same color as one next to it?

6-5

13. Find $_5P_3$ and $_5C_3$. Compare the two values.

14. Write the fourth row of Pascal's triangle in the following ways.

6-6

   a. Use numerical values.

   b. Use combination notation.

15. **Writing** Describe the relationship between Pascal's triangle and combinations.

16. **Baseball** Mathias successfully steals half of the stolen bases he attempts to steal. What is the probability that he will successfully steal exactly two of the next five bases he attempts to steal?

6-7

17. **Open-ended** Find an example of an event with two equal out-comes in everyday life and write a probability problem about it.

Aidan sees a movie on Friday nights 60% of the time. 6-8

18. Find *P*(Aidan sees a movie on exactly three of the next four Fridays).

19. Find *P*(Aidan sees a movie on at least three of the next four Fridays).

Write each power of a binomial in expanded form. 6-9

20. $(x + 2)^4$ **21.** $(x - 3)^5$ **22.** $(x + y)^3$ **23.** $(r - s)^3$

24. **Self-evaluation** How are counting methods used in probability? Which of the counting methods from this unit (tree diagram, organized list/table, combinations, permutations) makes the most sense to you? Why?

25. **Group Activity** Work in a group of three students. Read and discuss the following problem.

Stan Musial had a lifetime batting average of 0.331, which means he got a hit about one third of the times that he had an official at bat. What is the probability that he would not get exactly two hits in five consecutive at bats?

a. One student should draw a diagram of the problem. A second student should show how to use Pascal's triangle to solve the problem. The third student should draw and use a spinner to solve the problem experimentally.

b. Were all three results the same? Why or why not? Which method seemed to work best?

IDEAS AND (FORMULAS)=X^2

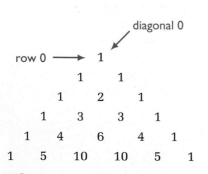

➤ **Problem Solving** Tree diagrams, tables, and organized lists are used to count small numbers of outcomes. *(pp. 296–298)*

➤ The multiplication counting principle is used to find the total number of outcomes of a series of selections. *(p. 303)*

➤ The number of arrangements (permutations) of *n* distinct objects is *n*!. *(p. 304)*

➤ The number of permutations of *n* different objects arranged *r* at a time ($r < n$) is given by this formula. When items are repeated, this formula does not necessarily apply. *(p. 304)*
$$_nP_r = \frac{n!}{(n - r)!}$$

➤ The number of combinations of *n* items selected *r* at a time ($r < n$) is given by this formula. With combinations, order does not matter. *(p. 329)*
$$_nC_r = \frac{n!}{(n - r)!r!}$$

➤ **Problem Solving** You can use Pascal's triangle to find combinations. The number in row *n*, diagonal *r*, is $_nC_r$. The sum of the numbers in row *n* is 2^n. *(p. 335)*

diagonal 0

row 0 ⟶ 1
1   1
1   2   1
1   3   3   1
1   4   6   4   1
1   5   10   10   5   1

STATISTICS & PROBABILITY

➤ To find the probability of mutually exclusive events A and B, add: $P(A \text{ or } B) = P(A) + P(B)$. *(p. 311)*

➤ The sum of the probabilities of complementary events is 1: $P(\text{event}) + P(\text{not the event}) = 1$. *(p. 312)*

➤ These ratios apply to equally likely outcomes. *(p. 314)*

$$\text{Probability of an event} = \frac{\text{number of favorable outcomes}}{\text{number of possible outcomes}}$$

$$\text{Odds in favor of an event} = \frac{\text{number of favorable outcomes}}{\text{number of unfavorable outcomes}}$$

$$\text{Odds against an event} = \frac{\text{number of unfavorable outcomes}}{\text{number of favorable outcomes}}$$

➤ To find the probability of independent events A and B, multiply the probabilities of the individual events: $P(A \text{ and } B) = P(A) \cdot P(B)$. *(p. 321)*

➤ To find the probability of dependent events A and B, multiply the probability of A by the probability of B after A: $P(A \text{ and } B) = P(A) \cdot P(B \text{ after } A)$. *(p. 323)*

➤ You can use Pascal's triangle or a probability tree diagram to find the probability of binomial events whether the two outcomes are equally likely or not. *(pp. 339–340, 345–346)*

GEOMETRY

➤ You can use area models to represent the probability of a compound event. *(pp. 321, 325)*

➤ You can use an area model to represent $(a + b)^2$ and a volume model to represent $(a + b)^3$. *(p. 351)*

ALGEBRA

➤ The binomial theorem is used to expand expressions of the form $(a + b)^n$, where n is a positive integer. The coefficients of the form $_nC_r$ are numbers in the nth row of Pascal's triangle. *(p. 353)*

$$(_nC_0)a^n b^0 + (_nC_1)a^{n-1}b^1 + (_nC_2)a^{n-2}b^2 + \cdots$$
$$\cdots + (_nC_{n-2})a^2 b^{n-2} + (_nC_{n-1})a^1 b^{n-1} + (_nC_n)a^0 b^n$$

Key Terms

- **tree diagram** (p. 296)
- **factorial, !** (p. 304)

- **complementary events** (p. 312)
- **independent events** (p. 320)
- **combination** (p. 329)
- **probability tree diagram** (p. 346)
- **expanded form** (p. 351)

- **outcome** (p. 296)
- **permutation** (p. 304)

- **odds in favor, odds against** (p. 314)
- **dependent events** (p. 320)
- **Pascal's triangle** (p. 334)
- **binomial** (p. 351)

- **binomial theorem** (p. 353)

- **event** (p. 296)
- **mutually exclusive events** (p. 311)
- **compound events** (p. 320)

- **sample space** (p. 320)
- **binomial experiment** (p. 339)
- **factored form** (p. 351)

unit 7

Logic and Proof

Mysteries

How good a detective are you? What clues can you find in this picture that could help you determine **WHODUNIT?** For instance, what day and time did the crime likely take place? Can you tell whether the writer was left-handed or right-handed? What do you think the message on the paper means? Does it look as if anything was removed from the desk?

The Daily News
Sunday Edition

whoDUNit?

Mystery stories have been popular in many countries for centuries. Among the mystery writers whose books have served as the basis for TV programs or movies are British author Agatha Christie and French author Maurice Leblanc. In their stories the mystery is solved by the police or by detectives like Jane Marple and Arsène Lupin.

AGATHA CHRISTIE

Arsène **LUPIN**
L'Aiguille creuse

Maurice Leblanc

Write a Mystery Story

Your project is to write a mystery story. To structure your story, you will need an outline that contains all the clues you give the reader. Your outline should show how the clues fit together to point to the solution of your mystery. As you outline your story, use two of the techniques of logical argument presented in the unit.

Also include in your story a travel itinerary and applications of at least two of the postulates and theorems about angles and parallel lines that you study in the unit.

When all the groups have completed their stories, have the members of another group read your group's story. Ask them to evaluate it according to the following criteria.

? Does the reader want to continue reading in order to solve the mystery?

? Does the reader have enough clues to solve the mystery?

? Does solving the mystery challenge, surprise, or inform the reader?

In **real life** not all mysteries are solved by amateur, police, or private detectives. Specialists in many fields use logic and reasoning to solve mysteries.

archaeology

Archaeologists dig for evidence of the existence of a mythic empire like the Toltec empire in central Mexico.

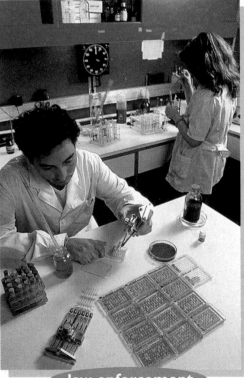

law enforcement

Forensic, or legal, scientists analyze the DNA in samples of blood or hair to determine if they came from a suspect in the case.

art history

Art historians are able to date paintings by determining the elements contained in the paint.

For this project you should work in a group of four students. Here are some ideas to help you get started.

☞ Decide where your story will take place and list the characters. The setting for your story could be a place you know, a place you read about, or even a place you make up.

Settings
- ~~school~~
- museum
- ~~boat~~
- ~~train~~
- apartment building
- ~~hospital~~
- woods

☞ Think of a mystery that you can write about. You might write about a missing object, a person who disappears, an unexplained sound, or an object that turns up in an unexpected place.

☞ Discuss possible clues to the solution of your mystery.

☞ Plan to meet later to discuss how you can: use logical arguments to develop an outline for your story; use a travel itinerary as a plot element; and apply theorems and postulates about angles or parallel lines.

Working on the Unit Project

Your work in Unit 7 will help you write your mystery story.

Related Exercises:

Section 7-1, Exercise 48
Section 7-2, Exercises 32, 33
Section 7-3, Exercise 29
Section 7-4, Exercise 43
Section 7-5, Exercise 24
Section 7-6, Exercise 24
Section 7-7, Exercise 24
Section 7-8, Exercise 27

Alternative Projects p. 423

Can We Talk Mysteries

➤ Why do you think mystery stories have been popular for so long in different cultures?

➤ Science is full of unsolved mysteries, such as why the dinosaurs became extinct. What other unsolved scientific mysteries have you heard about? What solutions have some scientists proposed?

➤ Which medium do you think is best for presenting a mystery story—books, movies, TV, or live theater? Why do you think so?

➤ What skills do you think private detectives, medical detectives, archaeologists, forensic scientists, and art historians have in common?

7-1

Using *And, Or, Not*

ConJunction

Bridget was researching part-time jobs for herself and some friends. She made a table of all the information she found. This type of organized listing is sometimes called a **database.**

Business	Job	Location	Hours/week	Hourly pay ($)
Cow Bar	ice cream server	South Mall	10	4.50
Bond's	filing clerk	South Mall	12	4.50
Food Stuff	stock clerk	South Mall	15	5.00
Lunch Bag	ice cream server	North Mall	20	4.75
Shop-All	stock clerk	North Mall	10	5.20
Great Lawns	yard worker	neighborhood	10	8.00
Pooch's	dog walker	neighborhood	15	4.00

Many people use databases in their work. Usually the information is stored in a computer.

You can search a database using the words *and, or,* and *not.*

Use Bridget's database.

a. Kayla is looking for a job that is for 15 or more hours per week *and* that pays over $4.50 per hour. Which jobs should Kayla consider?

b. Lucas wants a job that is for 15 or more hours per week *or* that pays over $4.50 per hour. Which jobs should Lucas consider?

c. Jason is willing to take any job but has no transportation to the North Mall. Which jobs should Jason consider?

Sample Response

Here are the conditions involved in parts (a)–(c).

15 or more hours per week   pay over $4.50   not at North Mall

Business	Job	Location	Hours/week	Hourly pay ($)
Cow Bar	ice cream server	South Mall	10	4.50
Bond's	filing clerk	South Mall	12	4.50
Food Stuff	stock clerk	South Mall	15	5.00
Lunch Bag	ice cream server	North Mall	20	4.75
Shop-All	stock clerk	North Mall	10	5.20
Great Lawns	yard worker	neighborhood	10	8.00
Pooch's	dog walker	neighborhood	15	4.00

a. Kayla wants a job that meets both conditions   *and*   . She should consider a job as a stock clerk at Food Stuff or as an ice cream server at Lunch Bag.

b. Lucas wants a job that meets condition   *or*   or both. He should consider the jobs at Food Stuff, Lunch Bag, Shop-All, Great Lawns, and Pooch's.

c. Jason wants a job that meets condition   . He should consider the jobs at Cow Bar, Bond's, Food Stuff, Great Lawns, and Pooch's.

Talk it Over

Use the database above. Recommend which job(s) each person should consider. Explain your reasoning.

1. Jean is willing to work as a stock clerk or to work at the North Mall.

2. Shenida wants a job that pays over $5 per hour and is for 20 or more hours per week.

Venn Diagrams for Logic

Statements involving *and*, *or*, and *not* have special names as described below.

Two statements connected by *and* form a **conjunction**. It is true when both statements are true.

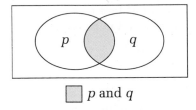

☐ *p* and *q*

Two statements connected by *or* form a **disjunction**. It is true when at least one statement is true.

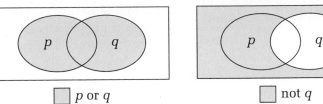

☐ *p* or *q*

A statement involving *not* is called a **negation**.

☐ not *q*

Reasoning with Or

In everyday language, *or* can mean two different things.

In the first situation *or* means at the library or on the field, *not both*. This is called an *exclusive or*.

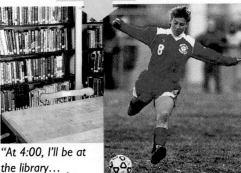

"At 4:00, I'll be at the library...

not both

...or on the playing field."

In the second situation *or* can mean being at the library, listening to music, or doing both. This is called an *inclusive or*.

"At 4:00, I'll be at the library or listening to music."

Logical statements in mathematics and in this book use the *inclusive or*.

······► Now you are ready for:
Exs. 1–20 on pp. 369–371

Talk it Over

Tell whether the *inclusive or* or the *exclusive or* is being used.

3. To meet graduation requirements Joe needs to take a writing course or a literature course next semester. He chooses to take creative writing and American literature.

4. Wakenda can afford to buy Bena either a classical music tape or a reggae tape for her birthday. Wakenda buys a reggae tape.

Logic with Graphs

Some mathematical statements involving a conjunction or a disjunction can be graphed on a number line or a coordinate plane.

MUSEUM ADMISSION

REGULAR	$7
ADULTS 65 YEARS & OVER	$6
CHILDREN 5 YEARS & UNDER	FREE

Sample 2

Use a mathematical statement and a number line to show the ages of people who pay the regular admission price at the art museum.

Sample Response

People who are over 5 *and* under 65 pay the regular admission price. Let a represent the ages of people who pay the regular admission price. Then $a > 5$ and $a < 65$.

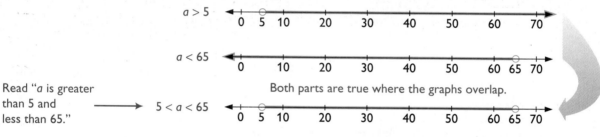

Read "a is greater than 5 and less than 65." $\longrightarrow$

Both parts are true where the graphs overlap.

Sample 3

Graph the disjunction $y \geq x$ or $x < 3$ on a coordinate plane. Tell which points are on the graph.

Sample Response

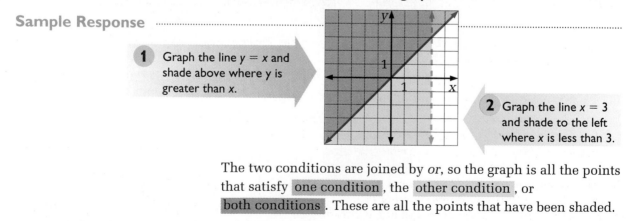

1 Graph the line $y = x$ and shade above where y is greater than x.

2 Graph the line $x = 3$ and shade to the left where x is less than 3.

The two conditions are joined by *or*, so the graph is all the points that satisfy one condition , the other condition , or both conditions . These are all the points that have been shaded.

Look Back

What is a conjunction? When is it true? What is a disjunction? When is it true? What is a negation?

▶ Now you are ready for: Exs. 21–48 on pp. 371–372

Unit 7 Logic and Proof

1. **Reading** What does the shaded portion of each Venn diagram on page 367 mean?

For Exercises 2–4, use this part of a database for the Museum of Fine Arts in Boston.

Detail from woven and embroidered Peruvian cloak, A.D. 50–100

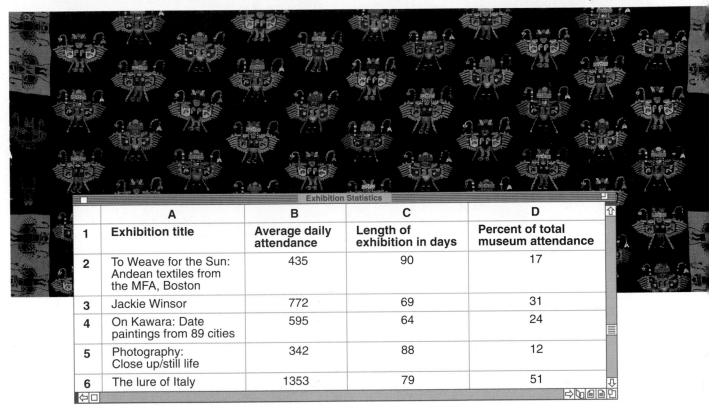

Exhibition Statistics

	A	B	C	D
1	Exhibition title	Average daily attendance	Length of exhibition in days	Percent of total museum attendance
2	To Weave for the Sun: Andean textiles from the MFA, Boston	435	90	17
3	Jackie Winsor	772	69	31
4	On Kawara: Date paintings from 89 cities	595	64	24
5	Photography: Close up/still life	342	88	12
6	The lure of Italy	1353	79	51

2. Which exhibition(s) lasted more than 75 days and had an average daily attendance greater than 500?

3. For which exhibition(s) was the average daily attendance over 600 or the percent of total museum attendance greater than 20?

4. **Writing** Describe two ways to search the database to find exhibitions that lasted more than 80 days and did not have a percent of total attendance less than 15.

For Exercises 5–8, use the Venn diagram showing seniors ( ) taking creative writing ( ). Match each letter W–Z with the student it represents.

5. Joan is a senior and is taking creative writing.

6. Sheila is a junior and is not taking creative writing.

7. Linh is a junior and is taking creative writing.

8. Lee is a senior and is not taking creative writing.

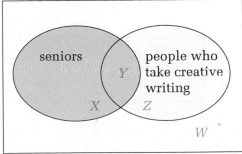

To make electrical current flow, a *circuit*, or continuous path for the current, is needed. These diagrams show the two main ways circuits can be connected.

Parallel Circuit

Series Circuit

9. Use the parallel circuit.

a. Will one light bulb stay lit if the other bulb is removed from its base?

b. Liz says that when one bulb or the other bulb is lit, current is flowing. She knows that current is flowing when both bulbs are lit. Is the *or* that Liz is using *inclusive* or *exclusive*?

10. Use the series circuit.

a. Will one light bulb stay lit if the other bulb is removed from its base?

b. Write a statement that describes the conditions for both bulbs to remain lit. Tell whether your statement is a *conjunction* or *disjunction*.

11. A red light bulb, a green bulb, and a yellow bulb are connected in a series circuit. Describe which bulbs must be in their bases for all the bulbs to be lit. Tell whether your statement is a *conjunction* or *disjunction*.

12. a. Use triangles *A–G*. Copy the table. Show where each triangle should be placed. Triangle *G* has been done for you.

	Acute	Right	Obtuse
Scalene	?	G	?
Isosceles	?	?	?
Equilateral	?		

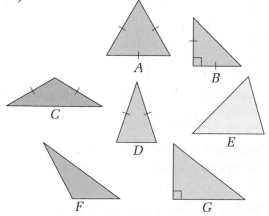

b. List the triangles that are isosceles and obtuse.

c. List the triangles that are isosceles or obtuse.

What conclusion can you reach from each set of conditions?

13. I am in the house or outside. I am not in the house.

14. The footprints are those of Caroline, Caitlin, or Kyra. The footprints are not Caroline's.

For Exercises 15 and 16, each conclusion is not justified. Explain why.

15. We are at the ball game or we are eating pizza. We are eating pizza. Conclusion: We are not at the ball game.

16. The person leaving a message on my recorder is Lily, Rose, or Talia. It is not Lily's voice. Conclusion: It is Talia's voice.

Thomas is at a food store. He says, "I will buy peanuts or I will buy raisins." For each situation, tell whether his statement was accurate.

17. He buys peanuts only.

18. He buys cashews only.

19. He buys a mixture of peanuts and raisins.

20. Suppose Thomas had said, "I will buy peanuts and raisins." He bought only peanuts. Was his statement accurate?

For Exercises 21–23, match each conjunction or disjunction with the letter of its graph.

21. $x > -20$ and $x \le 10$

22. $x < -20$ or $x \ge 10$

23. $x > -20$ or $x \ge 10$

A. 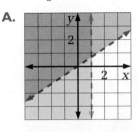   B. 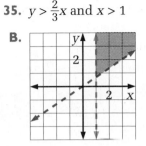   C.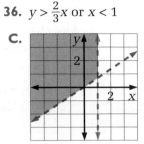

Graph each conjunction or disjunction on a number line.

24. $x \le 7$ or $x \ge 10$

25. $x > 7$ and $x < 10$

26. $x > 7$ and $x > 10$

27. $x < 7$ or $x > 10$

28. $x \le 7$ and $x < 10$

29. $x > 7$ or $x < 10$

30. Which of Exercises 24–29 can be written $7 < x < 10$?

Open-ended Write a conjunction or disjunction whose graph fits each description.

31. a segment

32. no points

33. the entire number line

Match each conjunction or disjunction with the letter of its graph.

34. $y > \frac{2}{3}x$ and $x < 1$

35. $y > \frac{2}{3}x$ and $x > 1$

36. $y > \frac{2}{3}x$ or $x < 1$

A. 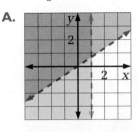   B. 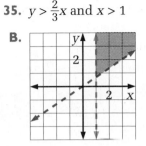   C.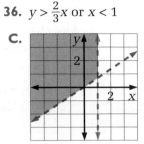

Graph each conjunction or disjunction on a coordinate plane. Tell which points are on the graph.

37. $y \ge 2x$ and $y > 5$

38. $y > x + 4$ or $y \le x - 3$

39. $y < 2x$ or $y < 5$

40. $y > -x$ and $y < -x - 1$

41. Open-ended Represent two situations involving inequalities as in Sample 2. Make one situation a conjunction and one a disjunction. Label each one and draw its graph on a number line.

42. Write $(x + 3)^3$ in expanded form. *(Section 6-9)*

Use the Museum of Fine Arts database from Exercises 2–4. Suppose you choose an exhibition at random. Find each probability. *(Section 6-3)*

43. P(exhibit lasts more than 60 days)

44. P(exhibit lasts less than 70 days)

45. P(the average daily attendance is greater than 500 and the percent of total attendance is greater than 30)

46. P(the average daily attendance is greater than 500 or the percent of total attendance is greater than 30)

47. Draw a Venn diagram that shows the relationships among quadrilaterals, parallelograms, and rectangles. *(Section 5-1)*

Working on the Unit Project

You can use a database to store information about the characters in your story.

48. a. Use the clues about Characters A, B, and C to complete this database. Write *Yes* or *No* in each box.

> **Clue 1** Each character is on only one team.

> **Clue 2** Each character is from only one country.

> **Clue 3** Character A has never been to Thailand.

> **Clue 4** Character B is allergic to the chlorine used in swimming pools.

> **Clue 5** The character who plays volleyball is from Ireland.

> **Clue 6** Character C plays basketball.

b. Tell which team each character plays on and which country each character comes from.

	A	B	C
Basketball	?	?	?
Volleyball	?	?	?
Swimming	?	?	?
Ireland	?	?	?
Thailand	?	?	?
Costa Rica	?	?	?

Implications

Mind Your P's and Q's

Biologists use classifications to organize information.

All prairie dogs are rodents.

There are several other ways to say
the same thing. Examples are given
below. The Venn diagram represents
them all.

> If an animal is a prairie dog, then it is a rodent.
> Every prairie dog is a rodent.
> The fact that an animal is a prairie dog implies that it is
> a rodent.
> An animal is a prairie dog only if it is a rodent.

You can represent these statements with symbols.

BY THE WAY...

Prairie dogs are not dogs, and
guinea pigs are not pigs. They
are both rodents, which are
characterized by large front
teeth used to gnaw. Mice,
beavers, chinchillas, and porcu-
pines are rodents, too.

Read "p implies q" or "if p, then q."

$$p \rightarrow q$$

Let p represent the "if" part or
hypothesis "an animal is a prairie dog." —

Let q represent the "then" part or
conclusion "an animal is a rodent."

Statements that can be written in the form $p \rightarrow q$ are called
implications or **conditionals.**

Use the implication "All rectangles have congruent diagonals."

a. Rewrite the implication in four different ways.

b. Tell whether the implication is *True* or *False*. If it is true, draw a Venn diagram for the implication. If it is false, give a counterexample.

c. Suppose $p \rightarrow q$ represents the implication. What do p and q represent in this case?

d. Write the *converse* of the implication. Tell whether it is *True* or *False*. If it is false, give a counterexample.

Sample Response

hypothesis ⌐   ⌐ conclusion

a. If a figure is a rectangle, **then** it has congruent diagonals.

Every rectangle has congruent diagonals.

The fact that a figure is a rectangle implies that it has congruent diagonals.

A figure is a rectangle only if it has congruent diagonals.

figures with congruent diagonals

rectangles

b. True. (See page 281.)

c. p means "a figure is a rectangle." q means "a figure has congruent diagonals."

d. The converse is "If a figure has congruent diagonals, then it is a rectangle." The converse is false. Here is a counterexample.

This trapezoid has congruent diagonals, but it is not a rectangle.

NORTH AMERICA

Canada

United States

Mexico

Talk it Over

1. Use the implication "I am in Canada only if I am in North America." Write the implication in if-then form. Then represent the implication with a Venn diagram.

2. Use this implication, "$x + 5 = 9$ implies that $x = 4$."

   a. Tell whether the implication is *True* or *False*.

   b. Write the converse of the implication.

   c. Tell whether the converse is *True* or *False*. If it is false, give a counterexample.

Cautions with If-then

Here is another way you can write the implication in the Sample.

If a figure is a rectangle , then it has congruent diagonals.

A figure has congruent diagonals if it is a rectangle .

This new type of translation is not the converse. This sentence is still symbolized $p \rightarrow q$, since the "if" part is still the same.

Remember, *"p only if q"* says the same thing as "If *p*, then *q*."

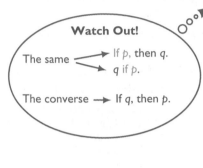

Watch Out!

The same → If *p*, then *q*.
             q if *p*.

The converse → If *q*, then *p*.

Talk it Over

3. Write "An animal is a chinchilla only if it is a rodent" in if-then form.

4. Draw a Venn diagram for the implication.

5. Is it possible to be in the *chinchilla* loop of your diagram without being in the *rodent* loop?

6. Is it possible to be in the *rodent* loop of your diagram without being in the *chinchilla* loop?

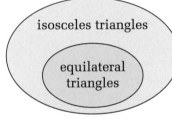

isosceles triangles

equilateral triangles

Look Back ◄

Write at least four equivalent implications for this Venn diagram. Write the converse of one of your statements. Tell whether the converse is *True* or *False*.

7-2 Exercises and Problems

1. **Reading** Which part of an implication is the hypothesis?

2. What are four translations of $p \rightarrow q$?

3. Use symbols to write the converse of $p \rightarrow q$.

For Exercises 4–7:

a. **Suppose $p \rightarrow q$ represents each implication. What do p and q represent in each case?**

b. **Rewrite each implication in an equivalent form using the key word(s) indicated.**

c. **Draw a Venn diagram for each implication.**

4. If a figure is a rhombus, then its diagonals are perpendicular. (*all*)

5. A figure is a square only if it is a rhombus. (*implies*)

6. Whenever it is Saturday, it is a day of the weekend. (*every*)

7. If a figure is a cylinder, then the formula for its volume is $V = Bh$. (*only if*)

For Exercises 8–13:

a. **Rewrite each implication in if-then form. Tell whether each implication is *True or False*. If it is false, give a counterexample.**

b. **Write the converse of each implication. Tell whether each converse is *True or False*. If it is false, give a counterexample.**

8. Whenever the probability of an event is zero, the event is impossible.

9. Rectangles are parallelograms.

10. The New England states are east of the Mississippi River.

11. This month is February if today is Valentine's Day.

12. A number ending in 0 implies that it is divisible by 2.

13. Cleo is a golden retriever only if Cleo is a dog.

PERIODIC TABLE

☐ Alkali metals
☐ Alkaline earth metals
☐ Transition metals
☐ Lanthanide series
☐ Actinide series
☐ Other metals
☐ Nonmetals
☐ Noble gases

connection to **CHEMISTRY**

Many of the elements that make up the substances in the universe are classified as metals. One category of metals is *transition metals*. Examples of transition metals include copper, silver, nickel, and gold.

1 H																	2 He
3 Li	4 Be											5 B	6 C	7 N	8 O	9 F	10 Ne
11 Na	12 Mg											13 Al	14 Si	15 P	16 S	17 Cl	18 Ar
19 K	20 Ca	21 Sc	22 Ti	23 V	24 Cr	25 Mn	26 Fe	27 Co	28 Ni	29 Cu	30 Zn	31 Ga	32 Ge	33 As	34 Se	35 Br	36 Kr
37 Rb	38 Sr	39 Y	40 Zr	41 Nb	42 Mo	43 Tc	44 Ru	45 Rh	46 Pd	47 Ag	48 Cd	49 In	50 Sn	51 Sb	52 Te	53 I	54 Xe
55 Cs	56 Ba		72 Hf	73 Ta	74 W	75 Re	76 Os	77 Ir	78 Pt	79 Au	80 Hg	81 Tl	82 Pb	83 Bi	84 Po	85 At	86 Rn
87 Fr	88 Ra		104 Unq	105 Unp	106 Unh	107 Uns	108 Uno	109 Une	110 Uun								

57 La	58 Ce	59 Pr	60 Nd	61 Pm	62 Sm	63 Eu	64 Gd	65 Tb	66 Dy	67 Ho	68 Er	69 Tm	70 Yb	71 Lu
89 Ac	90 Th	91 Pa	92 U	93 Np	94 Pu	95 Am	96 Cm	97 Bk	98 Cf	99 Es	100 Fm	101 Md	102 No	103 Lr

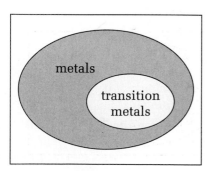

For Exercises 14–17, tell whether each implication is represented by the Venn diagram. Write *Yes* or *No*.

14. A transition metal is one type of metal.

15. All transition metals are metals.

16. If an element is a metal, then it is a transition metal.

17. An element is a transition metal only if it is a metal.

18. Does the fact that tin is a metal imply that it is a transition metal?

19. Does the fact that copper is a transition metal imply that it is a metal?

The piece of jewelry shown is a *tabzimt*. It is worn by Kabyle women of northern Algeria. A woman wears it at her neck if it is in her dowry when she marries. She wears it on her forehead if it is given by her husband on the birth of their first son.

20. Write each of the two conditionals in the above paragraph in if-then form.

21. Suppose a married Kabyle woman with a son wears a tabzimt at her neck. Explain why she may be wearing it there.

22. Is this statement *True* or *False*? If the materials in the tabzimt shown include silver, coral, and enamel, then the tabzimt has a transition metal in it. (See Exercises 14–19.)

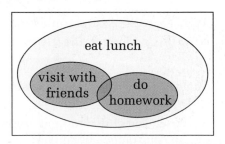

23. A *chord* is a segment whose endpoints are on a circle.

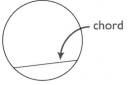

    a. Is a diameter of a circle a chord?

    b. Write an implication about chords and diameters.

    c. **Writing** Write the converse of your implication. Is it true? Explain.

24. **Games** In the game *tick-tack-toe*, players take turns putting Xs and Os in a 3-by-3 grid. Three of the same symbol in a row wins. The game at the right is in progress. The numbers below the letters tell the order in which they were played. Player X went first.

X_1	O_2	
		X_3

    a. Assume that each player blocks a win whenever the other player has two in a row. Show how this game will finish.

    b. **Writing** Explain how each move is an example of an implication.

Ongoing **ASSESSMENT**

25. **Writing** Rewrite one statement from each of the previous six units as an implication. Use as many different forms of implications as you can.

Review **PREVIEW**

26. Graph the conjunction $y < 4$ and $y < \frac{3}{2}x$ on a coordinate plane. *(Section 7-1)*

The Venn diagram shows how students responded to a survey on three specific activities done during lunch time. Tell whether each statement about the students in the survey is *True* or *False*. *(Section 1-6)*

27. If a student eats lunch, then the student does not do homework.

28. All students who eat lunch do homework.

29. Some students visit with friends and do homework.

30. Murphy's Market charges these prices for the brands of peanut butter it sells. *(Section 3-5)*

    a. Write the prices in the table as a 3 × 3 matrix.

    b. Use scalar multiplication to write a matrix representing a 7% increase in peanut butter prices.

	12 oz	18 oz	40 oz
Jem	$1.69	$2.29	$3.89
MJ's	$1.75	$2.49	$4.19
Susan's Best	$2.19	$2.79	$4.99

31. Writing Use the Venn diagram to write three true statements, one each using *and*, *or*, and *not*. *(Section 7-1)*

SCIENTISTS
Marie Curie

Leonardo Da Vinci

ARTISTS
Georgia O'Keeffe
Diego Rivera

SCULPTORS
Auguste Rodin
Jackie Winsor

Working on the Unit Project

For Exercises 32 and 33, use this excerpt from Michael Crichton's book *The Andromeda Strain*. The characters are trying to solve a mystery about an infection.

"The child was normal," Hall said. "It could cry, and disrupt its acid-base balance. That would prevent the Andromeda Strain from getting into its bloodstream....Sooner or later it would stop....Then it would be vulnerable to Andromeda....When the child stopped crying, either the organism was no longer there–or else the organism–"

"Changed," Stone said. "Mutated."

"Yes. Mutated to a noninfectious form. And perhaps it is still mutating. Now it is no longer directly harmful to man,..."

32. Identify at least two implications in the excerpt and write each in if-then form.

33. Writing The child stopped crying. Do you think it was harmed by the Andromeda organism?

Valid and Invalid Arguments

PREMISES, *Premises*

EXPLORATION

(*Who*) *is going to the party?*

- **Work in a group of four students.**

Clue 1 If Don is going, then Eve is going.

Clue 2 Ben is not going to the party.

How often have you heard friends say, "I'll go if you'll go"? You will use these clues to determine who is going to the party:

Clue 3 If Al is going, then Ben is going.

Clue 4 If Carla is going, then Don is going.

In your group, discuss which clues can lead you to an answer to each of these questions. Then agree on an answer.

1. Is Ben going to the party?
2. Is Al going to the party?
3. Is Carla going to the party?
4. Is Don going to the party?
5. Is Eve going to the party?
6. List the students who are going to the party. Compare your list with another group's list. If there are any differences, try to convince the others that your reasoning is valid.

Clue 5 Al or Carla is going to the party.

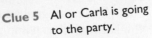

In the Exploration you may have used patterns of reasoning called *rules of logic*. Each rule of logic shown below involves two given statements called **premises** and produces a statement called a **conclusion.**

When both premises are true, the conclusion *must* be true. Such reasoning produces a **valid argument**.

RULES OF LOGIC

X shows what is true.

Direct Argument

If p is true, then q is true.
p is true.
_____
Therefore, q is true.

$p \rightarrow q$
p
_____
$\therefore q \leftarrow$ Read "Therefore q."

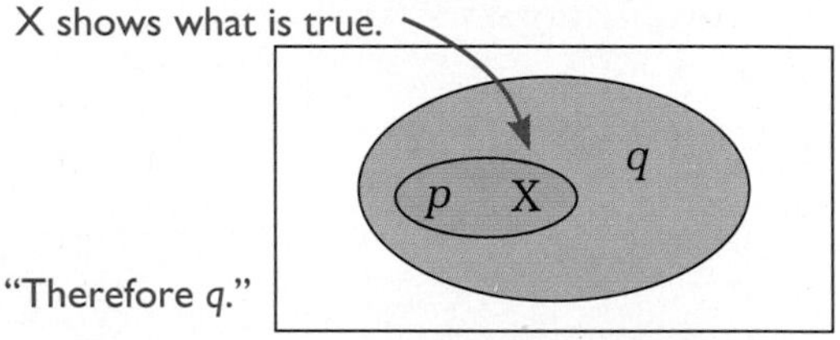

Indirect Argument

If p is true, then q is true.
q is not true.
_____
Therefore, p is not true.

$p \rightarrow q$
not q
_____
$\therefore$ not p

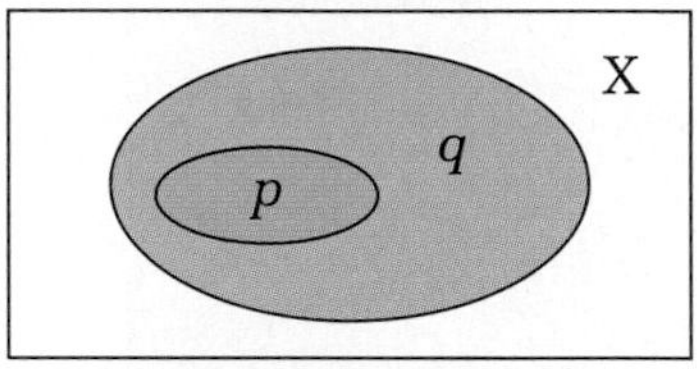

Chain Rule

If p is true, then q is true.
If q is true, then r is true.
_____
Therefore, if p is true, then r is true.

$p \rightarrow q$
$q \rightarrow r$
_____
$\therefore p \rightarrow r$

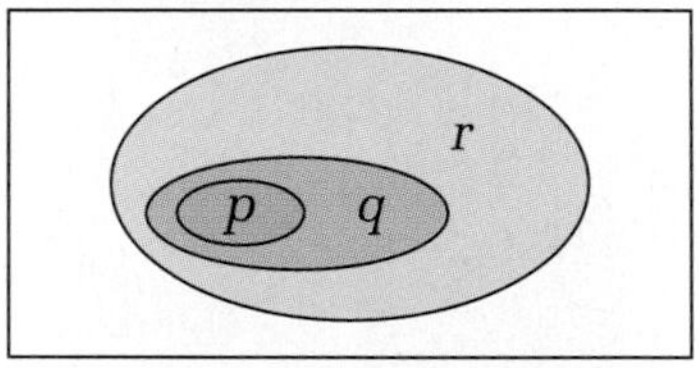

Or Rule

p is true or q is true.
p is not true.
_____
Therefore, q is true.

p or q
not p
_____
$\therefore q$

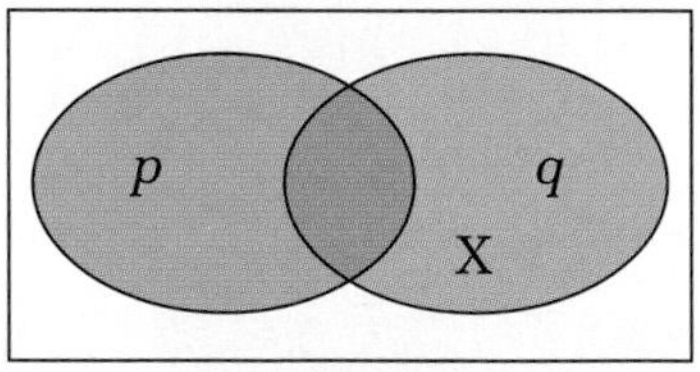

Talk it Over

Tell which rule of logic is used in these valid arguments.

1. John is in his room or John is in the kitchen. John is not in the kitchen. Therefore, John is in his room.

2. If I take the Number 10 bus, then I can get to the mall. If I can get to the mall, then I can go to the movies. Therefore, if I take the Number 10 bus, then I can go to the movies.

3. If Manuela has eaten guacamole, then she has tasted avocado. Manuela has eaten guacamole. Therefore, she has tasted avocado.

What conclusion can you reach when both premises are true?

a. Premise 1: If an animal is an insect, then it has exactly six legs.
   Premise 2: A spider does not have exactly six legs.

b. Premise 1: If a polygon is a square, then it is a rectangle.
   Premise 2: If a polygon is a rectangle, then it is a parallelogram.

Sample Response

Translate each premise into its symbolic form.

a. *insect* → *six legs*   These are the premises $p \to q$
   not *six legs*   of an indirect argument.   not q
                                                           ∴ not p

   Conclusion: A spider is not an insect.

b. *square* → *rectangle*   These are the premises $p \to q$
   rectangle → *parallelogram* of a chain rule argument. $q \to r$
                                                              ∴ $p \to r$

   Conclusion: Therefore, if a polygon is a square,
   it is a parallelogram.

Invalid Arguments

Arguments that do not use rules of logic are considered errors,
or **invalid arguments.**

Decide if each argument is *valid* or *invalid*. Explain your reasoning.

a. All multiples of 20 are multiples of five.
   Sam's locker number is a multiple of five.
   Therefore, Sam's locker number is a multiple of 20.

b. Every member of a youth hostel club (YHC) likes to travel.
   Indira is not a member of a youth hostel club.
   Therefore, Indira does not like to travel.

- . *Continued on next page.*

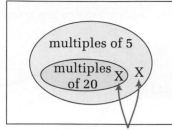

multiples of 5

multiples of 20 X X

Sam's locker number?

Write the premises as if-then statements. Then use symbols and Venn diagrams to examine the argument.

a. If a number is a multiple of 20, then it is a multiple of 5. $p \rightarrow q$
Sam's locker number is a multiple of 5. q
_____
Therefore, Sam's locker number is a multiple of 20. $\therefore p$

This argument is invalid. It does not use a rule of logic and assumes that the converse of every statement is true. This is called a *converse error*. An example of a multiple of 5 that is not a multiple of 20 is 10.

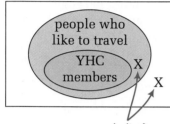

people who like to travel

YHC members X

X

Indira?

b. If a person is a member of YHC,
then the person likes to travel. $p \rightarrow q$
Indira is not a member of YHC. not p
_____
Therefore, Indira does not like to travel. $\therefore$ not q

This argument is invalid. It does not use a rule of logic and is called an *inverse error*. The diagram shows that it is possible that Indira likes to travel.

Talk it Over

Do you think each argument is valid? Why or why not?

4. If we visit Hong Kong, then we will eat well.
   If we visit Hong Kong, then we will see Victoria Harbor.
   Therefore, if we eat well, then we will see Victoria Harbor.

5. If $x = 5$, then $2x + 3 = 13$.
   $2x + 3 \neq 13$.
   Therefore, $x \neq 5$.

Look Back

Look again at the rules of logic on page 380. In each argument, tell whether each statement is a premise or a conclusion.

7-3 Exercises and Problems

1. **Reading** What does "$\therefore q$" mean?

For Exercises 2–5, what conclusion can you reach when both premises are true?

2. If an animal has a backbone, it is a vertebrate. A horse has a backbone.

3. If a triangle is isosceles, then it has at least two angles equal in measure.
   $\triangle ABC$ does not have at least two angles equal in measure.

4. If $2x + 3 = 21$, then $2x = 18$.
   If $2x = 18$, then $x = 9$.

5. If $P(A) = 0$, then A is an impossible event.
   A is not an impossible event.

6. For each of steps 2–5 in the Exploration, you used rules of logic to find out which students were going to the party. For each student, name the rule of logic you used.

connection to **HISTORY**

For Exercises 7 and 8, what conclusion can you reach when both premises are true? For each exercise, the first premise is from an amendment to the Constitution.

7. "The right of citizens . . ., who are 18 years of age or older, to vote shall not be denied . . . ." Kerry is a citizen and is 19 years old.

8. "No person shall be elected to the office of the President more than twice . . . . ." Ronald Reagan was elected President twice.

Decide if each argument is *valid* or *invalid*. Explain your reasoning.

9. $q \rightarrow r$	10. s or t	11. $v \rightarrow w$
not r	not s	w
$\therefore$ not q	$\therefore$ not t	$\therefore v$

connection to **LITERATURE**

In *A Case of Identity*, a Sherlock Holmes mystery story, James Windibank has tried unsuccessfully to disguise himself as Hosmer Angel. Sherlock Holmes explains how he uncovered the deception.

> ...Then the fact that the two men were never together, but that the one always appeared when the other was away, was suggestive. So were the tinted spectacles and the curious voice, which both hinted at a disguise, as did the bushy whiskers. My suspicions were all confirmed by his peculiar action in typewriting his signature, which of course inferred that his handwriting was so familiar to her [Angel's stepdaughter] that she would recognize even the smallest sample of it....these isolated facts, together with many minor ones, all pointed in the same direction.

For Exercises 12 and 13, decide if each argument is *valid* or *invalid*. Explain your reasoning.

12. If a person wears tinted glasses, then he may be wearing a disguise. James Windibank wears tinted glasses. Conclusion: James Windibank may be wearing a disguise.

13. If James and Hosmer appear together, they are different people. James and Hosmer did not appear together. Conclusion: James and Hosmer are not different people.

14. Write a valid argument based on Sherlock Holmes's remarks.

Decide if each argument is *valid* or *invalid*. Explain your reasoning.

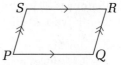

15. If a polygon is a rhombus, then it is a parallelogram.
PQRS is a parallelogram. Therefore, *PQRS* is a rhombus.

16. If today is Monday, then I go to school.
Today is not Monday.
Therefore, I do not go to school.

17. Jim Burks or Lonnie Foy dropped the pass.
Lonnie Foy did not drop the pass.
Therefore, Jim Burks dropped the pass.

18. All pyramids are polyhedrons.
All polyhedrons have polygonal faces.
Therefore, all pyramids have polygonal faces.

19. If Amy hits a home run, then she is credited with an RBI.
Amy is not credited with an RBI.
Therefore, Amy did not hit a home run.

20. Geology If minerals are hematite, then
they leave rust-colored streaks.
Therefore, these minerals are hematite.

21. **Research** Find three examples of valid
or invalid arguments in advertisements,
comics, or newspaper articles. Explain
the error in reasoning or the rule of
logic used.

Ongoing **ASSESSMENT**

22. **Open-ended** Write an advertisement that uses
a valid argument to convince someone to buy
Sparkle Flakes. Identify the rule of logic it uses.

Review **PREVIEW**

For Exercises 23–25: *(Section 7-2)*

a. Rewrite each implication in if-then form.
Tell whether each implication is *True* or
False. If it is false, give a counterexample.

b. Write the converse of each implication. Tell
whether the converse of each implication is
True or *False*. If it is false, give a counterexample.

23. An angle is obtuse only if the measure of the angle is between
90° and 180°.

24. The fact that $x = 5$ implies that $x < 8$.

25. You are in a state bordering the Pacific Ocean if you are in California.

Find the probability of each event. *(Section 6-7)*

26. getting no heads when two coins are tossed

27. getting exactly three heads when three coins are tossed

28. getting exactly three heads when four coins are tossed

Working on the Unit Project

You may want to create a series of valid arguments as a framework for your mystery story. You can use the arguments to write clues.

29. A painting credited to Francisco de Zurbarán (1598–1664) contained the pigments cadmium sulfide yellow and chromium oxide green. Tests showed that graphite filled the cracks of the painting like dust. The graphite had been applied all at once.

Use any of these clues to write an argument to convince someone that the painting is a fake.

Clue 1 Dust accumulates over centuries.

Clue 2 Graphite can look like dust but is actually different from it.

Clue 3 Cadmium sulfide yellow and chromium oxide green pigments were invented after 1863.

Unit 7 **CHECKPOINT**

1. **Writing** Suppose you want to convince a friend to apply to become an astronaut. Write a valid argument using three implications and the chain rule.

Graph each conjunction or disjunction on a coordinate plane. Tell which points are on each graph. 7-1

2. $x < 5$ and $y \geq 2$ 3. $y < x$ or $y \geq x$

4. Use a mathematical statement and a number line to show the ages of people who pay the adult admission price at the movies.

| Adults: $6.50 | Children 13 and under: $3.00 | Seniors 55 or over: $4.00 |

For Exercises 5–7, rewrite each implication in if-then form. 7-2

5. Corey is a high school student only if he is a teenager.

6. Every multiple of 4 is also a multiple of 2.

7. All matrices with 4 columns and 3 rows have the dimensions 3×4.

8. What conclusion can you reach when both premises are true? If Jana scores 85 or less, she lowers her average. Jana did not lower her average. 7-3

9. Decide if this argument is *valid* or *invalid*. Explain your reasoning.

If a figure is a parallelogram, then it has two pairs of parallel sides. A square is a parallelogram. Therefore, a square has two pairs of parallel sides.

Biconditionals and Good Definitions

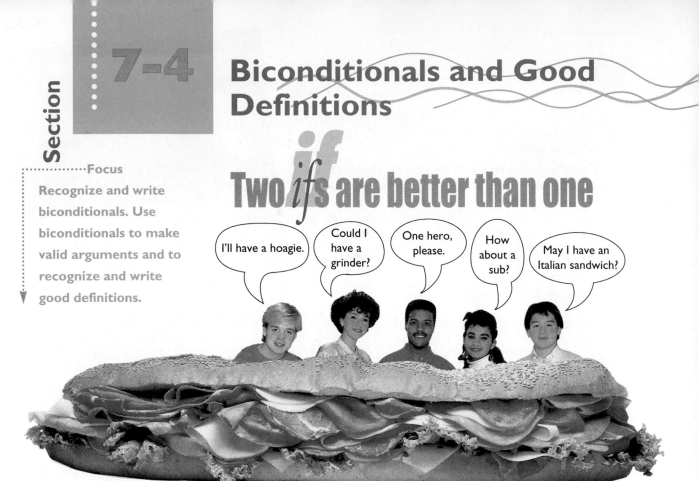

Two *if*s are better than one

I'll have a hoagie.

Could I have a grinder?

One hero, please.

How about a sub?

May I have an Italian sandwich?

Talk it Over

1. What communication problem does the photo suggest?
2. Describe the sandwich they are all ordering.

Biconditionals

For people to communicate, they must agree on the meanings of words.

If a sandwich is a hoagie , then it is a grinder .

and

If a sandwich is a grinder , then it is a hoagie .

When a conditional and its converse are true, the conjunction of the two conditionals is a true statement called a **biconditional.**

You can also write a biconditional using the phrase "if and only if."

A sandwich is a hoagie *if and only if* it is a grinder.

A biconditional is true when both of its conditionals are true.

You can use Venn diagrams to show the relationship between a hoagie and a grinder.

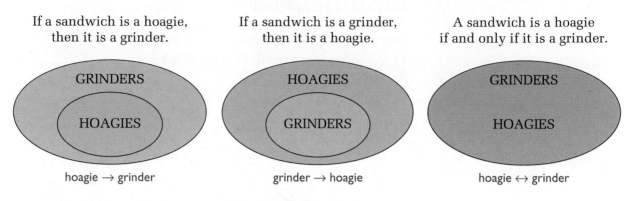

| If a sandwich is a hoagie, then it is a grinder. | If a sandwich is a grinder, then it is a hoagie. | A sandwich is a hoagie if and only if it is a grinder. |

hoagie → grinder grinder → hoagie hoagie ↔ grinder

You can represent "if and only if" symbolically by a double arrow.

$q \rightarrow p$ and $p \rightarrow q$
p is true if q is true and
p is true only if q is true.

$$p \leftrightarrow q$$

p is true if and only if q is true.

Sample 1

Write the pair of conditionals as a biconditional using "if and only if."

If an angle has a measure of 90°, then it is a right angle.

If an angle is a right angle, then it has a measure of 90°.

Sample Response

An angle has a measure of 90° if and only if it is a right angle.

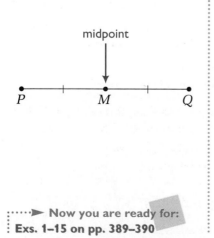

midpoint

$P \quad M \quad Q$

Talk it Over

3. For each statement in parts (a) and (b), identify the hypothesis and conclusion.

   a. A point on a segment is the same distance from each endpoint if it is the midpoint of the segment.

   b. A point on a segment is the same distance from each endpoint only if it is the midpoint of the segment.

4. Write the pair of conditionals in question 3 as a biconditional using "if and only if."

5. a. Write the two implications represented by this biconditional: A quadrilateral is a rectangle if and only if the quadrilateral is a parallelogram.

   b. Is the biconditional in part (a) *True* or *False*?

······► Now you are ready for:
Exs. 1–15 on pp. 389–390

Good Definitions

You can use biconditionals to write definitions. A good definition is built from a true conditional with a true converse. For example, consider this definition of a rectangle:

A *rectangle* is a parallelogram with four right angles.

This definition asserts two true conditionals:

If a figure is a rectangle, then it is a parallelogram with four right angles.

If a figure is a parallelogram with four right angles, then it is a rectangle.

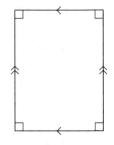

Sample 2

Rewrite this definition using "if and only if":

A *square* is a rectangle with congruent sides.

Sample Response

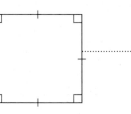

A figure is a *square* if and only if it is a rectangle with congruent sides.

Sample 3

Writing Tell what is wrong with each attempted definition and give a good definition.

a. An angle is *acute* if the measure of the angle is 85°.

b. The number b is a *square root* of a if and only if $b = \sqrt{a}$.

Sample Response

a.

> Peter Wong
>
> The statement is true but it is not a biconditional.
>
> Here is a good definition: An angle is acute if and only if the measure of the angle is between 0° and 90°.

b.

> Karen Miller
>
> The biconditional is not true because one of its conditionals is not true.
>
> For example, the square roots of 4 are 2 and -2, but the symbol √ means the positive square root. √4 = 2
>
> Here is a good definition: the number b is a square root of a if and only if b² = a.

6. What is wrong with this definition?
   A polygon is a *rhombus* if it is a square.

7. Give a good definition of a rhombus.

This is a Hmong textile from Laos. Do you think it is a square?

Biconditionals and Valid Arguments

You can make valid arguments using biconditionals just as you do with implications.

A figure is a square if and only if it is a rectangle with four congruent sides.
$p \leftrightarrow q$
QRST is a rectangle with four congruent sides.
q

Therefore, QRST is a square.
$\therefore p$

This is a special case of direct argument.
If either p or q is true, the other is true.

You can also use biconditionals in indirect arguments.

$x = 12$ if and only if $3x = 36$ $p \leftrightarrow q$
$x \neq 12$ not p

Therefore, $3x \neq 36$. $\therefore$ not q

This is a special case of indirect argument.
If either p or q is false, the other is false.

Now you are ready for:
Exs. 16–43 on pp. 390–393

Look Back

Describe several different ways of representing biconditionals.

7-4 Exercises and Problems

1. **Reading** What does "*p* if and only if *q*" mean?

Write each pair of conditionals as a biconditional using "if and only if."

2. If it is my birthday, then I was born on this date.
   If I was born on this date, then it is my birthday.

3. If $5x = 20$, then $x = 4$.
   If $x = 4$, then $5x = 20$.

4. A polygon is a quadrilateral if it has four sides.
   A polygon has four sides if it is a quadrilateral.

For Exercises 5–7:

a. **Are the implications converses of each other?**

b. **Is each implication true?**

c. **If you answered yes to parts (a) and (b), rewrite the pair of implications as a biconditional.**

5. If $\frac{x}{2} = 7$, then $x = 14$.

   If $x = 14$, then $\frac{x}{2} = 7$.

6. A quadrilateral is a square only if it is a rectangle.
   If a quadrilateral is a square, then it is a rectangle.

7. A space figure is a cube if it has six faces.
   A space figure has six faces if it is a cube.

Tell whether each biconditional is *True* or *False*. Explain your reasoning.

8. I can afford a snack that costs $.40 if and only if I have $1.

9. An animal is a bird if and only if it flies.

10. A quadrilateral is a square if and only if all of its sides are equal in measure.

11. A figure is a rectangle if and only if it is a parallelogram with four right angles.

12. An instrument is a stringed instrument if and only if it is a violin.

Represent each statement by a Venn diagram.

13. If Tim is awake, then he is talking. (Label one circle "Tim is awake" and the other "Tim is talking.")

14. A basketball is a sphere only if it is inflated.

15. If Sandy is tired, then she yawns; and if Sandy yawns, then she is tired.

Rewrite each definition using "if and only if."

16. In a set of data, the *mean* is the sum of the items divided by the number of items.

17. A *scalene* triangle has three sides that are not equal in measure.

18. The *probability* of an event E is the ratio of the number of outcomes favoring E divided by the total number of equally likely outcomes.

19. An angle is *obtuse* if and only if the measure of the angle is 150°.

20. The number b is a *square root* of a if and only if $b = \pm\sqrt{a}$.

21. Two lines are *perpendicular* if and only if they intersect to form a right angle.

22. *Perpendicular* lines intersect to form at least two congruent angles.

23. Here is a good definition of a square:
    "A *square* is a rectangle with four congruent sides."
    Write the two implications that make up this definition.

Writing For Exercises 24–26, decide whether each statement can be rewritten using "if and only if" to make a good definition. If so, rewrite it. If not, explain why not.

24. A figure with four sides equal in measure is a *parallelogram.*

25. A *parallelogram* is a polygon with two pairs of opposite sides parallel.

26. A *parallelogram* is a quadrilateral with at least one pair of parallel sides.

27. Write a good definition of *parallelogram.*

28. People in different parts of the country call the same kind of drink "soda," "pop," "soda pop," "tonic," or "soft drink." What do you call this drink? Write a good definition for the word you use.

Decide whether each argument is *valid* or *invalid*.

29. A figure is a rhombus if and only if it is a quadrilateral with four congruent sides.

    Quadrilateral *PQRS* is not a rhombus.

    Therefore, *PQRS* does not have four congruent sides.

30. A quadrilateral is a kite if and only if it has two pairs of consecutive sides equal in measure. These pairs do not have a side in common.

    DEFG is a quadrilateral with two pairs of consecutive sides equal in measure. These pairs do not have a side in common.

    Therefore, *DEFG* is a kite.

31. $x - 4$ if and only if $\frac{x}{4} = 1$
    $x \neq 4$
    $\therefore \frac{x}{4} \neq 1$

The yew and rhododendron are common plants.

Rhododendrons are shrubs with simple, alternating leaves. They can be evergreen, semi-evergreen, or deciduous. The flowers are usually white, pink, or red and are shaped like bells or funnels. Rhododendrons originated in northern India and China.

Yews are evergreen trees and shrubs with reddish brown bark that is thin and scaled. Flat, needle-like leaves, about one inch long, are dark green above and yellowish beneath. The hard green to black seeds are exposed in a fleshy red cup.

32. a. What is wrong with this definition of a yew?
A *yew* is a tree or shrub with reddish brown bark and needle-like leaves.

b. Write a better definition of a yew.

c. Is your definition a good definition? Why or why not?

33. Which plant do you think would be easier to identify if you have never seen it before? Explain.

34. Tell whether the following argument is *valid* or *invalid*. Explain.

If a plant is a rhododendron, then it is a shrub with simple, alternating leaves.

All rhododendrons originated in northern India and China.

Therefore, if a plant is a shrub with simple, alternate leaves, then it originated in northern India and China.

Ongoing **ASSESSMENT**

35. Open-ended Write good definitions for three mathematical terms. Make a convincing case that all three of your definitions are good.

Review **PREVIEW**

Decide if each argument is *valid or invalid.* *(Section 7-3)*

36. If today is Tuesday, then I am going to the dentist.
I am not going to the dentist today.
Therefore, today is not Tuesday.

37. x is greater than 3.
3 is greater than y.
Therefore, y is greater than x.

Simplify. *(Toolbox Skill 12)*

38. $\sqrt{36}$

39. $\sqrt{50}$

40. $3\sqrt{7} \cdot 4\sqrt{14}$

What can you conclude from each statement? *(Section 7-3)*

41. Fran is taller than Danielle and Abby is shorter than Danielle.

42. $x = -4 + 10$ and $-4 + 10 = 6$

Working on the Unit Project

43. **Research** Read one or more of these mysteries to get ideas for characters, plot elements, settings, or clues for your story. As you read, you may want to take notes on ideas to help your story.

Suggested Bibliography

➤ *The Adventures of Sherlock Holmes* by Arthur Conan Doyle

➤ *Coyote Waits* by Tony Hillerman

➤ "Euclid's Crop Circles; Off the Beat" by Ivars Peterson *Science News,* February 1, 1992

➤ "It ain't over till it's over. . . cold fusion" by Jerry E. Bishop *Popular Science,* August 1993

➤ *Miss Marple: The Complete Short Stories* by Agatha Christie

➤ *Pigeon Blood* by Alexander Gary

➤ *The Vandermark Mummy* by Cynthia Voigt

➤ *Too Close to the Edge* by Susan Dunlap

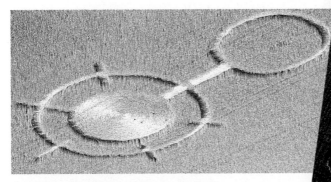

Crop circles like these in Wiltshire, England, intrigue scientists and investigators.

Introduction to Proof

·······Focus

Become familiar with key
elements of proof and
formats for two-column,
paragraph, and flow proofs.

Go with the flow

Suppose you are a ticket agent for Euclid Airlines. Your specialty is planning routes, or itineraries, between the most populous cities of the world. The map shows the available flights and flight numbers.

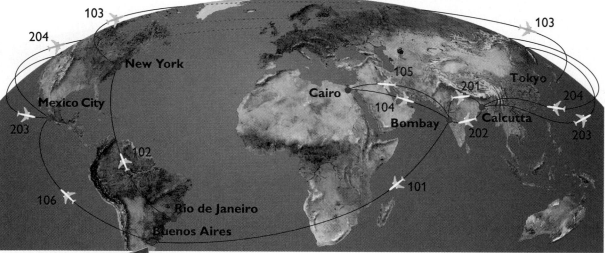

Here is a sample itinerary for a trip from Bombay to Mexico City.

City	Flight
Bombay	Departure point
Buenos Aires	Flight 101: Bombay → Buenos Aires
Mexico City	Flight 106: Buenos Aires → Mexico City

Read as "to."

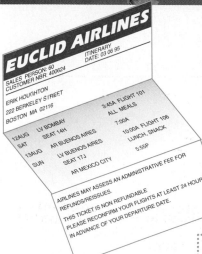

Talk it Over

1. a. What is the first flight taken?

   b. How do you know that it goes *from* Bombay?

2. Use the map to plan a different itinerary to make the trip from Bombay to Mexico City. Write it in the same form as above.

3. Write an itinerary for a trip from Mexico City to Bombay.

Proofs and Itineraries

The itinerary on page 394 shows that it is possible to fly from Bombay to Mexico City on Euclid Airlines. A logical demonstration such as this itinerary is called a *proof*.

BY THE WAY...

Because of time zone differences, it is possible to arrive before the time you leave. You may leave Atlanta at 1:39 P.M. and arrive in Birmingham at 1:25 P.M.

Sample 1

Write a proof of this statement: You can fly from Bombay to Mexico City.

Sample Response

Given You are in Bombay. ◄—— State what is given.

Prove You can fly to Mexico City. ◄—— State what you want to prove.

Plan Ahead ◄—— Plan your strategy.

You can connect to Mexico City by going through Buenos Aires.

Show Your Reasoning

Justify each statement.

Statements	Justifications
1. You are in Bombay.	1. Given
2. You can fly to Buenos Aires.	2. Flight 101: Bombay → Buenos Aires
3. You can fly to Mexico City.	3. Flight 106: Buenos Aires → Mexico City

Notice these similarities between itineraries and proofs.

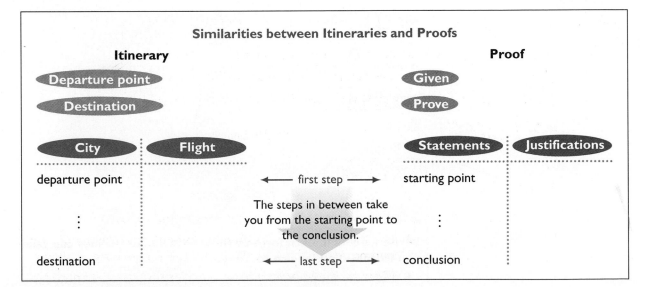

Similarities between Itineraries and Proofs

Itinerary — Departure point / Destination — City / Flight

Proof — Given / Prove — Statements / Justifications

departure point ◄—— first step ——► starting point

The steps in between take you from the starting point to the conclusion.

destination ◄—— last step ——► conclusion

······► Now you are ready for:
Exs. 1–6 on pp. 397–398

4. Write a proof of this statement: You can fly from Buenos Aires to Calcutta. Use the map on page 394.

5. Can there be more than one itinerary for a trip? Do you think there can be more than one proof of a statement? Explain.

Forms of Proofs

There are many forms of proofs. The form you just used is called a **two-column proof** because of the layout of the chart.

Another form is a **paragraph proof**. Here is a paragraph proof of the Bombay-Mexico City itinerary:

Notice that the statements of the proof are written in sentences to form a paragraph.

> It is possible to fly from Bombay to Mexico City. From Bombay you can fly to Buenos Aires because Flight 101 goes from Bombay to Buenos Aires. From Buenos Aires you can fly to Mexico City because Flight 106 goes from Buenos Aires to Mexico City.

Justifications are written where needed.

Another form of proof is a **flow proof.** It is a diagram using arrows to show how to get from one statement to the next.

Statements

Circled numbers refer to the justifications for the statements of the proof.

Bombay $\xrightarrow{\text{①}}$ Buenos Aires $\xrightarrow{\text{②}}$ Mexico City

Justifications

① Flight 101   ◄—— Justifications are given in a numbered list.
② Flight 106

Talk it Over

Write a proof in each form to show that Euclid Airlines can take you from Rio de Janeiro to Tokyo.

6. two-column form   7. paragraph form   8. flow form

Rules of Logic and Proofs

You can think of the statements of a proof as using rules of logic in a different format.

Tell which rule of logic is used to go from statement 1 to statement 2 on page 395. Then tell which rule of logic is used to go from statement 1 to statement 2 to statement 3.

Sample Response

Rewrite the statements as premises and a conclusion.

Itinerary	Logic
If you are in Bombay, then you can fly to Buenos Aires.	$p \to q$
You are in Bombay.	p
Therefore, you can fly to Buenos Aires.	$\therefore q$

Direct argument is used to go from statement 1 to statement 2.

If you are in Bombay, then you can fly to Buenos Aires.	$p \to q$
If you are in Buenos Aires, then you can fly to Mexico City.	$q \to r$
Therefore, if you are in Bombay, then you can fly to Mexico City.	$\therefore p \to r$

The chain rule is used to go from statement 1 to statement 2 to statement 3.

Look Back

How are the three forms of proof in this section alike? How are they different?

▶ Now you are ready for:
Exs. 7–24 on pp. 398–400

7-5 Exercises and Problems

1. **Reading** List some of the similarities between itineraries and proofs.

2. Fill in the missing parts of this nonsense proof.

Given You are here.

Prove You can go someplace.

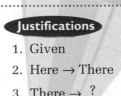

Statements	Justifications
1. You are here.	1. Given
2. You can go _?_.	2. Here → There
3. You can go wherever.	3. There → _?_
4. You can go someplace.	4. _?_ → _?_

For Exercises 3–5, use the map on page 394.

3. Write an itinerary showing that it is possible to fly on Euclid Airlines from Calcutta to Buenos Aires.

4. Rewrite the itinerary you wrote in Exercise 3 as a two-column proof.

5. Explain why it is impossible to fly on Euclid Airlines from Tokyo to New York City.

6. **Group Activity** Work with another student.

   a. Each of you should plan your own itinerary on Euclid Airlines. Do not show them to each other. On a separate piece of paper, write your starting point and destination.

   b. Trade papers. Try to find itineraries for each other's trips. Discuss your results.

For Exercises 7–9, use this proof.

Given You are in Cairo.

Prove You can fly to Calcutta.

Statements	**Justifications**
1. You are in Cairo.	1. Given
2. You can fly to Bombay.	2. Flight 104: Cairo → Bombay
3. You can fly to Calcutta.	3. Flight 201: Bombay → Calcutta

7. Tell which rule of logic is used to go from statement 1 to statement 2.

8. Tell which rule of logic is used to go from statement 1 to statement 2 to statement 3.

9. Rewrite the proof as a flow proof.

10. **Writing** Write a paragraph proof showing that you can fly on Euclid Airlines from Mexico City to Cairo.

11. **Games** Here is an example of a word game.
    Change WARM to COLD. Rule: Form a real word at each step by changing just one letter at a time.
    Solution: WARM → WORM → WORD → CORD → COLD

    a. Use the rules to change the word CAT into the word DOG.

    b. Use the rules to change the word TRY into the word WIN.

    c. **Writing** How is this puzzle like planning an itinerary?

12. **Open-ended** Create your own word puzzle like those in Exercise 11. Use five-letter words and at least four steps.

13. a. Rewrite each power as a number: $7^0, 7^1, 7^2, 7^3, 7^4, 7^5, 7^6, 7^7, 7^8, 7^9$

    b. Describe any pattern you find in the unit's digit in part (a).

    c. Write a paragraph proof to prove that the pattern you described in part (b) holds for all powers of 7.

    d. **Writing** What is the unit's digit in 7^{100}? Explain.

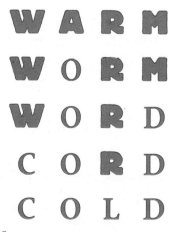

14. a. The drawing at the right shows five squares. Use logical reasoning to find the lengths of the sides of squares *A*, *B*, and *C*.

b. How is the way you solved this puzzle like writing proofs?

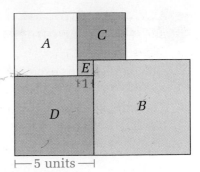

├── 5 units ──┤

The Mesozoic Era is divided into three periods. The periods can be used to describe the age of fossils and rocks.

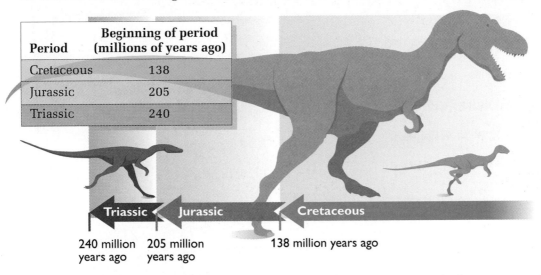

Period	Beginning of period (millions of years ago)
Cretaceous	138
Jurassic	205
Triassic	240

Triassic ◀ Jurassic ◀ Cretaceous

240 million years ago   205 million years ago   138 million years ago

15. Write a paragraph proof that a rock formed in the Cretaceous period did not exist in the Triassic period.

16. Tell which rule of logic you used in your proof.

Ongoing ASSESSMENT

17. Open-ended Plan your own itinerary on Euclid airlines. Write your itinerary in two different forms of proof. See page 394 for flights.

Review PREVIEW

For Exercises 18 and 19, tell whether each definition is a good definition, then write the two conditionals it uses. If it is not a good definition, tell why not. *(Section 7-4)*

18. A quadrilateral is a rhombus if and only if it has four congruent sides.

19. A quadrilateral is a rhombus if and only if it is a square.

20. Solve this system of equations by substitution. $x + y = 7$ *(Section 3-2)*
$2x + 3y = 28$

Solve each equation. *(Toolbox Skill 13)*

21. $n - 3 = 40$ **22.** $60 = 15x$ **23.** $24 = -3(a - 10)$

As you complete this exercise, you will learn about one way to include a travel itinerary in your mystery story.

24. Zoe wants to add an early twentieth century European flavor to her mystery story. She researches the routes of the Orient-Express and creates this itinerary.

ORIENT EXPRESS

O-E 301: Paris → Vienna

O-E 302: Paris → Milan

O-E 410: Venice → Rome

O-E 412: Venice → Belgrade

O-E 701: Bucharest → Istanbul

O-E 503: Innsbruck → Munich

O-E 602: Milan → Venice

O-E 111: Vienna → Innsbruck

O-E 812: Belgrade → Istanbul

O-E 900: Munich → Vienna

a. Zoe could have her heroine take the Orient-Express from Paris directly to Istanbul but decides to make things more interesting by having a stop in Italy. Write a smaller itinerary that allows the heroine to go from Paris to Istanbul via Milan, Venice, or Rome.

b. Write a paragraph proof of the itinerary you wrote in part (a).

ORIENT EXPRESS
NEAR CONSTANTINOPLE

BY THE WAY...

The Orient-Express originated in 1883 to provide train service from Paris to Constantinople (now Istanbul). It actually was many connected train systems and included several destinations.

Section 7-6

Postulates and Proofs in Algebra

Focus

Use postulates of algebra to write proofs.

Created Equal

At the beginning of the Declaration of Independence, the colonists explained why they wanted to break their ties with Great Britain.

> When in the course of human events, it becomes necessary for one people to dissolve the political bands which have connected them with another, … they should declare the causes which impel them to the separation. We hold these truths to be self-evident, that all men are created equal, …

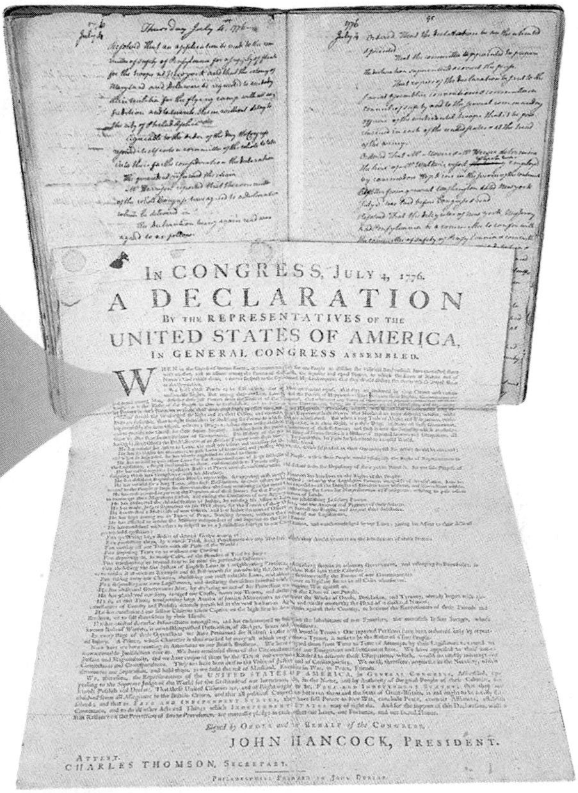

Talk it Over

1. What did the colonists mean by the phrase "We hold these truths to be self-evident . . ."?
2. The colonists "declare the causes" for separation from Great Britain. What part of a mathematical proof is this similar to?
3. At the end of the Declaration, the colonists say "We, therefore … declare, That these United Colonies are, and of Right ought to be Free and Independent States. . . ." What part of a proof in mathematics is this similar to?

Xab

In any logical argument, some statements must be assumed to be true to begin. These assumptions are called **postulates.**

SOME POSTULATES OF ALGEBRA

1. **Addition Property of Equality** — If the same number is added to equal numbers, the sums are equal. — $a = b \rightarrow a + c = b + c$

2. **Subtraction Property of Equality** — If the same number is subtracted from equal numbers, the differences are equal. — $a = b \rightarrow a - c = b - c$

3. **Multiplication Property of Equality** — If equal numbers are multiplied by the same number, the products are equal. — $a = b \rightarrow ac = bc$

4. **Division Property of Equality** — If equal numbers are divided by the same nonzero number, the quotients are equal. — $a = b \text{ and } c \neq 0 \rightarrow \dfrac{a}{c} = \dfrac{b}{c}$

5. **Reflexive Property of Equality** — A number is equal to itself. — $a = a$

6. **Substitution Property** — If values are equal, one value may be substituted for the other. — $a = b \rightarrow a$ may be substituted for b.

7. **Distributive Property** — An expression of the form $a(b + c)$ is equivalent to $ab + ac$. — $a(b + c) = ab + ac$

When you solve an equation in algebra, you are writing the steps of a proof. Here is how you solve $3x + 8 = 29$:

$$3x + 8 = 29 \quad \longleftarrow \text{Given}$$
$$3x - 21 \quad \longleftarrow \text{Subtraction property of equality}$$
$$x = 7 \quad \longleftarrow \text{Division property of equality}$$

Sample 1

Prove that if $3x + 8 = 29$, then $x = 7$.

a. Write a flow proof. b. Write a paragraph proof.

Sample Response

a. **Given** $3x + 8 = 29$ **Prove** $x = 7$

Plan Ahead

Get $3x$ alone on one side of the equation. Divide to find x.

Show Your Reasoning

Statements

$3x + 8 = 29$ ①→ $3x = 21$ ②→ $x = 7$

Justifications

① Subtraction property of equality
② Division property of equality

b.

Given: 3x + 8 = 29   Prove: x = 7
You can use the subtraction property of equality to subtract
8 from both sides of 3x + 8 = 29. Therefore, 3x = 21.
        Then you can use the division property of equality to divide
both sides by 3. Therefore, x = 7.

Definitions can also be reasons in proofs. The following definition is used in Sample 2. A **square root** of a number is one of two equal factors of the number.

$$a^2 = n \leftrightarrow a = \pm\sqrt{n}$$

Sample 2

One fourth of the area of a square field is 16 square units. Prove that if $\frac{s^2}{4} = 16$, then $s = 8$.

Sample Response

Given $\frac{s^2}{4} = 16$ **Prove** $s = 8$

Plan Ahead

Get s alone on one side of the equation. Use the definition of a square root. Remember that the length of a field is positive.

Show Your Reasoning

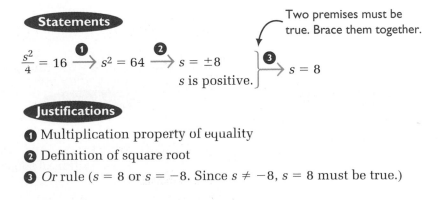

Statements

$\frac{s^2}{4} = 16$ ①→ $s^2 = 64$ ②→ $s = \pm 8$
                                        s is positive. } ③→ $s = 8$

Two premises must be true. Brace them together.

Justifications

① Multiplication property of equality
② Definition of square root
③ *Or* rule ($s = 8$ or $s = -8$. Since $s \neq -8$, $s = 8$ must be true.)

Look Back

Give a numerical example of each of the postulates of algebra on page 402.

7-6 Exercises and Problems

Reading **Identify which postulate or definition is used in each implication.**

1. If $3x + 2 = 8$, then $3x = 6$.

2. If $3x = 6$, then $x = 2$.

3. If $x^2 = 9$, then $x = 3$ or $x = -3$.

4. If $5x = 15$, then $5x + 3 = 18$.

connection to **HISTORY**

The Woman's Rights Convention held in Seneca Falls, New York, in 1848 issued the first formal appeal for the right of women to vote. About 300 people approved a "Declaration of Sentiments."

5. The Declaration begins, "We hold these truths to be self-evident: that all men and women are created equal. . . ." How is this statement like a postulate?

6. The Declaration later states, ". . . let facts be submitted to a candid world." A listing of supporting reasons is similar to what part of a proof in mathematics?

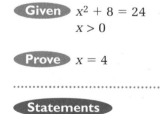

Engraving of the convention

BY THE WAY...

Frederick Douglass, famous reformer and author, wrote, "If there is no struggle, there is no progress."

7. Copy and complete the two-column proof.

Given $x^2 + 8 = 24$
$x > 0$

Prove $x = 4$

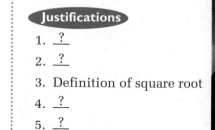

Statements	**Justifications**
1. $x^2 + 8 = 24$	1. ?
2. $x^2 = 16$	2. ?
3. ?	3. Definition of square root
4. $x > 0$	4. ?
5. ?	5. ?

8. Copy and complete the flow proof.

Given $2x - 15 = 25$

Prove $x = 20$

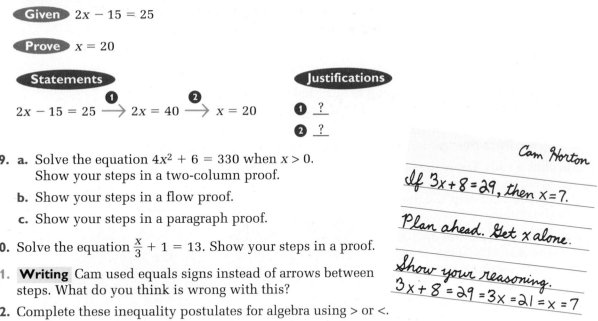

Statements

$2x - 15 = 25 \xrightarrow{\;1\;} 2x = 40 \xrightarrow{\;2\;} x = 20$

Justifications

❶ _?_

❷ _?_

9. a. Solve the equation $4x^2 + 6 = 330$ when $x > 0$. Show your steps in a two-column proof.

  b. Show your steps in a flow proof.

  c. Show your steps in a paragraph proof.

10. Solve the equation $\frac{x}{3} + 1 = 13$. Show your steps in a proof.

11. Writing Cam used equals signs instead of arrows between steps. What do you think is wrong with this?

Cam Horton

If $3x + 8 = 29$, then $x = 7$.

Plan ahead. Get x alone.

Show your reasoning.
$3x + 8 = 29 = 3x = 21 = x = 7$

12. Complete these inequality postulates for algebra using > or <.

  a. If $a < b$, then $a + c \;\underline{?}\; b + c$.   **b.** If $a < b$, then $a - c \;\underline{?}\; b - c$.

  c. If $a < b$ and $c > 0$, then $ac \;\underline{?}\; bc$.   **d.** If $a < b$ and $c < 0$, then $ac \;\underline{?}\; bc$.

13. a. Writing Why do you think there are two inequality postulates involving multiplication in Exercise 12? Give examples to explain your reasoning.

  b. Write two postulates involving inequalities and division.

14. In solving quadratic equations you have used this postulate: If $ab = 0$, then $a = 0$ or $b = 0$.

  a. Write the postulate in words.

  b. How is this postulate different from the others you have studied?

  c. If $ab = 0$, can both a and b equal zero?

3-by-3 square

15. There are surprising numerical relationships on calendars.

  a. Use any month. Take any nine numbers that form a 3-by-3 square. What do you notice about their average?

  b. Let the number in the center of any 3-by-3 square be n. Prove that the average of the nine numbers equals the center number.

16. Camille proposed this postulate for squaring with inequalities:

If $a < b$, then $a^2 < b^2$.

a. Give an example that shows when this is a true statement.

b. Give a counterexample.

c. **Writing** Did Camille write a postulate? Explain.

17. **Group Activity** Work in a group of four students.

a. Use a large copy of the postulates on page 402. Cut it up to make 21 cards, each showing a postulate in words or symbols or its name. Turn the "cards" face down and mix them.

b. Pick a card. Name the postulate and give it in words and symbols. You get one point for each correct answer. Let one person who does not play be the checker.

c. Return the card to the table and scramble again. Play several rounds, so each person gets a chance to be the checker. High score wins.

18. **a.** **Writing** Explain why any even number can be represented by $2n$ and why any odd number can be represented by either $2n + 1$ or $2n - 1$.

b. Complete this paragraph proof that the product of two consecutive numbers is an even number.

> I am given two consecutive numbers. Then one must be even and the other one odd.
> Let $2n$ be the even number and $2n + 1$ or $2n - 1$ be the odd number.
> Then the product is $2n(2n + 1)$ or $2n(2n - 1)$.
> The product has a factor of _?_, so the product must be an _?_ number.

Ongoing ASSESSMENT

19. **Open-ended** Write and solve your own equation. Present the solution as a flow proof or as a two-column proof.

20. Name and describe three forms of proof. *(Section 7-5)*

21. Arturo does a survey of attitudes about his school's sports program. He distributes the survey to every student he sees and asks that it be completed. Describe the problems in this method of surveying. *(Section 1-4)*

Tell if each definition is a good definition. If it is not, rewrite it so that it is a good definition. *(Section 7-4)*

22. A figure is a parallelogram if and only if the figure has two pairs of parallel sides.

23. A figure is a kite if it is a quadrilateral.

Working on the Unit Project

24. **Research** Edgar Allan Poe may be best known for his horror stories, including "The Pit and the Pendulum," and for his poetry, including "The Raven." He is also highly regarded as a literary theorist and as a short story writer.

Edgar Allan Poe set out guidelines for the use of ratiocination in what was to become the modern detective story. Find out what he meant by *ratiocination* and how he used it in mystery stories such as "The Murders in the Rue Morgue."

Unit 7   CHECKPOINT

1. **Writing** Explain why you need to plan ahead when writing a proof.

For Exercises 2 and 3, refer to this statement: 7-4
A quadrilateral is a rectangle with parallel sides.

2. Write the statement as a biconditional.

3. Is the biconditional true? Explain.

4. Is the reasoning *valid* or *invalid*? Explain.
$16 + x = 12 \leftrightarrow x = -4$
$16 + x \neq 12$
Therefore, $x \neq -4$

For Exercises 5 and 6, replace each __?__ with the correct   7-5
word or phrase.

5. A __?__ is a diagram using arrows to show how to get from one statement to the next.

6. The destination of an itinerary is similar to the __?__ of a proof.

7. Prove that if $7x - 3 = 25$, then $x = 4$. Write a   7-6
two-column proof.

7-6 Postulates and Proofs in Algebra   **407**

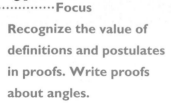
Proofs for Angles

····Focus

Recognize the value of
definitions and postulates
in proofs. Write proofs
about angles.

Lawyers need to prove things in the courtroom. They cannot just say, "It is clear the defendant is guilty!"

The same is true in mathematics. When you make a conjecture, it needs to be proved.

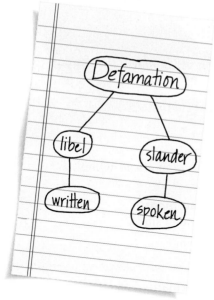

Talk it Over

1. Write a good definition of **complementary angles** and a good definition of **supplementary angles.**

2. a. Think of two angles of the same measure. Find the *supplement* of each. What is true about the supplements?

   b. Make a conjecture about the supplements of angles equal in measure. Can you test your conjecture for all angles? Would a proof about angle supplements apply to all angle supplements?

In this book, you write $m \angle A = 30°$ to show that the measure of $\angle A$ is 30°. You write $m \angle A = m \angle B$ to show that the two angles are equal in measure. You write $\angle A \cong \angle B$ to show that $\angle A$ is congruent to $\angle B$.

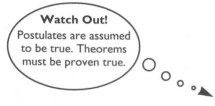

Watch Out!
Postulates are assumed
to be true. Theorems
must be proven true.

Important statements you can prove are called **theorems.** To prove a statement, you can use rules of logic, postulates, definitions, given information, and proven theorems as justifications.

Prove that supplements of the same angle are equal in measure.

Sample Response

If two angles are supplements of the same angle, then they are equal in measure.

← It helps to rewrite the statement in if-then form.

Given ∠1 is supplementary to ∠2.
∠3 is supplementary to ∠2.

← Make and label a diagram to represent the situation.

Prove $m \angle 1 = m \angle 3$ ← State what is given and what you need to prove.

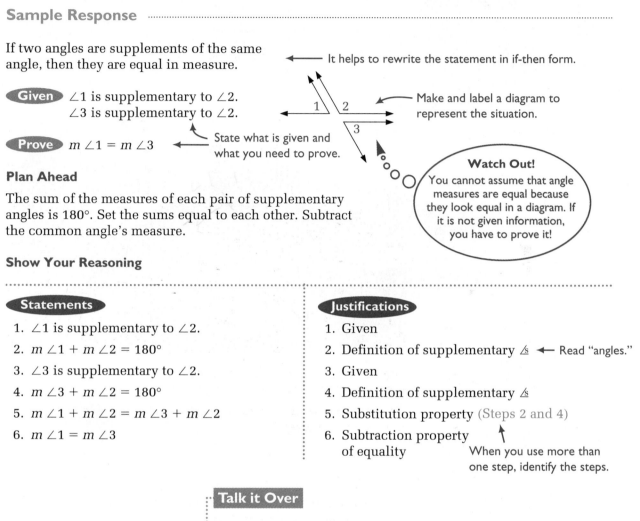

Watch Out!
You cannot assume that angle measures are equal because they look equal in a diagram. If it is not given information, you have to prove it!

Plan Ahead

The sum of the measures of each pair of supplementary angles is 180°. Set the sums equal to each other. Subtract the common angle's measure.

Show Your Reasoning

Statements

1. ∠1 is supplementary to ∠2.
2. $m \angle 1 + m \angle 2 = 180°$
3. ∠3 is supplementary to ∠2.
4. $m \angle 3 + m \angle 2 = 180°$
5. $m \angle 1 + m \angle 2 = m \angle 3 + m \angle 2$
6. $m \angle 1 = m \angle 3$

Justifications

1. Given
2. Definition of supplementary ∡ ← Read "angles."
3. Given
4. Definition of supplementary ∡
5. Substitution property (Steps 2 and 4)
6. Subtraction property of equality

When you use more than one step, identify the steps.

Talk it Over

3. Rewrite the proof in flow form.

4. Prove in paragraph form that *complements* of the same angle are equal in measure.

X Lab

SUPPLEMENTS AND COMPLEMENTS OF ANGLES

Theorem 7.1 If two angles are supplements of the same angle, then they are equal in measure.

Theorem 7.2 If two angles are complements of the same angle, then they are equal in measure.

Two angles formed by intersecting lines and facing in opposite directions are **vertical angles.** To prove theorems about vertical angles, you need two more postulates.

∠**1** and ∠**3** are vertical angles.
∠**2** and ∠**4** are vertical angles.

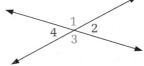

STRAIGHT ANGLE POSTULATE

Postulate 8   If the sides of an angle form a straight line, then the angle is a straight angle with measure 180°.

180°

$m \angle APC = 180°$

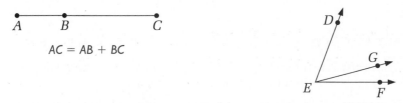

The bottom edge of this fan forms a straight angle with measure 180°. The sum of the measures of the smaller angles is 180°.

Watch Out!

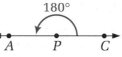

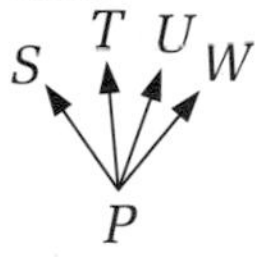

The parts must not overlap!
$m \angle SPW \neq m \angle SPU + m \angle TPW$

WHOLE AND PARTS POSTULATE

Postulate 9   For any segment or angle, the measure of the whole is equal to the sum of the measures of its non-overlapping parts.

$AC = AB + BC$

$m \angle DEF = m \angle DEG + m \angle GEF$

Prove that vertical angles are equal in measure.

Sample Response

Given $\angle 1$ and $\angle 2$ are vertical angles.

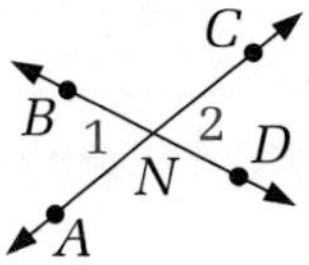

Prove $m\angle 1 = m\angle 2$

Plan Ahead

Use the straight angle postulate to show that $m\angle 1 + m\angle 3 = m\angle 2 + m\angle 3$. Then use the subtraction property of equality.

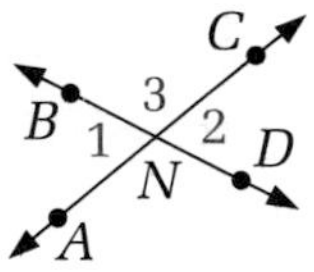

Show Your Reasoning

Statements

Lines AC and BD intersect at N ❶ to form vertical angles 1 and 2. →

$m\angle ANC = 180°$
$m\angle BND = 180°$ ❷

$m\angle ANC = m\angle BND$ ❸

$m\angle ANC = m\angle 1 + m\angle 3$
$m\angle BND = m\angle 2 + m\angle 3$ ❹

$m\angle 1 + m\angle 3 = m\angle 2 + m\angle 3$ ❺ → $m\angle 1 = m\angle 2$

Justifications

❶ If the sides of an angle form a straight line, then the angle is a straight angle with measure 180°.

❷ Substitution property

❸ For any angle, the measure of the whole is equal to the sum of the measures of its non-overlapping parts.

❹ Substitution property

❺ Subtraction property of equality

X · Lab

VERTICAL ANGLES THEOREM

Theorem 7.3 Vertical angles are equal in measure.

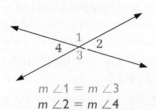

$m\angle 1 = m\angle 3$
$m\angle 2 = m\angle 4$

Look Back ←
What kinds of statements can be used
as justifications in proofs?

7-7 Exercises and Problems

Reading Identify each type of statement as one or more of the
following: a *definition*, a *postulate*, or a *theorem*.

1. a statement that is a biconditional

2. a statement that you assume is true, but do not prove

3. a statement that you may use as a justification in a proof

4. a statement that you can prove

**In Exercises 5–7, state a conclusion that can be made in one
step from the given information. Give a reason.**

5. *Given:* $\angle Q$ is supplementary to $\angle R$.

6. *Given:* $\angle R$ and $\angle T$ are vertical angles.

7. *Given:* $\angle G$ is supplementary to $\angle H$. $\angle G$ is supplementary to $\angle J$.

8. Copy and complete the proof.

> **Given** Line r intersects lines l and k.
> $m \angle 1 = m \angle 2$
>
> **Prove** $m \angle 3 = m \angle 2$

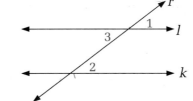

> **BY THE WAY...**
>
> The words *theorem* and *theater*
> both come from the same Greek
> root *to see*. At a theater you see
> a performance. In a theorem you
> see that a statement is true.

Statements	**Justifications**
1. l and r are intersecting lines.	1. Given
2. $\angle 1$ and $\angle 3$ are vertical angles.	2. ?
3. ?	3. Vertical ∡ are = in measure.
4. $m \angle 1 = m \angle 2$	4. ?
5. ?	5. Substitution property (Steps 3 and 4)

9. Laurie wants to double the area of a square. She first
doubles each side. This gives her a square four times as
large. Then she cuts each of the four squares in half.

   a. Is the area of the new figure twice the area of the
   original square?

   b. **Writing** How do you know for sure that the sides
   of the new figure are equal in measure? Explain
   your reasoning.

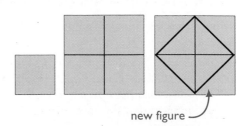

new figure

10. Copy and complete the proof.

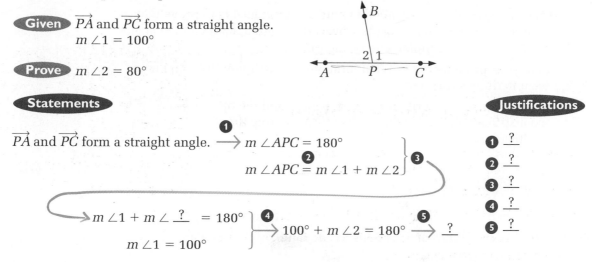

Given $\overrightarrow{PA}$ and $\overrightarrow{PC}$ form a straight angle.
$m\angle 1 = 100°$

Prove $m\angle 2 = 80°$

Statements

$\overrightarrow{PA}$ and $\overrightarrow{PC}$ form a straight angle. $\longrightarrow$ ❶ $m\angle APC = 180°$

❷ $m\angle APC = m\angle 1 + m\angle 2$ ❸

❹ $m\angle 1 + m\angle \underline{?} = 180°$

$m\angle 1 = 100°$ $\longrightarrow$ ❹ $100° + m\angle 2 = 180°$ $\longrightarrow$ ❺ $\underline{?}$

Justifications

❶ $\underline{?}$

❷ $\underline{?}$

❸ $\underline{?}$

❹ $\underline{?}$

❺ $\underline{?}$

11. Write a flow proof: If $\angle 1$ and $\angle 2$ are complementary and $m\angle 1 = 75°$, then $m\angle 2 = 15°$.

12. Write a paragraph proof: If $\angle 1$ and $\angle 2$ form a straight angle and $m\angle 1 = 25°$, then $m\angle 2 = 155°$.

13. **Law** Do you think the statement "A person is innocent until proven guilty" is closer to a definition, a postulate, or a theorem?

14. What is the converse of Postulate 8? Is it true?

15. Write a proof of the following:

Given $\angle ABC$ is a straight angle.
$m\angle ABF = m\angle FBE$
$m\angle EBD = m\angle DBC$

Prove $\angle FBD$ is a right angle.

the salchow jump

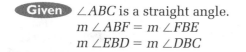

Mathematics and the law have their own vocabularies and rules. So do many sports and games. All players must understand the terms and play by the same rules.

16. **Research** Choose two of the following terms. Find sports or games that use your terms. Write a good definition of each of your terms using a biconditional.

foul	starboard	netball	goal
salchow	stroke	out	checkmate

17. **Open-ended** Choose a game or a sport you know. Make up a situation where the players might have a dispute. Use the rules and definitions for your game or sport to decide on a ruling.

BY THE WAY...

Ulrich Salchow won the first men's figure skating event in the Olympics in 1908. He also won ten World and nine European Championships, representing Sweden.

18. Group Activity Work with another student. Your goal is to prove that if ∠1 and ∠2 are supplementary angles and ∠1 and ∠3 are vertical angles, then ∠2 and ∠3 are supplementary angles.

  a. Plan your proof together. What form of proof will you use? You may want to draw a diagram.

  b. One of you should write the first statement and the other should write the justification. Then switch. Take turns writing the statements and justifications.

Review **PREVIEW**

19. Write a proof of the following: If $2(x + 7) = 3x$, then $x = 14$. *(Section 7-6)*

Tell whether each system of equations has *no solution*, *one solution*, or *many solutions*. *(Section 3-3)*

20. $y = 3x + 2$
      $y = -2x - 5$

21. $y = x - 1$
      $7y = 7x - 7$

22. $y = 2x - 2$
      $y = 2x + 2$

23. Name three kinds of quadrilaterals that are parallelograms. *(Section 5-1)*

Working on the Unit Project

24. Doctors, scientists, and engineers are sometimes called on to solve medical mysteries. When thousands of American Legionnaires met for a convention in Philadelphia in 1976, more than 200 came down with an unexplained illness. The symptoms were high fever, chest pains, and difficulty breathing.

Doctors found that blood samples showed a high level of a particular enzyme. Other samples revealed a bacterial infection. Six months after the convention, these clues led to finding the bacterium that causes Legionnaires' disease.

To solve your mystery story, readers need all the clues. List the clues that you plan to use in the order you will reveal them.

DISEASE DETECTIVES AT WORK

ATLANTA, GEORGIA—Officials at the U.S. Centers for Disease Control recently announced that their researchers have pieced together clues to discover the organism that caused Legionnaires' disease in Philadelphia. Physicians, biologists, chemists, bacteriologists, and microbiologists examined samples collected by investigators. They finally found that a previously unknown bacillus, newly named *Legionella pneumophilia*, caused the disease.

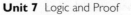

Proofs about Parallel Lines

Know all the Angles

EXPLORATION

How are angles and parallel lines related?

- **Materials: ruler or straight edge, protractor, lined notebook paper, blank paper**
- **Work in a group of four students.**

① Use lined notebook paper. Use a ruler to darken two parallel lines. Draw a dark line intersecting both parallel lines, but not perpendicular to them.

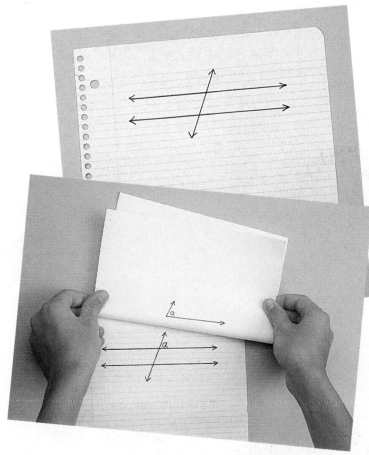

② Place a blank sheet of paper over your drawing. Trace one acute angle and label it *a*. Find all other angles of equal measure. Put a small *a* inside each angle with that measure.

③ Trace an obtuse angle and label it *o*. Find all other angles of equal measure. Put a small *o* inside each angle with that measure.

④ **a.** How many different angles did you find?

   b. How are the acute and obtuse angles related to one another?

   c. Describe any patterns you see in the results.

⑤ Can you find a pair of parallel lines and a transversal for which your observations do not hold?

⑥ Suppose all your classmates agree on relationships among the angles. What sort of reasoning are you using? Does this prove the relationships?

Transversals and Special Angle Pairs

It is helpful in talking about intersecting lines to agree on some terms.

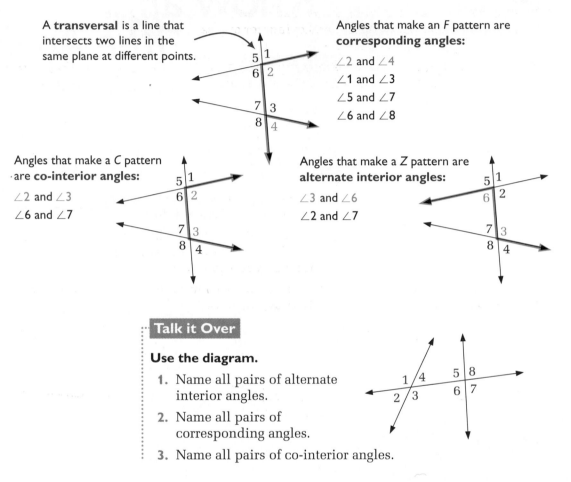

A **transversal** is a line that intersects two lines in the same plane at different points.

Angles that make an *F* pattern are **corresponding angles:**

∠2 and ∠4
∠1 and ∠3
∠5 and ∠7
∠6 and ∠8

Angles that make a *C* pattern are **co-interior angles:**

∠2 and ∠3
∠6 and ∠7

Angles that make a *Z* pattern are **alternate interior angles:**

∠3 and ∠6
∠2 and ∠7

Talk it Over

Use the diagram.

1. Name all pairs of alternate interior angles.

2. Name all pairs of corresponding angles.

3. Name all pairs of co-interior angles.

When lines are parallel, a transversal creates special angle pairs. As the Exploration suggests, some pairs are equal in measure and others are supplementary. If you assume Postulate 10, then you can prove that other relationships must be true.

X ◁*ab*

A POSTULATE ABOUT PARALLEL LINES

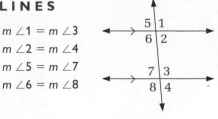

Postulate 10 If two parallel lines are intersected by a transversal, then corresponding angles are equal in measure.

$m \angle 1 = m \angle 3$
$m \angle 2 = m \angle 4$
$m \angle 5 = m \angle 7$
$m \angle 6 = m \angle 8$

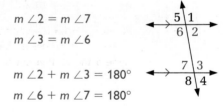

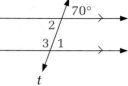

X : lab

Here are statements of other patterns you may have observed in the Exploration.

THEOREMS ABOUT PARALLEL LINES

Theorem 7.4 If two parallel lines are intersected by a transversal, then alternate interior angles are equal in measure.

$m \angle 2 = m \angle 7$

$m \angle 3 = m \angle 6$

Theorem 7.5 If two parallel lines are intersected by a transversal, then co-interior angles are supplementary.

$m \angle 2 + m \angle 3 = 180°$

$m \angle 6 + m \angle 7 = 180°$

Talk it Over

4. In the diagram at the right, how do you know that $m \angle 1 = 70°$?

5. $\angle 1$ and $\angle 2$ are alternate interior angles. What are their measures? How do you know?

⋯⋯► **Now you are ready for:**
Exs. 1–11 on pp. 419–420

6. $\angle 2$ and $\angle 3$ are co-interior angles. What are their measures? How do you know?

Parallel Lines in Proofs

The symbol ∥ is read either as "parallel" (two ∥ lines) or as "is parallel to" ($m \parallel n$).

Sample 1

Prove that if two parallel lines are intersected by a transversal, then alternate interior angles are equal in measure. (Theorem 7.4)

Sample Response

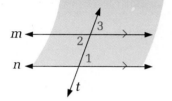

Given Lines m and n are parallel.
Transversal t intersects lines m and n.

Prove $m \angle 1 = m \angle 2$

Plan Ahead

Think about which angle pairs are equal in measure. Show that $\angle 1$ and $\angle 2$ are both equal in measure to $\angle 3$. Then $\angle 1$ and $\angle 2$ are equal in measure.

Continued on next page.

Show Your Reasoning

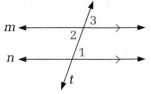

Statements

$$m \parallel n \xrightarrow{\textbf{①}} \left. \begin{array}{l} m \angle 1 = m \angle 3 \\ \textbf{②} \\ m \angle 2 = m \angle 3 \end{array} \right\} \xrightarrow{\textbf{③}} m \angle 1 = m \angle 2$$

Justifications

① If two ∥ lines are intersected by a transversal, then corresponding △ are = in measure.

② Vertical △ are = in measure.

③ Substitution property

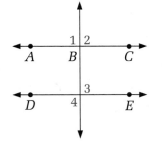

There are some things you can assume from a diagram and some you cannot. In this diagram you *can* assume:

All points shown are in the same plane.

Points *A*, *B*, and *C*, are on the same line.

∠3 and ∠4 are vertical angles.

Here you *cannot* assume:

$\overleftrightarrow{AC}$ is parallel to $\overleftrightarrow{DE}$.

$m \angle 1 = m \angle 2$

$AB = BC$

Sample 2

Prove that if a quadrilateral is a parallelogram, then consecutive angles are supplementary.

Sample Response

Given parallelogram *ABCD*

Prove ∠1 is supplementary to ∠2.

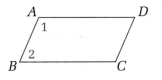

Plan Ahead

Find parallel lines intersected by a transversal for which ∠1 and ∠2 are co-interior angles. Then ∠1 is supplementary to ∠2.

Show Your Reasoning

Statements

1. *ABCD* is a parallelogram.
2. $\overline{AD}$ is parallel to $\overline{BC}$.
3. ∠1 is supplementary to ∠2.

Justifications

1. Given
2. Definition of a parallelogram
3. If two ∥ lines are intersected by a transversal, then co-interior △ are supplementary.

PARALLELOGRAM ANGLE THEOREMS

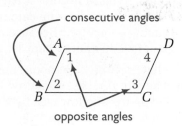

consecutive angles

opposite angles

Theorem 7.6 If a quadrilateral is a parallelogram, then consecutive angles are supplementary.

$m \angle 1 + m \angle 2 = 180°$ $m \angle 2 + m \angle 3 = 180°$

$m \angle 3 + m \angle 4 = 180°$ $m \angle 4 + m \angle 1 = 180°$

Theorem 7.7 If a quadrilateral is a parallelogram, then opposite angles are equal in measure.

$m \angle 1 = m \angle 3$ $m \angle 2 = m \angle 4$

Talk it Over

7. Write a plan to prove that if a quadrilateral is a parallelogram, then opposite angles are equal in measure.

Look Back

What postulate was assumed in this lesson? What theorems could be deduced from this postulate and previous theorems and definitions?

······► **Now you are ready for:**
Exs. 12–27 on pp. 420–422

7-8 Exercises and Problems

For Exercises 1–6, use the diagram.

1. Name four pairs of corresponding angles.
2. Name two pairs of alternate interior angles.
3. Name two pairs of co-interior angles.
4. Name at least ten pairs of supplementary angles.
5. What might be a good name for the pair of angles numbered 1 and 4?
6. Suppose $m \angle 3 = 100°$. Find the measure of each angle.

   a. $\angle 1$ b. $\angle 2$ c. $\angle 4$ d. $\angle 5$

   e. $\angle 6$ f. $\angle 7$ g. $\angle 8$

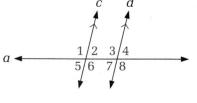

7. *ABCD* is a trapezoid.

   a. What type of angles are $\angle 1$ and $\angle 2$?

   b. What can you conclude about their measures?

   c. What is your justification?

Eratosthenes lived in northeast Africa in the 3rd century B.C. Exercises 8–10 show how he calculated the circumference of Earth using geometry. (Because the sun is so far from Earth, its rays can be considered parallel.)

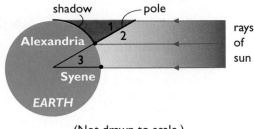

(Not drawn to scale.)

He saw that on June 21 at noon, the sun cast no shadow in Syene. The sun *did* cast a shadow in Alexandria, north of Syene. Using the shadow cast by a pole, Eratosthenes found that the measure of $\angle 1$ was 7.2°.

8. How are $\angle 1$ and $\angle 2$ related? $\angle 2$ and $\angle 3$? **9.** What is the measure of $\angle 3$?

10. a. Eratosthenes estimated the distance between Alexandria and Syene to be 5000 stadia. (One *stadium* is about 607 ft.) Use this proportion to estimate the circumference of Earth:

$$\frac{m \angle 3}{360°} = \frac{5000 \text{ stadia}}{\text{Earth circumference}}$$

 b. What is the estimate in feet?

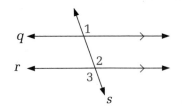
Pin goes through both straws.

11. Using Manipulatives You will need four straws, four straight pins, scissors, and blank paper.

 a. Hold two straws parallel, a few inches apart. Lay a straw across them and pin the intersections. Lay a fourth straw parallel to the third. Pin the intersections.

 b. Writing Gently shift the parallelogram so that the angles change size. Describe how consecutive pairs of angles are affected. Describe how opposite pairs of angles are affected.

12. Write a paragraph proof of Theorem 7.4: If two parallel lines are intersected by a transversal, then alternate interior angles are equal in measure.

13. Write a two-column proof of Theorem 7.5: If two parallel lines are intersected by a transversal, then co-interior angles are supplementary.

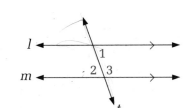

14. a. Given: Lines *q* and *r* are parallel.
 Prove: $m \angle 1 = m \angle 3$

 b. Write the conclusion of part (a) as a theorem using words.

15. *PQRS* is a parallelogram. What is the relationship between each pair of angles?

 a. $\angle P$ and $\angle Q$ **b.** $\angle P$ and $\angle R$

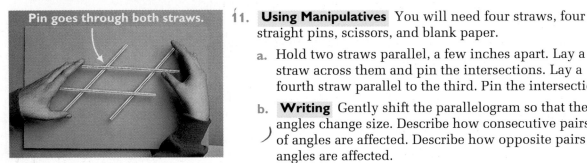

16. In parallelogram *ABCD*, $m \angle A = x°$.

 a. Write an expression for the measure of each of the other angles.

 b. Write an expression for the sum of the measures of the angles.

 c. Use your answer in part (b) to make a conjecture about the sum of the angles of a parallelogram.

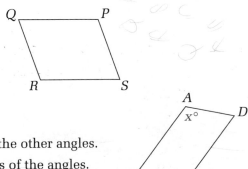

17. Copy and complete this proof.

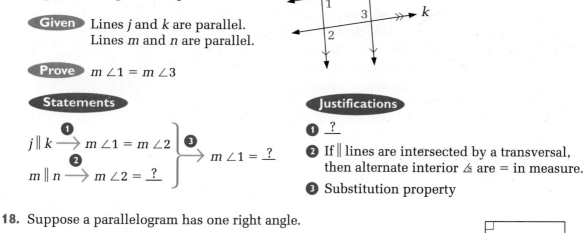

Given Lines *j* and *k* are parallel.
Lines *m* and *n* are parallel.

Prove $m \angle 1 = m \angle 3$

Statements

$j \parallel k \xrightarrow{\;①\;} m \angle 1 = m \angle 2$ ③
$m \parallel n \xrightarrow{\;②\;} m \angle 2 = \underline{?}$ } → $m \angle 1 = \underline{?}$

Justifications

① $\underline{?}$

② If $\parallel$ lines are intersected by a transversal, then alternate interior $\angle$s are = in measure.

③ Substitution property

18. Suppose a parallelogram has one right angle.

   a. What can you conclude about the angles consecutive to this angle? Why?

   b. What can you conclude about the angle opposite this angle? Why?

   c. What special parallelogram is this?

   d. **Writing** Decide whether this is a good definition: A parallelogram is a rectangle if and only if it has at least one right angle. Explain why or why not.

19. In parallelogram *QRST*, $m \angle Q = 123°$. Find the measures of the other angles.

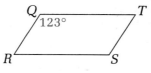

20. Physicians and physical therapists use a tool called a *goniometer* to measure range of motion.

   a. The goniometer indicates that the range of motion of the knee shown is 30°. The arms of the goniometer make a 150° angle. What do you think "range of motion" measures?

   b. Find the center of the goniometer. Compare the angle formed by the lines through the center with the angle formed by the inside edges of the tool. Write a proof of why these angles must be equal in measure.

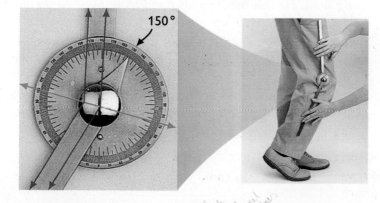

150°

21. a. Open-ended Lines q and r are parallel. Transversal s intersects lines q and r. Create a reasonable name for a pair of angles positioned like $\angle 1$ and $\angle 2$.

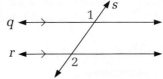

b. How do you think the measures of $\angle 1$ and $\angle 2$ are related?

c. Prove your conjecture using two different forms of proof (paragraph, flow, or two-column).

Review **PREVIEW**

22. The measure of $\angle 1$ is 40°. What are the measures of $\angle 2$, $\angle 3$, and $\angle 4$? *(Section 7-7)*

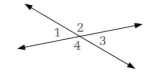

Solve. *(Section 4-3)*

23. $2x^2 + 7 = 17$

24. $(x - 2)^2 + 5 = 21$

25. $4(x - 3)^2 - 1 = 15$

26. Write the converse of this statement: "If an animal has feathers, then it is a bird." *(Section 1-6)*

 Working on the Unit Project

27. In the following situation, Carl claims he did not see Rowena waiting for him at 8:00. Suppose you are Carl. Explain why you did not see her. Make a sketch to support your argument.

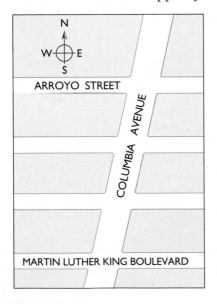

Rowena calls Carl. She says, "On the evening of the reunion, I will wait for you on the southeast corner of Columbia Avenue and Arroyo Street. I will stand on the north side of the block. If you are not there by 8:00, I'll take a taxi."

"OK," Carl answers, "I will be there on time if my car is running."

At 7:00 P.M. on the evening of the reunion, Carl is still fixing his car. He works under the hood for so long that he gets a stiff neck. He can not turn his head more than 70° in either direction.

At last the car starts! Carl drives northeast on Columbia Avenue. As he checks the time, he crosses Martin Luther King Boulevard.

At 8:00 P.M. Carl drives across the intersection of Columbia Avenue and Arroyo Street. He turns his head but does not see Rowena. He drives on to the reunion alone.

Completing the Unit Project

Complete your mystery story. Your finished project should include these things:

➤ an outline that contains valid logical arguments leading to the solution of your mystery. Include at least two types of logical argument.

➤ an interesting mystery story with a plot that involves a travel itinerary and applications of at least two of the geometry postulates and theorems from this unit

➤ a written report of readers' reactions to your story

Look Back

How could you revise your story to make it more interesting? to make the mystery more challenging to solve?

Alternative Projects

Project 1: Testing the Validity of Arguments in the News Media

Collect examples of implications in advertisements, newspaper or magazine editorials, and news stories presenting various points of view on a controversial issue. Analyze the implications in the advertisements, editorials, and news stories. Identify arguments based on these implications. (If there are none, write some of your own.) Determine whether or not the arguments are valid. Discuss your reasoning.

Project 2: Analyzing a Mystery Story

Read a mystery story or watch a mystery movie or TV program. List the clues that are given to the reader or viewer. Identify the important premises and implications in the story. Write an outline of the story in the form of a series of valid arguments.

Tanya is working on a science project on the construction of balls used in different sports. She made this database.

7-1

Ball	Diam. (cm)	Mass (g)	Interior Construction	Exterior Construction
baseball	7.3	145	rubber or cork wrapped with yarn	leather cover
basketball	24.0	596	inflated rubber	leather or rubber cover
lacrosse	6.4	143	solid rubber	solid rubber cover
soccer	22.0	425	inflated shell	leather cover
tennis	6.5	57	hollow	cloth cover
volleyball	21.0	270	inflated rubber	leather or rubber cover

For Questions 1 and 2, find every ball that makes each statement true.

1. The ball has a diameter less than 10 cm and a mass greater than 140 g.

2. The ball has a diameter less than 10 cm or a mass greater than 140 g.

3. Use a mathematical statement and a graph to describe the range of diameters that are greater than that of a lacrosse ball and less than that of a basketball.

4. For Exercises 1 and 2, which statement is an example of a conjunction? a disjunction?

5. Is this statement *True* or *False* for the balls in the database? Each ball with a leather cover has a mass over 100 g.

7-2

6. Write the converse of the statement in Question 5 and decide if it is *True* or *False*. If it is false, give a counterexample.

7. Draw a Venn diagram for the statement in Question 5.

For Questions 8 and 9, decide if the argument is *valid* or *invalid*. If the argument is valid, tell which rule of logic was used. If the argument is invalid, tell why.

7-3

8. If a triangle is equilateral, then it is equiangular.
   Triangle *QRS* is not equiangular.
   Therefore, triangle *QRS* is not equilateral.

9. I will be home this afternoon or I will be at work. I will be at work. Therefore, I will not be home this afternoon.

10. **Open-ended** Write a valid argument using the chain rule.

11. Write the two implications in this biconditional using symbols and using words: $x^2 = 36 \leftrightarrow x = 6$

7-4

12. Is the biconditional in Question 11 *True* or *False*? If it is false, rewrite it so it is true.

13. **Writing** Tell how you know that a biconditional is true.

14. Use the flight schedule to prove this statement: **7-5**
You can fly from Cairo to Mexico City.

   a. Write a paragraph proof.

   b. Write a two-column proof.

   c. Tell which rule of logic is used in
   the two-column proof in part (b).

15. Prove this statement:
If $3a^2 - 5 = 43$ and a is positive, then $a = 4$.   **7-6**

   a. Write a flow proof.

   b. Write a two-column proof.

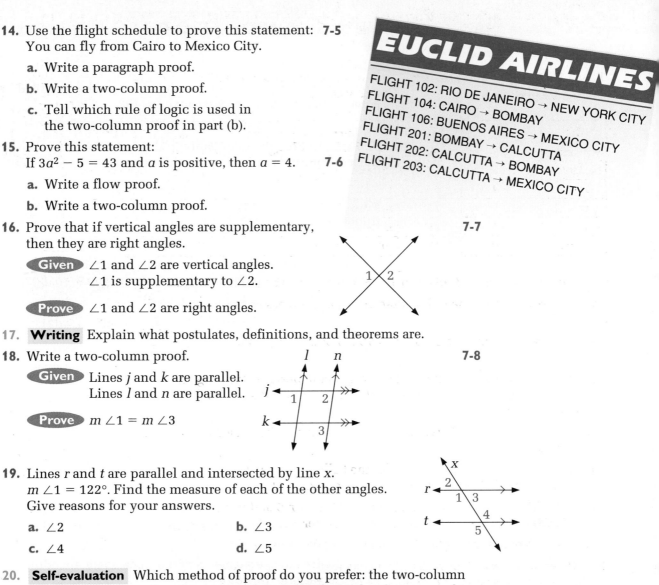

EUCLID AIRLINES

FLIGHT 102: RIO DE JANEIRO → NEW YORK CITY
FLIGHT 104: CAIRO → BOMBAY
FLIGHT 106: BUENOS AIRES → MEXICO CITY
FLIGHT 201: BOMBAY → CALCUTTA
FLIGHT 202: CALCUTTA → BOMBAY
FLIGHT 203: CALCUTTA → MEXICO CITY

16. Prove that if vertical angles are supplementary,   **7-7**
then they are right angles.

   Given ∠1 and ∠2 are vertical angles.
   ∠1 is supplementary to ∠2.

   Prove ∠1 and ∠2 are right angles.

17. **Writing** Explain what postulates, definitions, and theorems are.

18. Write a two-column proof.   **7-8**

   Given Lines j and k are parallel.
   Lines l and n are parallel.

   Prove $m \angle 1 = m \angle 3$

19. Lines r and t are parallel and intersected by line x.
$m \angle 1 = 122°$. Find the measure of each of the other angles.
Give reasons for your answers.

   a. ∠2   **b.** ∠3

   c. ∠4   **d.** ∠5

20. **Self-evaluation** Which method of proof do you prefer: the two-column
proof, the flow proof, or the paragraph proof? Why? What features make
your preferred form easier for you?

21. **Group Activity** Work in a group of three students. Each student should
prove the statements in parts (a)–(c), one student by two-column proof, one
student by flow proof, and one student by paragraph proof. Each student
should use each method once.

   a. If $9x - 10 = -1$, then $x = 1$.

   b. If $\angle V$ and $\angle W$ are supplementary
   and $m \angle V = 75°$, then $m \angle W = 105°$.

   c. If lines l and k are parallel and
   intersected by line n, then $m \angle 1 = m \angle 3$.

   d. For each statement, discuss which method
   seems easiest to follow. Is there a way to
   decide which method to use before you start?

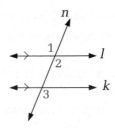

IDEAS AND (FORMULAS) $=X^2$

$_5P_5$

Postulates of Algebra

➤ **Addition Property of Equality:** If the same number is added to equal numbers, the sums are equal. *(p. 402)*

$$a = b \rightarrow a + c = b + c$$

➤ **Subtraction Property of Equality:** If the same number is subtracted from equal numbers, the differences are equal. *(p. 402)*

$$a = b \rightarrow a - c = b - c$$

➤ **Multiplication Property of Equality:** If equal numbers are multiplied by the same number, the products are equal. *(p. 402)*

$$a = b \rightarrow ac = bc$$

➤ **Division Property of Equality:** If equal numbers are divided by the same nonzero number, the quotients are equal. *(p. 402)*

$$a = b \text{ and } c \neq 0 \rightarrow \frac{a}{c} = \frac{b}{c}$$

➤ **Reflexive Property:** A number is equal to itself. *(p. 402)*

$$a = a$$

➤ **Substitution Property:** If values are equal, one value may be substituted for the other. *(p. 402)*

$$a = b \rightarrow a \text{ may be substituted for } b.$$

➤ **Distributive Property:** An expression of the form $a(b + c)$ is equivalent to $ab + ac$. *(p. 402)*

$$a(b + c) = ab + ac$$

Postulates and Theorems of Geometry

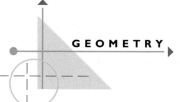

➤ If two angles are supplements of the same angle, then they are equal in measure. *(p. 409)*

➤ If two angles are complements of the same angle, then they are equal in measure. *(p. 409)*

➤ If the sides of an angle form a straight line, then the angle is a straight angle with measure 180°. *(p. 410)*

➤ For any segment or angle, the measure of the whole is equal to the sum of the measures of its non-overlapping parts. *(p. 410)*

➤ Vertical angles are equal in measure. *(p. 411)*

➤ If two parallel lines are intersected by a transversal, then:
  • corresponding angles are equal in measure. *(p. 416)*
  • alternate interior angles are equal in measure. *(p. 417)*
  • co-interior angles are supplementary. *(p. 417)*

➤ If a quadrilateral is a parallelogram, then:
  • consecutive angles are supplementary. *(p. 419)*
  • opposite angles are equal in measure. *(p. 419)*

$p \leftrightarrow q$

LOGICAL
if - then **REASONING**

➤ A database stores information and may be searched using *and*, *or*, and *not*. *(p. 365)*

➤ A conjunction is true when both statements are true. A disjunction is true when at least one statement is true. *(p. 367)*

➤ Implications can be represented by Venn diagrams. *(p. 367)*

➤ There are several ways to state an implication: *(p. 373)*

If p, then q.	Every p is a q.	$p \rightarrow q$
p implies q.	All p are q.	p only if q.
q if p. *(p. 375)*		

➤ Direct Argument: If p is true, then q is true.
　　　　　　　　　　p is true.
　　　　　　　　　　Therefore, q is true. *(p. 380)*

➤ Indirect Argument: If p is true, then q is true.
　　　　　　　　　　　q is not true.
　　　　　　　　　　　Therefore, p is not true. *(p. 380)*

➤ Chain Rule: If p is true, then q is true.
　　　　　　　If q is true, then r is true.
　　　　　　　Therefore, if p is true, then r is true. *(p. 380)*

➤ *Or* Rule: p is true or q is true.
　　　　　　p is not true.
　　　　　　Therefore, q is true. *(p. 380)*

➤ Arguments that do not use rules of logic are invalid. *(p. 381)*

➤ The converse of a true implication is not necessarily true. *(p. 382)*

➤ A biconditional is true when both of its conditionals are true. *(p. 386)*

➤ Good definitions are made of true biconditionals. *(p. 388)*

➤ Proofs may be presented in two-column form, paragraph form, or flow form. *(p. 396)*

➤ The steps of a proof use rules of logic. *(p. 397)*

········· **Key Terms**

- **database** (p. 365)
- **negation** (p. 367)
- **implication** (p. 373)
- **valid argument** (p. 380)
- **indirect argument** (p. 380)
- **invalid argument** (p. 381)
- **paragraph proof** (p. 396)
- **square root** (p. 403)
- **m ∠A** (p. 408)
- **transversal** (p. 416)
- **co-interior angles** (p. 416)

- **conjunction** (p. 367)
- **hypothesis** (p. 373)
- **conditional** (p. 373)
- **∴** (p. 380)
- **chain rule** (p. 380)
- **biconditional** (p. 386)
- **flow proof** (p. 396)
- **complementary angles** (p. 408)
- **theorem** (p. 408)
- **corresponding angles** (p. 416)
- **‖** (p. 417)

- **disjunction** (p. 367)
- **conclusion** (pp. 373, 380)
- **premise** (p. 380)
- **direct argument** (p. 380)
- **or rule** (p. 380)
- **two-column proof** (pp. 395–396)
- **postulate** (p. 402)
- **supplementary angles** (p. 408)
- **vertical angles** (p. 410)
- **alternate interior angles** (p. 416)

Similar and Congruent Triangles

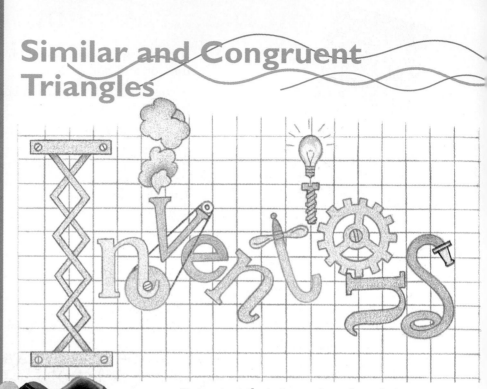

One day over fifty years ago, a Swiss mountain climber walked through some prickly bushes. As he struggled to remove the tiny thorns that stuck to his pants and socks, the idea for that sticky fastening tape today used on everything from athletic shoes to picture hangers popped into his head.

To protect their inventions from being copied, many inventors apply for a patent. A **patent** gives an inventor the exclusive right to make and sell a product for a period of time. To receive a patent, an inventor must prove to the patent office that an invention works and that it is both new and useful.

Inventions

come about in many ways. Below are a few stories of how some everyday things began.

hooks — loops

This roller skate curiously resembles the popular in-line skates of today.

1823

Levi Strauss invented blue jeans for the miners of California.

1873

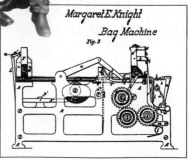

First century A.D.

Sneakers originated when the Mayans of Central America coated the soles of their feet with the sap of rubber trees.

1870

Brown paper bags are the result of machinery invented by Margaret Knight, who, starting at the age of 12, created over 27 inventions.

Margaret E. Knight Bag Machine Fig. 3

Patent Your Idea

Your project is to invent a tool and write a patent application for it. The tool you design may combine and/or modify features of the tools you read about as you complete the "Working on the Unit Project" exercises.

Use at least two of these ideas in the construction or operation of your tool:

➤ properties of parallel lines

➤ the triangle sum theorem

➤ properties of similar triangles

➤ minimum conditions for congruent triangles

➤ right triangle trigonometry

In your patent application you should:

➤ Describe your invention clearly and completely.

➤ Explain how to make your invention.

➤ Explain how to use your invention.

➤ Include sketches and diagrams.

When all the groups have completed their patent application, have each group make a presention to the class. The class should decide whether to award a patent to each group.

The future

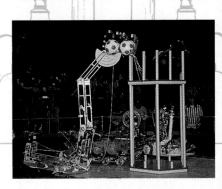

The U.S. FIRST tournament makes heros out of inventors. In this **technological superbowl** the competing teams consist of working engineers paired with students from high schools across the nation. The 1994 games were won by the "orange cannon" robot designed by the team from Walnut High School in Cincinnati.

Dedicated inventors working on two continents worked at perfecting the light bulb before Thomas Edison patented it.

1880

1910

The flying plastic disks so popular today originated when students at Yale University began tossing around pie tins.

429

Getting Started

For this project you should work in a group of four students. Here are some ideas to help you get started.

☞ You may wish to obtain a book or article about patents in order to review some existing patents.

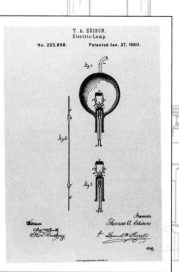

☞ In your group discuss how you will use words and pictures in your patent application to help make your explanations clear and complete. You may wish to look over some car repair manuals or assembly instructions to get ideas that you could apply in your patent application.

☞ Plan to meet later to discuss the features of the tool and which ideas from geometry will be applied in building or using it.

These pages are from the patent issued to Thomas A. Edison for the "electric lamp" on January 27, 1880.

Working on the Unit Project

Your work in Unit 8 will help you design a tool and apply for a patent.

Related Exercises:

Section 8-1, Exercise 28
Section 8-2, Exercise 44
Section 8-3, Exercise 27
Section 8-4, Exercises 21, 22
Section 8-5, Exercise 19
Section 8-6, Exercise 32
Section 8-7, Exercise 30
Section 8-8, Exercise 38

Alternative Projects p. 497

Can We Talk

Inventors

➤ What characteristics do you think successful inventors may have in common?

➤ Some inventions remain "trade secrets." Do you think it is better to keep an invention secret or to patent it? Why?

➤ New products are being invented all the time. What new inventions have you heard or read about lately?

➤ Fewer than one out of a hundred patented inventions ever reach the market. What factors do you think may be responsible for this?

➤ The U.S. FIRST tournament is a competition modeled on a sporting event. It was created as a way of increasing respect for science and scientists. What other ways can you think of to accomplish the same goal?

Converses and Parallel Lines

T for Two

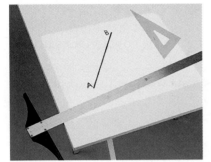

T-squares and triangles are drafting tools used to draw lines and angles. The methods for using the tools are based on relationships from geometry.

With a T-square and a triangle, you can draw a line *CD* parallel to another line *AB*.

1 Draw line *AB*.

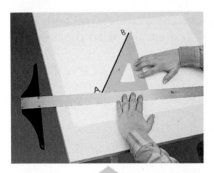

2 Position the tools so that the hypotenuse of the triangle lines up with line *AB*.

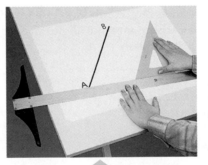

3 Slide the triangle along the T-square.

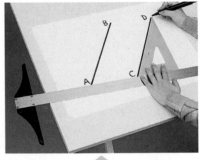

4 Draw line *CD* parallel to line *AB*.

The method assumes that when corresponding angles are equal in measure, the lines will be parallel. This assumption is true and is stated as a postulate.

X Lab

A POSTULATE ABOUT PARALLEL LINES

Postulate 11   If two lines are intersected by a transversal and corresponding angles are equal in measure, then the lines are parallel.

1. In steps 1–4 on page 431, line *CD* is drawn parallel to line *AB*. Where are the corresponding angles that are equal in measure?

2. **a.** State the converse of Postulate 11.

    b. Look back at page 416 of Unit 7. Does your converse match Postulate 10?

3. **a.** State the converse of Theorem 7.4: If two parallel lines are intersected by a transversal, then alternate interior angles are equal in measure.

    b. State the converse of Theorem 7.5: If two parallel lines are intersected by a transversal, then co-interior angles are supplementary.

Watch Out!

The converse of a postulate or theorem is not necessarily true, but it is worthwhile to investigate converses. You may discover another theorem.

You can use Postulate 11 to investigate whether the converses you stated above are true.

Sample 1

Prove that if two lines are intersected by a transversal and alternate interior angles are equal in measure, then the lines are parallel.

Sample Response

Given Transversal *t* intersects lines *k* and *l*.

$m \angle 1 = m \angle 2$

Prove $k \parallel l$

State what is given and what you need to prove about your diagram.

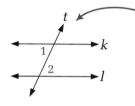

Make and label a diagram to represent the situation.

Plan Ahead

The lines are parallel if a pair of corresponding angles are equal in measure. Show that corresponding angles 1 and 3 are equal in measure.

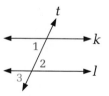

Show Your Reasoning

Method **1** Write a two-column proof.

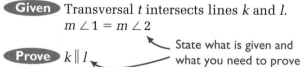

Statements	Justifications
1. $m \angle 1 = m \angle 2$	1. Given
2. $m \angle 2 = m \angle 3$	2. Vertical ⧄ are = in measure.
3. $m \angle 1 = m \angle 3$	3. Substitution property (Steps 1 and 2)
4. $k \parallel l$	4. If two lines are intersected by a transversal and corresponding ⧄ are = in measure, then the lines are ∥.

Method ❷ Write a paragraph proof.

Alternate interior angles ∠1 and ∠2 are equal in measure (given). Since ∠2 and ∠3 are vertical angles, they are also equal in measure. Substitute m ∠3 for m ∠2 in the statement m ∠1 = m ∠2, and ∠1 must be equal in measure to ∠3. Since the corresponding angles ∠1 and ∠3 are equal in measure, the lines intersected by the transversal are parallel, so k ∥ l.

Sample 1 proves the first theorem below. You will prove the second theorem in Exercise 12.

THEOREMS ABOUT PARALLEL LINES

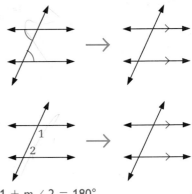

Theorem 8.1 If two lines are intersected by a transversal and alternate interior angles are equal in measure, then the lines are parallel.

Theorem 8.2 If two lines are intersected by a transversal and co-interior angles are supplementary, then the lines are parallel.

$$m \angle 1 + m \angle 2 = 180°$$

······▶ **Now you are ready for:**
Exs. 1–14 on pp. 435–437

Drafters may also use perpendicular lines to draw parallel lines. The triangle tool is a right triangle.

1 Place a leg of the right triangle along the T-square.

2 Draw line *EF* along the other leg.

3 Slide the right triangle along the T-square.

4 Draw line *GH*. Then line *GH* is parallel to line *EF*.

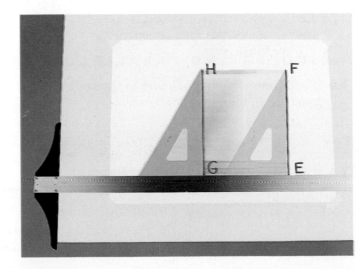

8-1 Converses and Parallel Lines

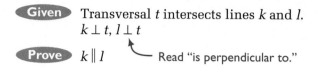
Write a flow proof to prove that if two lines are perpendicular to the same transversal, then they are parallel.

Sample Response

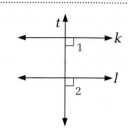

Given Transversal t intersects lines k and l.
$k \perp t, l \perp t$

Prove $k \parallel l$ — Read "is perpendicular to."

Plan Ahead

The lines are parallel if a pair of corresponding angles are equal in measure. Show that angles 1 and 2 are equal in measure.

Show Your Reasoning

Statements

$$k \perp t \xrightarrow{\;①\;} m \angle 1 = 90°$$
$$l \perp t \xrightarrow{\;①\;} m \angle 2 = 90° \Bigg\} \xrightarrow{\;②\;} m \angle 1 = m \angle 2 \xrightarrow{\;③\;} k \parallel l$$

Justifications

① Definition of perpendicular lines

② Substitution property

③ If two lines are intersected by a transversal and corresponding $\angle$s are = in measure, then the lines are $\parallel$.

The statement proved in Sample 2 is stated as Theorem 8.3. Theorem 8.4 is related and will be proved in Exercise 15.

$X_{\bigcirc} \triangle ab$

PERPENDICULAR AND PARALLEL LINES

Theorem 8.3 If two lines are perpendicular to the same transversal, then they are parallel.

Theorem 8.4 If a transversal is perpendicular to one of two parallel lines, then it is perpendicular to the other one also.

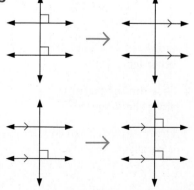

······► Now you are ready for:
: Exs. 15–28 on pp. 437–438

Look Back ◄──────────────

Two lines are intersected by a transversal. Describe the angle relationships that can be used to decide whether the two lines are parallel.

Exercises and Problems

1. **Reading** How were corresponding angles used in Sample 1 to prove Theorem 8.1 about alternate interior angles?

For each figure, state a postulate or theorem that could be used to prove that lines *l* and *m* are parallel.

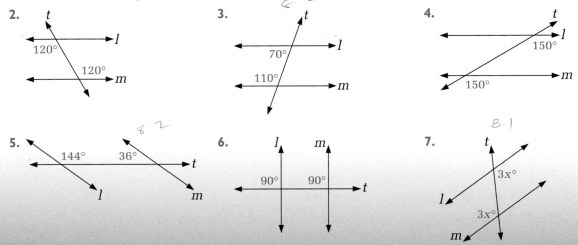

2.
t
120° → *l*
120° → *m*

3.
6. 2
t
70° → *l*
110° → *m*

4.
t
150° → *l*
150° → *m*

5.
8 2
144°   36° → *t*
l   *m*

6.
l   *m*
90°   90° → *t*

7.
8.1
t
3x°
l
3x°
m

In the Arctic, the prevailing winds blow the snow to form parallel ridges called sastrugi. For centuries the Inuits have used this natural phenomenon to give them direction as they traveled along the frozen Arctic plain.

For each of Exercises 8–11, use the given angle measures to decide whether lines *v* and *w* are parallel. Write Yes or No.

8. $m\angle 1 = 24°$, $m\angle 2 = 156°$

9. $m\angle 1 = 35°$, $m\angle 2 = 35°$ NO

10. $m\angle 1 = 3x°$, $m\angle 2 = (180 - 3x)°$

11. $m\angle 1 = y°$, $m\angle 2 = (90 - y)°$ NO

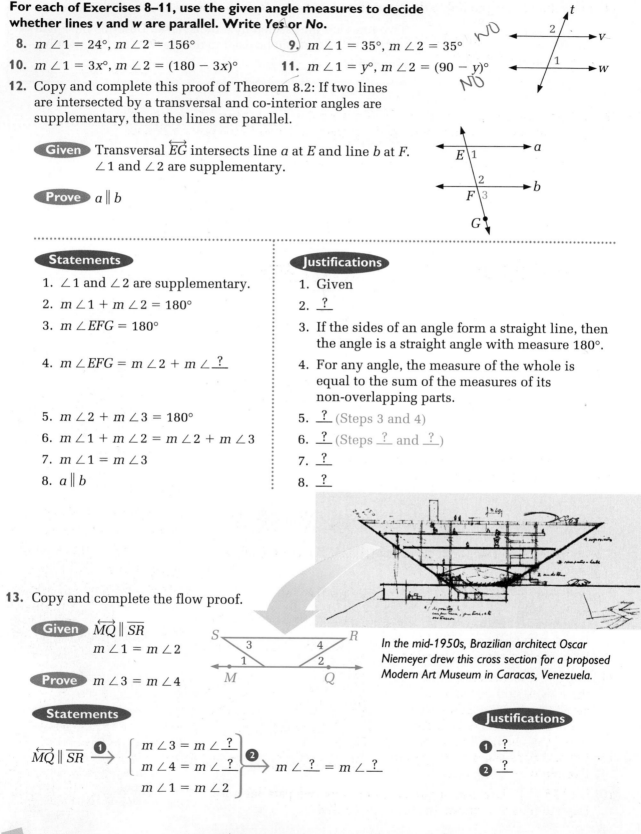

12. Copy and complete this proof of Theorem 8.2: If two lines are intersected by a transversal and co-interior angles are supplementary, then the lines are parallel.

   Given Transversal $\overleftrightarrow{EG}$ intersects line *a* at *E* and line *b* at *F*. $\angle 1$ and $\angle 2$ are supplementary.

   Prove $a \parallel b$

Statements	Justifications
1. $\angle 1$ and $\angle 2$ are supplementary.	1. Given
2. $m\angle 1 + m\angle 2 = 180°$	2. ?
3. $m\angle EFG = 180°$	3. If the sides of an angle form a straight line, then the angle is a straight angle with measure 180°.
4. $m\angle EFG = m\angle 2 + m\angle \underline{?}$	4. For any angle, the measure of the whole is equal to the sum of the measures of its non-overlapping parts.
5. $m\angle 2 + m\angle 3 = 180°$	5. ? (Steps 3 and 4)
6. $m\angle 1 + m\angle 2 = m\angle 2 + m\angle 3$	6. ? (Steps ? and ?)
7. $m\angle 1 = m\angle 3$	7. ?
8. $a \parallel b$	8. ?

13. Copy and complete the flow proof.

   Given $\overleftrightarrow{MQ} \parallel \overline{SR}$
   $m\angle 1 = m\angle 2$

   Prove $m\angle 3 = m\angle 4$

In the mid-1950s, Brazilian architect Oscar Niemeyer drew this cross section for a proposed Modern Art Museum in Caracas, Venezuela.

Statements

$\overleftrightarrow{MQ} \parallel \overline{SR}$ ➊ $\left\{ \begin{array}{l} m\angle 3 = m\angle \underline{?} \\ m\angle 4 = m\angle \underline{?} \\ m\angle 1 = m\angle 2 \end{array} \right.$ ➋ $\rightarrow m\angle \underline{?} = m\angle \underline{?}$

Justifications

➊ ?

➋ ?

14. Prove that lines parallel to the same line are parallel to each other.

> **Given** Transversal t intersects lines a, b, and c.
> $a \parallel b$, $c \parallel b$

> **Prove** $a \parallel c$

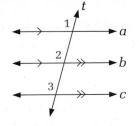

15. a. Copy and complete this proof of Theorem 8.4: If a transversal is perpendicular to one of two parallel lines, then it is perpendicular to the other one also.

> **Given** Transversal t intersects lines k and l.
> $k \parallel l$, $t \perp l$

> **Prove** $t \perp k$

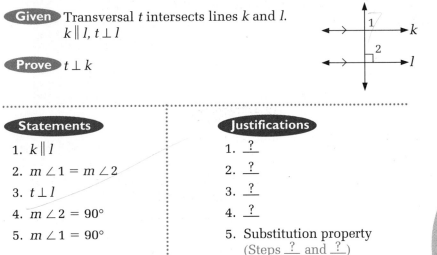

Statements	**Justifications**
1. $k \parallel l$	1. _?_
2. $m \angle 1 = m \angle 2$	2. _?_
3. $t \perp l$	3. _?_
4. $m \angle 2 = 90°$	4. _?_
5. $m \angle 1 = 90°$	5. Substitution property (Steps _?_ and _?_)
6. $t \perp k$	6. _?_

b. Rewrite the two-column proof in part (a) as a paragraph proof.

---

connection to INDUSTRIAL TECHNOLOGY

A drafting student places a T-square parallel to the bottom edge of a rectangular sheet of paper.

16. The student then draws a line by placing a leg of a right triangle against the T-square and drawing along the other leg. How does the student know that the line drawn will be parallel to the left and right edges of the paper?

17. Suppose the student places the hypotenuse of the triangle along the T-square and draws a line along one leg. Will the line drawn be parallel to the left and right edges of the paper? Explain why or why not.

18 TECHNOLOGY Use drawing software to draw two parallel lines. Explain how you know that they are parallel.

19. **Given** $\overline{GH} \perp \overline{HJ}$
$m \angle KJH = 90°$

Prove $\overline{GH} \parallel \overline{KJ}$

20. **Given** $\overleftrightarrow{LM} \parallel \overrightarrow{PQ}$
$m \angle MRS = 90°$

Prove $\overrightarrow{PQ} \perp \overleftrightarrow{RS}$

21. Prove that a quadrilateral with four right angles is a parallelogram.

22. **Writing** In Section 7-8, Exercise 18 stated that every parallelogram with at least one right angle is a rectangle. Is it accurate to say that every quadrilateral with at least one right angle is a rectangle? Explain.

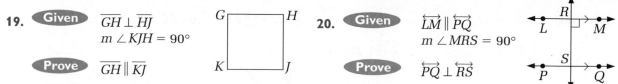

Ongoing ASSESSMENT

23. **Open-ended** Write a statement for an angle relationship that you think produces parallel lines but has not been discussed in this section. Prove your statement using a flow proof.

Review PREVIEW

24. In a parallelogram *ABCD*, $m \angle D = 75°$. Find the measures of the other angles. *(Section 7-8)*

For Exercises 25 and 26, tell whether each implication is *True* or *False*. If it is false, give a counterexample. *(Sections 5-1, 7-2)*

25. If a figure has four sides, then it is a parallelogram.

26. All squares are kites.

27. Solve $5x + 2x + 40 = 180$. *(Toolbox Skill 13)*

> **BY THE WAY...**
>
> Woven fabric will not stretch very much if it is pulled along a weft thread or along a warp thread. Fabric that is pulled along the bias, however, will stretch.

Mademoiselle Madeleine Vionnet, a dressmaker in Paris, introduced the bias cut. The dress shown was designed by Vionnet in 1926.

Working on the Unit Project

As you complete Exercise 28, think about how you can include properties of parallel and perpendicular lines in the tool you design.

28. A *parallel ruler* is an instrument used by navigators to draw parallel lines on navigation charts. It consists of two rulers joined by two clips. The clips rotate at the points where they are attached. This allows the two rulers to move apart while still remaining parallel.

a. What properties of parallel lines could the tool-maker use when fastening the clips to the rulers? Can the tool-maker check only one property to verify that the rulers are parallel, or should all the properties be checked?

b. The rulers are parallel in any position. What conjecture can you make about the clips in any position?

c. What would you need to know to prove your conjecture from part (b)?

The Triangle Sum Theorem

---Focus

Prove the triangle sum theorem and apply it to numerical problems and proofs of other theorems.

On the Level

The airplane instrument shown is called an *artificial horizon*, or *attitude indicator*. The instrument shows the position of the plane with respect to the horizon. There is only one position at which the plane is flying level and the plane's wings are parallel to the horizon.

— horizon line

— planes's wings

The photo shows that the left wing of the plane is up (the plane is "banking" to the right).

Talk it Over

1. **a.** On a piece of paper, draw any line and any point not on the line.

   b. Do you think there is a line through your point that is parallel to the line you drew?

   c. Do you think there is more than one parallel line through your point?

X ⬦ab

THE UNIQUE PARALLEL POSTULATE

Postulate 12 Through a point not on a given line, there is one and only one line parallel to the given line.

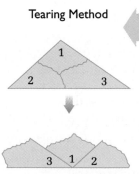

Folding Method

Tearing Method

In an earlier course, you probably explored the relationship between angles in triangles by folding or tearing paper triangles.

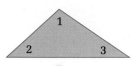

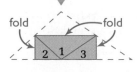

Inductive reasoning led you to the conjecture that the sum of the measures of the angles of a triangle is 180°. The unique parallel postulate will help you prove this by deductive reasoning.

Prove that the sum of the measures of the angles of a triangle is 180°.

Sample Response

Given $\triangle ABC$

Prove $m\angle 1 + m\angle 2 + m\angle 3 = 180°$

Plan Ahead

Draw a helping line through B parallel to $\overline{AC}$. Then use alternate interior angles and the whole and parts postulate to show that the sum of the measures of the angles of a triangle equals the sum of the measures of the parts of a straight angle.

Show Your Reasoning

Statements	**Justifications**
1. ABC is a triangle.	1. Given
2. Draw helping line $\overleftrightarrow{DE}$ through B so that $\overleftrightarrow{DE} \parallel \overline{AC}$.	2. Through a point not on a given line, there is one and only one line parallel to the given line.
3. $m\angle DBE = 180°$	3. If the sides of an angle form a straight line, then the angle is a straight angle with measure 180°.
4. $m\angle DBE = m\angle 4 + m\angle 2 + m\angle 5$	4. For any angle, the measure of the whole is equal to the sum of the measures of its non-overlapping parts.
5. $m\angle 4 + m\angle 2 + m\angle 5 = 180°$	5. Substitution property (Steps 3 and 4)
6. $m\angle 1 = m\angle 4; m\angle 3 = m\angle 5$	6. If two $\parallel$ lines are intersected by a transversal, then alternate interior $\angle$s are $=$ in measure.
7. $m\angle 1 + m\angle 2 + m\angle 3 = 180°$	7. Substitution property (Steps 5 and 6)

THE TRIANGLE SUM THEOREM

Theorem 8.5 The sum of the measures of the angles of a triangle is 180°.

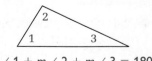

$m\angle 1 + m\angle 2 + m\angle 3 = 180°$

Write a paragraph proof to prove that the sum of the measures of the angles of a quadrilateral is 360°.

Sample Response

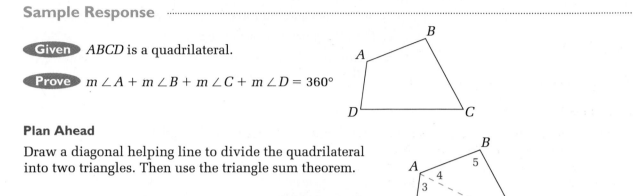

Given *ABCD* is a quadrilateral.

Prove $m \angle A + m \angle B + m \angle C + m \angle D = 360°$

Plan Ahead

Draw a diagonal helping line to divide the quadrilateral into two triangles. Then use the triangle sum theorem.

Show Your Reasoning

Draw the diagonal $\overline{AC}$ to form $\triangle ABC$ and $\triangle CDA$. The angles of the quadrilateral ABCD are made up of the angles of the two triangles. The sum of the angle measures of each triangle is 180°. The sum of the measures of the angles of the quadrilateral is 180° + 180°, which equals 360°.

The statement proved in Sample 2 can be used to prove other theorems about quadrilaterals. You will prove Theorem 8.7 in Exercise 17.

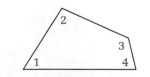

QUADRILATERAL THEOREMS

Theorem 8.6 The sum of the measures of the angles of a quadrilateral is 360°.

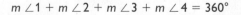

$$m \angle 1 + m \angle 2 + m \angle 3 + m \angle 4 = 360°$$

Theorem 8.7 If both pairs of opposite angles of a quadrilateral are equal in measure, then the quadrilateral is a parallelogram.

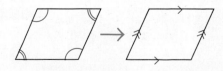

2. **a.** Write an equation that represents the sum of the measures of the angles of $\triangle ABC$.

   b. Solve the equation for x.

   c. Find the measures of the angles.

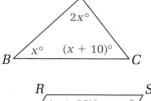

3. **a.** Write an equation for the sum of the measures of the angles of quadrilateral $RSTU$.

   b. Find the measures of the angles.

   c. Explain why $RSTU$ is a parallelogram.

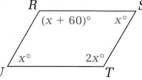

····▶ Now you are ready for:
Exs. 1–25 on pp. 443–446

EXPLORATION

(How) *do the interior angles of a triangle relate to an exterior angle?*

- **Materials: geometric drawing software or protractors**
- **Work with another student.**

$\angle CAD$ is an exterior angle.

$\angle B$ and $\angle C$ are the **remote interior angles** for $\angle CAD$.

① Draw any $\triangle ABC$. Extend $\overline{BA}$ through a point D to form an exterior angle of $\triangle ABC$.

② Measure $\angle CAD$, $\angle B$, and $\angle C$ for your triangle. Complete the first row of the table.

	$m \angle CAD$	$m \angle B$	$m \angle C$	$m \angle B + m \angle C$
△ 1	?	?	?	?
△ 2	?	?	?	?
△ 3	?	?	?	?
△ 4	?	?	?	?
△ 5	?	?	?	?

③ Repeat steps 1 and 2 for four other triangles. Use a variety of types of triangles and choose different locations for the exterior angle.

④ Look at the completed table. Describe any patterns you see.

◀·········

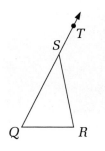

Talk it Over

4. In the Exploration, why do you think ∠B and ∠C are called *remote* interior angles?

5. Which angles in the figure at the left are the remote interior angles for exterior ∠RST?

6. Suppose you extend $\overline{RS}$ through S to a point V. What are the remote interior angles for ∠QSV?

7. Do you think an exterior angle of a triangle can be acute? Why or why not?

In the Exploration, you may have seen the relationship described in Theorem 8.8. You will prove this theorem in Exercise 34.

X ⚠ lab

EXTERIOR ANGLE THEOREM

Theorem 8.8 An exterior angle of a triangle is equal in measure to the sum of the measures of its two remote interior angles.

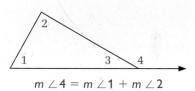

$$m \angle 4 = m \angle 1 + m \angle 2$$

Look Back

:·····► **Now you are ready for:**
: **Exs. 26–44 on pp. 447–448**

Summarize the ideas developed in this section about angle measures.

8-2 Exercises and Problems

1. Reading How was the unique parallel postulate used in the proof of the triangle sum theorem in Sample 1?

For Exercises 2–7, find each unknown angle measure.

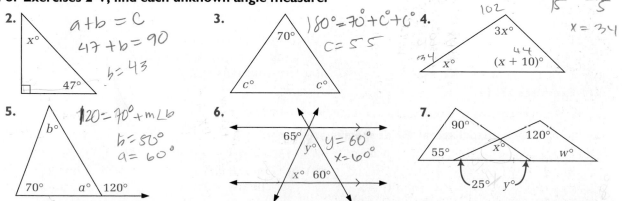

handwritten work:
$X + 3x + (x + 10°) = 180°$
$5x + 10° = 180°$
$-10° = -10°$
$\frac{5x}{5} = \frac{170°}{5}$
$x = 34$

2. $a + b = c$; $47 + b = 90$; $b = 43$; $x°$; $47°$

3. $180° = 70° + c° + c°$; $c = 55$; $70°$; $c°$ $c°$

4. 102; $3x°$; 34; $x°$; 44; $(x + 10)°$

5. $120 = 70° + m\angle b$; $b = 50°$; $a = 60°$; $b°$; $70°$ $a°$ $120°$

6. $65°$; $y° $ $y = 60°$; $x = 60°$; $x°$ $60°$

7. $90°$; $120°$; $55°$; $x°$; $w°$; $25°$ $y°$

Surveying The highest point on Earth is the summit of Mount Everest on the border of Nepal and China. In 1852, a government survey of India established the height of this mountain as 29,002 ft. Surveyors used a series of six triangles and averaged the results to find the distance between the peak and some inaccessible point directly below the summit. Calculations in the 1950s resulted in the official height accepted now, 29,028 ft.

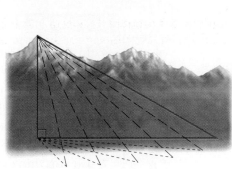

The tool used to measure angles from the plain to the summit is called a *theodolite.*

8. Suppose the angle measured at *B* for one triangle is 5°. What is the measure of ∠*A*?

9. Suppose in another triangle that *m* ∠*ADN* = 176°. What is the measure of ∠*A*?

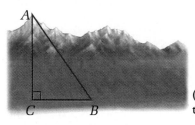

(Not drawn to scale.)

10. Which group of angle measures does not form a triangle? Explain your reasoning.

Group 1	Group 2	Group 3
35°, 72°, 83°	35°, 72°, 73°	27°, 38°, 115°

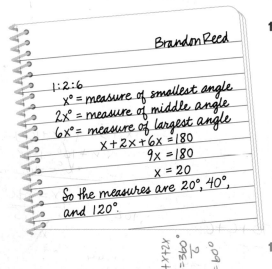

11. **a.** How did Brandon use the triangle sum theorem in his solution to the following question?

   "The measures of the angles of a triangle are in a ratio of 1:2:6. What are the measures of the three angles?"

   b. Use Brandon's method to find the measures of the three angles of a triangle where the angles are in a ratio of 1:3:5.

   c. Repeat part (b) for the angle measure ratio of 2:4:9.

   d. The measures of the angles of △*CDE* are in the ratio of 1:1:2. Is △*CDE* an *acute*, an *obtuse*, or a *right* triangle?

12. **Writing** Robin says that a triangle can have only one right angle. Do you agree or disagree with her? Explain your reasoning.

For Exercises 13–16:

a. Find the measure of each angle of quadrilateral *ABCD.*

b. Identify each quadrilateral. Be as specific as you can.

13. $m \angle A = x°$
    $m \angle B = x°$
    $m \angle C = x°$
    $m \angle D = x°$

14. $m \angle A = x°$
    $m \angle B = 2x°$
    $m \angle C = x°$
    $m \angle D = 2x°$

15. $m \angle A = 2x°$
    $m \angle B = 4x°$
    $m \angle C = 3x°$
    $m \angle D = 3x°$

16. $m \angle A = x°$
    $m \angle B = 2x°$
    $m \angle C = 4x°$
    $m \angle D = 3x°$

17. Copy and complete this proof of Theorem 8.7: If both pairs of opposite angles of a quadrilateral are equal in measure, then the quadrilateral is a parallelogram.

> **Given** $JKLM$ is a quadrilateral.
> $m \angle J = m \angle L$, $m \angle K = m \angle M$

> **Prove** $JKLM$ is a parallelogram.

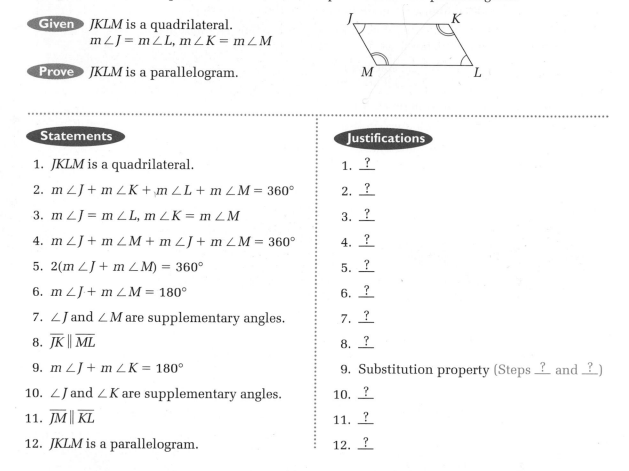

Statements	**Justifications**
1. $JKLM$ is a quadrilateral.	1. ?
2. $m \angle J + m \angle K + m \angle L + m \angle M = 360°$	2. ?
3. $m \angle J = m \angle L$, $m \angle K = m \angle M$	3. ?
4. $m \angle J + m \angle M + m \angle J + m \angle M = 360°$	4. ?
5. $2(m \angle J + m \angle M) = 360°$	5. ?
6. $m \angle J + m \angle M = 180°$	6. ?
7. $\angle J$ and $\angle M$ are supplementary angles.	7. ?
8. $\overline{JK} \parallel \overline{ML}$	8. ?
9. $m \angle J + m \angle K = 180°$	9. Substitution property (Steps ? and ?)
10. $\angle J$ and $\angle K$ are supplementary angles.	10. ?
11. $\overline{JM} \parallel \overline{KL}$	11. ?
12. $JKLM$ is a parallelogram.	12. ?

For Exercises 18 and 19, use this information.

A *tessellation* is a pattern formed when polygons cover a plane without gaps or overlaps.

18. a. Quadrilateral $ABCD$ has been tessellated to cover a plane. What is the sum of the measures of the angles of $ABCD$?

b. What is the sum of the measures of the angles at any vertex not on the boundary of the tessellation?

c. **Writing** Describe any tessellations you see in the quilt at the right.

Thinking of Winter by Carol Gersen

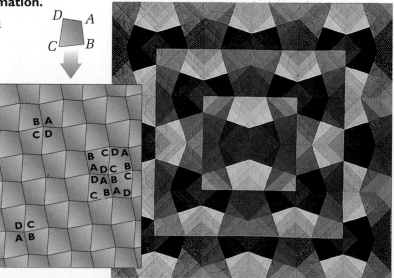

19. a. **Using Manipulatives** Draw any quadrilateral and make a tessellation with it. Make a sketch of the tessellation or cut out several copies of your quadrilateral and arrange them to model the tessellation.

b. What is the sum of the measures of the angles in your tessellation at any vertex not on the boundary?

c. Explain why the following statement is true.
"Any quadrilateral will tessellate a plane."

20. Use the figure at the right to prove the triangle sum theorem.

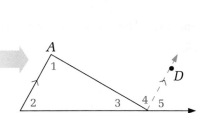

21. a. Write the following statement in if-then form.

"The acute angles of a right triangle are complementary."

b. Prove the statement from part (a).

22. **Writing** Suppose you are tutoring a student. Describe how helping lines are used in the proofs of some theorems in this section.

connection to **LITERATURE**

Alfonsina Storni (1892–1938) was an Argentinian poet and teacher. Her emotional poetry is known for its symbolism, but she wrote about everyday life in everyday language.

23. a. **Group Activity** Work in a group of four students. Translate this poem from Spanish into English.

CUADRADOS Y ÁNGULOS

Casas enfiladas, casas enfiladas,
Casas enfiladas.
Cuadrados, cuadrados, cuadrados.
Casas enfiladas.
Las gentes ya tienen el alma cuadrada,
Ideas en fila
Y ángulo en la espalda.
Yo misma he vertido ayer una lágrima,
Dios mio, cuadrada.
—Alfonsina Storni, 1918

This oil painting by Chilean artist Nemesio Antúnez is entitled New York, New York 10008 (1967).

b. How does Alfonsina Storni use squares and angles to express her feelings about the world she lived in?

24. **Writing** What feelings do the simple geometric shapes in the painting give you about New York?

25. **Writing** Think of a situation in your life that makes you think of angles, triangles, or quadrilaterals. Write a short paragraph about it.

Name the remote interior angles for each exterior angle.

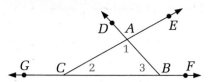

26. $\angle DAC$

27. $\angle EAB$

28. $\angle FBA$

29. $\angle GCA$

For Exercises 30–33, find each unknown angle measure.

30.　　　　　31.　　　　　32.　　　　　33.

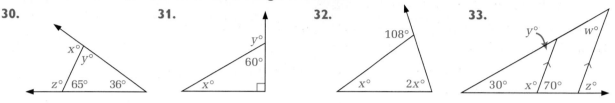

34. Copy and complete this proof of Theorem 8.8: An exterior angle of a triangle is equal in measure to the sum of its two remote interior angles.

Given △ABC with exterior $\angle 4$

Prove $m\angle 4 = m\angle 1 + m\angle 2$

Statements

① $m\angle BCD = 180°$ **③**
② $m\angle BCD = m\angle 3 + m\angle 4$

$m\angle 3 + m\angle 4 = 180°$
$m\angle 1 + m\angle 2 + m\angle 3 = 180°$ **④** **⑤**

$m\angle 3 + m\angle 4 = m\angle 1 + m\angle 2 + m\angle 3$ **⑥**

$m\angle 4 = m\angle 1 + m\angle 2$

Justifications

① ?

② ?

③ ?

④ ?

⑤ ?

⑥ ?

35. a. **Using Manipulatives** Draw a large △ABC. Place your pencil at A as shown in step 1. Slide the pencil along $\overline{AB}$ until the eraser is at B and then rotate it around B as shown in step 2. Now slide it to C and rotate it around C (step 3). Finally slide it back to A and rotate it around A (step 4).

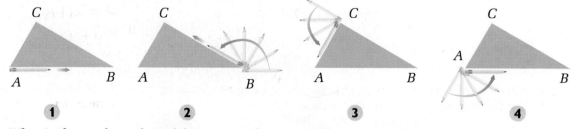

b. What is the total number of degrees you have rotated your pencil?

c. What conclusion about the exterior angles of a triangle is suggested above?

d. **Writing** Do you think that the same conclusion is true for quadrilaterals? pentagons? hexagons? 12-gons? n-gons? Explain.

Ongoing **ASSESSMENT**

36. Writing Describe two ways to find the measure of ∠ 2.

Review **PREVIEW**

For each of Exercises 37–40, use the given angle measures to decide whether lines *l* and *m* are parallel. Write Yes or No. *(Section 8-1)*

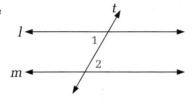

37. $m \angle 1 = 56°$, $m \angle 2 = 124°$ **38.** $m \angle 1 = 49°$, $m \angle 2 = 121°$

39. $m \angle 1 = 110°$, $m \angle 2 = 110°$ **40.** $m \angle 1 = 90°$, $m \angle 2 = 90°$

41. Solve this system of equations: $5x + y = 30$ *(Section 3-4)*
$$3x - 4y = 41$$

42. Explain how to solve the proportion $\frac{8}{5} = \frac{12}{x}$. *(Toolbox Skill 17)*

43. What do the markings in the diagram indicate? *(Toolbox Skill 27)*

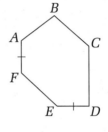

Working on the Unit Project

44. Research Read about how some everyday or unusual tools were created, how they work, and how they were patented. See how words and diagrams work together to explain an invention. Here are some books that contain information:

➤ *Blacks in Science: Ancient and Modern* by Ivan Van Sertima, ed.

➤ *Black Pioneers of Science & Invention* by Louis Haber

➤ *Extraordinary Origins of Everyday Things* by Charles Panati

➤ *Mothers of Invention* by Ethlie A. Vare and Greg Ptacek

➤ *Panati's Browser's Book of Beginnings* by Charles Panati

➤ *The Real McCoy: African-American Invention & Innovation, 1619–1930* by Portia James

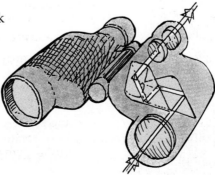

➤ *Steven Caney's Invention Book* by Steven Caney

➤ *The Way Things Work* by David Macaulay

Similar Triangles

Focus

Apply the properties of
similar triangles. Prove that
triangles are similar.

SCALE THE HEIGHTS

The John Hancock Center in Chicago is the fifth tallest sky-scraper in the United States. The interesting patterns of *congruent* and *similar* triangles on the sides of the building offer excellent strength and support.

Talk it Over

1. Two triangles are **congruent** if and only if their vertices can be matched up so that the *corresponding parts* (angles and sides) of the triangles are equal in measure.

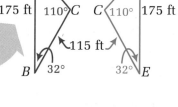

   a. What angle of △*ABC* is equal in measure to ∠*D*?

   b. What side of △*DEC* is equal in measure to $\overline{AC}$?

   c. Explain why △*ABC* ≅ △*DEC*.

   d. Vertices are named in the order that they correspond. Complete: △*BCA* ≅ __?__.

2. Two triangles are **similar** if and only if their vertices can be matched up so that corresponding angles are equal in measure and corresponding sides are *in proportion* (that is, the ratios of their measures are all equal).

   a. Are the angles of △*DEC* and △*FGH* equal in measure?

   b. Find the ratios $\frac{DE}{FG}$, $\frac{EC}{GH}$, and $\frac{DC}{FH}$. What do you notice?

   c. Explain why △*DEC* ~ △*FGH*.

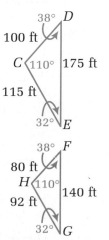

Read "is similar to."

449

Two triangles are similar by definition when *all* corresponding angles are equal in measure and *all* corresponding sides are in proportion. To prove that two triangles are similar, however, you only need to show that *two* pairs of angles are equal in measure.

X.Lab

TRIANGLE SIMILARITY POSTULATE

Postulate 13 If two angles of one triangle are equal in measure to two angles of another triangle, then the two triangles are similar. (AA Similarity)

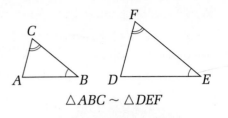

$\triangle ABC \sim \triangle DEF$

Sample 1

For each pair of triangles, tell whether the triangles are similar. Write *Yes* or *No*. Explain.

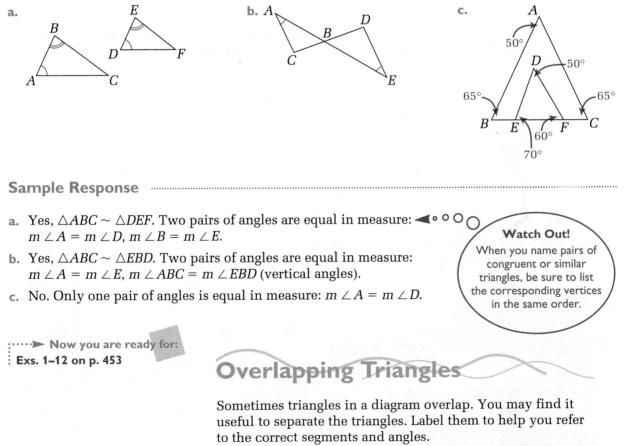

a.

b.

c.

Sample Response

a. Yes, $\triangle ABC \sim \triangle DEF$. Two pairs of angles are equal in measure: $m \angle A = m \angle D$, $m \angle B = m \angle E$.

b. Yes, $\triangle ABC \sim \triangle EBD$. Two pairs of angles are equal in measure: $m \angle A = m \angle E$, $m \angle ABC = m \angle EBD$ (vertical angles).

c. No. Only one pair of angles is equal in measure: $m \angle A = m \angle D$.

> **Watch Out!**
> When you name pairs of congruent or similar triangles, be sure to list the corresponding vertices in the same order.

⋯▶ **Now you are ready for:**
Exs. 1–12 on p. 453

Overlapping Triangles

Sometimes triangles in a diagram overlap. You may find it useful to separate the triangles. Label them to help you refer to the correct segments and angles.

Unit 8 Similar and Congruent Triangles

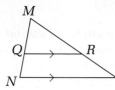

△**MQR** and △**MNP** are similar. Name the pairs of corresponding parts.

Sample Response

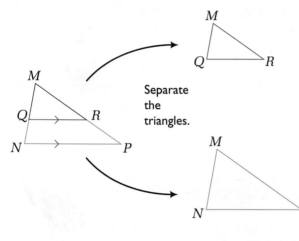

Separate the triangles.

Corresponding parts	
Angles	**Sides**
$\angle M, \angle M$	$\overline{MQ}, \overline{MN}$
$\angle MQR, \angle MNP$	$\overline{QR}, \overline{NP}$
$\angle MRQ, \angle MPN$	$\overline{MR}, \overline{MP}$

Prove that a line drawn from a point on one side of a triangle parallel to another side forms a triangle similar to the original triangle.

Sample Response

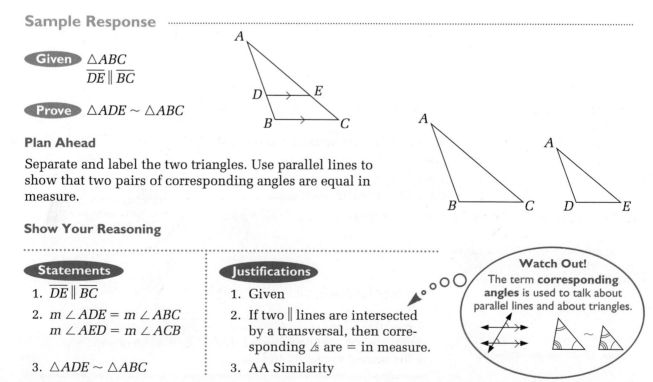

Given △ABC
$\overline{DE} \parallel \overline{BC}$

Prove △$ADE \sim$ △ABC

Plan Ahead

Separate and label the two triangles. Use parallel lines to show that two pairs of corresponding angles are equal in measure.

Show Your Reasoning

Statements

1. $\overline{DE} \parallel \overline{BC}$

2. $m \angle ADE = m \angle ABC$
   $m \angle AED = m \angle ACB$

3. △$ADE \sim$ △ABC

Justifications

1. Given

2. If two $\parallel$ lines are intersected by a transversal, then corresponding ⩜ are = in measure.

3. AA Similarity

Watch Out!
The term **corresponding angles** is used to talk about parallel lines and about triangles.

8-3 Similar Triangles

451

In Sample 3, a parallel line was drawn to form similar triangles. The parallel line drawn in a triangle may be parallel to any of the three sides. In each case, similar triangles are formed.

X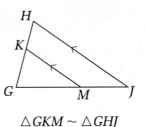

OVERLAPPING SIMILAR TRIANGLES

Theorem 8.9 If a line is drawn from a point on one side of a triangle parallel to another side, then it forms a triangle similar to the original triangle.

$$\triangle GKM \sim \triangle GHJ$$

Sample 4

Find the measure of $\overline{AD}$.

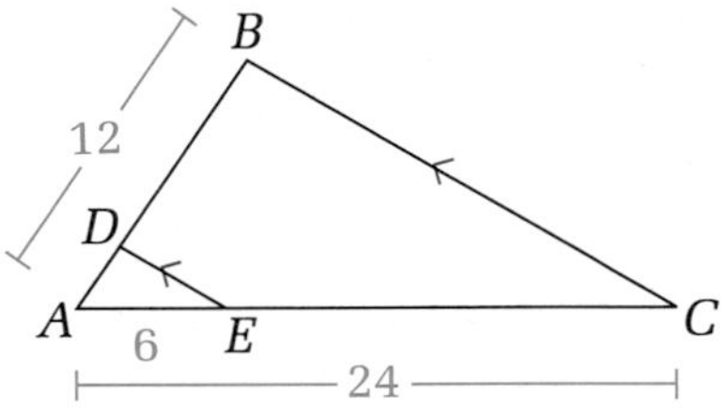

Sample Response

Use a proportion.
Since $\overline{DE} \parallel \overline{BC}$, $\triangle ADE \sim \triangle ABC$.

$$\dfrac{AD}{AB} = \dfrac{AE}{AC} \quad \longleftarrow \text{ Corresponding sides of similar triangles are in proportion.}$$

$$\dfrac{AD}{12} = \dfrac{6}{24} \quad \longleftarrow \text{ Substitute the measures you know.}$$

$$24(AD) = 72 \quad \longleftarrow \text{ Use cross products.}$$

$$AD = 3 \quad \longleftarrow \text{ Divide both sides by 24.}$$

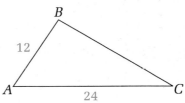

The measure of $\overline{AD}$ is 3 units.

······► Now you are ready for:
Exs. 13–27 on pp. 453–456

Look Back ◄────────

What should you look for to prove that two triangles are similar?

Exercises and Problems

Reading Use the similar triangles △*ABC* and △*DEF*.

1. Name the corresponding angles.

2. Name the corresponding sides.

3. If *m* ∠*A* = 35° and *m* ∠*E* = 70°, what are the measures of the remaining angles?

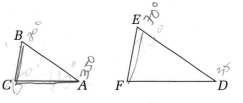

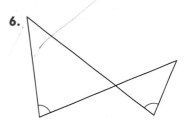

Explain why the triangles are similar.

4.

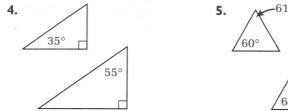

35°

55°

5.
61°
60°
60° 59°

6.

For Exercises 7 and 8, name the pairs of similar triangles.

7. *C*   *F*

A *B*

D   *E*

8.
W
150°   70°
X *Y*   *Z*

F
80°
70°
G   *H*

9. Write a paragraph proof.

Given $\overline{AB} \parallel \overline{DE}$

Prove △*ABC* ~ △*EDC*

A   *B*   *C*   *E*   *D*

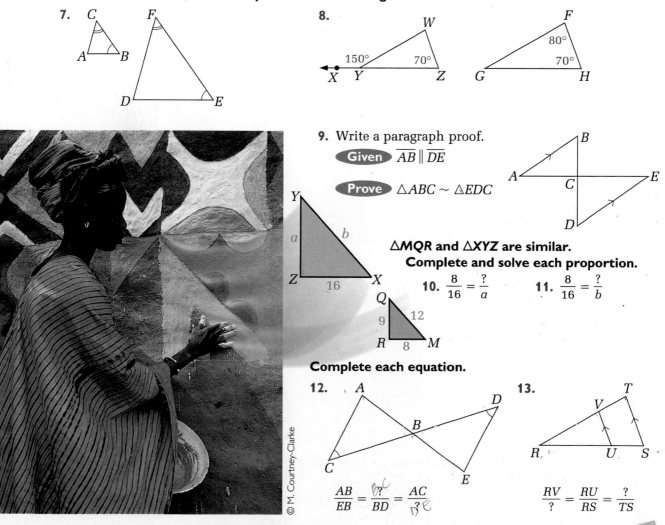

△*MQR* and △*XYZ* are similar.
Complete and solve each proportion.

10. $\frac{8}{16} = \frac{?}{a}$

11. $\frac{8}{16} = \frac{?}{b}$

Complete each equation.

12. *A*   *D*   *B*   *C*   *E*

$$\frac{AB}{EB} = \frac{?}{BD} = \frac{AC}{?}$$

13. *T*   *V*   *R*   *U*   *S*

$$\frac{RV}{?} = \frac{RU}{RS} = \frac{?}{TS}$$

© M. Courtney-Clarke

14. **a.** Why is $\triangle FGH \sim \triangle JKH$?

   b. Find the values of x and y.

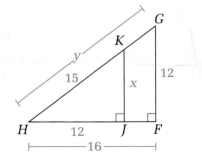

15. Prove that if a line is drawn from a point on one side of a triangle parallel to another side, then it divides the sides proportionally.

Given $\overline{BC} \parallel \overline{DE}$

Prove $\dfrac{AB}{BD} = \dfrac{AC}{CE}$

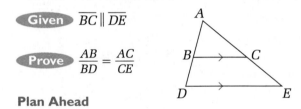

Plan Ahead

Show that $\triangle ABC$ and $\triangle ADE$ are similar and that the corresponding sides are in proportion. Then use $AD = AB + BD$ and $AE = AC + CE$.

---

connection to **ART**

Artists may use *perspective* to represent three-dimensional objects on a two-dimensional surface. In many early Renaissance paintings the lines on tiled floors seem to meet at a single point, the *vanishing point*, at the "back" of the painting. Artists used vanishing points to pull a viewer into the painting.

16. The actual lines on the plaza floor shown would be parallel, but in the painting they also seem to meet at a single point. Where do the lines all seem to meet?

17. The horizontal lines in the floor are called *transversals*. What would you need to know about the transversals to prove that $\triangle ABC \sim \triangle DEC$?

18. **Writing** Explain how the figure below was drawn starting with the vertical blue line and using two vanishing points.

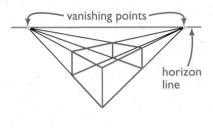

19. **Using Manipulatives** Work with another student. You can use a mirror to measure the height of a tree indirectly. When you see an image in a mirror, the angles of incidence and reflection are equal in measure ($m \angle 1 = m \angle 2$).

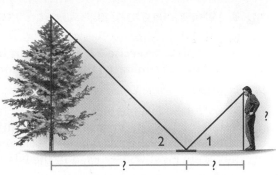

You will need a mirror and a tape measure. Place the mirror on the ground between the tree and yourself. Move away from the mirror until you see the top of the tree in the mirror. Use similar triangles to find the height of the tree (x).

20. If the ratio of the measures of the corresponding sides of two similar triangles is 1:1, what is the special relationship between the triangles?

21. **a.** Find the missing angle measures in each of the triangles.

    b. Suppose you choose one of the six triangles at random. What is the probability that the triangle is similar to △I? Explain.

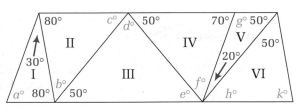

Ongoing **ASSESSMENT**

22. **Writing** Explain how each statement follows from the AA Similarity Postulate.

    a. If an acute angle of one right triangle is equal in measure to an acute angle of another right triangle, then the triangles are similar.

    b. If two triangles are similar to the same triangle, then they are similar to each other.

Review **PREVIEW**

23. In △CDE the measure of $\angle D$ is 37°. Find the measure of each numbered angle.
    (Section 8-2)

For Exercises 24 and 25, tell whether each product is defined. If so, find the product matrix. *(Section 3-7)*

24. $[\,4 \;\; 7 \;\; 11 \;\; 1.3\,] \begin{bmatrix} 1 & 52 \\ 9.7 & 4 \end{bmatrix}$ 25. $\begin{bmatrix} 1 & 2 & 3 \\ 2 & 5 & 6 \end{bmatrix} \begin{bmatrix} 1 \\ 2 \\ 3 \end{bmatrix}$

26. M is the midpoint of $\overline{AB}$. The coordinates of A and M are $A(-3, 7)$ and $M(0, 3)$.

    a. Find the coordinates of B. *(Section 5-3)*

    b. Find AB. *(Section 5-2)*

As you complete Exercise 27, think about how you can use the properties of similar triangles in the tool you design.

27. **Group Activity** Work with another student.

An astrolabe is a medieval instrument that was used to determine latitude by measuring the altitude of the sun and other stars. Although astrolabes were used in a variety of cultures, they were most widely used in the Islamic world.

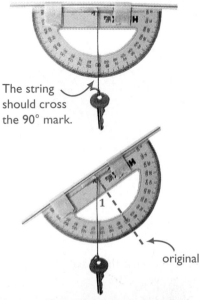

The string should cross the 90° mark.

original position

a. **Using Manipulatives** Make a simple astrolabe. You will need a protractor, a straw, a small weight or stone, and a piece of string about as long as the straw.

➤ Tie the weight to one end of the string. Tape the other end of the string to the center of the base of the protractor.

➤ Tape the straw to the base of the protractor.

b. Use your astrolabe to find your latitude.

➤ At night, look at the North Star through the straw.

➤ Have your partner note where the string crosses the protractor.

➤ Find the measure of the angle that the new position of the string makes with the original position of the string (∠ 1 at the left and in the diagram below).

The measure of ∠ 1 equals the measure of the angle of the North Star above the horizon (∠ 2) and is equal to your latitude.

c. Each degree of latitude is equal to 111.2 km along Earth's surface. How far are you from the equator? (The equator has 0° latitude.)

d. Are the two triangles in the diagram similar? Explain.

1. **Writing** Write at least three things you have learned in this unit about angles and triangles.

2. **Given** $m \angle 1 = 80°$
   $m \angle 2 = 100°$

   Prove $k \parallel l$

   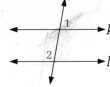

   8-1

3. Explain how you know that $t \perp a$.

   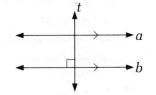

4. Find the value of x in each diagram.

   8-2

   a.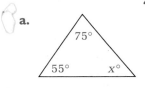

   b.

   c.

   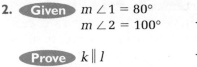

5. Is there enough information given to prove that the triangles below are similar? Why or why not?

   8-3

   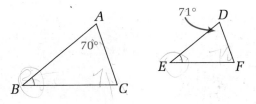

6. a. Name the similar triangles.

   b. Name the corresponding angles.

   c. Name the corresponding sides.

   d. Write a proportion that shows how the measures of the sides are related.

   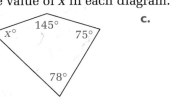

7. Find the value of x.

   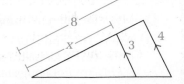

Congruent Triangles: ASA and AAS

AS Alike AAS can be

Use two angles and a side in proofs about congruent triangles.

EXPLORATION

How can you show that two triangles are congruent?

- **Materials: geometric drawing software or graph paper, rulers, and protractors**
- **Work with another student.**

① Draw any △ABC. Measure the angles and sides of your triangle.

EXAMPLE

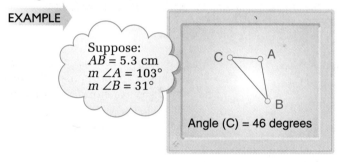

Suppose:
AB = 5.3 cm
m ∠A = 103°
m ∠B = 31°

Angle (C) = 46 degrees

② Use the measures you found in step 1 for AB, ∠A, and ∠B to draw △EFG.

Draw EF = AB = 5.3 cm.

Draw m ∠E = m ∠A = 103°.

Draw m ∠F = m ∠B = 31°.

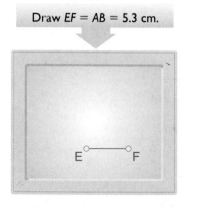

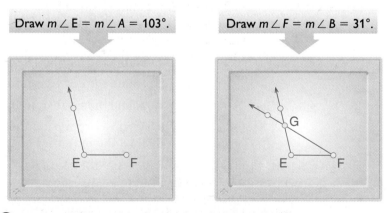

③ Measure the remaining angle and sides of △EFG.

④ Are △ABC and △EFG congruent? Do you think you could draw △EFG as instructed in step 2 so that △ABC and △EFG are not congruent? Explain why or why not.

5 Use the measures you found in step 1 for AB, $\angle A$, and $\angle C$ to draw $\triangle QRS$.

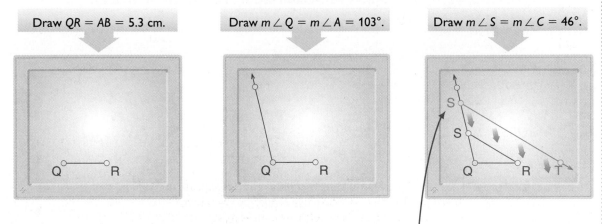

Draw $QR = AB = 5.3$ cm.   Draw $m\angle Q = m\angle A = 103°$.   Draw $m\angle S = m\angle C = 46°$.

6 Measure the remaining sides and angle of $\triangle QRS$.

7 Are $\triangle ABC$ and $\triangle QRS$ congruent? Do you think you could draw $\triangle QRS$ as instructed in step 5 so that $\triangle ABC$ and $\triangle QRS$ are not congruent? Explain why or why not.

Draw $\overrightarrow{ST}$ so that $m\angle QST = 46°$. Adjust the position of $\overrightarrow{ST}$ until it passes through R.

To show that two triangles are congruent, it is not necessary to show that *all* pairs of angles are equal in measure and *all* pairs of sides are equal in measure.

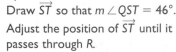

THEOREMS ABOUT CONGRUENT TRIANGLES

The sides between the marked angles are called *included sides*.

Theorem 8.10 If two angles and the included side of one triangle are equal in measure to the corresponding angles and side of another triangle, then the triangles are congruent. (ASA, angle-side-angle)

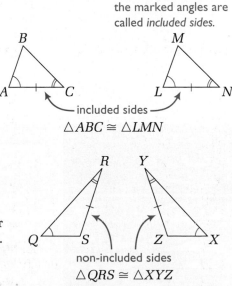

included sides

$\triangle ABC \cong \triangle LMN$

Theorem 8.11 If two angles and a non-included side of one triangle are equal in measure to the corresponding angles and side of another triangle, then the triangles are congruent. (AAS, angle-angle-side)

non-included sides

$\triangle QRS \cong \triangle XYZ$

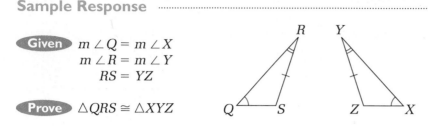

Use a two-column proof to prove Theorem 8.11.

Sample Response

Given $m \angle Q = m \angle X$
$m \angle R = m \angle Y$
$RS = YZ$

Prove $\triangle QRS \cong \triangle XYZ$

Plan Ahead

Prove that the triangles are similar. Show that the pairs of corresponding sides from the two triangles have a ratio of 1, so they are equal in measure.

Show Your Reasoning

Statements	Justifications
1. $m \angle Q = m \angle X$, $m \angle R = m \angle Y$	1. Given
2. $\triangle QRS \sim \triangle XYZ$	2. AA Similarity Postulate
3. $m \angle S = m \angle Z$	3. Definition of $\sim \triangle$ ←
4. $\dfrac{RS}{YZ} = \dfrac{SQ}{ZX} = \dfrac{QR}{XY}$	4. Definition of $\sim \triangle$ ←
5. $RS = YZ$	5. Given
6. $\dfrac{RS}{YZ} = 1$	6. Division property of equality
7. $1 = \dfrac{SQ}{ZX}$, $1 = \dfrac{QR}{XY}$	7. Substitution property (Steps 4 and 6)
8. $SQ = ZX$, $QR = XY$	8. Multiplication property of equality
9. $\triangle QRS \cong \triangle XYZ$	9. Definition of $\cong \triangle$ (Steps 1, 3, 5, and 8)

Read "similar triangles."

Read "congruent triangles."

Talk it Over

1. In any $\triangle ABC$, what side is included between $\angle B$ and $\angle C$?

2. What do ASA and AAS stand for?

3. How would a proof of Theorem 8.10 compare with the proof of Theorem 8.11?

4. Suppose Nadine wants to prove that $\triangle DEF \cong \triangle GHK$. What information does she need to know to use AAS in her proof?

The photo shows a portion of a wall painted by two Ndebele women of the Transvaal region of South Africa.

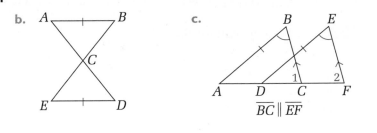
**For each pair of triangles, tell whether there is enough informa-
tion to prove that the triangles are congruent. Write Yes or No.
Explain.**

a.

b.

c.

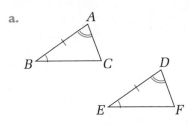

$\overline{BC} \parallel \overline{EF}$

Sample Response

a. Yes, $\triangle ABC \cong \triangle DEF$ by ASA. Two pairs of angles and the included sides are
equal in measure: $m \angle B = m \angle E$, $m \angle A = m \angle D$, $AB = DE$.

b. No. Only one pair of angles and one pair of sides are known to be equal in
measure: $m \angle ACB = m \angle DCE$ (vertical angles), $AB = DE$.

c. Yes, $\triangle ABC \cong \triangle DEF$ by AAS. Two pairs of angles and the corresponding
non-included sides are equal in measure: $m \angle B = m \angle E$, $m \angle 1 = m \angle 2$
(corresponding angles formed by parallel lines and a transversal), $AB = DE$.

·····▶ **Now you are ready for:**
Exs. 1–9 on pp. 462–463

Corresponding Parts of Congruent Triangles

You can prove relationships between the corresponding
parts of two triangles once you have proved that the triangles
are congruent. Use the statement *Corresponding parts of congruent triangles are equal in measure.*

Some people abbreviate
this statement as CPCTE.

Sample 3

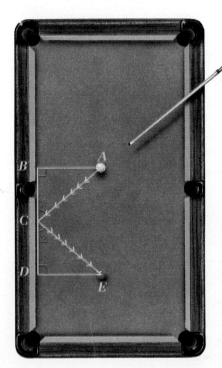

Given A billiard player plans to hit ball *E* by *banking* ball *A*
off the side at point *C*. The perpendicular distances *AB*
and *ED* to the side of the table are the same. The angles
made when a ball with no spin hits the side at medium speed are equal in measure: $m \angle 1 = m \angle 2$.

Prove *C* is the midpoint of $\overline{BD}$.

Continued on next page.

8-4 Congruent Triangles: ASA and AAS

461

Sample Response

Given $m \angle 1 = m \angle 2$
$AB = ED$
$\overline{AB} \perp \overline{BD}$ and $\overline{ED} \perp \overline{BD}$

Prove C is the midpoint of $\overline{BD}$.

Plan Ahead

Show that $\triangle ABC \cong \triangle EDC$. Then corresponding sides $\overline{BC}$ and $\overline{DC}$ will be equal in measure.

Show Your Reasoning

Statements

$\left.\begin{array}{l} \overline{AB} \perp \overline{BD} \\ \overline{ED} \perp \overline{BD} \end{array}\right\}$ **①** $\rightarrow$ $\left.\begin{array}{l} m \angle ABC = 90° \\ m \angle EDC = 90° \end{array}\right\}$ **②** $\rightarrow$ $\left.\begin{array}{c} m \angle ABC = m \angle EDC \\ m \angle 1 = m \angle 2 \\ AB = ED \end{array}\right\}$ **③**

④ **⑤**
$\rightarrow \triangle ABC \cong \triangle EDC \xrightarrow{} BC = DC \xrightarrow{} C$ is the midpoint of $\overline{BD}$.

Justifications

① Definition of perpendicular lines

② Substitution property

③ AAS

④ Corres. parts of $\cong$ $\triangle$ are $=$ in measure.

⑤ Definition of midpoint

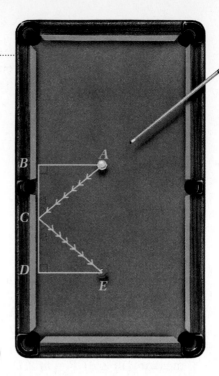

The U.S. patent in 1869 for the new material celluloid resulted from the game of billiards. A billiards ball manufacturer had offered $10,000 for an inexpensive substitute for ivory.

BY THE WAY...

Look Back

Explain why it may be necessary to first prove that two triangles are congruent in order to prove that certain sides or certain angles are equal in measure.

······▶ **Now you are ready for:**
Exs. 10–22 on pp. 464–465

8-4 Exercises and Problems

1. **Reading** Sketch a triangle XYZ. Copy and complete the table.

Sides	Included Angle
$\overline{XY}$ and $\overline{YZ}$	?
$\overline{YZ}$ and $\overline{ZX}$	?
$\overline{ZX}$ and $\overline{XY}$	?

In each of Exercises 2–4, the triangles are congruent. Trace the triangles so that they are side by side with corresponding vertices in the same position. Mark the parts that are equal in measure. An example is done for you.

Example

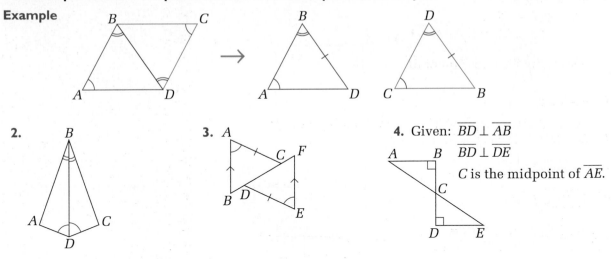

2.

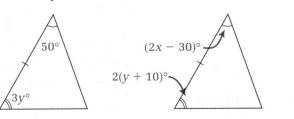

3. A

4. Given: $\overline{BD} \perp \overline{AB}$
$\overline{BD} \perp \overline{DE}$
C is the midpoint of $\overline{AE}$.

5. Use the triangles in the Exploration on pages 458–459. Choose the letter of the statement that correctly shows the relationship between the triangles.

   a. $\triangle ABC \cong \triangle RQS$ **b.** $\triangle ABC \cong \triangle QRS$ **c.** $\triangle ABC \cong \triangle SRQ$

6. Find the value of x and the value of y.

7. **Given** $m \angle TUW = m \angle VUW$
            $\overline{UW} \perp \overline{TV}$

    Prove $\triangle TUW \cong \triangle VUW$

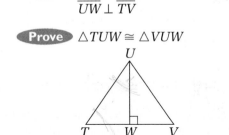

8. **Group Activity** Work with another student.

   a. Plot the points $J(1, 9)$, $K(3, 3)$, and $L(6, 4)$ on a coordinate plane. Connect them. Find the slopes of $\overline{JK}$ and $\overline{LK}$. What is the measure of $\angle K$?

   b. Plot the points $M(-2, -5)$, $N(-8, -3)$, and $P(-9, -6)$ on the same coordinate plane. Connect the points. Find the slopes of $\overline{MN}$ and $\overline{PN}$. What is the measure of $\angle N$?

   c. Use the distance formula to show that $JL = MP$.

   d. If $m \angle J = m \angle M$, what is the relationship between $\triangle JKL$ and $\triangle MNP$? Explain.

9. **Writing** Explain why two right triangles are congruent if the hypotenuse and an acute angle of one right triangle are equal in measure to the hypotenuse and an acute angle of the other right triangle.

For Exercises 10–12, suppose you had to prove each relationship given. What pair of triangles would you first need to prove congruent?

a. $m \angle 1 = m \angle 2$

b. $AB = CD$

10.

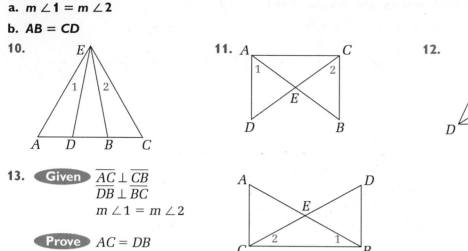

11.

12.

13. **Given** $\overline{AC} \perp \overline{CB}$
$\overline{DB} \perp \overline{BC}$
$m \angle 1 = m \angle 2$

Prove $AC = DB$

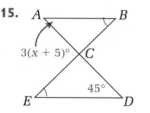

Find the value of x. If there is not enough information given, write *not enough information*.

14.

15.

16.

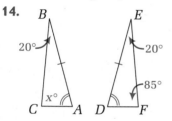

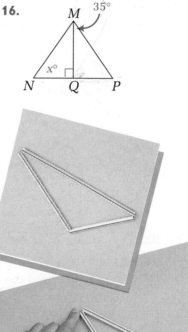

• • • • • • • • •
Ongoing **ASSESSMENT**

17. **Group Activity** Work with another student. You will need straws, string, a ruler, and a protractor.

   a. Each of you should cut straws into pieces. Cut lengths of 4 in., 5 in., and 7 in. Now thread string through your straw pieces and connect them tightly to form a triangle.

   b. Use the protractor to measure the angles of both triangles.

   c. What relationship exists between your two triangles? Explain.

   d. Compare your triangles to other groups' triangles. Does the relationship still hold?

   e. The theorems in this section indicate that when you know that two pairs of corresponding angles and a pair of corresponding sides are equal in measure, then you can say that the triangles are congruent. What other group of three pairs of corresponding parts did you use in steps (a)–(d) to also guarantee congruent triangles?

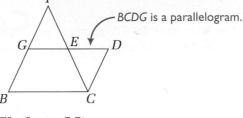
Review **PREVIEW**

18. Identify the similar triangles. Identify the postulates or theorems that support your answer. *(Section 8-3)*

19. The measure of one exterior angle of a triangle is 35°. What type of triangle is it? *(Section 8-2)*

20. What is the justification for the statement $PR = PQ + QR$? *(Section 7-7)*

Working on the Unit Project

As you complete Exercises 21 and 22, think about how you can include the properties of congruent triangles in the tool you design.

A common problem for many land surveyors is how to measure distances considered "inaccessible" because they cannot be measured directly, like the distance across a canyon. In Exercise 21, you will explore a tool used to find such distances.

21. **a.** **Using Manipulatives** Find a wooden pole a little taller than yourself. Nail a stick of wood about the size of a ruler to the pole at a height less than or equal to your eye level. This stick should be movable, but should not hang freely. Follow the directions at the right.

b. What can you say about the two triangles formed? Explain.

c. What can you say about the bases of the two triangles? Measure to confirm your answer.

1. Stand the pole so that it is perpendicular to the ground.

2. Adjust the stick so that it points to an object like the base of a goal post several feet away from where you are standing.

3. Without readjusting the stick, rotate the pole. Mark a point A, where the stick is now pointing.

22. How can a surveyor use a similar tool to find the distance across a canyon?

Congruent Triangles: SAS and SSS

Focus

Use two sides and an angle or three sides in proofs about congruent triangles.

Choosing  S I D E S

Structures that are made from triangles are stable. The angles in the structure cannot change without breaking the sides. A structure that is a quadrilateral, on the other hand, can be distorted. The angles can change while the measures of the sides stay the same.

One way to build two congruent triangles is to make them with sides of equal measures (SSS Postulate). You can also make two congruent triangles by making two pairs of sides and the angles between them equal in measure (SAS Postulate).

X ⟨ △ab

POSTULATES ABOUT CONGRUENT TRIANGLES

Postulate 14 If two sides and the included angle of one triangle are equal in measure to the corresponding sides and angle of another triangle, then the triangles are congruent. (SAS, side-angle-side)

The angles between the marked sides are called *included angles*.

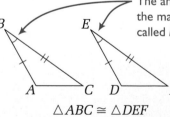

$\triangle ABC \cong \triangle DEF$

Postulate 15 If three sides of one triangle are equal in measure to the corresponding sides of another triangle, then the triangles are congruent. (SSS, side-side-side)

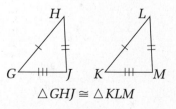

$\triangle GHJ \cong \triangle KLM$

For each pair of triangles, tell whether there is enough information to prove that the triangles are congruent. Write *Yes* or *No*.
Explain.

a.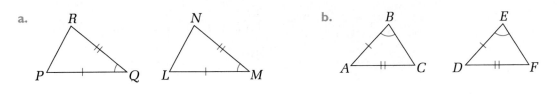

b.

Sample Response

a. Yes, $\triangle PQR \cong \triangle LMN$ by SAS: $RQ = NM$, $m \angle Q = m \angle M$, $PQ = LM$.

b. No. The congruent angles are not included angles. You would need to know
that the third pair of sides is also congruent, or that a second pair of angles
is congruent, to prove that $\triangle ABC \cong \triangle DEF$.

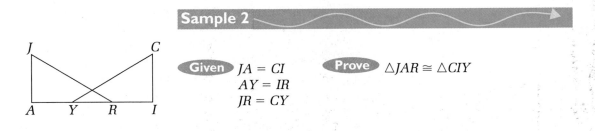

Given $JA = CI$ **Prove** $\triangle JAR \cong \triangle CIY$
$AY = IR$
$JR = CY$

Sample Response

Plan Ahead

Separate the triangles and mark the diagram
using the given information. Show that $AR = IY$
and then use SSS.

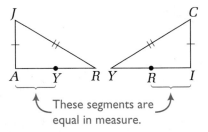

These segments are
equal in measure.

Show Your Reasoning

$JA = CI$, $JR = CY$ (given). The remaining sides of $\triangle JAR$ and
$\triangle CIY$ are $\overline{AR}$ and $\overline{IY}$. You know that $AY = IR$. Add YR to
both sides. This gives $AY + YR = IR + RY$ (add. prop. of =).
$AY + YR = AR$ and $IR + RY = IY$ (measure of whole equals
sum of measures of non-overlapping parts). By
substitution, $AR = IY$. Now $\triangle JAR \cong \triangle CIY$ by SSS.

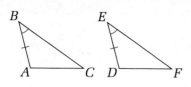

Tell what additional information you need in order to use each congruence postulate or theorem to show that △*ABC* ≅ △*DEF*.

1. SAS   2. SSS   3. ASA   4. AAS

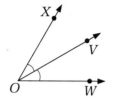

Bisectors

In the diagram at the left, $\overrightarrow{OV}$ bisects ∠ *WOX*. An **angle bisector** is a ray that begins at the vertex of an angle and divides the angle into two angles of equal measure.

Sample 3

Given $\overrightarrow{AD}$ bisects ∠ *BAC*.
$AB = AC$

Prove $BD = CD$

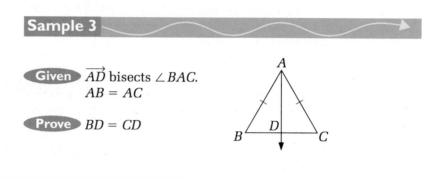

Sample Response

Plan Ahead

Show that △*BAD* ≅ △*CAD* by SAS. Then the corresponding parts $\overline{BD}$ and $\overline{CD}$ will be equal in measure.

Show Your Reasoning

Statements	Justifications
1. $AB = AC$	1. Given
2. $\overrightarrow{AD}$ bisects ∠ *BAC*.	2. Given
3. $m \angle BAD = m \angle CAD$	3. Definition of angle bisector
4. $AD = AD$	4. Reflexive property of equality
5. △*BAD* ≅ △*CAD*	5. SAS (Steps 1, 3, and 4)
6. $BD = CD$	6. Corres. parts of ≅ △ are = in measure.

> **Watch Out!**
> An angle bisector does not *always* bisect a side of a triangle. △*ABC* is a special case.

In Sample 3, $\overrightarrow{AD}$ bisects $\overline{BC}$. A **segment bisector** is a ray, line, or segment that divides a segment into two parts of equal measure. The bisector passes through the midpoint of the segment it bisects.

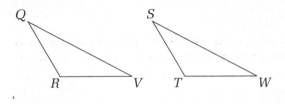

Look Back

What information would you need in order to decide whether these two triangles are congruent? (There is more than one answer.)

8-5 Exercises and Problems

For each pair of triangles, tell whether there is enough information to prove that the triangles are congruent. Write *Yes* or *No*. Explain.

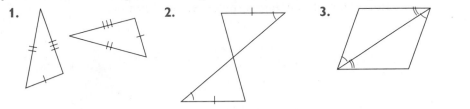

1.   **2.**   **3.**   **4.**

Copy each figure and mark any parts that are equal in measure. Identify the postulate or theorem you would use to prove that each pair of triangles is congruent.

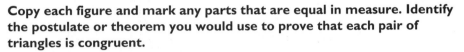

5. $\overline{AD} \perp \overline{AB}$, $\overline{BC} \perp \overline{CD}$
   $m \angle ABD = m \angle CDB$

$\triangle ABD \cong \triangle CDB$

6. $m \angle PQR = m \angle SRQ$
   $PQ = SR$

$\triangle PQR \cong \triangle SRQ$

7. $\overline{WZ} \parallel \overline{YX}$
   $WZ = YX$

$\triangle WZY \cong \triangle YXW$

8. a. Plot the points $G(2, 2)$, $H(7, 2)$, and $J(3, 5)$ on a coordinate plane. Connect the points to form $\triangle GHJ$.

   b. Plot the points $K(2, -1)$, $L(7, -1)$, and $M(3, -4)$ on a coordinate plane. Connect the points to form $\triangle KLM$.

   c. Use the distance formula to prove that $\triangle GHJ \cong \triangle KLM$.

9. If you are given only the measures $AC = 3.5$ ft, $m \angle A = 42°$, and $m \angle B = 23°$, you can draw a triangle that will automatically be congruent to the triangle in the diagram. If you are given only the three angle measures, you cannot.

Make an organized list of all the sets of three measures that provide enough information to draw a triangle that will automatically be congruent to $\triangle ABC$.

This building at Futuroscope, a science-based theme park in France, resembles a quartz crystal.

10. **Reading** How are segment bisectors and angle bisectors alike? How are they different?

11. $\overrightarrow{BD}$ bisects $\angle ABC$. Find x.

12. **Given** $\overline{PR}$ and $\overline{NS}$ bisect each other.

Prove $\triangle NPQ \cong \triangle SRQ$

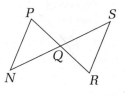

---

connection to INDUSTRIAL TECHNOLOGY

Drafters can duplicate line segments, angles, and geometric shapes using only a compass and a *straightedge* (a device for drawing straight lines that does not have marks for measuring).

13. **Using Manipulatives** Follow these steps to duplicate a triangle using only a compass and a straightedge.

a. Use a straightedge to draw any triangle and label it $\triangle ABC$.	
b. Draw a point and label it D. Adjust the compass so that it is open to the length of $\overline{AB}$. With this compass setting, put the compass point on D and draw an arc. Choose a point on the arc and label it E.	
c. Adjust the compass so that it is open to the length of $\overline{AC}$. With this compass setting, put the compass point on D and draw a second arc.	
d. Adjust the compass so that it is open to the length of $\overline{BC}$. Then put the compass point on E and draw a third arc that intersects the arc from part (c). Label the point where the two arcs intersect F.	
e. Connect the points to form $\triangle DEF$. Why is $\triangle DEF \cong \triangle ABC$?	

14. a. **Research** Find out if it is possible to bisect an angle using only a compass and straightedge. If so, describe how to do it.

b. **Research** Find out if it is possible to *trisect* an angle using only a compass and straightedge. If so, describe how to do it.

15. Writing Identify the theorem or postulate about congruent triangles that can be used to justify each statement. Explain your choice.

a. If the legs of one right triangle are equal in measure to the corresponding legs of another right triangle, then the triangles are congruent.

b. If any side and an acute angle of one right triangle are equal in measure to the corresponding side and acute angle of another right triangle, then the triangles are congruent.

16. **Given** $\overline{RS} \parallel \overline{VT}$
$RW = TW$

Prove $RS = TV$ *(Section 8-4)*

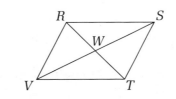

17. Joshua remembers that the last four digits of his friend's phone number are 3, 4, 6, and 8. Unfortunately he doesn't remember the order of the numbers. How many permutations of the four numbers are there? *(Section 6-2)*

18. Draw a Venn diagram for the implication "If a triangle is equilateral, then it is isosceles." *(Section 7-2)*

8 Working on the Unit Project

As you complete Exercise 19, think about how you can use the properties of congruent triangles in the tool you design.

19. Ruth Levinson is surveying a piece of property. She needs to measure the distance between *A* and *B* across a pond. She drives in a stake at any point *X*. Then she uses her steel tape to measure $\overline{AX}$ and $\overline{BX}$. After more measuring, she drives in stakes at points *Y* and *Z*.

a. How long do you think she makes $\overline{XY}$? How long do you think she makes $\overline{XZ}$?

b. Ruth was very careful to make sure that point *Y* lies on $\overleftrightarrow{AX}$ and point *Z* lies on $\overleftrightarrow{BX}$. She knew this would guarantee that $m \angle YXZ = m \angle AXB$. Explain her reasoning.

c. Ruth measures $\overline{YZ}$. She finds that $YZ = 53$ ft. What is *AB*? How do you know?

Surveyors may use a *steel tape* when finding distances across lakes, canyons, and other geographical features whose dimensions cannot be measured directly. The flexible steel tape is rolled up on a reel. The tape can be reeled in like a line on a fishing rod.

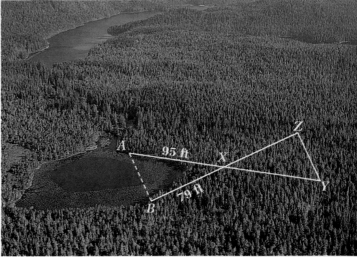

Congruence and Isosceles Triangles

UPON REFLECTION

Focus

Apply properties of isosceles triangles, equilateral triangles, and perpendicular bisectors.

BY THE WAY...

The internal spaces in a vulture's metacarpal bone approximate isosceles triangles. This bone structure in the wing is light-weight but very strong. The structure resembles the bridge structure on page 466.

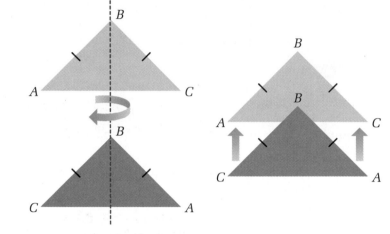

The diagram shows the image of isosceles $\triangle ABC$ after it has been reflected over its line of symmetry. The triangles are overlapped to show how the parts of the two triangles correspond.

Talk it Over

For question 1–5, use the figures above. For questions 1–3, tell which part of the image corresponds to each given part of the original triangle.

1. $\overline{AB}$ **2.** $\angle B$ **3.** $\overline{CB}$

4. What postulate or theorem can you use to prove that $\triangle ABC \cong \triangle CBA$?

5. Why must $\angle A$ and $\angle C$ be equal in measure?

6. What can you say about $\angle X$ and $\angle Z$ in isosceles $\triangle XYZ$?

Theorem 8.12 summarizes the results of the questions you just answered. You will prove this theorem in Exercise 14 and its converse, Theorem 8.13, in Exercise 15.

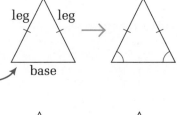

X c Lab

ISOSCELES TRIANGLE THEOREMS

Theorem 8.12 If two sides of a triangle are equal in measure, then the angles opposite those sides are equal in measure.

In an isosceles triangle, the sides of equal measure are called **legs** and the third side is called the **base**.

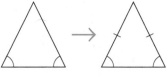

Theorem 8.13 If two angles of a triangle are equal in measure, then the sides opposite those angles are equal in measure.

The isosceles triangle theorems can help you find measures of sides and angles.

Sample 1

In a △GRE, GR = ER. The measure of ∠R is ten more than three times the measure of one of the other angles. Find the measures of all three angles.

Sample Response

Draw and label a diagram.

$GR = RE$, so $\triangle GRE$ is isosceles.

Let $x°$ = the measure of $\angle G$. Then $x°$ = the measure of $\angle E$, since $\angle G$ and $\angle E$ are angles opposite sides of equal measure.

Also, $(3x + 10)°$ = the measure of $\angle R$.

$$m \angle G + m \angle E + m \angle R = 180°$$ ← Use the triangle sum theorem.
$$x + x + 3x + 10 = 180$$
$$5x + 10 = 180$$
$$5x = 170$$
$$x = 34$$

Substitute 34 for x to find the measure of $\angle R$.

$$3x + 10 = 3(34) + 10 = 102 + 10 = 112$$

Then, $m \angle G = 34°$, $m \angle E = 34°$, and $m \angle R = 112°$.

This building is in the city of Sandakan in Malaysia.

On a coordinate plane, plot the points W(1, 5), Q(5, 5), and R(3, 1). Show that $m \angle W = m \angle Q$.

Sample Response

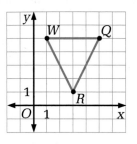

Use the distance formula $d = \sqrt{(x_2 - x_1)^2 + (y_2 - y_1)^2}$.

$$WR = \sqrt{(3 - 1)^2 + (1 - 5)^2} \qquad QR = \sqrt{(3 - 5)^2 + (1 - 5)^2}$$

$$= \sqrt{(2)^2 + (-4)^2} \qquad\qquad = \sqrt{(-2)^2 + (-4)^2}$$

$$= \sqrt{4 + 16} \qquad\qquad\qquad = \sqrt{4 + 16}$$

$$= \sqrt{20} \qquad\qquad\qquad\quad = \sqrt{20}$$

Since $WR = QR$, you can conclude that $m \angle W = m \angle Q$, because in a triangle that has two sides of equal measure, the angles opposite those sides are equal in measure.

Equilateral Triangles

Equilateral triangles have three sides of equal measure. They are a special type of isosceles triangle. You will investigate the following theorems about equilateral triangles in Exercise 17.

$X_{(\cdot)} \angle ab$

EQUILATERAL TRIANGLE THEOREMS

Theorem 8.14 If a triangle is equilateral, then it is also equiangular, with three 60° angles.

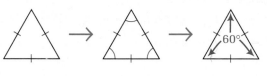

Theorem 8.15 If a triangle is equiangular, then it is also equilateral.

The angles of **equiangular** figures are all equal in measure.

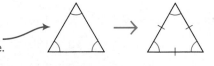

······▶ Now you are ready for:
Exs. 1–20 on pp. 476–477

Talk it Over

7. What is the measure of $\angle ABD$? Explain.

8. What is the perimeter of an equiangular triangle with one side of measure 8 cm?

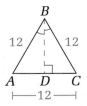

Perpendicular Bisectors

The **perpendicular bisector** of a segment is a line (or ray or segment) that bisects the segment and is perpendicular to it.

The diagrams below show how you can construct a perpendicular bisector using a straightedge and a compass.

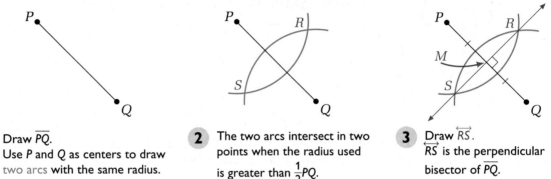

1 Draw $\overline{PQ}$.
Use P and Q as centers to draw two arcs with the same radius.

2 The two arcs intersect in two points when the radius used is greater than $\frac{1}{2}PQ$.

3 Draw $\overleftrightarrow{RS}$.
$\overleftrightarrow{RS}$ is the perpendicular bisector of $\overline{PQ}$.

The construction works because of the following theorem. You will prove Theorem 8.16 in Exercise 21.

PERPENDICULAR BISECTOR THEOREM

Theorem 8.16 If a point is the same distance from both endpoints of a segment, then it lies on the perpendicular bisector of the segment.

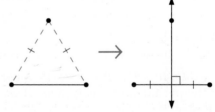

Talk it Over

9. $ABCD$ is a rhombus. Explain why $\overleftrightarrow{BD}$ is the perpendicular bisector of $\overline{AC}$.

10. Name at least four pairs of angles that are equal in measure in the diagram of the rhombus at the left.

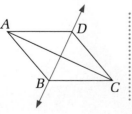

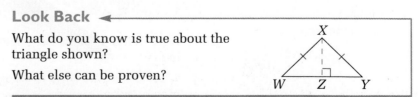

Look Back

What do you know is true about the triangle shown?

What else can be proven?

......▶ **Now you are ready for:**
Exs. 21–32 on pp. 478–480

For each figure, identify the isosceles triangle(s) and identify the pair(s) of angles that are equal in measure.

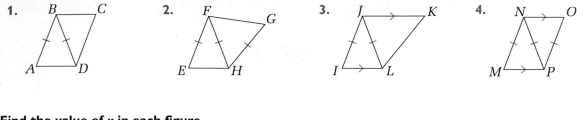

1.   2.   3.   4.

Find the value of *x* in each figure.

5.   6.   7.   8.

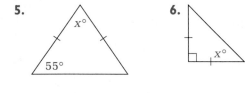
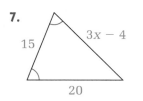
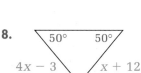

9. a.   **Using Manipulatives** Cut a large isosceles triangle out of a piece of paper and fold it so the sides that are equal in measure match up.

   b.   **Reading** What can you call the fold line?

   c.   Use the results of part (a) and (b). Draw as many conclusions as possible about the angles, sides, and their measures in the isosceles triangle.

Use the diagram at the right for Exercises 10 and 11.

10.   Identify two pairs of angles that are equal in measure.

11.   Suppose $m \angle A = 2(x - 5)°$ and $m \angle ACB = (x + 50)°$. Find the measure of each angle of each triangle.

12.   In $\triangle DEF$, $m \angle E = m \angle F$. Write an expression for the perimeter of the triangle if $DE = 2x + 3$ and $EF = 4x - 2$.

13.   A *golden triangle* has two angles of equal measure that are each twice as large as the third angle. Find the measure of the angles of a golden triangle.

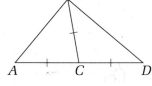

BY THE WAY...

In a golden triangle, the ratio of the lengths of a leg and the base is the golden ratio.

$$\frac{\text{leg}}{\text{base}} \approx 1.618$$

14. Copy and complete this proof of Theorem 8.12.

Given $GI = HI$

Prove $m \angle G = m \angle H$

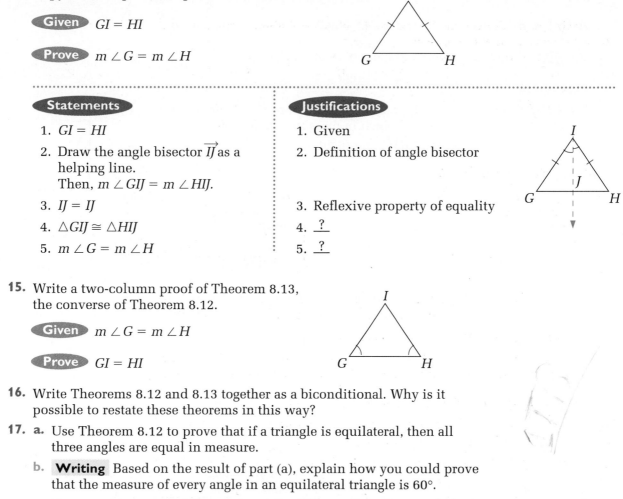

Statements	**Justifications**
1. $GI = HI$	1. Given
2. Draw the angle bisector $\overrightarrow{IJ}$ as a helping line. Then, $m \angle GIJ = m \angle HIJ$.	2. Definition of angle bisector
3. $IJ = IJ$	3. Reflexive property of equality
4. $\triangle GIJ \cong \triangle HIJ$	4. ?
5. $m \angle G = m \angle H$	5. ?

15. Write a two-column proof of Theorem 8.13, the converse of Theorem 8.12.

Given $m \angle G = m \angle H$

Prove $GI = HI$

16. Write Theorems 8.12 and 8.13 together as a biconditional. Why is it possible to restate these theorems in this way?

17. a. Use Theorem 8.12 to prove that if a triangle is equilateral, then all three angles are equal in measure.

b. **Writing** Based on the result of part (a), explain how you could prove that the measure of every angle in an equilateral triangle is 60°.

c. How would a proof of Theorem 8.15 be different from the proof of Theorem 8.14 in parts (a) and (b)?

18. a. On a coordinate plane, plot the points $P(4, 2)$, $E(3, 7)$, and $R(8, 6)$. Draw $\triangle PER$.

b. Find PE, ER, and PR. What type of triangle is $\triangle PER$?

c. Find the midpoint of $\overline{PR}$. Label this point S.

d. Find the slopes of $\overline{ES}$ and $\overline{PR}$. What is the relationship between these segments?

19. a. On a coordinate plane, plot the points $A(-2, 0)$, $B(0, \sqrt{12})$, and $C(2, 0)$. Draw $\triangle ABC$.

b. Show that $\triangle ABC$ is equiangular.

Student Resources Toolbox
p. 642 *Algebraic Expressions*

20. **Given** $LM = LO$
$m \angle 1 = m \angle 3$

Prove $MN = ON$

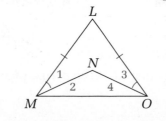

21. Copy and complete this two-column proof of Theorem 8.16.

Given $RP = RQ$

Prove R lies on the perpendicular bisector of $\overline{PQ}$.

Plan Ahead

Draw $\overleftrightarrow{RM}$ through M, the midpoint of $\overline{PQ}$. Then use congruent triangles to prove that angles 1 and 2 are equal in measure. Show that these angles are right angles. Then $\overleftrightarrow{RM}$ is perpendicular to $\overline{PQ}$.

Show Your Reasoning

Statements	Justifications
1. $RP = RQ$	1. ?
2. Draw a line from R passing through the midpoint M of $\overline{PQ}$ so that $PM = QM$.	2. Definition of midpoint
3. $\overleftrightarrow{RM}$ bisects $\overline{PQ}$.	3. ?
4. $RM = RM$	4. Reflexive property of equality
5. $\triangle PRM \cong \triangle QRM$	5. ? (Steps 1, 2, and 4)
6. $m \angle 1 = m \angle 2$	6. ?
7. $m \angle 1 + m \angle 2 = m \angle PMQ$	7. For any angle, the measure of the whole is equal to the sum of the measures of its non-overlapping parts.
8. $m \angle PMQ = 180°$	8. If the sides of an angle form a straight line, then the angle is a straight angle with measure 180°.
9. $m \angle 1 + m \angle 2 = 180°$	9. Substitution property (Steps ? and ?)
10. $m \angle 1 + m \angle 1 = 180°$	10. Substitution property (Steps ? and ?)
11. $2(m \angle 1) = 180°$	11. Distributive property
12. $m \angle 1 = 90°$	12. ?
13. $\overleftrightarrow{RM} \perp \overline{PQ}$	13. ?
14. $\overleftrightarrow{RM}$ is the perpendicular bisector of $\overline{PQ}$, so R lies on the perpendicular bisector of $\overline{PQ}$.	14. Definition of perpendicular bisector (Steps ? and ?)

22. **Writing** The proof in Exercise 21 has many steps. Explain what happened in steps 6–13.

23. a. On a coordinate plane, plot the points $H(-2, -1)$, $J(4, -1)$, $K(1, 3)$, and $L(1, -4)$. Draw $HKJL$, $\overleftrightarrow{KL}$, and $\overline{HJ}$.

b. Explain how you know that $\overleftrightarrow{KL}$ is the perpendicular bisector of $\overline{HJ}$.

connection to HISTORY

An arrangement of Mayan buildings at Uaxactun, Guatemala, may have been used for solar observations and keeping the solar calendar. An observer at one structure looking east across an open plaza would see three buildings. The center building is due east of the observer. The outside buildings are due south and due north of the center building and equidistant from it.

The sun rose approximately above the northernmost building on the first day of summer.

The sun passed directly over the central building on both equinox days.

The sun rose over the southernmost building on the first day of winter.

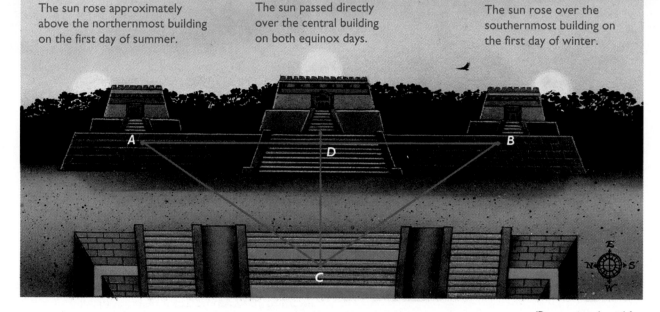

(Perspective altered for illustrative purposes.)

24. What information in the paragraph above tells you that $DA = DB$? What information tells you that $\angle ADC$ and $\angle BDC$ are right angles?

25. How can you prove that $\triangle ADC \cong \triangle BDC$?

26. Explain how you would know that $\overrightarrow{CD}$ is the perpendicular bisector of $\overline{AB}$?

Ongoing ASSESSMENT

27. **Open-ended** Draw any large triangle on a piece of paper. Construct the perpendicular bisector of each side using a straightedge and compass as shown on page 475. What do you notice about the three bisectors?

Review PREVIEW

28. Tell whether there is enough information to prove that $\triangle ABC \cong \triangle XYZ$. Write *Yes* or *No*. Explain. *(Section 8-5)*

29. Factor $x^2 + 5x - 84$. *(Section 4-4)*

30. Solve the proportion $\frac{3}{8} = \frac{9}{x}$. *(Toolbox Skill 17)*

31. Find the area of $\triangle DEF$. *(Toolbox Skill 28)*

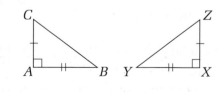

Working on the Unit Project

As you complete Exercise 32, think about how you can use the properties of isosceles triangles in the tool you design.

The ancient Egyptians used a tool called a *plumb level*. It was used to determine if a surface was level.

A *plumb level* consists of an A-frame and a weighted string that hangs from the vertex, B.

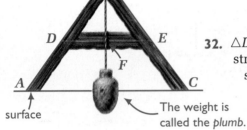

surface

The weight is called the *plumb*.

This temple for Queen Hatshepsut of Egypt was built at Dayr al-Bahri around 1460 B.C.

32. △DBE is isosceles with DB = EB, and AB = CB. The string is perpendicular to $\overline{DE}$ when the plumb level stands on a level surface—one that is not tilted. The Egyptians knew that if the surface was level, then the string would bisect $\overline{DE}$.

Prove that $\overline{DE} \parallel \overline{AC}$ when $\overleftrightarrow{BF}$ bisects $\overline{DE}$.

Unit 8 CHECKPOINT 2

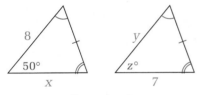

Exercise 2

1. **Writing** Describe how you might decide which method to use to show that two triangles are congruent.

2. Find the values of x, y, and z. Explain your reasoning.   8-4

For Exercises 3 and 4, identify the congruent triangles.   8-5
How do you know they are congruent?

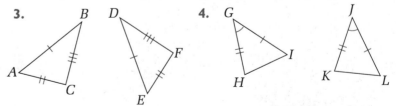

3.   4.

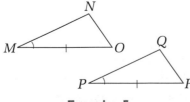

Exercise 5

5. Suppose you want to say that △MNO ≅ △PQR. What additional information do you need?

6. On a coordinate plane, plot the points S(1, 1),   8-6
   T(3, −4), and U(5, 1). What can you say about △STU?

7. In △ABC, AB = CB. The measure of ∠B is four less than twice the measure of ∠C. Find the measures of all three angles.

Similarity in Right Triangles

Identify similar right
triangles and apply right
triangle theorems. Find
geometric means.

Two rights rights make a right

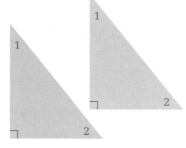

EXPLORATION

How can you make three similar triangles from one right triangle?

- **Materials: paper, rulers, scissors**
- **Work with another student.**

(1) Draw and cut out two congruent right triangles.

(2) On each triangle, label the corresponding acute angles "1" and "2." Mark the right angles.

(3) An **altitude** of a triangle is a segment from a vertex perpendicular to the line containing the opposite side.

a. On one of your triangles make a fold line that is the altitude to the hypotenuse.

b. Cut this triangle along the altitude, forming two new triangles.

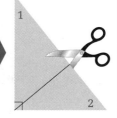

c. Mark the right angles on the two new triangles.

(4) Turn the small triangles over and label the angles on the other side also.

(5) Discuss how you know that the three triangles are similar.

481

In the Exploration you may have observed this relationship.

SIMILAR RIGHT TRIANGLES THEOREM

Theorem 8.17 If the altitude is drawn to the hypotenuse of a
right triangle, then the two triangles formed are
similar to the original triangle and to each other.

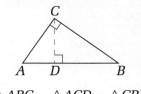

$$\triangle ABC \sim \triangle ACD \sim \triangle CBD$$

Similar right triangles may be used to prove one of the most
famous theorems in mathematics, the Pythagorean theorem. A
proof is shown in Exercise 5.

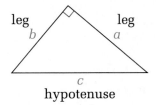

THE PYTHAGOREAN THEOREM

Theorem 8.18 In any right triangle, the square of the length of
the hypotenuse is equal to the sum of the squares
of the lengths of the legs.

$$c^2 = a^2 + b^2$$

Sample 1

**In $\triangle PQR$, $\overline{RS}$ is the altitude to hypotenuse $\overline{PQ}$. Identify the
similar triangles.**

Sample Response ·····

Sketch the large triangle and the two smaller triangles
formed by the altitude to the hypotenuse. Mark the angles
that are equal in measure.

Use the angle marks to write the corresponding vertices
in the same order for each triangle: $\triangle PQR \sim \triangle PRS \sim \triangle RQS$.

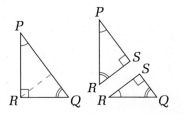

Talk it Over

1. Use the figure in Sample 1 to complete these statements.

   a. $\dfrac{QS}{RS} = \dfrac{?}{PS}$

   b. $\dfrac{QS}{QR} = \dfrac{?}{QP}$

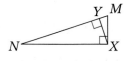

·····▶ **Now you are ready for:**
Exs. 1–9 on pp. 485–486

2. In $\triangle MNX$ at the left, $\overline{XY}$ is an altitude to hypotenuse $\overline{MN}$.
   Identify the similar triangles.

The Geometric Mean

When you complete the proportion in *Talk it Over* question 1(a) on page 482, notice that *RS* appears in two places. The length *RS* is the *geometric mean* between the lengths *QS* and *PS*.

If a, x, and b are positive numbers and

$$\frac{a}{x} = \frac{x}{b},$$

then x is called the **geometric mean** between a and b. The geometric mean is always positive.

Sample 2

Find the geometric mean between 2 and 32.

Sample Response

Let x = the geometric mean between 2 and 32.
Write a proportion and solve it.

$$\frac{2}{x} = \frac{x}{32}$$ ← Use the proportion $\frac{a}{x} = \frac{x}{b}$.

$$64 = x^2$$ ← Use cross products.

$$\sqrt{64} = x$$ ← The geometric mean is always positive. Find the positive square root.

$$8 = x$$

The geometric mean between 2 and 32 is 8.

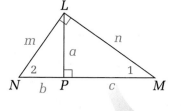

Talk it Over

Use the diagram below to complete each proportion.

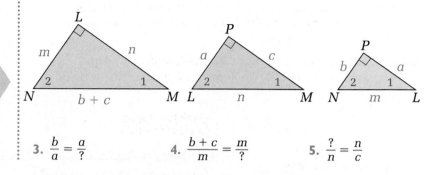

3. $\dfrac{b}{a} = \dfrac{a}{?}$

4. $\dfrac{b+c}{m} = \dfrac{m}{?}$

5. $\dfrac{?}{n} = \dfrac{n}{c}$

The results of *Talk it Over* question 3 can be generalized to Theorem 8.19, proved in Exercise 20. Questions 4 and 5 can be generalized to a theorem stated in Exercise 26.

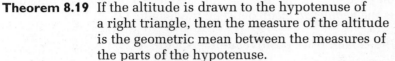

GEOMETRIC MEAN THEOREM

Theorem 8.19 If the altitude is drawn to the hypotenuse of a right triangle, then the measure of the altitude is the geometric mean between the measures of the parts of the hypotenuse.

$$\frac{AD}{CD} = \frac{CD}{BD}$$

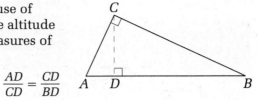

Sample 3

Find the lengths x, y, and z.

Sample Response

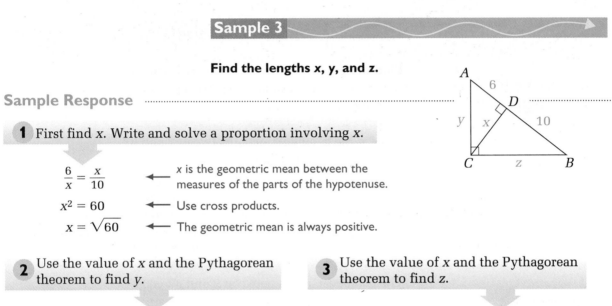

1 First find x. Write and solve a proportion involving x.

$$\frac{6}{x} = \frac{x}{10}$$ ⟵ x is the geometric mean between the measures of the parts of the hypotenuse.

$$x^2 = 60$$ ⟵ Use cross products.

$$x = \sqrt{60}$$ ⟵ The geometric mean is always positive.

2 Use the value of x and the Pythagorean theorem to find y.

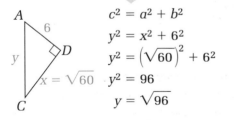

$$c^2 = a^2 + b^2$$
$$y^2 = x^2 + 6^2$$
$$y^2 = \left(\sqrt{60}\right)^2 + 6^2$$
$$y^2 = 96$$
$$y = \sqrt{96}$$

3 Use the value of x and the Pythagorean theorem to find z.

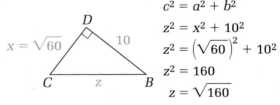

$$c^2 = a^2 + b^2$$
$$z^2 = x^2 + 10^2$$
$$z^2 = \left(\sqrt{60}\right)^2 + 10^2$$
$$z^2 = 160$$
$$z = \sqrt{160}$$

The lengths x, y, and z are $\sqrt{60}$, $\sqrt{96}$, and $\sqrt{160}$, or about 7.7, about 9.8, and about 12.6.

Look Back ◀

Altitude $\overline{ST}$ is drawn to the hypotenuse of right $\triangle QRS$. State two true relationships.

⋯▶ **Now you are ready for:**
Exs. 10–30 on pp. 486–488

For Exercises 1 and 2, draw and identify the similar triangles.

1.

2.

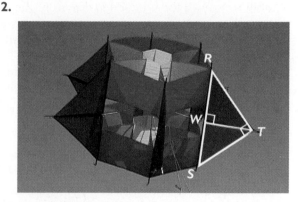

3. **Reading** What can you do to more easily identify angles that are equal in measure when similar triangles overlap?

4. In right $\triangle EFG$, $\overline{GH}$ is the altitude to the hypotenuse $\overline{EF}$. The measure of $\angle E$ is 65°. Draw $\triangle EFG$ and label the measures of all the angles.

5. Copy and complete this proof of the Pythagorean theorem.

> **Given** $\triangle ABC$ with right $\angle C$.
> $\overline{CD}$ is the altitude to the hypotenuse.

> **Prove** $c^2 = a^2 + b^2$

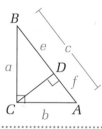

Statements	**Justifications**
1. In $\triangle ABC$, $\angle C$ is a right angle. $\overline{CD}$ is the altitude to the hypotenuse.	1. _?_
2. $\triangle ABC \sim \triangle CBD$; $\triangle ABC \sim \triangle ACD$	2. If the altitude is drawn to the hypotenuse of a right triangle, then the two triangles formed are similar to the original triangle and to each other.
3. $\dfrac{c}{a} = \dfrac{a}{e}$; $\dfrac{c}{?} = \dfrac{b}{f}$	3. Definition of similar triangles: corresponding sides are in proportion.
4. $ce = \underline{\ ?\ }$; $cf = \underline{\ ?\ }$	4. _?_
5. $ce + cf = \underline{\ ?\ } + \underline{\ ?\ }$	5. _?_
6. $c(e + f) = \underline{\ ?\ } + \underline{\ ?\ }$	6. _?_
7. $e + f = c$	7. _?_
8. $c(\underline{\ ?\ }) = a^2 + b^2$	8. _?_ (Steps 6 and 7)
9. $\underline{\ ?\ } = a^2 + b^2$	9. _?_

Notice which sides correspond in the three right triangles.

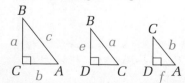

Find the measure of each unknown side.

6.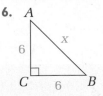

7.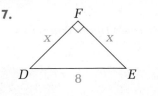

8.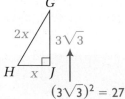

$(3\sqrt{3})^2 = 27$

9. A *Pythagorean triple* is a group of three integers that satisfy the equation $c^2 = a^2 + b^2$ and that can be the lengths of the sides of a right triangle.

   a. Show that 5, 12, 13 is a Pythagorean triple.

   b. **Open-ended** Name two other Pythagorean triples.

   c. Show that multiplying the integers in a Pythagorean triple by a constant produces another Pythagorean triple.

   d. Suppose the integers of a Pythagorean triple are the lengths of the sides of a right triangle. If you multiply the integers in the triple by 2 and form a new triangle, how will the triangles be related to each other?

Solve each proportion.

10. $\dfrac{4}{x} = \dfrac{5}{10}$ **11.** $\dfrac{3}{x} = \dfrac{x}{12}$ **12.** $\dfrac{5 + x}{x} = \dfrac{4}{3}$

Find the geometric mean between each pair of numbers.

13. 6 and 24   **14.** 27 and 3   **15.** 4 and 16   **16.** 45 and 5

17. 12 is the geometric mean between 3 and what other number?

18. 10 is the geometric mean between 25 and what other number?

Architecture Andrea Palladio (1508–1580), an Italian Renaissance architect, proposed a method for determining a pleasing height for a room. Palladio suggested that in rooms with flat ceilings, the height should be equal to the width. In square rooms with vaulted ceilings, the height should be one third greater than the width.

For many other rooms, Palladio suggested that the height should be equal to the geometric mean between the room's length and width.

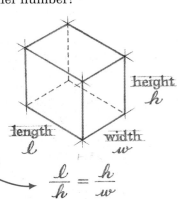

$\dfrac{l}{h} = \dfrac{h}{w}$

The basilica, or public building, in Vicenza, Italy, was designed by Palladio.

19. **Group Activity** Work with at least one other student.

   a. Is your classroom floor a square? Does the room have a flat ceiling? Which of Palladio's suggestions applies to your classroom?

   b. Measure the actual length and width of the room.

   c. Calculate the proper height for the room, based on Palladio's suggestions.

   d. Measure the actual height of your classroom. Is the room's proper height the same as the actual height?

20. Copy and complete this proof of Theorem 8.19.

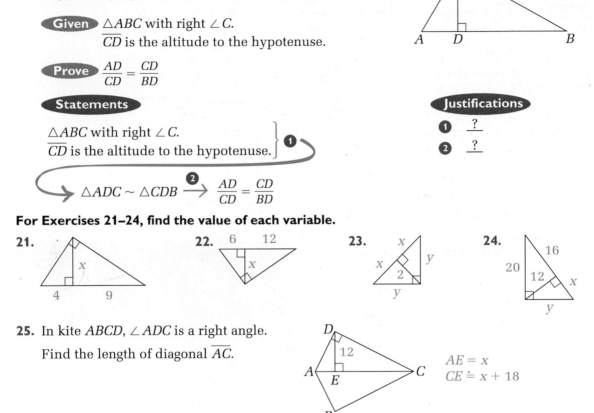

Given $\triangle ABC$ with right $\angle C$.
$\overline{CD}$ is the altitude to the hypotenuse.

Prove $\dfrac{AD}{CD} = \dfrac{CD}{BD}$

Statements

$\triangle ABC$ with right $\angle C$.
$\overline{CD}$ is the altitude to the hypotenuse. **①**

② $\triangle ADC \sim \triangle CDB \longrightarrow \dfrac{AD}{CD} = \dfrac{CD}{BD}$

Justifications

① $\underline{\quad ? \quad}$

② $\underline{\quad ? \quad}$

For Exercises 21–24, find the value of each variable.

21.

22. 6 12 x

23. x y 2 y

24. 16 20 12 x y

25. In kite $ABCD$, $\angle ADC$ is a right angle.
Find the length of diagonal $\overline{AC}$.

$AE = x$
$CE = x + 18$

```
.......... 
```
Ongoing **ASSESSMENT**

26. **Group Activity** Work with another student.

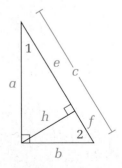

a. Cut out two congruent right triangles.

b. As in the Exploration on page 481, label the corresponding acute angles "1" and "2." Mark the right angles.

c. Label the measures of the sides of the triangles. Label the hypotenuse c, the longer leg a, and the shorter leg b.

d. On one of the triangles make a fold line that is the altitude to the hypotenuse. Cut the triangle along the altitude.

e. On the two new triangles, label the side that was the fold line h.

f. Label the remaining sides of the two triangles e or f, as appropriate.

g. **Writing** Use your similar triangles to explain how the proportions
$\dfrac{c}{a} = \dfrac{a}{e}$ and $\dfrac{c}{b} = \dfrac{b}{f}$ lead to this second geometric mean theorem:
If an altitude is drawn to the hypotenuse of a right triangle, then the measure of each leg is the geometric mean between the measure of the hypotenuse and the measure of the part of the hypotenuse that meets that leg.

27. **Given** △*ABD* is an equilateral triangle.
$\overline{BC} \perp \overline{AD}$

   a. What is the measure of $\overline{AC}$? *(Section 8-6)*

   b. What is the measure of ∠*ABD*? What is the measure of ∠*ABC*?

   c. What is the measure of $\overline{BC}$?

28. How many different four-letter arrangements can be made from the letters in the word WISH? Assume that a letter cannot be used more than once. *(Section 6-2)*

29. Draw and label a right △*JKL* so that
$$\tan K = \frac{\text{measure of leg opposite } \angle K}{\text{measure of leg adjacent to } \angle K} = \frac{5}{12}. \text{ (Toolbox Skill 29)}$$

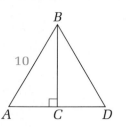

Working on the Unit Project

As you complete Exercise 30, think about how you can use the properties of similar right triangles in the tool you design.

30. A carpenter uses a tool called a *framing square* to measure and draw right angles. A square consists of two rulers that form an "L."

The framing square is in the shape of a right angle. Troy uses this right angled tool to estimate the height of a tree. The distance from the ground to Troy's eyes is 6 ft. He holds the corner of a framing square near his eye and moves back until he can see both the top and the bottom of the tree. Troy marks this spot and measures its distance from the tree.

   a. Which triangles are congruent? Which triangles are similar?

   b. Write a proportion and figure out the height of the tree.

   c. Why is it important that the angle held near Troy's eye is a right angle?

Special Right Triangles and Trigonometry

········Focus

Discover properties of 45°-45°-90° and 30°-60°-90° triangles. Review the trigonometric ratios: sine, cosine, and tangent.

THE **RIGHT RATIO**

Talk it Over

Refer to △ABC below.

1. △ABC is an *isosceles right triangle*. It is a right triangle with legs of equal measure. What can you say about $m \angle A$ and $m \angle B$?

2. Why do you think that an isosceles right triangle is also called a *45°-45°-90° triangle*?

3. Use the Pythagorean theorem to find the length of $\overline{AB}$. Leave your answer in radical form.

4. This tapestry was woven in Turkey in the 19th Century. Suppose the weaver had used an isosceles right triangle whose legs were both 8 cm long. Find the length of the hypotenuse of that triangle.

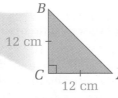

12 cm

C 12 cm A

You can use the patterns below to find the lengths of the sides of some special right triangles. You will verify the relationships in 45°-45°-90° triangles and 30°-60°-90° triangles in Exercise 32.

$\mathbf{X} \overset{\frown}{ab}$

RIGHT TRIANGLE RELATIONSHIPS

In a 45°-45°-90° triangle, the measure of the hypotenuse is $\sqrt{2}$ times the measure of a leg.

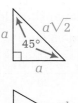

In a 30°-60°-90° triangle, the measure of the hypotenuse is twice the measure of the shorter leg. The measure of the longer leg is $\sqrt{3}$ times the measure of the shorter leg.

Find the exact measure of each unknown side in each triangle.

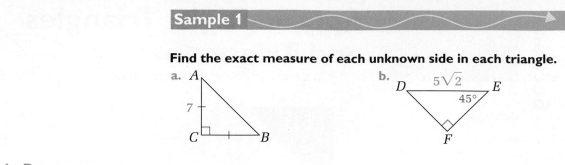

a.

b.

Sample Response

Use the relationships for an isosceles right, or 45°-45°-90°, triangle on page 489.

a. Substitute 7 for a in the diagram.

b. Substitute $5\sqrt{2}$ for $a\sqrt{2}$. Then solve for a.

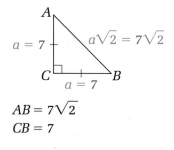

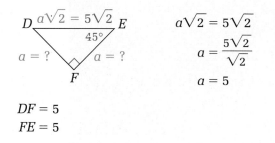

$AB = 7\sqrt{2}$

$CB = 7$

$DF = 5$

$FE = 5$

$$a\sqrt{2} = 5\sqrt{2}$$
$$a = \frac{5\sqrt{2}}{\sqrt{2}}$$
$$a = 5$$

Find the approximate measure of each unknown side in each triangle.

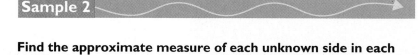

a.

b.

Sample Response

Use the relationships for a 30°-60°-90° triangle on page 489.

a. Substitute 5 for b in the diagram.

b. Substitute 7 for $b\sqrt{3}$. Then solve for b.

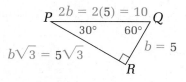

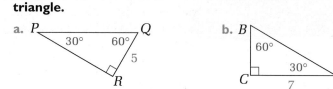

$PQ = 10$

$PR = 5\sqrt{3} \approx 8.7$

$BC \approx 4.0$

$AB \approx 2(4.04) \approx 8.1$

$$b\sqrt{3} = 7$$
$$b = \frac{7}{\sqrt{3}}$$
$$b \approx 4.04$$

······► **Now you are ready for:**
Exs. 1–18 on pp. 493–494

Talk it Over

5. Is △MNO isosceles? Explain.

6. Find MO and NO to the nearest tenth.

Trigonometry

The word *trigonometry* comes from the Greek language. It means *triangle measurement*. The Egyptians used trigonometry over 3800 years ago in constructing pyramids.

Each of the trigonometric ratios, **sine**, **cosine**, and **tangent**, compares the measures of two sides of a right triangle.

TRIGONOMETRIC RATIOS

$$\sin A = \frac{\text{measure of leg opposite } \angle A}{\text{measure of hypotenuse}} = \frac{BC}{AB}$$

$$\cos A = \frac{\text{measure of leg adjacent to } \angle A}{\text{measure of hypotenuse}} = \frac{AC}{AB}$$

$$\tan A = \frac{\text{measure of leg opposite } \angle A}{\text{measure of leg adjacent to } \angle A} = \frac{BC}{AC}$$

The symbols for the sine, cosine, and tangent are sin, cos, and tan.

You can use the relationships between the sides of special right triangles to find the sine, cosine, and tangent of the acute angles in each triangle. The ratios are given in the table below.

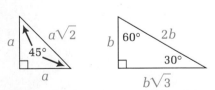

Watch Out!

The value of a trigonometric ratio depends only on the measure of the angle. No matter how large a 30°-60°-90° triangle is, $\cos 60° = \frac{1}{2}$.

Trigonometric Ratios for Special Right Triangles

	30° angle	45° angle	60° angle
sine = $\dfrac{\text{opposite}}{\text{hypotenuse}}$	$\dfrac{b}{2b} = \dfrac{1}{2}$	$\dfrac{a}{a\sqrt{2}} = \dfrac{1}{\sqrt{2}}$	$\dfrac{b\sqrt{3}}{2b} = \dfrac{\sqrt{3}}{2}$
cosine = $\dfrac{\text{adjacent}}{\text{hypotenuse}}$	$\dfrac{b\sqrt{3}}{2b} = \dfrac{\sqrt{3}}{2}$	$\dfrac{a}{a\sqrt{2}} = \dfrac{1}{\sqrt{2}}$	$\dfrac{b}{2b} = \dfrac{1}{2}$
tangent = $\dfrac{\text{opposite}}{\text{adjacent}}$	$\dfrac{b}{b\sqrt{3}} = \dfrac{1}{\sqrt{3}}$	$\dfrac{a}{a} = 1$	$\dfrac{b\sqrt{3}}{b} = \sqrt{3}$

Find the value of the variable in each figure.

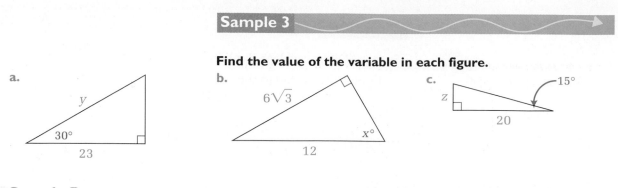

a.

b.

$6\sqrt{3}$

$x°$

12

c.

15°

z

20

Sample Response

Decide which side measure(s) you know and which you want to know: opposite, adjacent, or hypotenuse. Use the trigonometric ratio that involves those sides.

a. **Method ❶** Use the special triangle ratios. This is a 30°-60°-90° triangle.

$$\cos 30° = \frac{\text{adjacent}}{\text{hypotenuse}}$$

$$\frac{\sqrt{3}}{2} = \frac{23}{y}$$

$$y\sqrt{3} = 46 \quad \longleftarrow \text{ Use cross products.}$$

$$y = \frac{46}{\sqrt{3}} \approx 26.6$$

Method ❷ Use a calculator to find the trigonometric ratios.

$$\cos 30° = \frac{\text{adjacent}}{\text{hypotenuse}}$$

$$0.8660 \approx \frac{23}{y}$$

$$y \approx \frac{23}{0.8660}$$

$$y \approx 26.6$$

b. You know some side measures, but not the angle measure.

$$\sin x° = \frac{\text{opposite}}{\text{hypotenuse}} = \frac{6\sqrt{3}}{12} = \frac{\sqrt{3}}{2} \quad \text{Work backward.}$$

The measure of an angle with a sine of $\frac{\sqrt{3}}{2}$ is 60°. The value of x is 60.

c. A triangle with a 15° angle is not one of the special right triangles.

$$\tan 15° = \frac{\text{opposite}}{\text{adjacent}}$$

$$0.2679 \approx \frac{z}{20} \quad \longleftarrow \text{ Use the } \boxed{\text{TAN}} \text{ key.}$$

$$z \approx 5.4$$

Look Back ◄

Describe a way to remember the sine, cosine, and tangent of the acute angles of a 45°-45°-90° triangle. Describe a way to remember the sine, cosine, and tangent of each acute angle of a 30°-60°-90° triangle.

┈┈► **Now you are ready for:**
Exs. 19–38 on pp. 495–496

Find the exact measure of each unknown side in each triangle.

1.

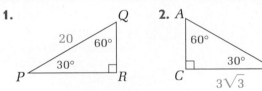

2. *A*
C ⌐ 60°
30°
3√3 *B*

3. *G* ——┼—— *E*
5 ⌐
F

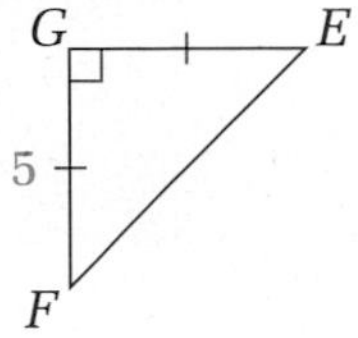

4. *M*
45° 14
O ⌐ *N*

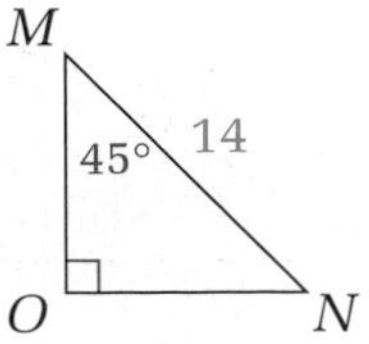

Find each measure to the nearest tenth.

5. the height of the parasailer above the ground

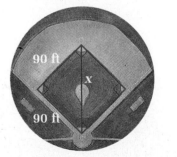

6. the length of a support in the skylight

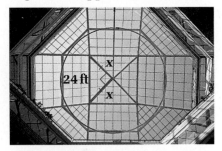

7. the distance from home plate to second base

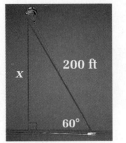

8. the length of the gangplank from the dock to the pier

9. Choose the letter of the triangle that must be an isosceles right triangle.

a.
2
1
⌐
√3

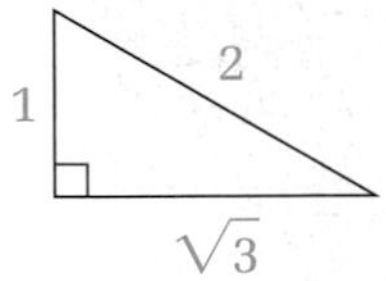

b. 45°
⌐

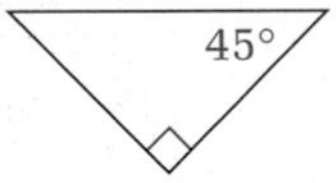

c. *a*   *a*

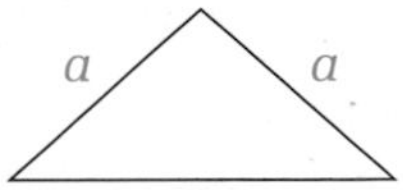

Find the measures of as many segments as possible in each figure.

10. *D* ——— *C*
45° ⌐
6 45°
A   *B*

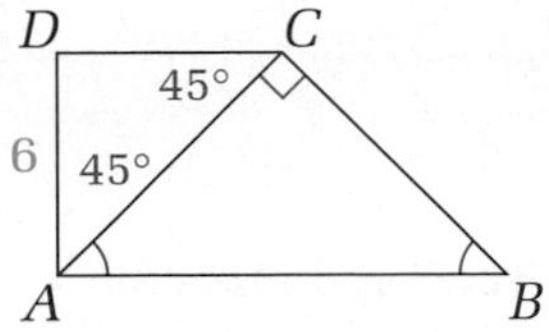

11. *S*
60° 4
V ⌐ *T*
U

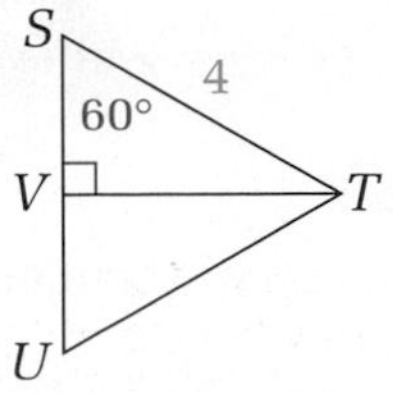

12. *N*
M 60° *P* ⌐ 60° *O*
|—— 18 ——|

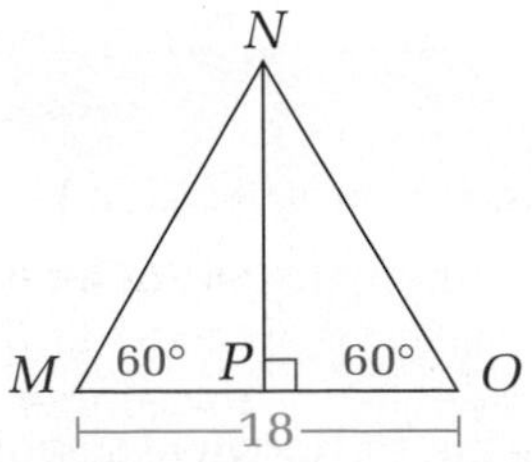

13. *L* —— 7 —— *M*
45° 4
K   *N*

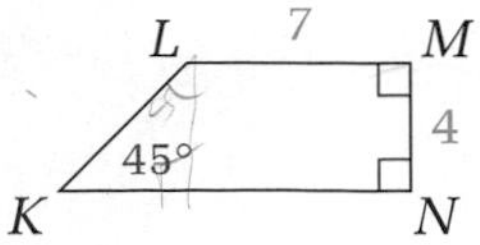

14. **Writing** Justify your answer to one of Exercises 10–13.

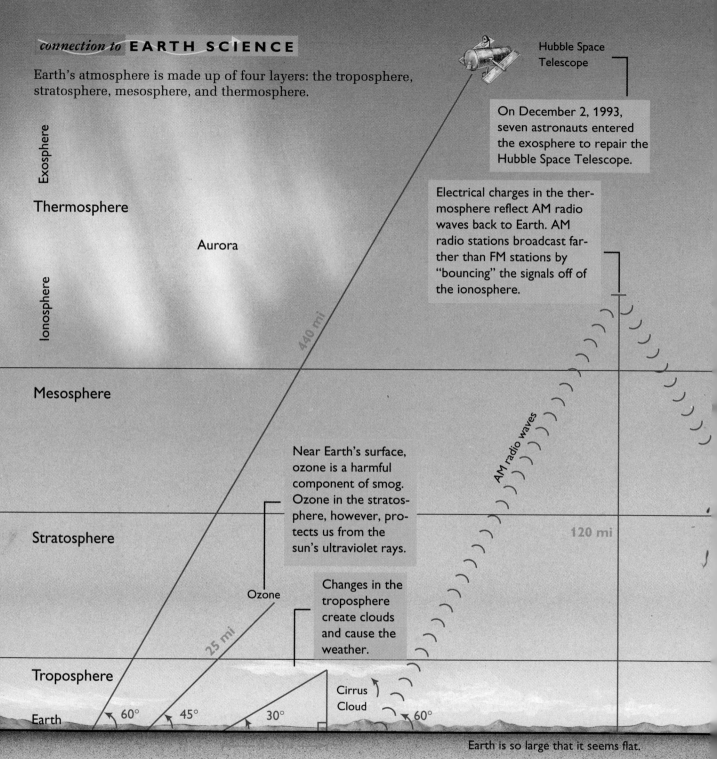

connection to **EARTH SCIENCE**

Earth's atmosphere is made up of four layers: the troposphere, stratosphere, mesosphere, and thermosphere.

Exosphere

Thermosphere

Aurora

Ionosphere

Hubble Space Telescope

On December 2, 1993, seven astronauts entered the exosphere to repair the Hubble Space Telescope.

Electrical charges in the thermosphere reflect AM radio waves back to Earth. AM radio stations broadcast farther than FM stations by "bouncing" the signals off of the ionosphere.

440 mi

Mesosphere

AM radio waves

Near Earth's surface, ozone is a harmful component of smog. Ozone in the stratosphere, however, protects us from the sun's ultraviolet rays.

Stratosphere

120 mi

Ozone

Changes in the troposphere create clouds and cause the weather.

25 mi

Troposphere

Cirrus Cloud

Earth   60°   45°   30°   60°

Earth is so large that it seems flat.

For Exercises 15–18, use the information in the diagram.

15. Estimate the height above ground of a cirrus cloud, one of the highest flying clouds.

16. Estimate the height above ground of the stratospheric ozone layer.

17. About how far does the radio wave travel before it is reflected?

18. How high above Earth did the astronauts go to reach the Hubble?

(Not drawn to scale.)

Reading Find the value of each variable.

19. $\cos x° = \dfrac{1}{2}$

20. $\sin y° = \dfrac{1}{\sqrt{2}}$

21. $\tan z° = 1$

22. $\sin w° = \dfrac{1}{2}$

Find the value of the variable in each figure.

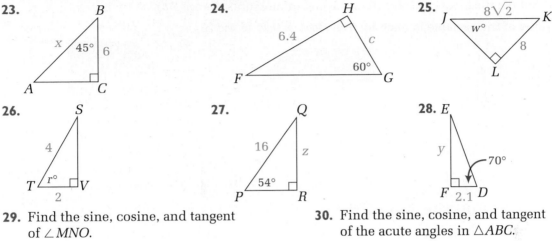

23.

24.

25.

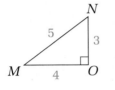

26.

27.

28.

29. Find the sine, cosine, and tangent of $\angle MNO$.

30. Find the sine, cosine, and tangent of the acute angles in $\triangle ABC$.

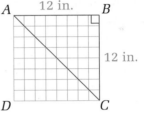

31. For parts (a)–(c), find each value.

   a. $\sin 60°$ and $\cos 30°$

   b. $\sin 30°$ and $\cos 60°$

   c. $\tan 60°$ and $\tan 30°$

   d. Find a pattern in your answers to parts (a)–(c). Make a conjecture. Support your conclusion.

. . . .
Ongoing **ASSESSMENT**

32. **Writing** Use the figures at the right.

   a. Explain why $\triangle ABC \sim \triangle DEF$. Are all 45°-45°-90° triangles similar?

   b. Use the Pythagorean theorem to find AB.

   c. What is the ratio of corresponding sides in $\triangle ABC$ and $\triangle DEF$?

   d. Explain why $DE = a\sqrt{2}$.

   e. $\triangle GHJ$ is an equilateral triangle with altitude $\overline{GK}$. What kind of special triangle is $\triangle GHK$?

   f. Suppose $HK = 1$ unit. Find HJ and HG. Show your reasoning.

   g. Use the Pythagorean theorem to find GK.

   h. Suppose that $\triangle LMN \sim \triangle GHK$ and $MN = b$ units. Use similar triangles to find LN and LM. Show your reasoning.

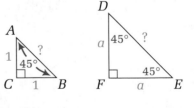

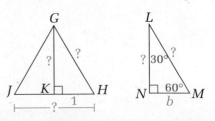

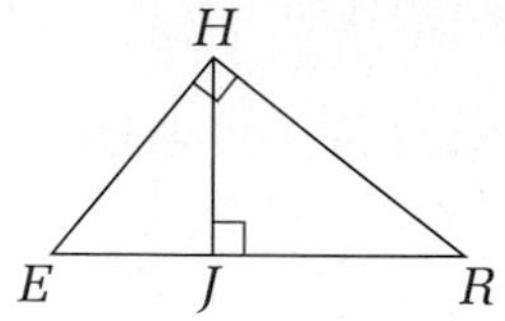

33. In △*EHR*, $\overline{HJ}$ is the altitude to hypotenuse $\overline{ER}$. Identify the similar triangles. *(Section 8-7)*

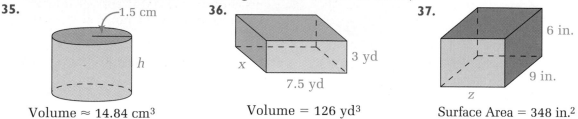

34. Quadrilateral *OBCD* has vertices *O*(0, 0), *B*(3, 5), *C*(7, 5), and *D*(10, 0). Show that the diagonals $\overline{OC}$ and $\overline{BD}$ are equal in measure. *(Section 5-6)*

Find the value of the variable in each figure. *(Toolbox Skills 15 and 28)*

35.

1.5 cm

h

Volume ≈ 14.84 cm³

36.

x

3 yd

7.5 yd

Volume = 126 yd³

37.

6 in.

9 in.

z

Surface Area = 348 in.²

Working on the Unit Project

As you complete Exercise 38, think about how you can use the properties of right triangles in the tool you design.

38. A *sextant* is a device that is normally used by navigators to help find a ship's position at sea. The instrument has two mirrors that allow a navigator to see the sun and horizon at the same time and to find the measure of the angle between them. This angle is always an angle of a right triangle.

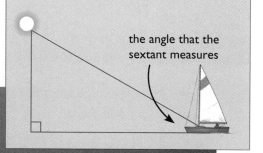

the angle that the sextant measures

This sextant from about 1810 was used by a ship's captain.

30°

Billie is out in a rowboat practicing using her sextant. When she sights the top and base of the lighthouse, the sextant gives Billie a reading of 30°. Suppose the lighthouse is 50 ft tall. About how far is Billie from the base? Round your answer to the nearest foot.

(Not drawn to scale)

Completing the Unit Project

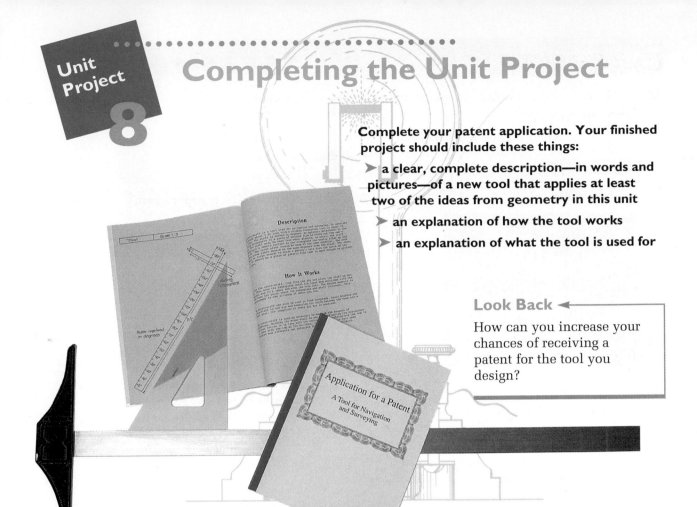

Complete your patent application. Your finished project should include these things:

➤ **a clear, complete description—in words and pictures—of a new tool that applies at least two of the ideas from geometry in this unit**

➤ **an explanation of how the tool works**

➤ **an explanation of what the tool is used for**

Look Back ◄

How can you increase your chances of receiving a patent for the tool you design?

Alternative Projects

Project 1: **Build the Tool You Design**

Design a tool according to the guidelines presented on page 429. Then build a working model of the tool.

Project 2: **A Pantograph**

A pantograph is a drawing tool used by mapmakers and artists to make an enlarged or reduced copy of an existing drawing. Find out how a pantograph is made. Explain how it works. Build your own pantograph and use it to enlarge or reduce a drawing.

Project 3: **CAD Software**

Many engineers use CAD (computer-aided design) software instead of hand-held drafting tools. If CAD software is available, use it to design a tool.

1. **Given** $\overline{AB} \parallel \overline{FC}$
$\angle B$ and $\angle F$ are right angles.

Prove $\overrightarrow{FE} \parallel \overrightarrow{CD}$

8-1

2. Find the measure of $\angle 1$.

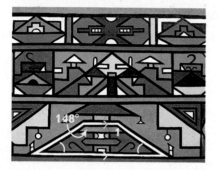

3. Is the quadrilateral a parallelogram? Why or why not?

8-2

The photos at left and above show two walls. The designs on the left wall were painted by an Ndebele woman in South Africa. The stone mosaic wall at the right is at Mitla, Oaxaca, Mexico.

4. Find the measure of $\angle 1$.

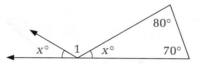

5. **Given** $\overline{AB} \parallel \overline{DC}$

Prove $\triangle AEB \sim \triangle CED$

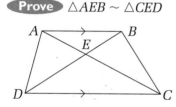

6. Find the values of x and y.

8-3

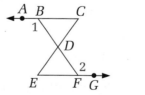

7. **Given** $m \angle 1 = m \angle 2$
$BD = DF$

Prove D is the midpoint of $\overline{CE}$.

8-4

8. **Open-ended** Name two everyday items that use triangles to give them rigidity.

8-5

9. **Given** B is the midpoint of $\overline{AE}$, $\overline{FC}$, and $\overline{GD}$.

Prove $\triangle ABG \cong \triangle EBD$

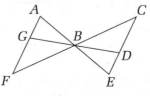

10. **Writing** Do you agree or disagree with the statement, "The base angles of every isosceles triangle are acute angles"? Explain.

8-6

11. Find the measures of the three angles in $\triangle QRS$.

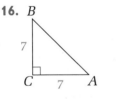

12. a. On a coordinate plane, plot the points $J(2, 2)$, $K(-3, 1)$, and $L(-1, 4)$. Draw $\triangle JKL$.

b. Show that $\triangle JKL$ is isosceles.

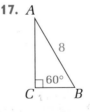

13. Explain how you know that $\overleftrightarrow{BD}$ is the perpendicular bisector of $\overline{AC}$.

14. Find the geometric mean between 100 and 4.

15. The logo shown is used by a shipbuilder. The artist drew the logo so that $\angle HKJ$ is a right angle. The measure of $\overline{HL}$ is 20 mm, and the measure of $\overline{LJ}$ is 16 mm.

a. Identify the similar triangles.

b. What is the measure of $\overline{KL}$?

c. What is the measure of $\overline{HK}$?

8-7

8-8

For Exercises 16 and 17:

a. Find the exact measure of each unknown side in each triangle.

b. Find the sine, cosine, and tangent of $\angle A$ in each triangle.

16. B

17. A

Find the approximate value of x in each figure.

18. **19.**

20. **Self-evaluation** What is some information you look for in diagrams involving lines intersected by a transversal or involving triangles? What are some questions you can ask yourself to help you think through a proof or problem?

21. **Group Activity** Work in a group of three students.

a. Each student should write "given(s)" and a "prove" statement for a proof about parallel lines, similar triangles, congruent triangles, isosceles triangles, or right triangles.

b. Trade your problem with another person in your group. Do the proof. Continue to trade until you have attempted each person's proof.

c. Could all the proofs be completed given what you know? Why or why not?

ALGEBRA)x^2

➤ The proportion $\frac{a}{x} = \frac{x}{b}$ can be written and solved to find the positive value x that is the geometric mean between two positive numbers a and b. *(p. 483)*

GEOMETRY

➤ Suppose two lines are intersected by a transversal. Then the lines are parallel under any of these conditions:
  • if corresponding angles are equal in measure *(p. 431)*
  • if alternate interior angles are equal in measure *(p. 433)*
  • if co-interior angles are supplementary *(p. 433)*

➤ If two lines are perpendicular to the same transversal, then they are parallel. *(p. 434)*

➤ If a transversal is perpendicular to one of two parallel lines, then it is perpendicular to the other one also. *(p. 434)*

➤ Through a point not on a given line, there is one and only one line parallel to the given line. (Unique Parallel Postulate) *(p. 439)*

➤ **Problem Solving** Drawing *helping lines* in a diagram can help you do a proof. *(p. 440)*

➤ **Measurement** The sum of the measures of the angles of a triangle is 180°. (Triangle Sum Theorem) *(p. 440)*

➤ **Measurement** The sum of the measures of the angles of a quadrilateral is 360°. *(p. 441)*

➤ If both pairs of opposite angles of a quadrilateral are equal in measure, then the quadrilateral is a parallelogram. *(p. 441)*

➤ **Measurement** An exterior angle of a triangle is equal in measure to the sum of the measures of its two remote interior angles. *(p. 443)*

➤ If two angles of one triangle are equal in measure to two angles of another triangle, then the two triangles are similar. (AA Similarity) *(p. 450)*

➤ If a line is drawn from a point on one side of a triangle parallel to another side, then it forms a triangle similar to the original triangle. *(p. 452)*

➤ Two triangles can be proven congruent when any of the following sets of corresponding parts are equal in measure:
  • two angles and the included side (ASA) *(p. 459)*
  • two angles and a non-included side (AAS) *(p. 459)*
  • two sides and the included angle (SAS) *(p. 466)*
  • three sides (SSS) *(p. 466)*

- You can prove that segments and angles are equal in measure if you can show that they are corresponding parts of congruent triangles. (CPCTE) *(p. 461)*

- If two sides of a triangle are equal in measure, then the angles opposite those sides are equal in measure. *(p. 473)*

- If two angles of a triangle are equal in measure, then the sides opposite those angles are equal in measure. *(p. 473)*

- A triangle is equilateral if and only if it is equiangular. An equiangular triangle has three 60° angles. *(p. 474)*

- If a point is the same distance from both endpoints of a segment, then it lies on the perpendicular bisector of the segment. *(p. 475)*

- In any right triangle, the square of the length of the hypotenuse is equal to the sum of the squares of the lengths of the legs. *(p. 482)*

- If the altitude is drawn to the hypotenuse of a right triangle:
  - then the two triangles formed are similar to the original triangle and to each other. *(p. 482)*
  - then the measure of the altitude is the geometric mean between the measures of the parts of the hypotenuse. *(p. 484)*

- **Measurement** The diagrams below show the relationships between the side measures in 45°-45°-90° triangles and 30°-60°-90° triangles. *(p. 489)*

- The trigonometric ratios for 30°, 45°, and 60° angles can be found by using the relationships between the measures of the sides of 30°-60°-90° and 45°-45°-90° triangles. *(p. 491)*

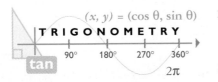

- The sine, cosine, and tangent ratios can be used to find the measure of an unknown side of a triangle. *(pp. 491–492)*

········· **Key Terms**

- ⊥ (p. 434)
- **similar triangles** (p. 449)
- **legs of an isosceles triangle** (p. 473)
- **perpendicular bisector** (p. 475)
- **sine, sin** (p. 491)

- **remote interior angles** (p. 442)
- **angle bisector** (p. 468)
- **base of an isosceles triangle** (p. 473)
- **altitude** (p. 481)
- **cosine, cos** (p. 491)

- **congruent triangles** (p. 449)
- **segment bisector** (p. 468)
- **equiangular** (p. 474)
- **geometric mean** (p. 483)
- **tangent, tan** (p. 491)

Polynomial and Rational Functions

ENERGY

Have you ever played hockey inside a mountain? At the 1994 Winter Olympics in Norway, hockey players went underground to take advantage of the insulating properties of a blanket of earth. An Olympic hockey stadium built deep inside a mountain uses 40% less energy than similar above-ground rinks.

underground

solar power

A thousand years ago, the Anasazi people of the American southwest built their houses out of heat-absorbing stones. These stones captured the warmth of the sun during the day and released it into their houses at night.

This kind of passive solar heating is still used today. An inside wall made of heat-absorbing material soaks up the sun's rays that stream in through large glass windows.

Air Your Opinion

Your project is to debate the pros and cons of using wind power to generate electricity. As you complete the "Working on the Unit Project" exercises, you will learn how to determine the power needs of a typical household in your area and what conditions influence the amount of power that can be produced by a wind machine in your area. You can use your findings to compile a list of the advantages and disadvantages of converting to wind power.

◄ Electric cars get their power from batteries and solar panels instead of gasoline. Many major car companies are developing electric cars in an effort to lower pollution.

sun

ENERGY

water

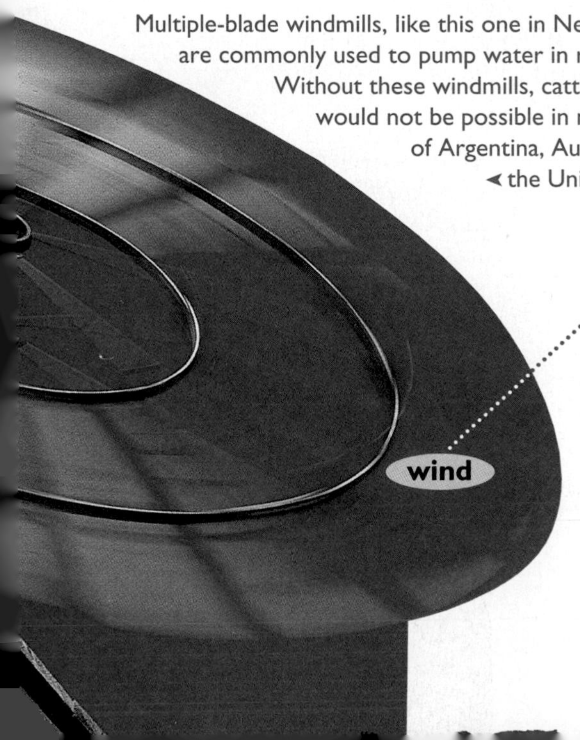

Multiple-blade windmills, like this one in New Mexico, are commonly used to pump water in rural areas. Without these windmills, cattle ranching would not be possible in many areas of Argentina, Australia, and ◄ the United States.

About 25% of the world's electricity is produced by water. Mountainous areas and large river valleys, like the Yangtze River valley in China, have good potential for hydropower. ►

wind

For this project you should work in a group of four students. Here are some ideas to help you get started.

☞ In your group, make a list of the electrical appliances used each day by a typical household in your area.

☞ Discuss ways to estimate the amount of wind available at a possible location for a wind turbine.

☞ Discuss whether you think wind speed measurements made at the nearest airport give an accurate picture of the wind at your location.

☞ Suppose you had an instrument to measure wind speed directly. Consider how many measurements you would need to compile an accurate wind profile at a location.

List of appliances used each day:

lights
TV   stereo
VCR   hair dryer
heat   oven
            air conditioning

Can We Talk ENERGY

Working on the Unit Project

Your work in Unit 9 will help you prepare for the debate.

Related Exercises:

Alternative Projects p. 549

Wind, sun, and water are sometimes called "alternative" energy sources. Today, most of the energy produced in the United States comes from the burning of fuels like oil, coal, and natural gas.

➤ Can you think of some important ways in which alternative energy sources are different from such fuels? What are some advantages and disadvantages of both types of energy sources?

➤ What do you think are the advantages of an electric car over a gasoline-powered car? What are some possible disadvantages?

➤ How do you think climate and geography influence the ability to use alternative sources of energy?

➤ Do you think your town or city would be a good location for a wind turbine? a dam? a solar house? Why or why not?

➤ Do you know of any place in your area that uses wind, sun, or water to generate power? If so, what is the power used for?

Polynomial and Rational Models

Focus

Model real-world situations with equations. Classify expressions.

On the Right Track

Heat makes metal expand. On hot days the rails of a railroad track get longer. If the ends of the rail cannot move, the middle of the rail may be pushed out of line. Some railroads have *expansion breaks* between sections of rail. On hot days the rails can expand into the breaks.

Sample 1

Suppose on a hot day, a 78 ft section of rail expands $\frac{1}{4}$ in. The middle of the rail curves out d inches. Write an equation to model the situation.

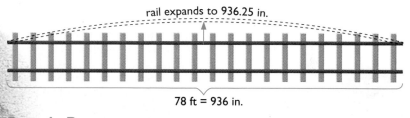

rail expands to 936.25 in.

78 ft = 936 in.

Sample Response

Let d = the distance (inches) that the middle of the rail curves out. Approximate the curve with two equal segments and form a right triangle. Use the Pythagorean theorem: $468^2 + d^2 = 468.125^2$

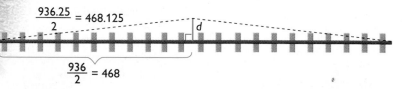

$\frac{936.25}{2} = 468.125$

d

$\frac{936}{2} = 468$

Talk it Over

1. Explain how to solve the equation $468^2 + d^2 = 468.125^2$.

2. Is it useful to use two line segments to model the expanded rail? Why or why not?

Kia wants to save $3500 for a trip to Africa after graduation. At the beginning of tenth grade, she puts $1000 into a savings account. She plans to save $1000 every year until she graduates. She wonders what yearly interest rate she must get to reach her goal. Model the situation with an equation.

Sample Response

Think about what happens to a deposit of $1000 in one year.

deposit + interest

$1000 + 1000r$ ←——— Let r = yearly interest rate.

$1000(1 + r)$ ←——— Use the distributive property.

$1000g$ ←——— Let $g = 1 + r$. The variable g is a *growth factor*.

> **BY THE WAY...**
>
> Africa has the world's longest river, the Nile (4145 mi), the world's largest desert, the Sahara (3.5 million mi²), and the world's longest freshwater lake, Tanganyika (420 mi). The climate varies widely. Within miles of each other there are ski slopes and deserts.

Use the growth factor g to find Kia's balance after graduation.

Kia starts tenth grade and deposits $1000.

$1000

Kia ends tenth grade and deposits another $1000.

$1000g   + $1000 ←——— This is her balance as she starts eleventh grade.

Kia ends eleventh grade and deposits another $1000.

$1000g \cdot g   + $1000g   + $1000 ←——— This is her balance as she starts twelfth grade.

Kia ends twelfth grade and graduates.

$1000g \cdot g \cdot g + $1000g \cdot g + $1000g

$1000g^3   + 1000g^2   + 1000g ←——— This is how much she has in her account for her trip.

The interest rate must be large enough so that Kia's balance is $3500.

$1000g^3 + 1000g^2 + 1000g = 3500$ ←——— This equation models the situation.

Polynomial Equations

The expression $1000g^3 + 1000g^2 + 1000g$ is an example of a *polynomial*. A **polynomial** is an expression that can be written as a monomial or sum of monomials with whole number exponents.

Each term is the product of a coefficient and a variable with a whole number exponent.

$$\overbrace{575x^3} - 12x^2 + 10x + 3 \qquad \longleftarrow \text{3 is the same as } 3x^0, \text{ since } x^0 = 1.$$

The **degree** of a polynomial is the largest exponent. This polynomial has degree 3.

The exponent of this variable is 1, because $x^1 = x$.

Polynomials	Not polynomials
$1000g^3 + 1000g^2 + 1000g$	$1000g^{-3} + 1000g^{-2} + 1000g^{-1}$
πr^2	$\pi r^{1/2}$
$\frac{1}{3}b - b^2 + b^3$	$3\left(\frac{1}{b}\right) - b^2 + b^3$
$y + 1$	$\frac{y}{y+1}$
$4x^2 + 3xy$	$\frac{4x^2}{y} + \frac{3x}{y}$

A **polynomial equation** is an equation that can be written with a polynomial as one side and 0 as the other side.

Polynomials are usually written in **standard form.** Reading from left to right, the exponents go from largest to smallest.

$$\begin{array}{cccc} 4 & 2 & 1 & 0 \end{array}$$
$$2x^4 - 15x^2 + 4x + 50 \qquad \longleftarrow \text{This polynomial is written in standard form.}$$

Talk it Over

3. Explain why each expression in the second column of the table is not a polynomial.

4. Is $2(x + 3)$ a polynomial? Explain why or why not.

5. The expression $\sqrt{2}\,x^3 - \pi x^4 + 30$ is a polynomial.

   a. What is the degree of the polynomial?

   b. How would the polynomial be written in standard form?

   c. What is the exponent of x for the last term? $(30x^? = 30)$

····▶ Now you are ready for:
Exs. 1–16 on pp. 509–510

Rational Equations

A rational number can be written as the quotient of two integers.

$$\frac{2}{3} \qquad \frac{3}{7} \qquad \frac{10}{5}$$

A **rational expression** is an expression that can be written as the quotient of two polynomials.

$$\frac{x+1}{2x+3}$$

A **rational equation** is an equation with only rational expressions on both sides.

$$\frac{x+1}{2x+3} = 10$$

Sample 3

Ken is mixing fruit punch. It is supposed to be 30% orange juice. So far Ken has mixed two pints of cranberry juice, one pint of orange juice, and one pint of ginger ale. Ken wonders how much orange juice to add. Write an equation to model the situation.

Sample Response

Step 1 Find out the percent of orange juice that is already in the punch.

$$\frac{\text{pints of orange juice}}{\text{pints of fruit punch}} = \frac{1}{4} = 0.25 \quad \longleftarrow \quad \begin{array}{l}\text{Ken has 4 pt of punch.}\\ \text{The punch is 25\% orange juice.}\end{array}$$

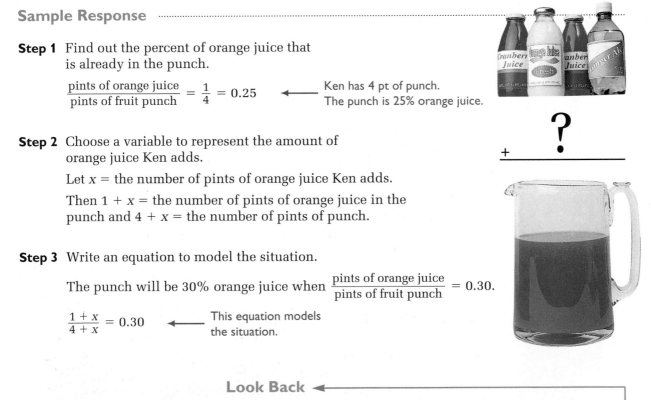

Step 2 Choose a variable to represent the amount of orange juice Ken adds.

Let x = the number of pints of orange juice Ken adds.

Then $1 + x$ = the number of pints of orange juice in the punch and $4 + x$ = the number of pints of punch.

Step 3 Write an equation to model the situation.

The punch will be 30% orange juice when $\dfrac{\text{pints of orange juice}}{\text{pints of fruit punch}} = 0.30$.

$$\frac{1+x}{4+x} = 0.30 \quad \longleftarrow \quad \begin{array}{l}\text{This equation models}\\ \text{the situation.}\end{array}$$

······► **Now you are ready for:**
Exs. 17–38 on pp. 511–512

Look Back

In Sample 2, Kia's savings were modeled by the polynomial equation $1000g^3 + 1000g^2 + 1000g = 3500$. Is this also a rational equation?

9-1 Exercises and Problems

1. **Reading** In Sample 2, what expression models Kia's savings account balance as she starts twelfth grade?

Write an equation to model the relationship among the measures in each figure.

2.

18 mi   30 mi

$x - 2$

3.

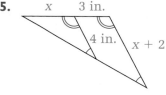

x

$x + 3$

Volume = 200π cm³

4.

x

6 in.

8 in.

Surface Area = 152 in.²

5.

x 3 in.

4 in. $x + 2$

6. Can all of your equations from Exercises 2–5 be written as polynomial equations? Explain.

7. Suppose there are no expansion breaks in a 500 m long straight railroad track. On a hot day, the rails expand 15 cm. The middle of one rail curves out d centimeters. Draw a sketch and write an equation to model the situation.

8. Maria is in tenth grade and wants to buy a $3000 used car after graduation. She plans to put $900 into a savings account every summer. She wonders what yearly interest rate she must get to have $3000 at the end of the summer after graduation. Model the situation with an equation.

9. The front of this Indonesian chest has dimensions in the golden ratio. The length of the chest is about 1.6 times the height. The width of the chest is equal to the height.

   a. An artist wants to create a replica of the chest with a volume of about 4500 in³. The artist wonders what the height should be. Write an equation to model the situation. Let x = the height of the replica.

   b. Is your equation from part (a) a polynomial equation? Explain why or why not.

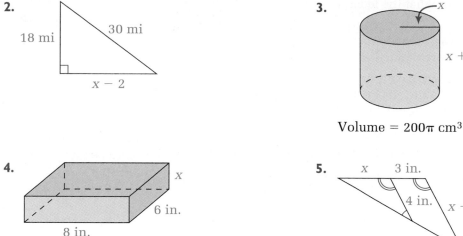

x

x

1.6x

Employment **For Exercises 10 and 11, assume that employees earn time and a half for any time worked over 40 hours in one week. *Time and a half* means that a worker earns 1.5 times his or her regular hourly wage.**

10. Linda Bowen worked 50 hours in one week. Her income before deductions was $325 for that week. Write an equation to model the situation. Let p = her regular hourly wage.

11. a. **Research** Find out what the federal minimum wage is in the United States.

    b. Find the hourly wage of an employee who works 54 hours in one week and earns $300 before deductions.

    c. Suppose someone earning minimum wage wants to earn $300 a week before deductions. Write an equation to model the situation. Let h = the number of hours of overtime worked.

For Exercises 12–15, use the polynomial $6x^9 + x^5 - 5x^2 + 2x - 15$.

12. What is the degree of the polynomial?

13. What is the coefficient of the third term from the left?

14. What is the exponent of the fourth term from the left?

15. Is the polynomial written in standard form? If not, rewrite it in standard form.

16. **Using Manipulatives** Use a $5\frac{1}{2}$ in. by 11 in. piece of paper, scissors, tape, and a ruler. Follow steps (a)–(c) to make a miniature pizza box.

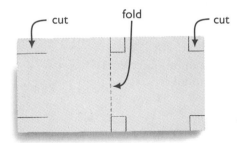

   a. Fold the paper in half. Cut four identical squares out of the corners of one of the halves as shown.

   b. Make two cuts on the uncut side as shown. Each cut should be twice as long as the squares from step (a).

   c. Fold along the dotted lines as shown.

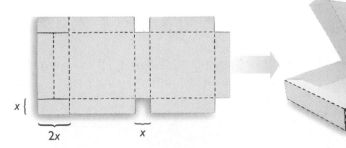 

   d. Measure the dimensions of your box. Find its volume.

   e. The employees at the Pizza Shop make their boxes out of 20 in. by 40 in. pieces of cardboard. Write an equation to model the volume of a Pizza Shop box. Let x = the length of the sides of the square cutouts and let V = the volume of the box.

**Tell whether each expression is a polynomial. Write *Yes* or *No*.
Give a reason for your answer.**

17. $3x^2 - 4x - 31$

18. $\dfrac{3}{x} + \dfrac{4}{x-2}$

19. $4x - 1$

20. $\dfrac{5}{3}r^3 - 3r - 2r^2 - 1$

21. $3x^{1/2} + 4x^3 + x^5$

22. $x^{-2} - 10x^{-1} + 2$

23. a. Is the equation $4x - 1 = 16$ linear?

   b. Are all linear equations also polynomial equations? Explain.

24. a. Is the equation $3x^2 - 4x - 31 = 0$ quadratic?

   b. Are all quadratic equations also polynomial equations? Explain.

25. Use cross products to solve the equation $\dfrac{1+x}{4+x} = 0.30$ from Sample 3.

26. Chemistry Laura Nyquist is a chemistry student. She mixes 5 mL acetic acid with 120 mL water to make a solution that should be 5% acid. Then she realizes she needs to add more acetic acid.

   a. Explain how Laura knows she needs to add more acetic acid.

   b. Laura wonders how much more acetic acid to add. Write an equation to model the situation.

   c. Is your equation in part (b) a rational equation?

27. Write an equation to model the relationship between the measures in the diagram.

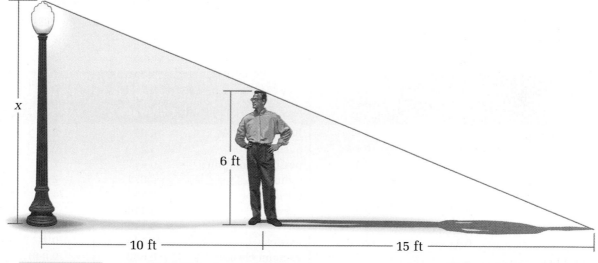

x   6 ft   10 ft   15 ft

28. Open-ended Write two rational equations.

29. a. Writing Tell what you think the graph at the right means.

   b. Let *n* represent the number of oranges available. Let *p* represent the price of an orange. Can this situation be modeled with a polynomial equation? Explain.

Price and Demand

Price (dollars)

p

10

0   10 n

Oranges (thousands)

30. a. Find the measures of as many segments as possible in △*MNO*.
(Section 8-8)

   b. Find the sine, cosine, and tangent of ∠*PNO*.

Simplify. *(Section 4-6)*

31. $3i - 6 - i^2 - 7i + 4$ **32.** $(2i)(5i)$ **33.** $(2 - i)(2 + i)$

34. Rewrite n^{-4} with a positive exponent. *(Section 2-6)*

35. Rewrite $\sqrt{x}$ with a fractional exponent. *(Section 2-6)*

36. What is the value of 2^0? of 99^0? of a^0? *(Section 2-6)*

Working on the Unit Project

The table shows the rate of electricity use for some common electrical appliances. It also shows the number of hours each appliance is typically used in one day. To find the amount of electricity used by each appliance in one day, you multiply the rate by the time.

rate of electricity use × average time of daily use = amount of electricity used in a day

   kilowatts (kW)   ×   hours (h)   =   kilowatt-hours (kW × h)

37. Use the table to estimate the total amount of electricity used in one day by a typical household in your area.

For appliances not in the table, read the power rating, in watts, on the appliance. Convert the rate to kilowatts by dividing by 1000. Then multiply by the estimated number of hours of daily use.

Appliance	Rate of Electricity Use (kilowatts)	Average Time of Daily Use (hours)	Appliance	Rate of Electricity Use (kilowatts)	Average Time of Daily Use (hours)
air conditioner	2	12	light bulb, 60 W	0.06	8
clock	0.002	24	oven	3.2	0.67
coffeemaker, drip	1.1	0.33	personal computer	0.44	2
curling iron	1.5	0.33	radio	0.071	2
dishwasher	1.201	0.43	refrigerator	0.29	24
dryer	5	0.5	stereo	0.110	3
electric blanket	0.177	8	TV	0.145	6
fan	0.2	12	toaster	1.146	0.1
hair dryer	1	0.25	vacuum cleaner	0.630	0.048
heating system	0.292	8	VCR	0.030	0.43
iron	1.1	0.17	water heater	4.5	3

38. Research Contact the company that supplies electricity in your area.

   a. Find out how much an average household in your area pays for electricity each month. How much is this per day? (Use 30 days for a month.)

   b. Find out the company's rate structure. Use it to estimate the daily cost of electricity for your group's typical household.

Power and Quotient Rules

Power Tools

Earth   Mars

Talk it Over

1. Complete. Describe any patterns you see.

   a. $x^3 \cdot x^2 = (x \cdot x \cdot x)(x \cdot x) = x^?$

   b. $x^4 \cdot x^2 = (x \cdot x \cdot x \cdot x)(x \cdot x) = x^?$

2. Write the product $x^{12} \cdot x^6$ as a power of x.

3. Complete. Describe any patterns you see.

   a. $\dfrac{a^5}{a^3} = \dfrac{\cancel{a} \cdot \cancel{a} \cdot \cancel{a} \cdot a \cdot a}{\cancel{a} \cdot \cancel{a} \cdot \cancel{a}} = a^?$

   b. $\dfrac{a^3}{a^5} = \dfrac{\cancel{a} \cdot \cancel{a} \cdot \cancel{a}}{\cancel{a} \cdot \cancel{a} \cdot \cancel{a} \cdot a \cdot a} = \dfrac{1}{a^?} = a^?$

   c. $\dfrac{a^5}{a^5} = \dfrac{\cancel{a} \cdot \cancel{a} \cdot \cancel{a} \cdot \cancel{a} \cdot \cancel{a}}{\cancel{a} \cdot \cancel{a} \cdot \cancel{a} \cdot \cancel{a} \cdot \cancel{a}} = 1 = a^?$

4. Write the quotient $\dfrac{x^7}{x^3}$ as a power of x.

The product of powers and quotient of powers rules describe the patterns you saw in questions 1–4.

BY THE WAY...

If you stood on Mars and looked at the sun, its diameter would look about 65% of the size you see from Earth.

$\dfrac{\text{distance of sun from Earth}}{\text{distance of sun from Mars}} \approx$

$\dfrac{1.5 \times 10^8 \text{ km}}{2.3 \times 10^8 \text{ km}} \approx 0.65$

X(. △ab

RULES OF EXPONENTS

For all positive, negative, zero, or fractional exponents: Examples

Product of Powers Rule	$a^m \cdot a^n = a^{m+n}$	$a^8 \cdot a^2 = a^{8+2} = a^{10}$
Quotient of Powers Rule	$\dfrac{a^m}{a^n} = a^{m-n}, \; a \neq 0$	$\dfrac{a^8}{a^2} = a^{8-2} = a^6$

Simplify. Write each answer without negative exponents.

a. $h^2 \cdot h^{-3} \cdot h$ b. $(-2x^{-5})(4x^8)$ c. $\dfrac{m^2 n^6}{n^9}$

Sample Response

a. $h^2 \cdot h^{-3} \cdot h = h^2 \cdot h^{-3} \cdot h^1$ ⟵ Rewrite h as h^1.

$\qquad\qquad = h^{2 + (-3) + 1}$ ⟵ Use the product of powers rule.

$\qquad\qquad = h^0$

$\qquad\qquad = 1$ ⟵ Use the zero exponent rule.

b. $(-2x^{-5})(4x^8) = (-2 \cdot 4)(x^{-5} \cdot x^8)$ ⟵ Group numbers and group powers with the same base.

$\qquad\qquad = (-2 \cdot 4)x^{-5 + 8}$ ⟵ Use the product of powers rule.

$\qquad\qquad = -8x^3$

c. $\dfrac{m^2 n^6}{n^9} = m^2 \cdot \dfrac{n^6}{n^9}$ ⟵ Think of each variable separately.

$\qquad\quad = m^2 \cdot n^{6 - 9}$ ⟵ Use the quotient of powers rule.

$\qquad\quad = m^2 \cdot n^{-3}$

$\qquad\quad = m^2 \cdot \dfrac{1}{n^3}$ ⟵ Rewrite using a positive exponent.

$\qquad\quad = \dfrac{m^2}{n^3}$

Watch Out!

The bases m and n are not the same, so $\dfrac{m^2}{n^3}$ cannot be simplified.

Factoring Polynomials

Drew hits a volleyball up from a point near the ground. The height h of the ball t seconds after being hit can be modeled by the polynomial equation $h = 32t - 16t^2$. You can write this equation in factored form:

$h = 32t - 16t^2$

$h = (2 \cdot 16)t - 16t^2$ ⟵ Notice that 16 is a common factor of 32 and 16.

$h = 16(2t - t^2)$ ⟵ Notice that t is a common factor of both terms in parentheses.

$h = 16t(2 - t)$ ⟵ The greatest common factor of $32t - 16t^2$ is $16t$.

To factor a polynomial completely, you first need to find the greatest common factor (GCF) of all the terms.

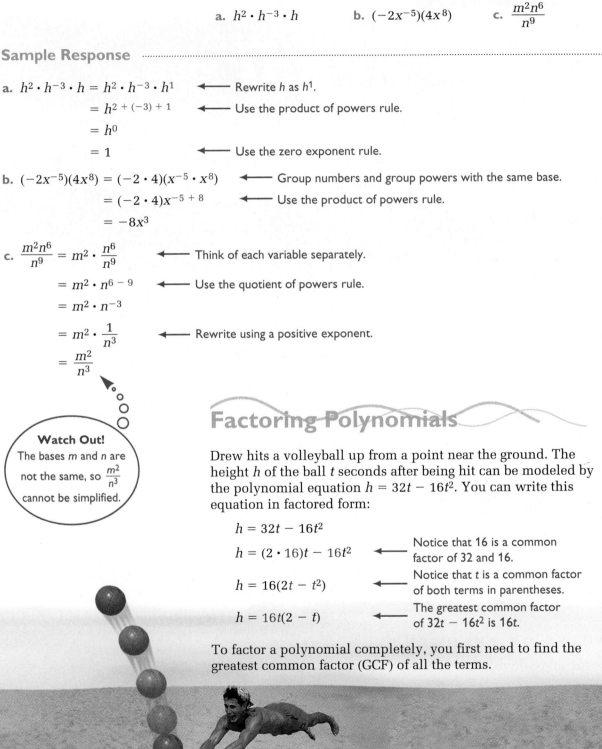

Sample 2

Factor $6x^5 - 8x^7 + 10x^2$ completely.

Sample Response

$$6x^5 - 8x^7 + 10x^2 = 6(x^2 \cdot x^3) - 8(x^2 \cdot x^5) + 10x^2$$

← Use the product of powers rule to find the GCF of the variable parts.

$$= 2x^2(3x^3) - 2x^2(4x^5) + 2x^2(5)$$

← The GCF of the coefficients is 2. The GCF of the variable parts is x^2.

$$= 2x^2(3x^3 - 4x^5 + 5)$$

Talk it Over

Complete.

5. $12x^5 = 4x^2 \cdot \underline{}$ 6. $16x^3y^5 = 4x^2y^3 \cdot \underline{}$ 7. $20x^2 = 4x^2 \cdot \underline{}$

8. Brian tried to factor the polynomial $3x^4 - 6x^3 - 45x^2$. He wrote $3x^2(x^2 - 2x - 15)$ as an answer. Has he factored the polynomial completely? If not, what else should he do?

······► Now you are ready for: Exs. 1–31 on pp. 517–518

More Rules of Exponents

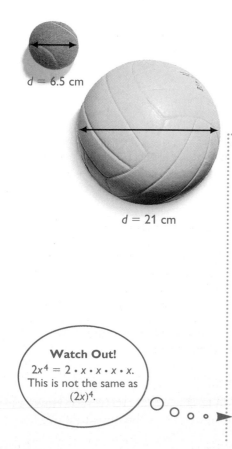

$d = 6.5$ cm

$d = 21$ cm

The ratio of the volumes of two spheres is equal to the ratio of the cubes of their diameters.

$$\frac{\text{volume of volleyball}}{\text{volume of tennis ball}} = \frac{(\text{diameter of volleyball})^3}{(\text{diameter of tennis ball})^3} = \frac{(21)^3}{(6.5)^3}$$

Talk it Over

9. Complete. Describe any patterns you see.

   a. $\left(\dfrac{21}{6.5}\right)^3 = \left(\dfrac{21}{6.5}\right)\left(\dfrac{21}{6.5}\right)\left(\dfrac{21}{6.5}\right) = \dfrac{21^?}{6.5^?}$

   b. $\left(\dfrac{2}{x}\right)^2 = \left(\dfrac{2}{x}\right) \cdot \left(\dfrac{2}{x}\right) = \dfrac{2^?}{x^?}$

10. Write $\left(\dfrac{a}{b}\right)^4$ as the quotient of a power of a and a power of b.

11. Complete. Describe any patterns you see.

   a. $(3^2)^3 = 3^? \cdot 3^? \cdot 3^? = 3^?$ b. $(2^5)^2 = 2^? \cdot 2^? = 2^?$

12. Write $(a^2)^7$ as a power of a.

13. Complete. Describe any patterns you see.

   a. $(3 \cdot 5)^2 = (3 \cdot 5)(3 \cdot 5) = (3 \cdot 3)(5 \cdot 5) = 3^? \cdot 5^?$

   b. $(2x)^4 = (2x)(2x)(2x)(2x) = 2^? \cdot x^? = \underline{}$

14. Write $(ab)^3$ as the product of a power of a and a power of b.

Watch Out!
$2x^4 = 2 \cdot x \cdot x \cdot x \cdot x$.
This is not the same as
$(2x)^4$.

RULES OF EXPONENTS

For all positive, negative, zero, or fractional exponents:

Examples

Power of a Power Rule $(a^m)^n = a^{mn}$ $(a^2)^3 = a^{2 \cdot 3} = a^6$

Power of a Product Rule $(ab)^n = a^n b^n$ $(ab)^2 = a^2 \cdot b^2 = a^2 b^2$

Power of a Quotient Rule $\left(\dfrac{a}{b}\right)^n = \dfrac{a^n}{b^n}, \; b \neq 0$ $\left(\dfrac{a}{b}\right)^3 = \dfrac{a^3}{b^3}$

Sample 3

Simplify. Write answers without negative exponents.

a. $(-2x^6)^4$ b. $(4b^{-5})^{-3}$ c. $\left(\dfrac{3y}{-2z}\right)^2$

Sample Response

a. $(-2x^6)^4 = (-2)^4 \cdot (x^6)^4$ ⟵ $-2x^6$ is the product of -2 and x^6. Use the power of a product rule.

$\qquad = 16 \cdot (x^6)^4$

$\qquad = 16 \cdot x^{(6 \cdot 4)}$ ⟵ $(x^6)^4$ is the fourth power of x^6. Use the power of a power rule.

$\qquad = 16x^{24}$

b. $(4b^{-5})^{-3} = 4^{-3} \cdot (b^{-5})^{-3}$ ⟵ $4b^{-5}$ is the product of 4 and b^{-5}. Use the power of a product rule.

$\qquad = \dfrac{1}{4^3} \cdot b^{(-5)(-3)}$ ⟵ Rewrite 4^{-3} with a positive exponent. Use the power of a power rule.

$\qquad = \dfrac{b^{15}}{64}$

c. $\left(\dfrac{3y}{-2z}\right)^2 = \dfrac{(3y)^2}{(-2z)^2}$ ⟵ Use the power of a quotient rule.

$\qquad = \dfrac{3^2 \cdot y^2}{(-2)^2 \cdot z^2}$ ⟵ Use the power of a product rule.

$\qquad = \dfrac{9y^2}{4z^2}$

Talk it Over

15. You know that $\sqrt{3} \cdot \sqrt{3} = 3$. Use the product of powers rule to show that $3^{1/2} \cdot 3^{1/2} = 3$.

16. Use the power of a power rule to show that $(x^{1/3})^3 = x$. How does this support the definition of $x^{1/3}$ as the cube root of x?

······► Now you are ready for:
Exs. 32–55 on pp. 518–519

Look Back ◄

Describe each rule of exponents in your own words. Give an example for each rule.

9-2 Exercises and Problems

1. **Reading** Which rule of exponents involves adding exponents? subtracting exponents?

Simplify. Write each answer without negative exponents.

2. $y^2 \cdot y^5 \cdot y^{-3}$

3. $x^{-6} \cdot x^2 \cdot t^3$

4. $x^{1/2} \cdot x^{1/2} \cdot x^2$

5. $(3t^4)(9t^0)$

6. $(5r^2)(-4r^{-3})$

7. $(8b^3)(2ab)(a^{-2})$

8. $\dfrac{m^6n^4}{mn^3}$

9. $\dfrac{d^{12}d^4}{d^8}$

10. $\dfrac{45u}{9u^5}$

11. $\dfrac{6a^{10}}{8a^2}$

12. $\dfrac{9jk^{12}}{3j^4k^2}$

13. $\dfrac{3x^8y^2}{x^2x^5}$

Simplify each pair of expressions. Compare the results.

14. $4^{(2+3)}$ and $4^2 + 4^3$

15. $2^{(3 \cdot 2)}$ and $2^3 \cdot 2^2$

16. $(5 \cdot 2)^3$ and $5 \cdot 2^3$

17. $(6-4)^2$ and $6^2 - 4^2$

18. 3^{-2} and $-(3^2)$

19. $\left(\dfrac{3}{4}\right)^2$ and $\dfrac{3^2}{4}$

20. **a.** Ferhan rewrote the product $(x+4)(x-2)(x+1)$ in expanded form. Explain each step of her solution.

b. Write the product $(y+2)(y-3)(y-5)$ in expanded form.

c. Use either Ferhan's method or the binomial theorem and Pascal's triangle to write $(z-4)^3$ in expanded form.

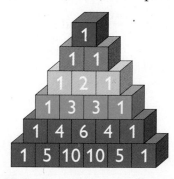

Ferhan G.

$(x+4)(x-2)(x+1)=[x\cdot x-2\cdot x+4\cdot x+4(-2)](x+1)$
$= (x^2-2x+4x-8)(x+1)$
$= (x^2+2x-8)(x+1)$
$= x^2\cdot x+x^2\cdot 1+2x\cdot x+2x\cdot 1-8\cdot x-8\cdot 1$
$= x^3+x^2+2x^2+2x-8x-8$
$= x^3+3x^2-6x-8$

Complete.

21. $8a^5 = 4a^2 \cdot \underline{\ ?\ }$

22. $18x^{15} = 3x^7 \cdot \underline{\ ?\ }$

23. $2a^6 = 2a \cdot \underline{\ ?\ }$

Factor completely.

24. $4x^5 - 2x^4 + 16x^2$

25. $x^4 - 2x^3 - 15x^2$

26. $6x^7 - 28x^6 + 16x^5$

27. $9p^3q + 15p^2$

28. $48u^5v^5 - 60u^3v^6w$

29. $49x^3y - 35x^2y^5$

Volleyball In the sport of volleyball, a ball is hit over a net into another team's court. The receiving team may hit the ball no more than three times before the ball is hit back to the other team's court. The ball cannot be hit by the same player twice in a row.

30. Derek hits a volleyball almost straight up. The equation $h = 32t - 16t^2$ models the height of the ball, in feet, t seconds after he hits it. How many seconds does his teammate have to hit the ball before it hits the ground?

31. Julie dives for a volleyball and hits it toward the net. The equation $h = 24t - 16t^2$ models the height of the ball, in feet, t seconds after she hits it.

    a. Write the equation in factored form. (Make sure it is completely factored.)

    b. Suppose nothing blocks the ball's path. After how many seconds will the ball hit the ground?

    c. The top of the net is about 8 ft from the ground. Suppose Julie's shot reaches the net one second after she hits it. Does the ball go over the net?

Simplify. Write each answer without negative exponents.

32. $(2y^{-5})^4$

33. $(8k^6)^{1/3}$

34. $(m^8)(m^{-2})^4$

35. $(8y^3)(2y^2)^{-1}$

36. $(a^2b)^3$

37. $(2n^3p^5)^3$

38. $\left(\dfrac{5}{x^2}\right)^3$

39. $\left(\dfrac{d^3}{c^4}\right)^2$

40. $\left(\dfrac{a^{-2}}{b^{-3}}\right)^{-1}$

41. $\left(\dfrac{6s^2}{4t^6}\right)^2$

42. $\dfrac{x^{-2}y^{-3}}{x^5y^{-4}}$

43. $\left(\dfrac{rs^{-5}}{s^{-7}}\right)^{-2}$

Simplify each pair of expressions. Compare the results.

44. $(3x)^2$ and $3x^2$

45. $(-5x^7)^2$ and $-5(x^7)^2$

46. $\dfrac{(-6a)^2}{3}$ and $\dfrac{-(6a^2)}{3}$

47. **Writing** Explain why it makes sense to use the fact that $\dfrac{a^3}{b^3} = \left(\dfrac{a}{b}\right)^3$ to simplify $\dfrac{12^3}{4^3}$.

Ongoing ASSESSMENT

48. **Writing** Devin wanted to understand why the expressions $1^0, 2^0, 3^0, \ldots, a^0$ are all equal to 1.

    a. Devin used the quotient of powers rule to show that $3^0 = 1$. Explain how his work helped him understand that $3^0 = 1$.

    b. Does Devin's method work for bases other than 3? Explain why or why not.

Devin

$3^4 \div 3^4 = 3^{4-4} = 3^0$

49. a. Write an equation to show how the measures in the
   diagram are related. *(Section 9-1)*

   b. Is your equation from part (a) a rational equation?

Solve each proportion. *(Toolbox Skill 17)*

50. $\dfrac{x}{8} = \dfrac{3}{4}$

51. $\dfrac{5}{y} = \dfrac{12}{31}$

52. $\dfrac{4.1}{8.2} = \dfrac{7}{t}$

53. $\dfrac{2}{3} = \dfrac{x+1}{9}$

54. Solve the quadratic equation $x^2 + x - 6 = 0$ by factoring. *(Section 4-4)*

Working on the Unit Project

**As you complete Exercise 55, think about how the weather, land, trees, and
buildings where you live might affect the power output from a wind machine
installed there.**

If you need to produce more power from a wind machine, you can install it
higher up, where the wind speed is greater. The physical features of the
region determine how much greater the wind speed is at greater heights.

This formula shows how wind speed increases with the height above the
ground. The diagram below contains values of *g*.

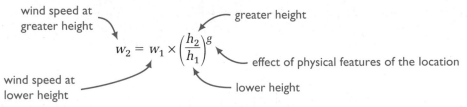

wind speed at greater height — greater height

$$w_2 = w_1 \times \left(\dfrac{h_2}{h_1}\right)^g$$

effect of physical features of the location

wind speed at lower height — lower height

55. Kaylie lives in a wooded area. She measures a wind speed of 10 mi/h at a
   height of 10 ft above the ground. What is the wind speed at the same location 50 ft above the ground?

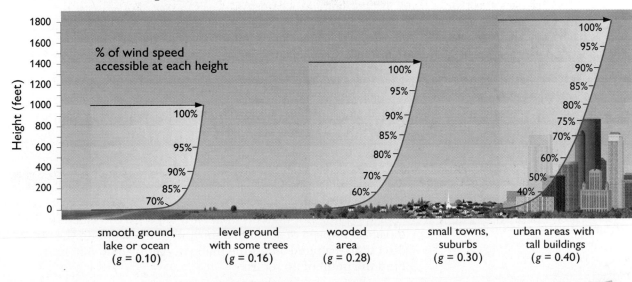

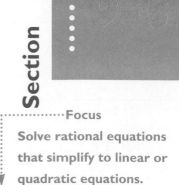

Solving Rational Equations

Against the Wind

Focus
Solve rational equations
that simplify to linear or
quadratic equations.

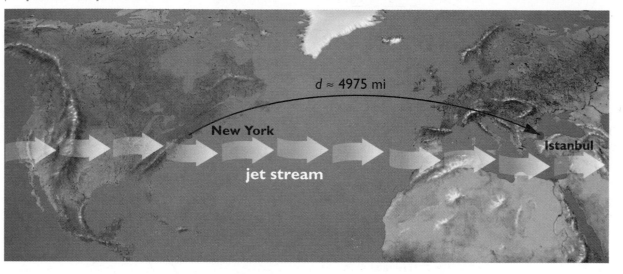

$d \approx 4975$ mi

New York

Istanbul

jet stream

A pilot flying over the ocean may need to know the *point of no return* in an emergency. This is the point where it would take the pilot as much time to return to the starting point as to continue on to the destination. Wind affects the point of no return.

BY THE WAY...

A jet stream is a strong wind current that occurs at higher altitudes. Jet streams move from west to east everywhere except for a region around part of the equator. There the jet stream moves from east to west.

Talk it Over

1. Rose takes a flight from New York City to Istanbul, Turkey. Tashiki takes a flight from Istanbul to New York City. Whose flight is faster? Why?

2. How many miles has the plane traveled when it is half way between the two cities?

3. Do you think the halfway point is the point of no return? Why or why not?

Sample 1

A plane flying the 4975 mi from New York City to Istanbul travels at a speed of about 675 mi/h with the wind. In the other direction, the wind slows the plane down to about 525 mi/h. Find the point of no return.

Sample Response

Problem Solving Strategy: Use a formula.

The point of no return occurs where the time to fly back to New York City is equal to the time to fly on to Istanbul. Use this formula: $\text{time} = \dfrac{\text{distance}}{\text{rate}}$.

$$\underbrace{\text{time needed to fly back to New York City}}_{} = \underbrace{\text{time needed to continue on to Istanbul}}_{}$$

distance from starting point ⟶
rate to fly back ⟶ $\quad \dfrac{d}{525} = \dfrac{4975 - d}{675} \quad$ ⟵ distance left to fly after d miles
⟵ rate to fly to destination

$$675d = 525(4975 - d) \quad \longleftarrow \text{ Use cross products.}$$

$$675d = 2{,}611{,}875 - 525d \quad \longleftarrow \text{ Use the distributive property.}$$

$$1200d = 2{,}611{,}875$$

$$d \approx 2177$$

The point of no return is about 2177 mi from the starting point.

Sample 2

Solve the equation $\dfrac{1}{x - 4} = \dfrac{2}{x^2 - 16}$.

Sample Response

$$\frac{1}{x - 4} = \frac{2}{x^2 - 16}$$

$$x^2 - 16 = 2(x - 4) \quad \longleftarrow \text{ Use cross products.}$$

$$x^2 - 16 = 2x - 8 \quad \longleftarrow \text{ Use the distributive property.}$$

$$x^2 - 2x - 8 = 0 \quad \longleftarrow \text{ Write the equation in standard form.}$$

$$(x + 2)(x - 4) = 0 \quad \longleftarrow \text{ Factor.}$$

$$x + 2 = 0 \quad or \quad x - 4 = 0 \quad \longleftarrow \text{ Use the zero-product property.}$$

$$x = -2 \qquad\qquad x = 4$$

Check Substitute the results in the original equation.

$$\frac{1}{-2 - 4} \overset{?}{=} \frac{2}{(-2)^2 - 16} \quad \longleftarrow \begin{array}{l}\text{Substitute } -2 \\ \text{for } x.\end{array}$$

$$\frac{1}{-6} \overset{?}{=} \frac{2}{-12}$$

$$\frac{1}{-6} = \frac{1}{-6} \checkmark \quad \longleftarrow \begin{array}{l}\text{This is a valid statement.} \\ -2 \text{ is a solution.}\end{array}$$

The solution is -2.

$$\frac{1}{4 - 4} \overset{?}{=} \frac{2}{4^2 - 16} \quad \longleftarrow \begin{array}{l}\text{Substitute } 4 \\ \text{for } x.\end{array}$$

$$\frac{1}{0} = \frac{2}{0} \quad \longleftarrow \begin{array}{l}\text{Division by zero is undefined.} \\ 4 \text{ is not a solution.}\end{array}$$

When a solution is not a solution of the original equation, it is called an **extraneous solution**.

·····▶ Now you are ready for:
Exs. 1–10 on p. 524

Using Common Multiples

Some rational equations cannot be solved using cross products. You need to eliminate the denominators. You can do this by multiplying both sides of the equation by a *common multiple* of the denominators.

Sample 3

Solve.

a. $\dfrac{3}{5} + \dfrac{4}{x - 3} = 7$

b. $\dfrac{d}{d + 2} + \dfrac{2}{d - 2} = \dfrac{d + 6}{(d - 2)(d + 2)}$

Sample Response

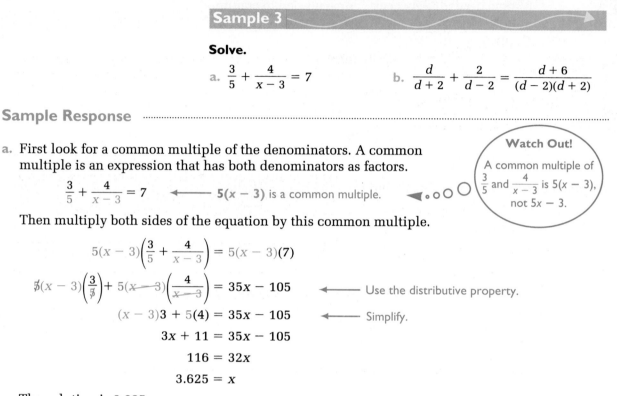

a. First look for a common multiple of the denominators. A common multiple is an expression that has both denominators as factors.

$\dfrac{3}{5} + \dfrac{4}{x - 3} = 7$ ⟵ $5(x - 3)$ is a common multiple. ◄•○○○

Watch Out!
A common multiple of $\dfrac{3}{5}$ and $\dfrac{4}{x - 3}$ is $5(x - 3)$, not $5x - 3$.

Then multiply both sides of the equation by this common multiple.

$$5(x - 3)\left(\dfrac{3}{5} + \dfrac{4}{x - 3}\right) = 5(x - 3)(7)$$

$$\cancel{5}(x - 3)\left(\dfrac{3}{\cancel{5}}\right) + 5(\cancel{x - 3})\left(\dfrac{4}{\cancel{x - 3}}\right) = 35x - 105 \quad \longleftarrow \text{Use the distributive property.}$$

$$(x - 3)3 + 5(4) = 35x - 105 \quad \longleftarrow \text{Simplify.}$$

$$3x + 11 = 35x - 105$$

$$116 = 32x$$

$$3.625 = x$$

The solution is 3.625.

b. Multiply both sides of the equation by a common multiple of the denominators: $(d - 2)(d + 2)$.

$$(d - 2)(d + 2)\left(\dfrac{d}{d + 2} + \dfrac{2}{d - 2}\right) = (d - 2)(d + 2)\left(\dfrac{d + 6}{(d - 2)(d + 2)}\right)$$

$$(d - 2)(\cancel{d + 2})\left(\dfrac{d}{\cancel{d + 2}}\right) + (\cancel{d - 2})(d + 2)\left(\dfrac{2}{\cancel{d - 2}}\right) = d + 6 \quad \longleftarrow \text{Use the distributive property.}$$

$$(d - 2)d + (d + 2)2 = d + 6 \quad \longleftarrow \text{Simplify.}$$

$$d^2 - 2d + 2d + 4 = d + 6$$

$$d^2 - d - 2 = 0$$

$$(d - 2)(d + 1) = 0 \quad \longleftarrow \text{Factor. Then use the zero-product property.}$$

$$d - 2 = 0 \quad \text{or} \quad d + 1 = 0$$

$$d = 2 \qquad\qquad d = -1$$

Watch Out!
Check both possible solutions. One solution may be extraneous. ○○○•►

The solution is −1.

Unit 9 Polynomial and Rational Functions

Talk it Over

4. In Sample 3, part (b), why is 2 an extraneous solution?
5. What is a common multiple of the denominators in
   the equation $4 + \dfrac{3}{y+2} = 5$?

Sample 4

Emily Johns has only six hours to make a pamphlet with eight pages of text and two pages of graphics. She knows her rate for producing graphics pages is one page per hour slower than her rate for producing text pages. At what rate will she need to make text pages?

Sample Response

Problem Solving Strategy: Use a table.

Let x = the rate in pages per hour for making text pages.

	Number of Pages	Rate (pages/hour)	Time (hours)
Text	8	x	$\dfrac{8}{x}$
Graphics	2	$x - 1$	$\dfrac{2}{x-1}$

Model the situation with an equation.

$$
\begin{array}{ccccc}
\text{time for making} & & \text{time for making} & & \text{total time for making} \\
\text{text pages} & + & \text{graphics pages} & = & \text{the pamphlet} \\
\dfrac{8}{x} & + & \dfrac{2}{x-1} & = & 6
\end{array}
$$

$$\text{time} = \frac{\text{number of pages}}{\text{rate}}$$

Multiply both sides of the equation by a common multiple of the denominators.

$$x(x-1)\left(\frac{8}{x} + \frac{2}{x-1}\right) = x(x-1)(6)$$

$$x(x-1)\left(\frac{8}{x}\right) + x(x-1)\left(\frac{2}{x-1}\right) = 6x^2 - 6x \qquad \longleftarrow \text{Use the distributive property.}$$

$$(x-1)8 + 2x = 6x^2 - 6x \qquad \longleftarrow \text{Simplify.}$$

$$8x - 8 + 2x = 6x^2 - 6x$$

$$0 = 6x^2 - 16x + 8$$

$$0 = 2(3x - 2)(x - 2) \qquad \longleftarrow \text{Factor.}$$

$$3x - 2 = 0 \quad or \quad x - 2 = 0 \qquad \longleftarrow \text{Use the zero-product property.}$$

$$x = \frac{2}{3} \qquad\qquad\quad x = 2$$

The solution $x = \dfrac{2}{3}$ makes no sense in this situation because it gives a negative pages/hour rate for making graphics pages. Emily Johns must make text pages at a rate of 2 pages/hour.

⋯⋯▶ Now you are ready for:
⋮ Exs. 11–38 on pp. 524–526

Look Back ◀────

Give two reasons why a solution of an equation may not be a solution of the original problem.

9-3 Exercises and Problems

1. **Reading** Why is one of the solutions in Sample 2 an extraneous solution?

Solve.

2. $\dfrac{12 - x}{4x} = \dfrac{1}{12}$

3. $\dfrac{1}{x} = \dfrac{4}{x - 2}$

4. $\dfrac{3}{y + 1} = \dfrac{y}{2}$

5. $\dfrac{2a + 5}{a - 1} = \dfrac{3a}{a - 1}$

6. $\dfrac{2}{c(c - 2)} = \dfrac{1}{c - 2}$

7. $\dfrac{3}{2x - 2} = \dfrac{2x - 1}{x}$

For Exercises 8–10, use the map.

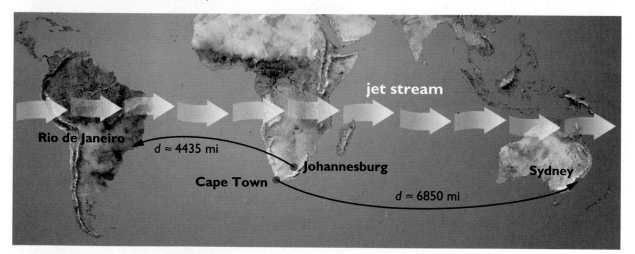

jet stream

Rio de Janeiro

$d \approx 4435$ mi

Johannesburg

Cape Town

$d \approx 6850$ mi

Sydney

8. A plane flying from Johannesburg, South Africa, to Rio de Janeiro, Brazil, travels at a speed of about 550 mi/h. In the other direction, the wind increases the plane's speed to 650 mi/h. Find the point of no return.

9. A plane is flying from Cape Town, South Africa, to Sydney, Australia. According to the cockpit readings, its speed relative to the ground is about 590 mi/h.

   a. The plane's speed is increased by a 45 mi/h wind. How fast is the plane really going?

   b. Suppose the plane has to fly back to Cape Town. Its speed is decreased by the 45 mi/h wind. What is its actual return speed?

10. Use the facts in Exercise 9. Find the point of no return for the flight to Sydney.

Solve.

11. $2 + \dfrac{3}{x} = x$

12. $\dfrac{1}{3} + \dfrac{1}{a} = 2a$

13. $\dfrac{6}{t} - \dfrac{2}{t - 1} = 1$

14. $\dfrac{x - 1}{x} + \dfrac{9}{4x} = 6$

15. $\dfrac{x}{x - 2} + \dfrac{30}{x + 2} = 9$

16. $\dfrac{1}{x + 1} - \dfrac{1}{x + 2} = \dfrac{1}{2}$

17. Reading In Sample 4, why is $x = \frac{2}{3}$ not a solution of the problem?

18. It takes Paul Lien five hours to type ten pages of text and create five pages of graphics. His rate for typing text pages is two pages per hour faster than his rate for creating graphics pages.

  a. How many text pages can Paul type in one hour?

  b. About how long does it take Paul to type one text page?

Find the unknown dimensions.

19.

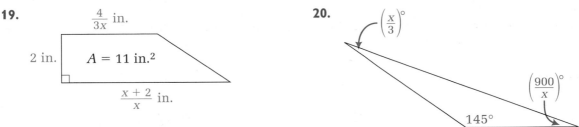

$\frac{4}{3x}$ in.

2 in. $A = 11$ in.^{2}

$\frac{x + 2}{x}$ in.

20.

$\left(\frac{x}{3}\right)^{\circ}$

$\left(\frac{900}{x}\right)^{\circ}$

145°

21. Jane can mow the lawn in 50 min. When she and her brother, Mike, work together, they can finish in 30 min. How long does it take Mike when he works alone?

Fuel Efficiency Use the information below for Exercises 22 and 23.

The yearly cost of fueling your car can be modeled by this equation:

$$\text{yearly fuel cost} = \frac{\text{distance traveled} \times \text{price per gallon}}{\text{car's fuel efficiency rate}}$$

22. Alice Volk drives about 10,000 mi each year. She pays an average of $1.15 per gallon of gasoline. Her yearly fuel cost is about $800. What is her car's fuel efficiency rate in miles per gallon?

23. Rob Scudder drives about 18,000 miles each year. He pays an average of $1.10 per gallon of gasoline. Rob wants to buy a new car with a better fuel efficiency rate.

  a. Write an expression to represent Rob's current yearly fuel cost.

  b. The new car Rob wants to buy travels eight more miles per gallon than his old car. Write an expression to represent his yearly fuel cost for the new car.

  c. Suppose Rob saves $400 in yearly fuel cost by buying the new car. Write and solve an equation to find the fuel efficiency rate for his old car and for his new car.

24. A marathon runner decides that any rate faster than 0.20 miles per minute can be maintained for only half of a 26.2 mile race.

Suppose the second half of a race will be run at 0.20 miles per minute. How fast does the runner need to run the first half to complete the race in under 2.5 hours?

25. **Open-ended** Determine the distance from your home to school. Assume you can walk at an average rate of four miles per hour. How much do you have to increase your speed so that it takes you one minute less time to walk to school?

Review **PREVIEW**

Simplify. Write each answer without negative exponents. *(Section 9-2)*

26. $(mn^2)^3$

27. $5\left(\dfrac{a}{b}\right)^{-3}$

28. $\left(\dfrac{x^2 y^3}{x^{-4}}\right)^2$

Find the measure of each unknown side in each figure. *(Section 8-8)*

29.

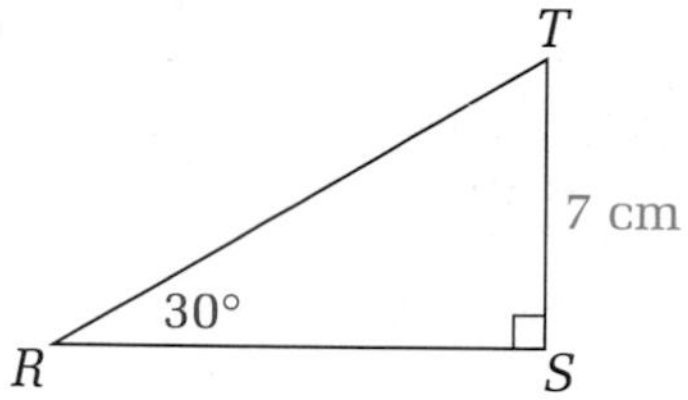

30.

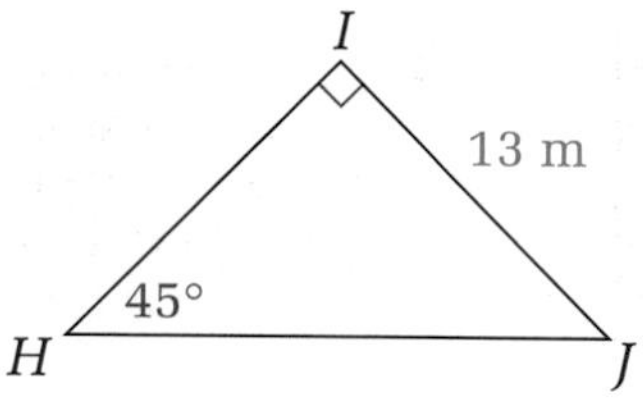

31.

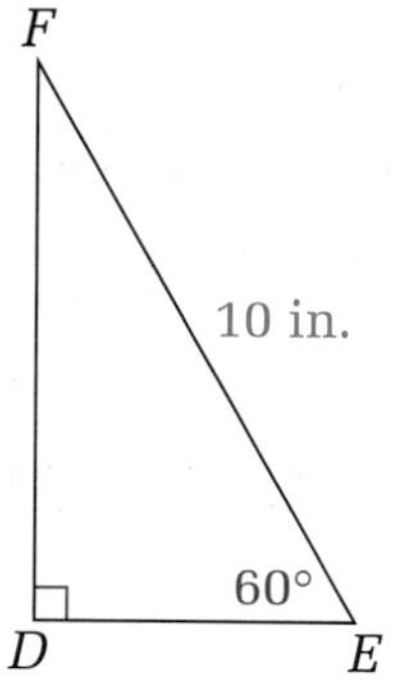

Graph each function. Find the x-intercepts. *(Section 4-1)*

32. $y = x^2 - 9$

33. $y = (x + 7)^2$

34. $y = x^2$

Working on the Unit Project

35. **Research** Look up the definitions of the words *power* and *energy*. Describe how they are related to one another. Can you have power without energy? Can you have energy without power?

36. **Research** Look up the definitions of *watt* and *kilowatt-hour*. Tell whether each is a unit of power or of energy.

37. **Research** Sometimes power is measured in *horsepower* (hp). What does 1 hp represent? How is horsepower related to watts?

38. Suppose an appliance has a power rating of P watts (W) and it uses E watt-hours (W · h) of electricity. The equation $P = \dfrac{E}{t}$ can be used to find the number of hours, t, that the appliance can operate. How long would a 2000 W air conditioner operate if it uses 150 W · h of electricity?

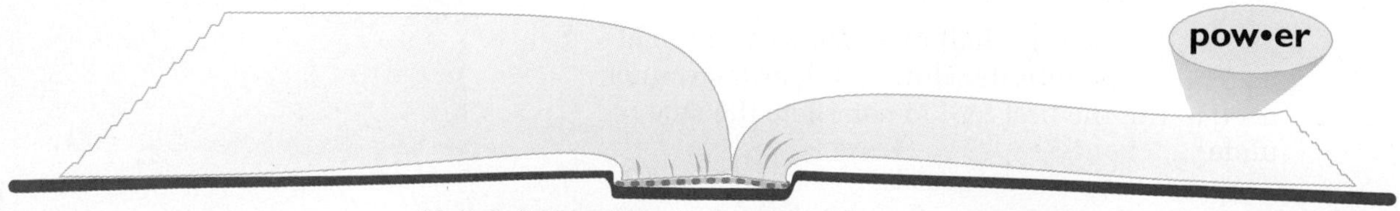

pow•er

1. **Writing** Explain what part exponents play in deciding whether or not an equation is a polynomial equation.

Estimated budget for buying a home		
	A	**B**
1	**Down Payment**	18,000
2	**Realtor's Fee**	6,000
3	**Appraisal**	250
4	**Credit Report**	50
5	**Escrow Waiver Fee**	125
6	**Settlement Fees**	200
7	**Underwriter Fee**	50
8	**Document Preparation**	100
9	**Title Insurance**	200
10	**Deed and Mortgage**	25
11	**Total**	25,000

2. Susan Duclos is planning to buy a house three years from now. She estimates she will need about $25,000 to cover a down payment and other costs. She deposits $7000 at the end of each year for three years. **9-1**

   a. Write an expression for the amount of money she will have at the end of the third year.

   b. Susan wonders what yearly growth rate she must get to meet her goal. Write an equation to model the situation.

Tell whether each expression is a polynomial. Write *Yes* or *No*. Give a reason for your answer.

3. $5x^2 - 3x - 7$

4. $3x^{1/2} - x - \frac{1}{4}$

5. $\frac{1}{2}x^3 + x$

6. $\frac{x - 1}{x^2 + 2}$

Simplify. Write each answer without negative exponents. **9-2**

7. $(yz^2)(y^{-3}z)$

8. $(m^2n^{-4})^3$

9. $(-10a^{-3})(5a^2)^{-1}$

10. $\frac{d^{-3}d^7}{d^{-1}d^9}$

11. $\left(\frac{8f^3}{2f^8}\right)^2$

12. $\frac{1}{2}\left(\frac{pq}{q^{-2}}\right)^3$

Solve. **9-3**

13. $\frac{2}{s + 3} - \frac{1}{s - 3} = 1$

14. $\frac{26}{r - 1} - \frac{26}{r} = 13$

15. Several members of a hiking club contributed equally to raise $60 to pay for a club picnic. When two members were unable to go, their money was refunded and the remaining members had to pay an extra dollar each. How many members went on the hike?

Graphing Cubic Functions

The **Third Degree**

------Focus

Analyze graphs of
polynomial functions
written in factored form.

TECHNOLOGY NOTE

Be sure to set an
appropriate window on your graphics calculator, especially when graphing cubic functions. You may miss
some characteristics of a graph if the
window is not set correctly. ◀

EXPLORATION

What does the graph of a polynomial function
of degree three look like?

• **Materials: graphics calculators or graphing software**

• **Work with another student.**

(1) Graph each quadratic function. What are the x-intercepts
of each graph? How can you use the factored form of the
function to predict the number of x-intercepts?

   a. $y = x^2$ **b.** $y = (x + 3)^2$ **c.** $y = (x + 3)(x - 1)$

(2) Graph each function listed below on a graphics calculator
or using graphing software. Make a sketch of each graph.
Record the number of x-intercepts for each graph. List the
x-intercepts.

Function	Graph	X-intercepts	Number of X-intercepts
$y = x^3$		0	1
$y = (x+2)^3$			
$y = (x-3)(x+1)^2$			
$y = (x-3)^2(x+1)$			
$y = x(x-3)(x+2)$			
$y = (x+2)(x-1)(x-4)$			

(3) If you write each function in the table in expanded form,
you get a polynomial of degree 3. A polynomial function
of degree 3 is called a **cubic function.**

Look for patterns in your table. How can you use the
factored form of a cubic function to predict the number
of x-intercepts? the behavior of the graph?

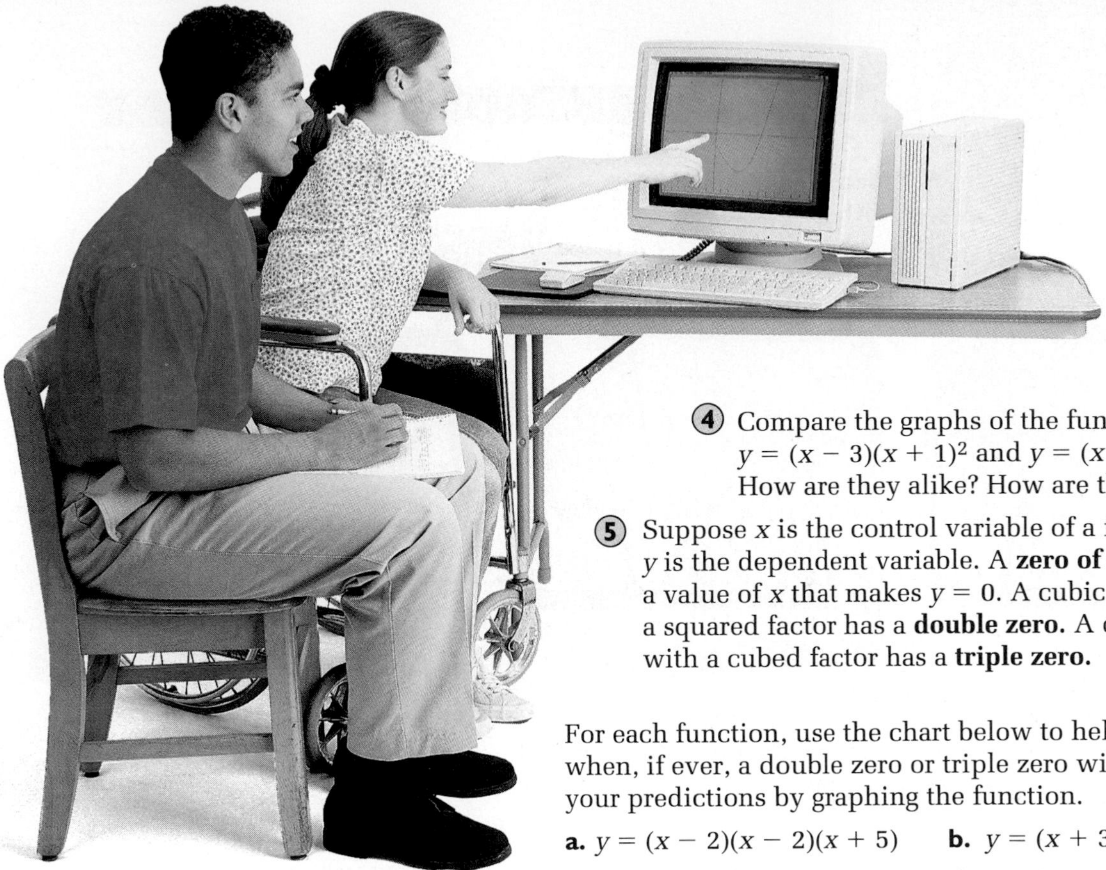

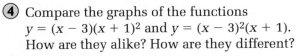

④ Compare the graphs of the functions
$y = (x - 3)(x + 1)^2$ and $y = (x - 3)^2(x + 1)$.
How are they alike? How are they different?

⑤ Suppose x is the control variable of a function and
y is the dependent variable. A **zero of a function** is
a value of x that makes $y = 0$. A cubic function with
a squared factor has a **double zero.** A cubic function
with a cubed factor has a **triple zero.**

For each function, use the chart below to help you predict
when, if ever, a double zero or triple zero will occur. Test
your predictions by graphing the function.

a. $y = (x - 2)(x - 2)(x + 5)$ **b.** $y = (x + 3)^3$

c. $y = (x + 1)^2(x - 2)$ **d.** $y = (x + 4)(x - 1)(x + 3)$

e. $y = (x + 1)(x - 5)^2$ **f.** $y = (x - 5)^3$

X Lab

GRAPHS OF CUBIC FUNCTIONS

Function	$y = (x - 2)^3$	$y = (x - 2)^2(x + 1)$	$y = (x - 2)(x + 1)(x + 4)$
Number of x-intercepts	1	2	3
x-intercepts	2	2, −1	2, −1, −4
Zeros	2 is a triple zero.	−1 and 2 are zeros. 2 is a double zero.	2, −1, and −4 are zeros.
Graph	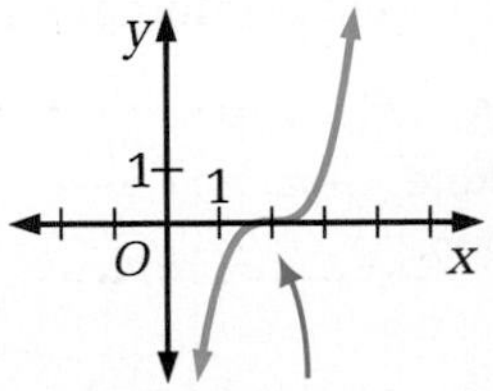 The graph flattens out and crosses the x-axis when $x = 2$ only.	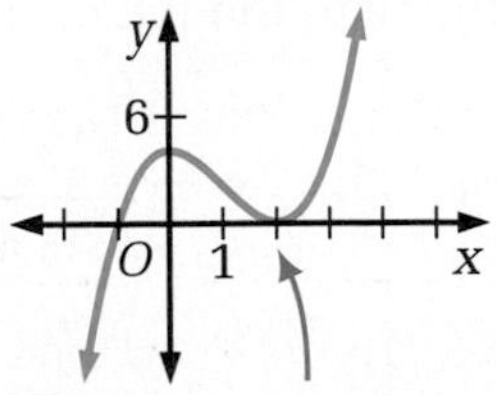 The graph touches the x-axis at two points but does not cross it when $x = 2$.	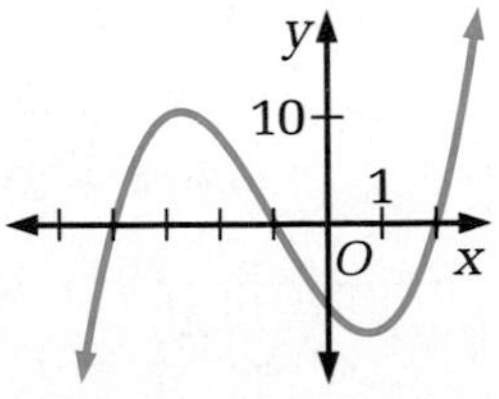 There are no multiple zeros, so the graph crosses the x-axis at three different points.

···▶ **Now you are ready for:**
Exs. 1–16 on p. 532

Match each function with its graph.

a. $y = (x - 2)^2(x + 3)$

b. $y = -(x - 2)^2(x + 3)$

c. $y = (x - 2)(x + 3)^2$

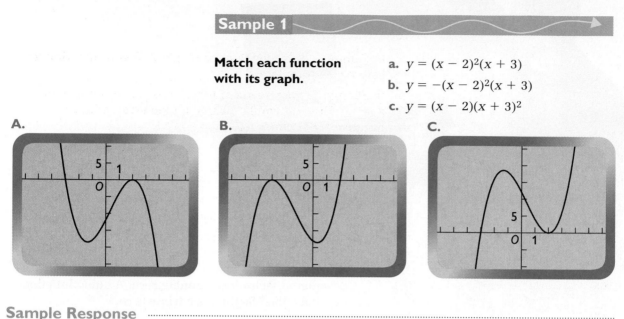

A. **B.** **C.**

Sample Response

Problem Solving Strategy: Break the problem into parts.

Step 1 Find the x-intercepts of the graph of each function.

a. $0 = (x - 2)^2(x + 3)$ **b.** $0 = -(x - 2)^2(x + 3)$ **c.** $0 = (x - 2)(x + 3)^2$

    2 and -3 2 and -3 2 and -3

In this case, all three functions cross the x-axis at $x = 2$ and at $x = -3$.

Step 2 Find any double or triple zeros.

All three functions have a squared factor, so all three functions have a double zero.

a. $0 = (x - 2)^2(x + 3)$ **b.** $0 = -(x - 2)^2(x + 3)$ **c.** $0 = (x - 2)(x + 3)^2$

    2 is a double zero.   2 is a double zero. -3 is a double zero.

The only graph that has a double zero of -3 is B.
Graph B matches function (c).

Step 3 Decide if the graph of the function starts above or below the x-axis.
Choose an x-coordinate to the left of the smallest x-intercept as a test point.

a. $y = (x - 2)^2(x + 3)$

    $= (-4 - 2)^2(-4 + 3)$ ⟵ The smallest x-intercept is -3. Substitute -4 for x in ⟶ each function.

    $= -36$

b. $y = -(x - 2)^2(x + 3)$

    $= -(-4 - 2)^2(-4 + 3)$

    $= 36$

The y-value of function (a) is negative. The graph starts below the x-axis.

Graph C matches function (a).

The y-value of function (b) is positive. The graph starts above the x-axis.

Graph A matches function (b).

1. In Sample 1, why can you match graph B with function (c) before you complete step 3?

2. In Sample 1, the *y*-value of function (a) is negative when $x = -4$. How do you know that all the *y*-values are negative for *x*-values less than -3?

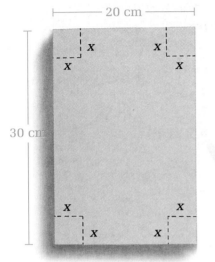

Sample 2

A box can be made from a rectangular piece of cardboard by cutting a square off of each corner. About how much should be cut off of each corner of the cardboard shown to make a box with the largest volume?

Sample Response

Problem Solving Strategy: Use a graph.

Let $x =$ the length of the square that is cut off of each corner. Write a function for the volume of the box in terms of *x*.

$$V = x(30 - 2x)(20 - 2x)$$ ◄───── Volume = length × width × height

Graph the function.

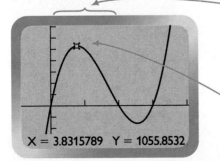

X = 3.8315789   Y = 1055.8532

You can only cut between 0 and 10 cm off of any corner. Trace the graph across this domain.

The maximum *y*-value represents the largest volume. It occurs when $x \approx 3.8$.

Cut a square about 3.8 cm × 3.8 cm off of each corner of the cardboard.

Look Back

What does the factored form of a cubic function tell you about its graph? What information do you need to find before you can sketch the graph of a function in factored form?

····► Now you are ready for:
Exs. 17–44 on pp. 532–535

Exercises and Problems

1. **Reading** How could you verify that the functions listed in the Exploration are cubic functions? Give an example of a cubic function that is not written in factored form.

For Exercises 2–10:

a. **Tell how many times the graph of each function intersects the x-axis.**

b. **List the x-intercepts.**

c. **List the zeros of the function. Tell which, if any, are double or triple zeros.**

2. $y = -x(x - 4)^2$ 3. $y = (x + 3)^3$ 4. $y = (x + 3)(x - 1)(x - 5)$

5. $y = (x + 8)^3$ 6. $y = (x + 2)(x - 3)(x + 1)$ 7. $y = (x - 1)^2(x + 4)$

8. $y = (x + 5)(x - 2)(x + 5)$ 9. $y = (x - 7)(x + 4)^2$ 10. $y = x^2(x + 2)$

Classify each function as *linear*, *quadratic*, or *cubic*.

11. $y = (x - 4)^2$ 12. $y = x^3 + 2x^2 - 3x + 1$ 13. $y = 3x - 5$

14. $y = (x + 2)(x - 3)(x + 1)$ 15. $y = -3x^2 + 8x - 2$ 16. $y = 3(x + 2)$

Match each function with its graph.

17. $y = x(x - 4)^2$ 18. $y = x^2(x - 4)$ 19. $y = (x - 1)(x + 4)^2$

20. $y = (x - 1)^2(x + 4)$ 21. $y = (x + 4)^3$ 22. $y = (x - 1)(x + 4)(x + 1)$

A.

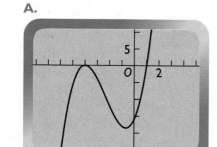

B.

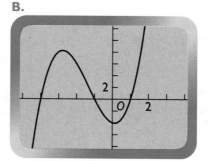

C.

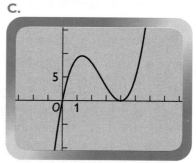

D.

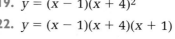

E.

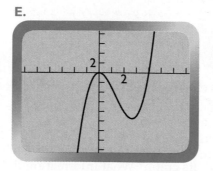

F.

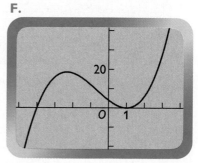

TECHNOLOGY For each function, predict the shape of its graph. Make a sketch of each prediction. Check your prediction using a graphics calculator or graphing software.

23. $y = x(x + 5)(x + 2)$ **24.** $y = (x + 3)(x - 3)^2$ **25.** $y = (x - 4)^3$

26. Michael and Kira each use a different method to determine whether the graph of $y = x(x - 3)(x + 12)$ starts above or below the x-axis.

Michael

The x-intercepts of the graph are -12, 0, and 3. The smallest x-intercept is -12.
Substitute x = -13 into the original equation.
$y = -13(-16)(-1)$
$y = -208$
The graph starts below the x-axis.

Kira

Since each factor of $y = x(x-3)(x+12)$ is negative for x-values smaller than -12, the graph starts below the x-axis.
$(\text{negative}) \times (\text{negative}) \times (\text{negative}) = $ a negative y-value.

a. Describe each person's method.

b. Which method do you think is easier? Why?

27. Group Activity Work with another student. You will need a graphics calculator.

a. Each of you should write down three numbers to represent the length, width, and height of a box. Multiply the three numbers to find the volume of the box.

b. Let w = the width of the box. Write expressions in terms of w for the length and height. Write a function in terms of w for the volume of the box.

c. Give your partner the volume you found in part (a) and the function you wrote in part (b). Graph the function you receive on a graphics calculator. What do the x-values represent? What do the y-values represent?

d. What part of your graph from part (c) applies to the volume of a box? Explain.

e. Use your graph to find the dimensions your partner wrote down in part (a). Check your answers with each other. Discuss any differences.

28 TECHNOLOGY The volume of a box is represented by the function $V = x^3 - 6x^2 + 3x + 10$, where x represents the length of the square that should be cut from each corner of a rectangular piece of cardboard to form the box.

   a. Use a graphics calculator to graph the function. Make a sketch of the graph.

   b. What are the x-intercepts of the graph?

   c. Use the graph to estimate the box's largest possible volume. What is the length of the square that should be cut from each corner to get the largest volume for the box?

29 TECHNOLOGY Use a graphics calculator or graphing software.

   a. Graph the functions $y = x^2$ and $y = x^3$. How are the graphs of the functions alike? How are they different?

   b. Graph each of the functions $y = x^4$, $y = x^5$, $y = x^6$, and $y = x^7$ on the same axes. Describe the similarities and differences among the graphs. Which ones are most alike?

   c. What do you think the graph of $y = x^{15}$ will look like? What about $y = x^{16}$? Graph the functions to check your predictions.

Ongoing **ASSESSMENT**

30. For each type of function, tell if a graph of this type can have only one x-intercept. If so, sketch a graph of that type through the x-intercept shown. If not, explain why not.

   a. linear function

   b. quadratic function

   c. cubic function

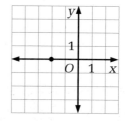

31. Repeat Exercise 30 for a graph having only the two x-intercepts shown.

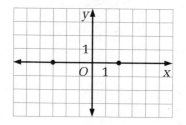

32. Repeat Exercise 30 for a graph having only the three x-intercepts shown.

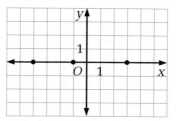

33. **Writing** How does the degree of a function relate to the number of zeros? to the possible number of x-intercepts? Explain your reasoning.

Review **PREVIEW**

Solve. *(Section 9-3)*

34. $\dfrac{5x + 2}{x + 7} = \dfrac{6x}{x + 7}$

35. $\dfrac{6}{t} - \dfrac{2}{t - 1} = 1$

36. $\dfrac{4}{x + 1} + \dfrac{1}{x - 2} = 2$

Complete each sentence so that it is a true statement. Be as specific as possible. *(Section 5-1)*

37. Every rectangle is also a _?_.   **38.** All _?_ are also rhombuses.

39. If a quadrilateral is a _?_, then it is also a kite.

Use the quadratic formula to find the solutions of each equation. *(Section 4-5)*

40. $-2x^2 + 5x + 3 = 0$ **41.** $x^2 - 3x + 3 = 0$ **42.** $6x^2 + 11x = 10$

· ·

Working on the Unit Project

Less than 60% of the wind's power can actually be converted to energy. Other factors, such as turbine design, further reduce the amount of energy produced. The equation $P = 0.25s^3$ can be used to estimate the speed of the wind, s, in miles per hour, needed to generate P watts of power for a wind machine that uses 25% of the available wind power.

43. **a.** Graph the function $P = 0.25s^3$.

  b. Explain why some portions of the graph do not apply to this situation.

  c. What values of s are reasonable for this situation?

44. Use your graph from Exercise 43 to determine the wind speed needed to operate each of these items.

  a. a radio that needs 70 watts of power

  b. a clock that needs 5 watts of power

  c. an electric oven that needs about 3200 watts of power

  d. a home heating system that needs about 12,000 watts of power

The students and faculty at the Tvind School in Denmark built one of the world's largest wind turbines. The Tvind machine provides enough power to supply the school with its electrical and heating needs.

Focus
Solve cubic equations by
various methods.

Solving Cubic Equations

Light the Way

Many public buildings have battery-operated emergency lights
that go on automatically during a power failure. There is always
a chance that an emergency light may fail to work. Because of
this, most rooms contain two or more emergency lights.

BY THE WAY...

A faulty setting at an electrical
plant near Niagara Falls has twice
resulted in a blackout of the
Northeastern United States and
Ontario, Canada. The only lights
seen in the normally bright city
skylines were from cars or
lights operating on emergency
systems.

Talk it Over

1. Let p = the probability that each emergency light will work.
   What is the probability that a light will not work?

2. In a room with three emergency lights, what is the
   probability that all three lights will not work?

3. Find the complement of the probability you wrote in question 2. What does the complement represent?

4. The reliability of a set of three emergency lights is given by
   the equation $r = 1 - (1 - p)^3$. Expand the right side of the
   equation to write a polynomial function to represent the
   reliability of the lighting system.

Suppose a building inspector requires an emergency lighting system to be 98% reliable. How reliable does each light need to be?

Sample Response

Problem Solving Strategy: Use a graph.

Use the expanded polynomial function you wrote in question 4 on page 536.

$$r = p^3 - 3p^2 + 3p$$

$$0.98 = p^3 - 3p^2 + 3p \quad \longleftarrow \text{The system needs to be 98\% reliable.}$$

$$0 = p^3 - 3p^2 + 3p - 0.98 \quad \longleftarrow \begin{array}{l}\text{Write the equation}\\ \text{in standard form.}\end{array}$$

Graph the related function $y = x^3 - 3x^2 + 3x - 0.98$.
The x-intercept tells you the value of x when y is zero.

The x-intercept is about 0.74.

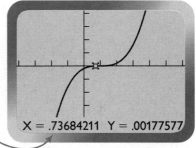

X = .73684211 Y = .00177577

Each light needs to be at least 74% reliable.

Solve $0 = p^3 - 3p^2 + 3p$.

Sample Response

$$0 = p^3 - 3p^2 + 3p$$

$$0 = p(p^2 - 3p + 3) \quad \longleftarrow \text{Factor out a } p \text{ from each term.}$$

$$p = 0 \quad or \quad p^2 - 3p + 3 = 0 \quad \longleftarrow \text{Use the zero-product property.}$$

$$p = -\frac{b}{2a} \pm \frac{\sqrt{b^2 - 4ac}}{2a} \quad \longleftarrow \text{Use the quadratic formula.}$$

$$= -\frac{(-3)}{2(1)} \pm \frac{\sqrt{(-3)^2 - 4(1)(3)}}{2(1)} \quad \longleftarrow \begin{array}{l}\text{Substitute } \mathbf{1} \text{ for } \boldsymbol{a}, -\mathbf{3} \text{ for } \boldsymbol{b},\\ \text{and } \mathbf{3} \text{ for } \boldsymbol{c}.\end{array}$$

$$= \frac{3}{2} \pm \frac{\sqrt{-3}}{2}$$

$$= 1.5 \pm \frac{i\sqrt{3}}{2}$$

$$p \approx 1.5 + 0.87i \quad or \quad p \approx 1.5 - 0.87i$$

The solutions are 0, about $1.5 + 0.9i$, and about $1.5 - 0.9i$.

5. All coordinates in an *x-y coordinate plane* are real numbers. Suppose you solved the equation in Sample 2 by graphing. Would you find all the solutions? Why or why not?

6. How can you solve the equation $x^3 + 3x^2 + 2x = 0$ without using a graph or the quadratic formula?

Look Back

How can you tell if you can use the zero-product property to solve a cubic equation?

9-5 Exercises and Problems

1. **Reading** Explain why the zero-product property could not be used to solve the equation in Sample 1.

Solve each equation without graphing.

2. $x^3 - 5x^2 + 6x = 0$

3. $x^3 + 2x^2 + 2x = 0$

4. $(x - 1)(x + 3)(3x - 1) = 0$

5. $x^3 + 3x^2 - 4x = 0$

6. $x^3 - 4x = 0$

7. $(x + 6)(x - 2)^2 = 0$

8. **Writing** Andrew solved the equation $x^3 - x^2 - 2x = 1$. Explain what is wrong with his solution.

If possible, factor and solve each equation *without graphing*. If it is not possible, write *solve by graphing*.

9. $x^3 + x + 2 = 0$

10. $x^3 + 7x^2 + 10x = 0$

11. $x^3 + 2x^2 - 3x = 1$

12. $x^3 - 2x^2 + 4x = 0$

13. $x^4 - 2x^3 - 15x^2 = 0$

14. $x^3 + x^2 = -4$

15. The equation $r = p^3 - 3p^2 + 3p$ can be used to find the reliability of a system of three lights. Micah wants to find the reliability of each light, p, when the system is 75% reliable.

a. Write an equation in standard form to represent the situation.

b. **Writing** Micah entered $y = x^3 - 3x^2 + 3x - 0.75$ on her graphics calculator. Explain how she can use the graph of this function to estimate p when $r = 0.75$.

You've made
a serious
mistake here!
Let's talk!   *Andrew Rose*

$x^3 - x^2 - 2x = 1$
$x(x^2 - x - 2) = 1$
$x(x - 2)(x + 1) = 1$
$x = 1$ or $x - 2 = 1$ or $x + 1 = 1$
$x = 1$ or $x = 3$ or $x = 0$

Check $x = 1$:
$1^3 - 1^2 - 2(1) \stackrel{?}{=} 1$
$-2 \neq 1$

Check $x = 3$:
$3^3 - 3^2 - 6 \stackrel{?}{=} 1$
$12 \neq 1$

Check $x = 0$:
$0^3 - 0^2 - 2(0) \stackrel{?}{=} 1$
$0 \neq 1$

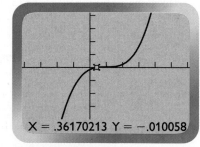

X = .36170213   Y = −.010058

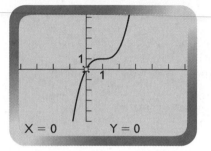

X = 0   Y = 0

16. **Writing** Rebecca tried to solve the equation in Sample 2 by using a graphics calculator. Describe the steps you think she followed.

17. In Sample 2 on page 506, Kia needs to find an investment that offers a yearly growth rate, g, so that $1000g^3 + 1000g^2 + 1000g = 3500$.

    a. Write an equation in standard form to represent the situation.

    b. Use the graph of the related function at the right to estimate g.

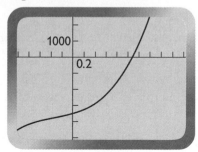

18 TECHNOLOGY The yearly profits for the Zavala family restaurant can be modeled by this equation:

$$y = -0.00135x^3 + 0.0125x^2 + 412x - 12{,}225$$

The average number of customers per month is represented by x and the profit for the year is represented by y.

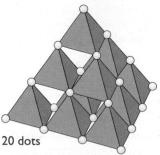

    a. About how many customers need to visit the restaurant each month in order for the restaurant to break even (profit = 0)?

    b. About how many customers does the restaurant need each month to make a $50,000 profit for the year?

19. The numbers 1, 4, 10, and 20 are called *tetrahedral numbers* because they are related to shapes called *tetrahedrons*.

1 dot

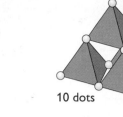

4 dots

10 dots

20 dots

    a. Count the number of dots on the base of each group of tetrahedrons. Any face can be the base. Look for a pattern. How many dots do you think there will be on the base of the fifth tetrahedron?

    b. How many dots in all do you think will be in the fifth tetrahedron?

    c. The formula $t = \frac{1}{6}n^3 + \frac{1}{2}n^2 + \frac{1}{3}n$ can be used to find the nth tetrahedral number. Use the formula to check your prediction from part (b).

    d. TECHNOLOGY Use a graphics calculator to decide if 100 is a tetrahedral number. If so, what is n?

20. **Writing** Write a note to someone who missed class explaining how to solve the equation $x^3 - x^2 - 6x = 0$. Describe two methods, one of which uses graphing.

Review **PREVIEW**

List the zeros of each cubic function. Tell which, if any, are double or triple zeros. *(Section 9-4)*

21. $y = (x + 1)(x + 3)^2$ **22.** $y = x(x - 2)(x + 3)$ **23.** $y = (x + 5)^3$

24. Is this statement a true biconditional? Explain why or why not. *(Section 7-4)*

    $(x - 1)(x + 2) = 0$ if and only if $x = 1$.

Solve each equation for t. *(Toolbox Skill 15)*

25. $x = 2(t + 2)$ **26.** $y = 2t - 4$ **27.** $x = -2(t - 1) + 16$

Working on the Unit Project

The power created by some wind turbines can be modeled by the equation
$$P = 0.2s(V - s)^2$$
where s = the blade speed in feet per second,
    V = the wind speed in feet per second, and
    P = the power in kilowatts (kW).

28. a. Copy the table. Multiply each wind speed by 1.47 to convert the units from mi/h to ft/s. Then write the equation for each wind speed. $\dfrac{5280 \text{ ft}}{3600 \text{ s}} \approx 1.47 \text{ ft/s}$

Wind speed (mi/h)	Wind speed (ft/s)	Function $P = 0.2s(V - s)^2$	Maximum Power (kW)
5	7.35	$P = 0.2s(7.35 - s)^2$	?
8	?	?	?
10	?	?	?
14	?	?	?

b. Find the zeros for each function you wrote in part (a). What do they represent in this situation?

c. Graph each function in part (a). Find the maximum amount of power this type of wind machine can generate at each speed. Complete the last column of the chart.

d. Approximate the wind speed needed for this type of wind turbine to supply all the electricity for your group's typical household.

e. Do you think this type of wind turbine is a practical alternative to buying electricity from the power company in your area? Why or why not?

This Savonius rotor has S-shaped blades that are made with split oil drums.

Parametric Equations

time travel

Focus

Graph parametric
equations to solve
problems.

EXPLORATION

Why does the path of a thrown ball look like
a parabola?

- **Materials: graphics calculators**
- **Work with another student.**

TECHNOLOGY NOTE

Choose parametric and simultaneous modes.

Use $0 \le t \le 1.2$ and increments of 0.1 for the *t*-values.

Use $0 \le x \le 7.6$ and increments of 0.8 for the *x*-values.

Use $-1.6 \le y \le 3.44$ and increments of 0.8 for the *y*-values.

1. To model tossing a ball straight up, graph $x_1 = 0.3$ and $y_1 = 6t - 4.9t^2$ on a graphics calculator. The *y*-values represent the height of the ball, in meters, *t* seconds after being tossed.

2. Trace along the graph to see the path of the ball. Record the values for *t* and *y* in a table.

3. A ball rolling along the ground moves forward at a constant speed as long as nothing slows it down. Model rolling a ball by graphing $x_2 = 0.3 + 6t$ and $y_2 = 0.1$. Trace along the graph to see the path of the ball. Record the values for *t* and *x* in a table.

4. When a ball is tossed at an angle, two things happen:
   ➤ Gravity pulls the ball toward Earth.
   ➤ The ball moves forward at a constant speed.

   Model throwing a ball at an angle by graphing $x_3 = 0.3 + 6t$ and $y_3 = 6t - 4.9t^2$. Trace along the graph to make a table of values for *t*, *x*, and *y*.

5. In step 4, the calculator graphs the path of the ball by using *t* to find *x* and *y*. To find *y* in terms of *x*, solve the equation $x = 0.3 + 6t$ for *t* and substitute your result into $y = 6t - 4.9t^2$. What kind of equation do you get?

6. Put your calculator in function mode. Graph your equation from step 5. How is this graph like the one you made in step 4? How is it different?

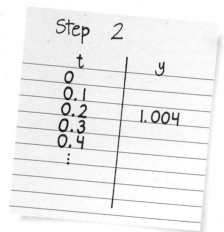

T = .2
X = .3   Y = 1.004

Step 2

t	y
0	
0.1	
0.2	1.004
0.3	
0.4	
⋮	

······► Now you are ready for:
Exs. 1–8 on pp. 544–545

The equations $x = 0.3 + 6t$ and $y = 6t - 4.9t^2$ are called **parametric equations** because both x and y are written in terms of a third value, t. The variable t is called the **parameter.**

Sample 1

Roger Wolverton is a warden pilot for the Maine Department of Fisheries and Wildlife. He stocks remote ponds with fish by flying overhead in his plane and dropping the fish into the pond. The path of the fish is modeled by these parametric equations:

$$x = 120t$$

The horizontal distance from the point of release, in meters, t seconds after the fish are released.

$$y = 80 - 4.9t^2$$

The height off the ground, in meters, t seconds after the fish are released.

a. How far from the center of the pond should the fish be released in order to land in the center?

b. Write an equation for y in terms of x.

Sample Response

a. **Method ❶**

Make a table of values for t, x, and y. Then find the horizontal distance the fish travel before they enter the water.

t	x = 120t	y = 80 − 4.9t²
0	0	80.0
1	120	75.1
2	240	60.4
3	360	35.9
4	480	1.6

At $t = 4$, the fish are only 1.6 m above the water.

Method ❷

Graph the parametric equations. Then trace to estimate the horizontal distance the fish travel before they enter the water.

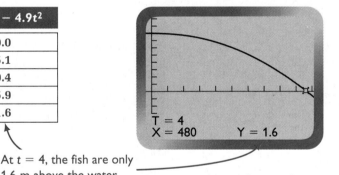

T = 4
X = 480   Y = 1.6

The fish should be released about 480 m from the center of the pond.

b. Solve $x = 120t$ for t.

$$x = 120t$$

$$\frac{x}{120} = t$$

Then substitute for t in the second equation.

$$y = 80 - 4.9t^2$$

$$y = 80 - 4.9\left(\frac{x}{120}\right)^2$$

Substitute $\frac{x}{120}$ for t in $y = 80 - 4.9t^2$.

$$y = 80 - 4.9\left(\frac{x^2}{14,400}\right)$$

Use the power of a quotient rule.

$$y = 80 - 0.00034x^2$$

During a football game, Tony held the ball on the 50 yard line while Bakham ran toward the goal line. After waiting 3 s, Tony threw the ball to Bakham.

Let x = the number of yards from the goal line
y = the number of yards from the sideline, and
t = the number of seconds that Bakham has been running.

These two equations describe Bakham's path:

$$x_1 = 42 - 6t \qquad\qquad y_1 = 45 - t \qquad\qquad 0 \le t \le 7.5$$

These two equations describe the ball's path as viewed from above:

$$x_2 = 50 - 22(t - 3) \qquad y_2 = 27 + 6(t - 3) \qquad 3 \le t \le 7.5$$

a. Graph Bakham's path.

b. Graph the ball's path as viewed from above.

c. Did Bakham catch the ball? Explain your reasoning. (Assume that the ball would have been at a reasonable height to be caught.)

Sample Response

TECHNOLOGY NOTE

The range for t is $0 \le t \le 7.5$. To graph the second pair of equations for $t \ge 3$, enter $x_2 = 50 - 22(t - 3)(t \ge 3)$, and $y_2 = 27 + 6(t - 3)(t \ge 3)$.

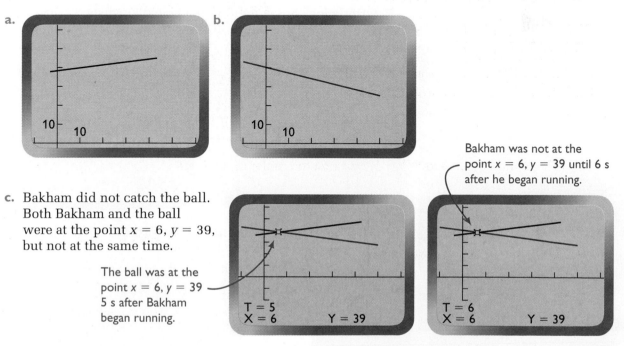

a.

b.

Bakham was not at the point $x = 6$, $y = 39$ until 6 s after he began running.

c. Bakham did not catch the ball. Both Bakham and the ball were at the point $x = 6$, $y = 39$, but not at the same time.

The ball was at the point $x = 6$, $y = 39$ 5 s after Bakham began running.

T = 5
X = 6   Y = 39

T = 6
X = 6   Y = 39

······► **Now you are ready for:**
: **Exs. 9–27 on pp. 545–548**

Look Back ◄

Explain how the path of a ball can be represented by parametric equations using three variables or by a single equation using two variables.

9-6 Exercises and Problems

1. **Reading** What is the control variable and what is the dependent variable for each equation in step 4 of the Exploration?

2. Suppose the path of a ball is described by the parametric equations $x = 7t$ and $y = 4t - 4.9t^2$. These equations are graphed below. Distance is measured in meters.

   a. How high is the ball a half second after it is released?

   b. About how long after the ball is thrown does it hit the ground?

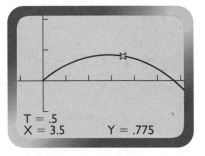

```
T = .5
X = 3.5        Y = .775
```

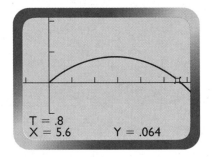

```
T = .8
X = 5.6        Y = .064
```

3. **Ornithology** Susan noticed that belted kingfishers pause in midair right before they dive into the water for fish. Susan modeled a bird's path on a calculator. Each interval is 1 m.

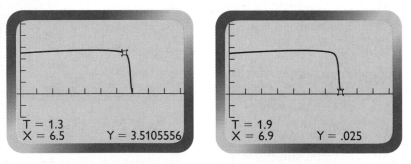

```
T = 1.3
X = 6.5        Y = 3.5105556
```

```
T = 1.9
X = 6.9        Y = .025
```

   a. According to Susan's model, how far above the water was the kingfisher when it began to dive?

   b. About how long did this bird fly before diving?

   c. When did the kingfisher enter the water?

4. **Writing** Write a note to someone who missed class. Explain what you learned from the Exploration.

For Exercises 5–7, write y in terms of x by following these steps:

a. Solve the first equation for t.

b. Substitute your answer to part (a) into the second equation and simplify.

5. $x = 4t - 3; y = 2t$

6. $x = 7t; y = 2t^2 - t + 4$

7. $x = 2 - t; y = \dfrac{t^2 - 1}{t}$

8. a. Graph the parametric equations $x = 1 - t$ and $y = t^3 - 1$.

   b. Write an equation for y in terms of x.

9. Wildlife Conservation When Roger Wolverton drops fish into ponds near mountains, he must fly at a higher altitude to avoid the trees and hills.

The path of the fish can be described by the parametric equations $x = 130t$ and $y = 150 - 4.9t^2$.

   a. How far from the center of the pond should the fish be released?

   b. About how long are the fish in the air?

10. Football In Sample 2, Tony threw a ball to Bakham.

   a. Bakham's path is described by the equations $x = 42 - 6t$ and $y = 45 - t$. How long after Bakham begins running does he cross the goal line?

   b. If Tony throws the ball at $t = 3$, the ball's path as viewed from above is described by $x = 50 - 22(t - 3)$ and $y = 27 + 6(t - 3)$. How long after Tony throws the ball does it cross the goal line?

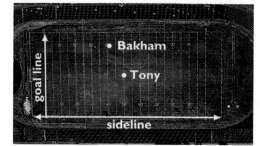

   c. How long must Tony wait before throwing the ball if he wants it to cross the goal line when Bakham does? Can Bakham catch it? Why or why not?

11. You can use the parametric equations in Sample 2 to write an equation for y in terms of x. Then Bakham's path is described by $y = 38 + \dfrac{x}{6}$ and

the ball's path as viewed from above is described by $y = \dfrac{447}{11} - \dfrac{3x}{11}$.

   a. Graph this system of equations.

   b. Can you tell from the graph whether Bakham caught the ball? Explain.

   c. What does the intersection of the lines represent?

200 ft/s

14 ft/s

12. a. Aviation Heidi Cohen is flying a small airplane at an altitude of 14,000 ft. When she begins her landing, she descends at a rate of 14 ft/s. Write an equation to model the plane's altitude t seconds after she begins her descent.

   b. Heidi is flying at a speed of 200 ft/s. She maintains this horizontal speed for most of her descent. Write an equation to describe the plane's horizontal position t seconds after she begins her descent.

   c. Graph your parametric equations from parts (a) and (b).

   d. About how far before the airport should Heidi begin her descent?

   e. Write an equation for y in terms of x.

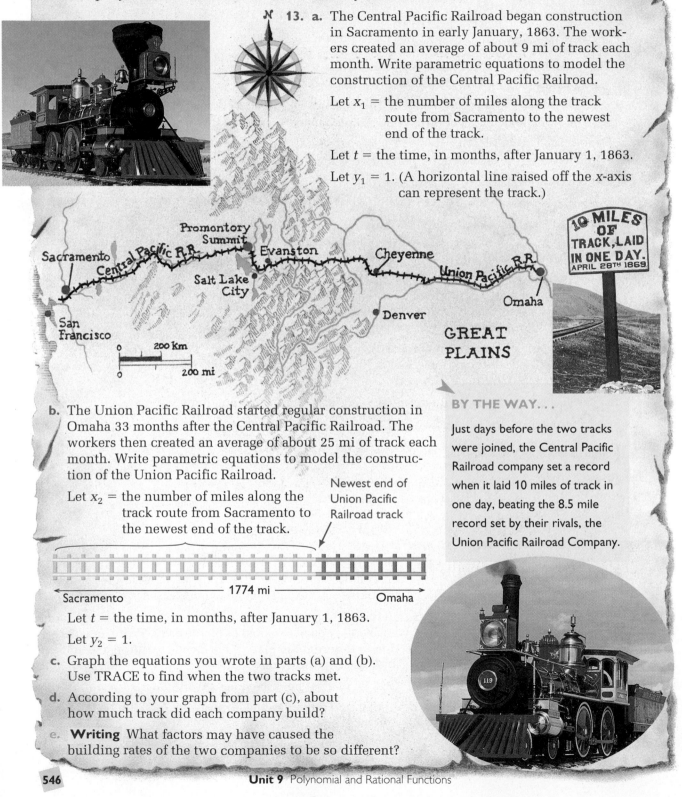

The Pacific Railroad was the first railroad to cross a continent. The Central Pacific Railroad Company and the Union Pacific Railroad Company laid the tracks that met at Promontory Summit, Utah.

N **13. a.** The Central Pacific Railroad began construction in Sacramento in early January, 1863. The workers created an average of about 9 mi of track each month. Write parametric equations to model the construction of the Central Pacific Railroad.

Let x_1 = the number of miles along the track route from Sacramento to the newest end of the track.

Let t = the time, in months, after January 1, 1863.

Let $y_1 = 1$. (A horizontal line raised off the x-axis can represent the track.)

b. The Union Pacific Railroad started regular construction in Omaha 33 months after the Central Pacific Railroad. The workers then created an average of about 25 mi of track each month. Write parametric equations to model the construction of the Union Pacific Railroad.

Let x_2 = the number of miles along the track route from Sacramento to the newest end of the track.

Newest end of Union Pacific Railroad track

1774 mi

Sacramento   Omaha

Let t = the time, in months, after January 1, 1863.

Let $y_2 = 1$.

c. Graph the equations you wrote in parts (a) and (b). Use TRACE to find when the two tracks met.

d. According to your graph from part (c), about how much track did each company build?

e. **Writing** What factors may have caused the building rates of the two companies to be so different?

BY THE WAY...

Just days before the two tracks were joined, the Central Pacific Railroad company set a record when it laid 10 miles of track in one day, beating the 8.5 mile record set by their rivals, the Union Pacific Railroad Company.

14. During the 1890s, a train to Omaha leaving Sacramento at 2 P.M. would travel at an average speed of 20 mi/h. A second train heading west from Omaha at 2:30 P.M. would travel at an average speed of 40 mi/h.

   a. Write parametric equations to model the motion of the train from Sacramento. (Let x_1 = the distance in miles of the train from Sacramento, t = the number of hours after 2:00 P.M., and $y_1 = 1$.)

   b. Write parametric equations to model the motion of the train from Omaha. (Let x_2 = the distance in miles of the train from Sacramento, t = the number of hours after 2:00 P.M., and $y_2 = 1.2$.)

   c. If neither train stops along the way, when will the trains pass each other? Use the map on page 546 to estimate where the trains will be when they pass each other.

15 TECHNOLOGY Use the figure at the right.

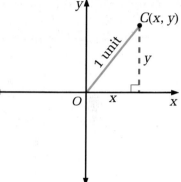

Let $C(x, y)$ = any point one unit away from the origin.

Let t = the measure of the angle $\overline{OC}$ makes with the x-axis.

   a. Use the sine ratio to write an equation for y in terms of t.

   b. Use the cosine ratio to write an equation for x in terms of t.

TECHNOLOGY NOTE

Use $0 \le t \le 360$, $-1.8 \le x \le 1.8$, and $-1.2 \le y \le 1.2$.

   c. Use a graphics calculator to graph the parametric equations from parts (a) and (b). What shape do you get?

   d. **Writing** Explain how you can use a graphics calculator to graph all points two units away from the origin.

16. **Open-ended** Think of a situation that could be modeled with parametric equations. Explain what x, y, and t represent.

Ongoing **ASSESSMENT**

17. **Writing** In Sample 2, suppose Tony waits 4 s to throw the ball instead of 3 s. The path of the ball as viewed from above can be described by the parametric equations $x_2 = 50 - 22(t - 4)$ and $y_2 = 27 + 6(t - 4)$ for $4 \le t \le 7.5$. Bakham's path is still described by the parametric equations $x_1 = 42 - 6t$ and $y_1 = 45 - t$. Can Bakham catch the ball, assuming that it is not too high or too low? Explain your reasoning.

Review **PREVIEW**

Solve. *(Section 9-5)*

18. $4x^3 - 12x^2 + 8x = 0$ **19.** $x^3 - 2x^2 = 7x$ **20.** $6x^4 + 10x^3 + 2x^2 = 0$

Simplify. *(Sections 3-5, 3-7)*

21. $\begin{bmatrix} 2 & 7 \\ -5 & 1 \end{bmatrix} + \begin{bmatrix} 3 & -3 \\ 4 & -2 \end{bmatrix}$ **22.** $2\begin{bmatrix} 3 \\ -1 \\ 0 \end{bmatrix} - \begin{bmatrix} -4 \\ 8 \\ 2 \end{bmatrix}$ **23.** $\begin{bmatrix} 1 & 1 \\ 0 & 3 \\ 2 & 9 \end{bmatrix}\begin{bmatrix} 5 & -1 & 7 \\ -2 & 1 & 0 \end{bmatrix}$

24. The measure of ∠1 is 40°. What are the measures of ∠2, ∠3, and ∠4?
(Section 7-7)

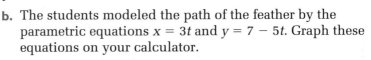

Complete each statement using *pyramid, prism, rectangles, triangles, base,* or *bases.* *(Toolbox Skill 28)*

25. A ⎯?⎯ has one ⎯?⎯. Its other faces are ⎯?⎯.

26. A ⎯?⎯ has two congruent ⎯?⎯ . Its other faces are ⎯?⎯.

Working on the Unit Project

27. Al, Ja-Wen, and Odessa did an experiment on their sports field to measure the speed of the wind. They measured the time (in seconds) that it took for a feather to fall to the ground from a height of 7 ft. They also measured the horizontal distance (in feet) that the feather traveled.

a. The three students say that the speed of the wind is the horizontal distance the feather traveled divided by the time it took to hit the ground. Explain their reasoning. What are the units of the wind speed they found?

b. The students modeled the path of the feather by the parametric equations $x = 3t$ and $y = 7 - 5t$. Graph these equations on your calculator.

c. According to this model, how long did it take the feather to reach the ground? When the feather lands, how far is it from the ladder?

d. Use your answers to part (c) to calculate the wind speed found by the students.

e. Do you think the graph in part (b) is a good model for the path of the feather? Why or why not?

Completing the Unit Project

Now you are ready to debate the pros and cons of using wind power to generate electricity in your area. You should include these points in your debate:

➤ the amount of electricity used by a typical household in your area

➤ the effect of the weather and geography in your area on the amount of electricity that can be produced by a wind turbine

➤ the feasibility of installing a wind turbine at a great enough height to generate sufficient electricity

➤ the cost of purchasing electricity from a local power company

➤ the effect on the environment

WIND POWER DEBATE

GROUP 4
"The WATTBUSTERS" present...
WILL WIND WORK?

Look Back

How could you make your point of view more persuasive in the debate about wind power? What additional information could you obtain in order to strengthen your argument?

Alternative Projects

Project 1: Other Alternative Energy Sources

Research other alternative sources of energy, such as hydropower, solar power, or geothermal power. Find out how they are used in various parts of the world, including South America, Asia, Africa, and Europe.

Project 2: Using Parametric Equations

Try the experiment described in "Working on the Unit Project" Exercise 27 in Section 9-6. You may use facial tissue in place of a feather. Use the distance formula to write parametric equations for the horizontal distance x and the height y in feet after t seconds. Compare your equations with the equations in Exercise 27. Explain any differences. Use your parametric equations to write an equation for y in terms of x.

For Questions 1 and 2, model each situation with an equation.   9-1
Do not solve the equation.

1. Cindra Bede has 1.75 lb cement, 7 lb gravel, and 3.25 lb sand to make concrete. She knows that 30% of the dry ingredients should be sand. How much more sand does she need?

2. Fred is planting a vegetable garden with an area of 120 ft². The length of the garden is along the side of his house. The length is 8 ft more than twice the width. Fred wants to put a fence around the other three sides. How much fence does he need?

Tell whether each expression is a polynomial. Write *Yes* or *No*.
Give a reason for your answer.

3. $\dfrac{x-3}{x}$

4. $3x^3 - x + 10$

5. $2x^{1/3} + 3x^{1/2}$

6. $x^{-5} + x^{-3}$

7. $\dfrac{x^{1/4} - 5}{2x^3 + 10}$

8. $\dfrac{1}{4}x^2 - 4x - 4$

Simplify. Write each answer without negative exponents.   9-2

9. $(4m^4)(3m^{-2})(2m)^2$

10. $(a^{-1}b)(ab)^{-1}$

11. $x^{-5}(2x^3y^{-5})$

12. $(rst)^6(rst)^{-3}$

13. $\dfrac{w^2w^{-4}w^5}{5w^{-3}}$

14. $\left(\dfrac{p^{-2}q^{-1}}{p^{-1}q^{-2}}\right)^3$

Solve.   9-3

15. $\dfrac{1}{x^2 - 4} = \dfrac{1}{x - 2}$

16. $\dfrac{z}{z-1} + \dfrac{1}{z} = 1$

17. $\dfrac{x-3}{x} - \dfrac{1}{x+2} = -1$

18. Carbonation Bottling Company installs a new machine that can cap 100 more bottles per hour than their old machine. This new machine takes one hour less than the old machine to cap 5600 bottles.

    a. Write an equation to model the situation.

    b. Solve the equation you wrote in part (a). What is the bottling speed of the new machine?

19. **Writing** In Exercise 18, there are two possible solutions to the equation. Explain why only one of the solutions is a solution to the problem.

List the zeros of each cubic function. Tell which, if any, are   9-4
double or triple zeros.

20. $y = x(x - 5)(x + 2)$

21. $y = (x + 3)^2(x - 1)$

22. $y = (x - 4)^3$

23. $y = (x - 2)(x + 6)^2$

24. **Open-ended** Write a cubic function that has a graph that crosses the x-axis at exactly two points.

Match each function with its graph.

25. $y = (x - 7)(x - 3)(x + 1)$

26. $y = \frac{1}{2}x^3$

27. $y = x(x - 2)^2$

28. $y = -(x - 7)(x - 3)(x + 1)$

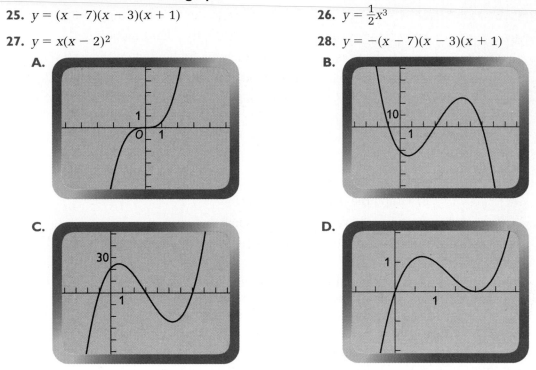

A.

B.

C.

D.

Solve.

9-5

29. $0 = x(x^2 - 4x + 1)$

30. $0 = (x + 3)(2x^2 + 7x - 4)$

31. $0 = 2x^3 - 12x^2 + 18x$

32. In three years, Al estimates he will need about $300 to update his music system. His savings account balance, s, after 3 years will be $s = 60g^3 + 60g^2 + 60g + 60$, where g is the yearly growth rate.

Use the graph of $y = 60x^3 + 60x^2 + 60x + 60 - 300$ to estimate the yearly growth rate he must get to reach his goal.

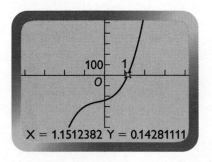

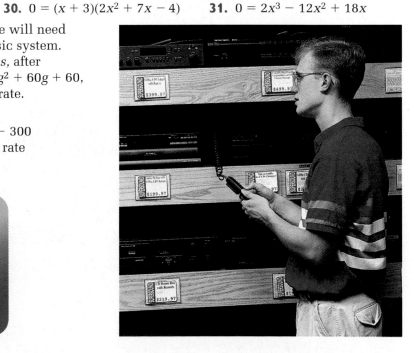

33. A fly lands on a spider's web and tries to move across it.

Let x = the horizontal distance from the fly's landing point.

Let y = the vertical distance from the fly's landing point.

Let t = the time, in seconds, since the fly landed on the web.

The fly's path can be described by these parametric equations:

$$x = 3 - 2t \qquad y = 6 + t \qquad 0 \le t \le 10$$

The spider sees the fly after 2 s and tries to catch the fly. The spider's path can be described by these parametric equations:

$$x = -2 - t \qquad y = -4 + 3t \qquad 2 \le t \le 10$$

a. Graph the path of the fly.

b. Graph the path of the spider.

c. Where do their paths intersect?

d. Does the spider catch the fly? If so, at what time? If not, why not?

34. Self-evaluation Think about the application problems you have solved in this unit. Do you find it more difficult to set up an equation or to solve the equation once you have set it up? How can you improve upon your problem solving skills?

35. Group Activity Work with another student.

a. One person should draw separate graphs of three different cubic functions:

➤ One graph should have only one x-intercept.

➤ One should have only two x-intercepts.

➤ One should have three different x-intercepts.

The other person should write three cubic functions:

➤ One should have a triple zero.

➤ One should have a double zero.

➤ One should have no multiple zeros.

b. Trade papers. The person who receives the functions should describe the graph of each function. The person who receives the graphs should write a function for each of the graphs.

c. Exchange papers and check each other's work. Discuss and resolve any differences.

d. Switch roles and repeat parts (a)–(c) using new graphs and functions.

IDEAS AND (FORMULAS) $= X^2$

ALGEBRA $)X^2$
$(X$

➤ **Problem Solving** Some situations can be modeled by polynomial equations or rational equations. *(pp. 505–508)*

➤ Expressions with positive, zero, or negative exponents can be simplified by using the rules of exponents. *(pp. 513–516)*

➤ Product of Powers Rule: $a^m \cdot a^n = a^{m+n}$ *(p. 513)*

➤ Quotient of Powers Rule: $\dfrac{a^m}{a^n} = a^{m-n}$, $a \neq 0$ *(p. 513)*

➤ Power of a Power Rule: $(a^m)^n = a^{m \cdot n}$ *(p. 516)*

➤ Power of a Product Rule: $(ab)^n = a^n \cdot b^n$ *(p. 516)*

➤ Power of a Quotient Rule: $\left(\dfrac{a}{b}\right)^n = \dfrac{a^n}{b^n}$, $b \neq 0$ *(p. 516)*

➤ To factor a polynomial completely, first you need to find the greatest common factor (GCF) of all the terms. *(p. 514)*

➤ Rational equations can be solved by cross multiplying or by using common multiples of the denominators. *(pp. 521–523)*

➤ Rational equations can have extraneous solutions that do not apply to the situations the equations model. *(pp. 521–523)*

➤ You can tell if a cubic function has a double or triple zero by analyzing the factored form or by graphing the function. *(p. 529)*

➤ **Problem Solving** To solve problems involving cubic equations, you can graph a related equation and find the *x*-intercepts. Some cubic equations can also be solved by factoring and using the quadratic formula. *(p. 537)*

➤ The path of a moving object can be described by parametric equations expressing horizontal and vertical position in terms of time. *(pp. 541–542)*

➤ You can analyze parametric equations by making a table of values for *x*, *y*, and *t* or by graphing the *x-y* pairs. *(p. 542)*

➤ You can use substitution to write a pair of parametric equations as a single equation in terms of *x* and *y*. *(p. 542)*

Key Terms

- **polynomial** (p. 507)
- **standard form of a polynomial** (p. 507)
- **extraneous solution** (p. 521)
- **double zero** (p. 529)
- **parameter** (p. 542)

- **degree** (p. 507)
- **rational expression** (p. 508)
- **cubic function** (p. 528)
- **triple zero** (p. 529)

- **polynomial equation** (p. 507)
- **rational equation** (p. 508)
- **zero of a function** (p. 529)
- **parametric equation** (p. 542)

10

Coordinates and Figures in Space

CONTAINERS

How much of a product's identity is associated with its container? Can you guess the contents of these containers just from the shape? To check your guesses, see the middle of page 556.

1

2

3

4

5

6

7

8

9

products

10

11

12

We demand a lot from the **packaging** for the things we buy! Packaging engineers and designers must develop packaging that protects products and meets our needs as consumers.

Over the ages, people throughout the world have found creative ways to make containers for carrying and storing water, food, and other materials. The beauty, strength, and **practicality** of these containers are still appreciated today.

bamboo

▲ In Southeast Asia, bamboo is used for making baskets. Reeds and grasses are commonly used in other regions.

Design and Build a Container

Your project is to design and build a container to hold an object, or group of objects, of your choice. Be sure to choose something you can bring to school. When your container is finished, you should place the object in it.

Your container should keep its shape when empty. At least one surface should be flat and shaped like a polygon or a circle. Other surfaces may be curved.

Clay pots have been used for thousands of years. The earliest pottery known was found in the Near East. ➤

Provide a written description of your container as well as a set of drawings showing its three-dimensional shape. In this unit you will learn several ways to represent three-dimensional shapes on paper. Use as many of these approaches as you can to draw your container.

CONTAINERS OF THE WORLD

◄ Chilkat, Tlingit, Apache, and Pueblo peoples were among those who developed techniques for weaving baskets with complex patterns.

The ancient Japanese art of origami is used to make decorative boxes by paper-folding, without scissors or glue. ▼

In parts of Africa and South America, gourds have been carved out for carrying liquids and storing grain. ▼

Getting Started

For this project you should work in a group of three students. Here are some ideas to help you get started.

☞ Discuss what object or objects you may choose to package.

☞ Will you package your object as a gift? for mailing? for sale? for storage?

☞ Discuss how the properties of the object may affect the design of the container.

☞ Think about what material you will use for your container. Consider its weight, strength, flexibility, cost, and disposal. What tools will you need to cut and assemble it?

☞ Plan to meet later to discuss which kinds of drawings you can use to represent your container on paper.

Answers to quiz on page 554:
1. milk; 2. takeout food or restaurant leftovers; 3. soda; 4. cereal; 5. pizza; 6. soup; 7. bandages; 8. hair spray; 9. deodorant; 10. toothpaste; 11. lip balm; 12. tuna or cat food

Can We Talk CONTAINERS

Working on the Unit Project

Your work in Unit 10 will help you design and build your container.

Related Exercises:

Section 10-1, Exercises 46–48

Section 10-2, Exercises 27, 28

Section 10-3, Exercises 28, 29

Section 10-4, Exercise 34

Section 10-5, Exercise 39

Section 10-6, Exercises 33–34

Alternative Projects p. 599

➤ What are some other natural containers like eggs and seed pods? How does their design suit their function?

➤ In a recent survey, 67% of people said fast-food packaging is "wasteful." What other products can you think of with wasteful packaging?

➤ Many food products are packaged in rectangular boxes. What other package shapes are common in grocery stores? Why do you think these shapes are used?

➤ Many snack foods are packaged in airtight bags that are difficult to tear open. Can you think of any other types of packaging for which protection of the contents leads to inconvenience for the consumer?

➤ In 1990 a major fast-food chain replaced its plastic foam containers with paper ones. What other changes in packaging have you noticed in recent years?

Figures in Space

Any Way You Look at

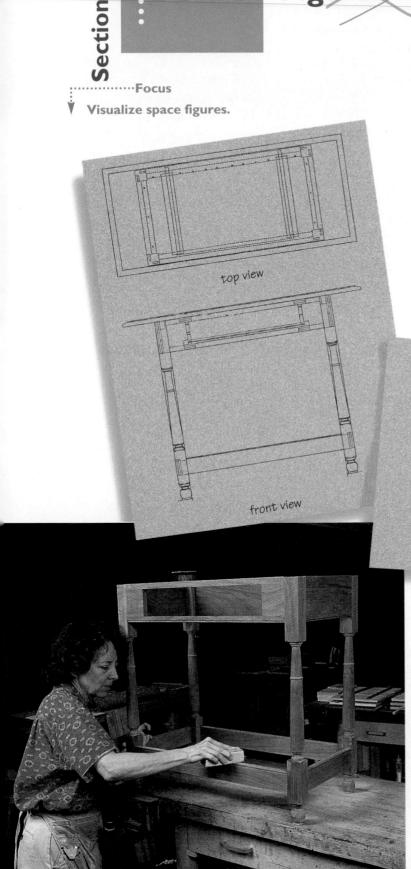

top view

front view

One way to represent a three-dimensional figure, or **space figure,** is to draw it as you would view it from different directions. Mary Conlan's plans for the table she is building include three views.

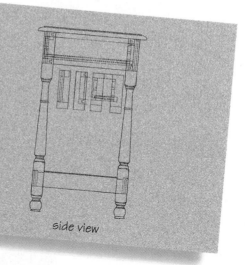

side view

Talk it Over

1. Describe Mary Conlan's table. How is it like tables you have seen? How is it different?

2. Do you think another furniture maker could build Mary Conlan's table given only the front view and the side view? Explain.

557

Triangular Prism

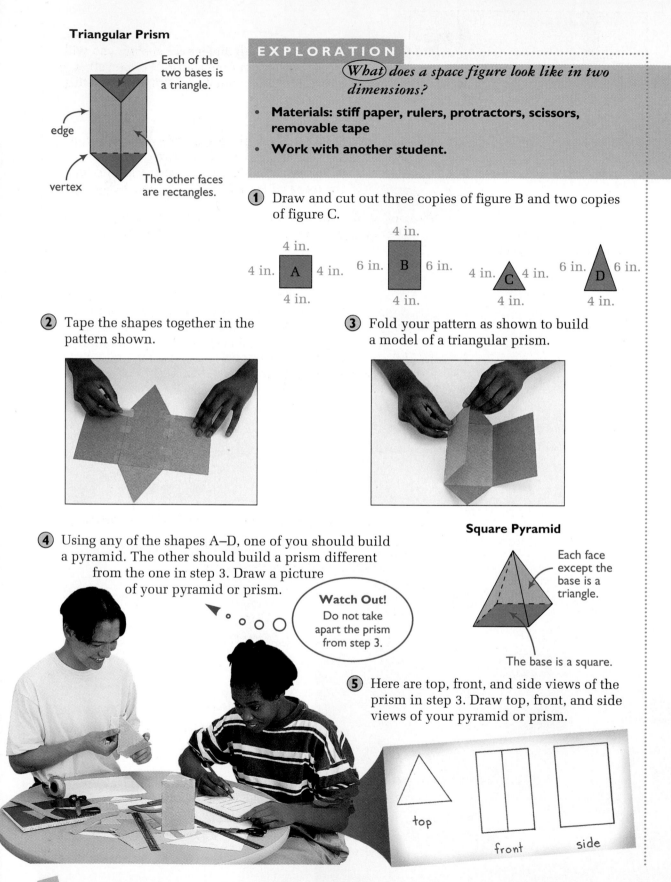

Each of the two bases is a triangle.

edge

vertex

The other faces are rectangles.

What *does a space figure look like in two dimensions?*

- **Materials: stiff paper, rulers, protractors, scissors, removable tape**

- **Work with another student.**

① Draw and cut out three copies of figure B and two copies of figure C.

4 in.

4 in. A 4 in.

4 in.

4 in.

4 in. B 6 in.

4 in.

4 in. C 4 in.

4 in.

6 in. D 6 in.

4 in.

② Tape the shapes together in the pattern shown.

③ Fold your pattern as shown to build a model of a triangular prism.

④ Using any of the shapes A–D, one of you should build a pyramid. The other should build a prism different from the one in step 3. Draw a picture of your pyramid or prism.

Watch Out!
Do not take apart the prism from step 3.

Square Pyramid

Each face except the base is a triangle.

The base is a square.

⑤ Here are top, front, and side views of the prism in step 3. Draw top, front, and side views of your pyramid or prism.

top

front   side

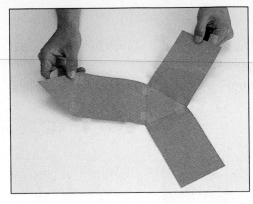

6 If you fold up the pattern shown, you will get the prism from step 3. Work together to unfold your model of the prism to get this pattern.

7 Draw two different patterns for your pyramid or prism from step 4. Draw two different patterns for your partner's pyramid or prism. Compare patterns for the same space figure.

8 Look at the figures other groups made. How many different pyramids and prisms did your class make?

······► **Now you are ready for:**
Exs. 1–19 on pp. 560–562

Cross Sections

Imagine the shape of a slice through a loaf of bread. You just pictured a *cross section* of the loaf. A **cross section** of a space figure is the intersection of a plane and the figure.

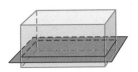 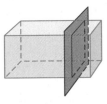

horizontal cross section   **vertical cross section**

Cross sections can be at any angle. Different space figures can have cross sections that are the same shape.

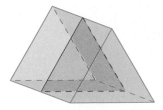         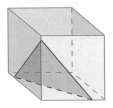

> **Talk it Over**
>
> **3.** Give an example and a counterexample of the statement "Parallel cross sections of a space figure are congruent."
>
> **4.** A slice of bread shows a cross section of a loaf of bread. What are some other everyday objects whose cross sections are easily seen?

10-1 Figures in Space

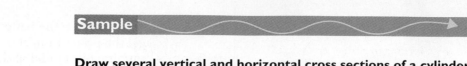
Draw several vertical and horizontal cross sections of a cylinder. Identify each shape.

Sample Response

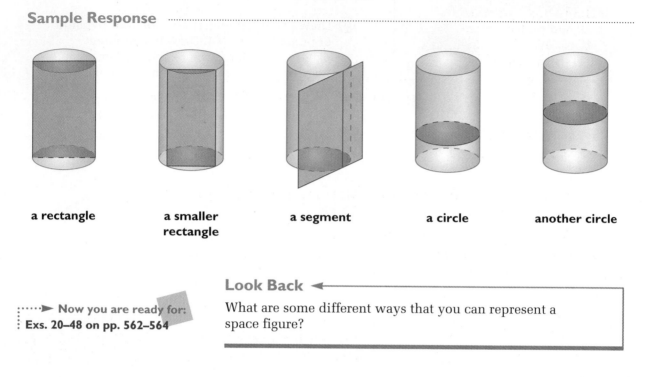

| a rectangle | a smaller rectangle | a segment | a circle | another circle |

Look Back

What are some different ways that you can represent a space figure?

:·····► Now you are ready for:
: Exs. 20–48 on pp. 562–564

10-1 Exercises and Problems

Using Manipulatives Draw and cut out copies of figures A–D in the Exploration to make the patterns shown. Fold each pattern into a space figure. Describe or draw each space figure.

1.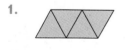

2.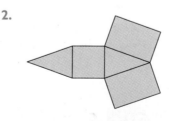

3.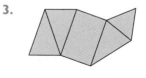

For Exercises 4 and 5, use one of your space figures from Exercises 1–3.

4. Draw a front view, side view, and top view of your space figure.

5. Draw a different pattern for your space figure.

6. Here are two patterns for a cube.

   a. Draw two other patterns that can be folded up to get a cube.

   b. Draw two patterns of six connected squares that cannot be folded up to get a cube.

7. **Open-ended** Find a simple object at school or at home that looks very different from two points of view. Describe or sketch the object from those views.

8. **Group Activity** Work with another student.

   a. Each of you should decide on a space figure. Draw a pattern for your figure.

   b. Exchange patterns with your partner. What space figure does your partner's pattern make? Draw it.

   c. Draw another pattern for the figure.

9. Four students are seated at the corners of a table, all looking at the same object. This is what they see.

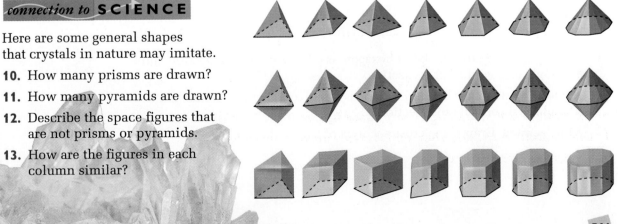

Jade's view   Keiko's view   Luisa's view   Miika's view

   a. How many cubes are in the object? It may help to build the object with sugar cubes or other cubes you have at home.

   b. Describe the order of the students around the table.

connection to **SCIENCE**

Here are some general shapes that crystals in nature may imitate.

10. How many prisms are drawn?

11. How many pyramids are drawn?

12. Describe the space figures that are not prisms or pyramids.

13. How are the figures in each column similar?

For Exercises 14–19, sketch each space figure. If not possible, give a reason.

14. a pyramid with exactly 10 faces

15. a prism with exactly 10 faces

16. a prism with exactly 10 edges

17. a pyramid with exactly 10 edges

18. a pyramid with exactly 7 vertices

19. a prism with exactly 7 vertices

20. **Reading** Can a space figure have more than one cross section?

connection to **GEOLOGY**

Cross sections are used by geologists. Examine the cross section of the Antarctic shown below.

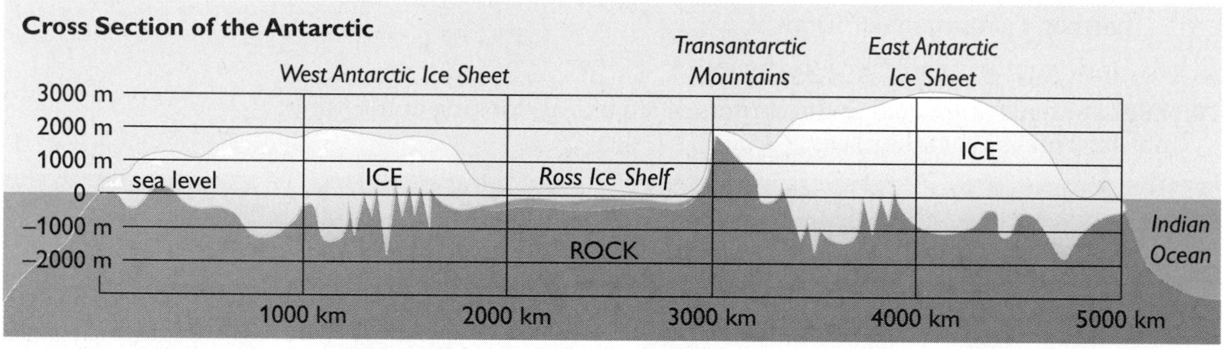

Cross Section of the Antarctic

21. About how far above sea level is the highest point of this region?

22. What information does the cross section tell you that you cannot get from an ordinary map?

23. Approximately what percent of the cross-sectional area above sea level is rock?

For Exercises 24–29, sketch a vertical and horizontal cross section of each object. Identify each shape.

24. a sharpened pencil

25. a ball

26. a bowl

27. a hexagonal prism

28. a cylinder

29. a square prism

30. Name a space figure that has a hexagon as a horizontal cross section and a triangle as a vertical cross section.

31. Name a space figure that has a circle as a horizontal cross section and a triangle as a vertical cross section.

32. **Open-ended** Draw three cross sections of a cube that are not squares.

33. **Research** Doctors use CAT scans to get cross-sectional images of the body. In what kinds of situations is a CAT scan an especially useful medical tool?

connection to **LITERATURE**

In Edwin A. Abbott's book *Flatland,* the narrator is a square who lives in a two-dimensional world inhabited by polygons. Confined to moving in a plane, he can see only the outlines of polygons, not their interiors. A sphere passes through Flatland and surprises the narrator by appearing as a circle that changes size.

FLATLAND

Stranger. You are living on a Plane. What you style Flatland is the vast level surface ... on ... the top of which you and your country-men move about, without rising above it or falling below it.

I am not a plane Figure, but a Solid. You call me a Circle; but in reality I am not a Circle, but an infinite number of Circles, of size varying from a Point to a Circle of thirteen inches in diameter, one placed on the top of the other. When I cut through your plane as I am now doing, I make in your plane a section which you, very rightly, call a Circle...

...You cannot indeed see more than one of my sections, or Circles, at a time; for you have no power to raise your eye out of the plane of Flatland; but you can at least see that, as I rise in Space, so my sections become smaller. See now, I will rise; and the effect upon your eye will be that my Circle will become smaller and smaller till it dwindles to a point and finally vanishes.

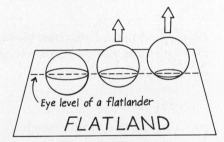

Eye level of a flatlander

FLATLAND

34. What is the radius of the sphere that speaks to the narrator in this passage?

For Exercises 35–38, suppose each space figure passes through Flatland. Describe how it might look to someone in Flatland. Draw some sketches.

35. cylinder 　　　　36. cone 　　　　37. square pyramid 　　　38. cube

39. **Writing** Explain how a Flatlander could tell the difference between a sphere and a cone passing through Flatland.

Open-ended Describe or draw two space figures that have each cross section.

40. a square

41. a circle

42. a triangle

43. Graph the parametric equations. *(Section 9-6)*

$x = 2t + 1$

$y = 2 - t$

44. Choose the letter of the equation that cannot be true if y varies inversely with x. *(Section 2-3)*

a. $x = \dfrac{7}{y}$

b. $xy = 7$

c. $y = \dfrac{7}{x}$

d. $y = 7x$

45. Find the volume of each space figure. *(Toolbox Skill 28)*

a. a cylinder with height 7 in. and radius 3 in.

b. a cone with height 7 in. and radius 3 in.

Working on the Unit Project

As you complete Exercises 46–48, think about how you can use cross sections and patterns to help you design and make your container.

46. The bottles at the right contain common household products.

a. Identify a product each bottle might hold.

b. Draw and describe two horizontal cross sections of each bottle.

c. Why do you think these bottles are shaped as they are?

47. Unfold a cardboard box. Draw a pattern that may have been used to make the box.

48. a. Measure the height and diameter of a twelve-ounce soft drink can.

b. List the dimensions of several possible boxes that could hold 24 twelve-ounce cans without allowing them to move. Which dimensions do you think are best? Why?

c. **Research** What are the dimensions of boxes used by grocery stores? What are the advantages of these dimensions? Are there any disadvantages?

Rotations in Space

Focus
Describe space figures that
are formed by rotating a
plane figure around a line.

This is an unopened
tissue party decoration.
It is made of tissue
paper sandwiched
between two
cardboard copies of
a two-dimensional
figure, or **plane figure.**

To open it, you rotate one of the cardboard ends
until it joins with the other cardboard end.

When you do this,
you are rotating a
plane figure around
a line to form a space
figure. The line is
called the **axis of rotation.**

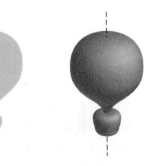

Talk it Over

1. You can think of each object below as
   the result of rotating a plane figure
   around an axis. Describe the
   plane figure. Where is the
   axis of rotation?

BY THE WAY...

The tin can was developed in
England in 1810. However, the
can opener was not invented
until 1858! The first cans came
with the instructions: "Cut
round on the top with a chisel
and hammer."

2. What other everyday objects can you think of as the result of
   rotating a plane figure around an axis?

3. Describe a horizontal and a vertical cross section of each
   object in question 1.

Describe the space figure formed when you rotate each rectangle around the y-axis. Do the same for rotation around the x-axis.

a.

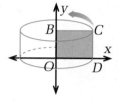

b.

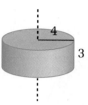

Sample Response

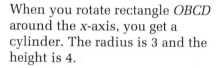

a. When you rotate rectangle *OBCD* around the *y*-axis, you get a cylinder. The radius is 4 and the height is 3.

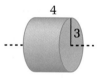

When you rotate rectangle *OBCD* around the *x*-axis, you get a cylinder. The radius is 3 and the height is 4.

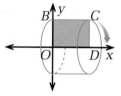

b. When you rotate rectangle *EFGH* around the *y*-axis, you get a cylinder. The radius is 4 and the height is 3.

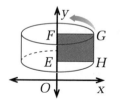

When you rotate rectangle *EFGH* around the *x*-axis, you get this ring shape. The radius of the outer cylinder is 5 and the height is 4. The radius of the inner cylinder is 2 and the height is 4.

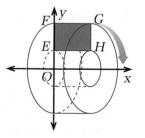
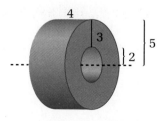

4. Explain how to find the surface area and volume of the first cylinder in Sample 1.

5. What space figure do you get if you rotate rectangle *EFGH* from Sample 1 around the line $y = 2$?

6. Describe a horizontal and a vertical cross section of each space figure in Sample 1.

Sample 2

a. Describe the space figure formed when $\triangle OBC$ is rotated around the *y*-axis. Do the same for rotation around the *x*-axis.

b. Which of the two space figures has the greater volume?

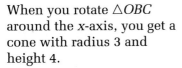

Sample Response

a. When you rotate $\triangle OBC$ around the *y*-axis, you get a cone with radius 4 and height 3.

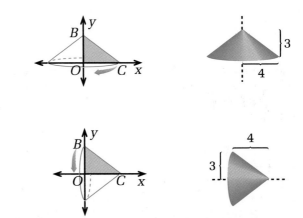

When you rotate $\triangle OBC$ around the *x*-axis, you get a cone with radius 3 and height 4.

b. The formula for the volume *V* of a cone is $V = \frac{1}{3}\pi r^2 h$, where *r* is the radius and *h* is the height.

Cone around the *y*-axis: $V = \frac{1}{3}\pi(4)^2(3) = 16\pi$ (cubic units)

Cone around the *x*-axis: $V = \frac{1}{3}\pi(3)^2(4) = 12\pi$ (cubic units)

The cone around the *y*-axis has the greater volume.

Look Back

Name two space figures you can get by rotating a plane figure around an axis. Describe a vertical and horizontal cross section for each space figure.

10-2 Exercises and Problems

1. **Reading** Suppose you rotate a plane figure around two different axes. Are the resulting two space figures necessarily the same?

2. **Using Manipulatives** You will need paper, scissors, tape, and a long pencil.

   a. Cut out a copy of the figure at the right.

   b. Tape the straight edge of the figure to the pencil as shown.

   c. Roll the pencil between your hands. If you spin the pencil quickly enough, the plane figure will blur and begin to look like a space figure. Sketch two different views of the space figure.

Describe or sketch the shape formed by rotating each figure around the indicated axis.

3.

4.

5.

Describe or sketch the space figure formed by each rotation.

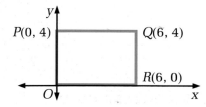

$P(0, 4)$ $Q(6, 4)$

$R(6, 0)$

O x

$P(0, 4)$

$R(6, 0)$

O x

6. Rotate $OPQR$ around the y-axis.

7. Rotate $\triangle OPR$ around the y-axis.

8. Rotate $OPQR$ around the x-axis.

9. Rotate $\triangle OPR$ around the x-axis.

10. Find the volume and surface area of the space figure in Exercise 6.

11. Find the volume of the space figure in Exercise 9.

12. a. Describe or sketch the cylinder formed by rotating rectangle $MNOP$ around $\overline{MN}$. Indicate the height and radius.

   b. Describe or sketch the cylinder formed by rotating rectangle $MNOP$ around $\overline{PM}$. Indicate the height and radius.

   c. Find the ratio of the volume of the cylinder in part (a) to the volume of the cylinder in part (b).

   d. Find the ratio of the surface area of the cylinder in part (a) to the surface area of the cylinder in part (b).

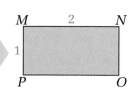

13. Repeat Exercise 12 with this rectangle.

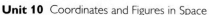

M b N

a

P O

14. Writing Which cylinder do you think has the greater volume? Explain your reasoning.

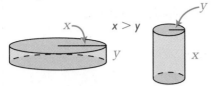

Tell whether each space figure can be formed by rotating a plane figure around an axis. Give a reason for your answer.

15. a cone   **16.** a pyramid   **17.** a sphere

Career Designers such as engineers and architects often use computer-aided design (CAD) programs in their work. Many computer 3-D graphics packages have a *surface revolution* tool. You draw a shape, and the surface revolution tool rotates it around an axis.

For Exercises 18 and 19, sketch the figure that is rotated to form the space figure. Indicate the axis of rotation.

18. 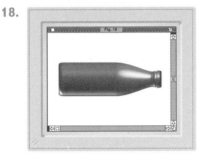   **19.**

Suppose you enter each plane figure into the computer and use the surface revolution tool to rotate it around the dashed line. Describe or sketch the space figure the computer will draw.

20. **21.** **22.**

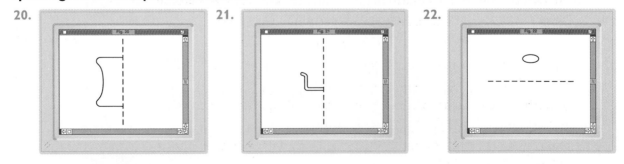

23. **Open-ended** Imagine an object you can design with a surface revolution tool. Draw the shape you will rotate and sketch what your finished object will look like.

24. Draw two different views of your mathematics book. *(Section 10-1)*

25. You roll a die three times. What is the probability of rolling a "1" exactly twice? *(Section 6-8)*

26. **Given** *P* is on the perpendicular bisector of $\overline{AB}$. *(Section 8-6)*

    Prove *PA* = *PB*

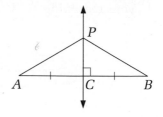

Working on the Unit Project

As you complete Exercises 27 and 28, think about how you can use rotations to help design your container.

27. Give several examples of containers that have an axis of rotation.

28. A fruit juice company designs a new can. The new can has the same height and diameter as the old can, but the bottom of the new can is indented about $\frac{5}{16}$ in.

old can   new can

$\frac{5}{16}$ in.

a. On a set of axes, draw a figure that can be rotated around the *y*-axis to model the old can. On a different set of axes, draw a figure that can be rotated around the *y*-axis to model the new can.

b. Will the new can hold as much juice as the old can?

c. Why do you think the new can was designed to have the same height and diameter as the old can?

d. Give other examples of containers that appear to hold more than they actually do.

Points That Fit Conditions

Focus

Describe or draw a set of points that meet one or more conditions.

It's Around Here Somewhere

On January 17, 1994, a large earthquake struck the western United States. The earthquake recording station at Topopah Spring, Nevada, recorded that the *epicenter* was located about 370 km away. The epicenter of a quake is the place on the surface of Earth above the focus of the quake.

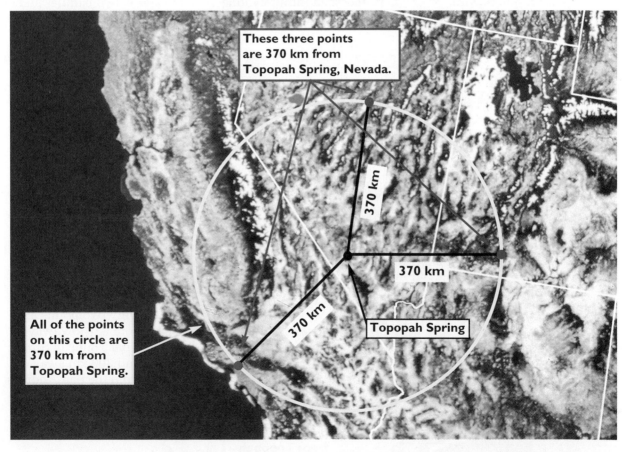

These three points are 370 km from Topopah Spring, Nevada.

370 km

370 km

370 km

Topopah Spring

All of the points on this circle are 370 km from Topopah Spring.

Earthquake stations record only the distance to the epicenter, not the direction. The location of the epicenter could be any point on a circle with radius 370 km centered at the recording station.

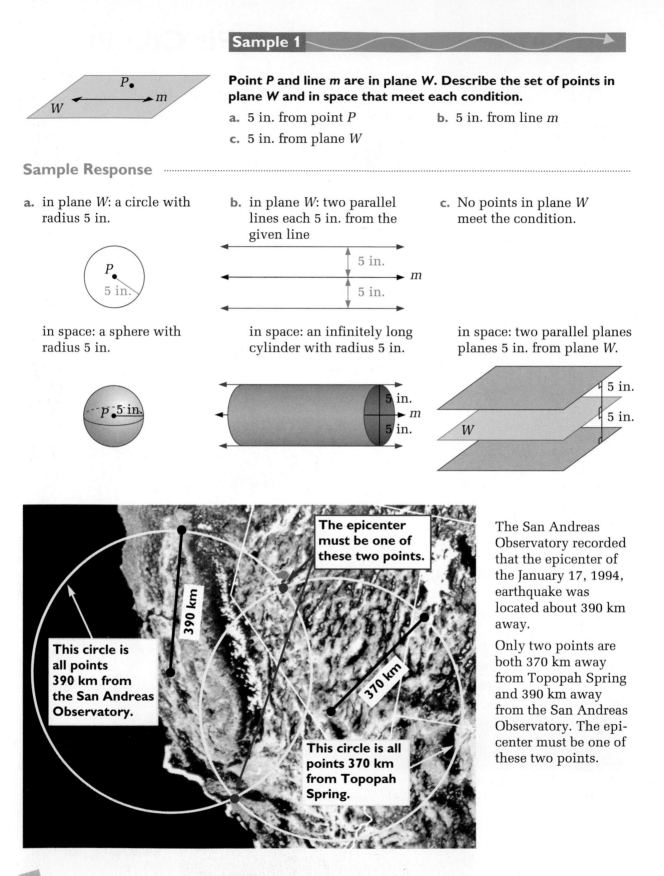

Point P and line m are in plane W. Describe the set of points in plane W and in space that meet each condition.

a. 5 in. from point *P*   **b.** 5 in. from line *m*

c. 5 in. from plane *W*

Sample Response

a. in plane *W*: a circle with radius 5 in.

b. in plane *W*: two parallel lines each 5 in. from the given line

c. No points in plane *W* meet the condition.

in space: a sphere with radius 5 in.

in space: an infinitely long cylinder with radius 5 in.

in space: two parallel planes planes 5 in. from plane *W*.

The epicenter must be one of these two points.

This circle is all points 390 km from the San Andreas Observatory.

390 km

370 km

This circle is all points 370 km from Topopah Spring.

The San Andreas Observatory recorded that the epicenter of the January 17, 1994, earthquake was located about 390 km away.

Only two points are both 370 km away from Topopah Spring and 390 km away from the San Andreas Observatory. The epicenter must be one of these two points.

1. How could you use data from a third recording station to decide which of the two points is the epicenter?

2. Do you know which of the two points was the epicenter?

Sample 2

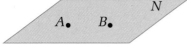
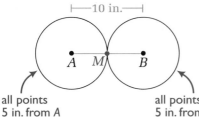

Points A and B are in plane N. For each condition, describe the set of points that are in plane N and 5 in. from both A and B.

a. *A* and *B* are 10 in. apart.

b. *A* and *B* are 8 in. apart.

c. *A* and *B* are 12 in. apart.

Sample Response

a. *M* is on both circles, so *M* is 5 in. from both *A* and *B*.

b. *P* and *Q* are 5 in. from both *A* and *B*.

c. No points are on both circles, so no points are 5 in. from both *A* and *B*.

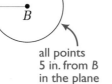

├──10 in.──┤

all points 5 in. from *A* in the plane

all points 5 in. from *B* in the plane

├──8 in.──┤

├──12 in.──┤

Talk it Over

3. In part (b) of Sample 2, explain why *P* and *Q* are on the perpendicular bisector of $\overline{AB}$.

4. If *A* and *B* are 10 in. apart, describe the set of points that are in space and 5 in. from *A* and *B*.

5. If *A* and *B* are 12 in. apart, describe the set of points that are in space and 5 in. from *A* and *B*.

A modern reconstruction of Chang Heng's earthquake detector of A.D. 132.

In Sample 2, point Q is the same distance from both A and B. It is said to be **equidistant** from A and B.

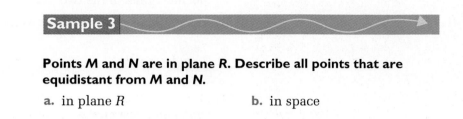

Sample 3

Points M and N are in plane R. Describe all points that are equidistant from M and N.

a. in plane R b. in space

Sample Response

a. In plane R, all the points on the perpendicular bisector of $\overline{MN}$ are equidistant from M and N.

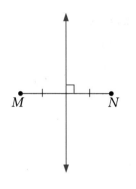

b. In space, all the points on the plane perpendicular to $\overline{MN}$ and halfway between M and N are equidistant from both points.

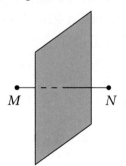

Look Back

Give an example of a condition that is met by a different set of points in a plane and in space.

10-3 Exercises and Problems

1. **Reading** If you want to locate the epicenter of an earthquake, why do you need more than one recording station?

2. What is the set of all points that are 1 m from the floor of the room you are in?

3. Imagine a point, P, on the floor of the room you are in.
   a. What is the set of all points on the floor that are 2 m from P?
   b. What is the set of all points in the room that are 2 m from P?

4. Imagine a line, $\overleftrightarrow{CD}$, down the middle of the floor of the room you are in.
   a. What is the set of all points on the floor that are 2 m from $\overleftrightarrow{CD}$?
   b. What is the set of all points in the room that are 2 m from $\overleftrightarrow{CD}$?

For Exercises 5–10, A and B are 6 cm apart in plane S. Describe or draw all points in plane S that meet each set of conditions.

5. 4 cm from both A and B

6. 2 cm from A and 4 cm from B

7. 2 cm from both A and B

8. 1 cm from A and 3 cm from B

9. 3 cm from both A and B

10. 4 cm from A and 5 cm from B

11. Describe the set of points 60 mi from the control room at the top of an airport's control tower.

12. **Writing** Suppose you are designing a track and field stadium. Why might you want to know the set of points where a shot putter's shot put can land?

13. **Writing** In a thunderstorm, if you hear thunder five seconds after you see lightning, then the lightning is about one mile away. Each second corresponds to about $\frac{1}{5}$ mi. Describe how the principle used to locate the epicenter of an earthquake can be used to locate lightning in a thunderstorm.

14. What is the set of all points equidistant from the floor and the ceiling of the room you are in?

15. Describe all points in a plane and in space that are 5 cm from a segment.

16. **Seismology** On April 18, 1993, many earthquake stations in South America recorded an earthquake. The Cocahabamba station in Bolivia is about 1200 km east and 1900 km south of the Cayambe station in Ecuador. The Cerro El Oso station in Venezuela is about 1100 km east and 1000 km north of the Cayambe station.

a. Plot the relative positions of the three recording stations on graph paper. Write a scale on your diagram.

b. The Cayambe station recorded that the epicenter of the quake was about 1300 km away. Sketch or use a compass to draw all the possible locations of the epicenter.

c. The Cocahabamba station also recorded that the epicenter was about 1300 km away. Sketch or use a compass to draw all the possible locations of the epicenter.

d. The Cerro El Oso station recorded that the epicenter was about 2500 km away. Estimate the location of the epicenter.

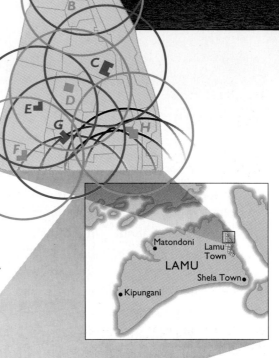

This map shows the locations of some of the mosques in the northernmost part of the town of Lamu, Kenya. Criers call from the mosques at dawn, at noon, in the afternoon, at nightfall, and after dark. The circles show how far away each crier can be heard.

17. Trace the part of Lamu Town shown.

   a. Shade the area where you can hear a crier calling from mosque *A*.

   b. With another color, shade the area where you can hear a crier calling from both mosque *A* and mosque *B*.

   c. **Open-ended** With another color, shade an area where you can hear a crier calling from each of three different mosques. Which mosques are they?

   d. With another color, shade an area where you cannot hear any criers from the mosques shown.

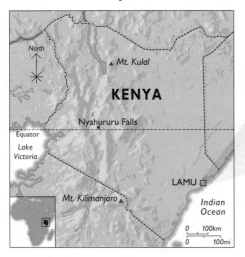

18. Trace the map of Kenya. Draw and label the points that fit each set of conditions.

   a. equidistant from Lamu and Mount Kilimanjaro

   b. equidistant from Lamu, Mount Kilimanjaro, and Mount Kulal

   c. 170 mi away from the equator and equidistant from Lamu and Mount Kilimanjaro

   d. equidistant from Lamu, Mount Kilimanjaro, Mount Kulal, and Nyahururu Falls

19. Describe the set of points in plane *F* and in space that are equidistant from two parallel lines in plane *F*.

20. Circle *D* is in plane *T*. Describe the set of points in plane *T* and in space that are equidistant from all the points on circle *D*.

21. **Research** The points on a parabola meet conditions related to the *focus* and *directrix* of the parabola. What are the focus and directrix? What conditions do the points on the parabola meet?

Ongoing ASSESSMENT

22. **Open-ended** For each answer, make up a problem like the ones in Samples 1, 2, or 3.

   a. Answer: a point   **b.** Answer: a line   **c.** Answer: no points

23. Describe or draw the space figure formed when you rotate △*MNO* around the *x*-axis. Find its volume. *(Section 10-2)*

24. What is wrong with the conclusion below? *(Section 1-7)*

If Marya gets a letter, then she will write a letter to her cousin. Marya writes a letter to her cousin. Conclusion: Marya got a letter.

Find the coordinates of the midpoint of the segment whose endpoints are given. *(Section 5-3)*

25. (0, 4) and (−3, 1) **26.** (−2, −5) and (8, −3) **27.** (0.5, 6) and (−4, 7)

Working on the Unit Project

28. Choose an object or objects that you will design your container to hold. Describe the object or objects.

29. a. Which of the following conditions should your container meet?

easy to open, unbreakable, resealable, waterproof, lightweight

b. What other conditions should your container meet?

Unit 10 CHECKPOINT

1. Writing Describe a sphere in terms of its cross sections, as a rotation in space, and as a set of points that fit a condition.

2. Draw a pattern for a pentagonal prism.   **10-1**

3. Draw two cross sections of a pentagonal prism.

Describe or sketch the space figure formed by rotating each plane figure around the y-axis. Indicate the height and radius.   **10-2**

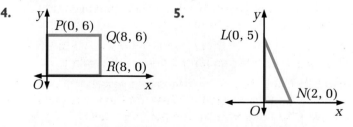

4.   **5.**

6. Points *A* and *B* are 6 in. apart in plane *W*. Describe all points in plane *W* that are 5 in. from *A* and *B*.   **10-3**

7. Points *C* and *D* are 5 in. apart in plane *W*. Describe all points in plane *W* that are 2 in. from *C* and *D*.

8. Points *E* and *F* are 4 in. apart in plane *W*. Describe all points in space that are equidistant from *E* and *F*.

Coordinates in Three Dimensions

Name That Point

Focus

Describe the location of points in space using three coordinates. Find midpoints of segments in three dimensions.

Value of Exports from Three Countries

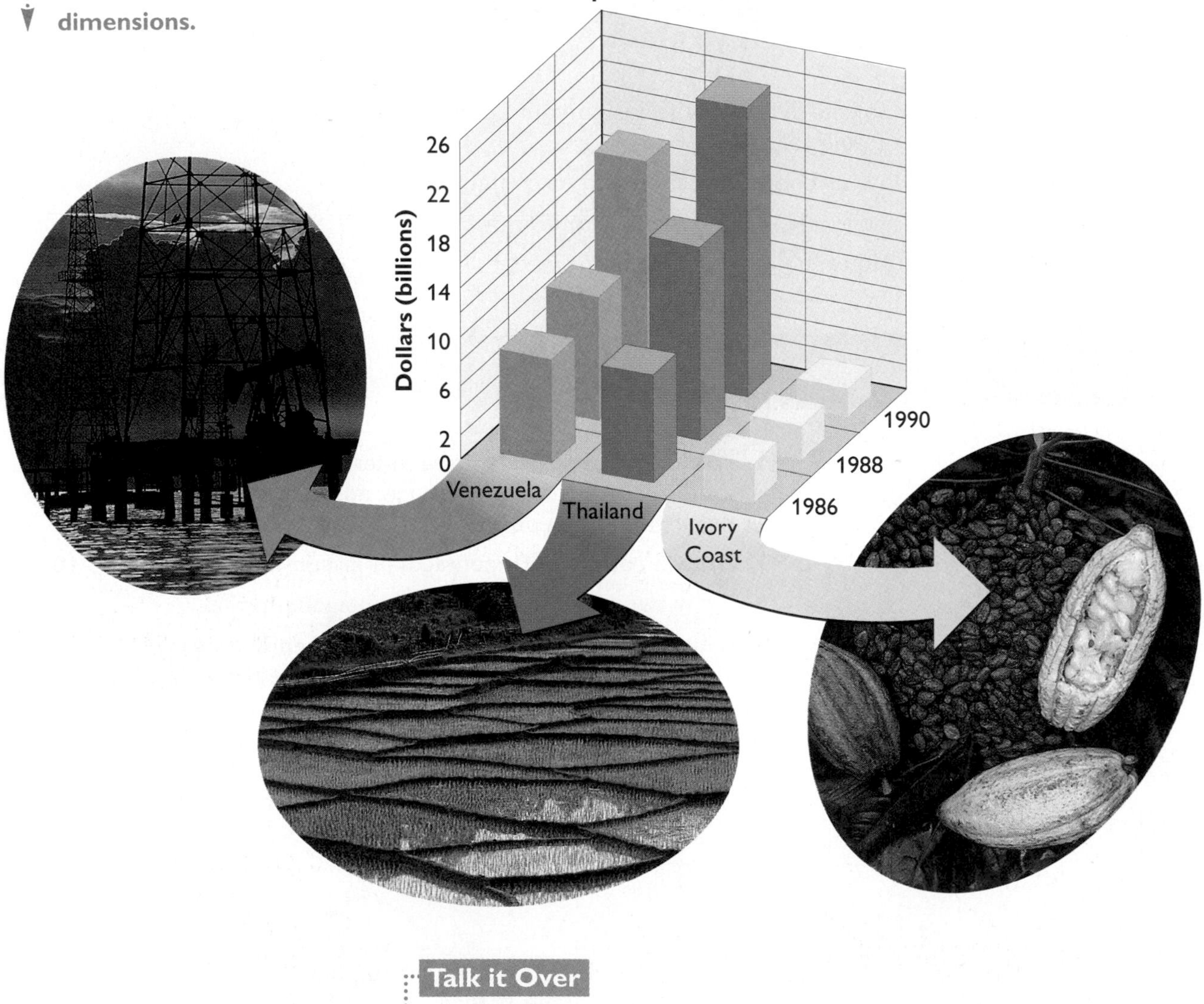

Talk it Over

1. Which country increased its earnings from exports the most from 1986 to 1990?

2. Which countries earned less than $20 billion in 1990?

3. About how much did Venezuela earn in exports in 1986?

The graph of exports is a model in three-dimensional space. To locate points in space, three coordinate axes are needed.

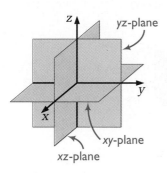

yz-plane

z

y

x

xy-plane

xz-plane

$(4, -2, 3)$ is an **ordered triple.**

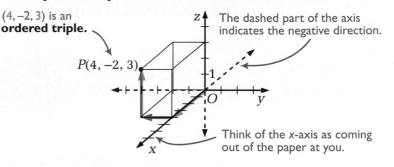

$P(4, -2, 3)$

The dashed part of the axis indicates the negative direction.

z

O

y

x

Think of the x-axis as coming out of the paper at you.

To locate point $P(4, -2, 3)$, start at the origin. Move 4 units toward you on the x-axis, 2 units to the left parallel to the y-axis, and 3 units up parallel to the z-axis.

Talk it Over

4. On which axis does the point (5, 0, 0) lie?

5. Describe how you would locate the point (6, 4, −1) in three dimensions.

6. Does it matter which axis you move along first to locate a point? Explain.

Sample 1

Coordinates of vertices D and F of the rectangular prism are given. Find the coordinates of vertices B, A, and H.

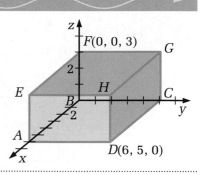

z

$F(0, 0, 3)$

G

2

E

H

B

C

y

−2

A

x

$D(6, 5, 0)$

Sample Response

B is at the origin. The coordinates of B are (0, 0, 0).

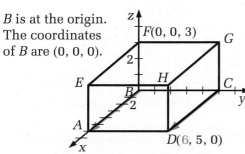

z

$F(0, 0, 3)$

G

2

E

H

B

C

y

−2

A

x

$D(6, 5, 0)$

A has the same x-coordinate as point D. The coordinates of A are (6, 0, 0).

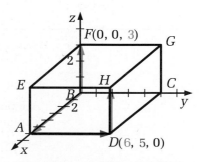

z

$F(0, 0, 3)$

G

2

E

H

B

C

y

−2

A

x

$D(6, 5, 0)$

H has the same x- and y-coordinates as point D and the same z-coordinate as F. The coordinates of H are (6, 5, 3).

Find the coordinates of the midpoint of $\overline{FD}$.

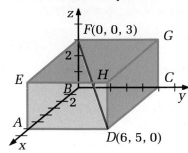

Sample Response

As in two dimensions, each of the coordinates of the midpoint of a segment is the mean of the corresponding coordinates of its endpoints.

$F(0, 0, 3)$
$D(6, 5, 0)$ } endpoints of $\overline{FD}$

$\left(\dfrac{0 + 6}{2}, \dfrac{0 + 5}{2}, \dfrac{3 + 0}{2} \right) = \left(3, \dfrac{5}{2}, \dfrac{3}{2} \right)$ ← midpoint of $\overline{FD}$

X $\cdot$ ab

THE MIDPOINT FORMULA FOR THREE DIMENSIONS

The midpoint of the segment with endpoints (x_1, y_1, z_1) and (x_2, y_2, z_2) has coordinates

$$\left(\dfrac{x_1 + x_2}{2}, \dfrac{y_1 + y_2}{2}, \dfrac{z_1 + z_2}{2} \right).$$

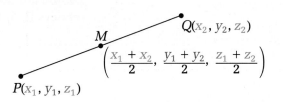

Look Back ←

Are point $F(1, 2, 3)$ and point $G(3, 2, 1)$ the same point? Explain.

1. In which year was the per capita consumption of bottled water the least?

2. Which drink lost popularity from 1980 to 1990?

3. Estimate the per capita consumption of soft drinks in 1990.

4. Do you think this graph accurately reflects your beverage consumption? Explain.

5. **Reading** What is an ordered triple?

6. Find the missing coordinates of each vertex.

    a. $O(0, 0, \underline{?})$

    b. $P(0, \underline{?}, \underline{?})$

    c. $Q(\underline{?}, 0, \underline{?})$

    d. $T(\underline{?}, \underline{?}, \underline{?})$

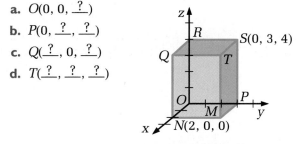

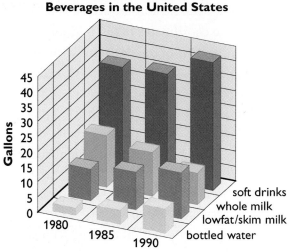

Per Capita Consumption of Beverages in the United States

7. **Group Activity** Work with another student. You will need a cardboard box at least 10 in. × 10 in. × 10 in., scissors, a large needle, thread, at least ten buttons or paper clips, and tape.

    a. Draw and label axes on three inside edges of the box as shown. The tick marks should be about 3 in. apart.

    b. Copy the x- and y-axes on the top of the box. Mark the xy-grid with holes as shown.

    c. Cut at least ten pieces of thread about 3 in. longer than your z-axis. Tie a button or paper clip to the end of each thread.

    d. Plot the point (1, 2, 3) by putting the thread through hole (1, 2) in the top of the box. Pull the button down inside until it is level with z = 3. Put tape over the hole to keep the rest of the thread from sliding through.

    e. List and plot at least ten ordered triples for which $x + y - z = 0$. Is the point (1, 2, 3) a solution of this equation?

    f. What do you notice about the solutions of $x + y - z = 0$?

For Exercises 8–10, use the rectangular prism at the right.

8. Find the coordinates of vertices *A* through *G*.

9. Find the volume and the surface area of the prism.

10. Find the coordinates of the midpoint of $\overline{BH}$.

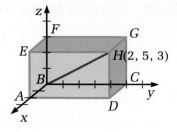

Find the midpoint of the segment with the given endpoints.

11. *L*(0, 0, 0) *P*(−2, −2, −2)   12. *R*(3, 6, 9) *S*(1, 5, 4)

13. *W*(2, 0, −3) *Z*(4, −1, 3)   14. *T*(−1, −1, −1) *V*(1, 1, 1)

15. **a.** Plot and connect the vertices of quadrilateral *ABCD*:
       A(0, 0, 0), *B*(5, 0, 0), *C*(5, −5, 0), *D*(0, −5, 0)

   b. On the same set of axes, plot quadrilateral *EFGH*:
       E(0, 0, 5), *F*(5, 0, 5), *G*(5, −5, 5), *H*(0, −5, 5)

   c. Draw $\overline{AE}$, $\overline{BF}$, $\overline{CG}$, and $\overline{DH}$.

   d. Describe the space figure.

16. **a.** How many different ordered triples contain each of the numbers 0, 1, and 2?

   b. Plot the ordered triples from part (a).

17. What is the *y*-coordinate of all points on the *z*-axis?

18. What is the *z*-coordinate of all points in the *xy*-plane?

19. What is the *z*-coordinate of all points 3 units below the *xy*-plane?

Career Archaeologists are studying a campsite near Boston that was used from 3000 years ago to 500 years ago by the Massachuseog people and their ancestors. They used the campsite when they came to the coast in the fall to gather supplies for the winter.

Archaeologists carefully remove dirt one layer at a time and record the locations of objects that they find.

For Exercises 20–24, use the diagram.

20. What object is at about this location: 3 cm from north wall, 10 cm from east wall, and 41 cm below surface?

21. What is the location of the stone ax?

22. **Writing** How is the method of recording three-dimensional locations in archaeology different from the method used in mathematics? Describe advantages and disadvantages of each method.

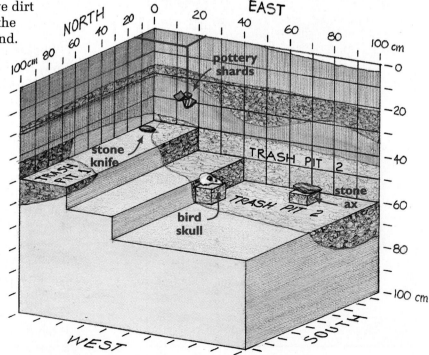

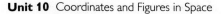

23. Which do you think was in the campsite longer, the pottery shards or the bird skull? Why?

24. Open-ended Why do you think archaeologists need to keep a record of the precise locations of objects?

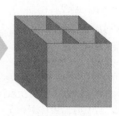

Ongoing **ASSESSMENT**

25. Open-ended Imagine your classroom in a three-dimensional coordinate system.

   a. Where would you place the origin?

   b. What distance would you use for one unit along each axis?

   c. Estimate the coordinates of the center of the classroom.

   d. Estimate the coordinates of two other points of interest in the room.

Review **PREVIEW**

26. Describe the set of points in space that are 12 in. from a line. *(Section 10-3)*

Simplify. *(Section 3-5)*

27. $6\begin{bmatrix} 3 & 5 \\ 4 & 6 \end{bmatrix}$

28. $-1\begin{bmatrix} 15 & 9 & 14 & 7 \\ 2 & 5 & 40 & 22 \\ 0 & 1 & 30 & 35 \end{bmatrix}$

29. $[2 \ 1 \ 6 \ 20] - [4 \ 0 \ 2 \ 6]$

Find the value of the variable in each figure. *(Section 8-7)*

30.
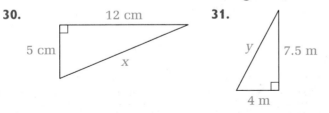

31.

Find the distance between each pair of points. *(Section 5-2)*

32. (0, 0) and (4, 7.5)

33. (2, 3) and (6, 10.5)

 Working on the Unit Project

34. a. Open-ended In a three-dimensional coordinate system, plot eight points that are the vertices of a rectangular prism.

   b. Suppose the prism in part (a) is a container and you want to divide it into four congruent spaces. You can use the midpoints of the top and bottom edges to help you place cardboard dividers. Write the coordinates of these midpoints.

The Distance Formula in Three Dimensions

Focus

Find the distance between two points in three dimensions.

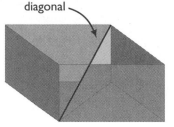

diagonal

(What) is the length of a diagonal of a box?

• **Materials: medium boxes (no larger than 14 in. × 14 in. × 14 in.), large sheets of heavy paper, rulers, protractors, scissors**

• **Work with another student.**

A **diagonal of a rectangular prism** is a segment that joins one vertex to the vertex that is farthest from it. In this Exploration you will make and measure a diagonal of a box.

① Choose a box.

② Measure and record the length and width of the inside of your box to the nearest eighth of an inch. Measure and record the height of your box.

③ On heavy paper, draw right $\triangle ABC$ so that AB is the width of your box, BC is the length of your box, and the right angle is at B. Label points A, B, and C inside the triangle.

④ Use the Pythagorean theorem to find AC. Record the result on your drawing. This is the length of a diagonal of the bottom face of your box.

⑤ Draw right $\triangle ACG$ so that CG is the height of your box and the right angle is at C. Label point G inside the triangle.

⑥ Use the Pythagorean theorem to find AG. This is the length of a diagonal of your box. Measure $\overline{AG}$. Are the two numbers close? Record AG on your drawing.

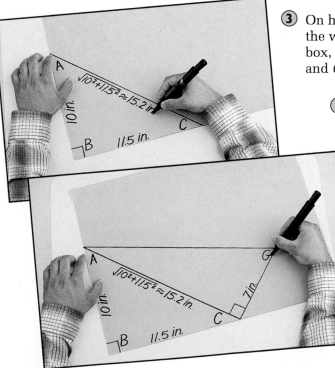

7 Cut out quadrilateral $ABCG$ and fold it along the line that passes through A and C.

8 Fit the folded quadrilateral into your box so that $\triangle ABC$ is flat on the bottom and $\overline{AG}$ shows a diagonal of the box.

> **Watch Out!**
> A diagonal of a face of a rectangular prism is not a diagonal of the prism.

Talk it Over

1. Do all diagonals of a rectangular prism have the same length?

2. In the Exploration, suppose x is the width, y is the length, and z is the height of a box. Use the Pythagorean theorem to show that

$$AG = \sqrt{\left(\sqrt{x^2 + y^2}\,\right)^2 + z^2} = \sqrt{x^2 + y^2 + z^2}.$$

LENGTH OF A DIAGONAL OF A RECTANGULAR PRISM

A rectangular prism with edges of length x, y, and z has a diagonal of length d, where

$$d = \sqrt{x^2 + y^2 + z^2}.$$

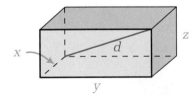

Sample 1

Find the length of a diagonal of a rectangular prism with edges of length 2 cm, 8 cm, and 5 cm.

Sample Response

Problem Solving Strategy: Use a formula.

Substitute 2 for x, 8 for y, and 5 for z in the formula for the length of a diagonal of a rectangular prism.

$$d = \sqrt{x^2 + y^2 + z^2} = \sqrt{2^2 + 8^2 + 5^2} = \sqrt{4 + 64 + 25} = \sqrt{93} \approx 9.64$$

The length of a diagonal is about 9.6 cm.

The Distance Formula

To find the distance from a point to the origin, imagine that the segment connecting the point and the origin is a diagonal of a rectangular prism. The distance to the origin is the length of the diagonal.

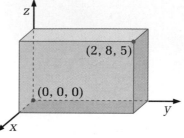

·······► Now you are ready for:
: Exs. 1–17 on p. 588

Talk it Over

Suppose the prism above is translated as shown below.

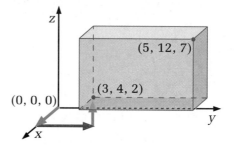

3. Do you think that translating the prism changes the length of the diagonal?

4. How can you find the lengths of the edges of the prism?

5. How can you find the length of the diagonal from (3, 4, 2) to (5, 12, 7)?

The distance between any two points in three dimensions can be found using a three-dimensional version of the distance formula.

X ⟨ △ab

THE DISTANCE FORMULA IN THREE DIMENSIONS

The distance, d, between the points (x_1, y_1, z_1) and (x_2, y_2, z_2) is

$$d = \sqrt{(x_2 - x_1)^2 + (y_2 - y_1)^2 + (z_2 - z_1)^2}.$$

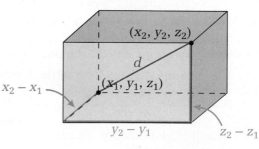

Find the distance between (3, 4, 2) and (5, 12, 7).

Sample Response

$$d = \sqrt{(x_2 - x_1)^2 + (y_2 - y_1)^2 + (z_2 - z_1)^2}$$ ◄——— Use the distance formula.

$$= \sqrt{(5 - 3)^2 + (12 - 4)^2 + (7 - 2)^2}$$ ◄——— Let $(x_1, y_1, z_1) = (3, 4, 2)$ and $(x_2, y_2, z_2) = (5, 12, 7)$.

$$= \sqrt{4 + 64 + 25}$$

$$= \sqrt{93}$$

$$\approx 9.64$$

The distance between the two points is about 9.6.

Tell whether the triangle formed by $P(4, 0, 0)$, $Q(0, 2, 0)$, and $R(3, 3, 5)$ is *scalene*, *isosceles*, or *equilateral*. Explain your answer.

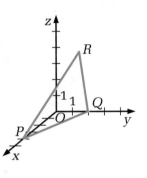

Sample Response

To classify the triangle as scalene, isosceles, or equilateral, find the lengths of the sides and compare them.

Use the distance formula to find PQ, QR, and RP.

$$PQ = \sqrt{(0 - 4)^2 + (2 - 0)^2 + (0 - 0)^2} = \sqrt{16 + 4 + 0} = \sqrt{20}$$

$$QR = \sqrt{(3 - 0)^2 + (3 - 2)^2 + (5 - 0)^2} = \sqrt{9 + 1 + 25} = \sqrt{35}$$

$$RP = \sqrt{(4 - 3)^2 + (0 - 3)^2 + (0 - 5)^2} = \sqrt{1 + 9 + 25} = \sqrt{35}$$

Since $QR = RP = \sqrt{35}$, the triangle is isosceles.
The triangle is not equilateral, because $PQ \neq \sqrt{35}$.

Look Back ◄———

······► Now you are ready for:
Exs. 18–39 on pp. 588–590

How is the distance formula in three dimensions like the distance formula in two dimensions? How is it different?

Use the Pythagorean theorem to calculate the lengths *AC* and *AG* in each figure to the nearest tenth.

1.

A, G
3 in., 5 in.
B, 4 in., C

2.

A, G
8 in., 8 in.
B, 8 in., C

3.

A, G
20 cm, 24 cm
B, 8 cm, C

Interior dimensions are given. Find the length of a diagonal of each prism. Will the object fit inside?

4.

10.5 in.

5.

28 in.

6.

79 in.

7 in.
5 in.
5 in.

9 in.
20 in.
25 in.

35 in.
18 in.
51 in.

7. **Open-ended** Find dimensions for two different boxes whose diagonals are 50 cm long. (*Hint*: choose lengths for two of the sides of each box and find the length of the third side.)

8. **Reading** How can you use a prism to help you find the distance from a point to the origin in three dimensions?

Find the distance from each point to the origin.

9. (1, 1, 1)
10. (2, 2, 2)
11. (−3, 3, 3)
12. (1, 2, 3)
13. (−1, 2, −3)
14. (1, 3, 5)
15. (2, 5, 7)
16. (3, 4, 12)

17. **Open-ended** Choose a point with three nonzero coordinates and find its distance from the origin.

Find the distance between each pair of points.

18. (4, 3, 6) and (6, 6, 1)
19. (2, 3, 4) and (2, 3, 7)
20. (−7, 8, 9) and (7, 8, 9)
21. (−1, 6, −5) and (3, −2, −7)

Tell whether each triangle is *scalene*, *isosceles*, or *equilateral*. Explain.

22. *A*(6, 1, 4), *B*(4, 3, 2), *C*(6, 4, 4)
23. *D*(0, 0, 0), *E*(3, 4, 5), *F*(3, 4, 0)
24. *P*(2, 3, 4), *Q*(3, 4, 2), *R*(4, 2, 3)
25. *L*(5, 9, 3), *M*(1, 11, 7), *N*(1, 5, 7)

Open-ended Find the three-dimensional coordinates of a point that is not on any axis and is the given distance from the origin.

26. $\sqrt{3}$
27. $\sqrt{14}$
28. $\sqrt{21}$

Product Evaluation The table gives the ratings by the editors of a magazine on three features of camcorders. A rating of 5 is the highest rating in each category.

Ratings of Camcorders			
Camcorder	Color accuracy	Low-Light performance	Picture clarity
Brand A	4	1	4
Brand B	3	5	2
Brand C	3	5	3
Brand D	4	3	4
Brand E	4	1	3
Brand F	3	1	2

Low Rating | High Rating

Low Rating | High Rating

picture clarity

color accuracy

low-light performance

(5, 5, 5)

d

A
E
F
D
C
B

For Exercises 29–31, use the table above.

29. **a.** Rank the camcorders by simply adding the three ratings. What is one disadvantage of this method?

   b. Rank the camcorders by using the distance formula to find each camcorder's "distance" from the perfect rating of (5, 5, 5).

   c. Do the ranking methods in parts (a) and (b) give the same results? Explain which ranking method you prefer.

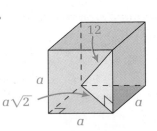

Low Rating | High Rating

30. Suppose you think "picture clarity" is more important than "color accuracy" or "low-light performance." How can you modify the distance formula you use in ranking the camcorders?

31. Suppose there are five features to consider in ranking the camcorders. How can you modify the distance formula?

32. The length of a diagonal of a cube is 12 in.

   a. Find the length of each side of the cube.

   b. Find the volume and the surface area of the cube.

12

a

$a\sqrt{2}$

a

a

33. **Writing** Describe the triangle whose vertices are (x, y, z), (y, z, x), and (z, x, y).

Review **PREVIEW**

34. Find the midpoint of the segment with endpoints $(0, 0, 0)$ and $(10, -2, 2)$. *(Section 10-4)*

35. Suppose you toss a coin and roll a die. Find the probability of getting heads on the coin and "3" on the die, or P(H and 3). *(Section 6-4)*

Tell how to translate the graph of $y = x^2$ in order to produce the graph of each function. *(Section 4-2)*

36. $y = (x - 4)^2$ 37. $y = (x + 2)^2$ 38. $y = x^2 - 7$

Working on the Unit Project

39. Steve wants to mail a rainstick to his pen pal in Hong Kong. The rainstick is 31.5 in. long. Steve finds these two rectangular boxes at home.

   a. Which box should Steve use? Why?

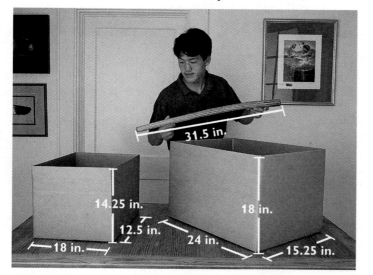

BY THE WAY...

Rainsticks are made from dead cactus branches. When a rainstick is rotated, the small stones within it travel down through a formation of sharp thorns, producing a soothing, rain-like sound. People in Chile and elsewhere have used rainsticks in ceremonies since ancient times. Many musicians today use the rainstick as a percussion instrument.

   b. **Open-ended** Design a long triangular prism box that can hold the rainstick. Draw the box on a three-dimensional grid with one edge of the box on the z-axis. Give the coordinates of the vertices. What are the advantages of your box over the box that Steve used? What are the disadvantages?

Circles and Spheres

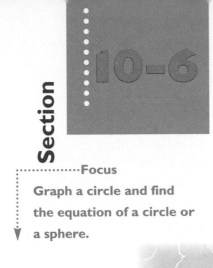

Journey to the Center

····Focus

Graph a circle and find
the equation of a circle or
a sphere.

possible location
of epicenter

(x, y)

900 km

Ajmer

0 200 km

On September 29, 1993,
a violent earthquake
shook the Ajmer record-
ing station in Rajasthan,
India. The station's
instruments showed that
the epicenter was about
900 km away.

Imagine that the Ajmer recording station is at the origin of
a coordinate system, and the epicenter is at some point
(x, y). You can use the distance formula to find an equation for all points (x, y) that are 900 km from the origin.

$$\sqrt{(x_2 - x_1)^2 + (y_2 - y_1)^2} = d$$

Recording station
is at (**0**, **0**).

$$\sqrt{(x - 0)^2 + (y - 0)^2} = 900$$ ← Distance is 900 km.

Epicenter is
at (**x**, **y**).

$$\sqrt{x^2 + y^2} = 900$$ ← Square both sides.

$$x^2 + y^2 = 810{,}000$$ ← An equation for
all points 900 km
from the origin.

Talk it Over

1. Explain why the graph of $x^2 + y^2 = 810{,}000$ is a circle.

2. How can you find an equation of a circle with center (0, 0)
   and radius 5?

3. Explain how you can use the three-dimensional
   distance formula to find an equation of the sphere
   with center (0, 0, 0) and radius 900.

X ᴄ∆ab

EQUATIONS OF CIRCLES AND SPHERES CENTERED AT THE ORIGIN

The equation of a circle with center $(0, 0)$ and radius r is $x^2 + y^2 = r^2$.

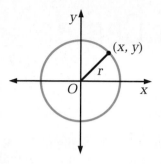

The equation of a sphere with center $(0, 0, 0)$ and radius r is $x^2 + y^2 + z^2 = r^2$.

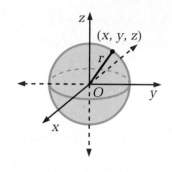

Sample 1

Graph the circle $x^2 + y^2 = 36$.

Sample Response

Method ❶ Use graph paper.

Since the equation is in the form $x^2 + y^2 = r^2$, the center is $(0, 0)$ and $r^2 = 36$.

Therefore, $r = \sqrt{36} = 6$.
The radius is 6.

From the origin, mark a radius of 6 on the x- and y-axes. Sketch the circle.

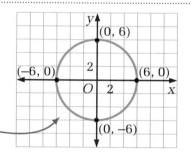

Method ❷ Use a graphics calculator.

Since $x^2 + y^2 = 36$ is not a function, graph two semicircles, each of which is a function.

$$x^2 + y^2 = 36$$
$$y^2 = 36 - x^2$$

Graph $Y_1 = \sqrt{36 - x^2}$.

Graph $Y_2 = -\sqrt{36 - x^2}$.

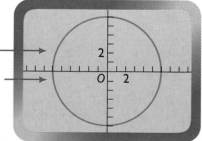

TECHNOLOGY NOTE

To make the graph appear circular, you may have to use the calculator feature that "squares" the screen. See Technology Handbook page 605.

a. Find an equation of the circle. The center is at the origin.

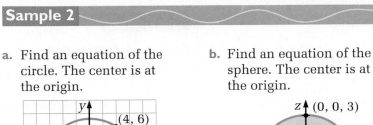

b. Find an equation of the sphere. The center is at the origin.

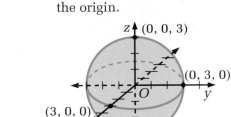

Sample Response

a. The center is (0, 0). The equation is of the form $x^2 + y^2 = r^2$.

The radius, r, is the distance between the points (0, 0) and (4, 6).

$$r = \sqrt{(4 - 0)^2 + (6 - 0)^2} = \sqrt{52}$$

An equation is $x^2 + y^2 = 52$. ⟵ $r^2 = (\sqrt{52})^2 = 52$

b. The center is (0, 0, 0) and the radius is 3. The equation is of the form $x^2 + y^2 + z^2 = r^2$. Substitute 3 for r.

An equation is $x^2 + y^2 + z^2 = 9$.

·····► **Now you are ready for:**
Exs. 1–16 on pp. 594–595

The Shillong earthquake recording station in Meghalaya, India, is about 1700 km east of the Ajmer station. The instruments at Shillong showed that the epicenter was about 1800 km away. Find an equation of a circle that describes all points 1800 km from the Shillong station.

Sample Response

Problem Solving Strategy: Use a formula.

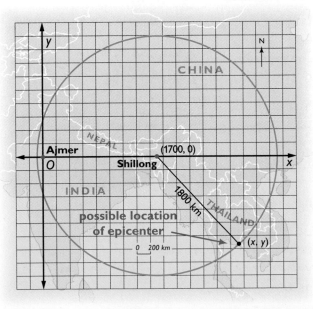

The distance from the Shillong station at (1700, 0) to the epicenter (x, y) is 1800. Use the distance formula.

$$\sqrt{(x_2 - x_1)^2 + (y_2 - y_1)^2} = d$$
$$\sqrt{(x - 1700)^2 + (y - 0)^2} = 1800$$
$$(x - 1700)^2 + y^2 = 3{,}240{,}000$$

An equation of the circle is
$$(x - 1700)^2 + y^2 = 3{,}240{,}000.$$

4. Use the map in Sample 3. The Lhasa recording station in Tibet, China, is about 400 km north of the Shillong station. The epicenter was about 2000 km from the Lhasa station.

   a. What would be the coordinates of the Lhasa recording station?

   b. What is an equation of the circle with its center at Lhasa that contains the epicenter (x, y)?

5. How can you use the equations of the circles with centers at Ajmer, Shillong, and Lhasa to find values for x and y?

EQUATIONS OF CIRCLES NOT CENTERED AT THE ORIGIN

The equation of a circle with center (h, k) and radius r is $(x - h)^2 + (y - k)^2 = r^2$.

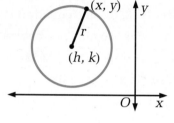

Look Back

Now you are ready for:
Exs. 17–34 on pp. 596–598

What information do you need to know about a circle to find its equation? What information do you need to know about a sphere to find its equation?

10-6 Exercises and Problems

For Exercises 1–7, write an equation of each circle or sphere.

1.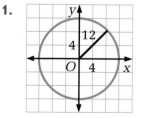

2.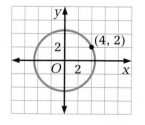

3.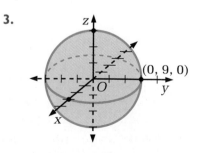

4. The center of the circle is $(0, 0)$. The radius is 2.5.

5. The center of the circle is $(0, 0)$. The endpoints of a diameter are $(5, 0)$ and $(-5, 0)$.

6. The center of the sphere is $(0, 0, 0)$. The radius is 6.

7. The center of the sphere is $(0, 0, 0)$. The radius is 4.

8. **Reading** Describe two methods you could use to graph the equation of a circle whose center is at the origin.

For Exercises 9–12, graph each circle.

9. $x^2 + y^2 = 25$ 10. $x^2 + y^2 = 100$ 11. $x^2 + y^2 = 15$ 12. $x^2 + y^2 = 3$

connection to **LANGUAGE ARTS**

Robin Mandel used ideas from geometry in his 1993 high school graduation speech at University School in Milwaukee, Wisconsin. Here is part of his speech.

"... Think of yourself as a point in space. Picture yourself hovering in three dimensions. Give yourself a radius, say arm's length, that you can reach out in all directions. Imagine that every time you think a new thought, or hear a different idea, or meet a new person, you reach out and touch another point. Learn about covalent chemical bonding, touch another point. Read a book about life as a teacher in rural New Mexico, touch another point. Keep reaching and accumulating points and a shape begins to emerge. In geometry, here at this very school, I learned the name of the shape defined by a set of points equidistant from a central point in all directions. It's called a sphere.

"Metaphorically speaking, then, *you* are the center point of the sphere of your life's experiences. The more points you can touch, the more complete your sphere becomes. As time goes on, you fill in the spaces of your sphere. And you have to remember to work in three dimensions and reach in all directions. Reach only one direction and you might end up a hemisphere, and those don't roll very far."

13. What is Robin trying to describe by using the idea of a sphere?

14. **Research** What is a *metaphor*? What does Robin mean by "metaphorically speaking"?

15. **Writing** Describe the sphere of your life or of the life of someone you know well. What is the radius of the sphere?

16. **Writing** Choose a different idea from the mathematics you have learned this year (such as *deductive reasoning, functions, transformations, modeling*). Write an essay about something in your life. Use the ideas and words of mathematics to help explain it.

Write an equation of each circle or sphere.

17. The center of the circle is (1, 3). The radius is 2.5.

18. The center of the circle is (−3, −2). The radius is 8.

19. The center of the sphere is (0, 0, 0). The radius is 4.

Write an equation of each circle.

20.

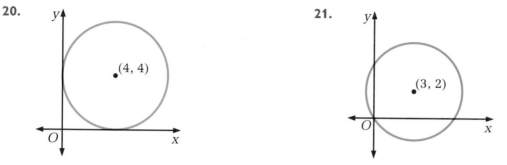

21.

22. **Agriculture** A *linear irrigation system* uses many sprinklers connected to a long water pipe on wheels. The spray from each sprinkler covers a circular area. As the water pipe moves across the field, the entire field can be watered.

   a. Suppose the sprinklers spray water 20 ft and are spaced along the water pipe every 40 ft. Write equations for circles *A*, *B*, and *C*.

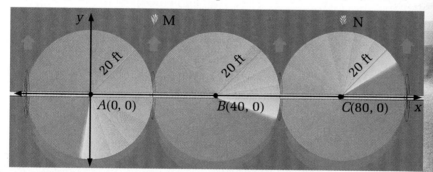

   b. Will plants M and N get the same amount of water? Explain.

   c. Suppose instead that the sprinklers are spaced along the water pipe every 35 ft. Write equations for circles *D*, *E*, and *F*.

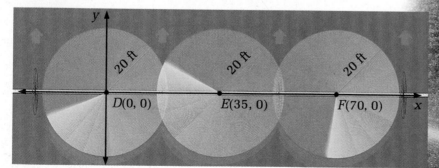

   d. Explain why a farmer might use the spacing in part (c) instead of the spacing in part (a).

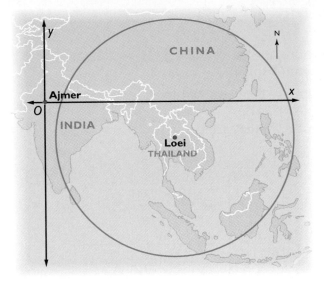

23. **Seismology** Use the diagram of earthquake recording stations.

    a. The Loei station in Thailand is about 2800 km east and 1000 km south of the Ajmer station. What are the coordinates of the Loei station?

    b. The epicenter of the September 29 earthquake was about 2600 km from the Loei station. Use your answer from part (a) to write an equation of the circle on which the epicenter lies.

Graph each circle.

24. $x^2 + (y - 1)^2 = 16$

25. $(x - 3)^2 + (y + 2)^2 = 49$

26. The equation of a circle is $(x - 8)^2 + (y + 4)^2 = 9$.

    a. Find the center and the radius of the circle.

    b. Is the point $(5, -5)$ inside or outside the circle? Use a drawing to explain.

27. The equation of a sphere is $(x - 8)^2 + (y + 4)^2 + (z - 5)^2 = 36$.

    a. Find the center and the radius of the sphere.

    b. **Open-ended** Find the coordinates of the endpoints of a diameter.

Career Investigators sometimes measure the marks tires leave on the road at the site of an accident. In some circumstances, knowing the radius of the circle on which the tire marks lie helps investigators estimate how fast a car was traveling when the tires began to slip.

(Not drawn to scale.)

28. a. The y-axis is perpendicular to the 33 m segment. Explain why the point $(16.5, r - 3.5)$ is on the circle.

    b. Substitute the coordinates $(16.5, r - 3.5)$ into the equation $x^2 + y^2 = r^2$.

    c. Solve the equation from part (b) for r to find the radius of the circle on which the tire marks lie.

    d. The equation $v = \sqrt{\mu g r}$ describes the speed of the car, where μ is the coefficient of friction (which depends on the road surface), g is the acceleration due to gravity, and r is the radius of the curve.

    Find the speed of the car in meters per second if $\mu = 0.8$, $g = 9.8$ m/s², and $r =$ the value you found in part (c).

29. a. Sketch the line $y = -x + 3$ and the circle with center $(0, 0)$ and radius 2. Do you think the two graphs intersect? Explain.

b. TECHNOLOGY Graph the circle and line from part (a) on a graphics calculator. Do they intersect? Use ZOOM if necessary.

c. How can you tell if the circle and line intersect without using a graphics calculator?

Ongoing **ASSESSMENT**

30. **Writing** Explain the steps you would take to write the equation of circle O and the equation of circle H. Then write each equation.

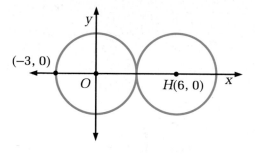

$(-3, 0)$

O $H(6, 0)$

Review **PREVIEW**

31. The diagonal $\overline{AB}$ of a rectangular prism has endpoints $(10, 2, 3)$ and $(6, 4, 4)$. Use the distance formula to find the length of $\overline{AB}$. *(Section 10-5)*

32. Use the implication "All squares are rectangles." *(Section 7-2)*

a. Tell whether the implication is *True* or *False*.

b. Write the converse of the implication. Tell whether it is *True* or *False*. If it is false, give a counterexample.

Working on the Unit Project

33. Write an equation for the edge of the bottom of the cylinder.

34. If your container has a circle in its design, draw it on a coordinate grid and write an equation for it.

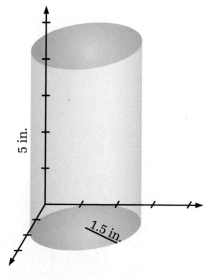

5 in.

1.5 in.

Completing the Unit Project

Now you are ready to complete your container.

Your completed project should include these things:

➤ **a container to hold an object or objects of your choice**

➤ **a written description of the container**

➤ **a set of drawings that represent the three-dimensional shape of the container in enough detail for another person to reconstruct it**

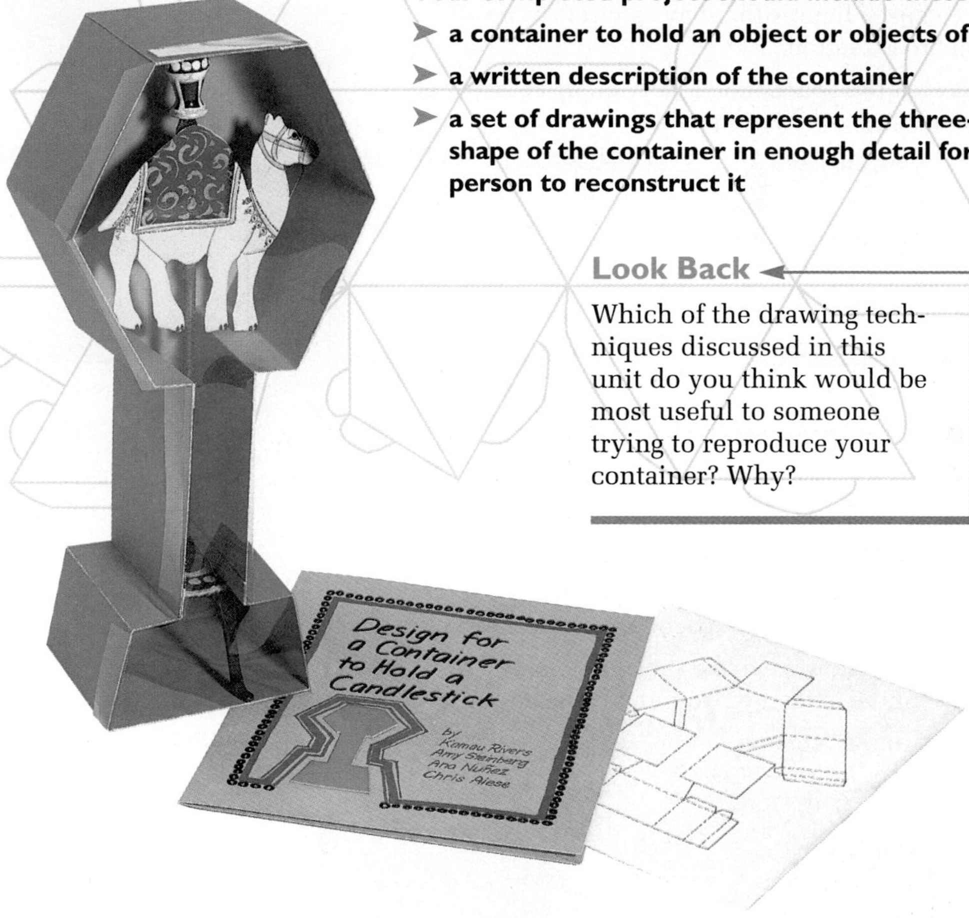

Look Back ◄

Which of the drawing techniques discussed in this unit do you think would be most useful to someone trying to reproduce your container? Why?

Design for a Container to Hold a Candlestick

by Komau Rivers
Amy Steinberg
Ana Nuñez
Chris Alesse

Alternative Projects

Project 1: Design a Birdhouse

Research the kinds of birdhouses that attract different kinds of birds. What shapes are common in birdhouses? Design a birdhouse and make drawings showing how to construct it.

Project 2: Make a Pop-up Book

Reading a book is usually a two-dimensional experience: the words lie flat on the page. But a pop-up book is three-dimensional. Look in the children's section of a bookstore to see how pop-up books work. Create a pop-up book that demonstrates some of the ideas about coordinates and figures in space that you learned in this unit.

1. What space figure does the pattern at the right represent?   **10-1**

2. Draw two different views of a cylinder.

3. Name three space figures that have a circle as a horizontal cross section.

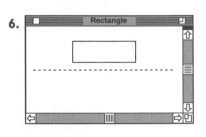

Describe or sketch the space figure formed by rotating each plane figure around the indicated line.   **10-2**

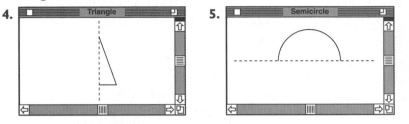

4. *Triangle*
5. *Semicircle*
6. *Rectangle*

7. **a.** **Open-ended** Draw a rectangle and label its length and width. Rotate the rectangle around its longer side. Sketch the space figure formed.

   b. Find the volume of the space figure.

8. Describe the set of points in space that are 6 cm from a point.   **10-3**

9. Describe the set of points in a plane that are 3 m from a line in the plane.

10. Describe the set of points in space that are equidistant from two points.

11. **Writing** Explain how to locate the epicenter of an earthquake if you know the distance of the epicenter from three earthquake recording stations.

12. Two vertices of the rectangular prism at the right are $E(5, 0, 4)$ and $C(0, 6, 0)$.   **10-4**

    a. Find the coordinates of the other six vertices.

    b. Find the midpoint of $\overline{EC}$.

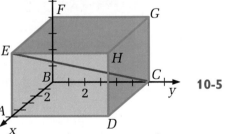

13. Find the length of a diagonal of a rectangular prism with sides of length 3, 6, and 9.   **10-5**

14. Is the triangle formed by $L(0, 3, 0)$, $M(5, 0, 0)$, and $N(2, 2, 2)$ *scalene*, *isosceles*, or *equilateral*? Explain.

15. Graph the circle $x^2 + y^2 = 49$.   **10-6**

Write an equation of each circle or sphere.

16. The center of the circle is $(2, -1)$ and the radius is 5.

17. The center of the sphere is $(0, 0, 0)$ and the radius is 6.

18. **a.** **Self-evaluation** Choose a radius and a height. Represent a cylinder with these dimensions as many ways as you can.

    b. **Group Activity** Exchange one of your representations with another student. Sketch each other's cylinder.

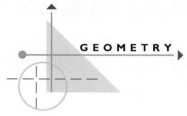

IDEAS AND (FORMULAS) $=x^2$

GEOMETRY

> Space figures are often represented by drawing several views. *(p. 557)*

> A pattern showing an "unfolded" space figure is another way to represent a space figure. *(p. 559)*

> Cross sections can help you visualize space figures. *(p. 559)*

> Some space figures are created by rotating a plane figure around a line called the axis of rotation. *(p. 565)*

> A circle can be considered the set of all points in a plane a given distance from a point. *(p. 571)*

> A sphere can be considered the set of all points in space a given distance from a point. *(p. 572)*

> If the set of points in a plane that meets one condition does not intersect the set of points in the same plane that meets another condition, then there are no points that meet both conditions. *(p. 573)*

> To locate points in three-dimensional space, three coordinate axes are needed. *(p. 579)*

ALGEBRA $)x^2$

> Each of the coordinates of the midpoint of a segment is the mean of the corresponding coordinates of its endpoints. If the endpoints have coordinates (x_1, y_1, z_1) and (x_2, y_2, z_2), the midpoint has coordinates
$$\left(\frac{x_1 + x_2}{2}, \frac{y_1 + y_2}{2}, \frac{z_1 + z_2}{2}\right).$$ *(p. 580)*

> The distance between the points (x_1, y_1, z_1) and (x_2, y_2, z_2) is
$$\sqrt{(x_2 - x_1)^2 + (y_2 - y_1)^2 + (z_2 - z_1)^2}.$$ *(p. 586)*

> The equation of a circle with center $(0, 0)$ and radius r is $x^2 + y^2 = r^2$. *(p. 592)*

> The equation of a sphere with center $(0, 0, 0)$ and radius r is $x^2 + y^2 + z^2 = r^2$. *(p. 592)*

> The equation of a circle with center (h, k) and radius r is $(x - h)^2 + (y - k)^2 = r^2$. *(p. 594)*

Key Terms

- **space figure** (p. 557)
- **axis of rotation** (p. 565)
- **diagonal of a rectangular prism** (p. 584)

- **cross section** (p. 559)
- **equidistant** (p. 574)

- **plane figure** (p. 565)
- **ordered triple** (p. 579)

Contents of Student Resources

Student Resources

Technology Handbook

Using a Graphics Calculator

This handbook introduces you to the basic features of most graphics calculators. Check your calculator's instruction manual for specific keystrokes and any details not provided here.

Performing Calculations

➤ The Keyboard

Look closely at your calculator's keyboard. Notice that most keys serve more than one purpose. Each key is labeled with its primary purpose, and labels for any secondary purposes appear somewhere near the key. You may need to press **2nd**, **SHIFT**, or **ALPHA** to use a key for a secondary purpose.

Examples of using the **X²** key:

Press **X²** to square a number.

Press **2nd** and then **X²** to take a square root.

Press **ALPHA** and then **X²** to get the letter I.

➤ The Home Screen

Your calculator has a "home screen" where you can do calculations. You can usually enter a calculation on a graphics calculator just as you would write it on a piece of paper.

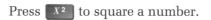

Shown below are other things to remember as you enter calculations on your graphics calculator.

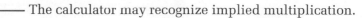

2(3)	
	6
3 − ⁻2	
	5
∛8	
	2

— The calculator may recognize implied multiplication.

— The calculator has a subtraction key, **−**, and a negation key, **(−)**. If you use these incorrectly, you will get an error message.

— You may need to get a cube root (or other operation that is not often used) from a **MATH** menu.

1. Use your calculator to find the value of each expression.

   a. $\sqrt[3]{64}$ **b.** 2^5 **c.** $\sin 75°$

2. Which of the following are true?

   a. $\sin 60° > \cos 30°$ **b.** $\tan 45° = \cos 45°$ **c.** $2\sin 30° = 1$

3. Find the value of each expression.

   a. $5!$ **b.** $\dfrac{5!}{3!}$ **c.** $\dfrac{5!}{(2!)(3!)}$

Displaying Graphs

➤ The Viewing Window

When you use a graphics calculator to display graphs, think of the screen as a "viewing window" that lets you look at a portion of the coordinate plane.

On many calculators, the standard viewing window uses values from −10 to 10 on both the *x*- and *y*-axes. You can adjust the viewing window by pressing the **RANGE** or **WINDOW** key and entering new values for the window variables.

```
RANGE
Xmin = −10
Xmax = 10
Xscl = 1
Ymin = −10
Ymax = 10
Yscl = 1
Xres = 1
```

The *x*-axis will be shown for $-10 \leq x \leq 10$.

The *y*-axis will be shown for $-10 \leq y \leq 10$.

With scale variables set to equal 1, tick marks will be 1 unit apart on both axes.

Some calculators have a resolution variable. This controls how "smooth" the graph will look.

➤ Entering and Graphing a Function

To graph a function, enter its equation in the form $y = ...$
If the equation does not use *x* and *y*, rewrite the equation.
Let *x* = the control variable and *y* = the dependent variable. Set the variables for an appropriate viewing window. The graph of $y = \frac{1}{2}x + 3$ is shown using the standard viewing window.

Use parentheses. If you enter $y = 1/2x + 3$ instead, the calculator may interpret the equation as $y = \frac{1}{2x} + 3$.

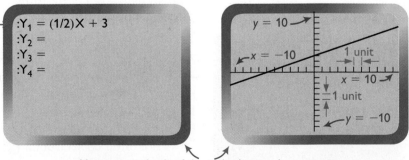

You can see both of these displays at the same time if your calculator has a split-screen mode.

➤ Squaring the Screen

A "square screen" is a viewing window with equal unit spacing on the two axes. For example, the graph of $y = x$ is shown for two different windows.

Standard Viewing Window

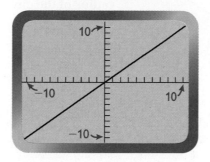

Square Screen Window

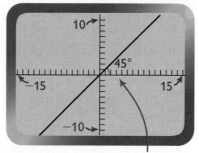

On a square screen, the line $y = x$ makes a 45° angle with the x-axis.

On many graphics calculators, the ratio of the screen's height to its width is about 2 to 3. Your calculator may have a feature that gives you a square screen. If not, choose values for the window variables that make the "length" of the y-axis about two-thirds the "length" of the x-axis:

$$(\text{Ymax} - \text{Ymin}) \approx \tfrac{2}{3}(\text{Xmax} - \text{Xmin})$$

Try This

4. Enter and graph each equation separately. Use the standard viewing window. You may need to put the equation in function form, $y = ...$, first.

   a. $y = 3x + 1$ **b.** $x + 2y = 4$ **c.** $y = |x|$ **d.** $y = \dfrac{5}{x}$

5. Find a good viewing window for the graph of $y = 65 - 3x$. Be sure your window shows where the graph crosses both axes.

6. Find a viewing window that will allow you to graph these two lines so that they appear to be perpendicular: $y = 2x + 1$ and $y = -0.5x - 2$.

Reading a Graph
➤ The TRACE Feature

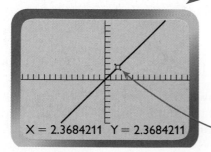

After a graph is displayed, you can use the calculator's TRACE feature. When you press [TRACE], a flashing cursor appears on the graph. The x- and y-coordinates of the cursor's location are shown at the bottom of the screen. Press the left- and right-arrow keys to move the TRACE cursor along the graph.

$X = 2.3684211$ $Y = 2.3684211$

The TRACE cursor is at the point (2.3684211, 2.3684211) on the graph of $y = x$.

Technology Handbook

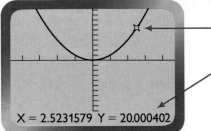

Suppose you want to find the radius of a circular hole with an area of 20 in². The formula for the area of a circle is $A = \pi r^2$. Rewrite the equation using x and y. Graph the equation $y = \pi x^2$.

Using the TRACE key, move the cursor along the graph until the y-value is approximately equal to 20. This will give you the value of x that is the radius of the circular hole.

Another way to solve the problem is to graph two equations on the same screen: $y = \pi x^2$ and $y = 20$. Use TRACE to move the cursor to the intersection of the two lines to find your answer.

➤ **Friendly Windows**

As you press the right-arrow key while tracing a graph, you may notice that the x-coordinate increases by "unfriendly" increments.

Your calculator may allow you to control the x-increment, ΔX, directly. If not, you can control it indirectly by choosing an appropriate Xmax for a given Xmin. For example, on a TI-82 graphics calculator, choose Xmax so that

$$\text{Xmax} = \text{Xmin} + 94\Delta X.$$

This number depends upon the calculator you are using.

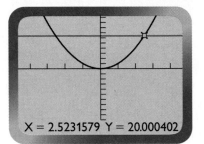

Suppose you want ΔX to equal 0.1. If Xmin $= -5$, then set Xmax equal to $-5 + 94(0.1)$, or 4.4. This gives a "friendly window" where the TRACE cursor's x-coordinate will increase by 0.1 each time you press the right-arrow key.

Try This

7. Graph the equation $y = x^2 + 2x - 1$. Choose a friendly window where $\Delta X = 0.1$. Use the TRACE feature to determine, to the nearest tenth, the x-coordinate of each of the two points where the graph crosses the x-axis.

Student Resources

➤ The TABLE Feature

Instead of tracing the graph of an equation, you may wish to examine a table of values. Not all calculators have a TABLE feature. Check to see if yours does.

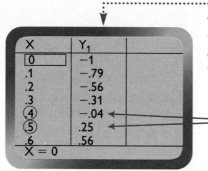

The screen shows a table of values for $y = x^2 + 2x - 1$. Here the value of x increases from a minimum of 0 in steps of 0.1. Some calculators have a table set-up feature that allows you to set the table minimum and the change in the control variable.

Notice that the y-values change sign between $x = 0.4$ and $x = 0.5$.

Taking a Closer Look at a Graph
➤ The ZOOM Feature

Suppose you are interested in the point where the graph of the equation $y = x^2 + 2x - 1$ crosses the positive x-axis. Tracing the graph shows that the x-coordinate of the point is between 0.4 and 0.5.

Move the TRACE cursor to a point just below the x-axis. The y-coordinate of this point is negative but close to 0.

Move the TRACE cursor to a point just above the x-axis. The y-coordinate of this point is positive but close to 0.

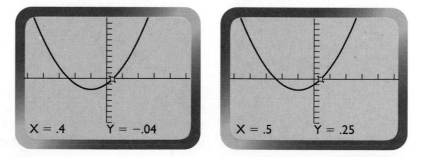

To get a closer look at the point of interest, you can use the ZOOM feature. Your calculator may have more than one way to zoom. A common way is to put a "zoom box" around the point. The calculator will then draw what's inside the box at full-screen size.

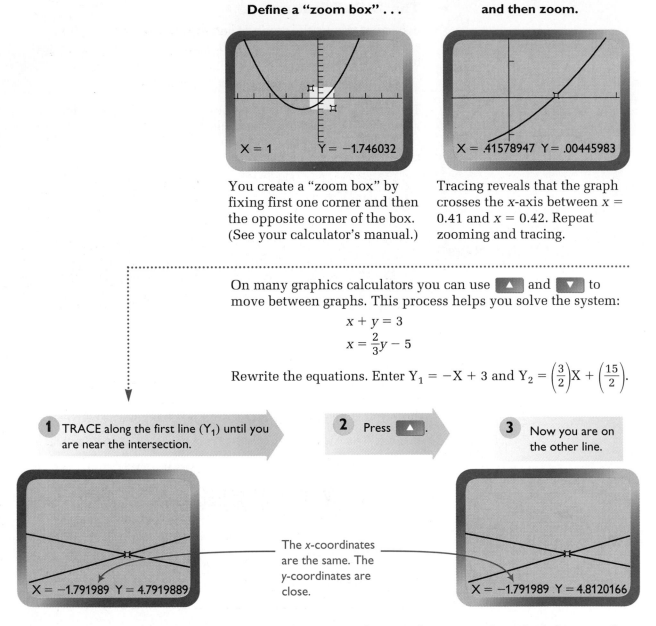

Define a "zoom box" . . .

X = 1   Y = −1.746032

You create a "zoom box" by fixing first one corner and then the opposite corner of the box. (See your calculator's manual.)

and then zoom.

X = .41578947 Y = .00445983

Tracing reveals that the graph crosses the x-axis between x = 0.41 and x = 0.42. Repeat zooming and tracing.

On many graphics calculators you can use ▲ and ▼ to move between graphs. This process helps you solve the system:

$$x + y = 3$$
$$x = \frac{2}{3}y - 5$$

Rewrite the equations. Enter $Y_1 = -X + 3$ and $Y_2 = \left(\frac{3}{2}\right)X + \left(\frac{15}{2}\right)$.

1 TRACE along the first line (Y_1) until you are near the intersection.

2 Press ▲.

3 Now you are on the other line.

X = −1.791989 Y = 4.7919889

The x-coordinates are the same. The y-coordinates are close.

X = −1.791989 Y = 4.8120166

You can ZOOM in and repeat the process described above until the y-coordinates are the same to the nearest tenth, hundredth, or any other decimal place. Some calculators have an intersection feature that lets you find the intersection after using TRACE.

Try This

8. Try zooming in on the point where the graph of $y = x^2 + 2x - 1$ crosses the negative x-axis. Between what two values, to the nearest hundredth, does the x-coordinate of the point lie?

9. Solve this sytem by graphing: $9x + 3y = 14$
$-3x + 2y = 8$

Comparing Graphs

➤ ## Using a List to Graph a Family of Curves

Some calculators allow you to enter a list as an element in an expression. The calculator can then plot a function for each value in the list and graph a family of curves.

$Y_1 = \{1, -2, 0.5\}X^2$
plots the family of functions
$y = x^2, y = -2x^2, y = 0.5x^2.$

$Y_2 = X^2 + \{-4, 5, 2\}$
plots the family of functions
$y = x^2 - 4, y = x^2 + 5, y = x^2 + 2.$

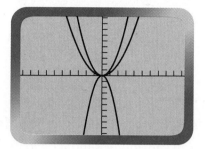
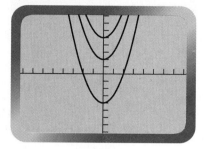

Using Matrices

➤ ## Entering and Multiplying a Matrix by a Number

Suppose you want to enter this table of sales data as a matrix on your calculator.

This Month's Sales by Age Group				
	VCRs	CD players	Faxes	Telephone answerers
Under 25	73	211	24	106
25–49	132	188	67	142
Over 49	89	55	46	98

Press the matrix function key. Select EDIT and choose matrix [A].

```
MATRIX [A] 3 × 4

[ 73   211  24  ...
[ 132  188  67  ...
[ 89   55   46  ...
```

Set the dimensions. The matrix has 3 rows and 4 columns of data.

Enter the elements of the matrix $\begin{bmatrix} 73 & 211 & 24 & 106 \\ 132 & 188 & 67 & 142 \\ 89 & 55 & 46 & 98 \end{bmatrix}$.

Suppose the data on page 609 are this month's sales in an electronics store you manage. You want to see what a projected increase of 14% in sales would be.

You have entered the data as matrix [A]. To increase each element by 14%, you can multiply [A] by 1.14.

First return to the home screen.

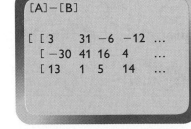

Press 1.14 [MATRX] [ENTER] on a TI-82 graphics calculator.

➤ Adding and Subtracting Matrices

You can add or subtract two matrices that have the same dimensions. You first enter each matrix. Suppose you enter two months' sales data as [A] and [B].

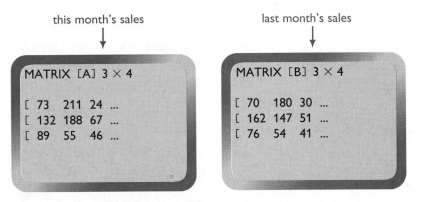

To compare the two data sets, you can subtract the matrices. The answer is a matrix with the same dimensions as the original matrices. Its elements are the sums or differences of elements in the same positions in [A] and in [B].

Press [MATRX] [ENTER] [−] [MATRX] 2 [ENTER].

➤ Finding the Product of Two Matrices

You can multiply two matrices when the number of columns of the first matrix is the same as the number of rows of the second matrix.

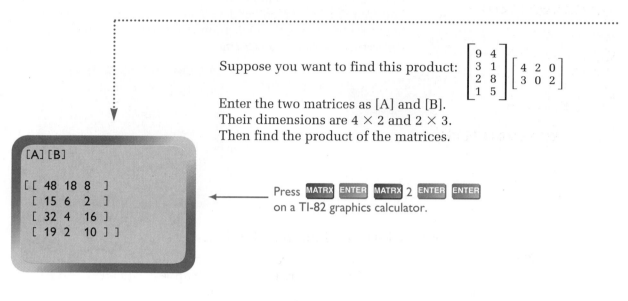

Suppose you want to find this product: $\begin{bmatrix} 9 & 4 \\ 3 & 1 \\ 2 & 8 \\ 1 & 5 \end{bmatrix} \begin{bmatrix} 4 & 2 & 0 \\ 3 & 0 & 2 \end{bmatrix}$

Enter the two matrices as [A] and [B].
Their dimensions are 4×2 and 2×3.
Then find the product of the matrices.

[A] [B]

[[48 18 8]
 [15   6 2]
 [32   4 16]
 [19   2 10]]

Press **MATRX** **ENTER** **MATRX** 2 **ENTER** **ENTER**
on a TI-82 graphics calculator.

➤ Finding the Inverse of a Matrix

You can use a graphics calculator to find the inverse of a matrix when the number of rows is the same as the number of columns.

Suppose you want to find the inverse of this matrix: $\begin{bmatrix} 3 & -1 \\ 4 & 0 \end{bmatrix}$

Enter the elements
of the matrix as [A].

To find [A]$^{-1}$ press
ENTER x^{-1} **ENTER**.

MATRIX [A] 2 × 2

[3 −1]
[4 0]

[A]$^{-1}$

[[0 .25]
 [−1 .75]]

Try This

Use matrices A, B, C, or D to find each answer. If a matrix does not exist, write *not defined*.

$A = \begin{bmatrix} 3 & 4 \\ 6 & 7 \end{bmatrix}$ $B = \begin{bmatrix} 5 & 11 \\ -3 & -7 \end{bmatrix}$ $C = \begin{bmatrix} 9 & 3 \\ 12 & 4 \end{bmatrix}$ $D = \begin{bmatrix} 2 & 0 & -8 & 1 \\ 5 & 7 & 3 & 9 \end{bmatrix}$

10. $A + B$ **11.** $B - C$ **12.** $2A$ **13.** AB

14. $C + D$ **15.** CD **16.** A^{-1} **17.** D^{-1}

Working with Statistics

➤ Histograms, Line Graphs, and Box-and-Whisker Plots

Many graphics calculators can display histograms, line graphs, and sometimes even box-and-whisker plots of data that you enter. For example, the histogram below displays the data about the readers of *Galaxy* magazine.

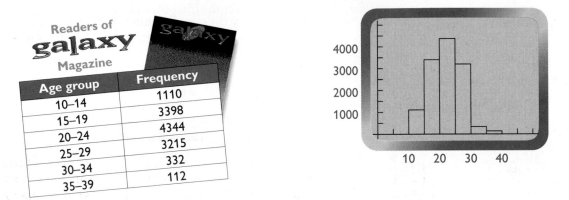

Readers of **galaxy** Magazine

Age group	Frequency
10–14	1110
15–19	3398
20–24	4344
25–29	3215
30–34	332
35–39	112

➤ Scatter Plots and Curve Fitting

Curve fitting is the process of finding an equation that describes a set of ordered pairs. Often, the first step is to graph the paired data in a scatter plot.

The scatter plot below displays the data for an Olympic event. It also shows a fitted line, called a *regression line*, that the calculator fit to the data.

Men's Winning Times in Olympic 400 m Freestyle Swimming		
Year	Years after 1960	Time (seconds)
1960	0	258.3
1964	4	252.2
1968	8	249.0
1972	12	240.27
1976	16	231.93
1980	20	231.31
1984	24	231.23
1988	28	226.95
1992	32	225.00

The equation of the regression line is $y = 2325 - 1.056x$ where x is the year and y is the winning time.

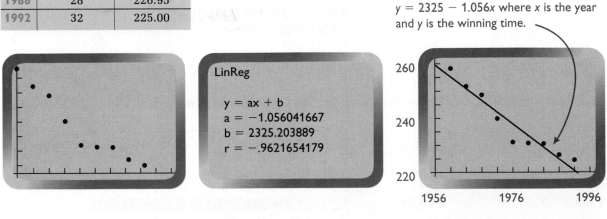

LinReg

$y = ax + b$
$a = -1.056041667$
$b = 2325.203889$
$r = -.9621654179$

Using a Spreadsheet

In addition to using a graphics calculator, you may want to use a computer with a spreadsheet program. A spreadsheet can help you solve a problem like this one: Suppose you want to buy a CD player that costs $195, including tax. You already have $37 and can save $9 per week. After how many weeks can you buy the player?

A spreadsheet is made up of cells named by a column letter and a row number, like A3 or B4. You can enter a label, a number, or a formula into a cell.

CD Savings

	A Week number	B Total saved
1	Week number	Total saved
2	0	37
3	= + A2 + 1	= + B2 + 9
4	= + A3 + 1	= + B3 + 9
5	= + A4 + 1	= + B4 + 9
6	= + A5 + 1	= + B5 + 9
7	= + A6 + 1	= + B6 + 9
8	= + A7 + 1	= + B7 + 9
9	= + A8 + 1	= + B8 + 9
10	= + A9 + 1	= + B9 + 9
11	= + A10 + 1	= + B10 + 9
12	= + A11 + 1	= + B11 + 9
13	= + A12 + 1	= + B12 + 9
14	= + A13 + 1	= + B13 + 9
15	= + A14 + 1	= + B14 + 9
16	= + A15 + 1	= + B15 + 9
17	= + A16 + 1	= + B16 + 9
18	= + A17 + 1	= + B17 + 9
19	= + A18 + 1	= + B18 + 9
20	= + A19 + 1	= + B19 + 9

Cell B1 contains the label "Total saved."

Cell B2 contains the number 37.

Cell B3 contains the formula "= +B2+9." This formula tells the computer to take the number in cell B2, add 9 to it, and put the result in cell B3. (Likewise, the formula in cell A3 tells the computer to take the number in cell A2, add 1 to it, and put the result in cell A3.)

Instead of typing a formula into each cell individually, you can use the spreadsheet's copy and fill commands.

CD Savings

	A Week number	B Total saved
1	Week number	Total saved
2	0	37
3	1	46
4	2	55
5	3	64
6	4	73
7	5	82
8	6	91
9	7	100
10	8	109
11	9	118
12	10	127
13	11	136
14	12	145
15	13	154
16	14	163
17	15	172
18	16	181
19	17	190
20	18	199

In this spreadsheet, the computer has replaced all the formulas with calculated values. You can have the computer draw a scatter plot with a line connecting the plotted points. As you can see, you will have enough money to buy the CD player after 18 weeks.

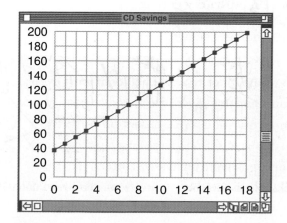

Technology Handbook

Extra Practice

Unit 1

In Exercises 1–4, estimate each amount. `1-1`

1. At a factory that makes compact discs, 2 out of a batch of 50 discs are found to be defective. Estimate the number of defective discs in a monthly output of 3,500 discs.

2. In a sample of wild bird food, 27 seeds out of a sample of 60 seeds are sunflower seeds. Estimate the number of sunflower seeds in a package of about 1500 seeds.

3. **a.** Roberto Rodriguez got 3 hits in 5 official trips to the plate in one baseball game. Based on this game, how many hits would he get in a season in which he has 400 official trips to the plate?

   b. Do you think this is a good method of predicting his record for the season? Why or why not?

4. Floyd Jefferson made 4 and missed 3 jump shots from outside the lane in yesterday's basketball game. Suppose he takes 56 jump shots from outside the lane in a season. Estimate the number of these he will make and the number he will miss.

5. Name a sample group from the population of all triangles. `1-1`

Use this simulation of random guessing on a test for Exercises 6–10. `1-2`

Suppose each question on a 10-question multiple-choice test has three answer-choices. A die is used to simulate random guessing on the test. Rolling a 1 or a 2 represents a correct answer. The results of six trials of rolling a die 10 times are shown.

Trial #	Numbers Rolled
First	2, 3, 5, 1, 6, 4, 2, 3, 2, 5
Second	4, 1, 2, 2, 5, 3, 6, 3, 6, 2
Third	1, 3, 4, 6, 4, 5, 3, 6, 3, 4
Fourth	3, 1, 2, 2, 5, 6, 4, 1, 3, 2
Fifth	4, 5, 3, 1, 5, 5, 2, 1, 2, 4
Sixth	5, 2, 4, 1, 6, 3, 4, 3, 3, 5

Use the table to estimate the probability of each event.

6. Exactly four questions were answered correctly.

7. Four or more questions were answered correctly.

8. Fewer than four questions were answered correctly.

9. All ten questions were answered correctly.

10. What is the mean number of questions answered correctly?

Suppose names are to be selected from a list of magazine subscribers to receive a special offer. Classify each sample as *random, convenience, stratified random, cluster,* or *systematic.* 1-3

11. Every fourth name in the list of subscribers is selected.

12. The first 200 names in the list are selected.

13. Subscribers having a ZIP code that begins with the digits 012 are selected.

14. The list is alphabetized, and the first 10 subscribers whose last names begin with each letter of the alphabet are selected.

15. The subscribers are numbered, the numbers are written on slips of paper, and 200 slips are drawn from a paper bag containing all the slips.

Use this dentist's survey in Exercises 16–18. 1-4

16. Can the dentist find the median of the answers to Question 2?

17. State a possible answer to Question 1 that is not one of the multiple choices.

18. What biases might be reflected in the results of the survey?

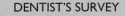

DENTIST'S SURVEY
1. How many times a day do you brush your teeth?
a. once
b. twice
c. three times
d. four or more times
2. How much time do you spend brushing on each occasion?
a. very little
b. 1 min
c. 2 min
d. a very long time

Predict the next number in each pattern. 1-5

19. 3, 6, 12, 24, _?_

20. 1, -2, 3, -4, _?_

21. 11, 101, 1001, 10,001, _?_

22. 1, 8, 27, 64, _?_

23. Suppose you take the product of four consecutive positive integers and add 1. For example, $(1 \cdot 2 \cdot 3 \cdot 4) + 1 = 25$. Try other examples and make a conjecture about the kind of number you always get.

Use the Venn diagram, which shows how students responded to a survey about after-school activities. Tell whether each statement about the students in the survey is *True* or *False*. 1-6

24. All the students in the glee club were involved in an indoor activity.

25. If a student attends an indoor activity, then the student is in the debating club.

26. No students are in both the glee club and the debating club.

27. If a student is on the school newspaper, then that student is also in the debating club.

28. Some students on the school newspaper are in the glee club.

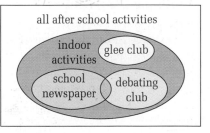

For Exercises 29–32: 1-7

 a. Tell whether or not each statement is true. If not, give a counterexample.

 b. Write the converse of each statement. Tell whether or not it is true. If not, give a counterexample.

29. If $x > 2$, then $x > 5$.

30. If $a + b = a + c$, then $b = c$.

31. If it is midnight, the sun is not out.

32. If $x + y = 5$, then $xy = 6$.

Tell whether each graph is an example of *linear growth, nonlinear growth, linear decay, nonlinear decay, a constant,* or *none of these.* 2-1

1.

2.

3.

4.

For each pair of points: 2-2

a. **Find the slope of the line that contains the points.**

b. **Describe the line as *increasing, decreasing,* or *constant.***

5. $(0, 4)$ and $(3, 0)$ **6.** $(-5, 2)$ and $(4, 5)$ **7.** $(7, 2)$ and $(-1, -10)$

8. $(-3, 6)$ and $(2, 6)$ **9.** $(-1, 8)$ and $(9, -7)$ **10.** $(1, -2)$ and $(6, -2)$

Write an equation for the line through each pair of points. 2-2

11. $(4, -3)$ and $(6, 7)$ **12.** $(0, -5)$ and $(-6, 4)$ **13.** $(2, 3)$ and $(-7, -9)$

14. $(-8, 5)$ and $(0, 11)$ **15.** $(1, 12)$ and $(-5, 9)$ **16.** $(-8, 6)$ and $(6, -1)$

For each equation: 2-2

a. **Identify the slope and the vertical intercept of the graph.**

b. **Draw the graph.**

c. **Write *increasing function, decreasing function,* or *constant function* to describe the graph.**

17. $y = \frac{1}{2}x$ **18.** $y = -2x + 3$ **19.** $y = -1.5$

20. $y = x - 1.5$ **21.** $y = \frac{2}{3}x - 1$ **22.** $y = -\frac{5}{2}x + 4$

Find y when x = 8. 2-3

23. $xy = 24$ **24.** $x = \frac{52}{y}$ **25.** $y = \frac{7.2}{x}$

Rewrite the equation in the $y = \frac{k}{x}$ form. 2-3

26. $xy = -28$ **27.** $\frac{13}{y} = x$ **28.** $-xy = 12$

Find the surface area and the volume of the sphere described. Leave your answer in terms of π. `2-4`

29. radius = 1.5

30. diameter = 9

31. diameter = 21

Find the radius of each sphere described. `2-4`

32. volume = 972π

33. surface area = 484π

34. volume = 7776π

Sphere Q has radius 15. Sphere R has radius 20. Find the ratio of each pair of measurements of the two spheres. `2-4`

35. the diameters

36. the surface areas

37. the volumes

For each equation: `2-5`

a. Find the value of y when $x = 10$.
b. Find the value of x when $y = 24$.

Round all decimal answers to the nearest tenth.

38. $y = 7x^3$

39. $y = \dfrac{\pi x^2}{5}$

40. $y = 0.008x^3$

41. $y = \dfrac{11}{25}x^2$

42. $y = 24{,}000x^3$

43. $y = \dfrac{1}{3}\pi x^2$

Evaluate each expression when $a = 64$. `2-6`

44. $(27a)^{1/3}$

45. $25a^{1/2}$

46. $(49a)^{1/2}$

47. $8a^{1/3}$

48. $\left(\dfrac{a}{125}\right)^{1/3}$

49. $\dfrac{16}{a^{1/2}}$

Rewrite each expression using fractional exponents. `2-6`

50. $15\sqrt{c}$

51. $\sqrt[3]{7x}$

52. $\sqrt[3]{\dfrac{b}{5}}$

Rewrite each expression in radical form. `2-6`

53. $(29pq)^{1/3}$

54. $\dfrac{y^{1/2}}{3x^{1/2}}$

55. $-(8v)^{1/2} \cdot \left(\dfrac{w}{2}\right)^{1/3}$

Use the equation $y = 15(2^x)$. Find the value of y for each value of x. `2-7`

56. $x = 6$

57. $x = 12$

58. $x = 15$

Use the equation $y = 16\left(\dfrac{1}{2}\right)^x$. Find the value of y for each value of x. `2-7`

59. $x = 4$

60. $x = 7$

61. $x = 10$

Unit 3

Solve each system of equations by graphing. 3-1

1. $y = x - 5$
$y = -2x - 2$

2. $y = \frac{1}{2}x + 4$
$y = 2x + 1$

3. $y = -x + 3$
$y = \frac{5}{2}x + 3$

4. $y = 2x + 3$
$y = \frac{1}{2}x$

5. $y = -3x + 8$
$y = -\frac{2}{3}x + 1$

6. $y = 0.4x - 6$
$y = -1.2x + 2$

Solve each system of equations by substitution. 3-2

7. $b = 2a + 11$
$a + b = 5$ $-2, 7$

8. $w = \frac{1}{3}v - 5$
$\frac{2}{3}v - w = 7$

9. $2c - d = 7$
$d = 3c - 11$

10. $q = \frac{1}{2}p - 7$
$-2p - q = 2$

11. $g - 3h = -4$
$-3g + 8h = 13$

12. $x = 5y - 2$
$\frac{1}{2}x + 2y = 8$

$-7, -1$

For each system of equations: 3-3

a. Without graphing, describe the relationship of the graphs of the equations.

**b. Tell whether the system has *no solution, one solution,* or *many solutions.*
Identify the system as *consistent* or *inconsistent*.**

13. $y = 5x + 2$
$y = -5x + 2$

14. $y = -2x + 5$
$y = -2x - 1$

15. $y = 3x - 7$
$-2y = -6x + 14$

16. $x - 4y = 18$
$3x - 12y = 18$

17. $2x + 3y = 12$
$2x + 3y = -12$

18. $3x - 6y = 9$
$5x - 10y = 15$

Write an equation of the line that fits each description. 3-3

19. The line goes through $(-4, 1)$ and is parallel to the line $y = -2x + 11$.

20. The line goes through $(6, 7)$ and is perpendicular to the line $y = 3x - 4$.

21. The line goes through $(-2, 5)$ and is perpendicular to the line $x = -1$.

22. The line goes through $(-3, -8)$ and is parallel to the line $x = 5$.

Use the addition-or-subtraction method to solve each system of equations. 3-4

23. $y + z = 5$
$2y - 3z = 15$

24. $3x - 5y = 9$
$-x + 4y = -10$

25. $4c - 3d = -5$
$5c - d = 13$

26. $4a + 2b = 12$
$7a - 4b = 21$

27. $j + 4k = 7$
$5j + 6k = -7$

28. $3p - 5q = 11$
$7p + 10q = 4$

29. $-7x + 3y = 3$
$\frac{1}{3}x + y = 9$

30. $2v - 3w = 9$
$3v - 7w = 11$

Simplify. 3-5

31. $\begin{bmatrix} -2 & 1 \\ 4 & 0 \end{bmatrix} + \begin{bmatrix} 3 & -1 \\ 3 & 1 \end{bmatrix}$

32. $\begin{bmatrix} 1 & 2 \\ -5 & 4 \\ -3 & 0 \end{bmatrix} - \begin{bmatrix} 1 & 6 \\ -2 & 0 \\ 4 & 5 \end{bmatrix}$

33. $2\begin{bmatrix} 7 & 2 & 0 \\ -3 & 1 & 1 \\ 4 & 2 & -1 \end{bmatrix}$

34. $\begin{bmatrix} -1 \\ 0 \\ 2 \\ 3 \\ -4 \end{bmatrix} - 3\begin{bmatrix} 3 \\ 5 \\ 7 \\ -10 \\ 2 \end{bmatrix}$

35. $-5\begin{bmatrix} 1 & -2 & -2 \\ 0 & 3 & -1 \end{bmatrix} + 2\begin{bmatrix} 3 & 1 & 6 \\ -5 & 2 & 0 \end{bmatrix}$

Find the coordinates of the vertices of △DEF after each transformation. Write your answer as a matrix. 3-6

36. a translation 1 unit left, 2 units up

37. a dilation with scale factor 3 and center at the origin

38. a translation 3 units right, 4 units down

39. a dilation with scale factor $\frac{1}{2}$ and center at the origin

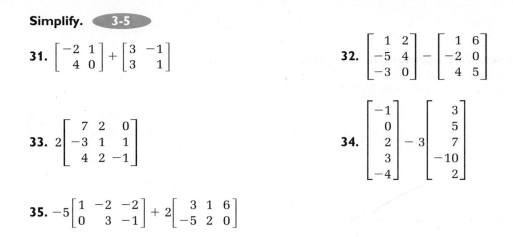

Find the product of each pair of matrices. 3-7

40. $\begin{bmatrix} 0 & -1 & 0.25 \\ 2 & -1 & 5 \end{bmatrix}\begin{bmatrix} 3 & 0 \\ 0.5 & 4 \\ 2 & -1 \end{bmatrix}$

41. $\begin{bmatrix} 4 & 2 & -3 & 0 & 1 \\ -1 & 2 & 0 & 5 & 3 \end{bmatrix}\begin{bmatrix} 1 \\ 1 \\ -1 \\ 2 \\ 3 \end{bmatrix}$

42. $\begin{bmatrix} 3 & 0 & -3 \\ 1 & 2 & 4 \\ -1 & 2 & 0 \end{bmatrix}\begin{bmatrix} 2 & 1 \\ -2 & 3 \\ -4 & 5 \end{bmatrix}$

43. $[7 \quad 10 \quad -11 \quad -3]\begin{bmatrix} 1 & 1 \\ 2 & -2 \\ 3 & 5 \\ -1 & 4 \end{bmatrix}$

Use a graphics calculator to find the inverse of each matrix, if it exists. Round each element to the nearest hundredth. 3-8

44. $\begin{bmatrix} 3 & 2 \\ -1 & 1 \end{bmatrix}$

45. $\begin{bmatrix} 7 & -3 \\ -9 & 4 \end{bmatrix}$

46. $\begin{bmatrix} 2 & 3 & 0 \\ -3 & 5 & -4 \\ -1 & 1 & -1 \end{bmatrix}$

Unit 4

For the graph of each function, find an equation of the line of symmetry and the coordinates of the vertex. Tell whether the value of the function at the vertex is a maximum or a minimum. 4-1

1. $y = -x^2 + 4x - 7$ **2.** $y = 2x^2 + 4x$ **3.** $y = -3x^2 - 18x + 5$

4. $y = 0.125x^2 - 2x - 6$ **5.** $y = -0.2x^2 + 6.4x - 1$ **6.** $y = 0.01x^2 + 0.5x - 2$

Find the y-intercept of each function. 4-1

7. $y = 4x^2 + x - 2$ **8.** $y = -x^2 - 6x + 10$ **9.** $y = 5x^2 - 2x$

Use the graph to estimate the x-intercepts. 4-1

10. $y = \frac{2}{3}x^2 - \frac{1}{3}x - 2$ **11.** $y = -x^2 + 4x + 1$ **12.** $y = 2x^2 + 5x - 4$

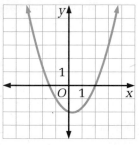
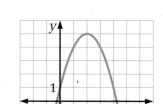
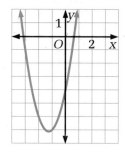

Tell how to translate the graph of $y = 0.5x^2$ in order to produce the graph of each function. 4-2

13. $y = 0.5(x + 3)^2 - 7$ **14.** $y = 0.5(x - 1)^2 - 4$

15. $y = 0.5(x - 6)^2 + 2$ **16.** $y = 0.5(x + 9)^2$

For the graph of each function: 4-2

a. Find the coordinates of the vertex.

b. Find the y-intercept.

17. $y = (x - 7)^2 - 1$ **18.** $y = -0.2(x + 5)^2 - 11$

19. $y = -5(x + 1)^2 + 14$ **20.** $y = 2.5(x + 6)^2 + 8$

Solve using algebra. 4-3

21. $4x^2 + 2 = 17$ **22.** $(x - 3)^2 = 15$

23. $(x + 1)^2 - 2 = 9$ **24.** $2(x - 3)^2 - 1 = 6$

25. $-3x^2 + 5 = -8$ **26.** $4(x - 5)^2 - 7 = 12$

27. $0.5(x + 4)^2 + 2 = 7$ **28.** $-0.25(x - 6)^2 + 3 = -14$

Factor. `4-4`

use quadratic formula

29. $x^2 - 4x - 21$

30. $2x^2 + 11x - 40$

31. $3x^2 - 13x + 14$

32. $7x^2 + 20x + 12$

33. $10x^2 + 19x - 15$

34. $12x^2 - 17x - 7$

35. $81x^2 - 25$

36. $a^2 - 144b^2$

37. $4 - 49x^2$

38. $x^2 - 12x + 36$

39. $9x^2 + 6x + 1$

40. $25x^2 - 20x + 4$

Solve by factoring. `4-4`

41. $x^2 - 8x = 33$

42. $2x^2 = 7x - 6$

43. $3x^2 - 4x + 1 = 5$

Solve using the quadratic formula. `4-5`

44. $x^2 - 11x + 7 = 0$

45. $x^2 + 6x - 2 = 0$

46. $x^2 - 2x - 14 = 0$

47. $3x^2 + 8x + 2 = 0$

48. $-5x^2 + 3x + 1 = 0$

49. $2x^2 + 8x - 7 = 0$

50. $0.5x^2 + 0.25x - 4 = 0$

51. $(x - 6)^2 + 3x = 29$

52. $2(x + 3)^2 - 5 = x$

For Exercises 53–58: `4-6`

a. Use the discriminant to tell whether each equation has *one solution,* *two solutions,* or *no solutions* in the set of real numbers.

b. Solve each equation that has at least one real-number solution. Graph the related quadratic function for each equation that has no real-number solutions.

53. $x^2 - x - 1 = 0$

54. $x^2 - 3x + 5 = 0$

55. $1.5x^2 + 3.5x + 2 = 0$

56. $2x^2 - 9x + 10 = 0$

57. $-x^2 + 4x - 5 = 0$

58. $2x^2 - 3x + 2 = 0$

Simplify. `4-6`

59. $(6 + 4i) - (7 + 2i)$

60. $-i(-3 + 5i)$

61. $(10 + 3i)(8 - i)$

Solve, using complex numbers. `4-6`

62. $x^2 + 6x + 10 = 0$

63. $x^2 - 2x + 11 = 0$

64. $-2x^2 + 6x - 7 = 0$

Solve each system by substitution. `4-7`

65. $y = 2x^2 + 5$
$y = 2x^2 - 4x - 7$

66. $y = -2x^2 - x + 7$
$y = -x^2 + x - 8$

67. $y = 4x^2 + 2x + 1$
$y = 3x^2 - 2x + 1$

Solve each system by graphing. `4-7`

68. $y = 0.5x^2 - 3x$
$y = -0.5x^2 + x - 4$

69. $y = x^2 - 2x - 3$
$y = -x^2 + 4x + 5$

70. $y = 2x^2 - 3$
$y = 2x^2 - 4x + 1$

Unit 5

Tell whether each statement is *True* or *False*. If it is false, explain why. `5-1`

1. All squares are rhombuses.
2. Every parallelogram is a rectangle.
3. If a quadrilateral is a kite, then it is a rhombus.
4. A quadrilateral is rhombus only if it is a kite.

Find the distance between each pair of points. `5-2`

5. $(-3, 5)$ and $(6, -7)$
6. $(5, -1)$ and $(8, -9)$
7. $(3, 11)$ and $(-4, -2)$

8. Use the distance formula to show that quadrilateral $ABCD$ with vertices $A(3, 1)$, $B(10, 2)$, $C(5, 7)$, and $D(-2, 6)$ is a rhombus. `5-2`

9. Use the distance formula to show that quadrilateral $PQRS$ with vertices $P(7, 2)$, $Q(3, 5)$, $R(-1, 2)$, and $S(3, -4)$ is a kite. `5-2`

Find the coordinates of the midpoint of each segment whose endpoint coordinates are given. `5-3`

10. $(-5, 2)$ and $(7, 8)$
11. $(4, -2)$ and $(-7, 9)$
12. $(11, 4)$ and $(-3, -6)$

13. $(3.25, 2.5)$ and $(-1.25, 5.5)$
14. $\left(\frac{2}{3}, \frac{5}{4}\right)$ and $\left(\frac{7}{3}, \frac{3}{4}\right)$

M is the midpoint of $\overline{AB}$. Find the coordinates of B. `5-3`

15. $A(-1, 7)$; $M(4, 2)$
16. $A(3, -5)$; $M(2, -1)$
17. $A(-1, 6)$; $M(-4, -7)$

For each transformation, tell what type of transformation is described. `5-4`

18. $(x, y) \to (5x, 5y)$
19. $(x, y) \to (-x, y)$
20. $(x, y) \to (y, -x)$

For each transformation, find the coordinates of the image of $\triangle ABC$. Sketch the original figure and the image figure on graph paper. `5-4`

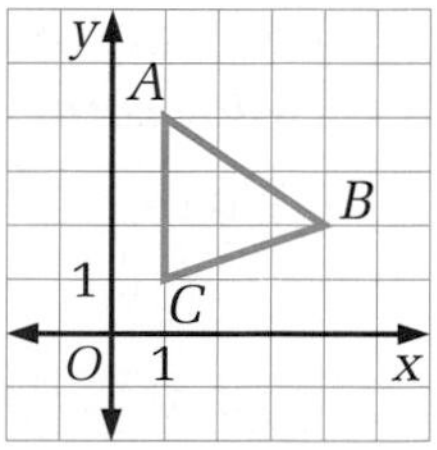

21. Shift the figure 3 units to the left and 1 unit down.
22. Reflect the figure over the y-axis.
23. Rotate the figure 90° counterclockwise.
24. Dilate the figure using a scale factor of 2 and using the origin as the center of dilation.

Name each missing coordinate without introducing a new variable. `5-5`

25.

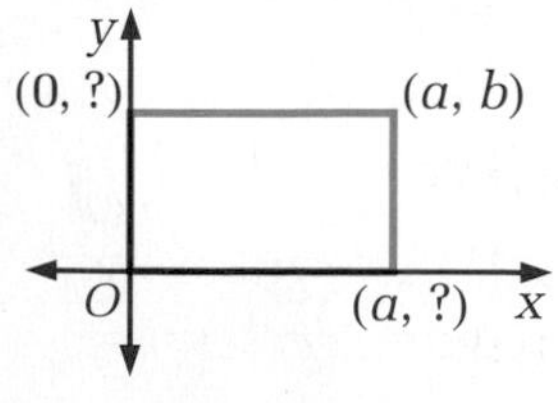

26.

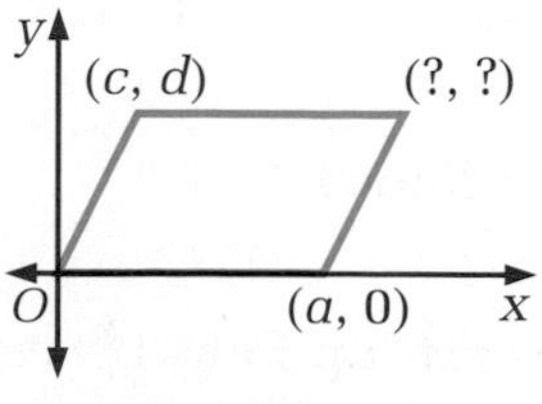

27.

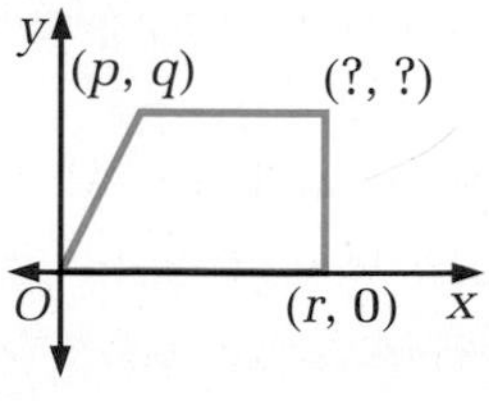

28. Quadrilateral *DEFG* has vertices *D*(0, 0), *E*(5, 0), *F*(7, 4), and *G*(2, 4). Use slopes to show that *DEFG* is a parallelogram.   5-6

Use the coordinates in the diagram to answer each question.   5-6

29. Is the figure a trapezoid? How do you know?

30. Find the coordinates of the midpoints of the diagonals. Do the diagonals have the same midpoint?

31. Find the lengths of the diagonals. Do the diagonals have the same length?

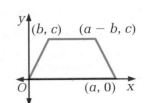

Unit 6

6-1

1. The math club has 7 members: 3 boys and 4 girls. One boy and one girl must be chosen to represent the school at a statewide math contest. In how many ways can the choice be made?

2. In how many ways can you form a numeral between 400 and 999 using only the digits 2, 3, 5, 6, 7, and 8 under each condition?

   a. Any digit may appear more than once.

   b. No digit may be repeated.

3. A ship has 4 different signal flags. How many different signals can be formed using from 1 to 4 of these flags placed vertically along the mast?

6-2

4. A store manager has chosen 7 items to put on sale: one item each week for seven weeks. In how many different ways can the manager choose the order in which the items go on sale?

5. How many four-letter sequences of letters can be formed using the letters of each word, without repeating any letters?

   a. HOUSE   **b.** FOLDER   **c.** FACTORIES

6-3

6. Suppose one card is drawn at random from a standard deck. What is the probability that the card is a heart or an ace?

7. Suppose you roll two dice. Find each probability.

   a. *P*(matching numbers)   **b.** *P*(sum is 5)   **c.** *P*(sum is 2 or 11)

8. Suppose a die is rolled and a coin is flipped.   6-4

   a. Are these two events independent?

   b. Find the probability that the die came up 5 and the coin came up tails.

9. Suppose the 13 diamonds from a standard deck of cards are placed face down on a table and two cards are turned over. Find each probability. `6-4`

   a. $P($ace and king$)$

   b. $P($both face cards$)$

   c. $P($both are even-numbered$)$

Find the value of each expression. `6-5`

10. $_5P_3$ **11.** $_7C_4$ **12.** $_6C_3$ **13.** $_8P_2$

Rita wants to choose 4 of her 10 insect specimens to display at the science fair. `6-5`

14. In how many ways can the choice of 4 be made?

15. In how many ways can she choose 4 specimens and display them in a row in a glass-topped case?

Find each value using Pascal's triangle. `6-6`

16. $_8C_1$ **17.** $_7C_2$ **18.** $_5C_4$ **19.** $_6C_6$

Use a row of Pascal's triangle to find the numbers of ways of answering a 6-question true-false test and getting each number of questions correct. `6-6`

20. 5   **21.** 2   **22.** 3   **23.** 4

At Three Corners, equal numbers of cars choose the left fork to Plainfield and the right fork to Centerville. Find the probability that, out of the next 5 cars, the given number will head toward Plainfield. `6-7`

24. 5   **25.** 1   **26.** 2   **27.** 3

28. For cars approaching a certain intersection in one direction, the traffic light cycles between a 55-second period of red and a 25-second period of green. Suppose you drive through this intersection in this direction at four random times during one week. `6-8`

   a. What is the probability that the light will be green exactly once?

   b. What is the probability that the light will be green exactly twice?

29. A die is rolled five times. What is the probability that a multiple of 3 comes up exactly twice? `6-8`

Use the binomial theorem to write each power of a binomial in expanded form. `6-9`

30. $(x + y)^5$ **31.** $(a - 3)^4$ **32.** $(10 - w)^3$ **33.** $(2c + d)^6$

Unit 7

Graph each conjunction or disjunction on a number line. `7-1`

1. $x > -1$ and $x < 3$

2. $x > 2$ or $x < 1$

3. $x > -3$ and $x > -1$

For Exercises 4–7, use the Venn diagram showing juniors on the school newspaper staff and in the Community Service Club. Match each letter A–D with the person it represents. `7-1`

4. Chu Hua is on the newspaper staff and is not in the Community Service Club.

5. Alvin is on the newspaper staff and is in the Community Service Club.

6. Lourdes is not in the Community Service Club and is not on the newspaper staff.

7. Terumi is in the Community Service Club and is not on the newspaper staff.

Graph each conjunction or disjunction on a coordinate plane. `7-1`

8. $y > 1$ and $y < 3$

9. $y < x$ or $y > 2$

10. $y < x + 1$ and $y > -x + 1$

For Exercises 11–13: `7-2`

a. Rewrite each implication in if-then form. Tell whether each implication is *True* or *False*. If it is false, give a counterexample.

b. Write the converse of each implication. Tell whether each converse is *True* or *False*. If it is false, give a counterexample.

11. $xy = xz$ implies that $y = z$.

12. Thanksgiving always falls on a Thursday.

13. An integer is evenly divisible by 10 only if its last digit is 0.

What conclusion can you reach when both premises are true? `7-3`

14. If you have two C's, you are not on the honor roll. Ji Sun is on the honor roll.

15. If our team plays the Tigers, we will win. If our team beats the Tigers, we will be in the semi-finals.

For Exercises 16–17, decide if each argument is *valid* or *invalid*. Explain your reasoning. `7-3`

16. If a quadrilateral is a rhombus, its diagonals are perpendicular.

The diagonals of *ABCD* are perpendicular.

Therefore, *ABCD* is a parallelogram.

17. If this month has 30 days, then it is not February.

This month is February.

Therefore, it does not have 30 days.

Tell whether each biconditional is *True* or *False*. Explain your reasoning. 7-4

18. A number is greater than 3 if and only if its square is greater than 9.

19. A quadrilateral is a parallelogram if and only if all four of its sides are congruent.

20. One team wins a baseball game if and only if that team outscores the other team.

21. A substance is transparent if and only if you can see through it.

22. Copy and complete this proof. 7-5

> **Given** Seattle
>
> **Prove** New York

Available Flights:
Flight 102: Denver → Cincinnati
Flight 104: Cincinnati → New York
Flight 103: Seattle → Denver

Statements	**Justifications**
1. Seattle	1. ?
2. Denver	2. ?
3. ?	3. Flight 102: Denver → Cincinnati
4. ?	4. ?

Identify the postulate used in each implication. 7-6

23. $3(x + 2) = 12 \rightarrow x + 2 = 4$

24. If $5x - 3 = 42$, then $5x = 45$

25. If $x = 4 + y$ and $y = 7$, then $x = 11$

26. If $x^2 = 36$, then $x = \pm 6$.

27. Write a paragraph proof for the solution of the equation $2x - 5 = 17$. 7-6

In Exercises 28 and 29, state a conclusion that can be made in one step from the given information. Give a reason. 7-7

28. $\angle R$ and $\angle S$ are complementary and $\angle R = 33°$.

29. $\angle A$ and $\angle B$ are supplementary angles.

30. Write a flow proof: If $m \angle 2 = m \angle 3$ and $m \angle 1 = 150°$, then $m \angle 3 = 30°$. 7-7

Use the diagram for Exercises 31–34. Justify each statement. 7-8

31. $m \angle 1 = m \angle 3$

32. $m \angle 1 = m \angle 4$

33. $m \angle 3 = m \angle 4$

34. $\angle 2$ and $\angle 3$ are supplementary

Write a flow proof. 8-1

1. **Given** ∠1 and ∠2 are supplementary.
   Prove $m \angle 3 = m \angle 4$

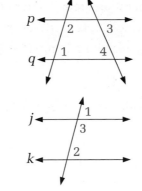

Use the given angle measures to decide whether lines *j* and *k* are parallel. 8-1

2. $m \angle 1 = 40°; m \angle 2 = 40°$
3. $m \angle 2 = (2x)°; m \angle 3 = (180 - 2x)°$

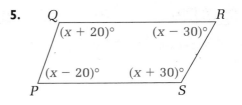

Find the measure of each angle. 8-2

4.

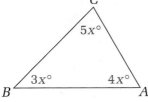

5.

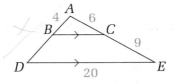

Find the measure of each side. 8-3

6. $\overline{AD}$
7. $\overline{BC}$

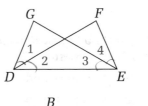

Write a paragraph proof. 8-4

8. **Given** $m \angle 1 = m \angle 4; m \angle 2 = m \angle 3$
   Prove $\triangle DEG \cong \triangle EDF$

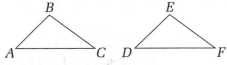

For Exercises 9–12, copy the triangles and mark any parts that are equal in measure. Identify the postulate or theorem you would use to prove that △*ABC* ≅ △*DEF*. 8-5

9. $AB = DE; m \angle B = m \angle E; BC = EF$

10. $m \angle A = m \angle D; m \angle B = m \angle E; m \angle C = m \angle F$

11. $m \angle A = m \angle D; BC = EF; m \angle C = m \angle F$

12. $AB = DE; BC = EF; CA = FD$

Write a two-column proof. 8-5

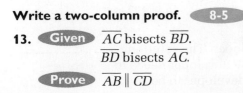

13. **Given** $\overline{AC}$ bisects $\overline{BD}$.
    $\overline{BD}$ bisects $\overline{AC}$.
    Prove $\overline{AB} \parallel \overline{CD}$

14. In $\triangle PQR$, $PQ = RQ$. The measure of $\angle Q$ is 9 less than 5 times the measure of $\angle P$. Find the measures of the three angles of the triangle. **8-6**

Write a two-column proof. **8-6**

15. **Given** $AC = BC$; $m \angle 1 = m \angle 2$.

Prove $AE = BD$

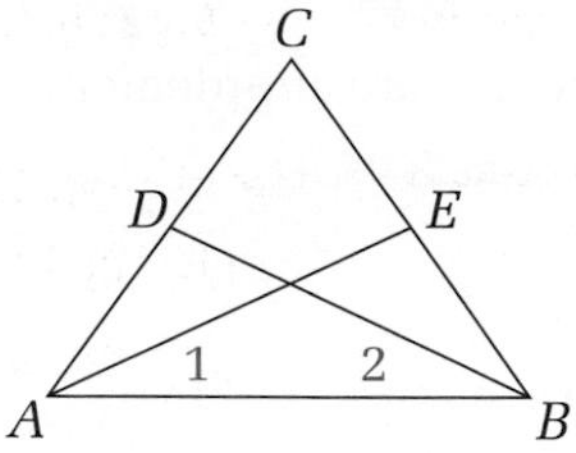

Find the measure of each unknown side. **8-7**

16.

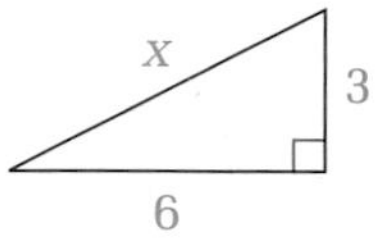

17.

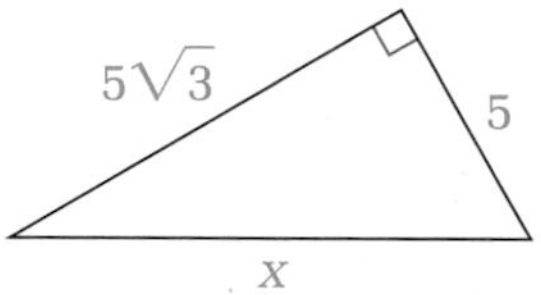

18.

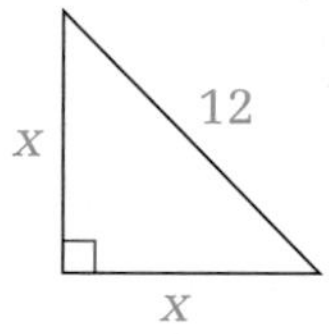

Solve each proportion. **8-7**

19. $\dfrac{6}{x} = \dfrac{4}{9}$

20. $\dfrac{x}{18} = \dfrac{8}{x}$

21. $\dfrac{2x + 3}{10} = \dfrac{x}{4}$

22. a. Find the length of the hypotenuse of $\triangle XYZ$. **8-8**

b. Find the sine, cosine, and tangent ratios for $\angle X$ in $\triangle XYZ$.

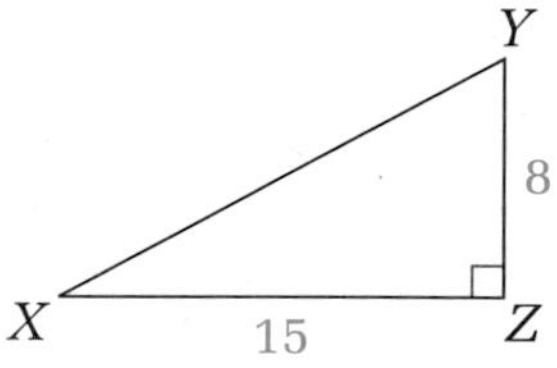

23. For parts (a)–(c), find the value of each sum. **8-8**

a. $(\sin 30°)^2 + (\cos 30°)^2$ **b.** $(\sin 60°)^2 + (\cos 60°)^2$ **c.** $(\sin 45°)^2 + (\cos 45°)^2$

d. Find a pattern in your answers to parts (a), (b), and (c). Make a conjecture.

Unit 9

In Exercises 1–4, write an equation to model each situation. **9-1**

1.

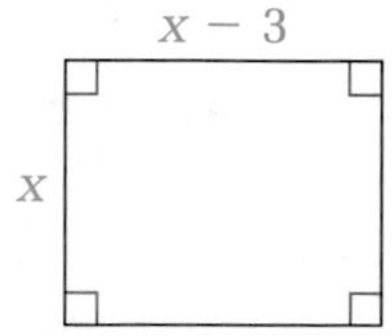

$A = 240$ in.^{2}

2.

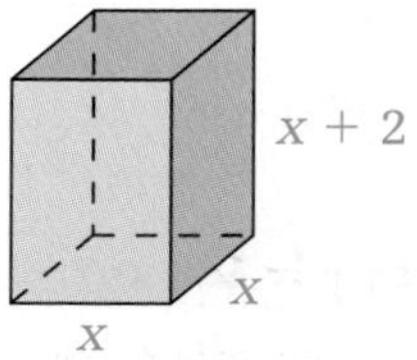

$V = 175$ in.^{3}

3.

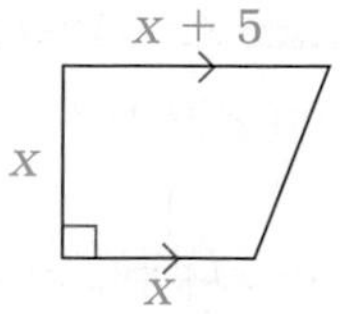

$A = 192$ cm^2

4. A photographic developing solution should be 16% developer. The solution now contains 42 mL of water and 3 mL of developer. Some developer needs to be added to make a 16% solution. Let $x =$ the amount of developer to be added.

Factor completely. 9-2

5. $3c^3d^5 - 6c^2d^6$

6. $7x^4y^2 - 28x^2y^4$

7. $2k^3 + 2k^2 - 40k$

8. $5u^2v^2 + 30uv^3 - 80v^4$

9. $21m^3n + 33mn^4$

10. $45a - 125ab^2$

Simplify. Write each answer without negative exponents. 9-2

11. $(25x^6y^8)^{1/2}$

12. $(2p^4q^{-5})^3(p^2q)$

13. $(r^{-2}s^4)^3(r^6s^3)^{-1}$

14. $\dfrac{v^{-5}w^{-7}}{v^3w^{-2}}$

15. $\left(\dfrac{15ab^{-3}}{25a^4b^{-1}}\right)^3$

16. $\left(\dfrac{d^3e^{-5}}{2d^{-1}e^{-2}}\right)^{-4}$

Solve. 9-3

17. $\dfrac{5}{b-3} = \dfrac{6}{b}$

18. $\dfrac{1}{2w} = \dfrac{5}{w+9}$

19. $\dfrac{6}{t(t+1)} = \dfrac{2}{t+1}$

20. $\dfrac{3}{2n+5} = \dfrac{4}{n}$

21. $\dfrac{x}{x-6} = \dfrac{3}{x-8}$

22. $\dfrac{5}{p+2} + \dfrac{3}{p-2} = 4$

23. $\dfrac{r-3}{2r} + \dfrac{9}{r} = 2$

24. $3 + \dfrac{5}{a-3} = -a$

25. $\dfrac{5y}{y+4} - \dfrac{2}{y+1} = 1$

List the zeros of each function. Tell which, if any, are double or triple zeros. 9-4

26. $y = x(x-3)(x+7)$

27. $y = (x+5)^2(x-8)$

28. $y = -x^2(x-5)$

29. $y = (x+9)^3$

30. $y = x(x+10)^2$

31. $y = -x^3$

Match each graph with one of the functions A–F. 9-4

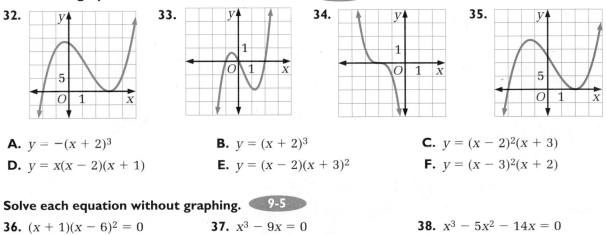

32.   **33.**   **34.**   **35.**

A. $y = -(x+2)^3$

B. $y = (x+2)^3$

C. $y = (x-2)^2(x+3)$

D. $y = x(x-2)(x+1)$

E. $y = (x-2)(x+3)^2$

F. $y = (x-3)^2(x+2)$

Solve each equation without graphing. 9-5

36. $(x+1)(x-6)^2 = 0$

37. $x^3 - 9x = 0$

38. $x^3 - 5x^2 - 14x = 0$

39. Use the parametric equations $x = 40t$ and $y = 7 - t^2$. 9-6

   a. Write y in terms of x by solving the first equation for t and substituting your answer into the second equation.

   b. Graph the parametric equations.

   c. Estimate the value of x for which $y = 0$.

Unit 10

Draw a vertical cross section and a horizontal cross section of each space figure. 10-1

1.

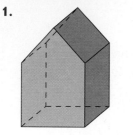

2.

3.

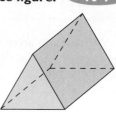

For Exercises 4–6: 10-2

a. Describe or sketch the shape given by rotating each figure around the given axis.

b. Find the volume of the space figure.

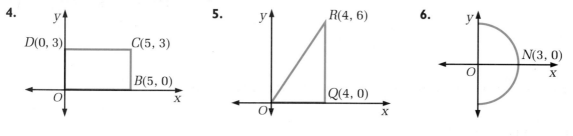

4.

$D(0, 3)$ $C(5, 3)$

$B(5, 0)$

O x

Rotate around y-axis

5.

$R(4, 6)$

$Q(4, 0)$

Rotate around x-axis

6.

$N(3, 0)$

O x

Rotate around y-axis

Draw the plane figure that is rotated to form each space figure. Indicate the axis of rotation. 10-2

7.

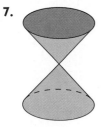

8.

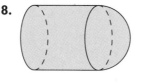

9.

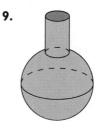

For Exercises 10–13, points _A_ and _B_ are 5 cm apart.
Describe the set of points that fit each condition. 10-3
a. in a plane containing _A_ and _B_
b. in space

10. 2 cm from point A

11. equidistant from A and B

12. 3 cm from the line through A and B

13. 2.5 cm from both A and B

With points *A* and *B* as in Exercises 10–13, describe the set of points in a plane containing *A* and *B* that fit each condition. 10-3

14. 3 cm from *A* and 4 cm from *B*

15. 2 cm from *A* and 1 cm from *B*

Give the coordinates of each point in the rectangular prism at the right. 10-4

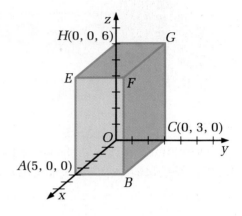

16. *B*   **17.** *E*

18. *F*   **19.** G

Find the midpoint of the segment with the given endpoints. 10-4

20. $(0, 0, 0), (-2, 6, 10)$

21. $(1, 3, -4), (5, -7, -2)$

22. $(-1, -8, 7), (1, 3, -4)$

Find the distance between each pair of points. 10-5

23. $(1, 4, 7)$ and $(3, -2, 4)$

24. $(5, -1, 2)$ and $(4, 3, -6)$

25. $(-1, -3, 2)$ and $(1, 11, 7)$

26. $(4, 7, -8)$ and $(1, -5, -4)$

Write an equation of each circle or sphere. 10-6

27. The center of the circle is $(0, 0)$. The points $(0, 4)$ and $(0, -4)$ are endpoints of a diameter.

28. The center of the circle is $(0, 0)$. The point $(5, 12)$ is on the circle.

29. The center of the sphere is $(0, 0, 0)$. The radius is 8.

30. The center of the sphere is $(0, 0, 0)$. The point $(7, 0, 0)$ is on the sphere.

Toolbox

➤ Statistics and Probability

Data Displays and Measures

Skill 1	Using a Fitted Line

A **fitted line** is a line that passes as close to as many data points on a scatter plot as possible.

Example The table shows sales of CDs at a record store that was trying out different weekly schedules with different numbers of hours of operation. Make a scatter plot of the data. Draw a fitted line. Predict sales for a 45-hour week.

Hours of operation	54	48	60	65	40	60	48	56
CDs Sold	710	530	850	940	520	740	630	750

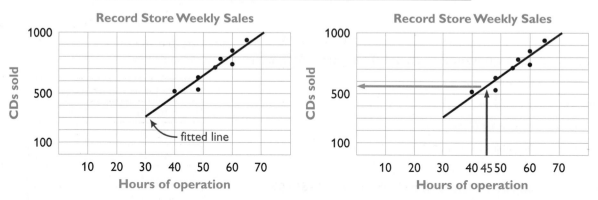

To predict sales for a 45-hour week, draw a vertical line from 45 on the horizontal axis to the fitted line. Then draw a horizontal line to the vertical axis. The point where the horizontal line meets the vertical axis is the prediction.

A 45-hour week should produce about 550 CD sales.

When two data sets increase together, their relationship is called a **positive correlation.** The points of a graph of the data *rise* to the right, as in the Example above. If the points of the graph of two data sets *fall* to the right, the graph shows a **negative correlation.**

1. Make a scatter plot using the data in the table below showing the use of a small beach on days with different high temperatures.

High temperature (°F)	65	72	90	85	85	72	100	95
Beach Users	20	60	120	90	110	85	150	130

2. Does your scatter plot show a *positive correlation*, a *negative correlation*, or *no correlation*?

3. Draw a fitted line for your scatter plot.

Use your fitted line to predict the number of beach users on days with each high temperature.

4. 80°F   **5.** 75°F   **6.** 105°F   **7.** 60°F

Skill 2   Using a Histogram and a Frequency Table

A **histogram** displays grouped data. Each group is defined by an interval on the horizontal axis. The height of the bar for an interval indicates the number of data items that fall in the group. This number is called a **frequency.**

Example The frequency table and the histogram show the number of supporters for candidate Kaoru Hirakawa in different age groups in her city.

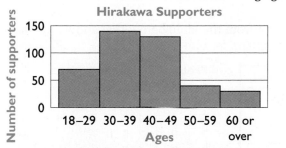

Age Group	Frequency
18–29	70
30–39	140
40–49	130
50–59	40
60 or over	30

Use the table or the histogram to answer each question.

a. How many Hirakawa supporters are between the ages of 50 and 59?

Histogram: The bar for the interval 50–59 has height 40.
Frequency table: The frequency for the age group 50–59 is 40.

There are 40 supporters between the ages of 50 and 59.

b. In which age groups does she have the greatest support and the least support?

Using the histogram, you see that the tallest bar is for the interval 30–39. She has the greatest support in this age group. The shortest bar is for the group "60 or over." She has the least support in this age group.

Use the histogram or the frequency table to answer each question.

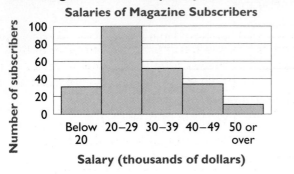

Salaries of Magazine Subscribers

Salary Range (thousand $)	Number of subscribers
Below 20	30
20–29	100
30–39	52
40–49	34
50 or over	11

How many subscribers make each salary?

1. Below $20,000   **2.** Between $20,000 and $29,000   **3.** $50,000 or over

4. Which salary range has the most subscribers? the least?

Skill 3   Making a Stem-and-Leaf Plot

A **stem-and-leaf plot** displays every data item but also groups the data by intervals, like a histogram.

The leaf is the last digit on the right. ———→

1 5 2

←——— The stem is the remaining digit or digits.

Example Make a stem-and-leaf plot from the table below that shows the daily protein intake of health club members for one day.

Protein Consumed (grams)				
63	68	69	82	84
43	84	87	70	72
52	75	71	68	44
56	57	63	76	64

Protein Consumed (grams)

```
4 | 3 4
5 | 2 6 7
6 | 3 3 4 8 8 9   ←— This row displays the numbers 63, 63, 64, 68, 68, 69.
7 | 0 1 2 5 6
8 | 2 4 4 7
```

1. In the Example, what data items do the numbers in the fourth row of the stem-and-leaf plot represent?

2. Make a stem-and-leaf plot of the data in the table at the right, showing times of runners in a 10 km road race.

3. In your stem-and-leaf plot, which interval contains the most data items? Which interval contains the fewest?

Finishing Times (minutes)				
52	34	45	63	71
45	41	32	50	62
52	44	43	51	46
51	66	65	66	58

Skill 4 Finding Mean, Median, Mode, and Range

mean: The sum of the data in a data set divided by the number of items.	**median:** The middle number or the mean of the two middle numbers in a data set when the data are arranged in order.
mode: The data item, or items, appearing most often. There may be more than one mode or no mode.	**range:** The difference between the smallest and largest data items.

Examples The following high temperatures were recorded on days in March:

42, 38, 56, 56, 60, 40, 65, 45, 48, 42, 56.

Find the mean, the median, the mode, and the range of the data.

Mean: There are 11 temperatures. Add the numbers. Divide the sum by 11.

$$\frac{42 + 38 + 56 + 56 + 60 + 40 + 65 + 45 + 48 + 42 + 56}{11} = 49.8$$

To the nearest tenth, the mean is 49.8.

Median: List the numbers in order. Find the middle number.

38 40 42 42 45 48 56 56 56 60 65

The median is 48.

Mode: Since 56 appears three times, and no other number appears more than twice, 56 is the mode.

Range: The smallest number is 38. The largest is 65. Subtract to find the range.

$$65 - 38 = 27$$

The range is 27.

Use the table at the right showing protein per serving of some foods.

1. Find the mean of the data.
2. Find the median of the data.
3. Find the mode of the data.
4. Find the range of the data.

Protein per serving (g)					
24	36	42	10	32	24
10	18	16	18	12	30

A **box-and-whisker plot** shows the median and range of data.

Example   Make a box-and-whisker plot of these scores:
68, 78, 93, 79, 72, 88, 44, 79, 75, 82, 71, 89, 75, 88, 73, 80, 66, 100, 75, 92.

Step 1   Write the scores in order from lowest to highest.

Step 2   Find the median, the *extremes,* and the *quartiles* of the ordered data set.

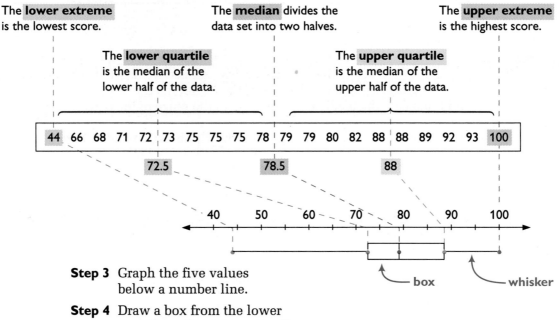

The **lower extreme** is the lowest score.

The **median** divides the data set into two halves.

The **upper extreme** is the highest score.

The **lower quartile** is the median of the lower half of the data.

The **upper quartile** is the median of the upper half of the data.

44 66 68 71 72 73 75 75 75 78 79 79 80 82 88 88 89 92 93 100

72.5   78.5   88

Step 3   Graph the five values below a number line.

Step 4   Draw a box from the lower quartile to the upper quartile. Draw a vertical line through the median.

Step 5   Draw line segments, or whiskers, from the box to the extremes.

You can see from the box-and-whisker plot that:

• About half the data are above 78.5.   • No data are below 44 or above 100.

• About 25% of the data are above 88.   • About 25% of the data are below 72.5.

1. Make a box-and-whisker plot of the data shown in the table at the right.

2. For what number is it true that about 25% of the data fall above the number?

3. For what number is it true that about 25% of the data fall below the number?

Fuel Economy (mi/gal)				
34	28	36	38	28
30	40	38	26	22
32	34	32	44	42
48	20	22	26	30

Probability

To describe how likely an event is, you use a number on a scale from 0 to 1. This number is called the **probability** of the event.

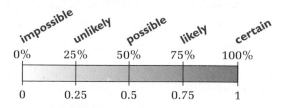

Probability that is based on the result of an experiment is called **experimental probability**. An **event** consists of one **outcome** or a group of outcomes of the experiment.

The experimental probability of an event E is the ratio:

$$P(E) = \frac{\text{number of times the event } E \text{ happened}}{\text{number of times the experiment was done}}$$

Example Janelle Franklin had 21 hits in her first 62 official at-bats for her high school softball team. What is the probability that she will get a hit?

The event E is "getting a hit."

$$P(E) = \frac{\text{hits}}{\text{at-bats}} = \frac{21}{62} \approx 0.339$$

The experimental probability of her getting a hit is about 0.34, or 34%.

Example Suppose Janelle has 20 more at-bats. How many hits can she expect?

Multiply the experimental probability by the number of future at-bats.

$(0.339)(20) = 6.78$

She can expect about 7 more hits.

The table shows how many of each different size of a particular style of sweatshirt were sold at one store last month. Find the probability that a sweatshirt sold will be each size.

1. Large
2. Medium
3. Extra Small
4. Extra Large
5. Suppose 150 sweatshirts are sold next year. How many will be Extra Large?

Size	Number Sold
Extra Small	12
Small	15
Medium	32
Large	44
Extra Large	14

When all outcomes of an experiment are equally likely, you can find the **theoretical probability** of an event without performing any trials of the experiment. The theoretical probability $P(E)$ is found by counting the ways the experiment can turn out.

$$P(E) = \frac{\text{number of favorable outcomes}}{\text{number of possible outcomes}}$$ ← "Favorable" means included in the event E.

Example   A spinner like the one shown at the right is spun. What is the probability that the spinner ends up pointing at a number greater than 3?

The event E is that a number greater than 3 will come up.
There are five possible outcomes: 1, 2, 3, 4, or 5 comes up.
There are two favorable outcomes: 4 or 5 comes up.

$P(\text{number greater than 3}) = \frac{2}{5} = 0.4$

The theoretical probability is $\frac{2}{5}$, or 0.4, or 40%.

A standard deck of playing cards has 52 cards, with 13 cards in each of four suits: clubs, spades, diamonds, and hearts. Face cards are jacks, queens, and kings.

Example   Suppose you pick a card at random from the 13 hearts of a standard deck. What is the probability that it is a face card?

There are 13 possible outcomes:

There are 3 favorable outcomes:

$P(\text{face card}) = \frac{3}{13} \approx 0.23$, or about 23%

Use the spinner above. Find each probability.

1. The pointer lands on 5.

2. The pointer lands on an odd number.

3. The pointer does not land on 1.

4. The pointer lands on a number less than 6.

A card is chosen at random from the 13 hearts of a standard deck.
Find each probability.

5. $P(\text{ace of hearts})$

6. $P(\text{queen or king of hearts})$

7. $P(2, 3, \text{ or } 4 \text{ of hearts})$

8. $P(\text{not a face card})$

9. $P(\text{a diamond})$

10. $P(\text{not a diamond})$

Geometric probability is probability based on areas and lengths.

Example Suppose in a one-hour TV program, 18 minutes are taken up by commercials. You tune in at a random time. What is the probability that you will tune in on a commercial?

Step 1 Model the situation with a number line. Use minutes as units.

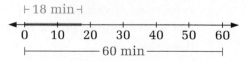

Step 2 Find the ratio of the length of the segment modeling commercial time to the length of the segment modeling total time.

$$P(\text{tuning in on a commercial}) = \frac{\text{commercial time}}{\text{total time}}$$

$$= \frac{18}{60} = \frac{3}{10}, \text{ or } 0.3, \text{ or } 30\%$$

If you can model the outcomes of an experiment by points in a plane, you can use geometric probability.

Example In a game, Trúc Ha hits a baseball over the park fence toward the wall of the house shown. Each window measures 2.5 ft by 4.5 ft. What is the probability that her hit will break a window?

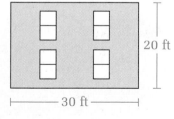

The area of the four windows is 4(2.5)(4.5) = 45 (ft²).

The wall area is (20)(30) = 600 (ft²).

$$P(\text{breaking a window}) = \frac{\text{area of 4 windows}}{\text{wall area}}$$

$$= \frac{45}{600} = \frac{3}{40}, \text{ or } 0.075, \text{ or } 7.5\%$$

1. In any 10-minute interval, a bus comes to the Eucalyptus Street stop and waits for 1.5 min. Suppose you arrive at the stop at a random time. What is the probability that a bus is waiting?

Find the probability that a point chosen at random in each figure is in the shaded region.

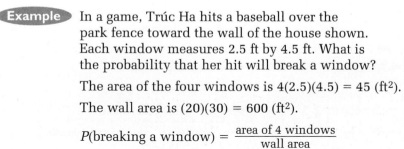

2.

3. 3 ... 1 2 ... 1

4. 120° 120° 120°

►Algebra and Graphing

Algebraic Expressions

People who work with mathematics follow a special **order of operations** so that they will agree on the value of a numerical expression. To simplify expressions such as $48 + (12 - 8)^2 \div 8$, you must carry out operations in the following order.

Parentheses	◄── Simplify inside parentheses.
Exponents	◄── Then calculate any powers.
Multiplication and Division	◄── Then do these as they appear from left to right.
Addition and Subtraction	◄── Then do these as they appear from left to right.

Example Simplify $48 + (12 - 8)^2 \div 8$.

$$48 + (12 - 8)^2 \div 8 = 48 + 4^2 \div 8 \quad ◄── \text{Simplify inside parentheses first.}$$
$$= 48 + 16 \div 8 \quad ◄── 4^2 \text{ means } 4 \cdot 4.$$
$$= 48 + 2 \quad ◄── \text{Do division next.}$$
$$= 50 \quad ◄── \text{Do addition last.}$$

Example Evaluate $7x^2 - 3x + 5$ when $x = -2$.

$$7x^2 - 3x + 5 = 7(-2)^2 - 3(-2) + 5 \quad ◄── \text{Substitute } -2 \text{ for } x.$$
$$= 7 \cdot 4 - 3(-2) + 5 \quad ◄── (-2)^2 \text{ means } (-2)(-2).$$
$$= 28 - (-6) + 5 \quad ◄── \text{Do multiplication next.}$$
$$= 28 + 6 + 5 \quad ◄── \text{To subtract } -6, \text{ add its opposite.}$$
$$= 39 \quad ◄── \text{Do addition last.}$$

Simplify each expression.

1. $12 \div 2^2 + 9$ **2.** $(13 - 5)^2 + 6 \div 2$ **3.** $4 + 5(7 - 9)$

4. $6 + 2^5 - 3 \cdot 5$ **5.** $7^2 - 4 \cdot 8 + 26 \div 13$ **6.** $(10 - 7)^4 + (5 - 1)^2 \div 8$

Evaluate each expression when $x = 3$.

7. $x^2 - 7x + 12$ **8.** $4x^3 - 5x + 1$ **9.** $15 - 4x^2$

10. $-2x^2 + 6x - 4$ **11.** $2x^5 - 4(x - 1)$ **12.** $(x - 5)^3 - 4(x + 1)^2$

Evaluate each expression when $a = -10$ and $b = 2$.

13. $3(a + b)$ **14.** $-a - b^2$ **15.** $-a^2 b$

16. $-4a^2 + b^2$ **17.** $-4(a^2 + b^2)$ **18.** $-4(a + b)^2$

You can simplify expressions like $3(x + 2)$ using the distributive property.

Distributive Property For all numbers a, b, and c,
$$a(b + c) = ab + ac \text{ and } a(b - c) = ab - ac.$$

Example
$$3(x + 2) = 3 \cdot x + 3 \cdot 2$$
$$= 3x + 6$$

Example
$$5(a - 7) = 5 \cdot a - 5 \cdot 7$$
$$= 5a - 35$$

To simplify some expressions, you use the fact that $-a = -1a$. Read $-a$ as "the opposite of a."

Example
$$-(y - 5) = -1(y - 5)$$
$$= (-1)y - (-1)(5) \quad \longleftarrow \text{ Use the distributive property.}$$
$$= -y - (-5)$$
$$= -y + 5$$

Example
$$9 - 2(x + 4) = 9 - (2x + 2 \cdot 4) \quad \longleftarrow \text{ Use the distributive property.}$$
$$= 9 - (2x + 8)$$
$$= 9 - 2x - 8 \quad \longleftarrow -1(2x + 8)$$
$$= -2x + 1$$

When you add expressions, each expression is a **term** of the sum. Terms with the same variables and powers are called **like terms**. You use the distributive property in reverse to **combine like terms**.

Example
$$2x^2 + 4xy - 5x^2 + 7xy = (2x^2 - 5x^2) + (4xy + 7xy) \quad \longleftarrow \text{ Group like terms.}$$
$$= (2 - 5)x^2 + (4 + 7)xy \quad \longleftarrow \text{ Use the distributive property.}$$
$$= -3x^2 + 11xy$$

Simplify.

1. $3(x + 4) - 5$ **2.** $-2(y - 7) + 3$ **3.** $4n - (3n + 5m)$

4. $5(-k + 3) - 2(k - 4)$ **5.** $4x^2 + 3x - x^2$ **6.** $4xy + 3yz - 7xy$.

7. $-a^2 + ab - 5a^2$ **8.** $-2hk + 4k^2 - k^2 + 5hk$ **9.** $3 + 9x^3 - 10 - 2x^3$

Toolbox

You can use the distributive property to expand a product.

Example $3x(x + 2) = 3x \cdot x + 3x \cdot 2$
$= 3x^2 + 6x$

Example $-2x(x - 5) = (-2x)x - (-2x)5$
$= -2x^2 - (-10x)$
$= -2x^2 + 10x$

Example $(x + 4)(x - 3) = (x + 4)x - (x + 4)3$ ⟵ Use the distributive property.
$= x^2 + 4x - (3x + 12)$ ⟵ Use the distributive property again.
$= x^2 + 4x - 3x - 12$
$= x^2 + x - 12$

Expand each product.

1. $x(2x + 3)$

2. $-4x(x - 5)$

3. $7a(-2a + 6)$

4. $(x + 5)(x - 9)$

5. $(y - 6)(y - 2)$

6. $(x - 3)(-x + 10)$

7. $(2x + 1)(x - 7)$

8. $(-3n + 7)(n + 5)$

9. $(4x - 2)(x - 5)$

10. $(3x - 4)(2x - 11)$

11. $(2x + 1)(7x - 8)$

12. $(-3k + 2)(-5k + 4)$

To simplify the square root of an integer, you first find the largest perfect-square factor of the integer. Then use the fact that for all nonnegative numbers a and b,

$\sqrt{}$ is the radical symbol. $\sqrt{ab} = \sqrt{a} \cdot \sqrt{b}$.

Example $\sqrt{18} = \sqrt{9 \cdot 2}$ ⟵ 9 is the largest perfect-square factor of 18. Write 18 as 9 · 2.
$= \sqrt{9} \cdot \sqrt{2}$ ⟵ Use the fact that $\sqrt{ab} = \sqrt{a} \cdot \sqrt{b}$.
$= 3\sqrt{2}$ ⟵ Write $\sqrt{9}$ as 3.

Note: It would *not* have been helpful to write $\sqrt{18}$ as $\sqrt{6 \cdot 3}$, because neither 6 nor 3 is a perfect square.

To simplify a product of radical factors, you use the fact that for all nonnegative numbers a and b,
$$\sqrt{a} \cdot \sqrt{b} = \sqrt{ab}.$$

Example
$$5\sqrt{3} \cdot \sqrt{2} = 5\sqrt{3 \cdot 2} \quad \longleftarrow \text{Use the fact that } \sqrt{a} \cdot \sqrt{b} = \sqrt{ab}.$$
$$= 5\sqrt{6}$$

Example
$$4\sqrt{5} \cdot 2\sqrt{15} = 4 \cdot 2 \cdot \sqrt{5} \cdot \sqrt{15} \quad \longleftarrow \text{Group radical terms.}$$
$$= 8\sqrt{5 \cdot 15} \quad \longleftarrow \text{Use the fact that } \sqrt{a} \cdot \sqrt{b} = \sqrt{ab}.$$
$$= 8\sqrt{75} \quad \longleftarrow \text{Simplify.}$$
$$= 8\sqrt{25 \cdot 3} \quad \longleftarrow \text{25 is the largest perfect square factor of 75.}$$
$$= 8\sqrt{25} \cdot \sqrt{3} \quad \longleftarrow \text{Use the fact that } \sqrt{ab} = \sqrt{a} \cdot \sqrt{b}.$$
$$= 8 \cdot 5\sqrt{3} \quad \longleftarrow \text{Write } \sqrt{25} \text{ as 5.}$$
$$= 40\sqrt{3}$$

Simplify.

1. $\sqrt{45}$ **2.** $\sqrt{300}$ **3.** $\sqrt{76}$ **4.** $5\sqrt{12}$ **5.** $12\sqrt{125}$

6. $\sqrt{6} \cdot \sqrt{7}$ **7.** $3\sqrt{5} \cdot \sqrt{2}$ **8.** $4.2\sqrt{11} \cdot \sqrt{3}$ **9.** $8\sqrt{2} \cdot 3\sqrt{3}$

10. $\sqrt{6} \cdot \sqrt{6}$ **11.** $\left(3\sqrt{3}\right)^2$ **12.** $2\sqrt{6} \cdot 3\sqrt{2}$ **13.** $4\sqrt{5} \cdot 3\sqrt{10}$

Solving Equations and Inequalities

Skill 13   Solving Linear Equations

You can solve some equations by *undoing* operations. Your goal is to get the variable alone on one side of the equation.

Example Solve $\frac{x}{2} + 7 = 40$.

$$\frac{x}{2} + 7 - 7 = 40 - 7 \quad \longleftarrow \text{Undo addition of 7. Subtract 7 from both sides.}$$

$$\frac{x}{2} = 33$$

$$2 \cdot \frac{x}{2} = 2 \cdot 33 \quad \longleftarrow \text{Undo division by 2. Multiply both sides by 2.}$$

$$x = 66$$

Example Solve $\dfrac{n-5}{3} = -11$.

$$3 \cdot \dfrac{n-5}{3} = 3(-11) \qquad \longleftarrow \text{Multiply both sides by 3.}$$

$$n - 5 = -33$$

$$n - 5 + 5 = -33 + 5 \qquad \longleftarrow \text{Add 5 to both sides.}$$

$$n = -28$$

When the variable appears on both sides of an equation, you will need to get the variable terms on the same side.

Example Solve $7x = 3(x + 1)$.

$$7x = 3x + 3 \qquad \longleftarrow \text{Use the distributive property.}$$

$$7x - 3x = 3x + 3 - 3x \qquad \longleftarrow \text{Subtract } 3x \text{ to get the variable terms on one side.}$$

$$4x = 3 \qquad \longleftarrow \text{Combine like terms.}$$

$$x = \dfrac{3}{4}, \text{ or } 0.75 \qquad \longleftarrow \text{Divide both sides by 4.}$$

Example Solve $\dfrac{2}{3}x = 4x - 10$.

$$\dfrac{2}{3}x - 4x = 4x - 10 - 4x \qquad \longleftarrow \text{Subtract } 4x \text{ from both sides.}$$

$$\dfrac{2}{3}x - 4x = -10$$

$$\dfrac{3}{2}\left(\dfrac{2}{3}x - 4x\right) = \dfrac{3}{2}(-10) \qquad \longleftarrow \text{Multiply both sides by } \dfrac{3}{2}, \text{ the reciprocal of } \dfrac{2}{3}.$$

$$x - 6x = -15 \qquad \longleftarrow \text{Use the distributive property.}$$

$$-5x = -15 \qquad \longleftarrow \text{Combine like terms.}$$

$$x = 3 \qquad \longleftarrow \text{Divide both sides by } -5.$$

Solve each equation.

1. $\dfrac{x}{6} = 12$

2. $\dfrac{n}{2} + 5 = 8$

3. $\dfrac{3}{4}x - 11 = 4$

4. $\dfrac{x+5}{3} = 10$

5. $\dfrac{x-7}{2} = 2$

6. $\dfrac{n-15}{2} = -5$

7. $\dfrac{w}{10} - 3.2 = 5.4$

8. $\dfrac{x-7}{2} + 4 = 2$

9. $3x = 2x - 5$

10. $-2x + 35 = 3x$

11. $\dfrac{x-7}{2} + 4 = 2x$

12. $5(x - 8) = 2x + 8$

13. $\dfrac{x}{3} - 5 = -4x$

14. $\dfrac{2}{3}n - 7 = n$

15. $\dfrac{2x+1}{5} = x$

To solve an inequality, you can use the same "undoing" operations that you used to solve equations.

Example Solve and graph the inequality $2x - 3 < 5$.   Read "is less than."

$2x - 3 < 5$

$2x - 3 + 3 < 5 + 3$ ← Undo subtraction of 3. Add 3 to both sides.

$2x < 8$

$\dfrac{2x}{2} < \dfrac{8}{2}$ ← Undo multiplication by 2. Divide both sides by 2.

$x < 4$

Draw a ray to the left to include all points less than 4.   Use an open circle to show that 4 is not included.

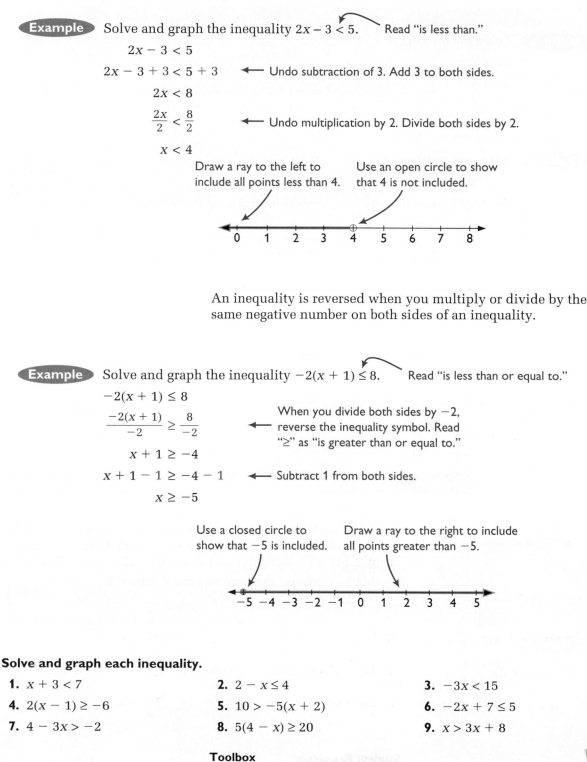

An inequality is reversed when you multiply or divide by the same negative number on both sides of an inequality.

Example Solve and graph the inequality $-2(x + 1) \le 8$.   Read "is less than or equal to."

$-2(x + 1) \le 8$

$\dfrac{-2(x + 1)}{-2} \ge \dfrac{8}{-2}$ ← When you divide both sides by -2, reverse the inequality symbol. Read "$\ge$" as "is greater than or equal to."

$x + 1 \ge -4$

$x + 1 - 1 \ge -4 - 1$ ← Subtract 1 from both sides.

$x \ge -5$

Use a closed circle to show that -5 is included.   Draw a ray to the right to include all points greater than -5.

Solve and graph each inequality.

1. $x + 3 < 7$

2. $2 - x \le 4$

3. $-3x < 15$

4. $2(x - 1) \ge -6$

5. $10 > -5(x + 2)$

6. $-2x + 7 \le 5$

7. $4 - 3x > -2$

8. $5(4 - x) \ge 20$

9. $x > 3x + 8$

Toolbox

645

Solving a formula or an equation for a variable means rewriting the formula or equation to get the variable alone on one side.

Example Solve the formula $A = lw$ for w.

$$A = lw$$

$$\frac{A}{l} = \frac{lw}{l} \quad \longleftarrow \text{ Undo multiplication by } l. \text{ Divide both sides by } l.$$

$$\frac{A}{l} = w$$

Example Solve the equation $3x + 2y = 10$ for y.

$$3x + 2y = 10$$

$$3x + 2y - 3x = 10 - 3x \quad \longleftarrow \text{ Undo addition of } 3x. \text{ Subtract } 3x \text{ from both sides.}$$

$$2y = 10 - 3x$$

$$\frac{1}{2} \cdot 2y = \frac{1}{2}(10 - 3x) \quad \longleftarrow \text{ Multiply both sides by the reciprocal of 2.}$$

$$y = 5 - \frac{3}{2}x \quad \longleftarrow \text{ Use the distributive property.}$$

Solve each equation for the variable shown in red.

1. $A = \frac{1}{2}bh$ **2.** $C = 2\pi r$ **3.** $A = \frac{1}{2}(a + b)$ **4.** $2x + y = 13$

5. $5x + 2y = 8$ **6.** $m = (n - 2)180$ **7.** $2x + y = 13$ **8.** $y = mx + b$

You can "undo" the squaring of a variable in an equation by taking the square root of both sides. Remember that every positive number has both a positive and a negative square root. The symbol $\sqrt{3}$ means "the *positive* square root of 3."

Example Solve $x^2 = 14$.

$$x^2 = 14$$

$$x = \pm\sqrt{14} \quad \longleftarrow \begin{array}{l}\text{Take the square root of both sides.} \\ \text{Use "±" to show that 14 has both a} \\ \text{positive and a negative square root.}\end{array}$$

$$x \approx \pm 3.74$$

Example Solve $x^2 + 16 = 81$.

$$x^2 + 16 - 16 = 81 - 16 \quad \longleftarrow \text{Undo addition of 16. Subtract 16 from both sides.}$$

$$x^2 = 65$$

$$x = \pm\sqrt{65} \quad \longleftarrow \text{Take the square root of both sides.}$$

$$x \approx \pm 8.06 \quad \longleftarrow \text{65 } \boxed{\text{INV}} \boxed{x^2}$$

You can undo the cubing of a variable in an equation by taking the cube root of both sides. Remember that a positive number has a positive cube root, and a negative number has a negative cube root. There is no "±" in the solution.

Example Solve $x^3 = 27$.

$$x = \sqrt[3]{27} \quad \longleftarrow \text{Take the cube root of both sides.}$$

$$x = 3 \quad \longleftarrow \text{27 } \boxed{\text{INV}} \boxed{y^x} \text{ 3 } \boxed{=}$$

Solve.

1. $x^2 = 49$ **2.** $x^2 = 19$ **3.** $x^3 = 8$ **4.** $x^3 = 64$

5. $x^3 = -125$ **6.** $x^2 + 25 = 36$ **7.** $x^2 - 16 = 81$ **8.** $49 - x^2 = 25$

Skill 17   **Solving Proportions**

You can solve some proportions by "undoing." If the variable is in the numerator of one of the equal fractions, you can use multiplication to undo the division.

Example Solve the proportion $\frac{x}{14} = \frac{8}{35}$.

$$\frac{x}{14} = \frac{8}{35}$$

$$14 \cdot \frac{x}{14} = 14 \cdot \frac{8}{35} \quad \longleftarrow \text{Multiply both sides by 14.}$$

$$x = \frac{16}{5} \quad \longleftarrow \text{Simplify.}$$

$$x = 3.2$$

Toolbox

You can solve any proportion by using the fact that the two cross products are equal.

Proportion: $\frac{a}{b} = \frac{c}{d}$ Cross products: $ad = bc$

Example   Solve the proportion $\frac{15}{x} = \frac{20}{21}$.

$$\frac{15}{x} = \frac{20}{21}$$

$15 \cdot 21 = x \cdot 20$ ⟵ Set the two cross products equal.

$315 = 20x$ ⟵ Simplify.

$\frac{315}{20} = \frac{20x}{20}$ ⟵ Divide both sides by 20.

$15.75 = x$ ⟵ Simplify.

Solve each proportion.

1. $\frac{x}{12} = \frac{13}{10}$ **2.** $\frac{18}{25} = \frac{z}{15}$ **3.** $\frac{y}{8} = \frac{14}{20}$ **4.** $\frac{24}{x} = \frac{15}{7}$

5. $\frac{28}{w} = \frac{16}{9}$ **6.** $\frac{11}{8} = \frac{5}{y}$ **7.** $\frac{17}{40} = \frac{q}{24}$ **8.** $\frac{12}{19} = \frac{33}{n}$

Skill 18   Using the Zero-Product Property

Zero-Product Property If a product of factors is zero, one or more of the factors must be zero.

Example   Solve the equation $(20 - x)(30 - 5x) = 0$.

$20 - x = 0$	or	$30 - 5x = 0$

⟵ At least one of the two factors must be 0.

$20 - x + x = 0 + x$ $30 - 5x + 5x = 0 + 5x$

$20 = x$ $30 = 5x$

$\frac{30}{5} = \frac{5x}{5}$

The solutions are 20 and 6. $6 = x$

Solve each equation.

1. $x(x + 10) = 0$ **2.** $2x(4 - x) = 0$ **3.** $-4x(x - 3) = 0$

4. $(x + 1)(x + 6) = 0$ **5.** $(x + 4)(x - 7) = 0$ **6.** $(2x - 1)(2x + 6) = 0$

Graphs, Equations, and Inequalities

A **function** is a relationship in which each value of the **control variable** determines exactly one value of the **dependent variable**.

Vertical Line Test: A graph with the control variable on the horizontal axis represents a function if no vertical line meets the graph in more than one place.

Example   To tell whether each graph is a function, imagine drawing vertical lines through it.

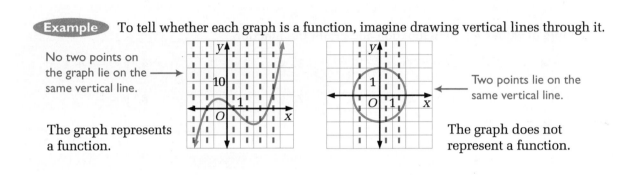

No two points on the graph lie on the same vertical line. →

The graph represents a function.

Two points lie on the same vertical line.

The graph does not represent a function.

Tell whether each graph represents a function when _x_ is the control variable.

1. 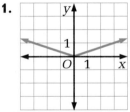   **2.** 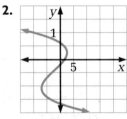   **3.** 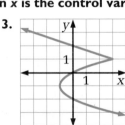   **4.**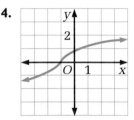

Example   Make a table of values and graph the function $y = 2x + 1$.

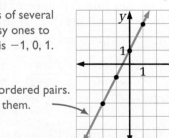

$y = 2x + 1$		
x	**y**	**(x, y)**
-2	-3	$(-2, -3)$
-1	-1	$(-1, -1)$
0	1	$(0, 1)$
1	3	$(1, 3)$

Find coordinates of several points. Some easy ones to find are when x is $-1, 0, 1$.

Plot the ordered pairs. Connect them.

Example Make a table of values and graph the function $y = x^2 - 3$.

Choose enough values to see the shape of the graph.

$y = x^2 - 3$		
x	**y**	**(x, y)**
-3	6	$(-3, 6)$
-1	-2	$(-1, -2)$
0	-3	$(0, -3)$
1	-2	$(1, -2)$
3	6	$(3, 6)$

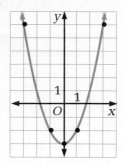

Make a table of values for each function and graph the function.

1. $y = x - 3$ **2.** $y = 3x - 4$ **3.** $y = -2x + 3$ **4.** $y = \frac{1}{2}x + 1$

5. $y = |x|$ **6.** $y = x^2 + 1$ **7.** $y = 2x^2 - 5$ **8.** $y = \frac{1}{x}$

Skill 21   Finding Slope

The **slope** of a line is the ratio of *rise* to *run*.

Example Find the slope of $\overline{AB}$.

$$\text{slope} = \frac{\text{rise}}{\text{run}} = \frac{4.8}{9.6} = 0.5$$

The slope is 0.5.

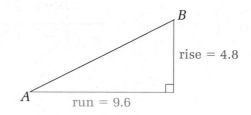

You can find the slope of a line in a coordinate system if you know two points on the line.

Example You can find the slope of the line shown using the points $(-2, 1)$ and $(3, 4)$.

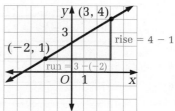

vertical change ⟶   ⟵ Subtract the y-coordinates.

$$\text{slope} = \frac{\text{rise}}{\text{run}} = \frac{4 - 1}{3 - (-2)} = \frac{3}{5} = 0.6$$

horizontal change ⟶   ⟵ Subtract the x-coordinates in the same order.

The slope of the line is 0.6.

The **slope of a horizontal line** is 0. The **slope of a vertical line** is undefined. A **negative slope** indicates that the line is "downhill" from left to right.

Example Find the slope of the line $y = 3$.

Two points on this line are $(0, 3)$ and $(4, 3)$.

slope $= \dfrac{3 - 3}{4 - 0} = \dfrac{0}{4}$, or 0

The slope is 0. (The line is horizontal.)

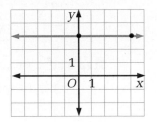

Find the slope of each line.

1.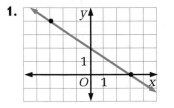

2. the line through $(1, -4)$ and $(3, 7)$

3. the line through $(-6, 2)$ and $(4, -2)$

4. the line through $(5, 0)$ and $(5, 5)$

Skill 22	Modeling Direct Variation

When the ratio of two variable quantities is a constant k, their relationship is called a **direct variation.** You can model a direct variation with an equation of the form $\dfrac{y}{x} = k$, or $y = kx$.

One quantity **varies directly with** another quantity.

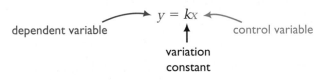

dependent variable $y = kx$ control variable

variation constant

Example The pressure on an underwater object varies directly with the depth of the object below the surface. Suppose the pressure on an object at a depth of 50 ft is 21.7 lbs/in.^{2} Find the pressure on an object at a depth of 85 ft.

Method ❶ Use a proportion. The ratio depth : pressure is constant.

depth $\longrightarrow$
pressure $\longrightarrow$ $\dfrac{50}{21.7} = \dfrac{85}{y}$

$50y = (21.7)(85)$ $\longleftarrow$ Set the cross products equal.

$y = \dfrac{(21.7)(85)}{50} = 36.89$

Continued on next page.

Method ❷ Use the equation $y = kx$.

Step 1 First find the variation constant.

Let x = the depth (ft) and y = the pressure (lbs/in.²).

$y = kx$ ←— Write the general form of the equation.

$21.7 = k \cdot 50$ ←— Substitute 50 for x and 21.7 for y.

$k = \dfrac{21.7}{50} = 0.434$ ←— Solve for k, the variation constant.

Step 2 $y = kx$ ←— Write the general form of the equation.

$y = (0.434)(85)$ ←— Substitute 0.434 for k and 85 for x.

$y = 36.89$

The pressure is 36.89 lbs/in.²

1. The distance a car travels at a constant speed varies directly with time. Suppose the car goes 92 miles in 2 h. How far would it go in 3.5 h?

2. The bounce height of a rubber ball varies directly with the drop height. A ball dropped from a height of 6.5 ft bounces to a height of 5.2 ft. How high will the ball bounce if dropped from 5.5 ft?

Skill 23 **Using y = mx + b**

One form of the equation of a line is **slope-intercept form:**

$$y = mx + b$$

slope ——→ vertical intercept

Example Find the slope and the vertical intercept of the line $y = \dfrac{2}{3}x - 5$.

The line is in the form $y = mx + b$. Therefore, the slope is $\dfrac{2}{3}$, and the vertical intercept is -5.

Example Write an equation for the line shown at the right.

Step 1 Use $(-3, 4)$ and $(3, 0)$ to find the slope m.

$$m = \frac{0 - 4}{3 - (-3)} = \frac{-4}{6} = -\frac{2}{3}$$

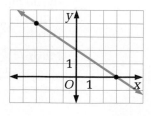

Step 2 The graph crosses the vertical axis at $(0, 2)$, so $b = 2$.

Step 3 Substitute the values in $y = mx + b$: $y = -\dfrac{2}{3}x + 2$.

Student Resources

Find the slope and the vertical intercept of each line.

1. $y = 3x - 4$ **2.** $y = -2.5x + 11.2$ **3.** $y = 6 - 7x$ **4.** $y = 4x$

Write an equation of each line in the form $y = mx + b$.

5. 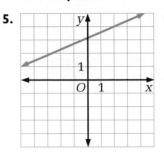   **6.** 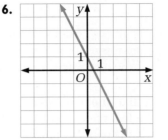   **7.**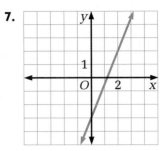

Skill 24   Using Intercepts to Graph

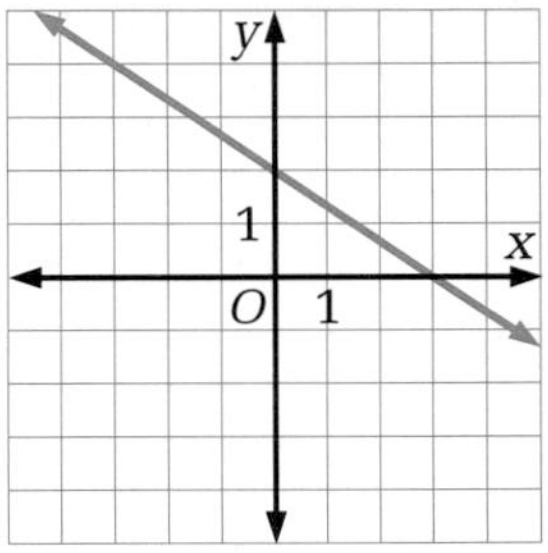

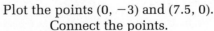

The **horizontal intercept** of a graph is the x-coordinate of the point where the graph crosses the x-axis. The **vertical intercept** is the y-coordinate of the point where the graph crosses the y-axis.

The graph at the left crosses the horizontal axis at $(3, 0)$ and the vertical axis at $(0, 2)$.

The horizontal intercept of the graph is 3.

The vertical intercept of the graph is 2.

If you know the equation of a line, one way to graph the line is to use the intercepts.

Example   Use the intercepts to graph the line $2x - 5y = 15$.

To find the vertical intercept, substitute 0 for x:

$$2x - 5y = 15$$
$$2(0) - 5y = 15$$
$$-5y = 15$$
$$y = -3$$

To find the horizontal intercept, substitute 0 for y:

$$2x - 5y = 15$$
$$2x - 5(0) = 15$$
$$2x = 15$$
$$x = 7.5$$

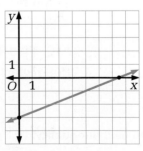

Plot the points $(0, -3)$ and $(7.5, 0)$. Connect the points.

Use the vertical and horizontal intercepts to graph each equation.

1. $3x + y = 6$

2. $5x - 2y = 10$

3. $-3x + 3y = 9$

4. $4x = y + 8$

5. $y = 2x - 3$

6. $y = -2.5x + 5$

Skill 25 Graphing an Inequality in Two Variables

To graph a **linear inequality** in two variables, such as $y > x + 2$, you shade a region on a coordinate plane whose edge is a line. The edge is called a **boundary line.** The shaded part of the graph of a linear inequality is the **solution region.**

Example Graph the inequality $y > x + 2$.

First graph the boundary line: $y = x + 2$.
Since the inequality symbol is ">," you use a dashed line for the boundary line.
Each point on the boundary line has y-coordinate $x + 2$. Therefore, the points for which $y > x + 2$ will lie *above* the boundary line. Shade this region.

Example Graph the inequality $x + 2y \le 6$.

First rewrite the inequality in slope-intercept form.

$$x + 2y \le 6$$

$$x + 2y - x \le 6 - x \qquad \longleftarrow \text{Subtract } x \text{ from both sides.}$$

$$2y \le 6 - x$$

$$\frac{1}{2} \cdot 2y \le \frac{1}{2}(6 - x) \qquad \longleftarrow \text{Multiply both sides by } \frac{1}{2}.$$

$$y \le 3 - \frac{1}{2}x$$

Graph the boundary line $y = 3 - \frac{1}{2}x$.

Since the symbol in the inequality is "$\le$," the boundary line is a solid line.

Each point on the boundary line has y-coordinate $3 - \frac{1}{2}x$. Therefore, the solution region lies *below* and includes the boundary line. Shade this region.

Graph each inequality.

1. $y > -x + 3$

2. $y \le 2x - 4$

3. $y < \frac{1}{2}x + 1$

4. $2x + 3y \ge 6$

5. $x - 3y > 3$

6. $3x + 2y \le 9$

654 **Student Resources**

➤Geometry and Measurement

Formulas and Relationships

Skill 26   Finding Unknown Angle Measures

An angle whose measure is 90° is called a **right angle.** An angle whose measure is 180° is called a **straight angle.**

Two angles whose measures add up to 90° are **complementary.**
Two angles whose measures add up to 180° are **supplementary.**

A mark like this indicates a right angle.

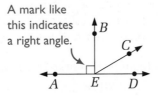

∠AEB is a right angle.
∠BEC and ∠CED are complementary.

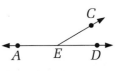

∠AED is a straight angle.
∠AEC and ∠CED are supplementary.

Example ▶ Find the unknown angle measure in the figure.

The sum of the measures of the angles of a triangle is 180°.

$x + 40 + 30 = 180$

$x = 180 - 70$

$= 110$

The unknown angle measure is 110°.

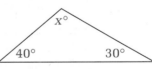

Example ▶ Find the unknown angle measures in the figure.

Vertical angles are equal in measure.

∠AOD and ∠BOC are vertical angles, so $y = 55$.

∠AOB and ∠BOC are supplementary, so $x = 180 - 55 = 125$.

The angle measures are 125° and 55°.

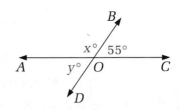

Find each unknown angle measure.

1.

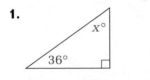

2.

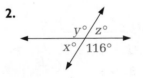

3.

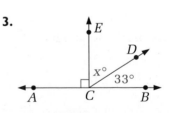

Toolbox

655

Certain marks in a geometry diagram indicate special relationships between lines, segments, and angles.

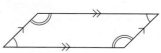

A small
square
indicates a
right angle.

Tick marks
indicate sides
that are equal
in measure.

Arcs indicate
angles that
are equal in
measure.

Arrowheads
indicate
parallel lines
or segments.

Example   List all the relationships indicated by marks in the figure.

Angles   Since ∠ *TOP* is marked with a small square,
∠ *TOP* is a right angle.

Since ∠ *T* and ∠ *Q* both have one arc,
∠ *T* and ∠ *Q* are equal in measure.

Sides   Since sides *TO* and *OP* both have one tick
mark, side *TO* ≅ side *OP*.

Since sides *SR* and *RQ* both have two tick
marks, side *SR* ≅ side *RQ*.

Since sides *RQ* and *TO* both have one arrowhead,
side *RQ* is parallel to side *TO*.

Since sides *PQ* and *ST* both have two arrowheads,
side *PQ* is parallel to side *ST*.

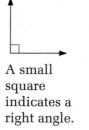

List all the relationships indicated by marks in each figure.

1.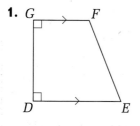

2.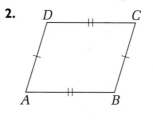

3.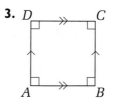

4.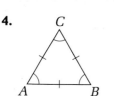

5.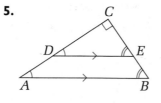

6.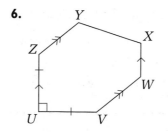

In formulas from geometry:

A = area   S.A. = surface area V = volume

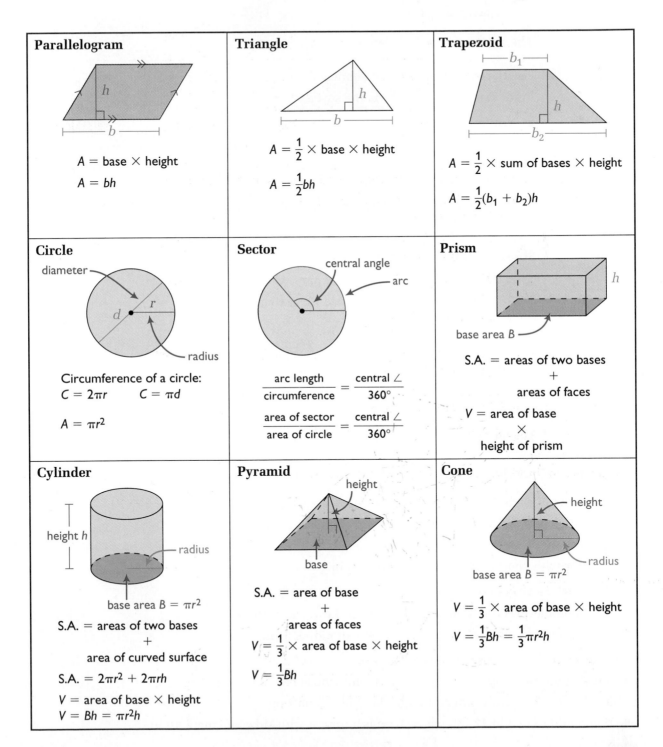

Parallelogram

A = base × height

$A = bh$

Triangle

$A = \frac{1}{2}$ × base × height

$A = \frac{1}{2}bh$

Trapezoid

$A = \frac{1}{2}$ × sum of bases × height

$A = \frac{1}{2}(b_1 + b_2)h$

Circle

diameter

radius

Circumference of a circle:

$C = 2\pi r$ $C = \pi d$

$A = \pi r^2$

Sector

central angle

arc

$\dfrac{\text{arc length}}{\text{circumference}} = \dfrac{\text{central } \angle}{360°}$

$\dfrac{\text{area of sector}}{\text{area of circle}} = \dfrac{\text{central } \angle}{360°}$

Prism

base area B

S.A. = areas of two bases
+
areas of faces

V = area of base
×
height of prism

Cylinder

height h

radius

base area $B = \pi r^2$

S.A. = areas of two bases
+
area of curved surface

S.A. $= 2\pi r^2 + 2\pi rh$

V = area of base × height

$V = Bh = \pi r^2 h$

Pyramid

height

base

S.A. = area of base
+
areas of faces

$V = \frac{1}{3}$ × area of base × height

$V = \frac{1}{3}Bh$

Cone

height

radius

base area $B = \pi r^2$

$V = \frac{1}{3}$ × area of base × height

$V = \frac{1}{3}Bh = \frac{1}{3}\pi r^2 h$

Example Find the area of the trapezoid shown.

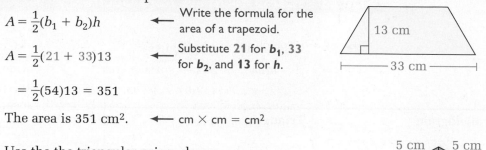

$A = \frac{1}{2}(b_1 + b_2)h$ ← Write the formula for the area of a trapezoid.

$A = \frac{1}{2}(21 + 33)13$ ← Substitute **21** for b_1, **33** for b_2, and **13** for h.

$= \frac{1}{2}(54)13 = 351$

The area is 351 cm². ← cm × cm = cm²

Example Use the the triangular prism shown.

Find: **a.** the volume   **b.** the surface area

a. Volume of a prism = area of base × height of prism.

Step 1 Find the area of the triangular base of the prism.

$B = \frac{1}{2}bh$ ← Write the formula for the area of a triangle.

$= \frac{1}{2}(6)(4)$ ← Substitute **6** for b and **4** for h.

$= 12$

Step 2 Find the volume of the prism.

$V = Bh$ ← Write the formula for the volume of a prism.

$= 12 \cdot 10$ ← Substitute **12** for B and **10** for h.

$= 120$

The volume of the prism is 120 cm³. ← cm × cm × cm = cm³

b. Surface area of a prism = area of two bases + area of three faces

S.A. = $\overbrace{12 + 12}$ $+ \overbrace{6 \cdot 10 + 5 \cdot 10 + 5 \cdot 10}$

$= 184$

The surface area is 184 cm².

Find the area of each figure.

1. a parallelogram of height 10 ft with a base of length 16 ft

2. a trapezoid of height 3 in. with bases of length 5 in. and 8 in.

3. a sector with central angle 40° and radius 9 in.

Find the surface area of each space figure.

4. a rectangular prism with dimensions 18 in., 12 in., and 4.5 in.

5. a cylinder of height 20 cm and with a base of radius 5 cm

Find the volume of each space figure.

6. a triangular prism whose height is 8 cm and whose base area is 25 cm²

7. a cylinder of height 8.5 m and with a base of radius 2 m

8. a pyramid of height 12 in., whose base is a square with sides of length 10 in.

Trigonometry

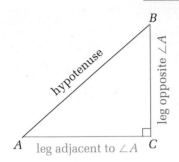

Suppose $\angle A$ is one of the acute angles of a right triangle. The **trigonometric ratios** for $\angle A$ are ratios of the measures of the sides of the triangle.

Sine of $\angle A$ $\sin A = \dfrac{\text{leg opposite } \angle A}{\text{hypotenuse}} = \dfrac{BC}{AB}$

Cosine of $\angle A$ $\cos A = \dfrac{\text{leg adjacent to } \angle A}{\text{hypotenuse}} = \dfrac{AC}{AB}$

Tangent of $\angle A$ $\tan A = \dfrac{\text{leg opposite } \angle A}{\text{leg adjacent to } \angle A} = \dfrac{BC}{AC}$

Example Write each trigonometric ratio as a fraction and as a decimal rounded to the nearest hundredth.

  a. $\sin P$ **b.** $\cos P$ **c.** $\tan P$

  d. $\sin Q$ **e.** $\cos Q$ **f.** $\tan Q$

a. $\sin P = \dfrac{\text{leg opposite } \angle P}{\text{hypotenuse}} = \dfrac{15}{17} \approx 0.88$

b. $\cos P = \dfrac{\text{leg adjacent to } \angle P}{\text{hypotenuse}} = \dfrac{8}{17} \approx 0.47$

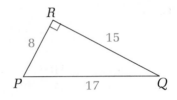

c. $\tan P = \dfrac{\text{leg opposite } \angle P}{\text{leg adjacent to } \angle P} = \dfrac{15}{8} \approx 1.88$

d. $\sin Q = \dfrac{\text{leg opposite } \angle Q}{\text{hypotenuse}} = \dfrac{8}{17} \approx 0.47$

e. $\cos Q = \dfrac{\text{leg adjacent to } \angle Q}{\text{hypotenuse}} = \dfrac{15}{17} \approx 0.88$

f. $\tan Q = \dfrac{\text{leg opposite } \angle Q}{\text{leg adjacent to } \angle Q} = \dfrac{8}{15} \approx 0.53$

Use the triangle at the right. Find the value of each trigonometric ratio.

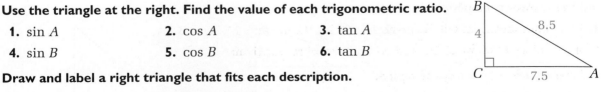

  1. $\sin A$ **2.** $\cos A$ **3.** $\tan A$

  4. $\sin B$ **5.** $\cos B$ **6.** $\tan B$

Draw and label a right triangle that fits each description.

  7. $\triangle ABC$ with $\sin A = \dfrac{\text{leg opposite } \angle A}{\text{hypotenuse}} = \dfrac{3}{5}$

  8. $\triangle XYZ$ with $\cos X = \dfrac{\text{leg adjacent to } \angle X}{\text{hypotenuse}} = \dfrac{5}{13}$

You can use the trigonometric ratios to find missing lengths in right triangles. The ratios are programmed into scientific calculators. There is a table of trigonometric ratios on page 668.

Example ▸ Find the missing length in the triangle at the right.

Since x is the measure of the leg opposite $\angle A$, and 24 is the measure of the hypotenuse of the right triangle, you use the sine ratio.

$$\sin \angle A = \frac{\text{length of leg opposite } \angle A}{\text{length of hypotenuse}}$$

$$\sin 32° = \frac{x}{24}$$

$$0.5299 \approx \frac{x}{24} \quad \longleftarrow \quad \text{Make sure your calculator is in degree mode. Use the } \boxed{\text{sin}} \text{ key.}$$

$$0.5299 \cdot 24 \approx \frac{x}{24} \cdot 24 \quad \longleftarrow \quad \text{Multiply both sides by 24.}$$

$$12.7 \approx x$$

Example ▸ Find the missing length in the triangle at the right.

Use the tangent ratio.

$$\tan 61° = \frac{49}{x}$$

$$1.804 \approx \frac{49}{x} \quad \longleftarrow \quad \text{Use the } \boxed{\text{tan}} \text{ key on your calculator.}$$

$$1.804 \cdot x \approx \frac{49}{x} \cdot x \quad \longleftarrow \quad \text{Multiply both sides by } x.$$

$$1.804x \approx 49$$

$$\frac{1.804x}{1.804} \approx \frac{49}{1.804} \quad \longleftarrow \quad \text{Divide both sides by 1.804.}$$

$$x \approx \frac{49}{1.804} \approx 27.2$$

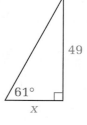

Find each missing length.

1.

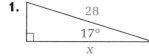

2.

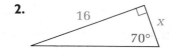

3.

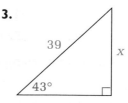

Student Resources

The Pythagorean Theorem

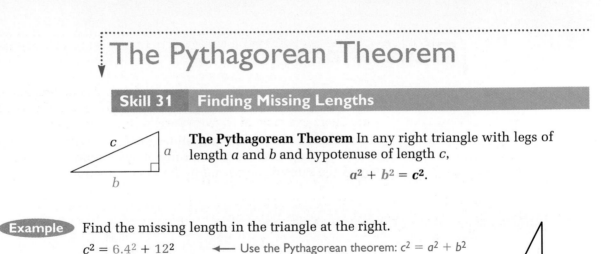

The Pythagorean Theorem In any right triangle with legs of length a and b and hypotenuse of length c,

$$a^2 + b^2 = c^2.$$

Example Find the missing length in the triangle at the right.

$c^2 = 6.4^2 + 12^2$ ⟵ Use the Pythagorean theorem: $c^2 = a^2 + b^2$

$c^2 = 40.96 + 144$

$c^2 = 184.96$

$c = \sqrt{184.96}$ ⟵ Find the positive square root.

$c = 13.6$

Find the missing length in the right triangle with legs a and b and hypotenuse c.

1. $a = 5$, $b = 12$, $c = ?$ **2.** $a = 10$, $c = 14.5$, $b = ?$ **3.** $b = 24$, $c = 75$, $a = ?$

If the lengths of the sides of a triangle satisfy the relationship $a^2 + b^2 = c^2$, the triangle is a right triangle with hypotenuse c.

Example Is the triangle with sides of the given lengths a right triangle?

a. 15, 20, 25   **b.** 8, 10, 13

If the triangle is a right triangle, the longest side must be the hypotenuse.

a. $a^2 + b^2 \stackrel{?}{=} c^2$ **b.** $a^2 + b^2 \stackrel{?}{=} c^2$

$15^2 + 20^2 \stackrel{?}{=} 25^2$ $8^2 + 10^2 \stackrel{?}{=} 13^2$

$225 + 400 \stackrel{?}{=} 625$ $64 + 100 \stackrel{?}{=} 169$

$625 = 625$ ✔ $164 \neq 169$

The triangle is a right triangle.   The triangle is not a right triangle.

Tell whether a triangle with sides of the given lengths is a right triangle.

1. 6, 8, 10   **2.** 2.1, 2.8, 3.5   **3.** 2.5, 6, 6.5   **4.** 10, 17.5, 20

Transformations

Skill 33 **Translating a Figure**

A **translation** of a plane figure slides the figure without changing its size or shape and without turning it. Each point of the figure moves the same distance and in the same direction.

Example Translate △ABC 4 units to the right and 1 unit down.

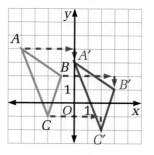

Step 1 Translate each vertex 4 units to the right and 1 unit down:

$A(-4, 4) \rightarrow A'(0, 3)$

$B(-1, 2) \rightarrow B'(3, 1)$

$C(-2, -1) \rightarrow C'(2, -2)$

Each translated vertex is labeled with a prime (′).

Step 2 Connect the vertices. The translated triangle is △A′B′C′.

Draw each translation of △DEF.

1. 3 units to the left.   **2.** 2 units down

3. 2 units to the right and up 3 units

4. 4 units to the left and down 1 unit

5. 1 unit to the right and down 4 units

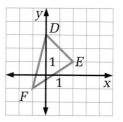

Skill 34 **Rotating a Figure**

A **rotation** moves each point of a figure through a circular arc about a common point, called the **center of rotation.** Each point of the figure is rotated by the same number of degrees.

Example Rotate △ABC 90° counterclockwise about the origin.

Imagine that △ABC is a paper triangle fixed to a stick, $\overline{OC}$. Suppose you press down on the stick at the center of rotation O and rotate the stick through a quarter of a circle (90°) counterclockwise. The rotated triangle is △A′B′C′.

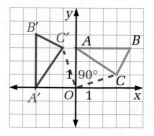

662   **Student Resources**

It is easier to draw a rotation on polar graph paper.

Example Rotate △*DEF* 60° counterclockwise about the origin.

Step 1 Move each vertex along its circle six lines in the counterclockwise direction. (From one line to the next is 10°, and 6 · 10° is 60°.) Label the new points *D'*, *E'*, *F'*.

Step 2 Connect the vertices. The rotated triangle is △*D'E'F'*.

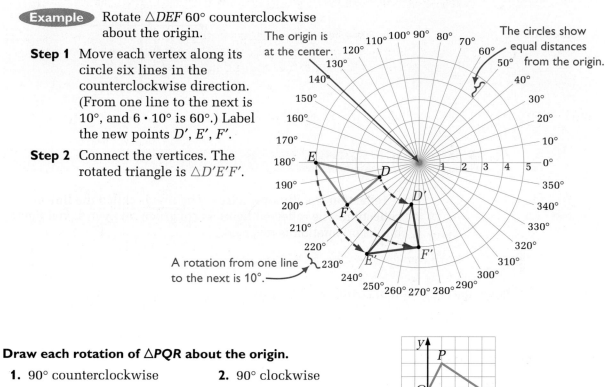

The origin is at the center.

The circles show equal distances from the origin.

A rotation from one line to the next is 10°.

Draw each rotation of △*PQR* about the origin.

1. 90° counterclockwise
2. 90° clockwise
3. 180° clockwise
4. 270° counterclockwise

Skill 35 | **Dilating a Figure**

A **dilation** transforms a figure into a similar figure. The ratio of any length in the transformed figure to the corresponding length in the original figure is the **scale factor.**

Example Draw a dilation of △*ABC*, with center *P*, in which the scale factor is 3.

Step 1 Draw rays from *P* through the vertices of △*ABC*.

Step 2 Measure the distance from *P* to each vertex of the original triangle along these rays. Mark points *A'*, *B'*, and *C'* on these rays that are 3 times as far from *P* as the corresponding vertex of the original figure.

Step 3 Connect the vertices. The dilated triangle is △*A'B'C'*.

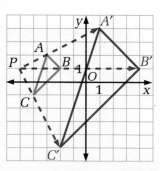

Draw a dilation of the parallelogram *JKLM* with each scale factor and with center *J*.

1. scale factor 2

2. scale factor $\frac{1}{2}$

3. scale factor $\frac{3}{2}$

4. scale factor $\frac{5}{2}$

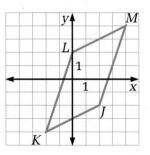

Skill 36 **Reflecting a Figure**

A **reflection** is a flip over a line. The line is called the **line of reflection.** The reflected figure is congruent to the original figure, but its orientation is reversed.

Example Draw the reflection of △*ABC* over the *x*-axis. Label the vertices with primes.

Point A is 3 units above the *x*-axis.

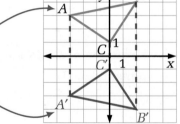

Point A′ is 3 units below the *x*-axis.

Notice in the sample that a reflection has these properties:

➤ Each segment connecting a vertex of the original figure with its corresponding vertex in the reflected figure is cut in half by the line of reflection, in this case, the *x*-axis.

➤ The vertices of the original figure in *clockwise* order correspond to the vertices of the reflected figure in counterclockwise order.

Draw a reflection of △*DEF* over each line.

1. the *x*-axis

2. the *y*-axis

3. the line $x = 1$

4. the line $y = -1$

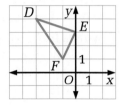

Student Resources

Table of Measures

Time

60 seconds (s) = 1 minute (min)
60 minutes = 1 hour (h)
24 hours = 1 day
7 days = 1 week
4 weeks (approx.) = 1 month

$\left.\begin{array}{l}\text{365 days} \\ \text{52 weeks (approx.)} \\ \text{12 months}\end{array}\right\}$ = 1 year

10 years = 1 decade
100 years = 1 century

Metric

Length

10 millimeters (mm) = 1 centimeter (cm)

$\left.\begin{array}{l}\text{100 cm} \\ \text{1000 mm}\end{array}\right\}$ = 1 meter (m)

1000 m = 1 kilometer (km)

Area

100 square millimeters = 1 square centimeter
(mm²)   (cm²)

10,000 cm² = 1 square meter (m²)

10,000 m² = 1 hectare (ha)

Volume

1000 cubic millimeters = 1 cubic centimeter
(mm³)   (cm³)

1,000,000 cm³ = 1 cubic meter (m³)

Liquid Capacity

1000 milliliters (mL) = 1 liter (L)

1000 L = 1 kiloliter (kL)

Mass

1000 milligrams (mg) = 1 gram (g)

1000 g = 1 kilogram (kg)

1000 kg = 1 metric ton (t)

Temperature Degrees Celsius (°C)

0°C = freezing point
of water

37°C = normal body
temperature

100°C = boiling point
of water

United States Customary

Length

12 inches (in.) = 1 foot (ft)

$\left.\begin{array}{l}\text{36 in.} \\ \text{3 ft}\end{array}\right\}$ = 1 yard (yd)

$\left.\begin{array}{l}\text{5280 ft} \\ \text{1760 yd}\end{array}\right\}$ = 1 mile (mi)

Area

144 square inches (in.²) = 1 square foot (ft²)

9 ft² = 1 square yard (yd²)

$\left.\begin{array}{l}\text{43,560 ft}^2 \\ \text{4840 yd}^2\end{array}\right\}$ = 1 acre (A)

Volume

1728 cubic inches (in.³) = 1 cubic foot (ft³)

27 ft³ = 1 cubic yard (yd³)

Liquid Capacity

8 fluid ounces (fl oz) = 1 cup (c)

2 c = 1 pint (pt)

2 pt = 1 quart (qt)

4 qt = 1 gallon (gal)

Weight

16 ounces (oz) = 1 pound (lb)

2000 lb = 1 ton (t)

Temperature Degrees Fahrenheit (°F)

32°F = freezing point
of water

98.6°F = normal body
temperature

212°F = boiling point
of water

Table of Symbols

Symbol		Page	Symbol		Page
$=$	equals, is equal to	5	$x^{1/3}$	cube root of x	100
$\dfrac{1}{a}$	reciprocal of a	8	$\overline{AB}$	segment AB	112
$P(E)$	probability of event E	8	$A \to A'$	point A goes to point A' after a transformation	160
$>$	is greater than	15	A^{-1}	inverse of matrix A	174
$<$	is less than	15	$\cos A$	cosine of $\angle A$	192
$\geq$	is greater than or equal to	15	$\pm$	plus-or-minus sign	200
$\leq$	is less than or equal to	15	i	$\sqrt{-1}$	225
a^n	nth power of a	15	$\cong$	congruent, is congruent to	243
$-a$	opposite of a	15	AB	the length of $\overline{AB}$	251
$^\circ$	degree(s)	33	$!$	factorial	304
$|a|$	absolute value of a	34	$_nP_r$	permutation	304
$\cdot$	$\times$ (times)	35	$_nC_r$	combination	329
$\neq$	is not equal to	43	$p \to q$	p *implies* q, or *if* p, *then* q	373
$\triangle ABC$	triangle ABC	43	$\therefore$	therefore	380
π	pi, a number approximately equal to 3.14	65	$p \leftrightarrow q$	p *if and only if* q	387
(x, y)	ordered pair	68	$m\angle A$	measure of angle A	408
m	slope	68	$\parallel$	is parallel to	417
k	variation constant	70	$\angle\!\!\!s$	angles	418
$\overleftrightarrow{AB}$	line AB	73	$\perp$	is perpendicular to	434
$\tan A$	tangent of $\angle A$	73	$a : b$	ratio of a to b	444
$\approx$	is approximately equal to	85	$\sim$	similar, is similar to	449
$\sqrt[3]{a}$	cube root of a	86	$\triangle\!\!\!s$	triangles	460
$\sqrt{a}$	nonnegative square root of a	93	$\overrightarrow{AB}$	ray AB	468
a^{-n}	$\dfrac{1}{a^n}, a \neq 0$	99	$\sin A$	sine of $\angle A$	491
$x^{1/2}$	square root of x	100	(x, y, z)	ordered triple	579

Table of Squares and Square Roots

No.	Square	Sq. Root	No.	Square	Sq. Root	No.	Square	Sq. Root
1	1	1.000	51	2,601	7.141	101	10,201	10.050
2	4	1.414	52	2,704	7.211	102	10,404	10.100
3	9	1.732	53	2,809	7.280	103	10,609	10.149
4	16	2.000	54	2,916	7.348	104	10,816	10.198
5	25	2.236	55	3,025	7.416	105	11,025	10.247
6	36	2.449	56	3,136	7.483	106	11,236	10.296
7	49	2.646	57	3,249	7.550	107	11,449	10.344
8	64	2.828	58	3,364	7.616	108	11,664	10.392
9	81	3.000	59	3,481	7.681	109	11,881	10.440
10	100	3.162	60	3,600	7.746	110	12,100	10.488
11	121	3.317	61	3,721	7.810	111	12,321	10.536
12	144	3.464	62	3,844	7.874	112	12,544	10.583
13	169	3.606	63	3,969	7.937	113	12,769	10.630
14	196	3.742	64	4,096	8.000	114	12,996	10.677
15	225	3.873	65	4,225	8.062	115	13,225	10.724
16	256	4.000	66	4,356	8.124	116	13,456	10.770
17	289	4.123	67	4,489	8.185	117	13,689	10.817
18	324	4.243	68	4,624	8.246	118	13,924	10.863
19	361	4.359	69	4,761	8.307	119	14,161	10.909
20	400	4.472	70	4,900	8.367	120	14,400	10.954
21	441	4.583	71	5,041	8.426	121	14,641	11.000
22	484	4.690	72	5,184	8.485	122	14,884	11.045
23	529	4.796	73	5,329	8.544	123	15,129	11.091
24	576	4.899	74	5,476	8.602	124	15,376	11.136
25	625	5.000	75	5,625	8.660	125	15,625	11.180
26	676	5.099	76	5,776	8.718	126	15,876	11.225
27	729	5.196	77	5,929	8.775	127	16,129	11.269
28	784	5.292	78	6,084	8.832	128	16,384	11.314
29	841	5.385	79	6,241	8.888	129	16,641	11.358
30	900	5.477	80	6,400	8.944	130	16,900	11.402
31	961	5.568	81	6,561	9.000	131	17,161	11.446
32	1,024	5.657	82	6,724	9.055	132	17,424	11.489
33	1,089	5.745	83	6,889	9.110	133	17,689	11.533
34	1,156	5.831	84	7,056	9.165	134	17,956	11.576
35	1,225	5.916	85	7,225	9.220	135	18,225	11.619
36	1,296	6.000	86	7,396	9.274	136	18,496	11.662
37	1,369	6.083	87	7,569	9.327	137	18,769	11.705
38	1,444	6.164	88	7,744	9.381	138	19,044	11.747
39	1,521	6.245	89	7,921	9.434	139	19,321	11.790
40	1,600	6.325	90	8,100	9.487	140	19,600	11.832
41	1,681	6.403	91	8,281	9.539	141	19,881	11.874
42	1,764	6.481	92	8,464	9.592	142	20,164	11.916
43	1,849	6.557	93	8,649	9.644	143	20,449	11.958
44	1,936	6.633	94	8,836	9.695	144	20,736	12.000
45	2,025	6.708	95	9,025	9.747	145	21,025	12.042
46	2,116	6.782	96	9,216	9.798	146	21,316	12.083
47	2,209	6.856	97	9,409	9.849	147	21,609	12.124
48	2,304	6.928	98	9,604	9.899	148	21,904	12.166
49	2,401	7.000	99	9,801	9.950	149	22,201	12.207
50	2,500	7.071	100	10,000	10.000	150	22,500	12.247

Tables

Table of
Trigonometric Ratios

Angle	Sine	Cosine	Tangent	Angle	Sine	Cosine	Tangent
1°	.0175	.9998	.0175	46°	.7193	.6947	1.0355
2°	.0349	.9994	.0349	47°	.7314	.6820	1.0724
3°	.0523	.9986	.0524	48°	.7431	.6691	1.1106
4°	.0698	.9976	.0699	49°	.7547	.6561	1.1504
5°	.0872	.9962	.0875	50°	.7660	.6428	1.1918
6°	.1045	.9945	.1051	51°	.7771	.6293	1.2349
7°	.1219	.9925	.1228	52°	.7880	.6157	1.2799
8°	.1392	.9903	.1405	53°	.7986	.6018	1.3270
9°	.1564	.9877	.1584	54°	.8090	.5878	1.3764
10°	.1736	.9848	.1763	55°	.8192	.5736	1.4281
11°	.1908	.9816	.1944	56°	.8290	.5592	1.4826
12°	.2079	.9781	.2126	57°	.8387	.5446	1.5399
13°	.2250	.9744	.2309	58°	.8480	.5299	1.6003
14°	.2419	.9703	.2493	59°	.8572	.5150	1.6643
15°	.2588	.9659	.2679	60°	.8660	.5000	1.7321
16°	.2756	.9613	.2867	61°	.8746	.4848	1.8040
17°	.2924	.9563	.3057	62°	.8829	.4695	1.8807
18°	.3090	.9511	.3249	63°	.8910	.4540	1.9626
19°	.3256	.9455	.3443	64°	.8988	.4384	2.0503
20°	.3420	.9397	.3640	65°	.9063	.4226	2.1445
21°	.3584	.9336	.3839	66°	.9135	.4067	2.2460
22°	.3746	.9272	.4040	67°	.9205	.3907	2.3559
23°	.3907	.9205	.4245	68°	.9272	.3746	2.4751
24°	.4067	.9135	.4452	69°	.9336	.3584	2.6051
25°	.4226	.9063	.4663	70°	.9397	.3420	2.7475
26°	.4384	.8988	.4877	71°	.9455	.3256	2.9042
27°	.4540	.8910	.5095	72°	.9511	.3090	3.0777
28°	.4695	.8829	.5317	73°	.9563	.2924	3.2709
29°	.4848	.8746	.5543	74°	.9613	.2756	3.4874
30°	.5000	.8660	.5774	75°	.9659	.2588	3.7321
31°	.5150	.8572	.6009	76°	.9703	.2419	4.0108
32°	.5299	.8480	.6249	77°	.9744	.2250	4.3315
33°	.5446	.8387	.6494	78°	.9781	.2079	4.7046
34°	.5592	.8290	.6745	79°	.9816	.1908	5.1446
35°	.5736	.8192	.7002	80°	.9848	.1736	5.6713
36°	.5878	.8090	.7265	81°	.9877	.1564	6.3138
37°	.6018	.7986	.7536	82°	.9903	.1392	7.1154
38°	.6157	.7880	.7813	83°	.9925	.1219	8.1443
39°	.6293	.7771	.8098	84°	.9945	.1045	9.5144
40°	.6428	.7660	.8391	85°	.9962	.0872	11.4301
41°	.6561	.7547	.8693	86°	.9976	.0698	14.3007
42°	.6691	.7431	.9004	87°	.9986	.0523	19.0811
43°	.6820	.7314	.9325	88°	.9994	.0349	28.6363
44°	.6947	.7193	.9657	89°	.9998	.0175	57.2900
45°	.7071	.7071	1.0000				

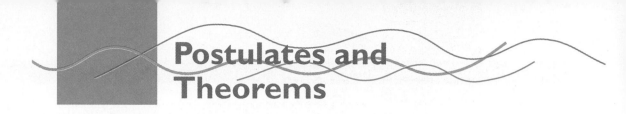

Postulates and Theorems

Postulates of Algebra

Postulate 1 **Addition Property of Equality** If the same number is added to equal numbers, then the sums are equal. *(p. 402)*

$$a = b \rightarrow a + c = b + c$$

Postulate 2 **Subtraction Property of Equality** If the same number is subtracted from equal numbers, then the differences are equal. *(p. 402)*

$$a = b \rightarrow a - c = b - c$$

Postulate 3 **Multiplication Property of Equality** If equal numbers are multiplied by the same number, then the products are equal. *(p. 402)*

$$a = b \rightarrow ac = bc$$

Postulate 4 **Division Property of Equality** If equal numbers are divided by the same nonzero number, then the quotients are equal. *(p. 402)*

$$a = b \text{ and } c \neq 0 \rightarrow \frac{a}{c} = \frac{b}{c}$$

Postulate 5 **Reflexive Property of Equality** A number is equal to itself. *(p. 402)*

$$a = a$$

Postulate 6 **Substitution Property** If values are equal, then one value may be substituted for the other. *(p. 402)*

$a = b \rightarrow a$ may be substituted for b.

Postulate 7 **Distributive Property** An expression of the form $a(b + c)$ is equivalent to $ab + ac$. *(p. 402)*

$$a(b + c) = ab + ac$$

Postulates and Theorems of Geometry

Angles

Theorem 7.1 If two angles are supplements of the same angle, then they are equal in measure. *(p. 409)*

Theorem 7.2 If two angles are complements of the same angle, then they are equal in measure. *(p. 409)*

Postulate 8 If the sides of an angle form a straight line, then the angle is a straight angle with measure 180°. *(p. 410)*

Postulate 9   For any segment or angle, the measure of the whole is equal to the sum of the measures of its non-overlapping parts. *(p. 410)*

Theorem 7.3   Vertical angles are equal in measure. *(p. 411)*

Theorem 8.5   The sum of the measures of the angles of a triangle is 180°. *(p. 440)*

Theorem 8.8   An exterior angle of a triangle is equal in measure to the sum of the measures of its two remote interior angles. *(p. 443)*

Theorem 8.12   If two sides of a triangle are equal in measure, then the angles opposite those sides are equal in measure. *(p. 473)*

Theorem 8.13   If two angles of a triangle are equal in measure, then the sides opposite those angles are equal in measure. *(p. 473)*

Theorem 8.14   If a triangle is equilateral, then it is also equiangular, with three 60° angles. *(p. 474)*

Theorem 8.15   If a triangle is equiangular, then it is also equilateral. *(p. 474)*

Parallel Lines

Postulate 10   If two parallel lines are intersected by a transversal, then corresponding angles are equal in measure. *(p. 416)*

Theorem 7.4   If two parallel lines are intersected by a transversal, then alternate interior angles are equal in measure. *(p. 417)*

Theorem 7.5   If two parallel lines are intersected by a transversal, then co-interior angles are supplementary. *(p. 417)*

Postulate 11   If two lines are intersected by a transversal and corresponding angles are equal in measure, then the lines are parallel. *(p. 431)*

Theorem 8.1   If two lines are intersected by a transversal and alternate interior angles are equal in measure, then the lines are parallel. *(p. 433)*

Theorem 8.2   If two lines are intersected by a transversal and co-interior angles are supplementary, then the lines are parallel. *(p. 433)*

Theorem 8.3   If two lines are perpendicular to the same transversal, then they are parallel. *(p. 434)*

Theorem 8.4   If a transversal is perpendicular to one of two parallel lines, then it is perpendicular to the other one also. *(p. 434)*

Postulate 12   Through a point not on a given line, there is one and only one line parallel to the given line. *(p. 439)*

Similar and Congruent Triangles

Postulate 13   If two angles of one triangle are equal in measure to two angles of another triangle, then the two triangles are similar. (AA Similarity) *(p. 450)*

Theorem 8.9   If a line is drawn from a point on one side of a triangle parallel to another side, then it forms a triangle similar to the original triangle. *(p. 452)*

Theorem 8.10   If two angles and the included side of one triangle are equal in measure to the corresponding angles and side of another triangle, then the triangles are congruent. (ASA) *(p. 459)*

Theorem 8.11   If two angles and a non-included side of one triangle are equal in measure to the corresponding angles and side of another triangle, then the triangles are congruent. (AAS) *(p. 459)*

Postulate 14   If two sides and the included angle of one triangle are equal in measure to the corresponding sides and angle of another triangle, then the triangles are congruent. (SAS) *(p. 466)*

Postulate 15   If three sides of one triangle are equal in measure to the corresponding sides of another triangle, then the triangles are congruent. (SSS) *(p. 466)*

Theorem 8.17   If the altitude is drawn to the hypotenuse of a right triangle, then the two triangles formed are similar to the original triangle and to each other. *(p. 482)*

Quadrilaterals

In a parallelogram, the diagonals have the same midpoint. *(p. 282)*

In a kite, the diagonals are perpendicular to each other. *(p. 282)*

In a rectangle, the diagonals are equal in measure. *(p. 282)*

In a parallelogram, opposite sides are equal in measure. *(p. 282)*

In a triangle, a segment that connects the midpoints of two sides is parallel to the third side and half as long. *(p. 283)*

Theorem 7.6   If a quadrilateral is a parallelogram, then consecutive angles are supplementary. *(p. 419)*

Theorem 7.7   If a quadrilateral is a parallelogram, then opposite angles are equal in measure. *(p. 419)*

Postulates and Theorems of Geometry (cont.)

Theorem 8.6 The sum of the measures of the angles of a quadrilateral is 360°. *(p. 441)*

Theorem 8.7 If both pairs of opposite angles of a quadrilateral are equal in measure, then the quadrilateral is a parallelogram. *(p. 441)*

Right Triangles

Theorem 8.18 In any right triangle, the square of the length of the hypotenuse is equal to the sum of the squares of the lengths of the legs. *(p. 482)*

Theorem 8.19 If the altitude is drawn to the hypotenuse of a right triangle, then the measure of the altitude is the geometric mean between the measures of the parts of the hypotenuse. *(p. 484)*

Lines

Theorem 8.16 If a point is the same distance from both endpoints of a segment, then it lies on the perpendicular bisector of the segment. *(p. 475)*

Student Resources

absolute value (p. 34) The distance that a number is from zero on a number line. An absolute value is a positive number or zero.

$$|-3| = 3 \quad |0| = 0 \quad |3| = 3$$

alternate interior angles (p. 416) Two interior angles on opposite sides of a transversal.

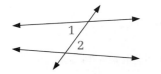

Angles 1 and 2 are alternate interior angles.

altitude of a triangle (p. 481) A segment drawn from a vertex perpendicular to the line containing the opposite side.

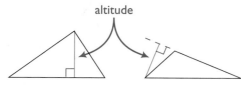

altitude

angle bisector (p. 468) A ray that begins at the vertex and divides the angle into two angles equal in measure.

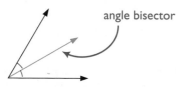

angle bisector

axis of rotation (p. 565) The line around which a plane figure is rotated to make a space figure.

biased sample (p. 17) A sample that over-represents or under-represents part of the population.

biconditional (p. 386) The conjunction of a true conditional and its true converse, usually written using the phrase "if and only if."

binomial (p. 351) An expression that can be written as the sum of two monomials.

binomial experiment (p. 339) An experiment with a fixed number of independent trials. For each trial there are two mutually exclusive, independent outcomes, success and failure. Each trial has the same $P(\text{success})$, and $P(\text{success}) + P(\text{failure}) = 1$.

binomial theorem (p. 353) If n is a positive integer, then $(a + b)^n$ is
$(_nC_0)a^nb^0 + (_nC_1)a^{n-1}b^1 + (_nC_2)a^{n-2}b^2 + ... + (_nC_{n-2})a^2b^{n-2} + (_nC_{n-1})a^1b^{n-1} + (_nC_n)a^0b^n$
where the coefficients $(_nC_r)$ are combinations found in the nth row of Pascal's triangle. *See also* Pascal's triangle.

boundary line (p. 654) A line that is the edge of a region of a graph of a linear inequality on a coordinate plane.

box-and-whisker plot (p. 636) A method for displaying the median, quartiles, and extremes of a data set.

center of dilation (p. 159) The point where lines drawn from corresponding points on the original figure and its image meet. *See also* dilation.

chain rule (p. 380) A rule of logic which states: If p is true, then q is true. If q is true, then r is true. Therefore, if p is true, then r is true.

cluster sample (p. 17) A sample that consists of items in a particular group.

coefficient (p. 352) A number multiplied by a variable in a term of an expression.

co-interior angles (p. 416) Two interior angles on the same side of a transversal.

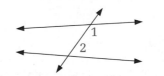

Angles 1 and 2 are co-interior angles.

combination (p. 329) A selection made from a group of items when order is not important. The number of ways to select r items from a group of n items is found in row n, diagonal r, of Pascal's triangle.

complementary angles (p. 655) Two angles whose measures have the sum 90°.

complementary events (p. 312) Two mutually exclusive events that together include all possibilities.

complex number (p. 225) A number of the form $a + bi$, where a and b are real numbers, and i is the imaginary unit $\sqrt{-1}$.

compound events (p. 320) Events made up of two or more events that can happen either at the same time or one after the other.

conclusion of an implication (p. 373) The *then* part of an *if-then* statement. *See also* implication.

conclusion of a logical argument (p. 380) A statement resulting from the premises of a logical argument.

conditional (p. 373) An *if-then* statement. *See also* implication.

congruent (p. 244) Having the same size and shape.

congruent triangles (p. 449) Two triangles whose vertices can be matched up so that corresponding parts (angles and sides) are equal in measure.

conjecture (p. 31) A statement, opinion, or conclusion based on observation.

conjunction (p. 367) Two statements connected by *and*. A conjunction is true when both statements are true.

consecutive angles (p. 419) In a polygon, two angles that share a side.

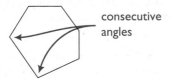

consecutive angles

consecutive sides (p. 244) In a polygon, two sides that share a vertex.

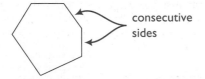

consecutive sides

consistent system (p. 136) A system of equations that has one or more solutions.

constant graph (p. 61) The graph of the function $y = c$ where c is any number.

convenience sample (p. 17) A sample that is chosen to make it easy to gather data.

converse (p. 39) A statement obtained by interchanging the *if* and *then* parts of an *if-then* statement.

corresponding angles (p. 416) Two angles in corresponding positions relative to two lines and their transversal.

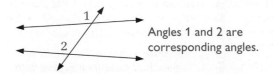

Angles 1 and 2 are corresponding angles.

counterexample (p. 33) An example that shows that a statement is not always true.

cross section (p. 559) The intersection of a plane and a space figure.

cubic function (p. 528) A polynomial function of degree three.

database (p. 365) An organized listing of information.

decay graph (p. 61) The graph of a decreasing function.

deductive reasoning (p. 38) Using facts, definitions, logic, and accepted rules and properties to reach conclusions.

degree of a polynomial (p. 507) The largest exponent of a polynomial.

dependent events (p. 320) A sequence of events where one event affects another event.

diagonal (p. 281) A segment joining two nonconsecutive vertices of a polygon.

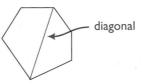

diagonal

diameter of a sphere (p. 85) A segment that joins two points on the surface of the sphere and passes through the center. Also, the length of such a segment.

dilation (p. 159) A transformation that results in a reduction or an enlargement of a figure. Lines drawn through the corresponding points on the original figure and its image meet at a point called the *center of dilation*.

dimensions of a matrix (p. 151) The number of rows and columns of a matrix. *See also* matrix.

direct argument (p. 380) A rule of logic that states: If p is true, then q is true. p is true. Therefore, q is true.

direct variation (p. 70) A linear function of the form $y = kx$, $k \neq 0$, where k is the *variation constant*.

direct variation with the cube (p. 94) A function of the form $y = kx^3$, $k \neq 0$, where y varies directly with x^3, and k is the *variation constant*.

direct variation with the square (p. 92) A function of the form $y = kx^2$, $k \neq 0$, where y varies directly with x^2, and k is the *variation constant*. The graph of this function is a *parabola*.

discriminant (p. 222) The expression under the radical sign of the quadratic formula, $b^2 - 4ac$. *See also* quadratic formula.

disjunction (p. 367) Two statements connected by *or*. A disjunction is true when at least one of the statements is true.

domain (p. 62) All the values of the control variable of a function. *See also* function.

double zero (p. 529) When a cubic function has a squared factor, the function has a double zero. At one point where $y = 0$, the graph of the function will just touch the x-axis but will not cross it. *See also* zero.

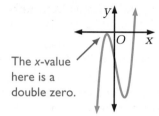

The x-value here is a double zero.

doubling period (p. 106) The amount of time it takes for a quantity to double.

element of a matrix (p. 151) Each entry in a matrix. *See also* matrix.

equiangular triangle (p. 474) A triangle in which all angles are equal in measure.

equidistant (p. 574) At the same distance.

event (p. 296) A set of outcomes. *See also* outcome.

expanded form (p. 351) When an expression is written as a sum, it is in expanded form.

experimental probability (p. 637) In an experiment, the ratio of the number of times an event occurs to the number of times the experiment is performed.

exponential decay (p. 108) A decreasing exponential function. An example is the function $y = a\left(\frac{1}{2}\right)^x$, $a \neq 0$, used to model halving.

exponential form (p. 100) When an expression is written as a power or a product of powers, it is in exponential form.

exponential function (p. 107) A function of the form $y = ab^x$, where $a > 0$, $b > 0$, and $b \neq 1$.

exponential growth (p. 107) An increasing exponential function. An example is the function $y = a \cdot 2^x$, $a \neq 0$, used to model doubling.

exterior angle (pp. 33, 442) An angle formed by extending a side of a polygon.

exterior angle

extraneous solution (p. 521) A solution of a simplified equation that is not a solution of the original equation.

factored form (p. 351) When an expression is written as a product of its factors, it is in factored form.

factorial (p. 304) The symbol ! after a positive integer. It means the product of all the positive integers from 1 to that number.

$$7! = 7 \cdot 6 \cdot 5 \cdot 4 \cdot 3 \cdot 2 \cdot 1$$

($0! = 1$ by definition.)

fitted line (p. 632) A line that passes as close to as many data points on a scatter plot as possible.

flow proof (p. 396) A proof written as a diagram using arrows to show the connections between statements. Numbers written over the arrows refer to a numbered list of the justifications for the statements.

frequency (p. 633) The number of times an event or data item occurs within an interval.

frequency table (p. 633) A table that displays the exact number of data items in an interval.

function (p. 60) A relationship where there is only one value of the dependent variable for each value of the control variable. All the values of the control variable are known as the *domain*. All the values of the dependent variable over the domain are known as the *range*.

geometric mean (p. 483) If a, b, and x are positive numbers, and $\frac{a}{x} = \frac{x}{b}$, then x is the geometric mean between a and b.

geometric probability (p. 639) Probability based on areas and lengths.

growth graph (p. 61) The graph of an increasing function.

half-life (p. 108) The amount of time it takes for a quantity to divide in half.

horizontal intercept (p. 122) The *x*-coordinate of the point where a graph intersects the *x*-axis. Also called *x*-intercept.

hyperbola (p. 77) The graph of a function of the form $y = \frac{k}{x}$, $x \neq 0$ and $k \neq 0$. *See also* inverse variation.

hypothesis (p. 373) The *if* part of an *if-then* statement. *See also* implication.

image (p. 159) The result of a transformation.

imaginary unit (p. 225) The number *i* such that $i = \sqrt{-1}$ and $i^2 = -1$.

implication (p. 373) A statement with an *if* part and a *then* part. The *if* part is the *hypothesis* and the *then* part is the *conclusion*. Also called a *conditional*.

inconsistent system (p. 136) A system of equations that has no solutions.

independent events (p. 320) A sequence of events where one event does not affect another event.

indirect argument (p. 380) A rule of logic which states: If *p* is true, then *q* is true. *q* is not true. Therefore, *p* is not true.

inductive reasoning (p. 31) A method of reasoning in which a conjecture is made based on several observations.

invalid argument (p. 381) An argument that does not use rules of logic.

inverse matrices (p. 174) Two 2 × 2 matrices whose product is the matrix $\begin{bmatrix} 1 & 0 \\ 0 & 1 \end{bmatrix}$. The symbol A^{-1} is used to represent the inverse of matrix *A*.

inverse variation (pp. 76, 77) A function of the form $xy = k$, or $y = \frac{k}{x}$, $x \neq 0$ and $k \neq 0$, where *y* varies inversely with *x*, and *k* is the *variation constant*. The graph of this function is a *hyperbola*.

isosceles triangle (p. 473) A triangle with two sides equal in measure.

kite (p. 244) A quadrilateral with two pairs of consecutive sides equal in measure. These pairs do not have a side in common.

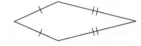

linear graph (p. 60) The graph of a linear function.

linear inequality (p. 654) An inequality whose graph on a coordinate plane is bounded by a line called a *boundary line*.

linear system (p. 121) Two or more linear equations stating relationships between the same variable quantities.

mathematical model (p. 67) An equation, table, graph, function, or inequality that represents a real-life situation.

matrix (p. 151) An arrangement of numbers, called *elements*, in rows and columns.

matrix equation (p. 175) An equation with a matrix term.

mean (p. 635) In a data set, the sum of the data divided by the number of items.

median (p. 635) In a data set, the middle number or the average of the two middle numbers when the data are arranged in numerical order.

midpoint (p. 259) The point halfway between the endpoints of a segment.

mode (p. 635) The most frequently occurring item, or items, in a data set.

monomial (p. 206) A number, a variable, or the product of a number and one or more variables.

mutually exclusive events (p. 311) Two events that cannot happen at the same time.

negation (p. 367) A statement involving *not*.

odds against (p. 314) The ratio of unfavorable outcomes to favorable outcomes of an event. The outcomes must be equally likely.

odds in favor (p. 314) The ratio of favorable outcomes to unfavorable outcomes of an event. The outcomes must be equally likely.

order of operations (p. 640) A set of rules that states the order in which you simplify an expression.

or rule (p. 380) A rule of logic which states: *p* is true or *q* is true. *p* is not true. Therefore, *q* is true.

ordered triple (p. 579) The ordered group of three numbers, (*x*, *y*, *z*), associated with each point in a three-dimensional coordinate system.

outcome (p. 296) One possible result. When each outcome of an event has the same chance of happening, the outcomes are *equally likely*. A set of outcomes is an *event*.

parabola (pp. 92, 187) The graph of $y = ax^2 + bx + c$, $a \neq 0$. The point where the curve turns is either the highest point or the lowest point and is called the *vertex*. *See also* direct variation with the square.

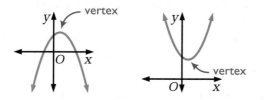

paragraph proof (p. 396) A proof whose statements and justifications are written in paragraph form.

parallelogram (p. 245) A quadrilateral with two pairs of parallel sides.

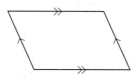

parametric equations (p. 542) Equations where two variables are expressed in terms of a third variable. This third variable is called the *parameter*.

Pascal's triangle (p. 334) A triangular arrangement of numbers. The number in row n, diagonal r, is the combination $_nC_r$. When you expand $(a + b)^n$, the coefficients are the numbers in row n. *See also* binomial theorem.

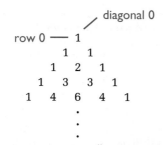

permutation (p. 304) The arrangement of any number of items in a definite order.

perpendicular bisector (p. 475) A line, ray, or segment that bisects a segment and is perpendicular to it.

plane (p. 559) A flat surface that extends without ending and has no thickness.

plane figure (p. 565) A two-dimensional figure.

polynomial (p. 507) An expression that can be written as a monomial or a sum of monomials. The monomials are called the *terms* of the polynomial.

polynomial equation (p. 507) An equation that can be written with a polynomial as one side and 0 as the other side.

population (p. 3) An entire group.

postulate (p. 402) A statement assumed to be true without proof.

premise (p. 380) A given statement in an argument. The resulting statement is called the *conclusion*.

probability tree diagram (p. 346) A tree diagram with the probability of each branch written on that branch.

pure imaginary number (p. 225) A number of the form bi, where i is the imaginary unit $\sqrt{-1}$ and b is any real number except zero.

Pythagorean theorem (p. 661) If the length of the hypotenuse of a right triangle is c and the lengths of the legs are a and b, then $c^2 = a^2 + b^2$.

quadratic equation (p. 201) Any equation that can be written in the form $0 = ax^2 + bx + c$, $a \neq 0$.

quadratic formula (p. 215) The formula
$$x = -\frac{b}{2a} \pm \frac{\sqrt{b^2 - 4ac}}{2a},$$ for the solutions of the equation $0 = ax^2 + bx + c$, $a \neq 0$.

quadratic function (p. 187) Any function that can be written in the form $y = ax^2 + bx + c$, $a \neq 0$.

quadratic system (p. 231) Two or more quadratic functions in the same variables.

quadrilateral (p. 245) A polygon with four sides.

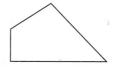

radical form (p. 100) When an expression is written using the symbol $\sqrt{}$, it is in radical form.

radius of a sphere (p. 85) A segment from the center of a sphere to its surface. Also, the length of such a segment.

random sample (p. 17) A sample in which each member of the population has an equally likely chance of being selected, and the members of the sample are chosen independently.

range of a data set (**p. 635**) The difference between the extremes in a data set.

range of a function (**p. 62**) All the values of the dependent variable over the domain. *See also* function.

rational equation (**p. 508**) An equation with only rational expressions on both sides.

rational expression (**p. 508**) An expression that can be written as the quotient of two polynomials.

real number (**p. 225**) A complex number of the form $a + bi$, where a is either a rational or irrational number and $b = 0$.

reciprocals (**p. 174**) Two numbers whose product is 1.

rectangle (**p. 245**) A quadrilateral with four right angles.

reflection (**p. 266**) A transformation involving flipping a figure over a line called *the line of reflection.*

remote interior angles (**p. 442**) In a triangle, the two angles that are not at the vertex where an exterior angle has been drawn.

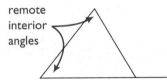

rhombus (**p. 244**) A quadrilateral with four sides of equal measure.

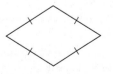

right angle (**p. 655**) An angle whose measure is 90°.

rotation (**p. 267**) A transformation involving turning a figure clockwise or counterclockwise around a point called *the center of rotation.*

sample (**p. 3**) A subset of the population on which a study or an experiment is being done.

sample space (**p. 320**) A set of all possible outcomes.

scalar multiplication (**p. 152**) Multiplication of a matrix by a number. The product matrix is the result of multiplying each element by the number.

scale factor (**p. 159**) The ratio of a length on an image to the corresponding length on the original figure of a dilation.

segment bisector (**p. 468**) A ray, line, or segment that divides a segment into two parts of equal measure.

similar triangles (**p. 449**) Two triangles whose vertices can be matched up so that corresponding angles are equal and corresponding sides are in proportion.

simulation (**p. 10**) Using an experiment based on a real-life situation to answer a question.

slope (**p. 68**) The measure of the steepness of a line given by the ratio of rise to run for any two points on the line.

slope-intercept form (**p. 68**) A linear equation written in the form $y = mx + b$, where m represents the slope and b represents the vertical intercept.

solution of a system of equations (**p. 122**) An ordered pair whose coordinates make all equations of the system true.

solution region (**p. 124**) The graph of the points that make all the inequalities of a system of inequalities true.

space figure (**p. 557**) A three-dimensional figure.

sphere (**pp. 84, 592**) The set of points in space that are equidistant from a point.

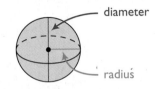

square (**p. 245**) A quadrilateral with four right angles and four sides of equal measure.

square root (**p. 403**) One of two equal factors of a number.

standard form of a quadratic function (**p. 187**) A quadratic function written in the form $y = ax^2 + bx + c$, $a \neq 0$.

standard form of a quadratic equation (**p. 201**) A quadratic equation written in the form $0 = ax^2 + bx + c, a \neq 0$.

standard form of a polynomial (**p. 507**) A polynomial written so that the term with the highest exponent is first, the term with the second highest exponent is second, and so on.

standard position (**p. 275**) The position of a polygon on a coordinate plane such that one vertex is at the origin and one side is on the x-axis. This placement makes calculations of slope and length easier.

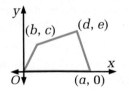

Student Resources

stem-and-leaf plot (p. 634) A display of data where each number is represented by a *stem* and a *leaf*.

straight angle (p. 655) An angle whose measure is 180°.

stratified random sample (p. 17) A sample chosen by dividing a population into subgroups with each population member in only one subgroup, and then selecting members randomly from each subgroup.

supplementary angles (p. 655) Two angles whose measures have the sum 180°.

systematic sample (p. 17) A sample chosen by using an ordered list of a population and then selecting members systematically from the list.

system of equations (p. 121) Two or more equations that state relationships between the same variable quantities.

system of inequalities (p. 124) Two or more inequalities that state relationships between the same variable quantities.

theorem (p. 408) A statement that is proven.

theoretical probability (p. 638) When all outcomes of an experiment are equally likely, the probability of an event is the ratio of favorable outcomes to the number of possible outcomes.

transformation (p. 159) A change in size or position made to a figure.

translation (pp. 161, 267) A transformation that moves each point of a figure the same distance in the same direction.

transversal (p. 416) A line that intersects two lines in the same plane at two different points.

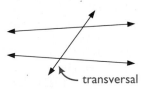
transversal

trapezoid (p. 245) A quadrilateral with one pair of parallel sides.

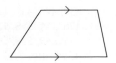

tree diagram (pp. 11, 296) A diagram that links items in different categories in all possible ways.

trial (p. 10) One run of an experiment.

trigonometric ratios (p. 659) The *sine, cosine,* and *tangent ratios* of an angle.

trinomial (p. 206) An expression that can be written as the sum of three monomials.

triple zero (p. 529) When a cubic function has a cubed factor, the function has a triple zero. The graph will flatten out and cross the *x*-axis one time only. *See also* zero.

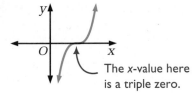
The *x*-value here is a triple zero.

two-column proof (p. 396) A proof written in two columns. Statements are listed in one column and justifications are listed in the other column.

valid argument (p. 380) An argument that uses rules of logic.

variation constant (p. 70) The nonzero constant k in a direct variation. *See also* direct variation.

Venn diagram (p. 38) A diagram used to show relationships between groups.

vertex of a parabola (p. 188) The maximum or minimum point of a parabola. *See also* parabola.

vertical angles (p. 410) Two angles formed by intersecting lines and facing in opposite directions.

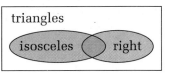

vertical intercept (p. 68) The *y*-coordinate of a point where a graph intersects with the *y*-axis. Also called *y*-intercept.

x-intercept (p. 189) The *x*-coordinate of a point where a graph intersects the *x*-axis (where $y = 0$). Also called a *horizontal intercept*.

y-intercept (p. 189) The *y*-coordinate of a point where a graph intersects the *y*-axis (where $x = 0$). Also called a *vertical intercept*.

zero of a function (p. 529) A value of the control variable of a function that makes the dependent variable equal 0.

zero-product property (p. 209) When a product of factors is zero, one or the more of the factors must be zero. If $ab = 0$, then $a = 0$ or $b = 0$.

System(s)
consistent, **136**
of linear equations, **121–123,
129–131, 135–139, 142–146,
175–177**
inconsistent, **136**
of inequalities, **124**
of quadratic equations, **230–233**
**Systematic list, making, 298, 305,
329**

Tables
of measures, **665**
of squares and square roots, **667**
of symbols, **666**
of trigonometric ratios, **668**
Tangent, 73, 491, 659, 660
Technology exercises
with calculator, **37** (Ex.
24), **42** (Ex.
13), **71** (Ex. **18**), **73** (Ex. **33**), **103**
(Ex. **33**), **111** (Ex. **15**), **177** (Exs.
3–6), **178** (Exs. **9–12**), **179** (Ex. **16**),
182 (Ex. **16**), **212** (Ex. **37**), **349** (Ex.
14), **533** (Exs. **23–25**), **534** (Exs. **28,
29**), **539** (Ex. **19**), **547** (Ex. **15**), **598**
(Ex. **29**)
with computer, **37** (Ex. **24**), **42** (Ex.
13), **103** (Ex. **33**), **284** (Ex. **7**), **437**
(Ex. **18**), **533** (Exs. **23–25**)
See also Calculator, Computer,
and Technology Handbook.
Technology Handbook, 603–613
Technology Notes
on calculator use
combinations key or menu, **330**
factorial key or menu, **305**
finding intersection point of
two graphs, **37, 123, 608**
finding inverse matrix, **175, 611**
graphing circles, **592**
order of operations on, **253**
parametric mode, **541, 543**
permutations key or menu, **305**
setting range, **528, 543, 604**
simulation mode, **541**
using scroll feature, **153**
using ZOOM feature, **123, 607**
See also Calculator, Computer.
Tessellation, 445
Testing, *See* Assessment.
Theorems, 408
*See pp. 669–672 for list of
theorems. See also* Proof.

Three dimensions
coordinates in, **578**
diagonal of a rectangular prism,
584, 585
distance formula in, **586**
equation of sphere centered at
the origin, **592**
midpoint formula, **580**
Toolbox
(examples and practice of previously learned skills), **632–664**
Transformation(s)
dilation, **159–161, 269, 663–664**
reflection, **266–268, 472, 664**
rotation, **267, 566, 567, 662–663**
slides, flips, turns, **266–268**
translation, **161–162, 193, 194,
267–268, 662**
Translation, 161–162, 662
of graphs of parabolas, **193, 194**
of images, **267–268, 662**
using matrix addition to represent, **161, 162**
Transversal, 416, 454
**Tree diagram, 11, 296, 302, 306,
325, 339, 346**
Trial, 10
Triangle(s)
altitude of, **481, 657**
base of isosceles, **473**
bisectors of, **468**
congruent, **449, 458–462, 466**
constructing copy of, **470**
equiangular, **474**
equilateral, **474**
generating a cone through rotation of, **567**
golden, **476**
isosceles, **473**
overlapping, **450**
overlapping similar, **452**
perpendicular bisector of, **475**
properties of, **283**
Pythagorean theorem, **251, 252,
482, 661**
right, *see* Right triangle(s).
segment through midpoints
property, **283**
similar, **449**
similar right, **482**
similarity postulate, **450**
in standard position, **275–276**
sum of angle measures, **439, 440**

Trigonometric ratios, 491, 659–660
Trinomial, 206
Two-column proof, 396

Unit Project, *See* Projects.

Variable expression
See Expressions.
Variation
constant, **70, 77, 651**
direct, **70, 651**
direct with cube, **94**
direct with square, **92**
inverse, **76, 77**
**Venn diagrams, 38, 39, 246, 367,
373–375, 380, 387**
Vertex, of a parabola, 188
Vertical angles, 410, 411, 655
Vertical intercept, 68
**Visual thinking, 11. 38, 40, 75, 90,
105, 122, 123, 137, 143, 194, 207,
245, 251, 280, 296, 312, 321, 335,
338, 351, 367, 380, 387, 415, 442,
456, 458, 465, 481, 558, 565, 584,
589**
See also Manipulatives.
Volume
using formulas, **84, 531, 567,
657–658**
similar spheres, **86–87, 515**
of a sphere, **84–85, 91**

Writing, *See under*
Communication.

***x*-intercept, 189**

***y*-intercept, 189**

Zero
division by, **46**
double, of a function, **529**
as exponent, **99**
of a function, **529**
triple, of a function, **529**
Zero-product property, 209, 648

Credits

DESIGN

Book Design: Two Twelve Associates, Inc.
Cover Design: Two Twelve Associates, Inc. Photographic collage by Susan Wides; student photography by Ken Karp.
Electronic Technical Art: American Composition & Graphics, Inc.

ACKNOWLEDGMENTS

20 From *The Crystal Desert*, by David G. Campbell. Boston: Houghton Mifflin Company, 1992. **50** From *The Phantom Tollbooth*, by Norton Juster. New York: Bullseye Books published by Alfred A. Knopf, Inc., 1961. **89** From *Journey to the Centre of the Earth*, by Jules Verne, translated by Robert Baldick. New York: Penguin Books, 1984. **220** From "An Aerial Reconnaissance" in *The Real Münchhausen*, retold by Angelita von Münchhausen, illustrated by Harry Carter. Copyright © 1960 by Angelita von Münchhausen. Copyright by Devin-Adair, Publishers, Inc., Old Greenwich, Connecticut, 06870. All rights reserved. **247** From *Our Town*, by Thorton Wilder. New York: HarperCollins, Publishers, 1957. **333** "The Old Method" by Chu Shih-Chieh. Originally appeared in a Chinese book entitled *Precious Mirror of the Four Elements* around A.D. 1303. **342** From *Rosencrantz & Guildenstern Are Dead* by Tom Stoppard. New York: Gove Press, Inc., 1967. **369** Source of data: Museum of Fine Arts, Boston, Massachusetts **378** From *The Andromeda Strain*, by Michael Crichton. New York: Dell Publishing, 1969. **383** From "A Case of Identity," by Arthur Conan Doyle. Originally appeared in Arthur Conan Doyle's *The Adventures of Sherlock Holmes*, published in 1892 by George Newnes, Limited. First U.S. edition also published in 1892. **446** "Cuadrados Y Angulos," from *De El Duce Daño*, by Alfonsina Storni. Buenos Aires: Sociedad Editora Latino America, 1988. **562** Adapted from *Global Atlas* published by Gage Educational Publishing Company. **563** From *Flatland, a Romance of Many Dimensions*, by Edwin A. Abbott. Originally published in 1884 by Seeley & Company, Ltd., London. **595** From "Time and Space," by Robin Mandel. Originally appeared in USM Today, published by the University School of Milwaukee, Summer 1993. **576** Adapted from "Figure 23: Sound Analysis" from *The Relationship Between Culture and Urban Forms in a Swahili Town* by Seyed Mohamed Maulana, a thesis submitted in 1988 to the University of Washington, Seattle, Washington.

STOCK PHOTOGRAPHY

vii Superstock; **ix** Peabody Essex Museum of Salem, MA. Photo by Mark Sexton.; **xi** © 1977 Robert Caputo/Aurora (t); Sabah Collection, Kuwait National Museum, Courtesy Aramco Services Co. (b); Photo by Oskar Prochnow, from *Formenkunst der Natur: Bildrafeln und Einfuhring,* published by Ernst Wasmuth Verlag, © 1934 (m); **xii** Glenn Dean/Renard Represents; **xiii** © Steve Nelson (b); Warren Morgen/Westlight (t); **xxvi** Coco McCoy/Rainbow (bl); © Earth Scenes/Mickey Gibson (br); Anthropology Dept., University of Arizona (tl); Pierre Mion/National Geographic Society (tr); **1** Richard Pasley/Stock Boston (t); © Alice Billings (bl); Mandana MacPherson/Used Rubber U.S.A. (br); Courtesy: Deja Shoes (m); **2** Patricia J. Bruno/Positive Images (b); **3** Wide World Photos; **5** Stamp Design © 1993 United States Postal Service, photo Wide World Photos; **6** Courtesy Michigan Biotechnology Institute; photo by Leavenworth Photography, Lansing, MI. (b); **7** National Archives (l); View of Thieving Lane, Now Bow Street, pub. 1807 (print) Royal Academy of Art Library, London/The Bridgeman Art Library (b); **10** Glenn Dean/Renard Represents; **12** The Bettmann Archive; **14** © Barrie Rokeach; **15** Dan McCoy/Rainbow; **20** © Earth Scenes/Doug Allan; **21** Philip Habib/Tony Stone Images/Chicago Inc.; **23** Warren Morgen/Westlight; **25** Superstock; **27** Copyright © 1993 NBA Properties, Inc. All rights reserved.; **28** Peter Menzel/Stock Boston; Bob Daemmrich/The Image Works; Stuart Franklin/Magnum Photos; Bryan Peterson/The Stock Market; **30** Charles Gupton/Stock Boston; **31** Bob Daemmrich (r); **36** Covent Garden: with St. Paul's Church by Nebot, Balthasar (fl. 1730–c.65), Guildhall Art Gallery, Corporation of London/The Bridgeman Art Library (l); E.W. Gilbert, "Pioneer Maps of Health and Disease in England," Geographical Journal, 124 (1958), 172–183. (r); **42** © Howard M. Paul; **48** L. Villota/The Stock Market; **53** Bob Daemmrich/Stock Boston; **56** © Arthur M. Greene (t); **56–57** Rod Planck/Photo Researchers, Inc. (b); **57** Gayle Dana/Desert Research Institute (bl); © Boyd Norton (br); **58** © Peter Essick; Courtesy Dept. of Parks and Recreation, California State Park System. (l); **59** Smithsonian Institution (bl); © David Jensen (mr); **62** Walter Hodges/Allstock; **65** Fotopic Int'l/Stock Imagery; **67** Charles Gupton/Stock Boston; **69** Bob Daemmrich/The Image Works; **73** © Nordic Track, the world's best aerobic exerciser. (tm); **74** Liane Enkelis/Mono Lake Committee (br); Georg Gerster/Comstock; **78** © 1990 Robert A. Tyrrell; **80** M.P. Kahl/Photo Researchers, Inc. (br); © Animals Animals/Geoff Kidd (br); **81** Courtesy Casio Inc. (mr); Mark Burnett/ Stock Boston (tl); **83** Bob Daemmrich/Stock Boston; **85** John Biever/Sports Illustrated; **86** © 1992 Mickey Pfleger; **87** Superstock; **88** From *Tents, Architecture of the Nomads* by Torvald Faegre, Bantam Doubleday Dell (br); David Rosenberg/Allstock (m); David Hiser/Tony Stone Images/Chicago Inc. (t); **93** © Steve Powell/Allsport (br); © Duomo 1991 (l); **94** Glen Allison/Tony Stone Images/Chicago Inc.; **96** Nick Gunderson/Allstock; **97** RKO (Courtesy Kobal Collection); **98** Comstock; **100** Photo reprinted courtesy of Texas Instruments, Inc. All Rights Reserved.; **101** Togo International (m); **103** John Lund/Tony Stone Images/Chicago Inc.; **104** © Larry Ford; **106** Michael Mu Po Shum/Tony Stone Images; **107** From *The Craft of the Japanese Sword* by Leon and Hiroko Kapp and Yoshinda Yoshihara. Photographed by Tom Kishida.

Levi Strauss & Co. Archives (br); © Earth Scenes/Holt Studios (bl); Courtesy of Wham-O (br); **429** © Michael Freeman (bl); Wm N. Fish/U.S. First (r & t); **430** U.S. Dept. of the Interior, National Park Service, Edison National Historic Site.; **435** © David Pelly; **436** Drawing by Oscar Niemeyer, copyright © Fundacao Oscar Niemeyer, Rio de Janeiro; **437** Courtesy of the Queens Borough Public Library (t); Photo courtesy of the Collection of Winifred Latimer Norman and the Queens Borough Public Library. (t); **438** Spencer Jones/FPG International (b); Courtesy Vogue. Copyright © 1926 (renewed 1954) by the Conde Nast Publications, Inc. (t); **439** The Science Museum, London, England. From the book Flying Machine published by Alfred A. Knopf, Inc., 1990.; **445** Detail from a studio art quilt, Thinking of Winter. © Carol H. Gersen 1984 Photo Credit: David Caras; **446** Nemesio Antúnez, New York, New York 10008, 1967. Oil on canvas, 22 x 24". Courtesy Courturier Gallery, Stamford, CT and Los Angeles, CA.; **448** Illustration © 1988 by David Macaulay from *The Way Things Work*. Reprinted by permission of Houghton Mifflin Company. All rights reserved.; **449** Don & Pat Valenti/Tony Stone Images/Chicago Inc.; **453** © Margaret Courtney-Clarke; **454** Scala/Art Resource; **455** Robert Semeniuk/The Stock Market; **456** Sabah Collection, Kuwait National Museum. Courtesy Aramco Services Co. (t); **460** © M. Courtney-Clarke; **465** © David Muench; **466** Vince Streano/Tony Stone Images/Chicago Inc. (l); © Gary Braasch (r); **469** Tony Craddock/Photo Researchers, Inc.; **471** Tom Bean/The Stock Market; **472** Photo by Oskar Prochnow, from *Formenkunst der Nature: Bildrafeln und Einfuhring*, published by Ernst Wasmuth Verlag, © 1934.; (c) 1977 Robert Caputo/Aurora (t); **473** Frank Viola/Comstock; © Animals Animals/Fred Whitehead; **479** James D. Nations/D. Donne Bryant Stock; **480** David Austen/Tony Stone Images/Chicago Inc.; **485** Dennis Hallinan/FPG International; © Alec Duncan (r); **486** Scala/Art Resource; **488** © Tony Freeman/Photo Edit; **489** Bertram Frauenknecht/Verlag Bertram Frauenknecht; **493** David C. Bitters/The Picture Cube (tr); © 1993 Alex Maclean/ Landslides (bl); Frank Siteman/Stock Boston (br); Superstock (tl); **496** Bryan F. Peterson/The Stock Market (r); Peabody Essex Museum Salem, MA. Photo by Mark Sexton. (l); **498** © Robert & Linda Mitchell (r); © M. Courtney-Clarke (l); **502** Nathan Bilow/Allsport (l & t); Hans Brox/Scan-Foto (r & t); **502–503** Bruce Berman/The Stock Market (b); **503** Sovfoto/Eastfoto; © Paul Agoglia; **504** Peter Menzel/Stock Boston; **505** © Ernest H. Robl; **509** Stan Musilek/Gump's By Mail; **514** Vic Bider/ProFiles West; **515** © Dan Paul; **518** © Tony Duffy/Allsport; **525** Allsport; **535** Tvindkraft; **536** Richard Howard/Black Star; **540** Arthur Tress/Photo Researchers, Inc.; **542** Bill Cross/Maine Dept. of Inland Fisheries; **543** © Alex Maclean/Landslides; **544** Heintges/Allstock; **545** Tom Bean/The Stock Market (bl); © Alex Maclean/Landslides (r); **546** Southern Pacific Lines (r); NPS/Golden Spike National Historic Site (r; Tom Hardin/Golden Spike Nat. Hist. Site (br); **550** Edward L. Miller/Stock Boston; **552** Camerique/EP Jones (tl); **554** Doranne Jacobson (b); **555** Terry E. Eiler/Stock Boston (tl); Chad Slattery/Tony Stone Images/Chicago Inc. (inset); Jeff Isaac Greenberg/Photo Researchers, Inc. (inset); Jacques Jengoux/Tony Stone Images/Chicago Inc. (inset); Ian Murphy/Tony Stone Images/Chicago Inc. (br); D. Weiss © 1992 (bl); Michael Newman/Photo Edit (inset); Stephen R.

Swinburne/Stock Boston (tr); **557** Courtesy Mary Conlan (m & r); **561** Dan McCoy/Rainbow; **563** Terry Qing/FPG International; **565** David Ball/The Stock Market (br); Smithsonian Institution (bl); **569** Dan McCoy/Rainbow; **571** U.S. Geological Survey/Science Photo Library/Photo Researchers, Inc.; **572** U.S. Geological Survey/Science Photo Library/Photo Researchers, Inc.; **573** Natural History Museum, London; **575** David Madison/Duomo (tl); U.S. Geological Society (br); **576** © Boyd Norton; **578** Superstock (tl); Wendy Stone/Odyssey/Chicago (bl); Jack Fields/Photo Researchers, Inc. (br); **583** Florence Hawley Ellis Archive; **589** © Kenji Kerins; **595** © Jane Barclay Mandel; **596** David Schultz/Tony Stone Images/Chicago Inc.; **597** Jim Pickerell/FPG International

ASSIGNMENT PHOTOGRAPHERS

Kindra Clineff xxvi (t), **xv**, **16**, **40**, **41**, **75**, **84**, **121**, **126**, **127**, **131**, **137** (tl), **141**, **144**, **173**, **180**, **186** (r), **242**, **243** (t), **256** (t,r), **280**, **287**, **297**, **298**, **306**, **327**, **329**, **330**, **331**, **332**, **358**, **362**, **367** (l), **367** (r), **383**, **415**, **420**, **423**, **424** (3rd from top), **428** (t), **456** (l), **456** (bl), **470**, **492**, **497**, **508**, **510**, **523**, **531**, **539**, **551**, **561**, **564**, **565** (tm), **565** (tl), **565** (bl)
Jeffrey Dunn **557** (bl)
Steve Greenberg vii, **266**
Richard Haynes v, viii, x, xiv, xv, **2** (t), **4**, **6** (t), **9**, **19**, **29**, **31**, **41**, **45**, **52**, **91**, **105**, **113**, **115**, **135**, **137**, **164**, **165**, **174**, **178**, **193**, **206**, **240**, **243** (b), **254**, **264**, **267**, **288–289**, **294**, **295**, **302**, **305**, **316**, **334** (l), **338** (l), **364**, **379**, **406**, **421**, **431**, **433**, **442**, **464**, **481**, **506**, **529**, **533**, **548**, **552** (br), **558**, **559**, **581** (b), **581** (m), **584**, **585**, **590**
Ken Karp **292** (t)
Tony Scarpetta **150**, **362** (t), **554** (t), **555** (m), **599**
Nancy Sheehan viii, xv, **197**, **221**, **235**
Tracey Wheeler v, **471**, **549**, **556**

ILLUSTRATIONS

Arnold Bombay **129**, **131** Jana Brenning **259**, **262** Dan Collins **428** (t) Chris Costello **184**, **400**, **405** (b), **428** (m), **444** (tr), **486**, **502** Steve Cowden **413**, **455** (t), **488**, **496**, **511** Christine Czernota xv, **52**, **180** (r), **198**, **204**, **218** (m), **229**, **235**, **236**, **287**, **358**, **563** (mr), **599** DLF Group **56**, **57**, **59** (t), **111**, **247**, **374**, **422**, **506**, **576**, **591**, **593**, **597** (t), **597** (b) Bob Doucet **479** Nancy Chandler Edwards **11**, **32**, **35**, **132**, **146**, **149**, **172**, **254**, **261**, **274** (b), **388**, **405** (t), **444**, **517**, **518**, **528**, **533**, **538** Glasgow & Associates **263** Robert Hynes **199** Piotr Kaczmareck **248**, **394**, **444** (tl), **513**, **519**, **520**, **524**, **561**, **596**, **597** Photo manipulations by Piotr Kaczmareck **505** Joe Klim **240–241**, **256** (m), **274** (t), **285**, **286**, **461**, **480**, **588** Ellen Kuzdro **546** Andrew Myer **35**, **50**, **119** (t), **128**, **253**, **272** Steve Patricia **582** (br) Deborah Perugi **119** (b), **456** (b), **465**, **499** Neil Pinchin **24**, **38** (b), **47** (t), **49** (t), **51**, **60**, **61**, **62**, **63**, **83**, **89**, **134**, **140**, **277**, **328**, **372**, **399**, **578**, **581** (tr), **589** Photo manipulations by Lisa Rahon **235**, **379**, **381**, **386**, **391**, **392**, **433**, **435**, **449**, **465**, **476**, **489**, **514**, **541** Patrice Rossi **494** Krystyna Stasiak **43** Rod Thomas **379** George Ulrich **213** (t), **234** (bm)

TYPOGRAPHIC TITLES

Frank Loose Design **3**, **9**, **16**, **23**, **31**, **38**, **45**, **59**, **67**, **75**, **84**, **91**, **99**, **105**, **121**, **129**, **135**, **142**, **151**, **159**, **165**, **174**, **187**, **193**, **199**, **206**, **214**, **222**, **230**, **243**, **251**, **259**, **266**, **274**, **280**, **295**, **302**, **310**, **319**, **328**, **333**, **338**, **345**, **351**, **365**, **373**, **379**, **386**, **394**, **401**, **408**, **415**, **431**, **439**, **449**, **458**, **466**, **472**, **481**, **489**, **505**, **513**, **520**, **528**, **536**, **541**, **557**, **565**, **571**, **578**, **584**, **591**

Selected Answers

Student Resources

Unit 1

Pages 3–5 Talk it Over

1. Answers may vary. An example is given. People may have expressed no preference for either design or wanted both issued as stamps. **2.** about 75%; about 25% **3.** Answers may vary. An example is given. Yes; both indicate that the young Elvis stamp is preferred by most people.
4. Answers may vary. **5–7.** Answers may vary. Examples are given. **5.** They are easy to compile and compare. **6.** b; A larger sample can more accurately reflect the diversity in the student body. **7.** (1) Can the information you are looking for be found by asking a yes-no or multiple-choice question? (2) How should you word the survey questions? (3) How should you interpret the results? (4) What size sample group would give you reasonable results? (5) How should you choose your sample group?

Pages 6–8 Exercises and Problems

1. about 0.45% **3.** a sample **5. a.** Answers may vary. Two examples are given. Choose one response to complete each question. (1) I would be willing to pay an average percent of increase of ? for recycled paper products. (a) 0% (b) 3% (c) 6% (d) 9% (2) Which percent shows how much more you would be willing to pay for a product made from recycled plastic packaging? (a) 2% or less (b) 4% (c) 6% (d) 8% **b.** No. My questions would give results for only two products, not all four. **7.** about 7200 people **9.** about 45 chicks **18.** 2 **19.** $-\frac{1}{2}$
20. -24 **21.**

x	y
-8	-4
-4	-3
0	-2
4	-1
8	0

slope = 0.25;
x-intercept = 8;
y-intercept = -2

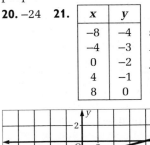

$y = 0.25x - 2$

22. $\frac{1}{6}$ **23.** $\frac{1}{2}$ **24.** $\frac{1}{3}$ **25.** 0

Pages 10–12 Talk it Over

1. Answers may vary, but should be reasonably close to 0.8. **2. a.** Yes; guessing on a true-false question involves two outcomes with equal probabilities, as does tossing a coin. **b.** No; spinning the spinner involves two outcomes with unequal probabilities. **c.** Yes; the possible outcomes (an even number or an odd number) have equal probabilities. **3.** less accurate **4.** There are only two possibilities: the light will be red or the light will not be red. The sum of the two possibilities is 1. $P(\text{red}) + P(\text{not red}) = 1$, so $P(\text{not red}) = 1 - P(\text{red}) = 1 - \frac{1}{3} = \frac{2}{3}$. **5.** No; you simply need an event with the same probability of getting a red light at the first traffic light. You could use any two numbers between 1 and 6.

Pages 12–15 Exercises and Problems

1. 25 trials; 100 trials; The greater the number of trials, the more accurate the results. **3. a.** Estimates may vary; about 60%. **b.** about 12 **c.** Answers may vary. **d.** Answers may vary. An example is given. No. A sample of 20 is quite small. **5.** No; that is much too small a sample. **7, 9.** Answers may vary. Answers are based on the results from Ex. 6. **7.** 0.4 **9.** 0.6 **13. a.** Answers may vary. Examples are given. Make a spinner and divide it into fourths. Mark $\frac{1}{4}$ "park close" and the other $\frac{3}{4}$ "park far." Then do trials to estimate the average time. **b.** about 1 out of 4 times **17.** about 113 mysteries **18.** $-5x + 5y + 7$ **19.** $12a^2 + 8b - 4ab$ **20.** $9n - 5mn$

21.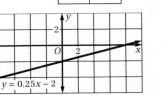

22.

23.

24.

Page 18 Talk it Over

1. people in her town who watch sports on television but who did not attend the baseball game
2. a. stratified random sample or cluster sample; Yes. Only one school and one classroom are represented, not all students from all grades in all schools. **b.** It would be better and less likely to be biased. There is

the underlying assumption that all the food in all the buildings is identical. The method offers a better cross-section of the population. However, the use of the cafeteria must be equally distributed among the entire student population of the district. **3.** The school or the class may be all male or the sports director could have chosen all males by chance. **4–6.** Answers may vary. Examples are given. **4.** Make a list of the social security numbers of all the members of the population, and then select every 50th number. **5.** Ask the first 20 people exiting a movie theater what they thought of the movie. **6.** Ask the people in a corner of a restaurant to evaluate the food they ate for their meal.

Pages 20–22 Exercises and Problems
1. a. Answers may vary. Examples: random, convenience, stratified random, cluster, systematic **b.** Descriptions may vary. An example is given. All of the methods involve choosing some smaller group to represent a larger group. The methods vary in how the members of the sample are related. The members may not be connected in any way or they may be connected by inclination or location, for example. **3. a.** cluster **b.** teenagers who do not read the magazine **7.** Answers may vary. An example is given. He may choose several locations, collect samples from each, and compare the number of healthy amphipods to the total number. **9.** Answers may vary. An example is given. The sample is a convenience sample. Whether the sample is a random sample depends on how the lunch schedule is arranged at the school. The first 50 students may all be the same age or may all be in the same class. Also, teachers may also use the cafeteria and they would not be represented. **11, 13.** For each type of sample, an example of a method for choosing the sample from a 250-word glossary is described. **11.** Open to a page. Choose the first 13 words on the page. **13.** Choose every tenth word. **15.** Answers may vary. An example is given. Assign each word in the glossary a number from 1 to n, where n is the number of words. Print each number on a piece of paper, mix the papers together in a bowl, and draw out 13 of them. Use the corresponding words in your sample. **19. a.** $-1, 1$ **b.** $\frac{2}{11} \approx 0.18$ **23.** Answers may vary. An example is given. Make a spinner divided into 8 sections. Shade one section for "below poverty level" and leave the other sections unshaded. Spin 50 times to approximate about 6 people below the poverty level. **24.** $-72m^2$ **25.** $-30wxy$ **26.** $7x - 6$ **27.** between 6700 and 7300 people

Pages 23–24 Talk it Over
1–4. Answers may vary. Examples are given. **1.** Both ask the same question. Both have an apparent built-in bias. The first raises the issue of personal civil rights, which might influence a positive response. The second raises the issue of public safety in a negative manner, perhaps influencing a negative response. **2.** Because of the issues raised in the answer to question 1, more "yes" answers might be expected to the first survey, more "no" answers to the second. **3.** Answers may vary. **4.** The survey should raise no issues other than the question at hand: "Should the city permit in-line skating on the sidewalk?" **5.** The choices in the box on the left are less precise. The phrases "sometimes" and "not very many" have no exact meaning. **6. a.** Yes; No; No. **b.** Yes; Yes; Yes.

Pages 26–29 Exercises and Problems
1. Answers may vary. It is reasonable to say that none of the questions is worded in such a way as to influence a response. **3, 5.** Answers may vary. Examples are given. **3.** Other questions might cover availability of sports programs, clubs, social activities, school facilities, availability and quality of food services, grading practices, or interaction between students and teachers. Questions: (5) How do you feel about the time allowed for each class period? (a) too long (b) never enough time (c) just right (d) occasionally not enough time (6) How do you feel about school lunches? (a) would like more variety of foods (b) usually can find something I like (c) always find something I like (d) never eat school lunches (7) How many extracurricular activities do you participate in? (a) 0 (b) 1 (c) 2 (d) 3 or more (8) How many sports activities do you participate in? (a) 0 (b) 1 (c) 2 (d) 3 or more **5.** The sample may be biased (that is, it was not randomly selected). Those interpreting the results may decide to ignore input from those in the sample who are in their first year at the school. The answers to Question 4 might be grouped into "satisfied" (those who selected "a") and "dissatisfied" (those who selected any other choice). **7.** Answers may vary. An example is given. If the question suggests a response conveying dissatisfaction, you may be more likely to get that response. For example, "Do you think the school requires too much homework?" would be biased. **9, 11, 13.** Answers may vary. Examples are given. **9.** People who choose not to participate may have strong positive or negative opinions. Why not eliminate those choosing not to respond from the sample, rather than assigning them a response they did not make? How large a group was surveyed? **11.** The sample is fairly small, considering results from at most 5000 viewers in a nation of 250 million people, most of whom watch television at some time. How were the 10,000 people selected?

What sort of information is collected in the diaries and how is it used? **13.** The graph does not give an accurate picture of team salaries. Five of the salaries under $500,000 are actually under $250,000. The graph would give a truer picture if the intervals were $0–$250,000, $250,001–$500,000, and so on. **18.** a cluster sample **19.** 13 m **20.** 16 in. **21.** 15 cm **22.** 0.5; 1.75 **23.** 0

Page 30 Checkpoint

1. Answers may vary. An example is given. A random sample chosen from the student population could be surveyed. Questions might include, "How often do you eat in the cafeteria? Would you buy this food if it were offered? Would having this food available make you more likely to use the cafeteria?"
2. about 190 students **3.** Answers may vary. Examples are given. Use a spinner with $\frac{2}{3}$ representing "at least 60" and $\frac{1}{3}$ representing "under 60." Use a die. If 1 or 2 is rolled, let that represent "under 60." If 3, 4, 5, or 6 is rolled, let that represent "at least 60."
4. random **5.** cluster **6. a.** Both parts of both questions give information that may influence the answers. **b.** Which shape is more appealing? (a) circular (b) rectangular; Which shape tastes better? (a) circular (b) rectangular

Pages 32–34 Talk it Over

1, 2. Answers and explanations may vary. Examples are given. **1.** No; there are infinitely many odd numbers, and there is no way to test every possible pair of them to check that all the sums are even. **2.** It is odd; the sum of two odd numbers is even, and when you add one more odd number to this even sum the result will be odd. **3, 4.** Answers may vary. Examples are given. **3.** No; the property you are testing might be unique to regular polygons. Also, if you test only regular polygons, your conjecture would apply only to them. **4.** No; for example, you already know the sum of the measures of the interior angles of a triangle is 180°. **5.** one **6.** You should test acute, obtuse, and scalene triangles. You may also test right, isosceles, and equilateral triangles, so long as you do not consider them exclusively.
7. The inequality is false; any number $x \geq 0$ provides a counterexample.

Pages 34–37 Exercises and Problems

3. Answers may vary. An example is given. A reasonable conjecture is that everyone called to the principal's office has been given some good news, so Shing should not be worried. **5. a–e.** Answers may vary. Examples are given. **a.** Marvin might conjecture that driving a red car increases your chances of getting a speeding ticket. **b.** No; they issue many tickets to all

different types of cars. **c.** He could observe a stretch of highway for a given period of time and record how many tickets are issued in general and how many to red cars. **d.** He may have been driving more, enjoying his new car. He may also have been showing off his new car, or feeling a sense of adventure that made him behave less responsibly. **e.** Some people might associate red cars with sportiness and speed. Others might see no connection. **7.** Beginning with the third number, each number in the pattern is the sum of the two previous numbers. The next number is 21.
9. Beginning with the second row, the digits of the square of an n-digit number with all of its digits 1 are the counting numbers in increasing order up to n, then in decreasing order back down to 1. The next row is 1111 · 1111 = 1234321. **11, 13.** Each conjecture is based on inductive reasoning. **11.** The product of two odd numbers is odd. **13.** If a triangle has its vertices on a circle and one side of the triangle is a diameter of the circle, the angle opposite the diameter is a right angle. **15.** False; any number $x \leq 0$ is a counterexample. **17.** True. **21.** 9 **23.** Based on the conjecture given, Dr. Snow might have increased access to clean water either by temporarily bringing water into the area or by extending the water-pumping system. **26.** Parents who work regular daytime jobs would be underrepresented. **27.** control variable: length of the test; dependent variable: amount of paper used **28.** control variable: number of people for whom she is fixing breakfast; dependent variable: number of eggs used **29.** 2 **30.** 5

Pages 39–40 Talk it Over

1. True. **2.** True. **3.** False. **4.** True. **5.** False.
6. All students who are not wearing a sweater are not wearing a blue sweater. **7.** Every student who is not wearing a sweater is not wearing a blue sweater.
8. Statements 4 and 5 are converses of each other.
9. a. $2a + 4b + 6 = 2(a + 2b + 3)$; Any integer that is the product of 2 and another integer is even.
b. $2a + 4b + 7 = (2a + 4b + 6) + 1$; $2a + 4b + 6$ was shown to be even in part (a) and any integer that is 1 more than an even integer is odd.

Pages 41–44 Exercises and Problems

3. True. **5.** False. **7.** True. **9.** True. **11.** Answers may vary. All students who work at a job watch TV. Some students who work at a job watch movies. No students who work at a job do volunteer work.
15. Open the person's airway and breathe slowly for the person if necessary. **17.** Rachel is older than Hector (or Hector is younger than Rachel). **19.** If the base angles of a triangle are equal in measure, then the sides opposite the base angles are equal in measure. **21. a.** No. **b.** Yes; $2x$ is even because any integer that is the product of 2 and another integer is

even. **c.** Yes; $2x + 1$ is odd, because $2x$ is even and any integer that is 1 more than an even integer is odd. **23.** physical education class will be held indoors **25.** $\triangle PQR$ is not isosceles **27.** $5x - 7 \le -17$ **29.** quadrilateral $MNOP$ is a rectangle **31.** Answer is based on the following facts. Any even number can be written as $2m$ for some integer m, and any odd number can be written as $2n + 1$ for some integer n. Also, any integer that is the product of 2 and another integer is even, and any integer that is 1 more than an even integer is odd. Let $2x + 1$ and $2y + 1$ be two odd numbers. Then $(2x + 1)(2y + 1) = 4xy + 2x + 2y + 1 = 2(2xy + x + y) + 1$, which is odd. **33.** Methods may vary. An example is given. Draw two intersecting lines and number the angles 1–4 in order so that $\angle 1$ and $\angle 3$ are vertical angles. $\angle 1$ and $\angle 2$ together form a straight angle, so $\angle 1 + \angle 2 = 180°$. But $\angle 2$ and $\angle 3$ together form a straight angle, so $\angle 2 + \angle 3 = 180°$, also. Then $\angle 1 + \angle 2 = \angle 2 + \angle 3$, and $\angle 1 = \angle 3$.
37. Answers may vary. An example is given. I think the inequality is true for all x. I will test some numbers.

x	$-x$	x^2	$-x \overset{?}{\le} x^2$	
2	−2	4	$-2 \le 4$	✓
0	0	0	$0 \le 0$	✓
−2	2	4	$2 \le 4$	✓
$-\frac{1}{2}$	$\frac{1}{2}$	$\frac{1}{4}$	$\frac{1}{2} \le \frac{1}{4}$	No.

The inequality is not true for $x = -\frac{1}{2}$, so it is not true for all x. **38.** cube; 600 in.^{2} **39.** triangular prism; 108 cm^2 **40.** cylinder; 96π in.^{2} **41. a.** slope = 2; vertical intercept = −1 **b.** $y = 2x - 1$ **42. a.** slope = −1; vertical intercept = 0 **b.** $y = -x$ **43. a.** Slope is undefined; there is no vertical intercept. **b.** $x = 3$

Pages 45–47 Talk it Over

1. Selbst getan ist wohl getan; Quien mucho abarca, poco aprieta. **2.** "It" refers to Earth. Recycling helps preserve the natural resources of Earth. **3.** No. The converse is "If you get another one free, then you buy two of something." The free item is conditional upon the purchase of the first two. **4.** Answers may vary. An example is given. If I live in California, then I live in San Fancisco. Converse: If I live in San Francisco, then I live in California. **5.** $0 = 0$ **6. a.** Gavin's prediction is more likely to be correct. The slope of the income line is $\frac{1}{3}$, while the slope of the expenses line is $\frac{2}{3}$. If things continue as they are now, the income and expenses will be equal in about 2 years. **b.** 1992; 1995 **c.** The reasonable answer is "Gavin's."

Pages 48–51 Exercises and Problems

3. a. False; $|-3| > 0$ for $n = -3$. **b.** If $n > 0$, then $|n| > 0$ for all n. **c.** True. **5. a.** True. **b.** If a triangle is isosceles, then two sides of the triangle are congruent. **c.** True. **7. a.** True. **b.** If a figure has four equal sides, then it is a square. **c.** False; it could be an octagon or a rhombus. **9.** No; they might have lost Friday's game but other teams who had to win may also have lost, or been eliminated in some other way.

28. **29.** **30.** **31.** Yes. **32.** Yes.

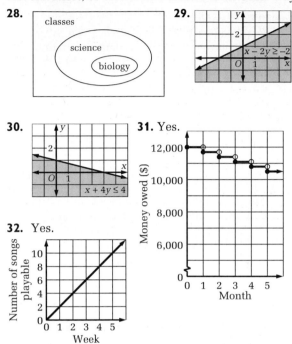

Pages 53–54 Unit 1 Review and Assessment

1. A survey is less expensive and requires less planning than a census. **2.** about 1440 **3.** about 90 min; Use a spinner divided into quarters. Each quarter represents a student from each class. **4.** No. **5.** Yes. **6.** No. **7.** Yes. **8.** Answers may vary. An example is given. A cluster sample consists of items in a group such as a neighborhood or household. Since the members of the group are not chosen independently of each other, they may share opinions and experiences to a greater extent than members of a random sample. This certainly might influence the results. **9.** Answers may vary. Examples are given. The manager is limiting the sample to those at home when the calls are made. Also, the audience includes many people outside that age group. Even if the manager has some reason to limit responses to those in that group, he or she has no way of knowing if a person giving a response is actually between 35 and 49. **10.** Answers may vary. Examples are given. How was the sample chosen? How was the survey worded? What were the actual responses?

11. No; it will bisect the base only if the triangle is isosceles. A counterexample is given.

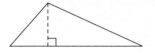

12. Yes. Let $4m$ and $4n$ be two different numbers that are both multiples of 4. Then $4m + 4n = 4(m + n)$, which is a multiple of 4. **13. a.** Answers may vary. An example is given. No; it is reasonable to assume that more than two students, or only one student, will get off at some bus stop. **b.** This would make her prediction more reasonable, since a brother and sister are likely to get off at the same stop. **14.** Let $2m$ and $2n$ be any two even numbers. Then $2m + 2n = 2(m + n)$, which is even, since any integer that is the product of 2 and an integer is even. **15.** False. **16.** True. **17.** False. **18.** None of the students in the Freshmen Singers is in the chorus. **19–21.** Counterexamples may vary. **19. a.** Most likely answer: True. **b.** If you sit in the front row at a movie, you arrived after most people. **c.** False; you may simply like to sit close to the screen. **20. a.** True. **b.** If two lines are perpendicular, they intersect to form right angles. **c.** True. **21. a.** False; $\frac{2}{3}$ is a rational number and $\frac{2}{3} = \frac{1}{\frac{1}{2}+1}$; $\frac{1}{2}$ is not an integer. **b.** If x is an integer, then $\frac{1}{x+1}$ is a rational number. **c.** False; -1 is an integer and $\frac{1}{-1+1} = \frac{1}{0}$ is not a rational number, it is undefined. **22.** Answers may vary. An example is given. A triangle can have at most one right angle. (The sum of the measures of the angles of a triangle is 180°. If a triangle contained two right angles, the sum of the three angle measures would have to be $90° + 90° + x = 180° + x$, which would be greater than 180°.)

Unit 2

Pages 59–62 Talk it Over
1. Answers may vary. An example is given. The path is downhill and bumpy at first, then downhill and straight until it becomes flat and straight. The graph then turns uphill and bumpy until it then becomes uphill and straight at the end. **2.** Answers may vary. An example is given. The graph is nonlinear decreasing from point A to point B, then linear decreasing from point B to point C. **3. a.** D and E or E and F **b.** B and C or E and F **c.** E and F **4. a.** A; B, C, D **b.** C; D; A **c.** A; B, C, D **5.** The checkout time during the first week in July remained constant. **6.** Answers may vary. An example is given. Yes. By looking at the water level change from September to October for the years 1983, 1984, 1985, and 1986,

you can make a reasonable estimate of the water level for October 1987. **7.** about 67 g **8.** Yes. The steepness of the graph can tell you how fast the temperature is changing at each depth. **9.** The graph is linear and decreasing from a depth of 0 to 10 meters, constant from a depth of 10 to 13 meters, linear and decreasing from 13 to 25 meters, and nonlinear and decreasing from 25 to 40 meters. **10.** Answers may vary. An example is given. Yes; no two points lie on the same vertical line (vertical-line test). **11.** 1979; 1992 **12.** $100,000; $1,400,000

Pages 63–66 Exercises and Problems
3. nonlinear and increasing on the interval from 1992 to 1994; linear and increasing on the interval from 1994 to 2000 **5.** linear and increasing on the interval from 10 to 20; constant on the interval from 20 to 25; linear and increasing on the interval from 25 to 35; constant on the interval from 35 to 40; linear and increasing on the interval from 40 to 50; constant on the interval from 50 to 55; nonlinear and increasing on the interval from 55 to 75; constant on the interval from 75 to 80; nonlinear and increasing on the interval from 80 to 100 **7.** No; a constant graph is a horizontal line and its slope is 0. The graph of $x = 4$ is a vertical line and its slope is undefined. **9.** It would be reasonable to advise her to invest because according to the graph in Ex. 3, the sale of cellular telephones should continue to increase through the year 2000. **11.** No; according to the graph in Ex. 5, the temperature can feel hotter or cooler, depending on the relative humidity. **13.** linear growth **15.** nonlinear decay **19. a.** circumference of a circle

b.
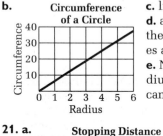

c. linear and increasing
d. a growth graph because the circumference increases as the radius increases
e. No; No; because the radius and the circumference cannot be negative.

21. a.
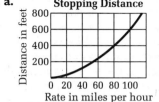

b. nonlinear and increasing **c.** a growth graph because stopping distance increases with increasing speed **d.** For every speed, there is one stopping distance and the graph passes the vertical-line test. **e.** domain: $0 \le s \le 110$; range: $0 \le d \le 715$ **26.** The survey did not claim that three out of four doctors recommend the medication, only that three out of four doctors who use it recommend it. Gabriel did not consider that the sample was biased.

27.

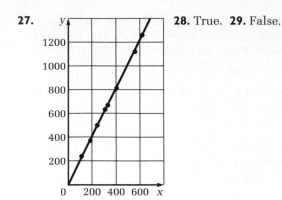

28. True. **29.** False.

b.

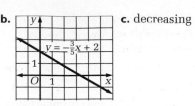

c. decreasing

27. A and D **34.** linear growth **35.** nonlinear decay
36. constant **37.** 48 **38.** −14 **39.** −25 **40.** $l = \dfrac{A}{w}$
41. $h = \dfrac{V}{B}$ **42.** $r = \dfrac{D}{t}$

Pages 67–70 Talk it Over

1. Maximum heart rate declines with age. **2.** −0.8a is always a negative number since a must be positive, so at any age −0.8a + 176 is less than 176.
3. a. Answers may vary. An example is given. $0 \le a \le 80$ **b.** Based upon the domain given in question 3(a), $112 \le h \le 176$. **4. a.** decreases by 8 **b.** linear **c.** decreasing **d.** decay graph; As a increases, h decreases. **5.** Direct variation is a linear function with y-intercept $b = 0$. **6.** 4 **7.** 0 **8.** The graph would not be as steep. It would rise 3 units for every positive 1 increase in x. **9.** The graph would have the same slope, but would be shifted up 2.5 units.

Pages 70–74 Exercises and Problems

1. 176 beats/min **3.** 0; constant **5.** 3; increasing
7. 0; constant **9.** $y = 3x − 2$ **11.** $y = −2x + 5$
13. $y = \dfrac{2}{3}x − 9$ **15.** c; $58.32 **17.** $m = \dfrac{d-0}{c-c} = \dfrac{d}{0} =$

undefined **21. a.** slope = 7; vertical intercept = 0

b.

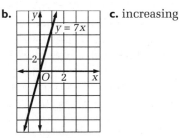

c. increasing

23. a. slope = 1; vertical intercept = 3.7

b.

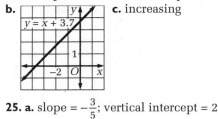

c. increasing

25. a. slope = $-\dfrac{3}{5}$; vertical intercept = 2

Pages 76–77 Talk it Over

1. a curve; The points on the scatter plot indicate a curve would fit to connect the points. **2.** Answers may vary. An example is given. The graph of an inverse variation is a curve and the graph of a direct variation is a line. In an inverse variation, the products of corresponding x- and y-values are constant. In a direct variation, the quotients are constant. **3.** the first quadrant **4.** the third quadrant **5.** For every ordered pair (x, y) for which $xy = 12$, it is also true that $(−x)(−y) = 12$. So, for every point of the graph in the first quadrant, there is a corresponding point in the third quadrant. **6.** Divide both sides of the equation $xy = k$ by x. **7.** The graph of $xy = −k$ is the image of $xy = k$ reflected over the vertical axis.
8. The smaller the value of k, the closer the curve lies to the axes. When k is larger, the curve lies farther out and its ends approach the axes more slowly.

Pages 79–82 Exercises and Problems

1. quadrant I **3. a.** Only one pair of dimensions is given for each pair of numbers; that is, a box w glasses wide and l glasses long is identical to one l glasses wide and w glasses long.

width	length
1	48
2	24
3	16
6	8

b. If x is the width and y is the length, the equation $xy = 48$ relates the width and length of each box.
5. No; $xy \ne$ constant.
9. $y = -\dfrac{7}{x}$ **11.** 12 **13.** $\dfrac{1}{2}$

15. a. The total needed for rent each month is $600. The more students sharing the apartment, the less each must pay. An equation would be share of rent $r = \frac{600}{s}$, where s is the number of students sharing the apartment. **b.** 5 **17.** 90 beats per second **19. a.** Let x be the rate of travel (in mph) and y the time it takes to get to the lake (in hours); $y = \frac{12}{x}$.

b.

Method of travel	x	y
backpacking	3	4
cross-country skiing	4	3
bicycling	10	1.2
car: slow & scenic	25	0.48
car: moderate	45	0.27
car: speed limit	55	0.22

c. Answers may vary. An example is given. $3 \le x \le 55$; The methods of travel given are the only feasible ones and the given rates are reasonable. **24.** b and d

25.

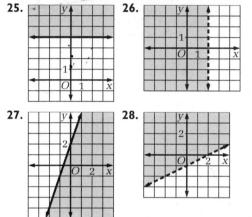

26.

27.

28.

29. S.A. = 248 cm²; V = 240 cm³ **30.** $V \approx 804.25$ m³
31. S.A. ≈ 70.69 ft²; $V \approx 42.41$ ft³

Page 83 Checkpoint

1. Answers may vary. An example is given. The graph represents the amount of money in a student's bank account over a series of months. The first drop is in August as the student buys back-to-school supplies and clothing. Then the amount in the account stays low as the student has no job for a few months and cuts back on expenditures. In December and January, the student gets a job at the mall during peak Christmas shopping and inventory times. He puts all money earned in the bank anticipating a big ski vacation in late winter. **2.** time; heart rate **3.** $0 \le t \le 80$; $70 \le h \le 105$ **4.** Over the interval $0 \le t \le 15$, the graph is nonlinear increasing. Over the interval $15 \le t \le 35$, the graph is constant. Over the interval $35 \le t \le 55$, the graph is linear decreasing. And over the interval $55 \le t \le 80$, the graph is constant. **5. a.** 8 **b.** −3 **c.** $y = 8x - 3$ **d.** 1.25 **6. a.** $y = \frac{10}{x}$

b.

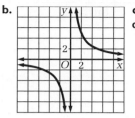

c. The graph is a hyperbola.
d. 4 **e.** 1.25

Pages 84–86 Talk it Over

1. Answers may vary. Examples are given. (1) Peel the orange carefully with the peeler, trying to make rectangular, triangular, or square pieces. Lay the pieces out and measure the area of each piece using the ruler. Add the areas to find the total surface area. (2) Wrap the string around the orange so that the entire surface is covered. Then arrange the string to form a rectangular region and calculate its area. (3) Wrap the orange with aluminum foil, cutting away the overlap. Unwrap the foil and use the ruler to measure the area of the foil that covered the orange. Find the area of this foil to find the surface area of the orange.
2. Answers may vary. Examples are given. (1) Cut six curved pieces off the orange so that you have a cube on the inside plus the six curved pieces. Measure the volume of the cube and estimate the volume of the six curved pieces. (2) Cut the orange into sections and carefully arrange the sections into a prism-like shape and find its volume. **3.** Answers may vary. An example is given. Use the string to find the circumference, $C = 2\pi r$. Divide the circumference by 2π to find r. **4.** $V = 2\pi r^3$; The sphere fills $\frac{2}{3}$ of the cylinder. **5.** Surface area is two-dimensional and so is measured in square units. Volume is three-dimensional and so is measured in cubic units.
6. Answers may vary. **7.** Diameter $d = 2r$, so use the formula S.A. $= 4\pi r^2 = 4\pi\left(\frac{d}{2}\right)^2 = \pi d^2$. **8. a.** Substitute 1810 for S.A. in the equation S.A. $= 4\pi r^2$. Using 12.57 as an estimate for 4π, divide both sides of the equation by 12.57 to get $143.99 \approx r^2$. Take the square root of 143.99 to estimate $r \approx 12.0$ cm. **b.** Answers may vary. An example is given. Sample 2 uses volume to find r and involves calculating a cube root. This problem uses surface area to find r and involves calculating a square root.
9. Yes. Using $d = 2r$, $\dfrac{(d_1)^2}{(d_2)^2} = \dfrac{(2r_1)^2}{(2r_2)^2} = \dfrac{4(r_1)^2}{4(r_2)^2} = \dfrac{(r_1)^2}{(r_2)^2}$.

10. Yes. Using $d = 2r$, $\dfrac{(d_1)^3}{(d_2)^3} = \dfrac{(2r_1)^3}{(2r_2)^3} = \dfrac{8(r_1)^3}{8(r_2)^3} = \dfrac{(r_1)^3}{(r_2)^3}$.

3. S.A. $= 64\pi$ ft^2; $V = \frac{256\pi}{3}$ ft^3 **5.** S.A. $= 400\pi$ mi^2;

$V = \frac{4000\pi}{3}$ mi^3

	Type of Ball	Diameter (cm)	Radius (cm)	Surface Area (cm^2)	Volume (cm^3)
7.	soccer ball	22.0	11.0	1520.5	5575.3
9.	tennis ball	6.5	3.25	132.7	143.8
11.	table tennis ball	3.7	1.85	43.0	26.5

13. 3 cm **15.** 5 m **21.** Answers may vary. An example is given. the inner core since the crust is just a very thin layer and the core is a fairly large circle **23.** about 7 billion km^3 **25.** about 612 billion km^3 **27.** about 17 billion km^3 **29. a.** about $\frac{125.65}{1}$ or 125.65:1 **b.** about $\frac{1408.48}{1}$ or 1408.48:1 **34.** c and d **35.** $\frac{1}{4} = 0.25$ **36.** $\frac{3}{8} = 0.375$ **37.** $\frac{3}{8} = 0.375$ **38.** Yes; variation constant 196. **39.** No. **40.** Yes; variation constant 13. **41.** No.

Pages 92–94 Talk it Over
1. Changing the sign of k reflects the graph of $y = kx^2$ over the horizontal or x-axis. When k is positive, the graph is a parabola that opens up; when k is negative, the graph is a parabola that opens down. **2.** As k increases, the parabola becomes "narrower" or closer to the vertical or y-axis. Check students' graphs. **3.** Changing the sign of k reflects the graph of $y = kx^3$ over the vertical or y-axis. **4.** As k increases, the curve becomes "narrower" or closer to the vertical or y-axis. Check students' graphs.

Pages 96–98 Exercises and Problems
1. When k is positive, the graph is in quadrants I and II; when k is negative, the graph is in quadrants III and IV.

3. Answers may vary. An example is given.

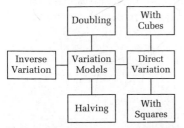

5. about 1.1; about −1.1 **7.** about 1.6; about −1.6

9. $E = ks^2$ **11.** 98 in.^{2} **15.** about 1.5 **17.** about 1.6 **19.** about 23.6 mi/h **21.** It is decreased to $\frac{1}{8}$ of the power generated by the original wind speed.
23. a. It is multiplied by 8. **b.** It is divided by 8.
26. S.A. $\approx$ 615.8 cm^2; $V \approx$ 1436.8 cm^3
27. S.A. $\approx$ 45.4 in.^{2}; $V \approx$ 28.7 in.^{3}
28. S.A. $\approx$ 48,305.1 cm^2; $V \approx$ 998,306.0 cm^3 **29.** 8
30. 12 **31.** 25 **32.** 23.4 **33.** 108 **34.** 972

Page 101 Talk it Over
1. 9 **2.** 3 **3.** −2 **4.** $a \cdot b^{1/2} = 36$; $(ab)^{1/2} = 12$; The values are different since in the first equation a is not raised to the $\frac{1}{2}$ power. **5.** $\sqrt{5x}$ **6.** $4n^{1/3}$

Pages 102–104 Exercises and Problems
1. when $x = 0$ **3.** $\frac{5}{u^5}$ **5.** $\frac{12}{m^2n^4}$ **7.** $4v^2$ **9.** $\frac{15p^4}{n^5}$
13. 8 **15.** −3 **17.** $-2x^{1/3}$ **19.** $s^{1/2}t^{1/3}$ **21.** $7(8x)^{1/2}$
23. $\left(\frac{s}{2}\right)^{1/2}$ **25.** $-6\sqrt[3]{w}$ **27.** $\sqrt{\frac{4}{r}}$ **35.** $A = kx^2$
36. $V = kr^3$ **37.** inductive **38.** deductive **39.** 144
40. 1920 **41.** 5625 **42.** 186,624

Pages 107–108 Talk it Over
1. a. 25,000 m^3 **b.** $n = -1$; $V = 25,000$ m^3
c. 12,500 m^3; the volume of the landfill 6 years before the newspaper report **2. a.** nonlinear; growth
b. present volume of the landfill **c.** No; if the graph were to intersect the horizontal axis, it would be at $V = 0$. Although at some point the actual volume of the landfill was zero, the value of the function $50,000(2^n)$ is never zero. **d.** Answers may vary. An example is given. The part of the graph that models the volume of the landfill is the portion for a few doubling periods before and after the year the report was written, that is, −3 or −2 ≤ n ≤ 2 or 3. Past doubling probably occurred only a few times. At some time in the future, the landfill will be completely filled up. Trash will be disposed of in some other manner. **3.** The area of the original piece in the data in Table 1 was 625.625 in.^{2}. After n tears, the area is $A = 625.625\left(\frac{1}{2}\right)^n$ in.^{2}. **4. a.** No; the dimensions of each sheet would get smaller and smaller but would never reach zero. **b.** The graph of the function never intersects the horizontal axis.

Integrated Mathematics

1. a. Let n be the number of tears and p the number of pieces; $p = 2^n$.

b.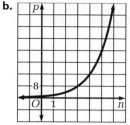

3. 3.2 million m³; This is one-fourth of the volume if the doubling period is three years. **5.** 1,856 **7.** 60,817,408 **9.** No; the graph intersects the horizontal axis. **17. a.** Let x be the number of 1600-year half-lives that have passed and y be the amount in grams of radium present; $y = 120\left(\frac{1}{2}\right)^x$. **b.** about 7336 years

19. a. Let x be the number of 9-year doubling periods and y be the population; $y = 345,000(2^x)$. **b.** 2024 **c.** Answers may vary. An example is given. No; it is not likely that the country's resources could indefinitely support a population that doubles every nine years. **22.** $\frac{36}{x^4}$ **23.** $\frac{7}{x^4 y^6}$ **24.** 1 **25.** 3 **26.** 0 **27.** $-\frac{1}{2}$ **28.** undefined **29.** right triangle **30.** rectangle **31.** trapezoid **32.** parallelogram

1. dependent variable: freshman enrollment; control variable: years **2.** domain: 1984–1991; range: about 392,000–425,000 **3.** The graph is drawn in linear segments. It is decreasing from 1984 to 1986; increasing from 1986 to 1988; and decreasing from 1988 to 1991. **4. a.** 3 **b.** 5 **c.** $y = 3x + 5$ **d.** 3 **e.** Let x represent the number of CD's ordered and y represent the total cost. Then $3x$ would be the cost for the CD's plus $5 handling charge to arrive at the equation $y = 3x + 5$. **5.** Explanations may vary. An example is given. direct variation; Each of the quotients $\frac{y}{x}$ is approximately equal to 1.1. **6.** Explanations may vary. An example is given. inverse variation; Each of the products xy is approximately equal to 12.26.

7. a. $y = \frac{144}{x}$ **b.** 7.2 **8.** about 113.1 in.³ **9. a.** 9:25 **b.** 36 ft² **10.** direct variation with the square **11.** about 15 km/h **12.** about 0.576 g/cm² **13.** $\frac{x^9}{y}$

14. g^2 **15.** $-\frac{20r}{t^3}$ **16.** $\frac{1}{64}$ **17.** 33.3 km/h

18. Descriptions may vary. An example is given. The graph of an exponential function with base 2 gets closer and closer to the horizontal axis but does not intersect it, yet it does intersect the vertical axis. As the value of the control variable increases, the value of the dependent value increases without bound.
19. a. 5,000 g **b.** about 17 days **c.** Let x be the number of 5-day half-lives that have passed and y be the amount (in grams) of the substance present; $y = 5000\left(\frac{1}{2}\right)^n$. **d.** 5.29×10^{-19} g

---

Unit 3

1.

Cost of Membership	FitnessPLUS	Bodyworks
5 months	350	400
10 months	650	575

2. FitnessPLUS costs less for 5 months; Bodyworks costs less for 10 months. **3.** FitnessPLUS: slope = 60, y-intercept = 50; Bodyworks: slope = 35, y-intercept = 225. The y-intercepts represent the initiation fee to join, and the slope represents the monthly dues or the rate at which the total cost is increasing.
4. FitnessPLUS: $470; Bodyworks: $470. After seven months, the costs have averaged out. However, you will be paying $25 more each month forever at FitnessPLUS. **5.** The x-coordinate is the number of months. The y-coordinate is the cost. **6.** Bodyworks; For every value of $n > 7$, the graph of the Bodyworks function is under the graph of the FitnessPLUS function, and therefore is less expensive since the y-axis represents the cost. **7.** From the graph, $n \approx 8.5$; $(n, c) \approx (8.5, 45)$. **8.** No. Since you cannot rent a locker for a portion of a month, you need to see only between which two months the solution lies. **9.** The maximum amount spent will be the cost of lunch and dinner and will be less than or equal to $50 (but no more than $50). The cost of the lunch and dinner is positive or zero for each. **10.** (10, 40), (20, 10), (0, 30), (30, 0), (−10, −10), and (−20, 10), for $l + d \le$ 50; (10, 40), (0, 30), (20, 10), (30, 0), and (50, 30), for $l \ge 0$; (30, 0), (−20, 10), (20, 10), (0, 30), (10, 40), and (50, 30), for $d \ge 0$. **11.** (10, 40), (0, 30), (30, 0), and (20, 10); The region is the triangle portion of the graph bounded by the equation $l + d = 50$, the l-axis, and the d-axis.

1. The solution of a system of equations is the ordered pair(s) for which both equations are true. The solution is the point of intersection of the graphs of the equations. **3.** about (−2, 4.5) **5.** (−3.75, −3.75) **7.** (−5, 3)

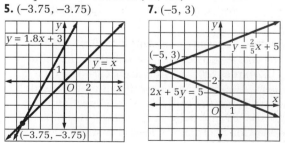

13. a. $c = 120 + 50n$ **b.** greatest slope: FitnessPLUS, where $c = 50 + 60n$; greatest intercept: Bodyworks, where $c = 225 + 35n$

c.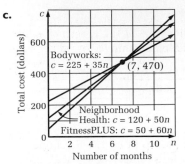

d. FitnessPLUS is cheapest for three months. At seven months, all plans have the same cost. The graph supports these answers since the line for Fitness-PLUS cost is below the other two lines at three months. All three graphs intersect at (7, 470), so all three plans cost $470 for seven months.

15.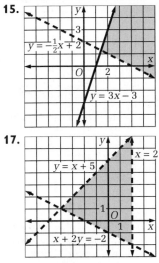

17.

21. trapezoid   **23.** rectangle

25. $y = 100\left(\frac{1}{2}\right)^n$, where n = the number of 1600-year half-lives.   **26.** $(8x)^{1/2}$ **27.** $-5t^{1/3}$ **28.** $(7m)^{1/3}$

29. $m = 7.5$ **30.** $a = -12$ **31.** $n = \frac{15}{7}$

Pages 129–130 Talk it Over
1. The cost to use one electronic bulb is the initial cost ($24) plus $.01/day for electricity. The total cost is $c = 24 + 0.01x$, where x = number of days used. The cost to use the equivalent in 100-watt bulbs is the cost of twenty bulbs at $.75 each ($15) plus $.04/day for electricity. The total cost is $c = 15 + 0.04x$, where x = number of days used.

2. about 301 days; At that point, the graphs of the two equations intersect and from there on the electronic bulb costs less in total cost.   **3.** No. It is a very close estimate, but although these two coordinates are on the graph of $y = 24 + 0.01x$, they are not *exactly* on the graph of $y = 15 + 0.04x$. The exact intersection point cannot be read all the time.   **4.** $x = 300$ days, as compared to 301 days solving by graphing and using TRACE   **5.** $y = 27$ **6.** $x - 2y = -11$ gives $-1 - 2(5) = -1 - 10 = -11$ ✓; $x + y = 4$ gives $-1 + 5 = 4$ ✓.
7. Graphing both equations on one set of axes, you find the graphs intersect at $(-1, 5)$, so $(-1, 5)$ is the solution of the system.

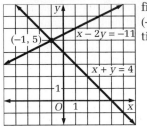

Pages 132–134 Exercises and Problems
1. a. 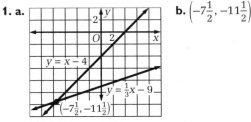   **b.** $\left(-7\frac{1}{2}, -11\frac{1}{2}\right)$

3. (3, 8)   **5.** (0, −1)   **7.** (0, −3)   **9. a.** Melissa solved for x in the first equation and substituted that expression into the second equation to solve for y. Bjorn solved the second equation for y and substituted that expression into the first equation to solve for x.
b. Yes. After solving for the first variable and then substituting into the original equation to solve for the second variable, both will get the same result. They just did it in different orders.   **c.** Answers may vary. An example is given. Melissa's method is easier for this system of equations. At different times, different methods are easier. It depends upon the equations as to which way is easiest.   **11.** $7\frac{1}{2}$ years   **13.** 112 general admission tickets; 207 student tickets
15. (104, 28)

20.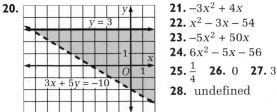

21. $-3x^2 + 4x$
22. $x^2 - 3x - 54$
23. $-5x^2 + 50x$
24. $6x^2 - 5x - 56$
25. $\frac{1}{4}$ **26.** 0   **27.** 3
28. undefined

1. $-\frac{1}{5}; \frac{4}{3}$ **2.** 0; undefined; No, because the slope of a vertical line is undefined.   **3.** The slope in the sample graph appears to be $\frac{1}{2}$ $\left(\frac{\text{rise}}{\text{run}} = \frac{2}{4}\right)$ and the y-intercept 2, so $\frac{1}{2}$ and 2 are reasonable values for m and b.   **4.** The slope will be the same, -2; substitute -6 for x, -1 for y, and -2 for m in the equation $y = mx + b$, so $-1 = (-2)(-6) + b$ and $b = -13$. The equation is $y = -2x - 13$.   **5.** $x = 4$

Pages 139–141 Exercises and Problems
3. a. parallel lines   **b.** no solution, inconsistent
5. a. intersecting lines   **b.** one solution, consistent
7. a. slopes: $\overline{AB} = -\frac{1}{8}$; $\overline{BC} = 3$; $\overline{CD} = -\frac{1}{8}$; $\overline{AD} = 3$
b. It is a parallelogram because opposite sides are parallel. It is not a rectangle because the slopes are not negative reciprocals of each other, and it is not a rhombus because the sides are not all the same length.   **9.** parallel   **11.** intersects   **17.** $-\frac{1}{3}$

19. $y = -4x - 10$ **21.** $y = 2$ **23.** $y = 3x + 12$
25. In both procedures, you use the slope-intercept form of an equation and substitute the slope of the line whose equation you are trying to find and the coordinates of the given point. Also, in both cases, you find the slope of the line from the slope of the given line. However, if you are finding an equation of a parallel line, you use the slope of the given line. If you are finding an equation of a perpendicular line, you use the negative reciprocal of the slope of the given line.   **27.** a rectangle since there are two pairs of parallel sides and two pairs of perpendicular sides
29. a. $m = 1$ **b.** $y = x + 1$; $y = x - 1$ **c.** no solution
31. $(20, -10)$ **32.** $(2, -5)$ **33.** $\left(\frac{1}{2}, 3\right)$ **34.** No; if $x = -1$, then -1 is not less than -2.   **35.** $y = \frac{3}{2}$ **36.** $x = 4$
37. $n = -\frac{3}{5}$

Pages 142–147 Talk it Over
1. The first column of rods (red, black, red) represent the numbers 4, -3, 11. The second column (black, red, black) represent -5, 2, -12.   **2.** red: positive; black: negative   **3.** Each column of the diagram represents an equation with the variables in the same position. Each equation is written in vertical form rather than in horizontal form; the Chinese method does not explicitly use variables.   **4.** because the coefficients of none of the variables is 1   **5.** $(-2, -1)$
6. The substitution method uses more steps than the addition-or-subtraction method. Answers may vary. An example is given. The addition-or-subtraction method is easier because it requires fewer steps.

7. In the first step, the scales remain balanced because equal amounts were added to each side. In the second step, the scales remain balanced because nothing was added or subtracted, just simplified.
8. The only difference is that you would add to eliminate the x-terms instead of subtracting. The result would be $1.6y = 29$ or $y = 18.125$.   **9.** If you want to eliminate y, multiply both sides of the first equation by 7.3 and subtract to eliminate the y-terms.
10. Multiply both sides of the first equation by 2 or by 3.   **11.** They are alike in that both last lines do not involve a variable. They are different in that one is true and the other is false. A false statement implies the system is inconsistent (parallel lines) and has no solution (or it is not true for any value of x).
12–14. Answers may vary. Examples are given.
12. substitution; One equation is already solved for c.
13. graphing; Both equations are in slope-intercept form.   **14.** subtraction; This will eliminate the x-term so that you can solve for y first.   **15.** They are the same line. The result, $-14 = -14$, is true for all values of c and d.

Pages 147–149 Exercises and Problems
3. $(8, -1)$ **5.** $\left(-\frac{33}{5}, -7\right)$ **7.** $(-6, -19)$ **9.** $(1, 4)$
13. $x = 147°$, $y = 33°$ **15.** 9 in., 17 in., 17 in.
19. $(-2, -4)$ **21.** $(-5, 2)$ **23. a.** t represents the number of tapes that are bought; c represents the number of CDs that are bought. The line labeled $6t + 12c = 200$ represents Cherub Records; the line labeled $8t + 10c = 200$ represents Flower's Music.
b. $(11, 11)$ **c.** $\left(11\frac{1}{9}, 11\frac{1}{9}\right)$ **d.** For $0 \le t \le 11$, it is cheaper to buy at Flower's Music. For $12 \le t \le 33$, you get more for your money at Cherub Records.
e. Answers may vary. An example is given. Graphing is visual and gives a better overall picture. The addition-or-subtraction method is more cumbersome.
25. addition-or-subtraction; It is easier to multiply both equations by a number than to solve one or both of the equations for a variable.   **27.** graphing; Both equations are in slope-intercept form and the lines are perpendicular.   **29.** no solution   **31.** $(1, 2)$
34. $y = -2x - 4$ **35.** about 0.55   **36.** about 0.20
37. about 0.26

Page 150 Checkpoint
1. one solution; Putting the second equation in slope-intercept form, $m = -\frac{1}{2}$. Since the two slopes are different, the lines intersect and there is one solution.
2. a. Let $c =$ costs and $t =$ tons of waste. Then the system of equations is $c = 400t$
$$c = 350 + 80t.$$

b.

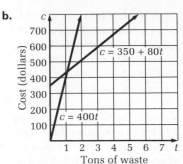

c. Direct disposal is cheaper for one ton of cardboard waste. Using a compactor is cheaper for two tons of cardboard waste. The point when the costs are equal is at slightly more than one ton of waste.

3.

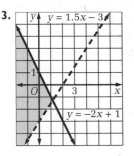

4. $\left(\frac{1}{2}, \frac{1}{2}\right)$ **5.** (225, 236)
6. $y = -3x + 11$ **7.** $y = \frac{1}{3}x + \frac{2}{3}$
8. (1, 1) **9.** infinitely many solutions **10.** (5, 16)
11. substitution, because one equation is already solved for y; The solution is (−3, 15).

Pages 152–155 Talk it Over
1. row 2, column 1 **2.** the price of shrimp kurma
3. 4×2 **4. a.** 1.04 is the same as 100% + 4% when you multiply by the price. **b.** 3×2 **5.** 65 **6.** 2×4; 2×4 **7.** Yes. You are multiplying each entry by a single number, or scalar, not another matrix. **8.** 652
9. a. how many more CDs and tapes were sold in February than in January **b.** Negative numbers mean the music store sold less in those categories in February than in January.

Pages 155–158 Exercises and Problems
1. 12 elements **3.** 3×5 **5.** 1×4
15. $\begin{bmatrix} 1.1 & -7.5 \\ -1.9 & 1.3 \\ -1.0 & 6.7 \end{bmatrix}$ **17.** $\begin{bmatrix} 14 \\ 26 \\ 51 \end{bmatrix}$ **25.** $\left(-4, -\frac{23}{4}\right)$
26. no solution **27.** $\left(-\frac{1}{3}, \frac{1}{3}\right)$ **28.** (4, −2) **29.** $\frac{d^4}{9c^5}$
30. $m^3 n^4$ **31.** $\frac{-18b^2}{a^3}$ **32.** $\frac{9}{x^3}$ **33.** translation
34. dilation

Pages 159–162 Talk it Over
1. the point in the upper right corner, where all the lines meet **2.** $\frac{2}{1}$ **3.** The coordinates are twice as large. **4.** $\begin{bmatrix} -3 \\ 8 \end{bmatrix}$ **5. a.** The first row represents the x-coordinate of each vertex in the polygon. The second row represents the y-coordinate of each vertex in the polygon. The four columns represent the four

vertices, P, Q, R, and S. **b.** $\begin{bmatrix} 1 & 5 & 5 \\ -2 & -2 & 1 \end{bmatrix}$
6. $J'(-7, 7)$, $K'(-3, 7)$, $L'(-3, 2)$, $M'(-6, 2)$
7.

Pages 162–164 Exercises and Problems
3. d **5.** $\begin{bmatrix} 4 & 12 & 4 \\ 12 & 2 & 6 \end{bmatrix}$ **7.** $\begin{bmatrix} \frac{2}{3} & 2 & \frac{2}{3} \\ 2 & \frac{1}{3} & 1 \end{bmatrix}$ **9.** $\begin{bmatrix} 1 & 3 & 2 & 0 \\ 5 & 2 & -1 & 0 \end{bmatrix}$
11. $\begin{bmatrix} -2 & 1 & -2 \\ 3 & 3 & -1 \end{bmatrix}$ **13.** dilation with center at the origin and scale factor 3 **15.** dilation with center at the origin and scale factor $\frac{1}{2}$ **20.** Both are 2×4.
21. a. $\begin{bmatrix} 74 & 61 & 34 & 61 \\ 213 & 130 & 210 & 205 \end{bmatrix}$ **b.** 34
22. a. $\begin{bmatrix} 112 & 196 & 210 & 119 \\ 441 & 140 & 280 & 35 \end{bmatrix}$ **b.** 140 **23.** $y = \frac{16}{3} - \frac{4}{3}x$
24. $x = \frac{5}{2}y - \frac{21}{2}$ **25.** $y = \frac{39}{4} - \frac{1}{4}x$

Pages 165–169 Talk it Over
1. $520 **2.** I multiplied the amount of carnations sold by the price of carnations, the amount of irises sold by the price of irises, and the amount of roses sold by the price of roses. Then the products were added together. **3.** $156 income from the sale of carnations, $204 income from the sale of irises, $160 income from the sale of roses, and $520 total income from all sales **4.** −17 **5.** No. If you multiply a 3×1 matrix by a 1×5 matrix, for example, you will have a 3×5 matrix, not a single number. **6.** Selections may vary. An example is given. Row 2 of L, column 3 of $R = -3 \cdot 6 + 4 \cdot 4 = -18 + 16 = -2$, which is in row 2, column 3 of P. ✓ **7.** Yes. In order for each row to be multiplied by a corresponding column and put in its proper place in the product matrix, the column number in the first matrix must match the row number in the second matrix. **8.** She was trying to multiply a 4×1 matrix by a 2×4 matrix. The number of columns of matrix A is not equal to the number of rows of matrix B. **9.** $AB = \begin{bmatrix} -18 & 3 \\ -30 & 2 \end{bmatrix}$; $BA = \begin{bmatrix} 2 & 2 \\ -45 & -18 \end{bmatrix}$;
$AC = \begin{bmatrix} 29 & 10 \\ 50 & 19 \end{bmatrix}$; $CA = \begin{bmatrix} 29 & 10 \\ 50 & 19 \end{bmatrix}$; $BC = \begin{bmatrix} -28 & 22 \\ -45 & -63 \end{bmatrix}$;

$CB = \begin{bmatrix} -48 & 23 \\ -30 & -43 \end{bmatrix}$ **10.** Yes. The result is dependent upon the order of matrices in multiplication. From question 9 above, $AB \neq BA$, $BC \neq CB$.

Pages 170–173 Exercises and Problems
3. -4 **5.** The number of columns of the first matrix (3) does not match with the number of rows of the second matrix (2). **11.** $AB = \begin{bmatrix} 7.45 & -0.99 \end{bmatrix}$

13. $\begin{bmatrix} -6 \\ 40 \\ 20 \end{bmatrix}$ **17.** Yes; 1×3. **20.** $P'(0, 3)$, $Q'(3, 3)$,

$R'(3, 0)$ **21.** $\frac{1}{4}a + 3b$ **22.** $-12m + 12n$

23. $-12y^2 + 6y$ **24.** $(-11, -58)$ **25.** infinitely many solutions **26.** $(-2, 1)$

Pages 175–176 Talk it Over

1. $AA^{-1} = \begin{bmatrix} -8 & 1 \\ -6 & 2 \end{bmatrix} \begin{bmatrix} -0.2 & 0.1 \\ -0.6 & 0.8 \end{bmatrix} = \begin{bmatrix} 1 & 0 \\ 0 & 1 \end{bmatrix} \checkmark$;

$A^{-1}A = \begin{bmatrix} -0.2 & 0.1 \\ -0.6 & 0.8 \end{bmatrix} \begin{bmatrix} -8 & 1 \\ -6 & 2 \end{bmatrix} = \begin{bmatrix} 1 & 0 \\ 0 & 1 \end{bmatrix} \checkmark$

2. $\begin{bmatrix} 0.1875 & 0.125 \\ -0.0625 & -0.375 \end{bmatrix}$ **3.** C^{-1} does not exist.

4. $\begin{bmatrix} -8 & 1 \\ -6 & 2 \end{bmatrix} \begin{bmatrix} x \\ y \end{bmatrix} = \begin{bmatrix} -8x + y \\ -6x + 2y \end{bmatrix}$ using matrix multiplication. **5.** Multiply both sides by the inverse matrix of $\begin{bmatrix} -8 & 1 \\ -6 & 2 \end{bmatrix}$.

6. $\begin{bmatrix} -0.2 & 0.1 \\ -0.6 & 0.8 \end{bmatrix} \begin{bmatrix} -8 & 1 \\ -6 & 2 \end{bmatrix} \begin{bmatrix} x \\ y \end{bmatrix} = \begin{bmatrix} -0.2 & 0.1 \\ -0.6 & 0.8 \end{bmatrix} \begin{bmatrix} 10 \\ 16 \end{bmatrix}$;

$\begin{bmatrix} x \\ y \end{bmatrix} = \begin{bmatrix} -0.4 & 6.8 \end{bmatrix}$; The solution is $(-0.4, 6.8)$.

7. $(-8)(-0.4) + 6.8 = 10 \checkmark$ and
$(-6)(-0.4) + (2)(6.8) = 16 \checkmark$

Pages 177–179 Exercises and Problems
1. $\begin{bmatrix} -3 & 9 \\ -6 & 4 \end{bmatrix}$ **18.** $\begin{bmatrix} 11 \\ 168 \end{bmatrix}$ **19.** $\begin{bmatrix} 63 & -88 \end{bmatrix}$ **20.** $\begin{bmatrix} 0 & 0 \\ -55 & 33 \end{bmatrix}$

21. If you are in Port Moresby, then you are south of the equator. **22.** 42 **23.** 14 **24.** 14 **25.** $16\frac{4}{9}$

Pages 181–182 Unit 3 Review and Assessment
1. a. $c = 93 + 42h$
    $c = 225$

b.
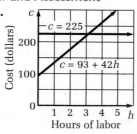

c. ABC Auto Repair is cheaper if repairs take 2 hours. Bob's Auto Shop is cheaper if the repairs take 4 hours. The graph shows a "break-even point" at slightly more than three hours.

2.
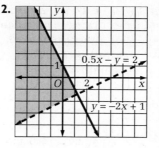

3. $2050 **4.** B and C because they are the same line (C is just twice B) **5.** A and C or A and B will be inconsistent. A and C both have $8x - 2y$ in common but different constants c when written in the form $ax + by = c$. So A and C are parallel lines and the system is inconsistent. If you multiply equation B by two, you obtain an equivalent equation to that of C, so A and B are also inconsistent. **6.** $y = -3x + 11$ **7.** infinitely many solutions **8.** $(3, -1)$ **9.** $(2, 13)$
10. Answers may vary. An example is given.
$\begin{bmatrix} 1.75 & 1.25 & 2.00 & 1.50 & 1.50 \\ 0 & 2.00 & 1.50 & 0 & 0 \\ 1.25 & 2.00 & 1.50 & 1.50 & 1.50 \end{bmatrix}$

11. a. $\begin{bmatrix} 2.40 & 3.00 & 4.00 \\ 7.00 & 8.00 & 10.00 \\ 8.00 & 8.00 & 10.00 \end{bmatrix}$; $\begin{bmatrix} 9.60 & 12.00 & 16.00 \\ 28.00 & 32.00 & 40.00 \\ 32.00 & 32.00 & 40.00 \end{bmatrix}$

b. $\begin{bmatrix} 9.60 & 12.00 & 16.00 \\ 28.00 & 32.00 & 40.00 \\ 32.00 & 32.00 & 40.00 \end{bmatrix} \checkmark$. They are the same.

12. $\begin{bmatrix} -1 & 1 & \frac{7}{3} \\ -1 & \frac{2}{3} & -\frac{1}{3} \end{bmatrix}$ **13.** $\begin{bmatrix} -4 & 2 & 6 \\ -5 & 0 & -3 \end{bmatrix}$ **14.** $BA = \begin{bmatrix} 62 & 0 \\ -2 & 10 \\ -11 & 24 \end{bmatrix}$

15.
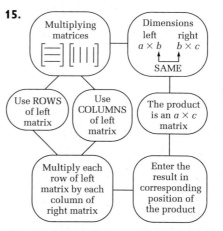

The map shows how to set up two matrices in order to multiply them. It also shows how to do the multiplication and the dimensions of the product.
16. about $(4.59, 0.412)$

Page 187 Talk it Over

1.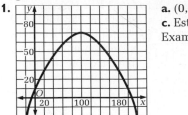

a. (0, 10) b. 70 ft
c. Estimates may vary.
Example: ≈208 ft

2. The graph still passes through (0, 10) but opens up instead of down and is shifted to the left.

Pages 190–192 Exercises and Problems

5. C 7. D 9. up 11. $x = \frac{3}{2}$ 13. $x = 1$ 15. (−2, −1);

minimum 17. Choice of parabola may vary. All parabolas are given.

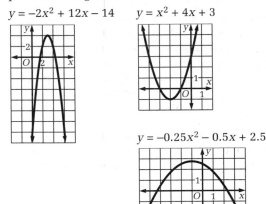

$y = -2x^2 + 12x - 14$ $y = x^2 + 4x + 3$

$y = -0.25x^2 - 0.5x + 2.5$

21. −3 23. −2 25, 27. Estimates may vary. Exact values are given. 25. 0 and 4; $\frac{1}{2}(0^2) - 2(0) = 0$;

$\frac{1}{2}(4^2) - 2(4) = 0$ 27. −4 and 5;

$0.2(-4)^2 - 0.2(-4) - 4 = 0$; $0.2(5)^2 - 0.2(5) - 4 = 0$

30. $\begin{bmatrix} 3 & 2 \\ 4 & -1 \end{bmatrix}\begin{bmatrix} x \\ y \end{bmatrix} = \begin{bmatrix} 5 \\ 3 \end{bmatrix}$ 31. $\begin{bmatrix} 4 & -2 \\ -3 & 5 \end{bmatrix}\begin{bmatrix} x \\ y \end{bmatrix} = \begin{bmatrix} 8 \\ -6 \end{bmatrix}$

32. $\begin{bmatrix} -3 & 1 \\ 2 & 1 \end{bmatrix}\begin{bmatrix} x \\ y \end{bmatrix} = \begin{bmatrix} -4 \\ 21 \end{bmatrix}$ 33. $r \approx 4$

34. $y = x^2 + 4$ 35. $y = (x - 4)^2$ 36. $y = (x + 4)^2$

Pages 194–196 Talk it Over

1. Yes. 2. No. 3. Yes. 4. Answers may vary. An example is given. You can tell if the graph has the same shape or position as a parabola with a simpler equation. You can determine the coordinates of the

vertex and tell whether the parabola opens up or down. 5. (0, 0); (0, 3); The vertex is translated 3 units up. 6. In equation (a), the vertex is translated down 2 units; in equation (b), the vertex is translated 4 units to the left; in equation (c), the vertex is translated 1 unit to the right and 3 units up. 7. Yes. Explanations may vary An example is given. According to the order of operations, the power should be simplified first. Then the expression can be multiplied by 3. If you distribute the 3 first and then simplify the power, you actually multiply each term by 3^2 or 9. 8. The equations have the same graph; they are equivalent equations.

Pages 196–198 Exercises and Problems

1. the graph in step 8, $y = (x - 7)^2 + 4$

3. $y = 5(x + 8)^2$, $y = \frac{2}{3}(x + 1)^2$, $y = 0.01(x - 3)^2$,

$y = 12(x - 5)^2$ 5. Move the graph 2 units to the right and 3 units up. 7. Move the graph 2 units to the left and 5 units up. 9. $y = \frac{1}{3}(x + 4)^2 - 3$ 13. (−6, 0); 36

15. (5, 2); 27 17. (1, 11); 16 22. (−6, −23);

minimum 23. $\left(-\frac{1}{5}, \frac{19}{5}\right)$; minimum 24. (3, 10);

maximum

25.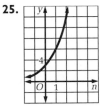

Since the equation $y = 3(2^n)$ is an exponential function with base 2, its graph represents exponential growth.

26. 13 and −13 27. 28 and −28 28. 8 and −8

Pages 200–202 Talk it Over

1. The number represented by the variable is a speed. A negative value would not make sense. 2. Yes; the solution set of an equation is not changed when both sides of the equation are divided by the same non-zero number. 3. Yes; $\frac{2\pi}{9.8}$ is a constant coefficient for

the x^2-term. 4. The x-intercepts are the solutions of the equation. 5. Both processes involve undoing. In Sample 1, since you are looking for a wavelength, you find only the positive square root. In Method 1 of Sample 2, since you do not know that the value you are looking for is positive, you find both square roots. **6.** Check by substituting both values for x in the original equation. **7.** Check by graphing the related equation $y = 2(x + 5)^2 - 22$ and finding the x-intercepts.

Pages 203–205 Exercises and Problems
3. -2 **5. a.** 3 **b.** $x = 3$ **c.** $x^2 - 6x + 5 = 0$ **d.** $x = -\frac{-6}{2} = 3$ **e.** The equation of the line of symmetry found from the graph and the equation found from the formula are the same, $x = 3$; and the mean of the solutions is also 3. **7.** $x \approx 57.58$ **9.** 40 and -40 **11.** 7 and -7 **13.** about 1.7, about -1.7; $\pm\sqrt{3}$ **15.** about 4.9, about -2.9; $1 \pm \sqrt{15}$ **17.** 2, -8 **19.** $3 \pm \sqrt{30}$; about 8.5, about -2.5 **21.** $6, -2$ **23.** $-23 \pm \sqrt{122}$; about -12, about -34 **32.** $(0, -1)$ **33.** $(-15, 0)$ **34.** $(2, 11)$ **35.** False. For example, Sarah might be in some other classroom, the cafeteria, or a hallway. **36.** $x^2 - 2x - 15$ **37.** $2y^2 - 20y + 32$ **38.** $36z^2 - 42z - 18$

Pages 207–209 Talk it Over
1. $(2x - 3)(x - 1)$ **2. a.** 1 and -3 or -1 and 3 **b.** $(2x + 1)(x - 3)$ **3. a.** 2 **b.** $2(2x^2 + 5x + 3)$ **c.** $2(2x + 3)(x + 1)$ **4.** b **5.** Substitute -1 and 1.25 for x in the original equation. **6.** about -1 and about 1.25 **7.** The x-intercepts of the graph of $y = 4x^2 - x - 5$ are the solutions of the equation $4x^2 - x - 5 = 0$.

Pages 210–212 Exercises and Problems
5. $(2x - 1)(x - 3)$ **7.** $(7n + 3)(n + 2)$ **9.** $(3x + 1)(4x - 3)$ **11.** $(4z + 1)(6z - 5)$ **13.** $3(x - 1)(2x - 7)$ **15.** $2(6d - 5)(d - 2)$ **21.** $(x - 7)^2$ **23.** $(x + 4)(x - 4)$ **25.** $(x - 5y)(x + 5y)$ **27.** $-1, \frac{1}{3}$ **29.** 1 **31.** $\frac{3}{2}, -\frac{1}{2}$ **33.** B **35.** A **39.** $3, -3$ **40.** $5 \pm \sqrt{5}$; about 7.2, about 2.8 **41.** $1, -5$ **42.** Let t be the time in hours and r be the rate in miles per hour; $rt = 150$ or $t = \frac{150}{r}$. **43.** 3 h **44. a.** $6x$ and 90 **b.** 15

Page 213 Checkpoint
1. No; there are some trinomials that cannot be factored. For example, $2x^2 + 3x + 5$ cannot be factored, so $2x^2 + 3x + 5 = 0$ cannot be solved by factoring. **2.** $(1, 4)$; minimum **3.** $\left(\frac{1}{2}, \frac{1}{4}\right)$; maximum **4.** 1 unit to the right, 5 units up **5.** 2 units to the left **6.** $\pm 2\sqrt{2}$; about 2.8, about -2.8 **7.** $-6 \pm \sqrt{11}$; about -2.7, about -9.3 **8.** 13, 3 **9.** $9, \frac{4}{3}$ **10.** $\frac{5}{3}, -\frac{5}{3}$ **11.** -3

Pages 214–216 Talk it Over
1. $\frac{1}{x} = \frac{x}{x + 1}$ **2.** $x + 1 = x^2$; No. To solve the equation $x^2 - x - 1 = 0$ by factoring, you consider the factors of the first term and the third term. The only possible factoring is $(x + 1)(x - 1)$, which does not produce the correct middle term. **3.** the numbers x for which $x + 1 = x^2$

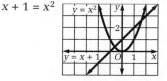

4. about -0.6 and about 1.6; The positive value is close to the golden ratio.
5. about -0.6 and about 1.6

6. The x-coordinates of the points of intersection are the x-intercepts of $y = x^2 - x - 1$. **7.** $a = 3$, $b = -2$, $c = 5$ **8.** There is no x-term so $b = 0$. **9. a.** When -1.72 is substituted for t in the original equation, the resulting statement is true. **b.** Since t represents a time, its value must be nonnegative. **c.** A valid mathematical solution must make sense in real terms in order to be a valid solution for a situation.
10. about $(0.15, 17.11)$; The vertex represents the maximum height the cliff diver reaches. The first coordinate indicates the time at which he reaches his maximum height above the water and the second coordinate indicates that height.

Pages 217–221 Exercises and Problems
5. $-7, -2$ **7.** 9, 3 **9.** $-1, -\frac{2}{3}$
11. Ex. 5: $x^2 + 9x + 14 = 0$; $(x + 7)(x + 2) = 0$; $x = -7$ or $x = -2$
Ex. 6: $x^2 + 7x + 12 = 0$; $(x + 3)(x + 4) = 0$; $x = -3$ or $x = -4$
Ex. 7: $z^2 - 12z + 27 = 0$; $(z - 9)(z - 3) = 0$; $z = 9$ or $z = 3$
Ex. 8: $2n^2 + 9n + 4 = 0$; $(2n + 1)(n + 4) = 0$; $n = -\frac{1}{2}$ or $n = -4$
Ex. 9: $3x^2 + 5x + 2 = 0$; $(3x + 2)(x + 1) = 0$; $x = -\frac{2}{3}$ or $x = -1$
Ex. 10: $2x^2 + x - 3 = 0$; $(2x + 3)(x - 1) = 0$; $x = -\frac{3}{2}$ or $x = 1$
13. about -3.1, about 8.1 **17.** $-3 + \sqrt{5}, -3 - \sqrt{5}$ **19.** $-5 + \sqrt{10}, -5 - \sqrt{10}$ **25.** about 1.4, about -0.24 **27.** $-1, \frac{1}{4}$ **29.** about -3.3, about 1.3

31. about −2.6, about 2.6   **33.** about 2.3, about 0.7
35. about 0.2, about −3.5   **45.** $(x-3)(x-2)$
46. $(2x+3)(x+4)$ **47.** $(3x-8)(x+1)$ **48.** systematic
49. $2x^2 - 3x$ **50.** $-5xy + 5x + 2y - 2$
51. $28k^2 + 55k - 18$

Page 227 Talk it Over

1. none   **2.** infinitely many; Every point on the graph
represents an ordered pair of real numbers that is a
solution of the equation.

Pages 227–229 Exercises and Problems

3. zero   **5.** negative   **7. a.** one solution **b, c.** 3
9. a. two solutions **b, c.** −1, −1.5
11. a, b. no solutions   **c.**

13. a, b. no solutions **c.**

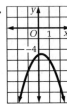

15. a. $k=6, k=-6$ **b.** $k>6$ or $k<-6$ **c.** $-6<k<6$
21. $0.5i$ **23.** $i\sqrt{83}$ or about $9.1i$ **25.** $6i$ **27.** $21-84i$
29. $-13+11i$ **31.** $78-36i$ **33.** 116   **35.** 1   **37.** i
39. about 0.5, about 0.2   **41.** −5   **43.** about $-0.5+0.3i$,
about $-0.5-0.3i$ **46, 47.** Solution methods may
vary. Examples are given.   **46.** undoing; about −2.8,
about −7.2   **47.** factoring; −1.5   **48.** the quadratic
formula; about 0.9, about −1.3   **49.** 32 students
50. (−3, 6)   **51.** infinitely many solutions   **52.** (1, −2)

Page 231 Talk it Over

1. Yes; the arcs intersect over the middle of the river
and 110 ft is halfway across.   **2.** Since x is the first
coordinate of the point of intersection, you will get
the same value for y from either equation.
3. $-0.006(110)^2 + 1.44(110) - 16.4 =$
$-72.6 + 158.4 - 16.4 = 69.4$ ✓
4. The solution should be about (110, 69.4).

Pages 233–235 Exercises and Problems

3. (2, 1), (−2, 1)   **5.** no real solutions   **7.** (−3, −3),
(3, −3)   **9.** (3, 3)
11. Sketches may vary.
An example is given.

13, 15. Estimates may vary. Examples are given.
13. (0.4, 2.3)

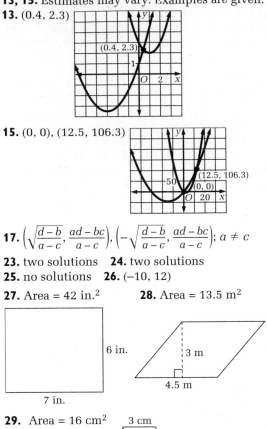

15. (0, 0), (12.5, 106.3)

17. $\left(\sqrt{\dfrac{d-b}{a-c}}, \dfrac{ad-bc}{a-c}\right), \left(-\sqrt{\dfrac{d-b}{a-c}}, \dfrac{ad-bc}{a-c}\right); a \neq c$
23. two solutions   **24.** two solutions
25. no solutions   **26.** (−10, 12)
27. Area = 42 in.²   **28.** Area = 13.5 m²

29. Area = 16 cm²

Pages 237–238 Unit 4 Review and Assessment

1. (0, 0); 0   **2.** (0, 4); 4   **3.** (−6, −8); 10   **4.** Answers
may vary. Example: $y = -x^2 - 6x - 9$ **5.** (3, −16);
down   **6.** (1, 1); down   **7. a, b.** Answers may vary.
Examples are given. **a.** $y = -x^2 + 6x - 5$
[or $y = -(x-3)^2 + 4$] **b.** $y = -\frac{1}{2}x^2 + 3x - \frac{1}{2}$
[or $y = -\frac{1}{2}(x-3)^2 + 4$] **c.** No; parabolas that are
translations of each other have the same shape.
8. C   **9.** A   **10.** D   **11.** B   **12.** 4

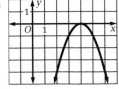

13. about 1.4, about −1.4

14. about 3.5, about −5.5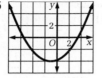

15. about 2.4, about −2.4 **16.** 10, −20 **17.** about 4.6, about −0.6 **18.** $(2x + 5)(x − 4)$ **19.** $(2n − 9)(2n + 9)$

20. $(4x − 3)^2$ **21.** $\frac{2}{3}$, 1 **22.** about −0.5, about −2.5

23. 1, −2.5 **24.** about 0.4, about 3.6 **25.** one solution **26.** two solutions **27.** no solutions **28.** $24 + 12i$ **29.** $−4 − 58i$ **30.** $56 + 34i$ **31.** about $0.5 + 0.76i$, about $0.5 − 0.76i$ **32.** about −0.3, about −11.7 **33.** about $−0.1 + 0.9i$, about $−0.1 − 0.9i$ **34.** (1.5, 5.25) **35.** (0, 1), (6, 79) **36.** about (−0.9, −1.5), about (0.9, −1.5)

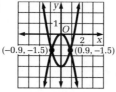

37. about (−3.9, 3.8), about (1.7, 0.7)

![graph]

Unit 5

Page 245 Talk it Over

1. Tyler must have assumed that a quadrilateral belongs to the family of quadrilaterals linked to it below. **2.** Yes; they satisfy the definition of a parallelogram.

Pages 246–250 Exercises and Problems

1. b **3.** True. **5.** True. **7.** False. **9.** No; the figure does not have two pairs of consecutive sides congruent. **11.** No; the figure does not have two pairs of consecutive sides congruent. **29.** quadrilateral **31.** rectangle; rhombus **33.** parallelogram **35. a.** 33.75 ft^2 **b.** 140 m^2; Yes. **c.** the family of trapezoids: trapezoids, isosceles trapezoids; the family of parallelograms: rhombuses, rectangles, squares **37.** about (−2.148, −0.308); about (2.148, −0.308) **38.** no solution **39.** (0, 2) **40.** $y = 2x − 4$ **41.** $x = −2$ **42.** $y = 4$ **43.** 25 cm

Pages 252–254 Talk it Over

1. Answers may vary. Let $O = P_1$ and $C = P_2$. Then $x_1 = 0$, $x_2 = 6$, $y_1 = 0$, and $y_2 = 8$. **2.** No; both

changes are squared. **3.** Since $x_2 − x_1 = −(x_1 − x_2)$, $(x_2 − x_1)^2 = [−(x_1 − x_2)]^2 = (x_1 − x_2)^2$. Similarly, $(y_2 − y_1)^2 = (y_1 − y_2)^2$. **4.** 0 **5.** Subtract the y-coordinates. **6.** 6 **7.** 6 **8.** Answers may vary. An example is given. $AB = \sqrt{(−3 − 3)^2 + (4 − 1)^2} = \sqrt{36 + 9} = \sqrt{45} = 3\sqrt{5}$; $BC = \sqrt{(3 − 6)^2 + (1 − (−5))^2} = \sqrt{9 + 36} = \sqrt{45} = 3\sqrt{5}$; $CD = \sqrt{(6 − 0)^2 + (−5 − (−2))^2} = \sqrt{36 + 9} = \sqrt{45} = 3\sqrt{5}$; $DA = \sqrt{(0 − (−3))^2 + (−2 − 4)^2} = \sqrt{9 + 36} = \sqrt{45} = 3\sqrt{5}$; since the four sides are equal in measure, $ABCD$ is a rhombus. **9.** Answers may vary. An example is given. Show that each pair of consecutive sides is perpendicular.

Pages 255–258 Exercises and Problems

3. the lower line **7.** $\sqrt{85} \approx 9.22$ **9.** 3 **11.** 5 **13.** $\sqrt{29} \approx 5.4$ **17.** slope of $\overline{VU}$ = slope of $\overline{WT}$ = 0; slope of $\overline{VW}$ = slope of $\overline{UT} = \frac{4}{3}$; $\overline{VU} \parallel \overline{WT}$ and $\overline{VW} \parallel \overline{UT}$ so $TUVW$ is a parallelogram. **19.** $LM = LK = KJ = JM = 5$; $\overline{LK}$ and $\overline{MJ}$ have 0 slope and $\overline{LM}$ and $\overline{KJ}$ have undefined slope, so $\overline{LK} \perp \overline{LM}$, $\overline{LK} \perp \overline{KJ}$, $\overline{MJ} \perp \overline{LM}$, and $\overline{MJ} \perp \overline{KJ}$. $JKLM$ has four congruent sides and four right angles, so $JKLM$ is a square. **21.** Two pairs of consecutive sides are congruent. **23.** All sides are congruent and consecutive sides are perpendicular. **27. a.** Measurements and answers may vary. The four sides of the figure are very close in length. **b.** $JM = KL = \sqrt{52} \approx 7.2$; $JK = ML = \sqrt{53} \approx 7.3$; $JKLM$ is not a rhombus because all four sides are not congruent. **c.** slope of $\overline{JM}$ = slope of $\overline{KL} = \frac{3}{2}$; slope of $\overline{JK}$ = slope of $\overline{ML} = \frac{2}{7}$; $\overline{JM} \parallel \overline{KL}$ and $\overline{JK} \parallel \overline{ML}$, so $JKLM$ is a parallelogram. **d.** Answers may vary. An example is given. Drawings may be deceptive; segments that appear to be congruent may not be and may be so close that even measuring will not establish the truth. For example, in a drawing, two segments that are 32.8 mm and 32.7 mm long will certainly appear to be congruent and could not be measured accurately with a ruler. **29. a.** trapezoid **b.** $AB = 8$; $BC \approx 5.1$; $CD = 4$; $AD \approx 5.8$ **c.** 30 square units **d.** about 22.9 **31.** False; if all four sides of a kite are not congruent, the kite is not a parallelogram. **32.** True. **33.** y is divided by 4. **34.** y is doubled. **35.** y is divided by 8. **36.** about 12.8°F **37.** 5.7 **38.** about 82.9

Page 259 Talk it Over

1. about (15, 5) **2.** 14; The average of 3 and 25 is 14. **3.** 5; The average of 7 and 3 is 5. **4.** (14, 5)

Pages 261–264 Exercises and Problems

3. $\left(2\frac{1}{2}, -3\frac{1}{2}\right)$ **5.** $(-1, 5)$ **7.** $\left(-2\frac{1}{2}, 5\right)$ **9.** $(1.65, 1.975)$

11. $D(4, 10)$ **13.** $D(6, 2)$

15. $PQ = \sqrt{(18-2)^2 + (14-4)^2} = \sqrt{256 + 100} = 2\sqrt{89}$; $PM = \sqrt{(10-2)^2 + (9-4)^2} = \sqrt{64 + 25} = \sqrt{89}$

25. $3\sqrt{5} \approx 6.71$ **26.** $8\sqrt{2} \approx 11.31$ **27.** 13 **28.** 4, −4

29. $5 \pm 2\sqrt{15}$; about 12.75, about −2.75 **30.** $x = -2 \pm \sqrt{15}$; about 1.87, about −5.87 **31.** dilation; $A'(0, 0)$; $B'(0, 4)$; $C'(6, 6)$; $D'(4, 0)$ **32.** translation; $A'(1, -6)$; $B'(3, -2)$; $C'(5, -2)$; $D'(5, -4)$ **33.** rotation; $A'(0, 0)$; $B'(-3, 2)$; $C'(-3, 4)$; $D'(-1, 4)$ **34.** reflection; $A'(-1, 1)$; $B'(-1, 3)$; $C'(-3, 3)$; $D'(-3, 0)$

Page 265 Checkpoint

1. two pairs of parallel sides; four right angles; four congruent sides; four congruent sides and four right angles; You would find the slope of a segment to determine if sides are parallel or if they meet at right angles. You would use the distance formula to show that the lengths of the sides are equal in measure.

2. a. slope of $\overline{AB}$ = slope of $\overline{DC} = \frac{2}{11}$; slope of $\overline{AD}$ = slope of $\overline{BC} = -\frac{5}{3}$ **b.** $ABCD$ is a parallelogram since it has two pairs of parallel sides. $ABCD$ is not a rectangle since the slopes of adjacent sides are not negative reciprocals. It is not a rhombus since it does not have four congruent sides. **3. a.** slope of $\overline{WX}$ = slope of $\overline{ZY} = 5$; slope of $\overline{XY}$ = slope of $\overline{WZ} = -\frac{1}{5}$

b. $WX = XY = YZ = WZ = \sqrt{26}$ **c.** $WXYZ$ is a square, since it is both a rectangle and a rhombus.

4. a. $2\sqrt{37} \approx 12.17$ **b.** $(-1, -1)$ **5. a.** $\sqrt{193} \approx 13.89$ **b.** $(-0.5, 6)$ **6. a.** $\sqrt{401} \approx 20.02$ **b.** $(2, -5.5)$ **7. a.** 5 **b.** $(4.5, -3)$ **8.** $(-8, -3)$ **9.** $(4, 1)$ **10.** $(7, -9)$ **11.** $(-2, 8)$

Pages 267–269 Talk it Over

1. $P'(6, 1)$, $Q'(5, 3)$, $R'(3, 4)$, $S'(1, -1)$ **2.** $AB = \sqrt{17}$; $A'B' = \sqrt{17}$; No; No. **3.** No; Yes. **4.** Yes. No; the slope of $\overline{AB}$ is positive and the slope of $\overline{A'B'}$ is negative. **5.** Yes; $\overline{BC}$ is another side in the same triangle. Therefore, it will be affected in the same manner as other sides of the triangle by a transformation.

Pages 270–273 Exercises and Problems

1. rotation of 90°, 180°, 270° **7. a.** a translation 5 units to the right, 3 units down **b.** To get the coordinates of the image of $\triangle QRS$, add 5 to the original x-coordinate and subtract 3 from the original

y-coordinate. $(x, y) \rightarrow (x + 5, y - 3)$ **9.** translation 2 units to the right, 5 units down

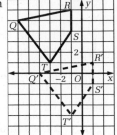

11. dilation with a scale factor of 3

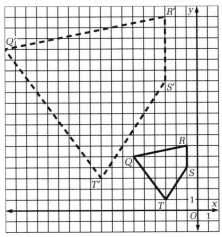

13. translation 4 units to the right

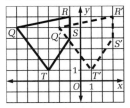

17. D **19.** C **21.** B

23.

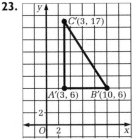

25.

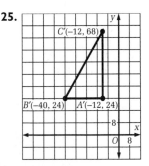

27.

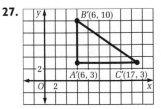

29. a. $\frac{11}{7}$ **b.** $-\frac{11}{7}; \frac{11}{7}; \frac{11}{7}; \frac{11}{7}; -\frac{7}{11}$ **c.** translation and dilation (Exs. 24–26); reflection (Ex. 23) and rotation (Ex. 27) **d.** Yes; translations, dilations preserve the orientation of the original image; reflections and most rotations do not preserve the orientation of the original image. All rotations of 180n, where n is an integer, will produce images, any of whose sides will have slope equal to the slope of the corresponding side in the original image. **37.** (50, –50) **38.** (4, 3) **39.** (–1.5, 2) **40. a.** $\frac{3}{49}$ or about 0.061 **b.** 6, –6 **41.** $AB = \sqrt{20} \approx 4.5$, $BC = 4$, $CD = \sqrt{32} \approx 5.7$, $AD = 10$

Pages 274–276 Talk it Over
1. 576.6 mi **2.** You will be able to read the miles traveled directly from the trip odometer.
3. a. Grace's; The arithmetic is simpler because more zeros are involved. **b.** No. **4.** $a = 4$, $b = 2$, $c = 3$
5. $a = 9$, $b = 2$, $c = 5$, $d = 6$, $e = 10$
6.

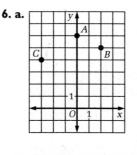

one variable

Pages 277–279 Exercises and Problems
9. a **11.** 0 **13.** 0 **15. a.** There are two possible answers: translate the triangle three units to the right or reflect the triangle over the y-axis.
b. translation: $J'(0, 0)$, $O'(3, 0)$, $L'(1, 3)$; reflection: $J'(3, 0)$, $O'(0, 0)$, $L'(2, 3)$ **17. a.** Translate the polygon one unit right and three units up. **b.** $L'(0, 0)$, $M'(3, 0)$, $N'(3, 2)$, $K'(0, 2)$ **19.** (–3a, 2a) **21.** –a
27. $A'(-1, -2)$, $B'(-3, 1)$, $C'(-2, 2)$ **28.** $A'(0, -3)$, $B'(2, 0)$, $C'(1, 1)$ **29.** $5i$ **30.** $i\sqrt{30}$ **31.** $24 + 6i$
32. $12 - 5i$ **33.** False; for example, when $x = \frac{1}{2}$, $\frac{1}{\frac{1}{2}} = 2$ which is greater than $\frac{1}{2}$.

Pages 282–283 Talk it Over
1. parallelograms, rectangles, rhombuses, squares
2. squares, kites, rhombuses **3.** rectangles, squares
4. parallelograms, rectangles, rhombuses, squares
5. three segments; Yes.

Pages 284–286 Exercises and Problems
1. The midpoint of $\overline{OV}$ is $\left(\frac{0 + 12}{2}, \frac{0 + 5}{2}\right) = \left(6, 2\frac{1}{2}\right)$.
The midpoint of $\overline{UW}$ is $\left(\frac{10 + 2}{2}, \frac{0 + 5}{2}\right) = \left(6, 2\frac{1}{2}\right)$.

3. Ex. 2; Ex. 1 merely provides an example, while Ex. 2 constitutes a proof for the general case.
5. a. midpoint of $\overline{OR} = \left(\frac{a + 0}{2}, \frac{a + 0}{2}\right) = \left(\frac{a}{2}, \frac{a}{2}\right)$;
midpoint of $\overline{QS} = \left(\frac{0 + a}{2}, \frac{a + 0}{2}\right) = \left(\frac{a}{2}, \frac{a}{2}\right)$
b. slope of $\overline{OR} = \frac{a - 0}{a - 0} = 1$; slope of $\overline{QS} = \frac{a - 0}{0 - a} = \frac{a}{-a} = -1$; Since the slope of $\overline{OR}$ is the negative reciprocal of the slope of $\overline{QS}$, $\overline{OR} \perp \overline{QS}$. **c.** $OR = a\sqrt{2}$ and $QS = a\sqrt{2}$, so the diagonals have the same length. **9. a.** $P(a, 2c)$; $Q(2a, c)$; $R(a, 0)$; $S(0, c)$
b. rhombus **c.** $PQ = \sqrt{(2a - a)^2 + (c - 2c)^2} = \sqrt{a^2 + c^2}$; $QR = \sqrt{(2a - a)^2 + (c - 0)^2} = \sqrt{a^2 + c^2}$;
$SR = \sqrt{(a - 0)^2 + (0 - c)^2} = \sqrt{a^2 + c^2}$;
$PS = \sqrt{(a - 0)^2 + (2c - c)^2} = \sqrt{a^2 + c^2}$; all four sides are equal in measure so $PQRS$ is a rhombus.
17. $(a, 0)$ **18.** $(a, 0)$ **19.** $(a + b, c)$ **20.** Carlos is taller than Ben. **21.** If Julie enters the race, then she will get a prize. **22.** $\frac{1}{80}$ **23.** $\frac{79}{80}$

Pages 288–289 Unit 5 Review and Assessment
1. True. **2.** True. **3.** True. **4.** True.
5.

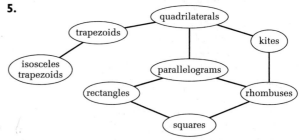

6. a.

b. C **c.** A **7.** The Pythagorean theorem tells how to find the square of the distance between the two endpoints of a hypotenuse of a right triangle: (distance)^2 = (change in x)^2 + (change in y)^2. Taking the same square root of both sides gives the distance formula: distance = $\sqrt{\text{(change in } x)^2 + \text{(change in } y)^2}$.
8. $FG = \sqrt{(-3 - 0)^2 + (0 - 2)^2} = \sqrt{13}$;
$HG = \sqrt{(-3 - 0)^2 + (0 - (-2))^2} = \sqrt{13}$;
$FJ = \sqrt{(2 - 0)^2 + (0 - 2)^2} = \sqrt{8}$;
$HJ = \sqrt{(2 - 0)^2 + (0 - (-2))^2} = \sqrt{8}$; Since $FGHJ$ has two pairs of adjacent congruent sides, $FGHJ$ is a kite.

9. slope of $\overline{MN} = \frac{3-5}{-1-(-5)} = -\frac{1}{2}$; slope of $\overline{PO} = \frac{2-0}{-4-0} =$ $-\frac{1}{2}$; slope of $\overline{MP} = \frac{5-2}{-5-(-4)} = -3$; slope of $\overline{NO} =$ $\frac{3-0}{-1-0} = -3$; slope of $\overline{MN} =$ slope of $\overline{PO}$ so $\overline{MN} \parallel \overline{PO}$; slope of $\overline{MP} =$ slope of $\overline{NO}$ so $\overline{MP} \parallel \overline{NO}$; since $MNOP$ has two pairs of parallel sides, $MNOP$ is a parallelogram.   **10. a.** $(3, -1)$ **b.** $(-12, -13)$

11. Answers may vary. An example is given. Suppose the coordinates $(1980, 1020)$ and $(1990, 980)$ represent two points on a fitted line that describes your school's enrollment from 1980 to the present. You can use the midpoint formula to estimate your school's enrollment in 1985:
$\left(\frac{1980 + 1990}{2}, \frac{1020 + 980}{2}\right) = (1985, 1000)$; your school's enrollment was about 1000 in 1985.

12. **13.**

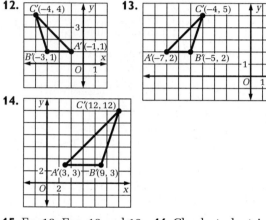

14.

15. Ex. 12; Exs. 12 and 13   **16.** Check students' sketches.   **a.** The image is a reflection over the y-axis.   **b.** The image is a 180° rotation.   **17.** No; a reflection over the x-axis maps (x, y) to $(x, -y)$. A 90° clockwise rotation maps (x, y) to $(y, -x)$.   **18.** 10   **19. a.** 6 or 0 **b.** 3   **20. a.**

b.

c. parallelogram

21. $OR = \sqrt{(2a - 0)^2 + (2c - 0)^2} = 2\sqrt{a^2 + c^2}$; $QR = \sqrt{(2a - 4a)^2 + (2c - 0)^2} = 2\sqrt{a^2 + c^2}$

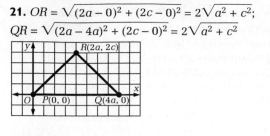

Unit 6

Pages 295–298 Talk it Over
1–3. Answers may vary. Examples are given.
1. a. Items to consider include the purpose of the trip, the weather, any special occasions to be attended, and so on. **b.** Draw a tree diagram with one column of branches for the shirts and one for the shorts or the jeans.   **2.** Draw a tree diagram with one column of branches for the first color and one for the second.   **3.** Both involve choosing a combination of items from a list of several items. There are more possible choices in question 2. Also, in question 2, the choices from the second category depend on the choice for the first.
4.

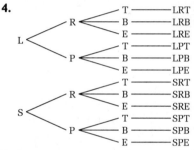

The meals are the same; the parts of the meal are listed in a different order.

5. Answers may vary. An example is given. You could make a chart with three columns, one for each choice. List one main dish in the first column, first row and one side dish in the second column, first row. Then list one drink choice in the third column, first row. Then with the same entries in the first two columns of the second row, list the next drink choice in the third column, second row. Proceed until all possible choices are listed. There will be twelve rows in the table.   **6. a.** 4 choices **b.** 6 choices
7. Answers may vary. An example is given. Without making a table, you may be able to think of the outcomes as ordered pairs with six different first coordinates and six different second coordinates.
8. 5 outcomes   **9.** 3 outcomes   **10.** 18 outcomes
11. In Sample 1, exactly one item is chosen from each category. In Sample 3, you do not have to choose an item from each category.   **12.** 15 accessory combinations

Pages 299–301 Exercises and Problems
1. 10 outcomes   **3.** 9 outcomes   **5.** white corded with built-in answering machine, white corded with

speakerphone, white cordless with built-in answering machine, white cordless with speakerphone, gray corded with built-in answering machine, gray corded with speakerphone, gray cordless with built-in answering machine, gray cordless with speakerphone, black corded with built-in answering machine, black corded with speakerphone, black cordless with built-in answering machine, black cordless with speakerphone   **7.** 8 ways (Let "H" indicate heads, and "T" tails, and the three letters indicate the position of the nickel, dime, and quarter in order from left to right. The possible outcomes are HHH, HHT, HTH, HTT, THH, THT, TTH, TTT.)   **9.** There are 36 possible results.   **11.** 16 ways   **21.** False.   **22.** True.
23. $\dfrac{50a^5}{b^2}$ **24.** $\dfrac{25x^4}{y^3}$ **25.** $\dfrac{36}{n^6}$

26.

Number of half-lives	Amount present (g)
0	600
1	300
2	150
3	75

Since the half-life is 8 days, there will be 100 g left after 16 days and before 24 days.   **27.** 6   **28.** 60   **29.** 3   **30.** −0.25

Pages 303–305 Talk it Over
1. a. 30 arrangements   **b.** Answers may vary. English examples: at, as; French examples: et, es   **2. a.** 120 arrangements   **b.** Answers may vary. English examples: rat, ate, sat; Spanish examples: ésa, ser   **3.** the number of arrangements when 8 are arranged 5 at a time   **4.** $(8 - 5)! = 3! = 6$ **5.** $_8P_5 = \dfrac{8!}{(8 - 5)!} = \dfrac{8!}{3!} = 8 \cdot 7 \cdot 6 \cdot 5 \cdot 4 = 6720$ **6.** There are four choices for the first letter, three for the second, and two for the third. By the multiplication counting principle, the number of arrangements is $4 \cdot 3 \cdot 2 = 24$. Using the permutations formula, $_4P_3 = \dfrac{4!}{(4 - 3)!} = \dfrac{4!}{1!} = 4 \cdot 3 \cdot 2 \cdot 1 = 24$. Both methods produce the same result.

Pages 306–309 Exercises and Problems
1. 9 factorial; $9 \cdot 8 \cdot 7 \cdot 6 \cdot 5 \cdot 4 \cdot 3 \cdot 2 \cdot 1 = 362,880$ **3.** 40,320 ways   **5. a.** 120 arrangements   **b.** 720 arrangements   **c.** Answers may vary. Examples are given. molds; models, seldom   **7.** 2   **9.** 5040   **17.** 6720   **19.** 5040   **21.** 120   **23.** 24   **25.** 24   **27.** 720   **32.** Lani, Eve, Derek, Peter; Lani, Eve, Peter, Derek; Lani, Derek, Eve, Peter; Lani, Derek, Peter, Eve; Lani, Peter, Derek, Eve, Lani, Peter, Eve, Derek; Eve, Lani, Derek, Peter; Eve, Lani, Peter, Derek; Eve, Derek, Lani, Peter; Eve, Derek, Peter, Lani; Eve, Peter, Derek, Lani; Eve, Peter, Lani, Derek; Derek, Eve, Lani,

Peter; Derek, Eve, Peter, Lani; Derek, Lani, Eve, Peter; Derek, Lani, Peter, Eve; Derek, Peter, Eve, Lani; Derek, Peter, Lani, Eve; Peter, Derek, Eve, Lani; Peter, Derek, Lani, Eve; Peter, Eve, Derek, Lani; Peter, Eve, Lani, Derek; Peter, Lani, Derek, Eve; Peter, Lani, Eve, Derek   **33.** $(2x + 3)(x - 2)$ **34.** $(3x - 5)(3x + 5)$ **35.** $(5x + 2)^2$ **36–39.** Answers may vary. Examples are given.   **36.** 0%; The sun rises every day.   **37.** 100%; I usually have cereal for breakfast.   **38.** 10%; Most of the ground is snow-covered now.   **39.** 50%; In New England, it is possible to have snow in December.

Pages 310–315 Talk it Over
1. 4   **2.** 26   **3.** 2   **4.** 12   **5.** 2 of diamonds, 2 of hearts   **6.** Jeannine's clue indicates her card is both a 2 and red; Chris's indicates his is one or the other. His will be harder to guess because his clue describes many more cards. Also, it is not clear if he means his card is not both.   **7.** No; each card has only one label.   **8.** No; there are three cards that are both spades and face cards.   **9. a.** 13; 39   **b.** Yes; a card cannot be a heart and not a heart at the same time.   **c.** 1   **10.** The events "no two people in a group of five people have the same birthday" and "at least two people in a group of five have the same birthday" are complementary. The probability that at least two of the five people have the same birthday is about $100\% - 97\%$ or 3%.   **11.** Find the probability that no two people in the group of six have the same birth date, and then subtract that probability from 1.   **12. a, b.** Answers may vary. For a class of 25 people, the probability that at least two people have the same birthday is about 57%.   **13.** 119:1   **14.** about 99%   **15.** 6:19; 19:6

Pages 315–318 Exercises and Problems
3. about 17%   **5.** about 67%   **7.** about 67%   **9.** rolling a 6 and rolling a prime   **11.** 25%   **13.** 98%   **23. a.** $\dfrac{1}{24}$ or about 4.17%   **b.** 1:23   **c.** $\dfrac{1}{12}$ **25.** 75%   **27.** 50%   **29.** 35:1   **41.** 120; 720   **42.** $9i$ **43.** $60i$ **44.** $34 + 22i$ **45.** $-3 + 15i$

46.

slacks color	yellow sweater	black sweater
blue	blue slacks, yellow sweater	blue slacks, black sweater
green	green slacks, yellow sweater	green slacks, black sweater

Pages 319–323 Talk it Over
1. Divide the number of entries the team has by the total number of entries.   **2.** about 0.152; about 0.015   **3.** dependent   **4.** dependent   **5.** independent   **6.** independent   **7.** In Sample 3, the list of possible

choices changes after the first choice. In Sample 2, the list does not change. In Sample 3, since songs do not repeat, the song chosen first is no longer a possible choice. There are only 49 possible choices remaining. **8. a.** independent; The choice of the first song has no effect on the choice of the second. **b.** 0.052

Pages 323–326 Exercises and Problems

1. about 0.016 **3.** about 0.063

5. a.

+	1	2	3	3
1	2	3	4	4
2	3	4	5	5
3	4	5	6	6
3	4	5	6	6

b. 2, 3, 4, 5, 6 **c.** 4; 0.3125 **d.** 0.25 **e.** The probability of an even sum is greater. P(even sum) = 0.625; P(odd sum) = 0.375 **15. a.** 0.09 **b.** about 0.067 **17.** about 0.000004 **19.** about 0.002 **25. a.** 0.4 **b.** 2:3 **26.** $P = \dfrac{I}{rt}$ **27.** $x = \dfrac{y + 40}{3}$ **28.** $y = \dfrac{p - mx}{n}$ **29. a.** the number of arrangements when 9 are arranged 2 at a time **b.** 72

Page 327 Checkpoint 1

1. First, determine how many sums are possible when two dice are rolled. Next, determine the probability of getting a total of 6 and the probability of getting a total of 9. Finally, multiply the two probabilities. **2. a.** JOHN, JONH, JHON, JHNO, JNOH, JNHO, OJHN, OJNH, OHJN, OHNJ, ONJH, ONHJ, HOJN, HONJ, HJON, HJNO, HNJO, HNOJ, NOJH, NOHJ, NJOH, NJHO, NHJO, NHOJ **b.** Answers may vary. An example is given. No; it may not be a good idea, since his four-letter name is an obvious choice and there are only 24 permutations. With three chances to guess the code, a thief would have a 12.5% chance of doing so. **3.** 5040 **4.** 1320 **5.** P(vowel) ≈ 0.429; P(consonant) ≈ 0.571 **6.** The events are mutually exclusive since none of the letters is both a vowel and a consonant. The events are complementary since they are mutually exclusive and together they include all the possibilities. **7.** 4:3 **8.** about 0.028 **9.** about 0.005

Pages 328–330 Talk it Over

1. Answers may vary. An example is given. The cones in the first column show all the ways the first three flavors can be arranged. The second column shows the ways the first two and the fourth can be combined, and so on. **2.** 60 cones

3. $_5P_3 = \dfrac{5!}{(5 - 3)!} = \dfrac{5!}{2!} = \dfrac{120}{2} = 60$ **4.** 6; $_3P_3$

5. 10 dishes **6.** $\dfrac{1}{6}$ **7.** 15 pairs **8.** 30 ways **9.** combinations; permutations

Pages 330–332 Exercises and Problems

1. the number of permutations of 7 items arranged 4 at a time **3.** the number of permutations of 8 items arranged 5 at a time **5.** $_8C_5$; 120 times; For every combination of 5 items, there are 120 arrangements of the 5 items. **7.** 1 **9.** 15 **11.** 84 **13.** 1680 **17.** combinations; 20 sets **25.** about 0.086 **26.** 90 ft^2 **27.** 4320 mm^2 **28.** 21 **29.** 405 **30.** 65,536x

Pages 333–335 Talk it Over

1. A line drawn through the center of the top circle and perpendicular to the opposite side of the triangle is an axis of symmetry. **2.** Summaries may vary. An example is given. The first and last symbols in each row are the same. The other symbols appear to be made by adding the number of marks on the two circles above a given symbol. **3.** 6 **4.** 10

5. $_4C_3 = \dfrac{4!}{3!1!} = \dfrac{24}{6} = 4$ **6.** $_4C_0 + {}_4C_1 + {}_4C_2 + {}_4C_3 = \dfrac{4!}{0!4!} + \dfrac{4!}{1!3!} + \dfrac{4!}{2!2!} + \dfrac{4!}{3!1!} = 1 + 4 + 6 + 4 = 15$

Pages 336–337 Exercises and Problems

1. a. one **b.** Given the first fifteen rows of Pascal's triangle, find the number in row 15, diagonal 5. Remember that the first row and diagonal are row 0 and diagonal 0. **c.** 1024 **5.** 10 **7.** 6 **9.** 7 **11.** 1 **13.** $n = 4, r = 2$; $n = 6, r = 1$; $n = 6, r = 5$ **15.** 3 ways **17.** 1 way **19.** 20 combinations

24. $_{120}C_2 = \dfrac{120!}{2!118!} = \dfrac{120 \cdot 119}{2!} = 7140$

25. slope: 4; vertical intercept: 0; increasing

26. slope: −2; vertical intercept: 3; decreasing

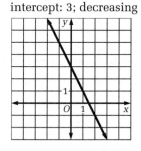

27. slope: 0; vertical intercept: −3; constant

28.

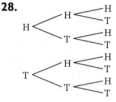

1. a. Answers may vary. I prefer Pascal's triangle, since it involves less work than making a diagram and it is not necessary to know what the actual out comes are. **b.** $_4C_2 = \frac{4!}{2!2!} = \frac{24}{2 \cdot 2} = 6$ **2.** 0.25
3. 0.3125 **4.** about 0.23

Pages 341–344 Exercises and Problems
3. 0.375 **5.** 0.3125 **7.** 0.3125 **18.** 15 ways
19. $Q'(-1, 0)$; $R'(1, 0)$; $S'(1, -4)$; $T'(-3, -3)$
20. $Q'(2, 4)$; $R'(6, 4)$; $S'(6, -4)$; $T'(-2, -2)$
21. a. about 0.167 **b.** 0.5 **c.** No; the events can happen at the same time since five is a prime number.

Page 344 Checkpoint
1. Find the number in row 5, diagonal 4. (5)
2. a. 126 groups **b.** 120 ways **3.** 1 3 3 1; Answers may vary. An example is given. The first and fourth numbers are 1. To find the second number, add the first and second numbers of row 2. To find the third number, add the second and third numbers of row 2.
4. $_4C_2$; 6 **5.** 0.125 **6.** 0.15625

Pages 346–347 Talk it Over
1. The probability of being left-handed is 0.1 and the probability of being right-handed is 0.9.
2. $_3C_2 = \frac{3!}{(3-2)!2!} = \frac{3 \cdot 2 \cdot 1}{1 \cdot 2 \cdot 1} = 3$ **3.** Answers may vary. An example is given. The number of left-handed students may be 0, 1, 2, or 3. Using the reasoning described, the probabilities would be 0 students: 0.729; 1 student: 0.081; 2 students: 0.009; 3 students: 0.001. The sum of those probabilities is only 0.82.
4. There is only one outcome for "no left-handed students" and $P(RRR) = 0.729$. Then P(at least one left-handed student) $= 1 - 0.729 = 0.271$. This method involves less computation and therefore less room for error than the other method. **5.** 0.028
6. about 0.167 **7.** about 0.833
8.

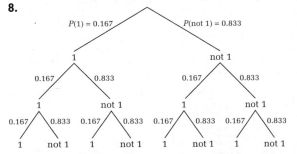

9. No; there are eight possible outcomes with varying probabilities. For example, $P(111) \approx 0.005$ and P(no 1's) ≈ 0.578.

Pages 347–350 Exercises and Problems
3. about 0.016 **5.** 0.15625 **7. a.** There are a limited number of trials. The two possible outcomes ("1" and "not 1") are mutually exclusive and $P(1) + P(\text{not } 1) = 1$. The trials are independent.
b. Solution method may vary. An example is given. Use the tree diagram shown in the answer for Talk it Over question 8. Since "rolling at least one 1" and "rolling no 1's" are complementary, find P(no 1's). The only favorable outcome is NNN with probability $\left(\frac{5}{6}\right)^3 \approx 0.579$. Then P(at least one 1) ≈ 0.421.
19. 0.3125 **20, 21.** Answers may vary. Examples are given. **20.** $(-2.7, 3.6)$ and $(0.7, 0.3)$ **21.** $(-0.5, 1)$ and $(0.5, 1)$ **22.** $V = 3a \cdot 3a \cdot 6a = 54a^3$
23. $V = 15x \cdot 10x \cdot 2y = 300x^2y$

Pages 351–354 Talk it Over
1. Both models have length $a + b$ and width $a + b$. The area of the figure on the left is $(a + b)^2$. The total area of the figures on the right is $a^2 + 2ab + b^2$.
2. $(a + b)(a + b) = (a + b)(a) + (a + b)(b) = a(a) + b(a) + a(b) + b(b) = a^2 + 2ab + b^2$ **3.** Each gold prism has a square base with side length equal to a, and a height equal to b, so the volume is $a \cdot a \cdot b = a^2b$.
4. Each green prism has a square base with side length equal to b, and a height equal to a, so the volume is $b \cdot b \cdot a = b^2a$. **5.** Answers may vary. Example: $(a + b)(a + b)(a + b) = (a + b)[(a + b)(a + b)] = (a + b)(a^2 + 2ab + b^2) = a(a^2 + 2ab + b^2) + b(a^2 + 2ab + b^2) = a(a^2) + a(2ab) + a(b^2) + b(a^2) + b(2ab) + b(b^2) = a^3 + 2a^2b + ab^2 + a^2b + 2ab^2 + b^3 = a^3 + 3a^2b + 3ab^2 + b^3$ **6.** The coefficients of $(a + b)^n$ are the numbers in row n of Pascal's triangle.
7. The exponents of the a variables in $(a + b)^n$ are decreasing consecutive integers from n to 0. The exponents of the b variables in $(a + b)^n$ are increasing consecutive integers from 0 to n. **8.** Yes.
9. $1a^3b^0 + 3a^2b^1 + 3a^1b^2 + 1a^0b^3$ **10. a.** 7 terms
b. $a^6 + 6a^5b + 15a^4b^2 + 20a^3b^3 + 15a^2b^4 + 6ab^5 + b^6$
11. $n + 1$ **12.** The second term of the binomial is a constant, not a variable, so the coefficients of Pascal's triangle are multiplied by the constant raised to the correct power. **13.** Even powers of negative numbers are always positive. **14.** because even and odd powers of negative numbers alternate signs

Pages 354–357 Exercises and Problems
1. $x^2 + 6x + 9$ **3. a.** $m^3 + 6m^2 + 12m + 8$ **b.** There is one block with volume m^3 and one with volume 8. There are three blocks with volume $2m^2$ and three with volume $4m$. **5.** $c^3 + 3c^2d + 3cd^2 + d^3$
7. $x^5 + 5x^4y + 10x^3y^2 + 10x^2y^3 + 5xy^4 + y^5$
9. $x^3 + 6x^2 + 12x + 8$ **11.** $y^4 - 8y^3 + 24y^2 - 32y + 16$
13. $x^3 + 9x^2 + 27x + 27$ **15.** $a^{10} + 10a^9 + 45a^8 + 120a^7 + 210a^6 + 252a^5 + 210a^4 + 120a^3 + 45a^2 + 10a + 1$ **17.** Yes; each term of the expansion has the

form $_6C_r p^{(6-r)}q^r$.   **19.** No; each term of the expansion has the form $_3C_r p^{(3-r)}(2q)^r$. When these terms are simplified, the coefficient of each term except the first is multiplied by a power of 2.   **26.** about 0.001
27. slope of $\overline{AB} = \frac{1+1}{2+3} = \frac{2}{5}$ and slope of $\overline{CD} = \frac{-1+3}{7-2} = \frac{2}{5}$; slope of $\overline{AD} = \frac{-3+1}{2+3} = -\frac{2}{5}$ and slope of $\overline{BC} = \frac{-1-1}{7-2} = -\frac{2}{5}$; $AB = \sqrt{(2+3)^2 + (1+1)^2} = \sqrt{29}$;
$BC = \sqrt{(7-2)^2 + (-1-1)^2} = \sqrt{29}$;
$CD = \sqrt{(7-2)^2 + (-1+3)^2} = \sqrt{29}$;
$AD = \sqrt{(2+3)^2 + (-3+1)^2} = \sqrt{29}$; Since $ABCD$ has two pairs of parallel sides and all four sides have the same measure, $ABCD$ is a rhombus.   **28.** True.
29. False.   **30.** True.   **31.** True.

Pages 359–360 Unit 6 Review and Assessment
1.

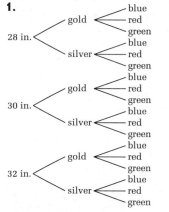

2. 6,084,000 plates   **3.** 2,948,400 plates   **4.** $_{15}P_{10} =$ 10,897,286,400   **5.** about 0.333   **6.** about 0.833
7. about 0.667   **8.** 1:2   **9.** 3:1   **10.** about 0.037
11. about 0.018   **12.** 495   **13.** $_5P_3 = 60$; $_5C_3 = 10$;
$_5C_3 = \frac{_5P_3}{_3P_3}$ **14.** 1, 4, 6, 4, 1; $_4C_0$, $_4C_1$, $_4C_2$, $_4C_3$, $_4C_4$
15. The number in row n, diagonal r of Pascal's triangle is equal to the number of combinations of n items selected r at a time.   **16.** 0.3125   **17.** Answers may vary. An example is given. For the event "a baby is born," $P(\text{boy}) = P(\text{girl})$. If twelve babies are born at a local hospital on one day, what is the probability that at least half of them are boys?   **18.** 0.3456
19. 0.4752   **20.** $x^4 + 8x^3 + 24x^2 + 32x + 16$
21. $x^5 - 15x^4 + 90x^3 - 270x^2 + 405x - 243$
22. $x^3 + 3x^2y + 3xy^2 + y^3$ **23.** $r^3 - 3r^2s + 3rs^2 - s^3$

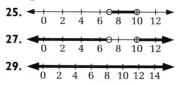

Pages 366–367 Talk it Over
1. stock clerk at Food Stuff or Shop-All, ice cream server at Lunch Bag; Jean wants a job as a shop clerk *or* to work at Northmall *or* both.   **2.** none; The only job that is for 20 or more hours per week pays less than $5.00.   **3.** inclusive *or*   **4.** exclusive *or*

Pages 369–372 Exercises and Problems
3. Jackie Winsor, The lure of Italy, On Kawara   **5.** *Y*
7. *Z*   **13.** I'm outside.   **15.** If the inclusive *or* is being used, the conclusion is not justified because it is possible to eat pizza while at a ball game. The conclusion would be justified only if the exclusive *or* were being used.   **17.** Yes.   **19.** Yes.   **21.** C   **23.** A

25.
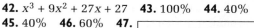

27.

29.

31, 33. Answers may vary. Examples are given.
31. $5 \le x \le 9$ **33.** $x > 5$ or $x < 7$ **35.** B
37.   **39.**

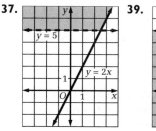
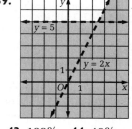

42. $x^3 + 9x^2 + 27x + 27$ **43.** 100%   **44.** 40%
45. 40%   **46.** 60%   **47.**

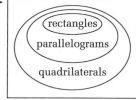

Pages 374–375 Talk it Over
1. If I am in Canada, then I am in North America.

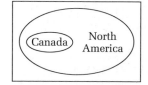

2. a. True.   **b.** If $x = 4$, then $x + 5 = 9$.   **c.** True.
3. If an animal is a chinchilla, then it is a rodent.

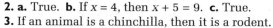

4.

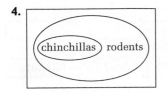

5. No.   **6.** Yes.

Pages 375–378 Exercises and Problems
1. the "if" part   **3.** $q \rightarrow p$ **5. a.** p: a figure is a square; q: a figure is a rhombus.   **b.** The fact that a figure is a square implies that it is a rhombus.

c.

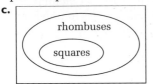

7. a. p: a figure is a cylinder; q: the formula for its volume is $V = Bh$.   **b.** A figure is a cylinder only if the formula for its volume is $V = Bh$.

c.

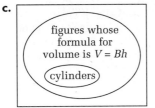

9. a. If a figure is a rectangle, then it is a parallelogram. True.   **b.** If a figure is a parallelogram, then it is a rectangle. False; a rhombus is also a parallelogram.   **11. a.** If today is Valentine's Day, then this month is February. True.   **b.** If this month is February, then today is Valentine's Day. False; it could be February 1 instead of February 14.   **13. a.** If Cleo is a golden retriever, then Cleo is a dog. True.   **b.** If Cleo is a dog, then Cleo is a golden retriever. False; Cleo could be an Irish setter.   **26.**

27. False.   **28.** False.   **29.** True.

30. a. $\begin{bmatrix} 1.69 & 2.29 & 3.89 \\ 1.75 & 2.49 & 4.19 \\ 2.19 & 2.79 & 4.99 \end{bmatrix}$ **b.** $\begin{bmatrix} 1.81 & 2.45 & 4.16 \\ 1.87 & 2.66 & 4.48 \\ 2.34 & 2.99 & 5.34 \end{bmatrix}$

31. Answers may vary. Examples are given. Leonardo Da Vinci was an artist and a scientist. Rodin was a sculptor or Marie Curie was a scientist. Diego Rivera was not a scientist.

Pages 380–382 Talk it Over
1. *or* rule   **2.** chain rule   **3.** direct argument   **4.** No; it has the form $p \rightarrow q$ and $p \rightarrow r$, $\therefore q \rightarrow r$, which is not a valid argument.   **5.** Yes; it is an indirect argument.

Pages 382–384 Exercises and Problems
1. therefore q **3.** $\triangle ABC$ is not isosceles.   **5.** $P(A) \neq 0$.   **7.** Kerry has the right to vote.   **9.** valid; indirect argument   **11.** invalid; It has the form $p \rightarrow q$; q; $\therefore p$, which is not a valid argument.   **23. a.** If an angle is obtuse, then it measures between 90° and 180°. True.   **b.** If an angle measures between 90° and 180°, then it is an obtuse angle. True.   **24. a.** If $x = 5$, then $x < 8$. True.   **b.** If $x < 8$, then $x = 5$. False; for example, x might be $3\frac{1}{2}$.   **25. a.** If you are in California, then you are in a state bordering the Pacific Ocean. True.   **b.** If you are in a state bordering the Pacific Ocean, then you are in California. False; you might be in Oregon, for example.   **26.** 25%   **27.** 12.5%   **28.** 25%

Page 385 Checkpoint
1. Answers may vary. An example is given. If you apply to the program, then you will get accepted. If you get accepted, you will be trained to fly on the space shuttle. If you fly on the space shuttle, you may get to walk in space. Therefore, if you apply to the program, you may get to walk in space.

2.   **3.**

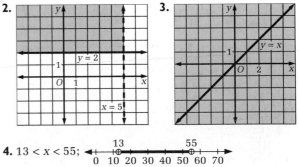

4. $13 < x < 55$;   **5.** If Corey is a high school student, then he is a teenager.   **6.** If a number is a multiple of 4, then it is also a multiple of 2.   **7.** If a matrix has 4 columns and 3 rows, then the dimensions of the matrix are 3×4.   **8.** Jana scored higher than 85.   **9.** valid; direct argument

Pages 386–389 Talk it Over
1. All the talking heads are using different names for the same thing.   **2.** The sandwich usually consists of sandwich meats with lettuce, tomato, and dressing, and may also have onions, peppers, and other vegetables.   **3. a.** hypothesis: A point is the midpoint of a segment. conclusion: The point is the same distance from each endpoint of the segment.   **b.** hypothesis:

A point on a segment is the same distance from each endpoint. conclusion: The point is the midpoint of the segment.   **4.** A point on a segment is the midpoint of the segment if and only if the point is the same distance from each endpoint.   **5. a.** If a quadrilateral is a rectangle, then it is a parallelogram. If a quadrilateral is a parallelogram, then it is a rectangle. **b.** False; it is not true that if a quadrilateral is a parallelogram, then it is a rectangle.   **6.** The statement is true, but it is not biconditional.   **7.** Wording may vary. An example is given. A figure is a rhombus if and only if it has four congruent sides.

Pages 389–393 Exercises and Problems

1. Answers may vary. Examples are given. If p, then q and if q, then p; $p \rightarrow q$ and $q \rightarrow p$; or $p \leftrightarrow q$.
3. Biconditionals may be written $p \leftrightarrow q$ or $q \leftrightarrow p$. One order is given. $5x = 20$, if and only if $x = 4$.
5. a. Yes. **b.** Yes **c.** $\frac{x}{2} = 7$ if and only if $x = 14$.
7. a. Yes. **b.** No. **c.** not possible   **9.** False; both conditionals are not true.   **11.** True; the two conditionals "If a figure is a parallelogram with four right angles, then it is a rectangle" and "If a figure is a rectangle, then it is a parallelogram with four right angles" are both true.

13. **15.**

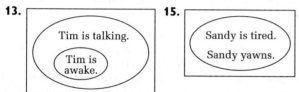

17. A triangle is *scalene* if and only if it has three sides that are not equal in measure.   **19.** No; the conditional "If an angle is obtuse, then the measure of the angle is 150°" is not true.   **21.** Yes; the conditionals "If two lines are perpendicular, they intersect to form a right angle" and "If two lines intersect to form a right angle, then the lines are perpendicular" are both true.   **23.** If a figure is a square, then it is a rectangle with four congruent sides. If a figure is a rectangle with four congruent sides, then the figure is a square.   **29.** valid   **31.** valid   **36.** valid   **37.** invalid
38. 6   **39.** 7.07 to the nearest hundredth   **40.** $84\sqrt{2}$
41. Fran is taller than Abby.   **42.** $x = 6$

Pages 394–396 Talk it Over

1. a. Flight 101 from Bombay to Buenos Aires
b. Bombay is the departure point.
2.

City	Flight
Bombay	Departure point
Calcutta	Flight 201: Bombay → Calcutta
Mexico City	Flight 203: Calcutta → Mexico City

3.

City	Flight
Mexico City	Departure point
Calcutta	Flight 204: Mexico City → Calcutta
Bombay	Flight 202: Calcutta → Bombay

4. *Given:* Buenos Aires
Prove: Buenos Aires to Calcutta
Statements (Justifications):
1. Buenos Aires (Given)
2. Mexico City (Flight 106: Buenos Aires → Mexico City)
3. Calcutta (Flight 204: Mexico City → Calcutta)
5. Yes; Yes. There are often many ways to prove a statement just as there can be many ways to solve a problem.
6. *Given:* Rio de Janeiro
Prove: Tokyo
Statements (Justifications):
1. Rio de Janeiro (Given)
2. New York City (Flight 102: Rio de Janeiro → New York City)
3. Tokyo (Flight 103: New York City → Tokyo)
7. It is possible to fly from Rio de Janeiro to Tokyo. You can take Flight 102 from Rio de Janeiro to New York City. Then you can take Flight 103 from New York City to Tokyo.
8. Statements
Rio de Janeiro $\overset{\text{❶}}{\rightarrow}$ New York City $\overset{\text{❷}}{\rightarrow}$ Tokyo
Justifications
❶ Flight 102 ❷ Flight 103

Pages 397–399 Exercises and Problems

3.

City	Flight
Calcutta	Departure point
Bombay	Flight 202: Calcutta → Bombay
Buenos Aires	Flight 101: Bombay → Buenos Aires

5. It is impossible to go from Tokyo to New York City because Euclid Airlines does not have any flights out of Tokyo.   **7.** direct argument

9. Statements Cairo $\overset{\text{❶}}{\rightarrow}$ Bombay $\overset{\text{❷}}{\rightarrow}$ Calcutta
Justifications ❶ Flight 104 ❷ Flight 201
18. Yes. If a quadrilateral is a rhombus, then it has four congruent sides. If a quadrilateral has four congruent sides, then it is a rhombus.   **19.** No. If a quadrilateral is a rhombus, then the quadrilateral is a square. If a quadrilateral is a square, then the quadrilateral is a rhombus. If a quadrilateral is a rhombus, it is not necessarily a square.   **20.** (−7, 14)   **21.** $n = 43$
22. $x = 4$ **23.** $a = 2$

1. The colonists meant that these truths do not require a proof or explanation.   **2.** the statements **3.** the conclusion

Pages 404–407 Exercises and Problems
1. Subtraction property of equality   **3.** Definition of square root   **5.** It means that these truths, like a postulate, do not require a proof or explanation.
7. *Given:* $x^2 + 8 = 24$; $x > 0$
Prove: $x = 4$
Statements (Justifications):
1. $x^2 + 8 = 24$ (Given)
2. $x^2 = 16$ (Subtraction property of equality)
3. $x = 4$ or $x = -4$ (Definition of square root)
4. $x > 0$ (Given)
5. $x = 4$ (Or rule)
9. a. *Given:* $4x^2 + 6 = 330$; $x > 0$
Prove: $x = 9$
Statements (Justifications):
1. $4x^2 + 6 = 330$ (Given)
2. $4x^2 = 324$ (Subtraction property of equality)
3. $x^2 = 81$ (Division property of equality)
4. $x = 9$ or $x = -9$ (Definition of square root)
5. $x > 0$ (Given)
6. $x = 9$ (Or rule)
b. Statements
$4x^2 + 6 = 330 \overset{❶}{\to} 4x^2 = 324 \overset{❷}{\to} x^2 = 81 \overset{❸}{\to}$
$x = 9$ or $x = -9$, $x > 0 \overset{❹}{\to} x = 9$

Justifications ❶ Subtraction property of equality ❷ Division property of equality ❸ Definition of square root; given ❹ Or rule   **c.** If $4x^2 + 6 = 330$, use the subtraction property of equality to subtract 6 from both sides: $4x^2 = 324$. Then use the division property of equality to divide both sides by 4: $x^2 = 81$. Then use the definition of square root: $x = 9$ or $x = -9$. Since $x > 0$, $x = 9$.   **13. a.** Answers may vary. An example is given. There are two inequality postulates because when you multiply an inequality by a positive number the inequality sign stays the same, but when you multiply an inequality by a negative number, the inequality sign is reversed. For example, for the inequality $2 < 5$, when both sides are multiplied by 3, then $6 < 15$. But when both sides are multiplied by -3, then $-6 > -15$. **b.** If $a < b$ and $c > 0$, then $\frac{a}{c} < \frac{b}{c}$. If $a < b$ and $c < 0$, then $\frac{a}{c} > \frac{b}{c}$.   **20.** Two-column proof: The *given* and the *prove* are stated. The premises are listed in the left column, and the justifications are listed in the right column. The final step in the proof is the *prove*. Flow proof: The statements are written from left to right with arrows between the steps. The arrows are numbered, and the justifications for each step are listed below the statements. Paragraph proof: The *given* and the *prove* statements are written first. Then the procedure and the justification for each step is described in paragraph form.
21. Answers may vary. An example is given. Arturo's results may not be based on a random sample. The people he sees are not randomly selected; they just happen to pass the place where Arturo is.   **22.** No. A figure is a parallelogram if and only if the figure is a quadrilateral with two pairs of parallel sides.
23. No; a figure is a kite if and only if it has two pairs of consecutive sides congruent.

Page 407 Checkpoint
1. Answers may vary. An example is given. I need to plan ahead before I write a proof so that I can get from the premises to the conclusion in a straightforward, logical fashion.   **2.** A figure is a quadrilateral if and only if it is a rectangle with parallel sides.
3. No; any four-sided figure is a quadrilateral, not just rectangles.   **4.** valid; it is an indirect argument.
5. flow proof   **6.** conclusion
7. *Given:* $7x - 3 = 25$
Prove: $x = 4$
Statements (Justifications):
1. $7x - 3 = 25$ (Given)
2. $7x = 28$ (Addition property of equality)
3. $x = 4$ (Division property of equality)

Pages 408–409 Talk it Over
1. Two angles are complementary if and only if the sum of their measures equals 90°. Two angles are supplementary if and only if the sum of their measures equals 180°.   **2. a.** The two supplements also have the same measure.   **b.** If two angles are equal in measure, then their supplements are also equal in measure. No; an infinite number of cases cannot be tested. Yes.
3. Statements
$\angle 1$ is supplementary to $\angle 2$. $\overset{❶}{\to} m\angle 1 + m\angle 2 = 180°$ ❷
$\angle 3$ is supplementary to $\angle 2$. $\overset{❶}{\to} m\angle 3 + m\angle 2 = 180°$ $\to$
$m\angle 1 + m\angle 2 = m\angle 3 + m\angle 2 \overset{❸}{\to} m\angle 1 = m\angle 3$

Justifications ❶ Definition of supplementary angles ❷ Substitution property ❸ Subtraction property of equality
4. *Given:* $\angle 1$ is complementary to $\angle 2$; $\angle 3$ is complementary to $\angle 2$. *Prove:* $m\angle 1 = m\angle 3$

If two angles are complementary, then their sum is equal to 90°. Therefore, $m\angle 1 + m\angle 2 = 90°$ and $m\angle 2 + m\angle 3 = 90°$. Since the sums both equal 90°, you can say $m\angle 1 + m\angle 2 = m\angle 2 + m\angle 3$ by the substitution property. Then you can use the subtraction property of equality to subtract $m\angle 2$ from both sides of the equation. Therefore, $m\angle 1 = m\angle 3$.

1. definition   **3.** definition, postulate, theorem
5. $m \angle Q + m \angle R = 180°$; definition of supplementary angles   **7.** $m \angle H = m \angle J$; If two angles are supplements of the same angle, then they are equal in measure.   **9. a.** Yes.   **b.** The sides of the new figure are all diagonals of congruent squares. These diagonals are all congruent.
11. *Given:* $\angle 1$ and $\angle 2$ are complementary.
$$m \angle 1 = 75°$$
Prove: $m \angle 2 = 15°$
Statements
$\angle 1$ and $\angle 2$ are complementary. $\overset{\textbf{❶}}{\rightarrow}$
$\left. \begin{array}{l} m \angle 1 + m \angle 2 = 90° \\ m \angle 1 = 75° \end{array} \right\} \overset{\textbf{❷}}{\rightarrow} 75° + m \angle 2 = 90° \overset{\textbf{❸}}{\rightarrow}$
$m \angle 2 = 15°$
Justifications ❶ Definition of complementary ∡
❷ Substitution property ❸ Subtraction property of equality   **13.** postulate
15. Proof forms may vary. A two-column proof is given.
Statements (Justifications):
1. $\angle ABC$ is a straight angle. (Given)
2. $m \angle ABC = 180°$ (If the sides of an angle form a straight line, then the angle is a straight angle with measure 180°.)
3. $m \angle ABF + m \angle FBE + m \angle EBD + m \angle DBC = m \angle ABC$ (For any angle, the measure of the whole is equal to the sum of the measures of its non-overlapping parts.)
4. $m \angle ABF + m \angle FBE + m \angle EBD + m \angle DBC = 180°$ (Substitution property [Steps 2 and 3])
5. $m \angle ABF = m \angle FBE$; $m \angle EBD = m \angle DBC$ (Given)
6. $2(m \angle FBE) + 2(m \angle EBD) = 180°$ (Substitution property [Steps 4 and 5])
7. $m \angle FBE + m \angle EBD = 90°$ (Division property of equality)
8. $m \angle FBE + m \angle EBD = m \angle FBD$ (For any angle, the measure of the whole is equal to the sum of the measures of its non-overlapping parts.)
9. $m \angle FBD = 90°$ (Substitution property [Steps 7 and 8])
10. $\angle FBD$ is a right angle. (Definition of right angle)
19. *Given:* $2(x + 7) = 3x$
Prove: $x = 14$
Statements (Justifications):
1. $2(x + 7) = 3x$ (Given)
2. $2x + 14 = 3x$ (Distributive property)
3. $14 = x$ (Subtraction property of equality)
20. one solution   **21.** many solutions   **22.** no solutions   **23.** rhombus, rectangle, square

1. $\angle 3$ and $\angle 5$, $\angle 4$ and $\angle 6$ **2.** $\angle 1$ and $\angle 5$, $\angle 4$ and $\angle 8$, $\angle 2$ and $\angle 6$, $\angle 3$ and $\angle 7$ **3.** $\angle 4$ and $\angle 5$, $\angle 3$ and $\angle 6$ **4.** Corresponding angles are equal in measure. The angle measuring 70° and $\angle 1$ are corresponding

angles. Therefore, $m \angle 1 = 70°$.   **5.** Because $m \angle 1 = 70°$ (from question 4) and alternate interior angles are equal in measure, $m \angle 2 = m \angle 1 = 70°$.   **6.** $m \angle 2 = 70°$ (from question 5). Since co-interior angles are supplementary, $m \angle 2 + m \angle 3 = 180°$. By the substitution property, $70° + m \angle 3 = 180°$. Using the subtraction property of equality, $m \angle 3 = 110°$.
7. *Given:* parallelogram $ABCD$
Prove: $m \angle 1 = m \angle 3$
Plan: $\angle 1$ and $\angle 3$ are both supplementary to $\angle 2$ (Theorem 7.6). Thus, they are equal (Theorem 7.1).

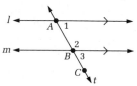

1. $\angle 1$ and $\angle 3$, $\angle 2$ and $\angle 4$, $\angle 5$ and $\angle 7$, $\angle 6$ and $\angle 8$
3. $\angle 2$ and $\angle 3$, $\angle 6$ and $\angle 7$ **5.** co-exterior angles
7. a. alternate interior angles   **b.** Their measures are equal.   **c.** If two parallel lines are intersected by a transversal, then alternate interior angles are equal in measure.   **9.** 7.2°
13. *Given:* Lines l and m are parallel and are intersected by line t. *Prove:* $\angle 1$ and $\angle 2$ are supplementary.
Statements (Justifications):
1. $l \parallel m$ (Given)
2. $m \angle 3 = m \angle 1$ (If two $\parallel$ lines are intersected by a transversal, then corresponding ∡ are = in measure.)
3. l, m, and t are lines. (Given)
4. $m \angle ABC = 180°$ (If the sides of an angle form a straight line, then the angle is a straight angle with measure 180°.)
5. $m \angle 2 + m \angle 3 = m \angle ABC$ (For any angle, the measure of the whole is equal to the sum of the measures of its non-overlapping parts.)
6. $m \angle 2 + m \angle 3 = 180°$ (Substitution property [Steps 4 and 5])
7. $m \angle 1 + m \angle 2 = 180°$ (Substitution property [Steps 2 and 6])
8. $\angle 1$ and $\angle 2$ are supplementary. (Definition of supplementary angles)
15. a. supplementary   **b.** equal in measure
17. *Given:* Lines j and k are parallel. Lines m and n are parallel.   *Prove:* $m \angle 1 = m \angle 3$
Statements
$\left. \begin{array}{l} j \parallel k \overset{\textbf{❶}}{\rightarrow} m \angle 1 = m \angle 2 \\ m \parallel n \overset{\textbf{❷}}{\rightarrow} m \angle 2 = m \angle 3 \end{array} \right\} \overset{\textbf{❸}}{\rightarrow} m \angle 1 = m \angle 3$

Justifications ❶ If two $\parallel$ lines are intersected by a transversal, then corresponding ∡ are equal in measure. ❷ If $\parallel$ lines are intersected by a transversal, then alternate interior ∡ are = in measure.
❸ Substitution property

19. $m \angle T = 57°$; $m \angle S = 123°$; $m \angle R = 57°$
22. $m \angle 2 = 140°$; $m \angle 3 = 40°$; $m \angle 4 = 140°$
23. $\sqrt{5}, -\sqrt{5}$ **24.** $-2, 6$ **25.** $1, 5$ **26.** If an animal is a bird, then it has feathers.

Pages 424–425 Unit 7 Review and Assessment
1. baseball, lacrosse ball **2.** baseball, lacrosse ball, tennis ball, basketball, soccer ball, volleyball
3. $6.4 < x < 24$

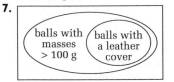

4. Ex. 1; Ex. 2 **5.** True. **6.** If a ball has a mass over 100 g, then it has a leather cover. False; the lacrosse ball is 143 g and has a solid rubber cover.
7.

```
 _____
|  _____    _____        |
| / balls \  / balls \        |
| / with  \ / with    \       |
| | masses  | a leather  |     |
| \ > 100 g / \ cover    /     |
|  _____/   _____/       |
|_____|
```

8. valid; indirect argument **9.** invalid; assumes exclusive *or* **10.** Answers may vary. An example is given. Premise: If I go to school, then I will take the history exam. If I take the history exam, then I will pass it. Conclusion: If I go to school, then I will pass the history exam. **11.** $x^2 = 36 \rightarrow x = 6$; $x = 6 \rightarrow x^2 = 36$; If the square of a number is 36, then the number is 6; if a number is 6, then its square is 36.
12. False; $x^2 = 36 \leftrightarrow x = 6$ or $x = -6$. **13.** A biconditional is true when both of its conditionals are true.
14. a. It is possible to fly from Cairo to Mexico City. From Cairo you can fly to Bombay because Flight 104 goes from Cairo to Bombay. From Bombay you can fly to Calcutta because Flight 201 goes from Bombay to Calcutta. From Calcutta you can fly to Mexico City because Flight 203 goes from Calcutta to Mexico City.
b. Statements (Justifications):
1. Cairo (Given)
2. Bombay (Flight 104: Cairo $\rightarrow$ Bombay)
3. Calcutta (Flight 201: Bombay $\rightarrow$ Calcutta)
4. Mexico City (Flight 203: Calcutta $\rightarrow$ Mexico City)
c. chain rule
15. a. *Given:* $3a^2 - 5 = 43$; $a > 0$ *Prove:* $a = 4$
Statements
$3a^2 - 5 = 43 \xrightarrow{\textbf{1}} 3a^2 = 48 \xrightarrow{\textbf{2}} a^2 = 16 \xrightarrow{\textbf{3}}$

$\left.\begin{array}{l} a = 4 \text{ or } a = -4 \\ a > 0 \end{array}\right\} \xrightarrow{\textbf{4}} a = 4$

Justifications ❶ Addition property of equality ❷ Division property of equality ❸ Definition of square root ❹ *Or* rule

b. *Given:* $3a^2 - 5 = 43$; $a > 0$
Prove: $a = 4$
Statements (Justifications):
1. $3a^2 - 5 = 43$ (Given)
2. $3a^2 = 48$ (Addition property of equality)
3. $a^2 = 16$ (Division property of equality)
4. $a = 4$ or $a = -4$ (Definition of square root)

5. $a > 0$ (Given)
6. $a = 4$ (*Or* rule [Steps 4 and 5])
16. Statements (Justifications):
1. $\angle 1$ and $\angle 2$ are vertical $\angle$s. (Given)
2. $m \angle 1 = m \angle 2$ (Vertical $\angle$s are = in measure.)
3. $\angle 1$ is supplementary to $\angle 2$. (Given)
4. $m \angle 1 + m \angle 2 = 180°$ (Definition of supplementary angles)
5. $m \angle 1 + m \angle 1 = 180°$ (Substitution property [Steps 2 and 4])
6. $2(m \angle 1) = 180°$ (Combine like terms.)
7. $m \angle 1 = 90°$ (Division property of equality)
8. $m \angle 2 = 90°$ (Substitution property [Steps 2 and 7])
9. $\angle 1$ and $\angle 2$ are right angles. (Definition of right angles)
17. Postulates are statements that are assumed to be true; definitions are biconditionals that give necessary and sufficient conditions for clarification; theorems are statements that are proved using previously proved theorems, definitions, and postulates.
18. *Given:* Lines j and k are parallel. Lines l and n are parallel.
Prove: $m \angle 1 = m \angle 3$
Statements (Justifications):
1. $l \parallel n$ (Given)
2. $m \angle 1 = m \angle 2$ (If two $\parallel$ lines are intersected by a transversal, then corresponding $\angle$s are = in measure.)
3. $j \parallel k$ (Given)
4. $m \angle 2 = m \angle 3$ (If two $\parallel$ lines are intersected by a transversal, then corresponding $\angle$s are = in measure.)
5. $m \angle 1 = m \angle 3$ (Substitution property [Steps 2 and 4])
19. a. 58°; $\angle 2$ and $\angle 1$ form a straight line and so are supplementary angles. **b.** 58°; $\angle 3$ and $\angle 1$ form a straight line and so are supplementary angles.
c. 122°; $\angle 4$ and $\angle 1$ are alternate interior angles.
d. 122°; $\angle 5$ and $\angle 1$ are corresponding angles.

Unit 8

Page 432 Talk it Over
1. $\angle BAC$ and the angle adjacent to $\angle DCA$
2. a. If two parallel lines are intersected by a transversal, then corresponding angles are equal in measure.
b. Yes. **3. a.** If two lines are intersected by a transversal and alternate interior angles are equal in measure, then the lines are parallel. **b.** If two lines are intersected by a transversal and co-interior angles are supplementary, then the lines are parallel.

Pages 435–438 Exercises and Problems
3. Theorem 8.2; If two lines are intersected by a transversal and co-interior $\angle$s are supplementary, then the lines are $\parallel$. **5.** Theorem 8.2; If two lines are intersect-

ed by a transversal and co-interior $\angle$s are supplementary, then the lines are ‖.   **7.** Theorem 8.1; If two lines are intersected by a transversal and alternate interior $\angle$s are = in measure, then the lines are ‖.
9. No.   **11.** No.   **13.** *Given:* $\overleftrightarrow{MQ} \parallel \overline{SR}$; $m\angle 1 = m\angle 2$
Prove: $m\angle 3 = m\angle 4$
Statements

$\overleftrightarrow{MQ} \parallel \overline{SR}$ ❶$\underset{\rightarrow}{\Big\{} \begin{array}{l} m\angle 3 = m\angle 1 \\ m\angle 4 = m\angle 2 \\ m\angle 1 = m\angle 2 \end{array} \Big\}$❷ $\rightarrow m\angle 3 = m\angle 4$

Justifications ❶ If two ‖ lines are intersected by a transversal, then alternate interior $\angle$s are = in measure. **❷** Substitution property
15. a. *Given:* Transversal t intersects lines k and l. $k \parallel l$, $t \perp l$
Prove: $t \perp k$
Statements (Justifications):
1. $k \parallel l$ (Given)
2. $m\angle 1 = m\angle 2$ (If two ‖ lines are intersected by a transversal, then corresponding $\angle$s are = in measure.)
3. $t \perp l$ (Given)
4. $m\angle 2 = 90°$ (Definition of perpendicular lines)
5. $m\angle 1 = 90°$ (Substitution property [Steps 2 and 4])
6. $t \perp k$ (Definition of perpendicular lines)
b. It is given that lines k and l are parallel lines. Therefore, $m\angle 1 = m\angle 2$ since if two ‖ lines are intersected by a transversal, then corresponding $\angle$s are = in measure. It is also given that line $t \perp l$, so $m\angle 2 = 90°$ by the definition of perpendicular lines. Substitute $m\angle 1$ for $m\angle 2$ in the equation $m\angle 2 = 90°$, and $m\angle 1 = 90°$. By definition of perpendicular lines, $t \perp k$.
19. *Given:* $\overline{GH} \perp \overline{HJ}$; $m\angle KJH = 90°$
Prove: $\overline{GH} \parallel \overline{KJ}$
Statements (Justifications):
1. $\overline{GH} \perp \overline{HJ}$; $m\angle KJH = 90°$ (Given)
2. $\overline{KJ} \perp \overline{HJ}$ (Definition of $\perp$ lines)
3. $\overline{GH} \parallel \overline{KJ}$ (If two lines are $\perp$ to the same transversal, then they are ‖.)
21. *Given:* Quadrilateral $ABCD$; $\angle A$, $\angle B$, $\angle C$, and $\angle D$ are right angles. *Prove:* Quadrilateral $ABCD$ is a parallelogram. Since $\angle A$ and $\angle B$ are right angles, $\overline{DA} \perp \overline{AB}$ and $\overline{CB} \perp \overline{AB}$. Then by Theorem 8.3, $\overline{AD} \parallel \overline{BC}$. Similarly, both $\angle A$ and $\angle D$ are right angles, so $\overline{CD} \perp \overline{DA}$ and $\overline{BA} \perp \overline{DA}$, then by Theorem 8.3, $\overline{DC} \parallel \overline{AD}$. Then, by definition, quadrilateral $ABCD$ is a parallelogram.   **24.** $m\angle A = m\angle C = 105°$; $m\angle B = 75°$ **25.** False; counterexamples may vary. An example is given. A kite is a four-sided figure that is not a parallelogram.   **26.** True.   **27.** $x = 20$

Pages 439–443 Talk it Over
1. a. Check students' work.   **b.** Yes.   **c.** No.
2. a. $x + 2x + (x + 10) = 180°$ **b.** 42.5°
c. $m\angle B = 42.5°$, $m\angle A = 85°$; $m\angle C = 52.5°$
3. a. $(x + 60) + x + 2x + x = 360°$ **b.** $m\angle R = 120°$, $m\angle S = 60°$; $m\angle T = 120°$, $m\angle U = 60°$ **c.** Both pairs of opposite angles are equal in measure. By Theorem 8.7, $RSTU$ is a parallelogram.   **4.** Answers may vary. An example is given. The angles are remote to, that is distant from, $\angle CAD$.   **5.** $\angle Q$ and $\angle R$ **6.** $\angle Q$ and $\angle R$ **7.** Yes. If the angle adjacent to the exterior angle is obtuse, then the exterior angle must be acute because the two angles form a straight angle which measures 180°.

Pages 443–448 Exercises and Problems
3. $c° = 55°$ **5.** $a° = 60°$, $b° = 50°$ **7.** $w° = 35°$, $x° = 120°$, $y° = 35°$ **13. a.** $m\angle A = 90°$, $m\angle B = 90°$, $m\angle C = 90°$, $m\angle D = 90°$ **b.** rectangle
15. a. $m\angle A = 60°$, $m\angle B = 120°$, $m\angle C = 90°$, $m\angle D = 90°$ **b.** trapezoid
17. *Given:* $JKLM$ is a quadrilateral. $m\angle J = m\angle L$, $m\angle K = m\angle M$
Prove: $JKLM$ is a parallelogram.
Statements (Justifications):
1. $JKLM$ is a quadrilateral. (Given)
2. $m\angle J + m\angle K + m\angle L + m\angle M = 360°$ (The sum of the measures of the $\angle$s of a quadrilateral is 360°.)
3. $m\angle J = m\angle L$, $m\angle K = m\angle M$ (Given)
4. $m\angle J + m\angle M + m\angle J + m\angle M = 360°$ (Substitution property [Steps 2 and 3])
5. $2(m\angle J + m\angle M) = 360°$ (Distributive property)
6. $m\angle J + m\angle M = 180°$ (Division property of equality)
7. $\angle J$ and $\angle M$ are supplementary angles. (Definition of supplementary angles)
8. $\overline{JK} \parallel \overline{ML}$ (If two lines are intersected by a transversal and co-interior $\angle$s are supplementary, then the lines are ‖.)
9. $m\angle J + m\angle K = 180°$ (Substitution property [Steps 3 and 6])
10. $\angle J$ and $\angle K$ are supplementary angles. (Definition of supplementary angles)
11. $\overline{JM} \parallel \overline{KL}$ (If two lines are intersected by a transversal and co-interior $\angle$s are supplementary, then the lines are ‖.)
12. $JKLM$ is a parallelogram. (Definition of parallelogram)
27. $\angle 2$ and $\angle 3$ **29.** $\angle 1$ and $\angle 3$ **31.** $x° = 30°$, $y° = 120°$ **33.** $x° = 110°$, $y° = 40°$, $z° = 70°$, $w° = 40°$
37. No.   **38.** No.   **39.** Yes.   **40.** Yes.   **41.** $x = 7$, $y = -5$ **42.** Multiply $8 \cdot x$ and $5 \cdot 12$ to get the equation $8x = 60$. Divide both sides by 8 to obtain $x = 7.5$.
43. $AF = DE$

Page 449 Talk it Over

1. a. $\angle A$ **b.** $\overline{DC}$ **c.** $m \angle B = m \angle E$; $m \angle C = m \angle C$; $m \angle A = m \angle D$; $AB = DE$; $AC = DC$; $BC = EC$; Since three pairs of sides are equal in measure and three pairs of angles are equal in measure, $\triangle ABC \cong \triangle DEC$ by definition. **d.** $\triangle ECD$ **2. a.** Yes. **b.** $\dfrac{DC}{FH} = \dfrac{5}{4}$; $\dfrac{EC}{GH} = \dfrac{5}{4}$; $\dfrac{DE}{FG} = \dfrac{5}{4}$; They are all equal. **c.** $m \angle D = m \angle F$; $m \angle E = m \angle G$; $m \angle C = m \angle H$; $\dfrac{DC}{FH} = \dfrac{EC}{GH} = \dfrac{DE}{FG}$; Since three pairs of angles are equal in measure and three pairs of sides are in proportion, $\triangle DEC \sim \triangle FGH$ by definition.

Pages 453–455 Exercises and Problems

1. $\angle A$ and $\angle D$; $\angle B$ and $\angle E$; $\angle C$ and $\angle F$ **3.** $\angle B = 70°$, $\angle C = 75°$, $\angle D = 35°$, $\angle F = 75°$ **5.** Angles of both triangles are $59°$, $60°$, and $61°$. **7.** $\triangle ABC$, $\triangle DEF$

9. *Given:* $\overline{AB} \parallel \overline{DE}$
Prove: $\triangle ABC \sim \triangle EDC$
Since $\overline{AB} \parallel \overline{DE}$, $m \angle A = m \angle E$ and $m \angle B = m \angle D$ because if two parallel lines are intersected by a transversal, then alternate interior angles are equal in measure. Then $\triangle ABC \sim \triangle EDC$ by the AA Similarity Postulate.

11. $\dfrac{8}{16} = \dfrac{12}{b}$ **13.** $\dfrac{RV}{RT} = \dfrac{RU}{RS} = \dfrac{VU}{TS}$

15. *Given:* $\overline{BC} \parallel \overline{DE}$
Prove: $\dfrac{AB}{BD} = \dfrac{AC}{CE}$
Statements (Justifications):
1. $\overline{BC} \parallel \overline{DE}$ (Given)
2. $m \angle ABC = m \angle ADE$ (If two $\parallel$ lines are intersected by a transversal, then corresponding $\angle$ are $=$ in measure.)
3. $m \angle A = m \angle A$ (Reflexive property of equality)
4. $\triangle ABC \sim \triangle ADE$ (AA Similarity)
5. $\dfrac{AB}{AD} = \dfrac{AC}{AE}$ (Corresponding sides of similar triangles are in proportion.)
6. $AD = AB + BD$; $AE = AC + CE$ (For any segment, the measure of the whole is equal to the sum of the measures of its non-overlapping parts.)
7. $\dfrac{AB}{AB + BD} = \dfrac{AC}{AC + CE}$ (Substitution property [Steps 5 and 6])
8. $AB(AC + CE) = AC(AB + BD)$ (Multiplication property of equality)
9. $AB \cdot AC + AB \cdot CE = AB \cdot AC + AC \cdot BD$ (Distributive property)
10. $AB \cdot CE = AC \cdot BD$ (Subtraction property of equality)
11. $\dfrac{AB}{BD} = \dfrac{AC}{CE}$ (Division property of equality)

21. a. I: $a° = 70°$; II: $b° = 50°$, $c° = 50°$; III: $d° = 80°$, $e° = 50°$; IV: $f° = 60°$; V: $g° = 110°$; VI: $h° = 50°$, $k° = 80°$ **b.** $\dfrac{1}{6}$ since $\triangle I$ is similar only to itself and not to any of the other 5 triangles. **23.** $m \angle 1 = 53°$, $m \angle 2 = 37°$, $m \angle 3 = 53°$, $m \angle 4 = 53°$, $m \angle 5 = 37°$

24. Product is not defined. **25.** $\begin{bmatrix} 1 & 2 & 3 \\ 2 & 5 & 6 \end{bmatrix} \begin{bmatrix} 1 \\ 2 \\ 3 \end{bmatrix} = \begin{bmatrix} 14 \\ 30 \end{bmatrix}$
26. a. $(3, -1)$ **b.** 10 units

Page 457 Checkpoint

1. Answers may vary. Examples are given. The sum of the measures of the angles of a triangle is $180°$. Any exterior angle of a triangle is equal in measure to the sum of the measures of its two remote interior angles. If two angles of one triangle are equal in measure to two angles of another triangle, then the two triangles are similar.
2. Format and approach of proof may vary. An example is given.
Given: $m \angle 1 = 80°$;
$m \angle 2 = 100°$
Prove: $k \parallel l$
Statements (Justifications):
1. $m \angle 1 = 80°$; $m \angle 2 = 100°$ (Given)
2. $m \angle 1 + m \angle 2 = 180°$ (Addition property of equality)
3. $\angle 1$ and $\angle 3$ are vertical angles. (Definition of vertical angles.)
4. $m \angle 1 = m \angle 3$ (Vertical $\angle$ are $=$ in measure.)
5. $m \angle 2 + m \angle 3 = 180°$ (Substitution property [Steps 2 and 4])
6. $\angle 2$ and $\angle 3$ are supplementary. (Definition of supplementary angles)
7. $k \parallel l$ (If two lines are intersected by a transversal and co-interior $\angle$ are supplementary, then the lines are $\parallel$.)
3. If a transversal is perpendicular to one of two parallel lines, then it is perpendicular to the other. (Theorem 8.4) **4. a.** $x° = 50°$ **b.** $x° = 62°$ **c.** $x° = 65°$
5. There is not enough information given to prove that the triangles are similar or that they are not similar. $m \angle A \neq m \angle D$, so $\triangle ABC \not\sim \triangle DEF$, but it is possible that $\angle C = 71°$ and $\angle F = 70°$. Then $\triangle ABC \sim \triangle FED$ would be true. **6. a.** $\triangle GHI$ and $\triangle JLK$
b. $\angle G$ and $\angle J$; $\angle H$ and $\angle L$; $\angle I$ and $\angle K$ **c.** $\overline{GH}$ and $\overline{JL}$; $\overline{GI}$ and $\overline{JK}$; $\overline{HI}$ and $\overline{LK}$ **d.** $\dfrac{GI}{JK} = \dfrac{GH}{JL} = \dfrac{HI}{LK}$ **7.** $x = 6$

Page 460 Talk it Over

1. $\overline{BC}$ **2.** ASA: angle-side-angle; AAS: angle-angle-side **3.** The plan of the proof would be exactly the same. The proofs would differ only in that the sides used in Steps 5 and 6 would be the sides included between the congruent angles. If Theorem 8.11 were already proven, you would only need to show that the two triangles are similar and so the third pair of angles are equal in measure. Then you would have two angles and a non-included side all congruent, and you could use Theorem 8.11.   **4.** Nadine would need to know that two pairs of angles are congruent and that a pair of non-included sides are congruent.

Pages 462–465 Exercises and Problems

1.

Sides	Included Angle
$\overline{XY}$ and $\overline{YZ}$	$\angle Y$
$\overline{YZ}$ and $\overline{ZX}$	$\angle Z$
$\overline{ZX}$ and $\overline{XY}$	$\angle X$

3. 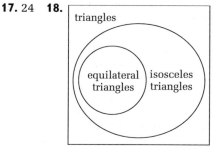   **5.** b

7. *Given:* $m \angle TUW = m \angle VUW$; $\overline{UW} \perp \overline{TV}$
Prove: $\triangle TUW \cong \triangle VUW$
Statements (Justifications):
1. $m \angle TUW = m \angle VUW$ (Given)
2. $UW = UW$ (Reflexive property of equality)
3. $\overline{UW} \perp \overline{TV}$ (Given)
4. $m \angle UWT = 90°$; $m \angle UWV = 90°$ (Definition of $\perp$ lines)
5. $m \angle UWT = m \angle UWV$ (Substitution property [Step 4])
6. $\triangle TUW \cong \triangle VUW$ (ASA)

11. a. $\triangle DEA \cong \triangle BEC$ **b.** $\triangle DAC \cong \triangle BCA$
13. *Given:* $\overline{AC} \perp \overline{CB}$; $\overline{DB} \perp \overline{BC}$; $m \angle 1 = m \angle 2$
Prove: $AC = DB$
Statements (Justifications):
1. $\overline{AC} \perp \overline{CB}$; $\overline{DB} \perp \overline{BC}$ (Given)
2. $m \angle ACB = 90°$; $m \angle DBC = 90°$ (Definition of $\perp$ lines)
3. $m \angle ACB = m \angle DBC$ (Substitution property [Step 2])
4. $m \angle 1 = m \angle 2$ (Given)
5. $BC = BC$ (Reflexive property of equality)
6. $\triangle ABC \cong \triangle DCB$ (ASA)
7. $AC = DB$ (CPCTE)
15. $x° = 10°$ **18.** $\triangle GEF \sim \triangle DEC$ by the AA Similarity Postulate (vertical angles at E, and $\angle EGF$ and $\angle EDC$ being alternate interior angles). $\triangle GEF \sim \triangle BCF$ by the Overlapping Similar Triangles Theorem ($\overline{GE} \parallel \overline{BC}$ because $GDBC$ is a parallelogram); $\triangle BCF \sim \triangle DEC$ by the AA Similarity Postulate (opposite angles B and D in the parallelogram and $\angle BCF$ and $\angle DEC$ being alternate interior angles).
19. obtuse   **20.** Whole and Parts Postulate: For any segment, the measure of the whole is equal to the sum of the measures of its non-overlapping parts.

Page 468 Talk it Over
1. $BC = EF$ **2.** $BC = EF$ and $AC = DF$
3. $m \angle A = m \angle D$ **4.** $m \angle C = m \angle F$

Pages 469–471 Exercises and Problems
1. Yes; SSS.   **3.** Yes; ASA.   **5.** AAS

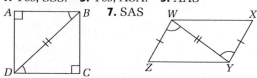   **7.** SAS

9. Using ASA: AC, $m \angle C$, $m \angle A$; AB, $m \angle A$, $m \angle B$; BC, $m \angle B$, $m \angle C$
Using SSS: AB, BC, AC
Using SAS: AC, AB, $m \angle A$; AB, BC, $m \angle B$; BC, AC, $m \angle C$
Using AAS: $m \angle A$, $m \angle B$, AC; $m \angle A$, $m \angle B$, BC; $m \angle B$, $m \angle C$, AB; $m \angle B$, $m \angle C$, AC; $m \angle A$, $m \angle C$, AB; $m \angle A$, $m \angle C$, BC
11. $x° = 45°$

16. *Given:* $\overline{RS} \parallel \overline{VT}$; $RW = TW$ *Prove:* $RS = TV$
Statements (Justifications):
1. $\overline{RS} \parallel \overline{VT}$ (Given)
2. $m \angle RSV = m \angle SVT$; $m \angle SRT = m \angle VTR$ (If two $\parallel$ lines are intersected by a transversal, then alternate interior $\angle\!\!\angle$ are = in measure.)
3. $RW = TW$ (Given)
4. $\triangle RSW \cong \triangle TVW$ (AAS)
5. $RS = TV$ (CPCTE)

17. 24   **18.**

triangles
equilateral triangles *isosceles triangles*

Pages 472–475 Talk it Over
1. $\overline{CB}$ **2.** $\angle B$ **3.** $\overline{AB}$ **4.** SAS   **5.** They are corresponding parts of congruent triangles.   **6.** They are equal in measure.   **7.** 30°; The triangle is equilateral and therefore equiangular having three 60° angles. Since $m \angle ABD = m \angle CBD$, both would be $\frac{1}{2}(60°) = 30°$.   **8.** 24 cm   **9.** A rhombus has four sides of equal measure. Thus, D is the same distance from A as from C (since $AD = DC$), and B is the same distance from A as from C (since $AB = BC$). Both B and D lie on the $\perp$ bisector of $\overline{AC}$ (Theorem 8.16), so $\overleftrightarrow{BD}$ is the perpendicular bisector of $\overline{AC}$.   **10.** $m \angle BAD = m \angle BCD$;

$m \angle ADC = m \angle ABC$; $m \angle ABD = m \angle CBD$;
$m \angle ADB = m \angle CDB$; $m \angle ABD = m \angle CDB$;
$m \angle ADB = m \angle CBD$; $m \angle ACD = m \angle BAC$;
$m \angle DAC = m \angle BCA$; $m \angle ACD = m \angle BCA$;
$m \angle DAC = m \angle BAC$

Pages 476–479 Exercises and Problems
1. $\triangle ABD$; $m \angle A = m \angle BDA$ **3.** $\triangle IJL$; $m \angle I =$
$m \angle ILJ = m \angle LJK$ **5.** $x° = 70°$ **7.** $x = 8$ **11.** $m \angle A =$
$m \angle ABC = 50°$; $m \angle ACB = 80°$; $m \angle BCD = 100°$;
$m \angle CBD = m \angle D = 40°$ **13.** $72°, 72°, 36°$
15. Given: $m \angle G = m \angle H$
Prove: $GI = HI$
Statements (Justifications):
1. $m \angle G = m \angle H$ (Given)
2. Draw the angle bisector $\overrightarrow{IJ}$ as a
   helping line. Then $m \angle GIJ =$
   $m \angle HIJ$. (Definition of angle bisector)
3. $IJ = IJ$ (Reflexive property of equality)
4. $\triangle GIJ \cong \triangle HIJ$ (AAS)
5. $GI = HI$ (CPCTE)

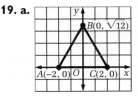

19. a. **b.** Using the distance formula gives $AB = 4$, $BC = 4$,
and $AC = 4$. Since $AB =$
$BC = AC = 4$, $\triangle ABC$ is
equilateral. Then $\triangle ABC$ is
equiangular as well be-
cause if a triangle is equi-
lateral, then it is equiangular, with three 60° angles.
21. Given: $RP = RQ$
Prove: R lies on the perpendicular bisector of $\overline{PQ}$.
Statements (Justifications):
1. $RP = RQ$ (Given)
2. Draw a line from R passing through the midpoint
   M of $\overline{PQ}$ so that $PM = QM$. (Definition of midpoint)
3. $\overleftrightarrow{RM}$ bisects $\overline{PQ}$. (Definition of a segment bisector)
4. $RM = RM$ (Reflexive property of equality)
5. $\triangle PRM \cong \triangle QRM$ (SSS)
6. $m \angle 1 = m \angle 2$ (CPCTE)
7. $m \angle 1 + m \angle 2 = m \angle PMQ$ (For any angle, the measure of the whole is equal to the sum of the measures of its non-overlapping parts.)
8. $m \angle PMQ = 180°$ (If the sides of an angle form a
   straight line, then the angle is a straight angle
   with measure 180°.)
9. $m \angle 1 + m \angle 2 = 180°$ (Substitution property
   [Steps 7 and 8])
10. $m \angle 1 + m \angle 1 = 180°$ (Substitution property
    [Steps 6 and 9])
11. $2(m \angle 1) = 180°$ (Distributive property)
12. $m \angle 1 = 90°$ (Division property of equality)
13. $\overleftrightarrow{RM} \perp \overline{PQ}$ (Definition of perpendicular)

14. $\overleftrightarrow{RM}$ is the perpendicular bisector of $\overline{PQ}$. R lies on
    the perpendicular bisector of $\overline{PQ}$. (Definition of
    perpendicular bisector [Steps 3 and 13])

23. a. **b.** Using the distance formula, $HK =$
$JK = 5$ and $HL = JL =$
$3\sqrt{2}$. Thus K is the
same distance from
H as from J, and L is
the same distance
from H as from J. By
Theorem 8.16, both

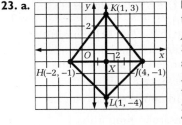

K and L lie on the $\perp$ bisector of $\overline{HJ}$, so $\overleftrightarrow{KL}$ is the $\perp$
bisector of $\overline{HJ}$. **25.** Since $\angle ADC$ and $\angle BDC$ are right
angles, $DA = DB$, and $DC = DC$, you know $\triangle ADC \cong$
$\triangle BDC$ by SAS. **28.** Yes; SAS. **29.** $(x - 7)(x + 12)$
30. $x = 24$ **31.** 30 square units

Page 480 Checkpoint
1. Summaries may vary. An example is given.
I would determine which sides and/or angles I knew
to be equal in measure and how they were related.
If I had two sides and an included angle, I would use
SAS. If I has two angles and an included side,
I would use ASA. If the side was not included,
I would use AAS. If I had three sides, I would use
SSS. **2.** The triangles are congruent by ASA, so
$x = 7$, $y = 8$, and $z° = 50°$ **3.** $\triangle ABC$ and $\triangle EDF$; SSS
4. $\triangle GHI$ and $\triangle JKL$; SAS **5.** $m \angle N = m \angle Q$, $m \angle O =$
$m \angle R$, or $\overline{MN} \cong \overline{PQ}$ **6.** $\triangle STU$ is isosceles since
$ST = TU$.

7. $m \angle A = m \angle C = 46°$; $m \angle B = 88°$

Pages 482–483 Talk it Over
1. a. RS **b.** QR **2.** $\triangle MXN \sim \triangle MYX \sim \triangle XYN$
3. c **4.** b **5.** $b + c$

Pages 485–488 Exercises and Problems
1.
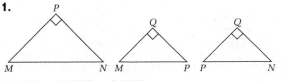
$\triangle MNP \sim \triangle MPQ \sim \triangle PNQ$
3. Sketch both triangles separately. Mark all angles
that are equal in measure.

5. *Given:* $\triangle ABC$ with right $\angle C$; $\overline{CD}$ is the altitude to the hypotenuse. *Prove:* $a^2 + b^2 = c^2$

Statements (Justifications):
1. $\triangle ABC$ with right $\angle C$; $\overline{CD}$ is the altitude to the hypotenuse. (Given)
2. $\triangle ABC \sim \triangle CBD$; $\triangle ABC \sim \triangle ACD$ (If the altitude is drawn to the hypotenuse of a right triangle, then the two triangles formed are similar to the original triangle and to each other.)
3. $\frac{c}{a} = \frac{a}{e}$; $\frac{c}{b} = \frac{b}{f}$ (Definition of similar triangles; corresponding sides are in proportion.)
4. $ce = a^2$; $cf = b^2$ (Multiplication property of equality)
5. $ce + cf = a^2 + b^2$ (Addition property of equality)
6. $c(e + f) = a^2 + b^2$ (Distributive property)
7. $e + f = c$ (For any segment, the measure of the whole is equal to the sum of the measures of its non-overlapping parts.)
8. $c(c) = a^2 + b^2$ (Substitution property [Steps 6 and 7])
9. $c^2 = a^2 + b^2$ (Definition of exponents)

7. $4\sqrt{2} \approx 5.7$ **11.** $x = 6$ or $x = -6$ **13.** 12 **15.** 8
17. 48 **21.** $x = 6$ **23.** $x = 2$, $y = 2\sqrt{2} \approx 2.8$
25. $AC = 30$ **27. a.** $AC = 5$ **b.** $m \angle ABD = 60°$; $m \angle ABC = 30°$ **c.** $BC = 5\sqrt{3} \approx 8.7$ **28.** 24
29.

(Either $\angle L$ or $\angle J$ can be the right angle.)

Pages 489–491 Talk it Over
1. $m \angle A = m \angle B = 45°$ **2.** because the angles of an isosceles right triangle always have measures of 45°, 45° and 90° **3.** $12\sqrt{2}$ cm **4.** $8\sqrt{2} \approx 11.3$ cm
5. Yes; the sum of the angle measures is 180°, so $\angle O = 45°$. If two angles of a triangle are equal in measure, then the sides opposite those angles are equal in measure. $\triangle MNO$ has two sides equal in measure, so it is isosceles by definition. **6.** $MO = NO \approx 7.1$

Pages 493–496 Exercises and Problems
1. $QR = 10$; $PR = 10\sqrt{3}$ **3.** $EG = 5$; $EF = 5\sqrt{2}$
5. 173.2 ft **7.** 127.3 ft **9.** b **11.** $SV = 2$; $VT = 2\sqrt{3}$
13. $KL = 4\sqrt{2}$; $KN = 11$ **19.** $x° = 60°$ **21.** $z° = 45°$
23. $x = 6\sqrt{2} \approx 8.5$ **25.** $w° = 45°$ **27.** $z \approx 12.9$
29. $\sin \angle MNO = \frac{4}{5} = 0.8$; $\cos \angle MNO = \frac{3}{5} = 0.6$;
$\tan \angle MNO = \frac{4}{3} \approx 1.33$ **31. a.** $\sin 60° = \cos 30° = \frac{\sqrt{3}}{2}$
b. $\sin 30° = \cos 60° = \frac{1}{2}$ **c.** $\tan 60° = \sqrt{3}$;
$\tan 30° = \frac{1}{\sqrt{3}}$ **d.** If $\angle A$ and $\angle B$ are complementary, then $\sin A = \cos B$ and $\tan A = \frac{1}{\tan B}$.

In $\triangle ABC$ with right $\angle C$, let $x° = m \angle A$ and $(90 - x)° = m \angle B$. Then $\sin x° = \sin A = \frac{BC}{AB}$, $\cos (90 - x)° = \cos B = \frac{BC}{AB}$, $\tan x° = \frac{BC}{AC}$,
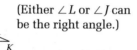

33. $\triangle EHR \sim \triangle HJR \sim \triangle EJH$ **34.** $OC = \sqrt{7^2 + 5^2} = \sqrt{49 + 25} = \sqrt{74}$; $BD = \sqrt{(10 - 3)^2 + (0 - 5)^2} = \sqrt{7^2 + (-5)^2} = \sqrt{49 + 25} = \sqrt{74}$ **35.** $h \approx 2.10$ cm
36. $x = 5.6$ yd **37.** $z = 8$ in.

Pages 498–499 Unit 8 Review and Assessment
1. *Given:* $\overline{AB} \parallel \overline{FC}$; $\angle B$ and $\angle F$ are right angles.
Prove: $\overline{FE} \parallel \overline{CD}$
Statements (Justifications):
1. $\overline{AB} \parallel \overline{FC}$ (Given)
2. $m \angle B = m \angle FCD$ (If two $\parallel$ lines are intersected by a transversal, then corresponding $\angle\!\!\angle$ are = in measure.)
3. $\angle B$ is a right angle. (Given)
4. $m \angle B = 90°$ (Definition of a right angle)
5. $m \angle FCD = 90°$ (Substitution property [Steps 2 and 4])
6. $\angle FCD$ is a right angle. (Definition of a right angle)
7. $\overline{FC} \perp \overline{CD}$ (Definition of perpendicular lines)
8. $\angle F$ is a right angle. (Given)
9. $\overline{FC} \perp \overline{FE}$ (Definition of perpendicular lines)
10. $\overline{FE} \parallel \overline{CD}$ (If two lines are $\perp$ to the same transversal, then they are $\parallel$.)
2. 148° **3.** Yes. If both pairs of opposite angles of a quadrilateral are = in measure, the quadrilateral is a parallelogram. **4.** $m \angle 1 = 120°$
5. *Given:* $\overline{AB} \parallel \overline{DC}$ *Prove:* $\triangle AEB \sim \triangle CED$
Statements (Justifications):
1. $\overline{AB} \parallel \overline{CD}$ (Given)
2. $m \angle BAE = m \angle DCE$ (If two $\parallel$ lines are intersected by a transversal, then alternate interior $\angle\!\!\angle$ are = in measure.)
3. $m \angle AEB = m \angle CED$ (Vertical $\angle\!\!\angle$ are = in measure.)
4. $\triangle AEB \sim \triangle CED$ (AA Similarity)
6. $x = 20$, $y = 25$
7. *Given:* $m\angle 1 = m \angle 2$; $BD = DF$
Prove: D is the midpoint of $\overline{CE}$.
Statements (Justifications):
1. $m \angle 1 = m \angle 2$ (Given)
2. $\overline{AC} \parallel \overline{EG}$ (If two lines are intersected by a transversal and alternate interior $\angle\!\!\angle$ are = in measure, then the lines are $\parallel$.)
3. $m \angle BCD = m \angle FED$ (If two $\parallel$ lines are intersected by a transversal, then alternate interior $\angle\!\!\angle$ are = in measure.)
4. $\angle BDC$ and $\angle FDE$ are vertical angles. (Definition of vertical angles)
5. $m \angle BDC = m \angle FDE$ (Vertical $\angle\!\!\angle$ are = in measure.)

6. $BD = DF$ (Given)

7. $\triangle BDC \cong \triangle FDE$ (AAS)

8. $ED = CD$ (CPCTE)

9. D is the midpoint of $\overline{CE}$. (Definition of midpoint)

8. Answers may vary. Examples are given. bridges, roofs, swing sets, tripods, braces under a folding table, geodesic domes, trusses in houses, stepladders **9.** *Given: B is the midpoint of $\overline{AE}$, $\overline{FC}$, and $\overline{GD}$.*

Prove: $\triangle ABG \cong \triangle EBD$

Statements (Justifications):

1. B is the midpoint of $\overline{AE}$, $\overline{FC}$, and $\overline{GD}$. (Given)

2. $AB = BE$; $GB = BD$ (Definition of midpoint)

3. $\angle ABG$ and $\angle EBD$ are vertical angles. (Definition of vertical angles)

4. $m \angle ABG = m \angle EBD$ (Vertical $\angle$s are = in measure.)

5. $\triangle ABG \cong \triangle EBD$ (SAS)

10. agree; A triangle can have at most one right or obtuse angle since the sum of the measures of the angles is 180°. Therefore, two angles of a triangle must be acute, and in an isosceles triangle, these are the base angles since they are equal in measure.
11. 35°, 35°, 110° **12. a.**

L(−1, 4) J(2, 2) K(−3, 1)

b. $JL = \sqrt{(2-(-1))^2 + (2-4)^2} = \sqrt{9+4} = \sqrt{13}$; $KL = \sqrt{(-3-(-1))^2 + (1-4)^2} = \sqrt{4+9} = \sqrt{13}$. Since sides JL and KL are equal in measure, $\triangle JKL$ is isosceles. **13.** Since point B is the same distance from points A and C, and D is the midpoint of $\overline{AC}$, $\overleftrightarrow{BD}$ is the perpendicular bisector of $\overline{AC}$ by Theorem 8.16.
14. 20 **15. a.** $\triangle HKJ \sim \triangle HLK \sim \triangle KLJ$ **b.** $8\sqrt{5} \approx 17.9$
c. about 26.8 **16.** $AB = 7\sqrt{2}$; $\sin A = \cos A = \frac{1}{\sqrt{2}}$;
$\tan A = 1$ **17.** $BC = 4$; $AC = 4\sqrt{3}$; $\sin A = \frac{1}{2}$;
$\cos A = \frac{\sqrt{3}}{2}$; $\tan A = \frac{1}{\sqrt{3}}$ **18.** $x = 5\sqrt{3} \approx 8.7$
19. $x \approx 26.5$

Unit 9

Pages 505–507 Talk it Over

1. First simplify 468^2 and 468.125^2, then subtract 468^2 from both sides of the equation. Undo the squaring on each side to find the positive square root.
2. It is useful because it simplifies the situation so that it can be easily modeled by using the Pythagorean theorem. The answer will only be an approximation, however, because a buckled railroad track is actually curved. **3.** None of the five expressions is a polynomial because each contains a term that is not a monomial. None of the following can be

written with a whole-number exponent: $1000g^{-3}$, $1000g^{-2}$, $1000g^{-1}$, $\pi r^{1/2}$, $3\left(\frac{1}{b}\right)$, $\frac{y}{y+1}$, $\frac{4x^2}{y}$, $\frac{3x}{y}$. **4.** Yes; $2(x + 3)$ is a polynomial because it can be written as a term or a sum of terms with exponents that are whole numbers: $2(x + 3) = 2x + 6$. **5. a.** 4 **b.** $-\pi x^4 + \sqrt{2}x^3 + 30$ **c.** zero

Pages 509–512 Exercises and Problems

3. $\pi x^2(x + 3) = 200\pi$ or $x^2(x + 3) = 200$

5. $\dfrac{x}{x+3} = \dfrac{4}{x+2}$

7. $\dfrac{50,015}{2} = 25,007.5$

$\dfrac{50,000}{2} = 25,000$

500 m = 50,000 cm

$25,000^2 + d^2 = 25,007.5^2$
13. −5 **15.** Yes. **17.** Yes; each term can be written with exponents that are whole numbers. **19.** Yes; each term can be written with exponents that are whole numbers. **21.** No; $3x^{1/2}$ cannot be written as a polynomial. **23. a.** Yes. **b.** Yes; all linear equations can be written in the form $ax + by = c$, which is a polynomial equation for all values of a, b, and c.

25. $\frac{2}{7}$ or about 0.29 **30. a.** $MN = 2\sqrt{2}$; $NO = 4$; $MP = 2$; $PO = 2\sqrt{3}$; $MO = 2 + 2\sqrt{3}$ **b.** $\sin PNO = \frac{\sqrt{3}}{2} \approx 0.8660$; $\cos PNO = 0.5$; $\tan PNO = \sqrt{3} \approx 1.732$

31. $-4i - 1$ **32.** -10 **33.** 5 **34.** $\frac{1}{n^4}$ **35.** $x^{1/2}$
36. 1; 1; 1

Pages 513–516 Talk it Over

1. a. 5 **b.** 6; The exponent of the product is the sum of the exponents of the quotient. **2.** x^{18} **3. a.** 2 **b.** 2; −2 **c.** 0; The exponent of the quotient is the difference of the exponents of the numerator and denominator.
4. x^4 **5.** $3x^3$ **6.** $4xy^2$ **7.** 5 **8.** No; he should factor $x^2 - 2x - 15$ as the product of two binomials, $x - 5$ and $x + 3$. **9. a.** 3; 3 **b.** 2; 2; The exponents of the numerator and denominator of the quotient on the right are both the same as the exponent of the quotient on the left. **10.** $\dfrac{a^4}{b^4}$ **11. a.** 2; 2; 2; 6

b. 5; 5; 10; The exponent on the right is the product of the exponents on the left. **12.** a^{14} **13. a.** 2; 2
b. 4; 4; $16x^4$; The exponent of each factor on the right is the same as the exponent of the product on the left.
14. a^3b^3 **15.** $3^{1/2} \cdot 3^{1/2} = 3^{(1/2 + 1/2)} = 3^1 = 3$
16. $(x^{1/3})^3 = x^{(1/3)(3)} = x^1 = x$; The cube root of x is the number whose cube is x. Since $(x^{1/3})^3 = x$, $x^{1/3}$ is the cube root of x.

1. product of powers rule; quotient of powers rule

3. $\frac{t^3}{x^4}$ 5. $27t^4$ 7. $\frac{16b^4}{a}$ 9. d^8 11. $\frac{3a^8}{4}$ 13. $3xy^2$

15. 64 and 32; $2^{(3 \cdot 2)} \neq 2^3 \cdot 2^2$ 17. 4 and 20;
$(6-4)^2 \neq 6^2 - 4^2$ 19. $\frac{9}{16}$ and $\frac{9}{4}$; $\left(\frac{3}{4}\right)^2 \neq \frac{3^2}{4}$ 21. $2a^3$

23. a^5 25. $x^2(x-5)(x+3)$ 27. $3p^2(3pq+5)$
29. $7x^2y(7x - 5y^4)$ 49. a. Equations may vary.

Example: $\frac{x}{x+2} = \frac{4}{5}$ b. Yes. 50. 6 51. $\frac{155}{12} = 12\frac{11}{12}$ or

about 12.9 52. 14 53. 5 54. $x = -3$ or $x = 2$

1. Rose's; From New York City to Istanbul, the plane is flying *with* the wind. The speed of the wind increases the plane's speed. From Istanbul to New York City, the plane is flying *against* the wind. The speed of the wind decreases the plane's speed.
2. 2487.5 miles 3. No; the point of no return is the point at which the flying *times* to the two cities are the same. The halfway point is the point at which the *distances* to the two cities is the same. Because of the effects of the wind, the plane flying from New York City to Istanbul reaches the point of no return before it reaches the halfway point, and the plane flying from Istanbul to New York reaches the point of no return after it reaches the halfway point. 4. When 2 is substituted into the original equation, it produces a fraction with a denominator of zero. Since division by zero is undefined, 2 is an extraneous solution.
5. $y + 2$

1. Substituting 4 in the original equation produces two fractions with denominators of zero. Since division by zero is undefined, 4 is not a solution of the original equation. 3. $-\frac{2}{3}$ 5. 5 7. 0.25, 2

9. a. about 635 mi/h b. about 545 mi/h 11. 3, −1
13. 2, 3 15. 3, 1 19. The bases are 4 in. long and 7 in. long. 21. 75 min 26. m^3n^6 27. $\frac{5b^3}{a^3}$

28. $x^{12}y^6$ 29. RT: 14 cm; RS: $7\sqrt{3}$ cm $\approx$ 12.1 cm
30. HI: 13 m; HJ: $13\sqrt{2}$ m $\approx$ 18.4 m 31. DE: 5 in.;
FD: $5\sqrt{3}$ in. $\approx$ 8.7 in.
32. $x = 3$ and −3 33. −7

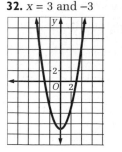   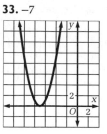

34. 0

1. If any term of an equation contains an exponent that is not a whole number, the equation is not a polynomial equation. 2. a. If g is the growth rate, the amount can be expressed as $7000 + 7000g + 7000g^2$. b. $7000 + 7000g + 7000g^2 = 25,000$ 3. Yes; each term can be written with exponents that are whole numbers. 4. No; $3x^{1/2}$ cannot be written with a whole-number exponent. 5. Yes; each term can be written with exponents that are whole numbers.
6. No; the term cannot be written with whole-number exponents. 7. $\frac{z^3}{y^2}$ 8. $\frac{m^6}{n^{12}}$ 9. $\frac{-2}{a^5}$ 10. $\frac{1}{d^4}$
11. $\frac{16}{f^{10}}$ 12. $\frac{p^3q^9}{2}$ 13. 0, 1 14. 2, −1
15. 10 members

1. It is the only graph that has a double zero of −3.
2. For all values of x less than −3, $x + 3$ is negative and $(x-2)^2$ is positive. The product of a negative number and a positive number is always a negative number.

3. a. once b. $x = -3$ c. −3; −3 is a triple zero.
5. a. once b. $x = -8$ c. −8; −8 is a triple zero.
7. a. twice b. $x = 1$ and $x = -4$ c. 1 and −4; 1 is a double zero. 9. a. twice b. $x = 7$ and $x = -4$ c. 7 and −4; −4 is a double zero. 11. quadratic 13. linear
15. quadratic 17. C 19. A 21. D 34. 2 35. 3, 2
36. $\frac{1}{2}$, 3 37. parallelogram 38. squares
39. rhombus 40. 3, $-\frac{1}{2}$ 41. $\frac{3+\sqrt{3}i}{2}, \frac{3-\sqrt{3}i}{2}$
42. $\frac{2}{3}, -\frac{5}{2}$

1. $1 - p$ 2. $(1-p)^3$ 3. $1 - (1-p)^3$; the probability that at least one light will work 4. $p^3 - 3p^2 + 3p$
5. No; two of the solutions, $1.5 + \frac{i\sqrt{3}}{2}$ and $1.5 - \frac{i\sqrt{3}}{2}$, are not real numbers. 6. You could solve this equation by factoring and using the zero-product property.

Pages 538–540 Exercises and Problems

1. The expression $p^3 - 3p^2 + 3p - 0.98$ cannot be written as a product of linear factors. **3.** $0, -1 + i,$ $-1 - i$ **5.** $0, -4, 1$ **7.** $-6, 2$ **9.** Solve by graphing. **11.** Solve by graphing. **13.** $0, 5, -3$ **21.** -1 and -3; -3 is a double zero. **22.** $0, 2,$ and -3; no multiple zeros **23.** -5; -5 is a triple zero. **24.** No; the conditional "If $(x - 1)(x + 2) = 0$, then $x = 1$" is not true since x can also be -2. **25.** $t = \frac{x}{2} - 2$ **26.** $t = \frac{y}{2} + 2$
27. $t = 9 - \frac{x}{2}$

Pages 544–548 Exercises and Problems

1. In the first equation, the control variable is t, and the dependent variable is x. In the second equation, the control variable is t, and the dependent variable is y. **3. a.** about 3.5 m **b.** about 1.3 s **c.** about 1.9 s after beginning its flight **5. a.** $t = \frac{x + 3}{4}$ **b.** $y = \frac{x + 3}{2}$

7. a. $t = 2 - x$ **b.** $y = \frac{3 - 4x + x^2}{2 - x}$ **9. a.** about 719 meters **b.** about 5.5 seconds

11. a.

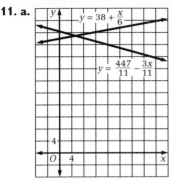

b. No. At (6, 39), Bakham has been running 6 s and the ball reaches this point in 5 s. Time is not indicated here. **c.** the point at which Bakham's path and the ball's path cross

13. a. $x_1 = 9t$; $y_1 = 1$ **b.** $x_2 = 1774 - 25(t - 33)$; $y_2 = 1$

c.

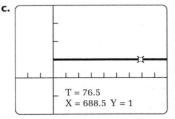

76.5 months after the start of the Central Pacific or May, 1869 **d.** The Central Pacific laid about 688.5 miles of track and the Union Pacific laid about 1087.5 miles of track.
e. Answers may vary. An example is given. The Central Pacific Railroad Company was laying track in the mountains, whereas the Union Pacific Railroad Company was laying track on flat land. **18.** $0, 1, 2$
19. $0, 1 + 2\sqrt{2}, 1 - 2\sqrt{2}$ **20.** $0, \frac{-5 + \sqrt{13}}{6}, \frac{-5 - \sqrt{13}}{6}$

21. $\begin{bmatrix} 5 & 4 \\ -1 & -1 \end{bmatrix}$ **22.** $\begin{bmatrix} 10 \\ -10 \\ -2 \end{bmatrix}$ **23.** $\begin{bmatrix} 3 & 0 & 7 \\ -6 & 3 & 0 \\ -8 & 7 & 14 \end{bmatrix}$

24. $m \angle 2 = 140°$; $m \angle 3 = 40°$; $m \angle 4 = 140°$
25. pyramid; base; triangles **26.** prism; bases; rectangles

Pages 550–552 Unit 9 Review and Assessment

1. $\frac{3.25 + x}{12 + x} = 0.30$ **2.** $w(2w + 8)$; fencing required will be $4w + 8$. **3.** No; $\frac{x - 3}{x}$ is a rational expression but is not a polynomial. **4.** Yes; it consists only of terms with whole-number exponents. **5.** No; both terms cannot be written with whole-number exponents. **6.** No; both terms cannot be written with whole-number exponents. **7.** No; the expression cannot be written as a monomial or a sum of monomials with whole number exponents. **8.** Yes; it consists only of terms with whole-number exponents.

9. $48m^4$ **10.** $\frac{1}{a^2}$ **11.** $\frac{2}{x^2 y^5}$ **12.** $r^3 s^3 t^3$
13. $\frac{w^6}{5}$ **14.** $\frac{q^3}{p^3}$ **15.** -1 **16.** $\frac{1}{2}$ **17.** $\sqrt{3}, -\sqrt{3}$
18. a. $\frac{5600}{x} - 1 = \frac{5600}{x + 100}$ **b.** 800 bottles per hour
19. The other solution, -800, does not make sense. The number of bottles capped per hour must be positive. **20.** $-2, 0,$ and 5; no multiple zeros **21.** -3 and 1; -3 is a double zero. **22.** 4; 4 is a triple zero. **23.** -6 and 2; -6 is a double zero. **24.** Answers may vary. Example: $y = x(x + 2)^2$ **25.** C **26.** A **27.** D **28.** B **29.** $0, 2 + \sqrt{3} \approx 3.7, 2 - \sqrt{3} \approx 0.27$ **30.** $-4,$ $-3, \frac{1}{2}$ **31.** $0, 3$ **32.** about 1.2

33. a, b.

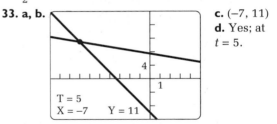

T = 5
X = –7   Y = 11

c. $(-7, 11)$ **d.** Yes; at $t = 5$.

Unit 10

Pages 557–559 Talk it Over

1. Mary Conlan's table is rectangular, has four legs and a drawer centered lengthwise beneath the top base. Many tables are designed this way. Mary's table is different from other tables in that its legs are connected near the bottom by wooden slats, and there is also some type of structure underneath the drawer.
2. Yes; the top view only shows that the top base is rectangular. A furniture maker can see the straight edges of the top base from the front and side views and determine that the top base must be rectangular with length given in the front view and width given in the side view. **3.** Answers may vary. An example is given. All parallel horizontal or vertical cross sections of a cube are congruent. Counterexample: Two parallel cross sections of a sphere may be circles with different diameters. **4.** Answers may vary. Examples: a page of a book, cards in a deck, coins in a pile

9. a. 9 cubes **b.** Jade, Luisa, Keiko, and Miika are in order clockwise. **11.** 7 pyramids **13.** Each column contains a pyramid, a double pyramid, and a prism made from the same base.

15. an octagonal prism **17.** a pentagonal pyramid

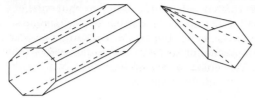

19. not possible; The number of vertices of a prism must be even. **21.** about 3000 m
23. Estimates may vary. Example: about 2%
25. **27.**

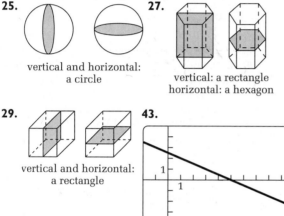

vertical and horizontal:
a circle

vertical: a rectangle
horizontal: a hexagon

29. **43.**

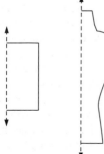

vertical and horizontal:
a rectangle

44. d **45. a.** about 198 cubic in.
b. about 66 cubic in.

1. For each figure, the axis is a line passing through the centers of the circles that form the top and bottom of the object. The drawings show the plane figure and the axis.

2. Answers may vary. Examples: a conical lamp shade, a ball, a glass jar, a funnel **3.** For each object, a horizontal cross section is a circle. A vertical cross section has the shape of the rotated plane figure along with its reflection across the axis of rotation.

4. Surface area $= 2\pi r^2 + 2\pi rh = 2\pi(4)^2 + 2\pi(4)(3) = 56\pi$; Volume $= \pi r^2 h = \pi(4)^2(3) = 48\pi$ **5.** a cylinder with radius 3 and height 4 **6.** Answers may vary. Examples are given. **a.** y-axis: A horizontal cross section is a circle with radius 4; a vertical cross section can be a rectangle 3 units high. x-axis: A horizontal cross section can be a rectangle 4 units wide; a vertical cross section can be a circle with radius 3. **b.** y-axis: A horizontal cross section is a circle with radius 4; a vertical cross section can be a rectangle 3 units high. x-axis: A horizontal cross section is a rectangle, a pair of rectangles or a segment 4 units long; a vertical cross section can be a ring.

3. cone **5.** a figure that looks like a cone with the top cut off. **7.** a cone with radius 6 and height 4
9. a cone with radius 4 and height 6 **11.** 32π
15. Yes; a triangle can be rotated around an axis to form a cone. **17.** Yes; a semicircle can be rotated around an axis to form a sphere.
19. **24.** Drawings may vary. Examples are given.

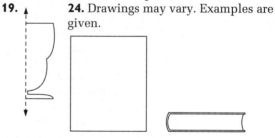

25. about 7%
26. Statements (Justifications):
1. P is on the perpendicular bisector of $\overline{AB}$. (Given)
2. $\triangle PCA$ and $\triangle PCB$ are right triangles. (Definitions of right $\triangle$s and perpendicular bisector)
3. $PC = PC$ (Reflexive)
4. $AC = BC$ (Definition of a bisector)
5. $\triangle PCA$ is congruent to $\triangle PCB$. (SAS)
6. $PA = PB$ (CPCTE)

1. The circle determined by the third station would intersect the first two circles at one of their intersection points. **2.** The 1994 earthquake was near the point in Los Angeles, California. **3.** If a point is the same distance from both endpoints of a line segment, then it lies on the perpendicular bisector of the segment. **4.** point M, the only point on both the sphere with radius 5 in. centered at A and the sphere with radius 5 in. centered at B. **5.** No points meet the condition.

3. a. a circle with center P and radius 2 m
b. a hemisphere with center P and radius 2 m

5. two points on the perpendicular bisector of $\overline{AB}$, each 4 inches from A and B **7.** No points meet the condition.   **9.** the midpoint of $\overline{AB}$ **11.** a dome-shaped space figure consisting of the points on a sphere with center at the control room and radius 60 mi that are on or above the intersection of the sphere and the plane of the ground (The ground is not actually a plane, nor is the control room a point.)   **15.** in a plane: a plane figure consisting of two parallel line segments each 5 cm from the given segment with their endpoints on each side of the given segment joined by a semicircle with center at the endpoint of the given segment and radius 5 cm; in space: a capsule-shaped figure consisting of a cylinder with radius 5 cm and length that of the segment with each end of the cylinder a hemisphere with center at the endpoint of the segment and radius 5 cm   **23.** a cone with height 2 and radius 5; $\frac{50\pi}{3}$ **24.** The conclusion assumes that the converse is automatically true, which may not be the case. Marya may have decided to write a letter to her cousin without having first received a letter herself. Her cousin may or may not write back.   **25.** $\left(-1\frac{1}{2}, 2\frac{1}{2}\right)$ **26.** $(3, -4)$ **27.** $\left(-1\frac{3}{4}, 6\frac{1}{2}\right)$

Page 577 Checkpoint
1. Any cross section of a sphere is a circle with a radius no bigger than the radius of the sphere. A sphere can be produced by rotating a semicircle about its diameter. A sphere is the set of all the points in space that are a given distance from a given point.

2.   **3.**

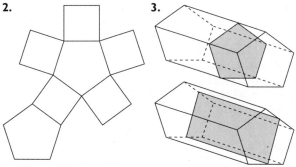

4. a cylinder with radius 8 and height 6   **5.** a cone with radius 2 and height 5   **6.** two points on the perpendicular bisector of $\overline{AB}$ each 5 in. from A and B **7.** No points meet the condition.   **8.** a plane that is perpendicular to $\overline{EF}$ and intersects $\overline{EF}$ at its midpoint

Pages 578–579 Talk it Over
1. Thailand   **2.** Venezuela and the Ivory Coast   **3.** about $8 billion   **4.** the x-axis   **5.** Start at the origin. Move 6 units toward you on the x-axis, 4 units to the right parallel to the y-axis, and -1 unit parallel to the z-axis.   **6.** No; the order in which you move will take you along a different path, but each path will lead you to the same point, provided you move the correct number of units along each axis as indicated by the coordinates of the ordered triple.

Pages 581–583 Exercises and Problems
1. 1980   **3.** about 42.5 gallons   **5.** An ordered triple (x, y, z) is three numbers that designate the position of a point in three-dimensional space. The x-coordinate, y-coordinate, and z-coordinate give the point's distance along each axis.   **9.** Volume = 30 cubic units; Surface area = 62 square units   **11.** $(-1, -1, -1)$ **13.** $\left(3, -\frac{1}{2}, 0\right)$

15. a–c.

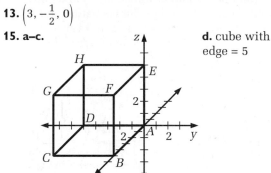

d. cube with edge = 5

17. 0   **19.** -3 **26.** an infinitely long cylinder with radius 12 in.

27. $\begin{bmatrix} 18 & 30 \\ 24 & 36 \end{bmatrix}$ **28.** $\begin{bmatrix} -15 & -9 & -14 & -7 \\ -2 & -5 & -40 & -22 \\ 0 & -1 & -30 & -35 \end{bmatrix}$

29. $\begin{bmatrix} -2 & 1 & 4 & 14 \end{bmatrix}$ **30.** 13 cm   **31.** 8.5 m   **32.** 8.5   **33.** 8.5

Pages 585–586 Talk it Over
1. Yes.   **2.** $\overline{AG}$ is the hypotenuse of a right triangle with legs of lengths $AC = \sqrt{x^2 + y^2}$ and $GC = z$; $AG = \sqrt{(\sqrt{x^2 + y^2})^2 + z^2} = \sqrt{x^2 + y^2 + z^2}$ **3.** No.   **4.** Subtract the x-coordinates of the endpoints of a width to find the width of the prism. Subtract the y-coordinates of a length to find the length of the prism. Subtract the z-coordinates of a height to find the height of the prism.   **5.** Find the change in x-coordinates, y-coordinates, and z-coordinates. Substitute these values for x, y, and z in the formula for a diagonal of a prism and simplify.

Pages 588–590 Exercises and Problems
1. $AC = 5$; $AG = 5\sqrt{2} \approx 7.07$ **3.** $AC = 4\sqrt{29} \approx 21.54$; $AG = 4\sqrt{65} \approx 32.25$ **5.** $d = \sqrt{1106} \approx 33.26$; Yes.   **9.** $\sqrt{3} \approx 1.73$ **11.** $3\sqrt{3} \approx 5.20$ **13.** $\sqrt{14} \approx 3.74$ **15.** $\sqrt{78} \approx 8.83$ **19.** 3   **21.** $2\sqrt{21} \approx 9.17$ **23.** isosceles; $EF = DF = 5$; not equilateral because $DE = 5\sqrt{2}$ **25.** isosceles; $LM = MN = 6$; not equilateral because $LN = 4\sqrt{3}$ **34.** $(5, -1, 1)$ **35.** $\frac{1}{12}$ or about 8.3%   **36.** Translate the graph 4 units to the right.   **37.** Translate the graph 2 units to the left.   **38.** Translate the graph down 7 units.

Pages 591–594 Talk it Over

1. The graph is the set of points 900 km from the origin. This set of points defines a circle with radius 900 km and center (0, 0).   **2.** Use the distance formula, substituting 0 for x_1 and y_1 and 5 for d. The equation of the circle is $x^2 + y^2 = 25$.   **3.** Substitute 0 for x_1, y_1, and z_1, and 900 for d. The equation of the sphere is $x^2 + y^2 + z^2 = 810,000$ **4. a.** (1700, 400)
b. $(x - 1700)^2 + (y - 400)^2 = 4,000,000$ **5.** Answers may vary. An example is given. Solve a system of two of the equations using substitution or addition-or-subtraction. For example, you could subtract the Shillong equation from the Lhasa equation and solve the resulting equation for y. You could verify your results by solving another system of two equations.

Pages 594–598 Exercises and Problems
1. $x^2 + y^2 = 144$ **3.** $x^2 + y^2 + z^2 = 81$ **5.** $x^2 + y^2 = 25$
7. $x^2 + y^2 + z^2 = 16$
9.

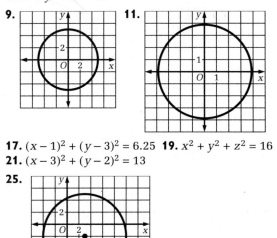

11.

17. $(x - 1)^2 + (y - 3)^2 = 6.25$ **19.** $x^2 + y^2 + z^2 = 16$
21. $(x - 3)^2 + (y - 2)^2 = 13$

25.

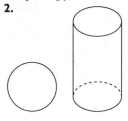

27. a. (8, –4, 5); 6   **31.** $\sqrt{21} \approx 4.6$ **32. a.** True.
b. All rectangles are squares; False. Counterexamples may vary. An example is given. The rectangle with length 4 units and width 2 units is not a square.

Page 600 Unit 10 Review and Assessment
1. square pyramid
2.

3. Answers may vary. Examples are given. a cylinder, a sphere, a cone   **4.** a cone   **5.** a sphere   **6.** a hollow cylinder   **7. a.** Answers may vary. An example is given.

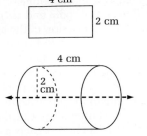

4 cm

2 cm

4 cm

2 cm

b. 16π cm³   **8.** a sphere with radius 6 cm   **9.** a pair of parallel lines each 3 m from the given line
10. a plane halfway between the two points and containing the perpendicular bisector of the line segment joining the two points   **11.** Each stations' recordings determine a circle. The intersection of the three circles is the epicenter of the quake.   **12. a.** A(5, 0, 0); B(0, 0, 0); D(5, 6, 0); F(0, 0, 4); G(0, 6, 4); H(5, 6, 4)
b. $(2\frac{1}{2}, 3, 2)$ **13.** $\sqrt{126} \approx 11.22$ **14.** scalene;
$LM = \sqrt{34}$, $MN = \sqrt{17}$, $LN = 3$
15.

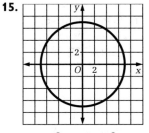

16. $(x - 2)^2 + (y + 1)^2 = 25$ **17.** $x^2 + y^2 + z^2 = 36$

Technology Handbook

Page 604 Try This
1. a. 4   **b.** 32   **c.** about 0.966   **2.** c   **3. a.** 120   **b.** 20
c. 10

Page 605 Try This
4. a.

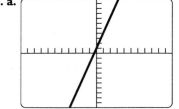

b.

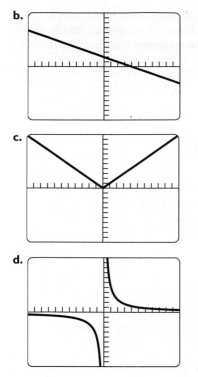

c.

d.

5. Answers may vary. An example is given. [−5, 30] and Xscl=5 for *x*, [−10, 75] and Yscl=5 for *y*.
6. Answers may vary. An example is given. [−7.5, 7.5] and Xscl=1 for *x*, [−5, 5] and Yscl=1 for *y*.

Page 606 Try This
7.

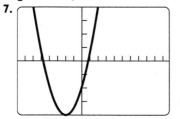

TI-82: window of [−4, 5.4] and Xscl=0.5 for *x*, and [−2, 2] and Yscl=0.5 for *y*. Graph crosses at 0.4 and −2.4. TI-81: window of [−4, 5.5] and Xscl=0.5 for *x*, and [−2, 2] and Yscl=0.5 for *y*. Graph crosses at 0.4 and −2.4.

Page 608 Try This
8. between −2.41 and −2.42
9.

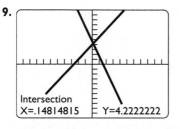

Intersection
X=.14814815   Y=4.2222222

Page 611 Try This
10.

[A]+[B]

[[8 15]
 [3 0]]

11.

[B]−[C]

[[−4   8]
 [−15 −11]]

12.

2[A]

[[6   8]
 [12 14]]

13.

[A][B]

[[3 5]
 [9 17]]

14. not defined
15.

[C][D]

[[33 21 −63 36]
 [44 28 −84 48]]

16.

[A]⁻¹

[[−2.33 1.33]
 [2   −1]]

17. not defined

Pages 614–615 Extra Practice Unit 1

1. 140 **3. a.** 240 **b.** No. The sample size is too small. **5.** all triangle types: isosceles, scalene, equilateral, right, acute, obtuse **7.** $\frac{2}{3}$ **9.** 0 **11.** systematic

13. cluster **15.** random **17.** 0 times **19.** 48 **21.** 100,001 **23.** You always get an odd perfect square. **25.** False. **27.** False. **29. a.** False; $x = 3$. **b.** If $x > 5$, then $x > 2$; the converse is true. **31. a.** True. **b.** If the sun is not out, then it is midnight. The converse is false. It could be cloudy or raining and the sun would not be out, or it could be 2 A.M.

Pages 616–617 Extra Practice Unit 2

1. nonlinear growth **3.** constant **5. a.** $-\frac{4}{3}$

b. decreasing **7. a.** $\frac{3}{2}$ **b.** increasing **9. a.** $-\frac{3}{2}$

b. decreasing **11.** $y = 5x - 23$ **13.** $y = \frac{4}{3}x + \frac{1}{3}$

15. $y = \frac{1}{2}x + \frac{23}{2}$ **17. a.** slope $= \frac{1}{2}$;

vertical intercept $= 0$

b. 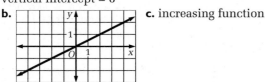 **c.** increasing function

19. a. slope $= 0$; vertical intercept $= -1.5$

b. 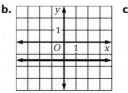 **c.** constant function

21. a. slope $= \frac{2}{3}$; vertical intercept $= -1$

b. **c.** increasing function

23. $y = 3$ **25.** $y = 0.9$

27. $y = \frac{13}{x}$ **29.** 9π; 4.5π **31.** 441π; 1543.5π **33.** 11

35. $3:4$ **37.** $27:64$ **39. a.** 62.8 **b.** 6.2; -6.2
41. a. 44 **b.** 7.4; -7.4 **43. a.** 104.7 **b.** 4.8; -4.8
45. 200 **47.** 32 **49.** 2 **51.** $7^{1/3}x^{1/3}$ or $(7x)^{1/3}$
53. $\sqrt[3]{29pq}$ **55.** $-\sqrt{8v} \cdot \sqrt[3]{\frac{w}{2}}$ **57.** 61,440

59. 1 **61.** 0.015625

Pages 618–619 Extra Practice Unit 3

1. $(1, -4)$ **3.** $(0, 3)$ **5.** $(3, -1)$ **7.** $(-2, 7)$ **9.** $(4, 1)$
11. $(-7, -1)$ **13. a.** lines intersecting **b.** one solution; consistent **15. a.** same line **b.** many solutions; consistent **17. a.** parallel lines **b.** no solution; inconsistent **19.** $y = -2x - 7$ **21.** $y = 5$ **23.** $(6, -1)$

25. $(4, 7)$ **27.** $(-5, 3)$ **29.** $(3, 8)$ **31.** $\begin{bmatrix} 1 & 0 \\ 7 & 1 \end{bmatrix}$

33. $\begin{bmatrix} 14 & 4 & 0 \\ -6 & 2 & 2 \\ 8 & 4 & -2 \end{bmatrix}$ **35.** $\begin{bmatrix} 1 & 12 & 22 \\ -10 & -11 & 5 \end{bmatrix}$

37. $\begin{matrix} D' & E' & F' \\ \begin{bmatrix} 15 & 6 & 0 \\ 3 & 18 & 9 \end{bmatrix} \end{matrix}$ **39.** $\begin{matrix} D' & E' & F' \\ \begin{bmatrix} 2.5 & 1 & 0 \\ 0.5 & 3 & 1.5 \end{bmatrix} \end{matrix}$

41. $\begin{bmatrix} 12 \\ 20 \end{bmatrix}$ **43.** $[-3 \ -80]$ **45.** $\begin{bmatrix} 4 & 3 \\ 9 & 7 \end{bmatrix}$

Pages 620–621 Extra Practice Unit 4

1. $x = 2$; $(2, -3)$; maximum **3.** $x = -3$; $(-3, 32)$; maximum **5.** $x = 16$; $(16, 50.2)$; maximum **7.** -2
9. 0 **11.** Estimates may vary. Examples are given.
$x = -\frac{1}{3}, 4\frac{1}{3}$ **13.** 3 units left, 7 units down

15. 6 units right, 2 units up **17. a.** $(7, -1)$ **b.** 48
19. a. $(-1, 14)$ **b.** 9 **21.** $x = \pm\frac{\sqrt{15}}{2}$ or about 1.94,

about -1.94 **23.** $x = \pm\sqrt{11} - 1$ or about -4.32, about

2.32 **25.** $x = \pm\sqrt{\frac{13}{3}}$ or about 2.08, about -2.08

27. $x = \pm\sqrt{10} - 4$ or about -7.16, about -0.84
29. $(x - 7)(x + 3)$ **31.** $(3x - 7)(x - 2)$
33. $(5x - 3)(2x + 5)$ **35.** $(9x + 5)(9x - 5)$
37. $(2 - 7x)(2 + 7x)$ **39.** $(3x + 1)^2$ **41.** $x = 11, -3$

43. $x = 2, -\frac{2}{3}$ **45.** $x = -3 \pm \sqrt{11}$ or about 0.32, about

-6.32 **47.** $x = \frac{-4 \pm \sqrt{10}}{3}$ or about -0.28, about -2.39

49. $x = -2 \pm \frac{\sqrt{30}}{2}$ or about 0.74, about -4.74

51. $x = \frac{9 \pm \sqrt{53}}{2}$ or about 8.14, about 0.86 **53. a.** two

solutions **b.** $x = \frac{1 \pm \sqrt{5}}{2}$ or about 1.62, about -0.62

55. a. two solutions **b.** $x = -1, -\frac{4}{3}$

57. a. no solutions
b.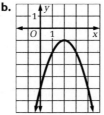

59. $-1 + 2i$ **61.** $83 + 14i$ **63.** $x = 1 \pm \sqrt{10}i$ or about $1 + 3.16i$, about $1 - 3.16i$ **65.** $(-3, 23)$ **67.** $(-4, 57)$, $(0, 1)$

69. $(-1, 0), (4, 5)$

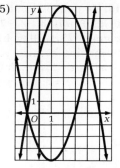

Pages 622–623 Extra Practice Unit 5

1. True. **3.** False, a kite may not have four sides of equal measure. **5.** 15 **7.** $\sqrt{218}$ **9.** $PQ = QR = 5$; $RS = SP = 2\sqrt{13}$ **11.** $(-1.5, 3.5)$ **13.** $(1, 4)$ **15.** $(9, -3)$ **17.** $(-7, -20)$ **19.** reflection over the y-axis

21. $A'(-2, 3)$; $B'(1, 1)$; $C'(-2, 0)$

23. $A'(-4, 1)$; $B'(-2, 4)$; $C'(-1, 1)$

25. $(0, b)$; $(a, 0)$ **27.** (r, q) **29.** Yes; two sides are parallel with slope = 0. **31.** $\sqrt{(a-b)^2 + c^2}$; $\sqrt{(a-b)^2 + c^2}$; Yes.

Pages 623–624 Extra Practice Unit 6

1. 12 **3.** 64 **5. a.** 120 **b.** 360 **c.** 3024 **7. a.** $\frac{1}{6}$ **b.** $\frac{1}{9}$ **c.** $\frac{1}{12}$ **9. a.** $\frac{1}{78}$ **b.** $\frac{1}{26}$ **c.** $\frac{5}{39}$ **11.** 35 **13.** 56 **15.** 5040 **17.** 21 **19.** 1 **21.** 15 **23.** 15 **25.** $\frac{5}{32}$ **27.** $\frac{5}{16}$ **29.** 0.329 **31.** $a^4 - 12a^3 + 54a^2 - 108a + 81$ **33.** $64c^6 + 192c^5d + 240c^4d^2 + 160c^3d^3 + 60c^2d^4 + 12cd^5 + d^6$

Pages 625–626 Extra Practice Unit 7

1.

3.

5. A **7.** B **9.**

11. a. If $xy = xz$, then $y = z$. False; $x = 0$, $y = 1$, $z = 2$. **b.** If $y = z$, then $xy = xz$. True. **13. a.** If an integer is evenly divisible by 10, then its last digit is 0. True. **b.** If an integer's last digit is 0, then it is evenly divisible by 10. True. **15.** If our team plays the Tigers, then we will be in the semi-finals. **17.** valid; indirect argument **19.** False; if four sides are congruent, the quadrilateral is a parallelogram; but not every parallelogram has four congruent sides. **21.** True; this is the definition of transparent. **23.** Division Property of Equality **25.** Substitution Property **27.** Given the equation $2x - 5 = 17$. Addition Property of Equality allows you to add 5 to both sides of the equation, leaving you with $2x = 22$. Then the Division Property of Equality allows you to divide both sides of the equation by 2, leaving you with $x = 11$. **29.** $m \angle A + m \angle B = 180°$; definition of supplementary **31.** If two $\parallel$ lines are intersected by a transversal, then alternate interior $\angle s$ are = in measure. **33.** Vertical $\angle s$ are = in measure.

Pages 627–628 Extra Practice Unit 8

1. ❶$\angle 1$ and $\angle 2$ are supplementary. ❷$\to p \parallel q$ ❸$\to$ $m \angle 3 = m \angle 4$

Justifications: ❶ Given ❷ If two lines are intersected by a transversal and co-interior $\angle s$ are supplementary, then the lines are $\parallel$. ❸ If two $\parallel$ lines are intersected by a transversal, then alternate interior $\angle s$ are = in measure.
3. Yes. **5.** $m \angle P = 70°$; $m \angle Q = 110°$; $m \angle R = 60°$; $m \angle S = 120°$ **7.** $BC = 8$ **9.** SAS **11.** AAS

13. *Given:* $\overline{AC}$ bisects $\overline{BD}$. $\overline{BD}$ bisects $\overline{AC}$.
Prove: $\overline{AB} \parallel \overline{CD}$
Statements (Justifications):
1. $\overline{AC}$ bisects $\overline{BD}$; $\overline{BD}$ bisects $\overline{AC}$. (Given)
2. $AX = CX$; $BX = DX$ (Definition of bisector)
3. $m \angle AXB = m \angle CXD$ (Vertical $\angle s$ are = in measure.
4. $\triangle AXB \cong \triangle CXD$ (SAS)
5. $m \angle DCX = m \angle BAX$ (CPCTE)
6. $\overline{AB} \parallel \overline{CD}$ (If two lines are intersected by a transversal and alternate interior $\angle s$ are = in measure, then the lines are $\parallel$.)

15. *Given:* $AC = BC$; $m \angle 1 = m \angle 2$.
Prove: $AE = BD$
Statements (Justifications):
1. $AC = BC$; $m \angle 1 = m \angle 2$ (Given)
2. $AB = AB$ (Reflexive property of equality)

Selected Ans wer

3. $m \angle DAB = m \angle EBA$ (If two sides of a triangle are = in measure, then the ≜ opposite those sides are = in measure.)
4. $\triangle DAB \cong \triangle EBA$ (ASA)
5. $AE = BD$ (CPCTE)
17. $x = 10$ **19.** $x = 13.5$ **21.** $x = 6$ **23. a.** 1 **b.** 1 **c.** 1
d. conjecture: $(\sin x)^2 + (\cos x)^2 = 1$

Pages 628–629 Extra Practice Unit 9

1. $x(x - 3) = 240$ **3.** $\frac{x(2x + 5)}{2} = 192$

5. $3c^2 d^5(c - 2d)$ **7.** $2k(k + 5)(k - 4)$

9. $3mn(7m^2 + 11n^3)$ **11.** $5x^3 y^4$ **13.** $\frac{s^9}{r^{12}}$ **15.** $\frac{27}{125a^9 b^6}$

17. $b = 18$ **19.** $t = 3$ **21.** $x = 9, x = 2$ **23.** $r = 5$
25. $y = 2, y = -1.5$ **27.** -5 (double), 8   **29.** -9 (triple)
31. 0 (triple)   **33.** D   **35.** C   **37.** $x = -3, x = 0, x = 3$

39. a. $y = 7 - \frac{x^2}{1600}$ **b.**
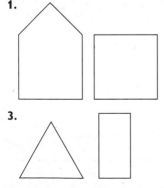
c. $x =$ about 106

Pages 630–631 Extra Practice Unit 10
1.
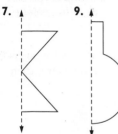
3.
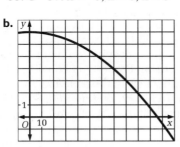

5. a. cone of height 4 and radius 6
   b. $V = 48\pi$ units^3

7.   **9.**

11. a. all points on the line perpendicular to $\overline{AB}$ at its midpoint **b.** all points on the plane perpendicular to $\overline{AB}$ at its midpoint   **13. a.** the midpoint of $\overline{AB}$ **b.** the

midpoint of $\overline{AB}$ **15.** No points meet the conditions.
17. (5, 0, 6)   **19.** (0, 3, 6)   **21.** (3, −2, −3)   **23.** 7
25. 15   **27.** $x^2 + y^2 = 16$ **29.** $x^2 + y^2 + z^2 = 64$

Toolbox Skills

Pages 632–633 Skill 1
1.
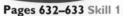
Use of a Small Beach
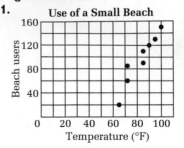

2. positive correlation
3–7. Answers may vary. Examples are given.
3.
Use of a Small Beach
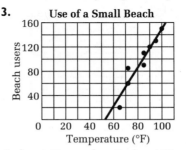

4. about 85 people   **5.** about 70 people
6. about 160 people   **7.** about 20 people

Pages 633–634 Skill 2
1. 30   **2.** 100   **3.** 11   **4.** $20,000–$29,000; $50,000 or over

Page 634 Skill 3
1. the numbers 70, 71, 72, 75, 76

2. Finishing Times (minutes)
```
3 | 2 4
4 | 1 3 4 5 5 6
5 | 0 1 1 2 2 8
6 | 2 3 5 6 6
7 | 1
```

3. 40–49 and 50–59; 70–79

Page 635 Skill 4
1. about 22.7   **2.** 21   **3.** 10, 18, and 24   **4.** 32

Page 636 Skill 5
1.   10 20 30 40 50   **2.** 38   **3.** 27

Integra *…matics*

Page 637 Skill 6
1. about 38% **2.** about 27% **3.** about 10%
4. about 12% **5.** about 18 sweatshirts

Page 638 Skill 7
1. 20% **2.** 60% **3.** 80% **4.** 100% **5.** about 8%
6. about 15% **7.** about 23% **8.** about 77% **9.** 0
10. 100%

Page 639 Skill 8
1. 15% **2.** 50% **3.** about 17% **4.** about 67%

Page 640 Skill 9
1. 12 **2.** 67 **3.** −6 **4.** 23 **5.** 19 **6.** 83 **7.** 0 **8.** 94
9. −21 **10.** −4 **11.** 478 **12.** −72 **13.** −24 **14.** 6
15. −200 **16.** −396 **17.** −416 **18.** −256

Page 641 Skill 10
1. $3x + 7$ **2.** $-2y + 17$ **3.** $n - 5m$ **4.** $-7k + 23$
5. $3x^2 + 3x$ **6.** $-3xy + 3yz$ **7.** $-6a^2 + ab$
8. $3k^2 + 3hk$ **9.** $7x^3 - 7$

Page 642 Skill 11
1. $2x^2 + 3x$ **2.** $-4x^2 + 20x$ **3.** $-14a^2 + 42a$
4. $x^2 - 4x - 45$ **5.** $y^2 - 8y + 12$ **6.** $-x^2 + 13x - 30$
7. $2x^2 - 13x - 7$ **8.** $-3n^2 - 8n + 35$ **9.** $4x^2 - 22x + 10$
10. $6x^2 - 41x + 44$ **11.** $14x^2 - 9x - 8$
12. $15k^2 - 22k + 8$

Pages 642–643 Skill 12
1. $3\sqrt{5}$ **2.** $10\sqrt{3}$ **3.** $2\sqrt{19}$ **4.** $10\sqrt{3}$ **5.** $60\sqrt{5}$
6. $\sqrt{42}$ **7.** $3\sqrt{10}$ **8.** $4.2\sqrt{33}$ **9.** $24\sqrt{6}$ **10.** 6
11. 27 **12.** $12\sqrt{3}$ **13.** $60\sqrt{2}$

Pages 643–644 Skill 13
1. $x = 72$ **2.** $n = 6$ **3.** $x = 20$ **4.** $x = 25$ **5.** $x = 11$
6. $n = 5$ **7.** $w = 86$ **8.** $x = 3$ **9.** $x = -5$ **10.** $x = 7$
11. $x = \frac{1}{3}$ **12.** $x = 16$ **13.** $x = \frac{15}{13}$ **14.** $n = -21$
15. $x = \frac{1}{3}$

Page 645 Skill 14
1. $x < 4$
2. $x \geq -2$
3. $x > -5$
4. $x \geq -2$
5. $x > -4$

6. $x \geq 1$
7. $x < 2$
8. $x \leq 0$
9. $x < -4$

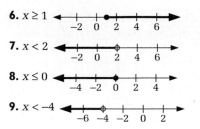

Page 646 Skill 15
1. $h = \frac{2A}{b}$ **2.** $r = \frac{C}{2\pi}$ **3.** $b = 2A - a$ **4.** $y = 13 - 2x$
5. $y = 4 - \frac{5}{2}x$ **6.** $n = \frac{m}{180} + 2$ **7.** $x = \frac{13}{2} - \frac{y}{2}$
8. $x = \frac{y - b}{m}$

Pages 646–647 Skill 16
1. $x = \pm 7$ **2.** $x \approx \pm 4.36$ **3.** $x = 2$ **4.** $x = 4$
5. $x = -5$ **6.** $x \approx \pm 3.32$ **7.** $x \approx \pm 9.85$ **8.** $x \approx \pm 4.90$

Pages 647–648 Skill 17
1. $x = 15.6$ **2.** $z = 10.8$ **3.** $y = 5.6$ **4.** $x = 11.2$
5. $w = 15.75$ **6.** $y = \frac{40}{11} \approx 3.64$ **7.** $q = 10.2$
8. $n = 52.25$

Page 648 Skill 18
1. $0, -10$ **2.** $0, 4$ **3.** $0, 3$ **4.** $-1, -6$ **5.** $-4, 7$
6. $\frac{1}{2}, -3$

Page 649 Skill 19
1. Yes. **2.** No. **3.** No. **4.** Yes.

Pages 649–650 Skill 20
1.

$y = x - 3$		
x	**y**	**(x, y)**
−3	−6	(−3, −6)
−2	−5	(−2, −5)
−1	−4	(−1, −4)
0	−3	(0, −3)
1	−2	(1, −2)
2	−1	(2, −1)
3	0	(3, 0)

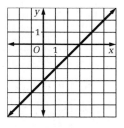

2.

y = 3x − 4		
x	**y**	**(x, y)**
−3	−13	(−3, −13)
−2	−10	(−2, −10)
−1	−7	(−1, −7)
0	−4	(0, −4)
1	−1	(1, −1)
2	2	(2, 2)
3	5	(3, 5)

3.

y = −2x + 3		
x	**y**	**(x, y)**
−1	5	(−1, 5)
0	3	(0, 3)
1	1	(1, 1)
2	−1	(2, −1)
3	−3	(3, −3)

4.

$y = \frac{1}{2}x + 1$		
x	**y**	**(x, y)**
−3	$-\frac{1}{2}$	$\left(-3, -\frac{1}{2}\right)$
−2	0	(−2, 0)
−1	$\frac{1}{2}$	$\left(-1, \frac{1}{2}\right)$
0	1	(0, 1)
1	$1\frac{1}{2}$	$\left(1, 1\frac{1}{2}\right)$
2	2	(2, 2)

5.

y = |x|		
x	**y**	**(x, y)**
−3	3	(−3, 3)
−2	2	(−2, 2)
−1	1	(−1, 1)
0	0	(0, 0)
1	1	(1, 1)
2	2	(2, 2)

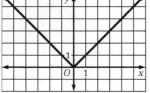

6.

y = x² + 1		
x	**y**	**(x, y)**
−3	10	(−3, 10)
−2	5	(−2, 5)
−1	2	(−1, 2)
0	1	(0, 1)
1	2	(1, 2)
2	5	(2, 5)
x	y	(x, y)

7.

y = 2x² − 5		
x	**y**	**(x, y)**
−3	13	(−3, 13)
−2	3	(−2, 3)
−1	−3	(−1, −3)
0	−5	(0, −5)
1	−3	(1, −3)
2	3	(2, 3)

8.

$y = \frac{1}{x}$		
x	**y**	**(x, y)**
−4	$-\frac{1}{4}$	$\left(-4, -\frac{1}{4}\right)$
−3	$-\frac{1}{3}$	$\left(-3, -\frac{1}{3}\right)$
−2	$-\frac{1}{2}$	$\left(-2, -\frac{1}{2}\right)$
−1	−1	(−1, −1)
$-\frac{1}{2}$	−2	$\left(-\frac{1}{2}, -2\right)$
0	—	—
$\frac{1}{2}$	2	$\left(\frac{1}{2}, 2\right)$
1	1	(1, 1)
2	$\frac{1}{2}$	$\left(2, \frac{1}{2}\right)$
3	$\frac{1}{3}$	$\left(3, \frac{1}{3}\right)$
4	$\frac{1}{4}$	$\left(4, \frac{1}{4}\right)$

Pages 650–651 Skill 21

1. $-\frac{2}{3}$ **2.** $\frac{11}{2}$ **3.** $-\frac{2}{5}$ **4.** undefined

Pages 651–652 Skill 22

1. 161 mi **2.** 4.4 ft

Pages 652–653 Skill 23

1. slope = 3; vertical intercept = -4 **2.** slope = $-\frac{5}{2}$ or -2.5; vertical intercept = $\frac{56}{5}$ or 11.2 **3.** slope = -7; vertical intercept = 6 **4.** slope = 4; vertical intercept = 0 **5.** $y = \frac{1}{2}x + 3$ **6.** $y = -2x + 1$

7. $y = \frac{5}{2}x - 3$

Pages 653–654 Skill 24

1. vertical intercept = 6; horizontal intercept = 2

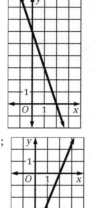

2. vertical intercept = -5; horizontal intercept = 2

3. vertical intercept = 3; horizontal intercept = -3

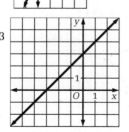

4. vertical intercept = -8; horizontal intercept = 2

5. vertical intercept = -3; horizontal intercept = $\frac{3}{2}$

6. vertical intercept = 5; horizontal intercept = 2

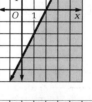

Page 654 Skill 25

1.

$y = -x + 3$		
x	y	(x, y)
0	3	$(0, 3)$
3	0	$(3, 0)$

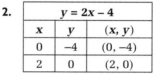

2.

$y = 2x - 4$		
x	y	(x, y)
0	-4	$(0, -4)$
2	0	$(2, 0)$

3.

$y = \frac{1}{2}x + 1$		
x	y	(x, y)
0	1	$(0, 1)$
-2	0	$(-2, 0)$

4.

$2x + 3y = 6$		
x	y	(x, y)
0	2	$(0, 2)$
3	0	$(3, 0)$

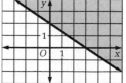

5.

x – 3y = 3		
x	**y**	**(x, y)**
0	–1	(0, –1)
3	0	(3, 0)

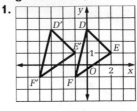

6.

3x + 2y = 9		
x	**y**	**(x, y)**
0	4.5	(0, 4.5)
3	0	(3, 0)

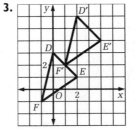

Page 655 Skill 26
1. 54°   **2.** x° = 64°, y° = 116°, z° = 64°   **3.** 57°

Page 656 Skill 27
1. ∠G and ∠D are right angles. Side GF is parallel to side DE.   **2.** Side AB ≅ side DC. Side AD ≅ side BC.
3. All angles are right angles. Side AD is parallel to side BC. Side DC is parallel to side AB.
4. Side AB ≅ side BC ≅ side AC. ∠A, ∠B, and ∠C are equal in measure.   **5.** Side AB is parallel to side DE. ∠A is equal in measure to ∠CDE. ∠B is equal in measure to ∠CED. ∠C is a right angle.   **6.** ∠ZUV is a right angle. Side ZY is parallel to side VW. Side ZU is parallel to side WX. Side UZ ≅ side UV.

Pages 657–658 Skill 28
1. 160 ft²   **2.** 19.5 in.²   **3.** 9π in.² ≈ 28.274 in.²
4. 702 in.²   **5.** 250π cm² ≈ 785.4 cm²
6. 200 cm³   **7.** 34π m³ ≈ 106.8 m³   **8.** 400 in.³

Page 659 Skill 29
1. $\frac{4}{8.5} \approx 0.47$ **2.** $\frac{7.5}{8.5} \approx 0.88$ **3.** $\frac{4}{7.5} \approx 0.53$
4. $\frac{7.5}{8.5} \approx 0.88$ **5.** $\frac{4}{8.5} \approx 0.47$ **6.** $\frac{7.5}{4} = 1.875$

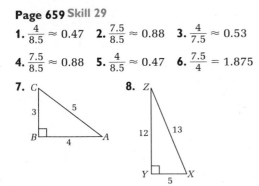

Page 660 Skill 30
1. x ≈ 26.8   **2.** x ≈ 5.8   **3.** x ≈ 26.6

Page 661 Skill 31
1. 13   **2.** 10.5   **3.** about 71.1

Page 661 Skill 32
1. Yes.   **2.** Yes.   **3.** Yes.   **4.** No.

Page 662 Skill 33
1. 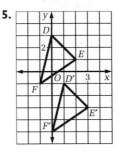   **2.**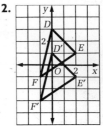

3.   **4.**
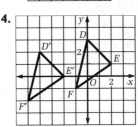

5.
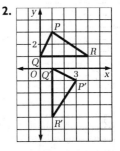

Pages 662–663 Skill 34
1. **2.**
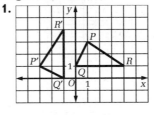

3.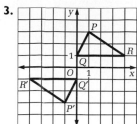

4.

Pages 663–664 Skill 35

1.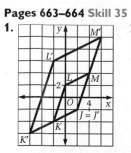

2.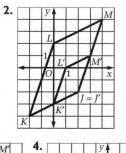

3.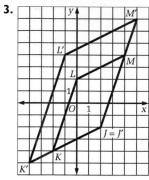

4.

Page 664 Skill 36

1.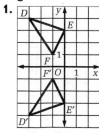

2.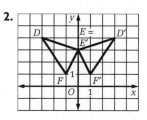

3.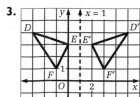

4.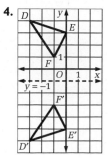